INTERNATIONAL   RUGBY   UNION

A Compendium
of Scotland's Matches

To the memory of my friend
A. M. C. (SANDY) THORBURN
The Scottish Rugby Union's first Historian

INTERNATIONAL RUGBY UNION

A Compendium
of Scotland's Matches

JOHN MCI. DAVIDSON

Honorary Historian and Librarian
Scottish Rugby Union

Based on an original volume by
A. M. C. THORBURN

Polygon
EDINBURGH

Published by Polygon
22 George Square
Edinburgh

Typeset in Monotype Photina and Helvetica
by Koinonia, Bury and printed and bound
in Great Britain by Page Bros Limited, Norwich

ISBN 0 7486 6186 7

The royalties earned from sales of this volume
are donated to the Murrayfield Centenary Fund
for Injured Players

Contents

Foreword

by

HER ROYAL HIGHNESS THE PRINCESS ROYAL

Patron of the Scottish Rugby Union

BUCKINGHAM PALACE

The very first rugby football international was played at Raeburn Place, Edinburgh, on Monday 27 March 1871. Scotland and England contested that first match and, excluding the disputes of 1885, 1888 and 1889, and the years of the two World Wars, these two countries have been competing on the rugby field on an annual basis ever since, 111 matches having been played to date. Scotland and England were eventually joined in annual encounter by Ireland in 1877, Wales in 1883 and France in 1910. The French connection eventually led to the formation of the Five Nations Championship.

In the meantime, Scotland first played New Zealand in 1905, South Africa in 1906 and New South Wales (later to become an international XV representing Australia) in 1927. Gradually, over the years, the fixture list was broadened to include many other countries and, to date, Scotland has played 433 full-cap internationals, and a representative XV has played 29 non-cap matches.

Alexander M. C. ('Sandy') Thorburn, the Scottish Rugby Unions's first Honorary Historian, recorded and documented international matches from 1871 to 1980 in his book *The History of Scottish Rugby*, published in 1981. In this volume, the Unions's present Historian, John McI. Davidson, brings the story of Scotland's international matches up to date, culminating with the two Tests played in Argentina in June 1994.

This new work is the result of the labours of love of the game by the Scottish Rugby Union's first two Honorary Historians. That all of Scotland's international rugby matches are recorded in detail in volume is worthwhile in itself. That the royalties resulting from the writers' endeavours are to be donated to the Murrayfield Centenary Fund for Injured Players is a bonus which reflects the dedication and application of the authors.

Key to Abbreviations

GENERAL
A Albion
Acads. Academicals
Coll. College
FP Former Pupils
GS Grammar School
HS High School
Inst. Institution
OB Old Boys
RWC Rugby World Cup
UC University College
Univ. University

SCOTLAND
DHSFP Dundee High School Former Pupils
Fet.-Lor. Fettesian-Lorettonians
GH-K Glasgow High–Kelvinside
KOSB King's Own Scottish Borderers
London Scot. London Scottish
RE Royal Engineers
RHS Royal High School
SFU Scottish Football Union
SRU Scottish Rugby Union
Stewart's FP Stewart's College Former Pupils

ARGENTINA
CASI Club Atletico, San Isidro
CUBA Club Universitario, Buenos Aires

ENGLAND
Bradford N Bradford Northern
Guy's Guy's Hospital
Hull KR Hull Kingston Rovers
Marl. Nomads Marlborough Nomads
N Durham North Durham
Newcastle N Newcastle Northern
OMT Old Merchant Taylors
RIEC Royal Indian Engineering College
RMA Royal Military Academy (Woolwich)
RMC Royal Military College (Sandhurst)
RN Royal Navy
RNAS Royal Naval Air Service
RNEC Royal Naval Engineering College
Bart's St Bartholomew's Hospital
St Thomas's St Thomas's Hospital

Un. Services United Services

FRANCE
A Bayonnais Aviron Bayonnais
BEC Bordeaux Etudiants Club
CASG Club Athlétique des Sports Généraux
Castres O Castres Olympique
Lyon OU Lyon Olympique Universitaire
PUC Paris Université Club
RCF Racing Club de France
SBUC Stade Bordelais Université Club
SCUF Sporting Club Universitaire de France
SF Stade Français
TOEC Toulouse Olympique Employés Club

IRELAND
CIYMS Church of Ireland Young Men's Society
Cork Const. Cork Constitution
Lond. Irish London Irish
NIFC North of Ireland Football Club
QC Cork Queen's College Cork

NEW ZEALAND
RNZAF Royal New Zealand Air Force

SOUTH AFRICA
B Border
EN Transvaal Eastern and Northern Transvaal
EP Eastern Province
GW Griqualand West
NE Cape North Eastern Cape
NT Northern Transvaal
Orange FS Orange Free State
SA Services South African Services
SWA South West Africa
T Transvaal
WP Western Province
WT Western Transvaal

WALES
Carmarthen TC Carmarthen Technical College
Pontypridd CS Pontypridd County School

Foreword to the First Edition

It might pay the Scottish Tourist Board to make Sandy Thorburn's inner sanctum at his pleasantly secluded Edinburgh home an official tourist attraction! The sanctum I refer to is his own special room in which he stores all his Rugby Union and cricket records. I still remember my feeling of awe on the memorable occasion when I was first privileged to enter that Holy of Holies.

That sanctum, and the wealth of information it houses, bear rich testimony to Sandy Thorburn's feel for sporting history and his meticulous attention to detail in setting down on record facts figures and anecdotes. When that experienced Welsh television producer, Dewi Griffiths, sought to trace the history of the Rugby Union game in Scotland for a series of programmes covering the world scene, Sandy Thorburn fascinated him and the interviewer, John Reason, with the depth of his knowledge and his gift for making the dry bones of history come alive with interest and vitality.

So it seems entirely appropriate that the task of recording the development of Rugby Union in Scotland should have been undertaken by Sandy Thorburn, whose greatest claim to fame, of course, is that he is a Hawick man! As another product of that blessed place, I also feel privileged to have been invited to write this foreword.

Scotland has been badly in need of a composite written record of her Rugby Union fortunes and of the distinctive contribution made by Scots to the game at large. Nowhere. for instance until now, has one come across complete coverage under one cover, of every single match which Scotland have played. In thus providing details of teams, score, scorers and play, Sandy Thorburn has supplied the means of settling thousands of friendly disputes in office and factory for the next hundred years.

As one turns the pages, memories come flooding back. One of my boyhood idols was that remarkable personality, Jock Beattie. There is his name in the complete list of Scottish captains, which is just one of several very interesting appendices to this book. It was in his very last international, the Calcutta Cup match at Twickenham in 1936, that Jock was captain of Scotland. On that day I was at Twickenham for the very first time, a twelve-year-old schoolboy on one of the famous Cook's tours by rail along with my father and some of his factory friends. Another of my Hawick heroes, Rob Barrie, was carried off with a broken collar bone early in the game. My heart was broken too, for Scotland lost. Two years later I was lucky enough to be back at Twickenham for 'Wilson Shaw's match' and Scotland's Triple Crown and Championship success. What a thrill to read about both these games in this book.

Life is constantly subject to change. It is important that Rugby Union, too, stays abreast of the times. Yet there is so much to be learned from the past, not least that all change is not necessarily for the good, that many of the old values and attitudes are still essential in the game today. It is good for us to be reminded, every now and again, of the rich heritage that has been handed on by the great pioneers and, indeed, of the huge part played by some of the famous former pupils' clubs which have fallen recently on hard times. Nor is there much in the modern game that is really new. Coaching, for instance, has brought about a minor revolution in preparation and play method over the past decade. Yet it is fascinating to read in the following pages that as long ago as 1859 the first seeds of coaching were being sown, as Merchistonians made the point that order and organisation had been brought to their game, 'each player now having a place assigned to him for which he is most suited...' And in the same school magazine reference to the then Merchiston captain surely stresses to those who watch the modern game the similarities between then and now: 'His way of ridding himself of those who press upon him too closely in the maul by stamping on their toes, is admirable!'

By his care in research and his attention to detail, Sandy Thorburn has produced a most valuable addition to rugby literature whilst underlining the part Scots have played in the game's evolution. There are those who contend that had it been left to the Scottish Rugby Union, handling in rugby would never have been legalized! Yet one of the stories that will give infinite pleasure to the thousands of Scots who will read this book is of Harry Stevenson (Edinburgh Academicals), capped fifteen times as a back in 1888 to 1893, quietly informing a group of Englishmen that rugby had been played in Scotland long before William Webb Ellis first picked up the ball and ran with it at Rugby School in 1823. They were doing that, he said, at the High School of Edinburgh in 1810. Even at the outset, Scotland led the way!

Bill McLaren

Preface

It was at Jock's Lodge that I first met Sandy Thorburn – a highly-respected rugby and cricket historian. Sandy was the Scottish Rugby Union's first Honorary Historian and was also rugby and cricket historian for RHSFP as well as Honorary Historian to the Scottish Cricket Union. He had researched and published a book, *The History of Scottish Rugby* in 1980. A career move in 1965 had seen me move from Aberdeen to Edinburgh. My appetite for rugby was satisfied by watching and supporting Royal High School FPs at Jock's Lodge. Upon that club going 'open', I became one of the first non-FP members.

Following the publication of Sandy's book, I was invited to join a small sub-committee set up to explore the possibility of preparing for publication an official history of the SRU, to be written by Sandy. From that time, Sandy and I worked closely together: Sandy researched and wrote, I edited, designed and produced the finished book. During that period we became good friends.

When the SRU decided to set up their Rugby Library and Museum at Murrayfield, I joined the working party which planned, researched and developed the idea. The Library and Museum was opened in December 1986 and was available to the public until June 1992 when the old West Stand at Murrayfield had to be demolished as part of the development of the stadium.

It was during that period, when the Library and Museum was being prepared, that Sandy put me on the spot by asking if I would be interested in 'learning the ropes' of rugby history and, perhaps, eventually succeeding him as Honorary Historian to the Union. I was both flattered and staggered: the idea had never crossed my mind and I stalled for several months before giving an answer. In time, working alongside Sandy, I came to realise that this was something that I found fascinating: something that stimulated and stretched the intellect. I was 'hooked'! Following Sandy's death in 1988, I had the honour and good fortune to be invited by the Scottish Rugby Union to fill the post of Honorary Historian.

The History of Scottish Rugby, by Sandy Thorburn, traced the story of Scotland's international rugby up to the end of season 1979-80. The volume has been out-of-print for some years now. There has been steady interest in, and a demand for, the book and so I undertook the formidable task of bringing the story up to date and, in doing so, researching and re-writing much of the original material as well as introducing some new features. This activity has resulted in the present volume.

My thanks are due to Her Royal Highness The Princess Royal, Patron of the Scottish Rugby Union, for writing the Foreword, despite a heavy work schedule.

The successful research, preparation and publication of this book would not have been possible without the assistance and encouragement of my wife, Margaret, and without the kind co-operation of the following people: Mrs Netta Thorburn; Kathryn McLean, Pamela O'Connor and Marion Sinclair of Polygon; the staff of the University of Edinburgh Library; Graham Law, Harry Pincott, Andrew Harton and Bill Brady of Scotsman Publications; Bill McMurtrie of *The Herald*; and my good friend Adam Robson, Past-President of the SRU and a former Scotland international player. Thanks are due, too, to the following colleagues and friends at the SRU: Ken Smith, President; Bill Hogg, Chief Executive; Gordon Alston and Mrs Carolyn Goodlad – each of whom assisted me toward the completion of the work. My friend, the late Bob Munro, Senior Vice-President of the SRU, is especially remembered for his encouragement when my enthusiasm threatened to flag.

Special mention must be made of Mrs Audrey Anderson, secretary to the Chief Executive, for her forbearance and friendly helpfulness when dealing with my many unscheduled requests for assistance and advice: for this I am especially grateful.

There are many others, too numerous to mention by name, to whom I am indebted. Without the encouragement and enthusiasm of all these good friends this book may not have been completed.

JOHN McI. DAVIDSON
Edinburgh, September 1994

I

The Formation of the Rugby Union Game: its Development in Scotland

Recreational pastimes have formed part of peoples lives since time immemorial and the populations of Scotland have been no exception. It is recorded that Roman soldiers in Britain found relaxation in *harpastum* – a hard-ball game which, it is claimed in some quarters, led eventually to the Border Ba' games. Although conjecture, a strong case can be made for this belief when it is recognised that the main Roman route into Scotland was across the Cheviots, past Jedburgh and Ancrum, and on to Newstead near Melrose. The Romans were encamped there for more than a century and it is almost inevitable that local communities were influenced by and acquired and developed some of their customs.

Harpastum was apparently played within a rectangular area which had a 'centre line'. Two teams were involved, the object of the game being to try to force the small hard ball over the line at the far end of the opposing team's half. The game featured running, passing and throwing the ball, and tackling opponents was allowable. With knowledge of these criteria, it is understandable that comparisons have been made with the game of rugby and conclusions drawn and claims made that *harpastum* was, indeed, a strong contender for the basis of the formation of the modern handling game.

Border Ba' Games

Evolving Border Ba' games formed the basis of football in Scotland. Local people divided themselves into two teams with no maximum number of participants being specified. There were few formal rules and no organised playing fields: the games were sometimes played in the streets. The team divisions were usually along local geographical criteria – e.g., the 'Uppies' (from the upper part of the town or village) against the 'Doonies' (from the opposite end). The object of the game was to carry the ba', mostly by sheer brute force (little finesse was exercised), to touch some agreed target, a wall perhaps, at the far end of the opposition's area. It would seem that kicking was not an option: the mass of struggling bodies

1

ruled that out – and such folly of action could have resulted in the would-be kicker injuring himself. The ba' used was quite small, about the size of a modern tennis ball and, being made from leather, it was quite hard. An annual symbolic game is still played in some areas, e.g., in Jedburgh.

The decline and rise of ball games

Some Town Councils in Scotland permitted an annual Fair game but they became increasingly concerned with the amount of damage done to property, caused by unruly participants and their boisterous play in the streets. However, by the end of the 18th and early 19th centuries, the popularity of the game of football had dwindled: it was no longer the popular pastime it had been previously. The upsurge of industrial work at that time was almost certainly responsible for the game's decline. Scottish people worked for six long days each week, leaving them with little desire or energy for football. It was saved from total extinction by being taken up in some schools, and in the universities, as an acceptable recreation.

These educational institutions developed kicking and/or handling games along lines, and with rules, to suit their own needs. There is recorded evidence of a handling game having been played at the High School in Edinburgh in 1810. Eventually, when they became former pupils and students, these gentlemen formed clubs and teams and they organised and governed the game in its formative years.

Attempts at uniformity

Several new schools were formed in Scotland during the first half of the nineteenth century, among them Edinburgh Academy (1824), Loretto (1827), Merchiston (1833), Glasgow Academy (1845) and Trinity College, Glenalmond (1847). Fettes College was founded in 1870 It is known that simple and crude forms of football were played at each of these schools, but it was in Edinburgh that the handling game first took root and spread to other areas of Scotland.

Meanwhile, in England, as in Scotland, there developed as many varieties of football as there were schools: each formed its own rules of play. Such diversity became only too obvious at the universities when players from different schools attempted to play football together. In some schools, running with the ball was unacceptable. The schools tended to play with a larger air-filled animal's bladder rather than the small hard leather ball. The air-filled ball could be kicked but only handled if caught directly from a kick. Play would then be momentarily halted whilst the catcher took a kick which could be charged by his opponents. However, handling and running with the ball slowly, but gradually, became accepted as a variation of the kicking game but it was not until the Rugby School Rules of Play, of 1846, that the practice became legalised.

2

Association Football and Rugby Football

Around the middle of the nineteenth century, the game of 'football' had many variations of play. Distinctions between a purely kicking game and one where ball-handling was allowed, became blurred. This, inevitably, resulted in confusion when teams, playing to different rules, met on the field of play. Something had to be done: either (a) a set of rules for one uniform game, or (b) rules for two different games.

England led the way in this respect. It is well known that, as an 18-year-old at Rugby School around 1823, William Webb Ellis became exasperated during a scoreless intra-school game. Seizing an opponent's punt, instead of heeling the ball for a free kick at goal, he ran helter skelter past his amazed team-mates and opponents alike and touched it down at the far end of the opposing side's area. Ellis outraged fellow students and officials and was severely censured for what was seen as an act of utter folly and bad sportsmanship – but he had planted the seed of an idea and running with the ball began to take hold at Rugby. However, there was no sudden desire to change to this new mode of play – neither at Rugby nor elsewhere. The acceptance was slow, gradual and fragmented.

In 1846, a meeting was called, at Cambridge, of representatives of all the schools and a code was drawn up in an attempt to unify the game of football. The representatives present took what they decided were the best points of the game as played at different schools – but the principle of running with the ball was rejected. Although no copy now exists of the set of rules drawn up at the 1846 conference, it had far-reaching effects. Rules at the various clubs remained somewhat individualistic but all except one club agreed that the game be restricted to a kicking code. Most clubs played 20-a-side and matches were decided by the number of goals scored – a goal being awarded when the ball was kicked under the bar and between the upright posts being defended by opponents. Thus did one form of football begin to emerge with almost-uniform rules and code of play.

Concurrently, the handling game also began to take shape. The Rugby School Rules of 1846 provided a code of play, albeit somewhat diffuse and confusing, which former pupils of the school could follow and show to others. These former pupils, when they proceeded to university or elsewhere, did their best to ensure that the rules and principles, as laid down, were firmly adhered to.

In 1863 representatives of several clubs, which were opposed to hacking, lengthy mauls and handling, produced a set of rules which excluded handling. This led to the formation of the Football Association. This new Association became remarkably active and it is surprising that another eight years were to pass before a somewhat similar Rugby Union was formed.

On December 1 1863, the Football Association published a set of rules which prohibited running with the ball. The Blackheath club, which had led the fight for running with the ball, withdrew from the conference and went its own independent way. Thus did the two divisions of football become delineated. The kicking game had the first set of uniform rules published under the title 'Rules of the London Football Association'. The kicking game eventually became known as 'soccer'.

Following the 1863 conference, more clubs joined Blackheath in playing the handling game. When football was introduced as a sport at Oxford, the Rugby game was favoured and the Oxford University club was formed in 1869 with Cambridge following in 1872. This spreading activity led to the foundation of the Rugby Football Union, as a governing body for the game, in 1871. The Scottish Football Union was formed in 1873.

The game comes to Scotland

In the Edinburgh area there were several boarding schools whose pupils were encouraged in physical exercise and sport. Cricket and football were played on the schools' own fields. The various forms of football being played allowed some handling of an air-filled ball. Intra-school matches were organised and recognised as an acceptable form of rivalry between young gentlemen.

Two young men, Francis and Alexander Crombie, came from Durham School to Edinburgh in 1854. Francis joined the Academy as a pupil but Alexander had already left school. Apparently, neither brother had played football at Durham but they took with them a knowledge of the rules of football as played at Rugby School and this they passed on. Francis is recorded as having been the first school football captain and Alexander became actively involved in the formation of the Edinburgh Academical Football Club. He qualified for membership under a rule which allowed relatives of school pupils to become members. In 1858 he became the first captain of the Football Club – a position he held for eight years.

During the same period, a boy named Hamilton came to the High School in Edinburgh (in 1856) from an English public school and brought with him the 'Rules of Rugby Football' as he had known them in the south. This document was instrumental in the High School's adapting their existing game to this new form.

The first-ever intra-school match recorded in Scotland was the High School *versus* Merchiston, played on 13 February 1858. The game suffered from lack of uniformity of both rule and ball. In the High School, in the early 1860s, football was played with '... monstrous inflated globes of vast circumference and ponderosity ...'. H. H. Almond, a master at both Loretto and Merchiston and a founding father of the game in Scotland, describing an incident in a Loretto *versus* Merchiston match, wrote: '... but so little did any of us, masters or boys, then know about it, that I remember how, when Lyall ran with the ball behind the Merchiston goal the resulting try was appealed against on the ground that no player may cross the line whilst holding the ball. The previous rule at Merchiston had been that he must let go of the ball and kick it over before he touched it down. It must be said in excuse for this and other similar sins of ignorance, that the only available rules were those printed for the use of Rugby School. They were very incomplete and presupposed a practical knowledge of the game'.

Gradually, over several years, the game approached that being played at Rugby. There were local variations which, inevitably, resulted in disputes. Almond again: '... well into the 1870s the only schools able to play each other on even terms were the Edinburgh Academy, Merchiston and the High School'.

Influential figures

As well as the school pupils, already mentioned, who brought the Rugby Rules to Edinburgh, there were three Scottish schoolmasters who greatly influenced the development of the game in Scotland.

Thomas Harvey, a native of Glasgow, was educated at Glasgow University and Balliol College, Oxford, before becoming a master at Edinburgh Academy between 1847 and 1856: he was there when Raeburn Place opened and the Crombie brothers arrived in Edinburgh. From 1856 until 1863 he was Headmaster at Merchiston and, from 1869 until 1888 he was Rector at the Academy.

John J. Rogerson was educated at Moffat Academy before graduating from the University of Edinburgh. Following short teaching spells at Loretto and Cheltenham, he came to Merchiston in 1858 and became Headmaster, following Thomas Harvey, in 1863, remaining in post until 1898.

Hely Hutchison Almond, a native of Glasgow, was a student at Glasgow University and Balliol College, Oxford. Following a year at Loretto, he came to Merchiston in 1858, returning to Loretto in 1862 as Headmaster and remained there until his death in 1902.

All three had been actively associated with football whilst in England and were together at Merchiston 1858-62. Each believed in the virtues of supervised outdoor exercise and encouraged their pupils to participate in intra-school matches.

Perhaps H. H. Almond was the best-known. He was once described as the 'great apostle of muscular Christianity in Scotland' because of the Spartan regime he established at Loretto where food, clothing, fresh air and outdoor sport were given equal importance with academic lessons and moral guidance. As both Master and Headmaster he took an active part in playing in some of the rugby and cricket matches: his name appears on the team lists over many seasons.

The formation of the clubs and early matches

By the late 1850s and early 1860s, senior (former pupils) clubs started to appear in both the Glasgow and Edinburgh areas. The Edinburgh Academy were first with a senior club in 1858. Their first match was against a team from the University of Edinburgh – and a most extraordinary affair it must have been! It was played over four Saturdays, starting on 26 December 1857 and finishing on 16 January 1858. At that time no formal University club existed: the team was probably made up from a group of students who were vacationing in the city. This seems to be the first recorded senior match in Scotland.

The rules drawn up for the match could be said to be eyebrow-raising. Each team consisted of 25 players and it was agreed that the match continue until the best of seven goals be scored. Day 1 saw the students score one goal. Days 2 and 3 were scoreless. On Day 4 the teams were increased to 30-a-side and, between the afternoon hours of 2 and 3.30, the Academicals had kicked four goals and thus won the long drawn-out encounter. The Academicals team, although outweighed by the students, owed much of its success to three or four of their players who had played the game in England and had learned how to drop kick. This seems to be the first reference to that rugby curiosity, the 'drop kick'.

By the mid-1860s the senior clubs were playing each other on a regular basis, making good use of the then new railways. In those early club matches play was often halted whilst captains and umpires tried to settle some point of difference. Such disputes and mix-ups were frequent.

Such a state of affairs could not continue indefinitely and a group of men from the Edinburgh Academical Football Club convened a series of meetings to discuss the possibility of drawing up a uniform set of rules. In 1868, with the agreement of the other schools and clubs, they set out and had printed rules for the game in Scotland. The resulting booklet, *Laws of Football as Played by the Principal Clubs in Scotland*, became known as 'The Green Book'. Alas, no copy survives but it is interesting to note that neither the clubs nor 'The Green Book' felt it necessary to include the word 'Rugby' in their title. Indeed, The Scottish Football Union, formed in 1873, did not alter its name to become the Scottish Rugby Union until 1924 – the year prior to the opening of Murrayfield.

II

The First International Match

Association football: England v. Scotland

The Football Association, having been formed at a meeting in London in 1863, formulated its rules of play, giving cognizance to the views which had been expressed at an earlier meeting in Cambridge the same year. However, clubs in the Sheffield area, which had been playing a form of football for at least five years, were not represented at the meeting nor were they consulted. In an effort to make amends for this seeming gaffe of omission, and to try to widen and strengthen its area of control, the FA arranged a match, in London, against the Sheffield clubs. This was so successful that other similar district matches were organised.

In March 1870 the FA arranged a match at the Oval cricket ground and titled it 'England v. Scotland'. The Scotland XI was made up of players living in the London area, some of whom had rather tenuous and extremely dubious Scottish qualifications. Unsubstantiated rumour had it that one player had Scottish ancestry, another had family connections with an estate north of the Border, another is supposed to have claimed qualification because of his admiration for whisky, and yet another because he went north every August for the 'Glorious Twelfth'!

Notwithstanding these seemingly false claims to Scottishness, the match went ahead and was a success, the England XI being victorious. The Secretary of the FA, C. W. Alcock, arranged another match, under the same heading, to be played in London in November 1870. However, on this occasion, Alcock wrote to several Scottish newspapers inviting clubs to nominate players for the Scotland XI. Only one player responded to the invitation. This is not surprising when it is realised that there were only four clubs (all in the Glasgow area) playing under FA rules: Queen's Park (1867), Thistle (1868), Hamilton (1869) and Airdrie (1870). The England team were again the winners, albeit by a solitary goal.

The Rugby Challenge

That second match triggered off a number of readers letters in *The Scotsman*, one of which, from a Glaswegian, suggested that Scottish (rugby) clubs should send ten players to join ten in London and challenge the FA. Alcock, in accepting the challenge, added a rider: 'More than eleven we do not care to play as with greater numbers it is our opinion that the game becomes less scientific and more a trial of charging and brute force'. This brought a rather ribald response in the form of a letter signed 'H. M.', (whom R. S. Phillips in his *History of Scottish Rugby*, identifies as H. H. Almond, Headmaster of Loretto): '... Mr Alcock is a very leading supporter of what is called the 'association game' which is to Rugby football or whatever its detractors may please to call it as moonlight unto sunlight and as water unto wine'.

Concurrently with this literary activity, the Scottish clubs had been discussing such matters among themselves. On 8 December 1870 there appeared in *Bell's Life in London* and in *The Scotsman*, the following letter which was to become historically famous in rugby annals. It was signed by the captains of five senior Scottish clubs:

Sir,
There is a pretty general feeling among Scotch football players that the football power of the old country was not properly represented in the late so-called International Football Match. Not that we think the play of the gentlemen who represented Scotland otherwise than very good – for that it was so is amply proved by the stout resistance they offered to their opponents and by the fact that they were beaten by only one goal – but that we consider the Association rules, in accordance with which the late game was played, not such as to bring together the best team Scotland could turn out. Almost all the leading clubs play by the Rugby code, and have no opportunity of practising the Association game even if willing to do so. We therefore feel that a match played in accordance with any rules other than those in general use in Scotland, as was the case in the last match, is not one that would meet with support generally from her players. For our satisfaction, therefore, and with a view of really testing what Scotland can do against an English team we, as representing the football interests of Scotland, hereby challenge any team selected from the whole of England, to play us a match, twenty-a-side, Rugby rules, either in Edinburgh or Glasgow on any day during the present season that might be found suitable to the English players. Let this count as the return to the match played in London on 19th November, or, if preferred, let it be a separate match. If it be entered into we can promise England a hearty welcome and a first-rate match. Any communications addressed to any one of us will be attended to.

We are, etc.
A. H. Robertson, West of Scotland FC
F. J. Moncreiff, Edinburgh Academical FC
B. Hall Blyth, Merchistonian FC
J. W. Arthur, Glasgow Academical FC
J. H. Oatts, St Salvador FC, St Andrews

The challenge taken up

Not unexpectedly perhaps, the letter was ignored by the FA but rugby-playing clubs in the London area felt that they could not but take up the challenge and B. H. Burns, Secretary of the oldest-established club, Blackheath, sent a letter of acceptance on their behalf. Following this, a committee of six was formed in Edinburgh to make the necessary arrangements: H. H. Almond (Loretto), J. W. Arthur (Glasgow Academicals), B. H. Blyth (Merchistonians), A. Buchanan (Royal High School FP), Dr J. Chiene and F. J. Moncreiff (Edinburgh Academicals). The match was fixed for Monday, 27 March 1871, to be played on the Academical ground at Raeburn Place. A decision was made to stage two trial matches: one in Glasgow on 11 March and the other in Edinburgh on 20 March.

In London, a committee was formed with B. H. Burns as its secretary. No trial match was held, the England team being made up of twelve from the London area and four each nominated by the two main clubs in the north: Liverpool and Manchester.

Prior to the match, there was some deliberation about, and chopping and changing of, the number of players in each team. The challenge had suggested twenty-a-side; by the end of February this had been reduced to fifteen but, by 15 March, B. H. Burns let it be known that he was, after all, able to bring twenty, which number was finally agreed upon.

On 25 March 1871 the *Glasgow Herald* reported that the match would be played using the rules of Rugby School with two minor alterations, both of which were customary in the London area:

1. The ball, on going into touch, is to be thrown into the ground again from the spot where it crossed the line, and not where it first pitched into touch.
2. For a try at goal, the ball is brought out in a straight line from where it was touched down. (This would eliminate the alternative choice of punting out after a touch down).

In the London area there was a generally-observed rule that a player could gather up a ball whether rolling or bounding. Scottish clubs only allowed it in the latter case and this was agreed for the first international.

Observations about some of the Scottish players make interesting reading: A. G. Colville (Merchistonians) had been playing with Blackheath since 1867 and so became the first Anglo-Scot. cap. The London committee had invited him to play in the England XX but he opted to play for Scotland.

J. H. L. Macfarlane (Edinburgh University) was born in Jamaica and educated at Craigmount and Edinburgh Institution and could be considered to be a first Colonial cap.

A. Clunies-Ross (St Andrews University) was a member of a famous Cocos Island family and was part-Scots, part-Malaysian. He was educated at Madras College before going on to study at St Andrews and Edinburgh Universities. He, too, could be considered a Colonial cap.

In the England XX, B. H. Burns filled a last-minute vacancy, so creating a precedent in this very first rugby international, for he was a Scot, born in Perthshire and educated at St Andrews and the Edinburgh Academy before going south to become a banker in London.

Four of the Scottish forwards, J. H. L. Macfarlane, A. Buchanan, W. Cross and F. J. Moncreiff were each more than competent performers at half-back for their clubs. Perhaps it was this that was in the mind of the writer of the following letter which appeared in *The Scotsman* on the morning of the match:

Sir,
Our Scottish team is a very heavy one and the play of the backs and half-backs is very fine. Will you allow me a corner of your columns to remind *some* of the rest of the Twenty that their proper place is 'forward' and that habitually. Assuming the positions as they did last Wednesday (i.e., at the Edinburgh Trial) of quarter backs and three quarter backs is an annoyance to the best players and very bad play. The business of a forward is not to hang about promiscuously waiting for something to turn up but to FOLLOW UP.

How often have we heard these sentiments expressed!

The letter of challenge had suggested either Glasgow or Edinburgh as possible venues for the match. This meant either Hamilton Crescent in Partick, or Raeburn Place in Edinburgh. The problem with Hamilton Crescent was that it lay some distance outside Glasgow and its then transport system. On the other hand, Raeburn Place was but a ten-minute cab ride from the New Town area where, almost certainly, the players would be lodged. Spectators would be able to use the local transport service to Stockbridge. The final choice made sense, too, from the players point of view: thirteen were resident in Edinburgh.

The Edinburgh Academical Cricket Club Committee (who controlled Raeburn Place) '... resolved by a majority that the ground be granted ...'. We know not what objections had been raised but the Committee were happier following the match: their Treasurer reported '... the large sum of £13 was obtained from the Football Fund, being balance of gate money on the day of the First International Match after deducting expenses.'

For the first international the pitch at Raeburn Place measured 120 yards by 55 yards, a narrowness which did not suit the England XX: their speedy backs preferred to take a semicircular path to the goal line.

Spectators paid 1 shilling (5p) to Mr J. H. A. Macdonald who sat at a deal table with an earthenware bowl to hold the takings. (Mr Macdonald, as Lord Kingsburgh, was to play an important part in the history of rugby football).

Scotland's other international grounds

Subsequent home internationals were to be played at Hamilton Crescent, Glasgow, four between 1873 and 1882; Hampden Park, Glasgow, two in 1896 and 1906; Powderhall, Edinburgh, two in 1897 and 1898. In 1897 land was purchased at Inverleith, Edinburgh. Thus the Scottish Football Union became the first of the Home Unions to own its ground. The first visitors were Ireland, on 18 February 1899: Scotland – 3 Ireland – 9.

International rugby was played at Inverleith until 1925. The SFU had purchased land, belonging to the Edinburgh Polo Club, at Murrayfield, in 1922. There they built the first Murrayfield Stadium which was opened on 21 March 1925, England being the visitors (Scotland – 14 England – 11).

III
International Match Summaries 1871–1994

Notes about the presentation of the match summaries
1. The back players are separated by semi-colons into their positions as fullbacks, backs and halves. Wing threequarters are named beside their centres but no attempt is made to be consistent in always naming, say, the right-wing pair first. Up to 1914 the half-backs are set out as a pair but, thereafter, the first named is that of the stand-off.
2. Up to 1914, the forwards are named alphabetically but from 1920 the named forwards indicate the scrum as front row, second row, back row. In this work, great assistance was rendered by Messrs D. S. Davies, A. C. Gillies, J. C. H. Ireland and D. J. McMyn.
3. Difficulty was experienced in naming clubs. Many university players played for London Scottish when in residence and then for some other club following the Inter-Varsity match in December. The Fettesian-Lorettonian players of the 1880s are examples: some played, in the same season, for their University, London Scottish, Fet.-Lor., and Edinburgh Wanderers.
4 In a number of cases, especially for away matches prior to 1914, doubts exist about the name of a scorer or goal kicker. In those cases the name accepted is that reported in *The Scotsman* and *The Glasgow Herald*.
5. Similar difficulties have been experienced in naming opponents. In this respect, acknowledgement is made to the painstaking research of Timothy Auty and Jean-Pierre Bodis, and to the information gleaned from the following publications: John Billot's *History of Welsh International Rugby*, various Rugby Football Union publications, Rothman's Year Books and the *FFR Annuaire*.
6. Team captains are indicated by an asterisk. The half-time interval is indicated thus: (H-T).

SCOTLAND: 1 goal, 1 try   Win
ENGLAND: 1 try
Raeburn Place
27 March 1871

Scotland: W. D. Brown (*Glas. Acads.*), T. Chalmers (*Glas. Acads.*), A. Clunies-Ross (*St Andrews Univ.*); T. R. Marshall (*Edin. Acads.*), J. W. Arthur (*Glas. Acads.*), W. Cross (*Glas. Acads.*); A. Buchanan (*RHSFP*), A. G. Colville (*Merchistonians*), D. Drew (*Glas. Acads*), J. F. Finlay (*Edin. Acads.*), J. Forsyth (*Edin. Univ.*), R. W. Irvine (*Edin. Acads.*), W. J. C. Lyall (*Edin. Acads.*), J. L. H. Macfarlane (*Edin. Univ.*), J. A. W. Mein (*Edin. Acads.*), F. J. Moncreiff* (*Edin. Acads.*), R. Munro (*St Andrews Univ.*), G. Ritchie (*Merchistonians*), A. H. Robertson (*West of Scot.*), J. S. Thomson (*Glas. Acads.*)

12

England: A. Lyon (*Liverpool*), A. G. Guillemard (*West Kent*), R. R. Osborne (*Manchester*); W. McLaren (*Manchester*); F. Tobin (*Liverpool*), J. E. Bentley (*Gipsies*), J. F. Green (*West Kent*); R. H. Birkett (*Clapham Rovers*), B. H. Burns (*Blackheath*), J. H. Clayton (*Liverpool*), C. A. Crompton (*Blackheath*), A. Davenport (*Ravenscourt Park*), J. M. Dugdale (*Ravenscourt Park*), A. S. Gibson (*Manchester*), A. St. G. Hamersley (*Marl. Nomads*), J. H. Luscombe (*Gipsies*), C. W. Sherrard (*Blackheath*), F. Stokes* (*Blackheath*), D. P. Turner (*Richmond*), H. J. C. Turner (*Manchester*)
Umpires: H. H. Almond, A. Ward

No scoring at half time. A. Buchanan scored and W. Cross converted; R. H. Birkett scored but F. Stokes failed; W. Cross scored but failed to convert.

Shortly after 3 pm Scotland kicked off from the Inverleith end with the slight north-easterly breeze behind them. Play was fairly even during the first half. Scotland carried the ball over the line once but the umpires decided on a hack-off at five yards as both sides claimed the touch. Turner narrowly missed a drop at goal from a free kick and McLaren, not permitted to pick up a rolling ball, tried but failed to kick a field goal from some 15 yards in front of the posts.

Early in the second half a maul formed about a yard from the English line and Ritchie with the ball was pushed over with half-a-dozen on top of him. One of his opponents also claimed the touch and as the two could not agree the umpires decided on a hack off at five yards. To the end of his days Ritchie maintained that he had scored. However, no sooner had the maul formed when the Scottish forwards drove the entire mass over the line where Buchanan with Macfarlane beside him, grounded the ball. This was loudly disputed on the grounds that the ball had not been put down before the surge was made, but the umpires were unable to make out the exact nature of the objection and so granted the try which was converted from near the east touch line by Cross.

Now the English backs began to show their speed and had some splendid runs, but hard tackling and the narrowness of the pitch halted their efforts. Green was particularly good but was so heavily tackled by Chalmers that he had to leave the field. Then H. J. C. Turner, catching a drop out after a touch down, passed the ball to Birkett who ran in close to touch. Stokes missed the long difficult kick across the wind.

Towards the end the better training of the Scots began to tell, and near full time their pack forced the ball into touch near the English line. From there a long throw in went beyond the forwards to Arthur who, attempting to catch the ball, knocked it forward over the heads of the defenders and Cross, following up quickly, touched down for a try which was at once disputed by the Englishmen who objected to the knock forward catching them out of position. But at this time such knocks were not illegal and the umpires, deciding that it was not intentional, gave the score. Cross failed to convert against the wind and the game finished some two minutes later, Scotland thus winning by the only goal.

Since both Scottish scores were disputed on the field and adversely spoken of in later years, some comments on the points of law involved must be made here.

The first score followed a hack off at five yards. For this a Scottish forward, holding the ball, was surrounded by the forwards of both sides, each standing upright, head in the air, shoulder to shoulder and facing his opponents' goal line. The ball was then pushed down onto the ground and all tried by pushing, hacking and kicking to force the ball forward through the mass. H. H. Almond later wrote: 'The ball had certainly been scrummaged over the line by Scotland and touched down first by a Scotchman. The try was vociferously disputed by the English team but upon what ground I was then unable to discover. Had the good rule of the Green Book been kept, viz. that no one except the captain should speak in any dispute unless appealed to, I should have understood that the point raised was that the ball had never been fairly grounded in the scrummage but had got mixed up among Scottish feet or legs. This I only learned afterwards. Indeed when the game was played twenty-a-side, the ball, at the beginning of a scrummage, was quite invisible to anyone outside, nor do I know how I could have decided the point had I known what it was.'

A study of the contemporary drawing of such a scrummage reveals the accuracy of Almond's observation and I would add that, having staged two old-style exhibition games, not only do I agree with Almond but am sure that in the scrummage only the holder of the ball could tell if it had been put down correctly. In view of Almond's initial remarks it may well have been the case that the Scots went into the maul so fast that they caught their opponents unprepared, for after all they did succeed in mauling the ball forward the five yards to the line for the score.

Almond's trenchant final comment on his decision has often been quoted: 'I must say, however, that when an umpire is in doubt, I think he is justified in deciding against the side which makes most noise. They are probably in the wrong.'

The second Scottish score raises no great problem. Undoubtedly by 1883 the try would have been disallowed as resulting from a knock on, but the original Rugby Football Union Laws which were approved in 1871 defined a knock on as 'deliberately hitting the ball with the hand' and so Arthur's unintentional deflection of the ball did not constitute a fault. It is recorded that in the 1879–80 season, H. T. Twynam, a Richmond cap, knocked the ball forward at the tail of a line out, followed up, caught the ball and scored against Oxford University. F. R. Adams, the Richmond captain and another cap, refused to admit that the knock on was deliberate and claimed the score. It is believed that the dead-lock that followed eventually caused the Union to amend the Law by omitting the word 'deliberately'.

Now while the Challenge Letter of 8 December 1870 certainly initiated a new stage in the history of the game, it may also have been the stimulus that prompted the English clubs to form their Rugby Union, for a letter over the names of the Blackheath and Richmond secretaries appeared on 26 December proposing a meeting of all rugby-playing clubs in order to produce an acceptable and uniform code of play. Such a meeting of 21 clubs took place in London on 26 January 1871, but the outcome was the formation of a Rugby Football Union with a constitution designed to produce and keep up to date the rules of the game and of the Union itself. The Committee of this Union duly produced a new set of Laws of play which were formally adopted at the first AGM in October 1871.

The Scottish clubs, who had worked by the Green Book since 1868, at once appreciated that this new code was more comprehensive and up-to-date, so accepted it by joining the new Union: West of Scotland, Glasgow Academicals and Edinburgh University in 1871 and Edinburgh Academicals, Royal High School FP and Edinburgh Wanderers in 1872. This immediate Scottish acceptance of the new Union as a Rule maker must be noted, and it could be recalled that a dispute over a try between Glasgow Academicals and West of Scotland in February 1870 had to be settled by referring the matter to the Editor of *Bell's Life in London*.

By November 1871 the Scottish clubs had received and accepted an invitation from the Rugby Football Union to repeat the International fixture in London and *The Scotsman* reported: 'It was now intended to make the event an annual affair to take place in Scotland and England alternately'. So the Scottish Committee met, arranged two trial games (rather ruined by the weather and the absence of nominated players) and eventually selected their XX. The Rugby Football Union asked each of their member clubs to nominate four players, reduced these to a pool of 40 and then ran two trials before picking their team, which at the Oval ground proved not only too heavy but too fit for their opponents.

Scotland once more included players from south of the Border: A. G. Colville (Blackheath), known as a very fast forward, adept at dribbling, was in again and there were three Army men in F. T. Maxwell, R. P. Maitland and H. W. Renny-Tailyour, the last two having made their names as fine back players while training at the R. M. A. Woolwich. This triggered off some discussion on the qualifications for inclusion in an International team: England favoured a residential basis but Scotland insisted on a birth qualification since they were losing so many players to business appointments down south, to the two Universities and to the Army. However, as we shall see this was a problem with so many facets that even today it is doubtful if a tidy answer has been found.

ENGLAND: 1 goal, 1 drop goal, 2 tries   Loss
SCOTLAND: 1 drop goal
Kennington Oval
5 February 1872

England: F. W. Mills (*Marl. Nomads*), W. O. Moberley (*Ravenscourt Park*), A. G. Guillemard (*West Kent*); H. Freeman (*Marl. Nomads*); J. E. Bendey (*Gipsies*), S. Finney (*RIEC*), P. Wilkinson (*Law Club*); T. Batson (*Blackheath*), J. A. Body (*Gipsies*), J. A. Bush (*Clifton*), F. I. Currey (*Marl. Nornads*), F. B. G. D'Aguilar (*Royal Engineers*), A. St. G. Hamersley (*Marl. Nomads*), F. W. Isherwood (*Ravenscourt Park*), F. Luscombe (*Gipsies*), J. E. H. Mackinlay (*St George's*), W. W. Pinching (*Guy's*), C. W. Sherrard (*Royal Engineers*), F. Stokes* (*Blackheath*), D. P. Turner (*Richmond*)
Scotland: W. D. Brown (*Glas. Acads.*), T. Chalmers (*Glas. Acads.*), L. M. Balfour (*Edin. Acads.*), T. R. Marshall (*Edin. Acads.*),

R. P. Maitland (*Royal Artillery*), J. W. Arthur (*Glas. Acads.*), W. Cross (*Glas. Acads.*), F. J. Moncreiff* (Edin. Acads.); J. W. Anderson (*West of Scot.*), E. M. Bannerman (*Edin. Acads.*), C. W. Cathcart (*Edin. Univ.*), A. G. Colville (*Merchistonians*), J. F. Finlay (*Edin. Acads.*), R. W. Irvine (*Edin. Acads.*), J. H. McClure (*West of Scot.*), J. L. H. Macfarlane (*Edin. Univ.*), W. Marshall (*Edin. Acads.*), F. T. Maxwell (*Royal Engineers*), J. A. W. Mein (*Edin. Acads.*), R. W. Renny-Tailyour (*Royal Engineers*)
Umpires: B. Hall Blyth, A. Rutter

C. W. Cathcart dropped a goal. A. St. C. Hamersley scored and F. W. Isherwood converted. (H. T.). H. Freeman dropped a goal. F. B. D'Aguilar scored and Isherwood failed. S. Finney scored and Isherwood failed.

Played in favourable weather before some 4000 spectators. The pitch measured 120 x 70 yards, an increase in width which suited the English backs. This year the English had prepared by several trial games and were much fitter than their opponents.

Scotland began well with a drop goal inside ten minutes but thereafter the English pack took charge. The nearest Scotland came to scoring again was from a free kick taken by L. M. Balfour from a 'fair catch' by T. Chalmers. The West Kent Club lent their goal posts and the touch lines were marked out by white flags borrowed from Union clubs. One Scot had his flannels torn off and was surrounded by the players until 'he was handed a macintosh in which he encased himself and amid considerable amusement repaired to the pavilion to obtain another garment'.

SCOTLAND: Nil   Draw
ENGLAND: Nil
Hamilton Crescent, Glasgow
3 March 1873

Scotland: J. L. P. Sanderson (*Edin. Acads.*), W. D. Brown (*Glas. Acads.*), T. Chalmers (*Glas. Acads.*); T. R. Marshall (*Edin. Acads.*), W. St. C. Grant (*Craigmount School*); G. B. McClure (*West of Scot.*), J. L. H. Macfarlane (*Edin. Univ.*), P. Anton (*St Andrews Univ.*) H. W. Allen (*Glas. Acads.*), E. M. Bannerman (*Edin. Acads.*), C. C. Bryce (*Glas. Acads.*), C. W. Cathcart (*Edin. Univ.*), J. P. Davidson (*RIEC*), R. W. Irvine (Edin. Acads.), J. A. W. Mein (*Edin. Acads.*), F. J . Moncreiff* (*Edin. Acads.*), A . G. Petrie (*RHSFP*), T. P. Whittington (*Merchistonians*), R. W. Wilson (*West of Scot.*), A. Wood (*RHSFP*)
England: F. W. Mills (*Marl. Nomads*), C. H. R. Vanderspar (*Richmond*), W. R. B. Fletcher (*Marl. Nornads*); H. Freeman (*Marl. Nornads*); C. W. Boyle (*Oxford Univ.*), S. Finney (*RIEC*), S. Morse (*Law Club*); J. A. Body (*Gipsies*), H. A. Bush (*Clifton*), E. C. Cheston (*Law Club*), A. St. G. Hamersley (*Marl. Nornads*), Hon. H. A. Lawrence (*Richmond*), F. Luscombe (*Gipsies*), J. E. H. Mackinlay (*St George's*), H. Marsh (*RIEC*), M. W. Marshall (*Blackheath*), C. H. Rickards (*Gipsies*), E. R. Still (*Oxford Univ.*), F. Stokes* (*Blackheath*), D. P. Turner (*Richmond*)
Umpires: B. Hall Blyth, A. G. Guillemard

A crowd of some 4000 saw the game played under the most disagreeable conditions for snow and frost had given way to heavy rain which fell throughout. There ensued a tremendous forward battle; the nearest to a score came from Freeman who, claiming a fair catch some 50 yards out, had a magnificent soaring drop kick which went so high that the umpires could only declare it 'a poster'.

Before the game the English players sent their boots to a local cobbler to have bars fixed to the soles. When the boots came back Boyle and Freeman found themselves one boot short and had to play with a dress boot on one foot.

A match card exists and shows Fletcher as a third back with Morse making a third half back.

ENGLAND: 1 drop goal   Loss
SCOTLAND: 1 try
Kennington Oval
23 February 1874

England: J. W. Batten (*Camb. Univ.*), M. J. Brooks (*Oxford Univ.*); H. Freeman (*Marl. Nomads*); W. H. Milton (*Marl. Nomads*), S. Morse (*Marl. Nomads*), W. E. Collins (*Old Cheltonians*); T. Batson (*Blackheath*), H. A. Bryden (*Clapham Rovers*), E. C. Cheston (*Richmond*), C. W. Cross (*Oxford Univ.*), F. L. Cunliffe (*RMA*), J. S. M. Genth (*Manchester*), A. St. G. Hamersley* (*Marl. Nomads*), E. Kewley (*Liverpool*), Hon. H. A. Lawrence (*Richmond*), M. W. Marshall (*Blackheath*), Hon. S. Parker

15

(*Liverpool*), W. F. H. Stafford (*RE*), D. P. Turner (*Richmond*), R. Walker (*Manchester*)
Scotland: W. D. Brown* (*Glas. Acads.*), T. Chalmers (*Glas. Acads.*); T. R. Marshall (*Edin. Acads.*),W. H. Kidston (*West of Scot.*), H. M. Hamilton (*West of Scot.*); W. St. C. Grant (*Craigmount School*), A. K. Stewart (*Edin. Univ.*); C. C. Bryce (*Glas. Acads.*), J. P. Davidson (*RIEC*), J. F. Finlay (*Edin. Acads.*), G. Heron (*Glas. Acads.*), R. W. Irvine (*Edin. Acads.*), J. A. W. Mein (*Edin. Acads.*), T. Neilson (*West of Scot.*), A. G. Petrie (*RHSFP*), J. Reid (*Edin. Wrs.*), J. K. Todd (*Glas. Acads.*), R. W. Wilson (*West of Scot.*), A. Wood (*RHSFP*), A. H. Young (*Edin. Acads.*)

J. F. Finlay scored but T. Chalmers failed. (H.T.). H. Freeman dropped a goal.

Another wet day for some 4000 spectators. Accidents to Macfarlane and Sanderson caused Scotland to alter their formation in the backs. One of the newcomers, A. K. Stewart, was noted as a pioneer of passing away from the mauls to the backs and during the day the 'chucking' between Stewart, Grant and Hamilton raised much comment. One report noted 'the Scotchmens' happy knack of "heeling" the ball out to their own quarterbacks several times stood them in good stead'.

Early on Stewart touched down between the posts, but the try was disallowed in the erroneous belief that he had played a dead ball. In the second half Morse nearly scored a field goal by kicking a rolling ball, but it was close to 'no side' when Freeman won the match with a tremendous drop kick estimated at 80 yards.

SCOTLAND: Nil   Draw
ENGLAND: Nil
Raeburn Place
8 March 1875

Scotland: W. D. Brown* (*Glas. Acads.*), T. Chalmers (*Glas. Acads.*); N. J. Finlay (*Edin. Acads.*), M. Cross (*Merchistonians*), H. M. Hamilton (*West of Scot.*); J. R. Hay-Gordon (*Edin. Acads.*), J. K. Tod (*Glas. Acads.*); A. Arthur (*Glas. Acads.*), J. W. Dunlop (*West of Scot.*), A. B. Finlay (*Edin. Acads.*), J. F. Finlay (*Edin. Acads.*), G. R. Fleming (*Glas. Acads.*), G. Heron (*Glas. Acads.*), R. W. Irvine (*Edin. Acads.*), A. Marshall (*Edin. Acads.*) J. A. W. Mein (*Edin. Acads.*), A. G. Petrie (*RHSFP*), J. Reid (*Edin. Wrs.*), D. Robertson (*Edin. Acads.*), A. Wood (*RHSFP*)
England: L. Birkett (*Clapham Rovers*), S. Morse (*Marl. Nomads*), A. W. Pearson (*Guy's*); W. A. D. Evanson (*Richmond*); W. E. Collins (*Old Cheltonians*), A. T. Mitchell (*Oxford Univ.*); F. R. Adams (*Richmond*), R. H. Birkett (*Clapham Rovers*), J. A. Bush (*Clifton*), E. C. Cheston (*Richmond*), W. R. B. Fletcher (*Oxford Univ.*), J. S. M. Genth (*Manchester*), H. J. Graham (*Wimbledon Hornets*), E. Kewley (*Liverpool*), Hon. H. A. Lawrence* (*Richmond*), F. Luscombe (*Gipsies*), M. W. Marshall (*Blackheath*), Hon. S. Parker (*Liverpool*), J. E. Paul (*RIEC*), D. P. Turner (*Richmond*)

A record crowd of 7000 watched in excellent conditions. The field had been increased to 130 x 85 yards. England had to make three changes, for R. Walker called off, whilst C. W. Cross and E. H. Nash were refused leave of absence by the Oxford University authorities. Ninian Finlay, who became one of the finest backs and drop kickers of his time, was still at school and joined his two brothers for this game. The Birketts were also brothers.

There were many near things, especially in the second half when the English backs continually dropped at goal. Finlay actually dropped a goal but it was disallowed 'because the ball had been called "down" by its possessor'. Once Cross fumbled a towering kick behind his line; Bush and Collins fell on him and claimed a touch down which, however, was not given. One account notes that R. H. Birkett came out of the maul and played in the backs.

ENGLAND: 1 goal, 1 try   Loss
SCOTLAND: Nil
Kennington Oval
6 March 1876

England: A. H. Heath (*Oxford Univ.*), A. W. Pearson (*Blackheath*); T. S. Tetley (*Bradford*), L. Stokes (*Blackheath*), R. H. Birkett (*Clapham Rovers*); W. E. Collins (*Old Cheltonians*), W. C. Hutchinson (*RIEC*); F. R. Adams (*Richmond*), J. A. Bush (*Clifton*), E. C. Cheston (*Richmond*), H. J. Graham (*Wimbledon Hornets*), W. Grey (*Manchester*), W. H. Hunt (*Preston Grasshoppers*), E. Kewley (*Liverpool*), F. H. Lee (*Oxford Univ.*), F. Luscombe* (*Gipsies*), M. W. Marshall (*Blackheath*), W. C. W. Rawlinson (*Blackheath*), G. R. Turner (*St George's*), R. Walker (*Manchester*)

16

Scotland: T. Chalmers (*Glas. Acads.*), J. S. Carrick (*West of Scot.*); M. Cross (*Glas. Acads.*), N. J. Finlay (*Edin. Acads.*); G. Q. Paterson (*Edin. Acads.*), A. K. Stewart (*Edin. Univ.*); A. Arthur (*Merchistonians*), W. H. Bolton (*West of Scot.*), N. T. Brewis (*Edin. Inst. FP*), C. W. Cathcart (*Edin. Univ.*), D. Drew (*Glas. Acads.*), G. R. Fleming (*Glas. Acads.*), J. H. S. Graham (*Edin. Acads.*), R. W. Irvine* (*Edin. Acads.*) J. E. Junor (*Glas. Acads.*), D. Lang (*Paisley*), A. G. Petrie (*RHSFP*), J. Reid (*Edin. Wrs.*),C. Villar (*Edin. Wrs.*), D. H. Watson (*Glas. Acads.*)
Referee: A. Rutter Umpires: H. M. Hamilton, C. D. Heatley

No scoring at half time. F. H. Lee scored and L. Stokes converted. W. E. Collins scored and L. Stokes failed.

About 4000 were present on a fine but cold and windy day. Early in the second half Scotland carried the ball inside the English 25 area and looked like scoring. However, Hutchinson seized a dropped pass and had a magnificent run to the Scottish 25 where he was tackled, but got a pass out to Lee who, noted for following up, was able to score between the posts. After this Watson was brought into the backs (his club position). This is the first team selection recorded in the SFU Minutes, and it had been decided to play six men behind the maul instead of the usual seven. R. H. Birkett had also started in the maul, but finished as a back. Scotland were outplayed at half where Stewart had dislocated a thumb and Paterson (8 st 12 lb) had not the physique to be effective in defence.

The Change to Fifteens

It is surprising to note that from 1846 when Rugby School first printed their Rules, no published set makes any mention of the number of players in a team until the Home Unions in their Rules of 1892 laid down: 'The game should be played by fifteen players on each side'.

Of course in the early days the public schools in their domestic games expected everyone to take part and in Scotland it was only after inter-scholastic matches began in 1858 that the playing of twenties became established. Right up to 1870 the schools were prepared to play twenties and the early Merchiston reports show their team structure to be: Goalkeepers four; Halfbacks four; Bulldogs twelve. One may recall the variations in numbers taking part in the Academical-University game of 1857-58 but the senior clubs, obviously short of players, soon settled down to play fifteens, generally placed as: Backs four; Half backs and Quarter backs two; Forwards nine. The letter file of the Edinburgh Academical FC for 1867 reveals that their Secretary was in touch with the West of Scotland FC asking: 'I presume you commence play about two. Please let me know as to this and also how many men you are to play'. He also wrote to Dr Almond at Loretto: 'I understand you used to play fifteen a side; please let me know if you still do so'.

Yet as we have seen the 1870 challenge to the English clubs suggested a game with twenties – a number that was finally accepted and maintained for the first six Internationals. However, the Scottish Football Union, after a Committee meeting in December 1875, wrote suggesting a change to fifteens but the Rugby Football Union decided that it was too late in the season to accept the proposal. The SFU repeated their suggestion after their AGM in October 1876 and this time the RFU agreed with the result that the English-Irish match at the Oval in February 1877 was the first to be played with fifteens. A fortnight later the Irish-Scottish match at Belfast saw Scotland field fifteen for the first time.

IRELAND: Nil Win
SCOTLAND: 4 goals, 2 drop goals, 2 tries
Ormeau, Belfast
19 February 1877

Ireland: H. Moore (*Windsor*), G. M. Shaw (*Windsor*); R. B. Walkington (*NIFC*), F. W. Kidd (*Lansdowne*); J. Heron (*NIFC*), T. G. Gordon (*NIFC*); W. H. Ash (*NIFC*), T. Brown (*Windsor*), H. L. Cox (*Dublin Univ.*), J. Currell (*NIFC*), W. Finlay (*NIFC*), H. C. Kelly (*NIFC*), J. A. Macdonald (*Windsor: Methodist Coll.*), H. W. Murray (*Dublin Univ.*), W. H. Wilson* (*Dublin Univ.*)
Scotland: H. H. Johnston (*Edin. Collegians*); M. Cross (*Glas. Acads.*), R. C. Mackenzie (*Glas. Acads.*); J. R. Hay Gordon (*Edin. Acads.*), E. J. Pocock (*Edin. Wrs.*); J. H. S. Graham (*Edin. Acads.*), R. W. Irvine* (*Edin. Acads.*), J. E. Junor (*Glas. Acads.*), D. Lang (*Paisley*), H. M. Napier (*West of Scot.*), A. G. Petrie (*RHSFP*), J. Reid (*Edin. Wrs.*), S. H. Smith (*Glas. Acads.*), C. Villar (*Edin. Wrs.*), D. H. Watson (*Glas. Acads.*)
Referee: A. Buchanan Umpires: A. R. Stewart, R. Bell

E. J. Pocock scored but Cross failed; R. C. Mackenzie dropped a goal: R. C. Mackenzie scored and Cross converted; (H.T.). R. C. Mackenzie dropped a goal; R. C. Mackenzie scored but Cross failed; R. W. Irvine scored and Cross converted; R. C. Mackenzie scored and Cross converted; J. Reid scored and Cross converted.

For this initial match against Ireland, Scotland for the first time played fifteen with a single fullback. There was a good attendance in spite of the unfavourable weather, rain falling throughout.

The Irish, averaging about a stone less, were outweighted and outplayed. Pocock (an Englishman educated at Clifton), a destructive runner against a weak defence, had a good match, but also note R. C. Mackenzie's tally of three tries and two drop goals.

The First Irish Matches

In 1877 Ireland had two Unions; the first, the Irish Football Union, being formed in Dublin in 1874 and the other, the Northern Football Union of Ireland, in Belfast in 1875. These two bodies, not without dissension, managed to cooperate and arrange matches against England, the third in February 1877 being the first ever to be played with XVs. The first against Scotland, also with XVs, was played in February 1877 but the offer of a return game in Glasgow in 1878 fell through because of further disagreements between the two Irish Unions who, however, eventually settled their differences by producing a single Irish Rugby Football Union during 1879 and this allowed the resumption of the fixture in that same year.

SCOTLAND: 1 drop goal Win
ENGLAND: Nil
Raeburn Place
5 March 1877

Scotland: J. S. Carrick (*Glas. Acads.*); H. H. Johnston (*Edin. Collegians*); M. Cross (*Glas. Acads.*), R. C. Mackenzie (*Glas. Acads.*); J. R. Hay Gordon (*Edin. Acads.*), E. I. Pocock (*Edin. Wrs.*); J. H. S. Graham (*Edin. Acads.*), R. W. Irvine* (*Edin. Acads.*), J. E. Junor (*Glas. Acads.*), H. M. Napier (*West of Scot.*), A. G. Petrie (*RHSFP*), J. Reid (*Edin. Wrs.*), T. J. Torrie (*Edin. Acads.*), C. Villar (*Edin. Wrs.*), D. H. Watson (*Glas. Acads.*)
England: L. Birkett (*Clapham Rovers*), A. W. Pearson (*Blackheath*); A. N. Hornby (*Preston Grasshoppers*), L. Stokes (*Blackheath*); W. A. D. Evanson (*Richmond*), P. L. A. Price (*Richmond*), C. C. Bryden (*Clapham Rovers*), H. W. T. Garnett (*Bradford*), G. Harrison (*Hull*), W. H. Hunt (*Preston Grasshoppers*), E. Kewley* (*Liverpool*), A. F. Law (*Richmond*), M. W. Marshall (*Blackheath*), R. Todd (*Manchester*), C. J. C. Touzell (*Camb. Univ.*)
Referee: W. Cross Umpire: A. Buchanan

No scoring at half time; M. Cross dropped a goal.

Scotland reverted to six behind the scrum to counter the strong running English backs. They held their own against the wind in the first half. Later the English were put under some pressure and only good defence by their backs prevented a score until close on time, when M. Cross dropped a great goal from near half way. Hay Gordon had a good match but Pocock, a good attacking player, proved too weak in defence so was put into the forwards, his place being taken by Watson who played half for his club.

ENGLAND: Nil   Draw
SCOTLAND: Nil
Kennington Oval
4 March 1878

England: A. W. Pearson (*Blackheath*), H. E. Kayll (*Sunderland*); L. Stokes (*Blackheath*), A. N. Hornby (Preston Grasshoppers); P. L. A. Price (*RIEC*), W. A. D. Evanson (*Richmond*); F. R. Adams (*Richmond*), J. M. Biggs (*Univ. Coll. Hospital*), H. Fowler (*Oxford Univ.*), F. D. Fowler (*RIEC*), E. T. Gurdon (*Richmond*), E. Kewley* (*Liverpool*), M. W. Marshall (*Blackheath*), G. T. Thomson (*Halifax*), G. F. Vernon (*Blackheath*)
Scotland: W. E. Maclagan (*Edin. Acads.*); M. Cross (*Glas. Acads.*), N. J. Finlay (*Edin. Acads.*); J. A. Campbell (*Merchiston Castle*), J. A. Neilson (*Glas. Acads.*); L. J. Auldjo (*Abertay*), N. T. Brewis (*Edin. Inst. FP*), J. H. S. Graham (*Edin. Acads.*), D. R. Irvine (*Edin. Acads.*), R. W. Irvine* (*Edin. Acads.*), J. E. Junor (*Glas. Acads.*), G. W. L. MacLeod (*Edin. Acads.*), H. M. Napier (*West of Scot.*), A. G. Petrie (*RHSFP*), S. H. Smith (*Glas. Acads.*)
Referee: A. G. Guillemard Umpires: A. R. Stewart, C. D. Heatley

Some 4000 watched in favourable weather. Scotland had the better of the first half; Campbell missing a scoring chance and Cross coming near with a drop. The call of half time halted a maul in goal between Napier and Pearson. Stokes was prominent in the second half narrowly missing a drop and scoring a try. Adams did touch down but the Scots had halted because of an infringement and the English captain 'was courteous enough to give way'. A score by Neilson was disallowed as he had picked up a dead ball. This was the last match played at the Oval.

IRELAND: Nil   Win
SCOTLAND: 1 goal, 1 drop goal, 1 try
Ormeau, Belfast
17 February 1879

Ireland: R. B. Walkington (*NIFC*), T. Harrison (*Cork*); R. N. Matier (*NIFC*), J. C. Bagot (*Dublin Univ.*); A. M. Whitestone (*Dublin Univ.*), W. J. Goulding (*Cork*); A. M. Archer (*Dublin Univ.*), W. E. A. Cummins (*QC Cork*), W. Finlay (*NIFC*), H. C. Kelly (*NIFC*), J. A. Macdonald (*Methodist Coll.*), W. C. Neville* (*Dublin Univ.*), H. Purdon (*NIFC*), G. Scriven (*Dublin Univ.*), J. W. Taylor (*NIFC*)
Scotland: W. E. Maclagan (*Edin. Acads.*), M. Cross (*Glas. Acads.*), N. J. Finlay (*Edin. Acads.*); W. H. Masters (*Edin. Inst. FP.*), I. A. Campbell (*Merchistonians*); R. Ainslie (*Edin. Inst. FP*), N. T. Brewis (*Edin. Inst. FP*), J. B. Brown (*Glas. Acads.*), J. H. S. Graham (*Edin. Acads.*), D. R. Irvine (*Edin. Acads.*), R. W. Irvine* (*Edin. Acads.*), H. M. Napier (*West of Scot.*), A. G. Petrie (*RHSFP*), E. R. Smith (*Edin. Acads.*), D. Somerville (*Edin. Inst. FP*)
Referee: Dr Chiene Umpires: A. R. Stewart, Mr Ball

J. B. Brown scored and M. Cross kicked a disputed goal. D. Somerville scored and M. Cross converted. (H.T.). M. Cross dropped a goal.

As Cross was about to convert Brown's try the Irish charged out and kicked the ball away, claiming that the rule concerning the taking out of the ball had been broken. After a long dispute Cross was allowed to take the kick but it was agreed to refer the matter to the Rugby Football Union who later decreed that the Irish action was correct. Apparently Irvine had lifted the ball to bring it out for the place kick and Cross took it out of his hands to show him the position in which it was to be held. The Irish maintained that under Rule 55 they could charge the instant that Irvine was about to place the ball since the kicker had also handled it.

The Scottish pack was too strong and Masters had a great game, being 'busy from start to finish'.

SCOTLAND: 1 drop goal   Draw
ENGLAND: 1 goal
Raeburn Place
10 March 1879

Scotland: W. E. Maclagan (*Edin. Acads.*); M. Cross (*Glas. Acads.*), N. J. Finlay (*Edin. Acads.*); J. A. Campbell (*Glas. Acads.*), J. A. Neilson (*Glas. Acads.*); R. Ainslie (*Edin. Inst. FP*), N. T. Brewis (*Edin. Inst. FP*), J. B. Brown (*Glas. Acads.*), E. N. Ewart (*Glas. Acads.*), J. H. S. Graham (*Edin. Acads.*), D. R. Irvine (*Edin. Acads.*), R. W. Irvine* (*Edin. Acads.*), J. E. Junor (*Glas. Acads.*), H. M. Napier (*West of Scot.*), A. G. Petrie (*RHSFP*)

England: H. Buth (*Huddersfield*), W J. Penney (*United Hospitals*); L. Stokes (*Blackheath*); W. A. D. Evanson (*Richmond*), H. H. Taylor (*St George's*); F. R. Adams* (*Richmond*), A. Budd (*Blackheath*), G. W. Burton (*Blackheath*), F. D. Fowler (*Manchester*), G. Harrison (*Hull*), N. F. McLeod (*RIEC*), S. Neame (*Old Cheltonians*), H. C. Rowley (*Manchester*), H. Springmann (*Liverpool*), R. Walker (*Manchester*).

Referee: G. R. Fleming Umpires: A. Buchanan, J. Maclaren

G. W. Burton scored and L. Stokes converted; (H.T.). N. J. Finlay dropped a goal.

This, the first contest for the beautiful Calcutta Cup, was watched in dull weather by a record crowd of 10,000. England, with the wind, started strongly. Their backs ran well and Stokes' drop kicking continually landed play near the Scottish line but powerful play by their pack returned play to the English half. Unfortunately on one occasion Cross miskicked and gave an easy run in for Burton. In the second half the Scottish pack again drove the ball down to the goal line only to be thwarted by a back stepping deliberately behind and touching down, a move that was loudly hissed by the crowd 'not because it lost a rare chance to Scotland but that it showed a want of pluck not normal with Britons'! However, later, both Stokes and Maclagan were loudly cheered for running the ball from behind the posts into play. The Scottish pack continued their pressure and eventually a passing run by Graham, Petrie and Ewart got the ball to Finlay who, although tackled near the line, managed to drop a goal. Throughout the match Maclagan's tackling was ferocious and he undoubtedly halted several scoring runs by the English backs.

A Decade of Development 1870-1880

At the beginning of this period play was largely confined to the forwards who, whenever play was halted, put the ball down in the middle of a maul and tried to force it forward through the mass. With 26 forwards involved this was almost entirely a matter of blind shoving enlivened by some hearty hacking if the ball was seen or felt at the feet. Once XVs were established there gradually developed a habit of stooping in the mauls so that the ball could be watched and be better controlled.

The quarter backs (the English term of half back was adopted at the turn of the century), usually two in number, stood some five yards back from the scrum, one on either side, watching for the ball to emerge. The player had then to swoop on to the ball, pick it up and make a run, finishing with a kick if his way was blocked and he had not been tackled. So the quarter backs had to be fast, alert players who did the bulk of the running and scoring.

The backs were basically defenders, tackling the runners or fielding the kicks and replying with a return kick. If circumstances were favourable they would drop at goal: N. J. Finlay, H. Freeman and L. Stokes were all famous for their successful long range drops at goal. Practically every kick was taken as a drop and indeed spectators were given to barracking a punt! The earlier, less pointed shape of the ball favoured both drop kicking and close dribbling but tended to slow up swift directed passing. In fact, an intentional long pass was sometimes achieved by throwing a ball that could be taken on the bounce.

The number and positioning of the back players also varied at this time but it appears that both countries up to 1876 played seven behind the maul. There is an SFU committee minute of 1876 which records their decision to play six behind in the approaching English match instead of seven as on previous occasions. However, during the actual game D. H. Watson was brought out of the forwards to play as a back, his usual club position. England frequently stationed one of their three full backs in a forward position as a three quarter back.

By 1880 the lowering of the heads in the mauls accompanied by linking with the arms had produced important variations in the manner of play. Thus instead of always trying to force the ball forward through the scrum, the players would steer it to the side (there was as yet no set scrum formation) and then break away in a dribbling rush. The Blackheath pack were famed for this wheeling manoeuvre while in Edinburgh the Merchiston forwards were constantly praised for their combined play which included fast breaking as a mass from the mauls.

The moving of the ball to the edge of the scrum produced another much debated trick. The *Lorettonian*, during 1880, commenting on the Fettes games notes: 'Just before the match began our Captain was informed by theirs that they played heeling out on their ground' (and later) 'I noticed a great deal of hoicking done by the Fettes forwards, that is, going to the side of the scrummage, thrusting in one leg and hoicking out the ball with it for the quarter back.' The Fettes captain concerned was A. R. Don Wauchope who, although one of the greatest individual scoring quarter backs of his age, was also deeply concerned to develop combined play amongst the college backs so naturally he had good reasons to get the ball back out of the scrums.

Such closer co-operation between the back players only became feasible after the schools began to use a formation of one full back three halves and two quarters. This set-up has been credited to the Fettes team of 1878-79 who took R. A. Carruthers out of the forwards into the backs to strengthen the defence against two dangerous Academy halves (A. P. Reid and F. T. Wright), but in fact both Merchiston and Fettes had experimented with the added half back during the previous season while the Academy and Loretto followed their example by 1880. Curiously enough it was at Loretto where deliberate attacking passing really began and developed. In the early '70s passing was despised as it rather suggested a lack of moral fibre in the passer. *The Scotsman*, reporting on an Academy-Loretto game in 1869, comments 'The Loretto players made some determined runs but were invariably collared and almost suffered their heads to be wrenched off ere they would deliver up the ball'. It was Almond, their Headmaster, who began the transformation.

A. S. Blair, a Blue in the Oxford XV of 1884, while discussing the part played by H. Vassall in producing a running game at Oxford during the early '80s, wrote: 'I have always thought it scarcely accurate to call Vassall the inventor of the modern game. To my mind he was rather the great genius who thought out and worked out for his own team ideas which already existed ... He was in truth the master builder, but without the straw he could not have made the bricks ... If by the modern game is meant the present fast open game with its quick passing, kicking and breaking up, I am inclined to think that Dr Almond... was perhaps the real inventor. At any rate most Lorettonians who were at School in the latter '70s and early '80s have vivid recollections of Almond in his quintuple capacity of Headmaster, captain, forward, umpire and coach, rushing about the field crying out to his boys "Pass, pass, pass," and "Kick, kick, kick" and there can be no doubt whatever that much of the phenomenal success of the Oxford teams in the early '80s was due to the Old Lorettonians in those teams.' As a matter of fact the Oxford XV of 1880 contained five Blues from Loretto while the 1884 team had seven, but while credit must be given to those from Loretto who brought their background of combined play, it must also be admitted that they found themselves in the company of gifted players who, realising its virtues, were at once able to adopt this new style of play. In particular there was A. Rotherham who arrived to partner the Lorettonian, A. G. G. Asher, at quarter back for three seasons, during which time that pair played a tremendous part in establishing the Oxford teams as the exponents of a new and superior style of aggressive, running rugby. One result of this was that the new style was taken up earlier by the English clubs than by the Scottish.

SCOTLAND: 1 goal, 2 drop goals, 2 tries   Win
IRELAND: Nil
Hamilton Crescent
14 February 1880

Scotland: W. E. Maclagan (*Edin. Acads.*); M. Cross (*Glas. Acads.*), N. J. Finlay (*Edin. Acads.*); W. H. Masters (*Edin. Inst. FP*), W. S. Brown (*Edin. Inst. FP*); R. Ainslie (*Edin. Inst. FP*), N. T. Brewis (*Edin. Inst. FP*), J. B. Brown (*Glas. Acads.*), E. N. Ewart (*Glas. Acads.*), J. H. S. Graham (*Edin. Acads.*), R. W. Irvine* (*Edin. Acads.*), D. McCowan (*West of Scot.*), A. G. Petrie (*RHSFP*), C. R. Stewart (*West of Scot.*), J. G. Tait (*Edin. Acads.*)
Ireland: R. B. Walkington (*NIFC*); J. C. Bagot (*Dublin Univ.*), T. Harrison (*Cork*); M. Johnston (*Dublin Univ.*), W. T. Heron (*NIFC*); A. P. Cronyn (*Lansdowne*), J. L. Cuppaidge (*Dublin Univ.*), W. Finlay (*NIFC*), A. J. Forrest (*Wanderers*), R. W. Hughes (*NIFC*), H. C. Kelly* (*NIFC*), A. Millar (*Kingston*), G. Scriven (*Dublin Univ.*), J. W. Taylor (*NIFC*), W. A. Wallis (*Wanderers*)
Referee: A Buchanan Umpires: H. W. Little, Dr Neville

N. J. Finlay dropped two goals; W. H. Masters scored and M. Cross converted (H.T.). E. N. Ewart scored two tries which Cross failed to convert.

The favourable weather suited the Scottish backs, Masters and Brown being especially brilliant, but it was the forwards who were highly praised for their rare combined play, dribbling and passing. The first try came from 'some of the prettiest chucking probably ever seen in Scotland', for the ball was passed via Stewart, Petrie, Graham and Ainslie to Brewis, who left Masters a clear run in. Ewart's two scores also came from strong forward play. In the first half Finlay dropped what appeared to be a second goal. The Irish disputed this and the umpires and referee were appealed to. Both umpires said they did not see the point and the referee thought it was a clear goal and it appears to have been accepted. However, the score was disallowed pending an appeal to the SFU. This was the first International match to be played on a Saturday.

ENGLAND: 2 goals, 3 tries   Loss
SCOTLAND: 1 goal
Whalley Range, Manchester
28 February 1880

England: T. W. Fry (*Queen's House*); L. Stokes* (*Blackheath*), C. M. Sawyer (*Broughton*); R. T. Finch (*Camb. Univ.*), H. H. Taylor (*St George's*); G. W. Burton (*Blackheath*), C. H. Coates (*Camb. Univ.*), C. Gurdon (*Richmond*), E. T. Gurdon (*Richmond*), G. Harrison (*Hull*), S . Neame (*Old Cheltonians*), C. Phillips (*Oxford Univ.*), H. C. Rowley (*Manchester*), G. F. Vernon (*Blackheath*), R. Walker (*Manchester*)
Scotland: W. E. Maclagan (*Edin. Acads.*); N. J. Finlay (*Edin. Acads.*), M. Cross (*Glas. Acads.*); W. H. Masters (*Edin. Inst. FP*), W. S. Brown (*Edin. Inst. FP*); R. Ainslie (*Edin. Inst. FP*), N. T. Brewis (*Edin. Inst. FP*), J. B. Brown (*Glas. Acads.*), D. Y. Cassels (*West of Scot.*), E. N. Ewart (*Glas. Acads.*), J. H. S. Graham (*Edin. Acads.*), R. W. Irvine* (*Edin. Acads.*); D. Macowan (*West of Scot.*); A. G. Petrie (*RHSFP*); C. R Stewart (*West of Scot.*)
Referee: A. G. Guillemard Umpires: A. R. Stewart, J. McLaren

H. H. Taylor scored twice but L. Stokes failed to convert. (H.T.). T. W. Fry scored and L. Stokes converted; W. S. Brown scored and M. Cross converted; E. T. Gurdon and G. W. Burton scored, L. Stokes converted the latter try.

This was the first English match to be played on a Saturday and the change to a venue in the north was a success. The conditions were reasonable and with the breeze in the first half the Scots had four near misses with drops but the somewhat slippery conditions affected the Scots backs more than the English whose superiority brought them five tries, one being the first to be run in by a full back.

This was 'Bulldog' Irvine's tenth successive, and last, match against England.

IRELAND: 1 drop goal   Loss
SCOTLAND: 1 try
Ormeau, Belfast
19 February 1881

Ireland: R. E. McLean (*Dublin Univ.*); J. C. Bagot (*Dublin Univ.*), W. W. Pike (*Kingstown*); M. Johnston (*Dublin Univ.*), H. F. Spunner (*Wanderers*); D. R. Browning (*Wanderers*), A. J. Forrest* (*Wanderers*), R. W. Hughes (*NIFC*), J. Johnston (*Belfast Albion*), J. A. Macdonald (*Methodist Coll.*), A. R. McMullan (*Cork*), H. B. Morell (*Dublin Univ.*), H. Purdon (*NIFC*), J. W. Taylor (*NIFC*), W. A. Wallis (*Wanderers*)
Scotland: T. A. Begbie (*Edin. Wrs.*); W. E. Maclagan (*Edin. Acads.*), N. J. Finlay (*Edin. Acads.*), R. C. Mackenzie (*Glas. Acads.*); J. A. Campbell (*Glas. Acads.*), P. W. Smeaton (*Edin. Acads.*); R. B. Allan (*Glas. Acads.*), J. B. Brown (*Glas. Acads.*), D. Y. Cassels (*West of Scot.*), J. H. S. Graham* (*Edin. Acads.*), J. E. Junor (*Glas. Acads.*), D. McCowan (*West of Scot.*), C. Reid (*Edin. Academy*), G. H. Robb (*Glas. Univ.*), A. Walker (*West of Scot.*)

No scoring at half time; J. H. S. Graham scored but T. A. Begbie failed; J. C. Bagot dropped a goal.

This match, the first International win by Ireland, is best told by quoting Jacques McCarthy, an Irish reporter with a colourful turn of phrase:

'They commenced fiercely but after Spunner and big Jock Graham had gotten black eyes, and a certain hot Scotsman had come second best out of an independent boxing match with Browning, milder methods were adopted. No tangible score was gained in the first half, but in the second McMullen making a miscatch at a long kick (... from Maclagan) placed the whole of the Scottish team onside, and Graham, who was leaning against the Irish goal post, rubbing his shin after a recent hack, leisurely limped over and touched the ball down ... some slight relief was forthcoming when Begbie missed the kick which was as easy as possible .... Only five minutes remained ... Taylor got possession after a drop out and ran and worried his way amidst frantic exhortations up to the Scottish 25 where he passed to Johnston who returned him the leather on the very verge of the Scottish line. Here it was heeled out to Johnston who amidst vociferous profanity missed his pick-up and Campbell shot the ball into touch ten yards down. Hughes, however, rapidly realised the situation and threw it out to Taylor before the Scotsmen could line up, and Taylor transferred to

Johnston, who quicker than you could think or write tossed to Bagot who dropped the ball over the goal.'

By 1880 club rivalries were well established and there was none fiercer than that between the Royal High School FPs and the Edinburgh Academicals which of course stemmed from the foundation of the Academy in 1824. Referring to some of their earlier matches a sports article in 1889 noted: 'It was never quite clear what the football was brought onto the field for, as after the first kick most of the players forgot it was there and they are said to have marched off the field one time and left the ball behind them'. (This must remind one of the spectator at the Hawick-Gala game who gave vent to the appeal 'Never mind the ba', get on wi' the game'.)

So when the XV to meet Ireland in 1881 was announced and it was seen that the captaincy held for the previous five years by R. W. Irvine had been passed to a relatively new cap in his clubmate, J. H. S. Graham, the indignation in certain areas that the senior cap in the High Scholar, A. G. Petrie, had been passed over, was tremendous. Phillips wrote that the lads met in crowds in their howffs and vented their displeasure on the Union. The outcome was a Special General Meeting which called for the resignation of the Union Committee, but after some considerable discussion the motion was withdrawn, the Committee having made some concessions which included a suggestion that the XV should be allowed to chose its own captain.

The affair then died down but there were two repercussions. Firstly the strong High School, Edinburgh Institution and Edinburgh University forward choices withdrew from the XV which lost to Ireland for the first time. Then at the next AGM of the Union there were wholesale changes in the Committee headed by the election of A. G. Petrie to the Presidency.

SCOTLAND: 1 goal, 1 try   Draw
ENGLAND: 1 drop goal, 1 try
Raeburn Place
19 March 1881

Scotland: T. A. Begbie (*Edin. Wrs.*); W. E. Maclagan (*Edin. Acads.*), N. J. Finlay (*Edin. Acads.*), R. C. Mackenzie (*Glas. Acads.*); A. R. Don Wauchope (*Camb. Univ.*), J. A. Campbell (*Glas. Acads.*); R. Ainslie (*Edin. Inst. FP*), T. Ainslie (*Edin. Inst. FP*), J. B. Brown (*Glas. Acads.*), J. W. Fraser (*Edin. Inst. FP*), J. H. S. Graham* (*Edin. Acads.*), D. McCowan (*West of Scot*), R. Maitland (*Edin. Inst. FP*), W. A. Peterkin (*Edin. Univ.*), C. Reid (*Edin. Acadamy*)

England: A. N. Hornby (*Manchester*); R. Hunt (*Manchester*), L. Stokes* (*Blackheath*); F. T. Wright (*Edin. Academy*), H. C. Rowley (*Manchester*); A. Budd (*Blackheath*), G. W. Burton (*Blackheath*), C. H. Coates (*Leeds*), C. W. L. Fernandes (*Leeds*), H. Fowler (*Walthamstow*), C. Gurdon (*Richmond*), E. T. Gurdon (*Richmond*), W. W. Hewitt (*Queen's House*), C. Phillips (*Birkenhead Park*), H. Vassall (*Oxford Univ.*)

Referee: C. H. Watson Umpires: J. Reid, J. McLaren

R. Ainslie scored but T. A. Begbie failed; (H.T.). L. Stokes dropped a goal; H. C. Rowley scored but L. Stokes failed; J. B. Brown scored and T. A. Begbie converted.

This match was twice postponed and J. E. Junor missed a cap as he had left for India. H. H . Taylor reported to the wrong station, saw no team mates and so went home. F. T. Wright, still at the Edinburgh Academy, was pulled into the team to replace him, so the Edinburgh Academy had two pupils playing in this match.

A temporary stand had been erected and 12,000 watched a fast and open game in good conditions. Scotland with the wind had the better of the first half but England, playing with ten forwards, dominated the second half.

R. Ainslie, who played magnificently both in defence and attack, opened the scoring but Begbie, taking a difficult kick, hit the post. C. Reid got over the line but lost a maul in goal to three opponents. Right on half time Campbell touched down at the north-east corner but the score was disputed and eventually yielded because he had knocked the corner flag down.

Midway through the second half L. Stokes dropped a historic 80 yards goal from the touchline sixteen yards inside his own half and then Rowley scored an unconverted try. Right on time Finlay broke away and after a long run dropped at goal but missed. J. B. Brown followed up, got the ball and although tackled, managed to touch down for Begbie to save the match by converting. This score was also disputed as some of the opponents raised a question of off-side but the claim was not accepted. This score rankled, for the President of the Rugby Football Union at their AGM was reported as saying 'They certainly did not win the Scotch match but that was no fault of theirs, for they sent a team that was fairly strong, but the Scotch team was strong also, their strength being in umpiring. Since that match, however, they had made such representation to the Scotch authorities that they hoped in future to have unbiassed referees who understood their duties.' Needless to say this more than upset the Scottish committee and some acrimonious correspondence followed but it must be noted that a neutral referee officiated for the first time in the 1882 game.

SCOTLAND: 2 tries   Win
IRELAND: Nil
Hamilton Crescent
18 February 1882

Scotland: T. Anderson (*Merchiston Castle*); W. E. Maclagan (*Edin. Acads.*), F. Hunter (*Edin. Univ.*); W. S. Brown (*Edin. Inst. FP*), A. G. G. Asher (*Oxford Univ.*); R. Ainslie* (*Edin. Inst. FP*), T. Ainslie (*Edin. Inst. FP*), J. B. Brown (*Glas. Acads.*), D. Y. Cassels (*West of Scot.*), A. F. C. Gore (*London Scot.*), D. McCowan (*West of Scot.*),G. W. L. McLeod (*Edin. Wrs.*), R. Maitland (*Edin. Inst. FP*), C. Reid (*Edin. Acads.*), D. Somerville (*Edin. Inst. FP*)
Ireland: R. B. Walkington (*NIFC*); R. E. McLean (*Dublin Univ.*), J. R. Atkinson (*Dublin Univ.*), J. W. R. Morrow (*QC Belfast*); W. W. Fletcher (*Kingstown*), J. Pedlow (*Bessbrook*); J. B. Buchanan (*Dublin Univ.*), W. Finlay (*NIFC*), R. W. Hughes (*NIFC*), J. Johnston (*Albion*), J. A. Macdonald (*Methodist Coll.*), R. Nelson (*QC Belfast*), A. C. O'Sullivan (*Dublin Univ.*), G. Scriven (*Dublin Univ.*), J. W. Taylor* (*NIFC*)
Referee: A. G. Petrie Umpires: W. Cross, R. D. Bell

W. S. Brown scored. (H.T.). D. McCowan scored; T. Anderson failed with both kicks.

The Irish team was weakened by some eight withdrawals yet managed to make a very even game of it . Scotland were clearly superior at quarter back where Asher had a good attacking match and Brown scored a typical solo try following on a forward rush. Tom Anderson, then nearly nineteen years old, was still at Merchiston and in September was capped for a Scottish Cricket Xl v. Australians.

ENGLAND: Nil   Win
SCOTLAND: 2 tries
Whalley Range, Manchester
4 March 1882

England: A. N. Hornby* (*Manchester*); E. Beswick (*Swinton*), W. N. Bolton (*Blackheath*); H. H. Taylor (*Blackheath*), J. H. Payne (*Broughton*); C. H. Coates (*York Wrs.*), H. G. Fuller (*Camb. Univ.*), C. Gurdon (*Richmond*), E. T. Gurdon (*Richmond*), J. T. Hunt (*Manchester*), P. A. Newton (*Blackheath*), H. C. Rowley (*Manchester*), W. M. Tatham (*Oxford Univ.*), G. T. Thomson (*Halifax*), H. Vassall (*Oxford Univ.*)
Scotland: J. P. Veitch (*RHSFP*); W. E. Maclagan (*Edin. Acads.*), A. Philp (*Edin. Inst. FP*); W. S . Brown (*Edin. Inst. FP*), A . R. Don Wauchope (*Camb. Univ.*); R. Ainslie (*Edin. Inst. FP*), T. Ainslie (*Edin. Inst. FP*), J. B. Brown (*Glas. Acads.*), D. Y. Cassels* (*West of Scot.*), D. McCowan (*West of Scot.*), R. Maitland (*Edin. Inst. FP*), C. Reid (*Edin. Acads.*), A. Walker (*West of Scot.*), J. G. Walker (*West of Scot.*), W. A. Walls (*Glas. Acads.*)
Referee: Mr Robinson (*Ireland*) Umpires: J. H. S. Graham, J. Maclaren

R. Ainslie scored a try in each half; J. G. Walker failed with both kicks.

This was the first match in which a neutral referee officiated and it was the first away win between the two countries. The game was badly interfered with, and nearly abandoned because of the spectators encroaching on the field. In the first half R. Ainslie took a pass from Don Wauchope and rushing against the crowd, managed to ground the ball over the goal line. The crowd were partly responsible for preventing J. H. Payne from scoring. The Scottish forwards were in tremendous form on a heavy greasy pitch and they fairly upset the strong English backs in the loose. R. Ainslie had a field day with two tries and also dealt severely with W. N. Bolton whenever he got on the move. A goal by Maclagan from a free kick was successfully disputed on the ground that he had not properly made his mark when claiming the free kick.

SCOTLAND: 3 goals   Win
WALES: 1 goal
Raeburn Place
8 January 1883

Scotland: D. W. Kidston (*Glas. Acads.*); W. E. Maclagan (*London Scot.*), D. J. McFarlan (*London Scot..*); A. R. Don Wauchope (*Camb. Univ.*), W. S. Brown (*Edin. Inst. FP*); T. Ainslie (*Edin. Inst. FP*), J. B. Brown (*Glas. Acads.*), D. Y. Cassels* (*West of Scot.*), J. Jamieson (*West of Scot.*), J. G. Mowat (*Glas. Acads.*), C. Reid (*Edin . Acads.*), D. Somerville (*Edin. Inst. FP*), A. Walker (*West of Scot.*), J. G. Walker (*West of Scot.*), W. A. Walls (*Glas. Acads.*)
Wales: C. P. Lewis* (*Llandovery*); C. H. Newman (*Newport*), W. B. Norton (*Cardiff*); W. F. Evans (*Rhymney*), G. F. Harding (*Newport*); A. Cattell (*Llanelli*), T. J. S. Clapp (*Newport*), R. Gould (*Newport*), A. Griffen (*Edin. Univ.*), J. A. Jones (*Cardiff*), T. B. Jones (*Newport*), J. H. Judson (*Llandovery*), H. S. Lyne (*Newport*), G. L . Morris (*Swansea*), F. T. Purdon (*Swansea*)
Referee: G. Rowland Hill (*England*)   **Umpires:** W. Cross, Mr Mullock

D. J. McFarlan scored and Maclagan converted. (H.T.). A. R. Don Wauchope and D. J. McFarlan scored and Maclagan converted both; J. H. Judson scored and C. P. Lewis converted.

The first Welsh match was played on a hard pitch before some 4000 spectators. Some confusion exists over R. H. Bridie (who came to Swansea from Greenock). He was selected for Wales, is named in one report but really seems to have been replaced by W. B. Norton. This is the first match where Wales played with a single full back. J. G. Walker and A. R. Don Wauchope were playing for the Fettesian-Lorettonians on Saturday, 6 January. Wauchope had a good game, his famous dodging play producing two tries, but J. G. Walker had to go off with a twisted knee within fifteen minutes of the start. Near the end a fine run by T. J. S. Clapp saw the ball pass to Gould, Cattell and Judson who scored.

IRELAND: Nil   Win
SCOTLAND: 1 goal, 1 try
Ormeau, Belfast
17 February 1883

Ireland: J. W. R. Morrow (QC *Belfast*); *W. W.* Pike (*Kingstown*), R. E. McLean (*NIFC*); S. R. Collier (*QC Belfast*), A. M. Whitestone (*Dublin Univ.*); S. A. M. Bruce (*NIFC*), F. S. Heuston (*Kingstown*), R. W. Hughes (*NIFC*), H. King (*Dublin Univ.*), J. A. Macdonald (*Methodist Coll .*), D. F. Moore (*Wanderers*), R. Nelson (*QC Belfast*), G. Scriven* (*Dublin Univ.*), J. W. Taylor (*NIFC*), W. A. Wallis (*Wanderers*)
Scotland: J. P Veitch (*RHSFP*); W. E. Maclagan (*London Scot.*), M. F. Reid (*Loretto School*); P. W. Smeaton (*Edin. Acads.*), G. R. Aitchison (*Edin. Wrs.*); T. Ainslie (*Edin. Inst. FP*), J. B. Brown (*Glas. Acads.*), D. Y. Cassels* (*West of Scot.*), J. Jamieson (*West of Scot.*), D. McCowan (*West of Scot.*), W. A. Peterkin (*Edin. Univ.*), C. Reid (*Edin. Acads.*), D. Somerville (*Edin. Inst. FP*), A. Walker (*West of Scot.*), W. A. Walls (*Glas. Acads.*)

No scoring at half-time; C. Reid and D. Somerville scored; W. E. Maclagan converted the second.

A dreadful week of rain had turned the pitch into a sea of slush and water and both players and spectators were well nigh blinded with the liquid mud flung up from the scrimmages. By the finish no one tried to pick up the ball but aimed flying kicks at it. Initially there was little between the sides but Ireland were terribly handicapped by injuries – Morrow was concussed and carried off, Wallis and Macdonald had to go off and Whitestone and Scriven finished quite crippled. Maclagan's defence was much praised. M. F. Reid, who was still at Loretto, was a very late replacement for D. J. McFarlan.

SCOTLAND: 1 try   Loss
ENGLAND: 2 tries
Raeburn Place
3 March 1883

Scotland: D. W. Kidston (*Glas. Acads.*); W. E. Maclagan (*London Scot.*), M. F. Reid (*Loretto School*); P. W. Smeaton (*Edin. Acads.*), W. S. Brown (*Edin. Inst. FP*), T. Ainslie (*Edin. Inst. FP*), J. B. Brown (*Glas. Acads.*), D. Y. Cassels* (*West of Scot.*), J. Jamieson (*West of Scot.*), D. McCowan (*West of Scot.*), J. G. Mowat (*Glas. Acads.*), C. Reid (*Edin. Acads.*), D. Somerville (*Edin. Inst. FP*), A. Walker (*West of Scot.*), W. A. Walls (*Glas. Acads.*)
England: H. B. Tristram (*Oxford Univ.*); W. N. Bolton (*Blackheath*), A. M. Evanson (*Richmond*), C. G. Wade (*Oxford Univ.*); A. Rotherham (*Oxford Univ.*), J. H. Payne (*Broughton*); H. G. Fuller (*Camb. Univ.*), C. Gurdon (*Richmond*), E. T. Gurdon* (*Richmond*), R. S. F. Henderson (*Blackheath*), E. J. Moore (*Oxford Univ.*), R. M. Pattison (*Camb. Univ.*), W. M. Tatham (*Oxford Univ.*), G. T. Thomson (*Halifax*), C. S. Wooldridge (*Oxford Univ.*)
Referee: Mr Kelly (*Ireland*)   **Umpires:** J. H. S. Graham: J. S. McLaren

A. Rotherham scored but J. H. Payne failed. (H.T.). C. Reid scored but W. E. Maclagan failed; W. N. Bolton scored but A. M. Evanson failed.

England, with seven Oxford men in the team played six backs against Scotland's five so that the game rather resolved itself into a trial between a fine fast-dribbling pack and backs who put on 'an exhibition of passing the like of which has never previously been seen here'. Rotherham, who did so much to establish the new passing style of play at Oxford, saw to it that the forwards slipped the ball out of the side of the scrum and that his backs were given the ball to run with. Scotland, without Don Wauchope and McFarlan, were weak at back but Maclagan, although not fully fit, showed what a tremendous defender he could be and England only led by a try at half time. After the restart C. Reid, who was really outstanding as a forward, scored a try which was disputed but eventually granted but a great solo run by the powerful Bolton produced the winning try. This score or the kick at goal was surprisingly hissed by the spectators – an action which produced an apology from an angry Scottish President at the evening dinner. W. S. Brown and P. W. Smeaton both took the ball over the line but did not get the score – a decision that Smeaton never accepted!

WALES: Nil   Win
SCOTLAND: 1 drop goal, 1 try
Rodney Parade, Newport
12 January 1884

Wales: C. P. Lewis (*Llandovery*); C. P. Allen (*Beaumaris*), C. G. Taylor (*Ruabon*), W. B. Norton (*Cardiff*); C. H. Newman* (*Newport*), W. H. Gwynn (*Swansea*); F. G. Andrews (*Swansea*), T. J. S. Clapp (*Newport*), R. Gould (*Newport*), T. B. Jones (*Newport*), H. S. Lyne (*Newport*), F. L. Margrave (*Llanelli*), G. L. Morris (*Swansea*), W. D. Phillips (*Cardiff*), H. J. Simpson (*Cardiff*)
Scotland: J. P. Veitch (*RHSFP*), W. E. Maclagan* (*London Scot.*), D. J. McFarlan (*London Scot.*), G. C. Lindsay (*Fet.-Lor.*); A. R. Don Wauchope (*Fet.-Lor.*), A. G. G. Asher (*Oxford Univ.*); T. Ainslie (*Edin. Inst. FP*), J. B. Brown (*Glas. Acad.*), J. Jamieson (*West of Scot.*), R. Maitland (*Edin. Inst. FP*), W. A. Peterkin (*Edin. Univ.*), C. Reid (*Edin. Acads.*), D. Somerville (*Edin. Inst. FP*), J. Tod (*Watsonians*), W. A. Walls (*Glas. Acads.*)
Referee: J. S. McLaren (*England*)   **Umpires:** J. A. Gardner, R. Mullock

No scoring at half time; A. G. G. Asher dropped a goal; T. Ainslie scored but McFarlan failed.

From a line out Reid passed to Asher who dropped a splendid goal from near half way. Don Wauchope, who played brilliantly throughout, had a typical run to near the line where he was tackled but got the ball away to Ainslie who scored at the corner. Both scores were disputed but not cancelled. The two Scottish quarter backs were in great form, and Maclagan's defence was very sound. Gwynn did well 'playing the passing game'. This match was originally meant to be played a week earlier.

SCOTLAND: 2 goals, 2 tries   Win
IRELAND: 1 try
Raeburn Place
16 February 1884

Scotland: J. P. Veitch (*RHSFP*); W. E. Maclagan* (*London Scot.*), E. T. Roland (*Edin. Wrs.*), D. F. McFarlan (*London Scot.*); A. R. Don Wauchope (*Fet.-Lor.*), A. G. G. Asher (*Oxford Univ.*); T. Ainslie (*Edin. Inst. FP*), C. W. Berry (*Fet.-Lor.*), J. B. Brown (*Glas. Acads.*), J. Jamieson (*West of Scot.*), D. McCowan (*West of Scot.*), W. A. Peterkin (*Edin. Univ.*), C. Reid (*Edin. Acads.*), J. Tod (*Watsonians*), W. A. Walls (*Glas. Acads.*)
Ireland: J. M. O'Sullivan (*Limerick*); R. E. McLean (*NIFC*), G. H. Wheeler (*QC Belfast*), L. M. McIntosh (*Dublin Univ.*); M. Johnson (*Dublin Univ.*), W. W. Higgins (*NIFC*); J. B. Buchanan (*Dublin Univ.*), A. Gordon (*Dublin Univ.*), T. H. M. Hobbs (*Dublin Univ.*), R. W. Hughes (*NIFC*), J. Johnston (*NIFC*), W. Kelly (*Wanderers*), J. A. Macdonald* (*Methodist Coll.*), J. F. Maguire (*Cork*), W. G. Rutherford (*Lansdowne*)
Referee: G. Rowland Hill (*England*)   **Umpires:** J. H. S. Graham, H. C. Kelly

L. McIntosh scored but R. E. McLean failed; W. A. Peterkin scored but C. W. Berry failed; J. Tod scored but C. W. Berry failed. (H.T.). A. R. Don Wauchope and A. G. G. Asher scored for C. W. Berry to convert both.

A temporary stand was set up along the east touch line and 8,000 watched in clear but cold weather. Ireland were handicapped by having to make eight changes and while their forwards did quite well their backs could not cope with a brilliant pair of quarter backs in Asher and Don Wauchope. The latter was at his elusive best, the second Scottish score coming 'by one of these unequalled wriggling runs for which he is famous. He went from near the centre through the Irish forwards and backs but when just on the line was tackled but Tod being in close attendance got hold and scored.' His own score came from a run in course of which he crossed from one side of the field to the other. Peterkin's score came from a long solo run and it should be recalled that at that time he was the Scottish 440 yards title holder. The Irish score, within five minutes of the start, was made by a good break by a forward who gave McIntosh a scoring pass.

ENGLAND: 1 goal   Loss
SCOTLAND: 1 try
Blackheath
1 March 1884

England: H. B. Tristram (*Oxford Univ.*); A. M. Evanson (*Richmond*), C. G. Wade (*Oxford Univ.*), W. N. Bolton (*Blackheath*); A. Rotherham (*Oxford Univ.*), H. T. Twynam (*Richmond*); C. Gurdon (*Richmond*), E. T. Gurdon* (*Richmond*), R. S. F. Henderson (*Blackheath*), R. S. Kindersley (*Exeter*), C. J. B. Marriott (*Blackheath*), E. L. Strong (*Oxford Univ.*), W. M. Tatham (*Oxford Univ.*), G. T. Thomson (*Halifax*), C. S. Wooldridge (*Blackheath*)
Scotland: J. P. Veitch (*RHSFP*); W. E. Maclagan* (*London Scot.*), E. T. Roland (*Edin. Wrs.*), D. J. McFarlan (*London Scot.*); A. R. Don Wauchope (*Fet.-Lor.*), A. G. G. Asher (*Fet.-Lor.*); T. Ainslie (*Edin. Inst. FP*), C. W. Berry (*Fet.-Lor.*), J. B. Brown (*Glas. Acads.*), J. Jamieson (*West of Scot.*), D. McCowan (*West of Scot.*), W. A. Peterkin (*Edin. Univ.*), C. Reid (*Edin. Acads.*), J. Tod (*Watsonians*), W. A. Walls (*Glas. Acads.*)
Referee: A Scriven (*Ireland*)   **Umpires:** J. H. S. Graham, J. McLaren

J. Jamieson scored but C. W. Berry failed. (H.T.). R. S. Kindersley scored and W. N. Bolton converted.

This was the first International to be played on the Rectory field at Blackheath. The excellence of the dribbling rushes by the Scots was matched by the strength of the English backs, the powerful Bolton always being dangerous. Asher and Don Wauchope, however, had a good match. Jamieson's try was the result of one hard forward rush. After the interval Kindersley scored a try which was to leave its mark on the history of the game. The Scots objected to the score and after a lengthy discussion allowed the kick to be taken under protest, the point to be referred to the Rugby Football Union Committee.

28

SCOTLAND: Nil   Draw
WALES: Nil
Hamilton Crescent
10 January 1885

Scotland: P. R. Harrower (*London Scot.*); W. E. Maclagan* (*London Scot.*), A. E. Stephen (*West of Scot.*), G. Maitland (*Edin. Inst. FP*); A. R. Don Wauchope (*Fet.-Lor.*), A. G. G. Asher (*Fet.-Lor.*); T. Ainslie (*Edin. Inst. FP*), C. W. Berry (*Fet.-Lor.*), J. Jamieson (*West of Scot.*), R. Maitland (*Edin. Inst. FP*), J. G. Mitchell (*West of Scot.*), W. A. Peterkin (*Edin. Univ.*), C. Reid (*Edin. Acads.*), G. H. Robb (*Glas. Acads.*), J. Tod (*Watsonians*)
Wales: A. J. Gould (*Newport*); C. G. Taylor (*Ruabon*), F. E. Hancock (*Cardiff*), H. M. Jordan (*Newport*); C. H. Newman* (*Newport*), W. H. Gwyn (*Swansea*), E. P. Alexander (*Brecon*), T. J. S. Clapp (*Newport*), S. Goldsworthy (*Swansea*), R. Gould (*Newport*), A. F. Hill (*Cardiff*), T. B. Jones (*Newport*), D. Morgan (*Swansea*), L. C. Thomas (*Cardiff*), W. H. Thomas (*Llandovery*)
Referee: G. Rowland Hill (*England*) **Umpires:** M. Cross, A. Duncan.

A soft ground and wet conditions hampered both teams. This and good tackling earned Wales their first drawn match, for the Scottish backs, particularly Don Wauchope, were full of running. Both sides also came near to scoring with drops at goal. W. H. Thomas aged nineteen, was still at Llandovery College. A. R. Don Wauchope, A. G. G. Asher and C. W. Berry played for the Fet.-Lor. XV against Glasgow Academicals on Thursday, 8 January.

IRELAND: Nil   Abandoned
SCOTLAND: 1 try
Ormeau, Belfast
21 February 1885

Ireland: J. W. R. Morrow (*QC Belfast*); R. E. McLean (*NIFC*), J. P. Ross (*Lansdowne*), D. J. Ross (*Albion*); J. C. Crawford (*Dublin Univ.*), R. G. Warren (*Lansdowne*); T. C. Allen (*NIFC*), H. M. Brabazon (*Dublin Univ.*), R. M. Bradshaw (*Wanderers*), J. Johnson (*Albion*), T. R. Lyle (*Dublin Univ.*), H. J. Neill (*NIFC*), W. G. Rutherford* (*Tipperary*), T. Shanahan (*Lansdowne*), R. G. Thompson (*Cork*)
Scotland: J. P. Veitch (*RHSFP*); W. E. Maclagan* (*London Scot.*), H. L. Evans (*Edin. Univ.*), G. C. Lindsay (*Fet.-Lor.*); A. R. Don Wauchope (*Fet.-Lor.*), P. H. Don Wauchope (*Fet.-Lor.*); T. Ainslie (*Edin. Inst. FP*), C. W. Berry (*Fet.-Lor.*), J. B. Brown (*Glas. Acads.*), T. W. Irvine (*Edin. Acads.*), J. Jamieson (*West of Scot.*), J. G. Mitchell (*West of Scot.*), W. A. Peterkin (*Edin. Univ.*), C. Reid (*Edin. Acads.*), J. Tod (*Watsonians*)
Referee: H. C. Kelly (*Ireland*) **Umpires:** J. H. S. Graham, J. W. Taylor

J. Jamieson scored before the game was abandoned.

After a clear morning a fearful storm broke out and when a start was made the Irish team on a waterlogged pitch was forced to face into an appalling gale force wind of sleet. No sensible football was possible and when after twenty minutes Jamieson scored and the Irish full back had to leave the field, the game by mutual consent was abandoned. In the evening it was agreed that this would stand as a win for Scotland unless Ireland played a second match in Edinburgh. This of course they did, so that this game stands as an abandoned match and surprisingly has been ignored in previous records.

SCOTLAND: 1 goal, 2 tries   Win
IRELAND: Nil
Raeburn Place
7 March 1885

Scotland: J. P. Veitch (*RHSFP*); W. E. Maclagan* (*London Scot.*), G. Maitland (*Edin. Inst. FP*), H. L. Evans (*Edin. Univ.*); A. R. Don Wauchope (*Fet.-Lor.*), P. H. Don Wauchope (*Fet.-Lor.*); T. Ainslie (*Edin. Inst. FP*), J. B. Brown (*Glas. Acads.*), T. W. Irvine (*Edin. Acads.*), J. Jamieson (*West of Scot.*), J. G. Mitchell (*West of Scot.*), W. A. Peterkin (*Edin. Univ.*), C. Reid (*Edin. Acads.*),

J. G. Tait (*Camb. Univ.*), J. Tod (*Watsonians*)
Ireland: J. W. R. Morrow (*Albion*); J. P. Ross (*Lansdowne*), D. J. Ross (*Albion*), E. H. Greene (*Dublin Univ.*); R. G. Warren (*Lansdowne*), D. V. Hunter (*Dublin Univ.*); R. M. Bradshaw (*Wanderers*), A. J. Forrest* (*Wanderers*), W. Hogg (*Dublin Univ.*), J. Johnstone (*Albion*), T. R. Lyle (*Dublin Univ.*), F. W. Moore (*Wanderers*), H. J. Neill (*NIFC*), T. Shanahan (*Lansdowne*), J. A. Thompson (*Queen's*)
Referee: H. C. Kelly (*Ireland*)   **Umpires:** M. Cross, W. A. Walls

C. Reid scored but J. P. Veitch failed. (H.T.). W. A. Peterkin and A. R. Don Wauchope scored; J. P. Veitch converted the latter try.

Both teams showed changes and in fact there is a doubt about the correct Irish XV, which, incidentally, played in white jerseys. A grandstand was erected along the east side of the pitch.

The Scottish pack dominated play and the first score came from a fine handling run by Reid, Ainslie, Peterkin, Tod and Jamieson which was finished off by Reid. Peterkin, already noted as the Scottish sprint champion in 1883, scored the second try by outpacing the Irish backs during a run up the touch line. A. R. Don Wauchope was at his elusive best, the last try coming after one of his typical dodging runs.

WALES: Nil   Win
SCOTLAND: 2 goals, 1 try
Cardiff
9 January 1886

Wales: D. H. Bowen (*Llanelli*); F. E. Hancock* (*Cardiff*), W. M. Douglas (*Cardiff*), A. J. Gould (*Newport*), C. G. Taylor (*Ruabon*); W. H. Stadden (*Cardiff*), A. A. Matthews (*Lampeter*); E. P. Alexander (*Camb. Univ.*), W. Bowen (*Swansea*), T. J. S. Clapp (*Newport*), A. F. Hill (*Cardiff*), D. H. Lewis (*Cardiff*), D. Morgan (*Swansea*), W. H. Thomas (*Llandovery Coll.*), G. A. Young (*Cardiff*)
Scotland: F. McIndoe (*Glas. Acads.*); W. F. Holms (*London Scot.*), D. J. Macfarlan (*London Scot.*), R. H. Morrison (*Edin . Univ.*); A . R. Don Wauchope (*Fet.-Lor.*), P. H. Don Wauchope (*Fet.-Lor.*); J. B. Brown* (*Glas. Acads.*), A. T. Clay (*Edin. Acads.*), J. French (*Glas. Acads.*), T. W. Irvine (*Edin. Acads.*), W. M. Macleod (*Edin. Wrs.*), C. J. B. Milne (*West of Scot.*), C. Reid (*Edin. Acads.*), J. Tod (*Watsonians*), W. A. Walls (*Glas. Acads.*)

A. T. Clay scored and W. M. Macleod converted. (H.T.). J. Tod and A. R. Don Wauchope scored; W. M. Macleod converted the second.

For the first time Wales began with four threequarters but the nine Scottish forwards so dominated play that D. H. Bowen was sent into the pack and A. J. Gould went to full back.

SCOTLAND: 3 goals, 1 drop goal, 2 tries Win
IRELAND: Nil
Raeburn Place
20 February 1886

Scotland: F. McIndoe (*Glas. Acads.*); A. E. Stephen (*West of Scot.*), D. J. Macfarlan (*London Scot.*), R. H. Morrison (*Edin. Univ.*); A. R. Don Wauchope (*Fet.-Lor.*), A. G. G. Asher (*Fet.-Lor.; Edin. Wrs.*); J. B. Brown* (*Glas. Acads.*), A. T. Clay (*Edin. Acads.*), T. W. Irvine (*Edin. Acads.*), D. A. Macleod (*Glas. Univ.*), W. M. Macleod (*Fet.-Lor.; Edin. Wrs.*), C. J. B. Milne (*West of Scot.*), C. Reid (*Edin. Acads.*), J. Tod (*Watsonians*), W. A. Walls (*Glas. Acads.*)
Ireland: J. W. R. Morrow (*Lisburn*); J. P. Ross* (*Lansdowne*), D. J. Ross (*Albion*), M. J. Carpendale (*Monkstown*); R. W. Herrick (*Dublin Univ.*), J. F. Ross (*NIFC*); J. Chambers (*Dublin Univ.*), J. McMordie (*QC Belfast*), F. H. Miller (*Wanderers*), F. W. Moore (*Wanderers*), V. C. Le Fanu (*Camb. Univ.*), H. J. Neill (*NIFC*), R. Nelson (*QC Belfast*), F. O. Stoker (*Wanderers*), J. Waites (*Bective Rangers*)
Referee: G. Rowland Hill (*England*)   **Umpires:** J. S. Carriek, Mayne

A. R. Don Wauchope scored twice but W. M. Macleod failed with both; R. H. Morrison scored twice and D. J. Macfarlan converted both. (H.T.). A. G. G. Asher dropped a goal; D. J. Macfarlan scored and converted.

The Irish team was badly weakened by withdrawals of players unable to travel and found themselves up against backs who were full of running. Straightaway Don Wauchope had two typical dodging 'deer-like runs' which brought tries. Then Morrison, the Edinburgh University sprinter, ran in another two before half time. In the second half the Scottish backs were still active but selfishness cost them scores. Apart from Asher, their tackling came in for some criticism. A grandstand, double the size of last year's one, was erected along the east side of the field.

SCOTLAND: Nil   Draw
ENGLAND: Nil
Raeburn Place
13 March 1886

Scotland: J. P. Veitch (*RHSFP*); W. F. Holms (*RIEC*), G. R. Wilson (*RHSFP*), R. H. Morrison (*Edin. Univ.*); A. R. Don Wauchope (*Fet.-Lor.*), A. G. G. Asher (*Fet.-Lor, Edin. Wrs.*), J. B. Brown* (*Glas. Acads.*), A. T. Clay (*Edin. Acads.*), T. W. Irvine (*Edin. Acads.*), M. C. McEwan (*Edin. Acads.*), D. A. MacLeod (*Glas. Univ.*), C. J. B. Milne (*West of Scot.*), C. Reid (*Edin. Acads.*), J. Tod (*Watsonians*), W. A. Walls (*Glas. Acads.*)

England: C. H. Sample (*Durham*); A. E. Stoddart (*Blackheath*), R. Robertshaw (*Bradford*), E. B. Brutton (*Camb. Univ.*); A. Rotherham (*Richmond*), F. Bonsor (*Bradford*); W. G. Clibborn (*Richmond*), C. Gurdon (*Richmond*), E. T. Gurdon* (*Richmond*), R. E. Inglis (*Blackheath*), G. L. Jeffery (*Camb. Univ.*), C. J. B. Marriott (*Blackheath*), N. Spurling (*Blackheath*), A. Teggin (*Broughton Rangers*), E. Wilkinson (*Bradford*)

Referee: H. Cook (*Ireland*)   **Umpires:** J. S. Carrick; G. Rowland Hill

In spite of the bitterly cold weather the resumption of the English fixture brought out a large crowd and the Railway Companies ran several special trains. A police force of 36 constables was reinforced for the first time by mounted police. This was a hard and fast game in which all the Scottish backs showed up well, but early on Bonsor hurt a knee which handicapped him throughout. As a result England was on the defensive for three-quarters of the game yet put in a tremendous finish. G. R. Wilson actually touched down but the score was disallowed as he was judged to have fumbled the ball in taking his pass. R. H. Morrison also crossed the line but was knocked into touch in goal before he could put the ball down. A. R. Don Wauchope and A. G. G. Asher were again very effective and Reid was very prominent and might have scored once but put out a pass which did not go to hand. R. Robertshaw played well at centre three quarter. A scene from this game is depicted in a painting by W. H. Overend and L. P. Smythe.

IRELAND: Nil   Win
SCOTLAND: 1 goal, 1 mark goal, 2 tries
Ormeau, Belfast
19 February 1887

Ireland: J. M. O'Sullivan (*Cork*); R. Montgomery (*Camb. Univ.*), D. F. Rambant (*Dublin Univ.*), C. R. Tillie (*Dublin Univ.*); R. G. Warren* (*Lansdowne*), J. H. McLoughlin (*Derry*); J. Chambers (*Dublin Univ.*), J. S. Dick (*QC Cork*), J. Johnston (*Albion*), T. R. Lyle (*Dublin Univ.*), J. Macaulay (*Limerick*), C. M. Moore (*Dublin Univ.*), H. J. Neill (*NIFC*), R. Stevenson (*Lisburn*), E. J. Walsh (*Lansdowne*)

Scotland: W. F. Holms (*London Scot.*); A. N. Woodrow (*Glas. Acads.*), W. E. Maclagan (*London Scot.*), D. J. Macfarlan (*London Scot.*); P. H. Don Wauchope (*Fet.-Lor.; Edin. Wrs.*), C. E. Orr (*West of Scot.*); C. W. Berry (*Edin. Wrs.*), A. T. Clay (*Edin. Acads.*), J. French (*Glas. Acads.*), T. W. Irvine (*Edin. Acads.*), H. T. Ker (*Glas. Acads.*), M. C. McEwan (*Edin. Acads.*), R. G. McMillan (*West of Scot.*), D. S. Morton (*West of Scot.*), C. Reid* (*Edin. Acads.*)

Referee: G. Rowland Hill (*England*) Umpires: J. S. Carrick, J. Pinion

C. W. Berry kicked a goal from a mark by D. J. Macfarlan; W. E. Maclagan scored: C. W. Berry converted. (H.T.). M. C. McEwan scored; C. W. Berry failed; D. S. Morton scored but the kick failed.

This game was played in fine weather on the NIFC ground at Ormeau. In the first half there was a lot of counter-kicking rather than running but Scotland held a clear advantage in the second half.

SCOTLAND: 4 goals, 8 tries   Win
WALES: Nil
Raeburn Place
26 February 1887

Scotland: A. W. Cameron (*Watsonians*); W. E. Maclagan (*London Scot.*), G. C. Lindsay (*London Scot.*), A. N. Woodrow (*Glas. Acads.*), P. H. Don Wauchope (*Edin. Wrs.*), C. E. Orr (*West of Scot.*); C. W. Berry (*Edin. Wrs.*), A. T. Clay (*Edin . Acads.*), J. French (*Glas. Acads.*), T. W. Irvine (*Edin. Acads.*), H. T. Ker (*Glas. Acads.*), M. C. McEwan (*Edin. Acads.*), R. G. Macmillan (*West of Scot.*), D. S. Morton (*West of Scot.*), C. Reid* (*Edin. Acads.*)
Wales: H. Hughes (*Cardiff*); D. Gwynn (*Swansea*), A. J. Gould (*Newport*), W. M. Douglas (*Cardiff*); G. E. Bowen (*Swansea*), O. J. Evans (*Cardiff*); A. F. Bland (*Cardiff*), W. Bowen (*Swansea*), T. J. S. Clapp (*Newport*), R. Gould* (*Newport*), T. W. Lockwood (*Newport*), D. Morgan (*Swansea*), E. S. Richards (*Swansea*), W. H. Thomas (*Camb. Univ.*), W. E. O. Williams (*Cardiff*)
Referee: F. I. Currey (*England*)   **Umpires:** J. S. Carrick, A. Duncan

P. H. Don Wauchope scored: C. W. Berry failed; G. C. Lindsay scored: C. W. Berry converted; C. E. Orr scored: C. W. Berry converted; G. C. Lindsay scored: M. C. McEwan failed. (H.T.). C. Reid and G. C. Lindsay scored: C. W. Berry failed with both; R. G. Macmillan scored: A. N. Woodrow converted; M. C. McEwan scored: A. N. Woodrow failed; G. C. Lindsay scored but failed to convert; W. E. Maclagan scored: C. W. Berry failed; D. S. Morton scored: A. W. Cameron failed; G. C. Lindsay scored: A. N. Woodrow failed.

This match originally set for January was postponed because of frost and both sides were forced to make changes. In particular G. C. Lindsay came in for D. J. Macfarlan, and his brilliant fast dodging running brought him five tries – an individual record which still stands. Scotland from the beginning were completely on top. Their forwards with Reid outstanding proved much too powerful, not only with foot rushes but with handling runs. McEwan's score came when he and Clay won a maul in goal with a lone Welsh forward . The backs too were in devastating form, their passing and combined play being a delight, and it seems that the Welsh tackling eventually cracked. It was reported, however, that they lost O. J. Evans through injury during the second half.

ENGLAND: 1 try   Draw
SCOTLAND: 1 try
Whalley Range, Manchester
5 March 1887

England: H. B. Tristram (*Richmond*); W. N. Bolton (*Blackheath*), R. Robertshaw (*Bradford*), R. E. Lockwood (*Dewsbury*), A. Rotherham* (*Richmond*), F. Bonsor (*Bradford*) C. R. Cleveland (*Oxford Univ.*), W. G. Clibborn (*Richmond*), J. H. Dewhurst (*Camb. Univ.*), J. L. Hickson (*Bradford*), G. L. Jeffery (*Blackheath*), R. L. Seddon (*Broughton Rangers*), H. H. Springmann (*Liverpool*), A. Teggin (*Broughton Rangers*), E. Wilkinson (*Bradford*)
Scotland: W. F. Holms (*London Scot.*); W. E. Maclagan (*London Scot.*), G. C. Lindsay (*London Scot.*), A. N. Woodrow (*Glas. Acads.*); P. H. Don Wauchope (*Edin. Wrs.*), C. E. Orr (*West of Scot.*); C. W. Berry (*Edin. Wrs.*), A. T. Clay (*Edin . Acads.*), J. French (*Glas. Acads.*), T. W. Irvine (*Edin. Acads.*), H. T. Ker (*Glas. Acads.*), M. C. McEwan (*Edin. Acads.*), R. G. Macmillan (*London Scot.*), D. S. Morton (*West of Scot.*), C. Reid* (*Edin. Acads.*)
Referee: J. Lyle (*Ireland*)   **Umpires:** J. S. Carrick, R. Stokes

G. L. Jeffery scored; W. N. Bolton failed. (H.T.). D. S. Morton scored; C. W. Berry failed.

The match was played in a fog so thick that at times it was difficult to see across the field. Scotland started confidently, Maclagan and Orr being seen in attacks as was Lockwood in defence but it was England who opened the scoring with a try by Jeffery whose play pleased the English critics. After half time England maintained their pressure but gradually Scotland got down to their 25 and Maclagan got over but was recalled before Morton scored the equaliser. Play appeared to be fairly even but five minutes from the end there came a tackle which is one of the game's legends. Maclagan slipped past Rotherham, knocked Lockwood over and although hemmed in on one side had only Tristram between himself and the goal line. He had no room to dodge so charged down on Tristram who sprang forward to meet him and the pair went down with a fearful crash – but no score for Scotland.

32

WALES: 1 try Loss
SCOTLAND: Nil
Newport
4 February 1888

Wales: E. J. Roberts (*Llanelli*); T. J. Pryce-Jenkins (*London Welsh*), A. J. Gould (*Newport*), G. E. Bowen (*Swansea*); W. H. Stadden (*Cardiff*), O. J. Evans (*Cardiff*); A. F. Bland (*Cardiff*), T. J. S. Clapp* (*Newport*), A. F. Hill (*Cardiff*), W. H. Howells (*Swansea*), T. D. Kedzli (*Cardiff*), J. Meredith (*Swansea*), R. W. Powell (*Newport*), W. H. Thomas (*London Welsh*), T. Williams (*Swansea*)
Scotland: H. F. T. Chambers (*Edin. Univ.*); W. E. Maclagan (*London Scot.*), H. J. Stevenson (*Edin. Acads.*), M. M. Duncan (*Camb. Univ.*); C. E. Orr (*West of Scot.*), C. J. P. Fraser (*Glas. Univ.*); C. W. Berry (*Fet.-Lor.*), A. T. Clay (*Edin. Acads.*), A. Duke (*RHSFP*), T. W. Irvine (*Edin. Acads.*), M. C. McEwan (*Edin. Acads.*), D. S. Morton (*West of Scot.*), C. Reid* (*Edin. Acads.*), L. E. Stevenson (*Edin. Univ.*), T. B. White (*Edin. Acads.*)
Referee: J. Chambers (*Ireland*) **Umpires**: W. S. Brown, A. Duncan

T. J. Pryce-Jenkins scored; T. D. Kedzli failed. (H.T.).

This was Wales' first win over Scotland who, however, were rather critical about the winning try. R. J. Phillips wrote later 'Pryce-Jenkins scored from a run remarkable in that a goodly part of its course was in touch. Some of the Scottish defenders allowed him to go and although his tracks were quite discernible, he got his try. Scotland were not so fortunate. Five times the ball was touched down over the Welsh line and on each occasion it was disallowed.' H. J. Stevenson left an equally blunt comment on those points for it was he, Duncan and Chambers who did not bother to put in a tackle. So Scotland put in a lot of pressure with no result. On the Welsh side A. J. Gould for once played well against Scotland.

SCOTLAND: 1 goal Win
IRELAND: Nil
Raeburn Place
10 March 1888

Scotland: H. F. T. Chambers (*Edin. Univ.*); W. E. Maclagan (*London Scot.*); H. J. Stevenson (*Edin. Acads.*), D. J. McFarlan (*LondonScot.*); A. R. Don Wauchope* (*Fet.-Lor.*), C. E. Orr (*West of Scot.*); C. W. Berry (*Edin. Wrs.*), A. Duke (*RHSFP*), T. W. Irvine (*Edin. Acads.*), H. T. Ker (*Glas. Acads.*), M. C. McEwan (*Edin. Acads.*), A. G. Malcolm (*Glas. Univ.*), D. S. Morton (*West of Scot.*), C. Reid (*Edin. Acads.*), T. B. White (*Edin. Acads.*)
Ireland: J. W. R. Morrow (*Lisburn*); C. R. Tillie (*Dublin Univ.*), A. Walpole (*Dublin Univ.*), M. J. Carpendale (*Monkstown*); R. G. Warren (*Lansdowne*), J. H. McLaughlin (*Derry*); W. Ekin (*QC Belfast*), V. C. Le Fanu (*Lansdowne*), R. H. Mayne (*Albion*), J. Moffatt (*Albion*), C. M. Moore (*Dublin Univ.*), W. A. Morton (*Dublin Univ.*), H. J. Neill* (*NIFC*), T. Shanahan (*Lansdowne*), E. W. Stoker (*Wanderers*)
Referee: J. McLaren (*England*) **Umpires**: W. S. Brown, E. McAllister

D. J. McFarlan scored and C. W. Berry converted. (H.T.).

This was a very even game where fast open play by both sides moved the ball from end to end and only good defence kept the score down to a single try. This was the result of wonderful passing between Don Wauchope, Stevenson and McFarlan who ran in for the score. Scotland lost Orr injured before half time but White who took over played very well. For Ireland, Le Fanu and Walpole frequently caught the eye. For the Scots, Don Wauchope did some fine saving by halting rushes by the Irish forwards; Stevenson again impressed as a centre half who could co-operate with his wingers but the biggest laugh of the afternoon came when Reid had a long run 'with the bulk of the Irish forwards hanging onto him'.

SCOTLAND: 2 tries   Win
WALES: Nil
Raeburn Place
2 February 1889

Scotland: H. F. T. Chambers (*Edin. Univ.*); W. F. Holms (*Edin. Wrs.*), H. J. Stevenson (*Edin. Acads.*), J. Marsh (*Edin. Inst. FP*); C. E. Orr (*West of Scot.*), C. F. P. Fraser (*Glas. Univ.*); W. Auld (*West of Scot.*), J. D. Boswell (*West of Scot.*), A. Duke (*RHSFP*), H. T. Ker (*Glas. Acads.*), M. C. McEwan (*Edin. Acads.*), W. A. Macdonald (*Glas. Univ.*), A. Methuen (*Camb. Univ.*), D. S. Morton* (*West of Scot.*), T. B. White (*Edin. Acads.*).
Wales: H. Hughes (*Cardiff*); R. M. Garrett (*Penarth*), J. E. Webb (*Newport*), E. H . Bishop (*Swansea*), H. M. Jordon (*Newport*); C. J. Thomas (*Newport*), R. Evans (*Cardiff*); W. Bowen (*Swansea*), D. W. Evans (*Cardiff*), J. Hannan (*Newport*), T. Harding (*Newport*), A. F. Hill* (*Cardiff*), S. H. Nicholls (*Cardiff*), R. L. Thomas (*London Welsh*), W. E. O. Williams (*Cardiff*).
Referee: A. McAllister (*Ireland*)   **Umpires:** A. R. Don Wauchope, A. Duncan

C. E. Orr scored; J. D. Boswell failed. (H.T.). H. T. Ker scored; M. C. McEwan failed.

The Welsh selectors ran into difficulties when some Cardiff and Llanelli players declined to travel as they wished to play in that local derby and eventually had to send a much altered team, which, however, used the four three quarter system that had been reintroduced for their match against the Maoris. The game was played in poor conditions snow falling at intervals and two half hours were played. Nevertheless both sets of backs ran well and the Welsh forwards were praised for some fine dribbling. Yet again Stevenson distinguished himself by fine attacking play. J. Marsh was an Englishman who went south and was later capped for England against Ireland, a unique distinction.

IRELAND: Nil   Win
SCOTLAND: 1 drop goal
Ormeau, Belfast
16 February 1889

Ireland: L. J. Holmes (*Lisburn*); R. A. Yeates (*Dublin Univ.*), T. B. Pedlow (*Queen's*), D. C. Woods (*Bessbrook*); J. Stevenson (*Lisburn*), R. G. Warren* (*Lansdowne*); H. W. Andrews (*NIFC*), T. M. Donovan (*QC Cork*), G. E. Forrest (*Wanderers*), J. S. Jameson (*Lansdowne*), J. Moffatt (*Albion*), L. C. Nash (*QC Cork*), C. R. R. Stark (*Dublin Univ.*), R. Stevenson (*Lisburn*), F. O. Stoker (*Wanderers*)
Scotland: H. F. T. Chambers (*Edin. Univ.*); W. F. Holms (*London Scot.*), H. J. Stevenson (*Edin. Acads.*), J. Marsh (*Edin. Inst. FP*); C. E. Orr (*West of Scot.*), D. G. Anderson (*London Scot.*); A. I. Aitken (*Edin. Inst. FP.*), J. D. Boswell (*West of Scot.*), A. Duke (*RHSFP*), T. W. Irvine (*Edin. Acads.*), M. C. McEwan (*Edin. Acads.*), J. G. McKendrick (*West of Scot.*), A. Methuen (*Camb. Univ.*), D. S. Morton* (*West of Scot.*), J. E. Orr (*West of Scot.*)
Referee: W. Phillips (*Wales*)   **Umpires:** J. A. Smith, J. Chambers

H. J. Stevenson dropped a goal. (H.T.).

On a soft ground Scotland started with the wind and sun at their backs and almost at once Anderson sent out a pass to Stevenson who dropped a fine goal down wind. After the restart Holms went off with an injured knee and Boswell took his place. In spite of this the Scottish forwards continued to dominate play and kept Ireland out. Yet again Stevenson was the outstanding back.

James Aikman Smith

1887-1890 – East Representative: 1890-1910 – Hon. Secretary & Treasurer: 1910-1914 – Hon. Secretary: 1915-1919 – Acting Secretary & Treasurer: 1914-1925 and 1927-1931 – Special Representative: 1925, 1926 and 1927 – Vice President & President.

The controversy over the captaincy which shook up the SFU in 1881 was merely one of several matters which had been causing concern. Another was the number of committee members who were voting themselves into the XV, e.g. in 1883 and 1884 there were five current caps among the six representatives and four during the next three seasons, but it is only fair to add that players such as A. R. Don Wauchope, C. Reid, T. Ainslie, J. B. Brown and J. Jamieson were practically automatic choices.

The RHSFP delegate to the AGMs, J. Aikman Smith, a Chartered Accountant by profession, had been most critical about the mode of presentation of information about the Union funds and finally had a motion carried that a proper printed summary must be produced by the Hon. Treasurer for the 1887 AGM.

The situation that developed after the 1884 dispute made it obvious that the committee should now contain men with the qualifications, ability and stature needed to formulate and establish the newly formed International Board. The sudden tragic death of the Hon. Secretary and Treasurer, J. A. Gardner, three weeks before the date of the 1887 AGM allowed his offices to be filled by A. S. Blair, WS, a splendid choice to handle the discussions over the IB that were now coming to a head.

The outspoken J. Aikman Smith was also elected as a new East representative and so began a period of unique service to the Union and the IB which only finished with his death in 1931. For 44 years his continued presence in a changing committee, his ability in office, his burning belief in the high quality and standing of rugby in Scotland, his bitter opposition to anything which smacked of professionalism allowed him to develop and exert a tremendous influence over the game, the players and clubs in Scotland.

He was not long in office before he had the real authority of the Union clearly established by a Special General Meeting in 1893 which endorsed a motion that the committee, so long as it worked within its Bye-Laws, had the power to formulate and enforce resolutions without prior consultation with the clubs. Barely a year later this authority was challenged when, following a complaint by a referee, the Union suspended play for the remainder of the season on the Gala field at Mossilee, severely censured and later suspended *sine die* the Gala captain. The latter, aided by a fund subscribed to by some well known club members, opened a law suit against the Union (and the referee) on the grounds that it had no powers to suspend. This action was firmly met and when it was dismissed the Union not only continued its suspension on the captain but also denied the privilege of membership of any Union club to the subscribers to the fund – a most convincing demonstration of the new authority of the Union.

Himself a product of Geo. Watson's College and the Royal High School, Aikman Smith saw the game develop as an amateur sport until the schism of 1895 in England which saw the formation of professional rugby in the North of England. A year later a proposed testimonial of considerable value raised for the great Welsh player, A. J. Gould, brought the Welsh Union into conflict with the IB and the subsequent complications were not smoothed over until January 1898, but since the Welsh Union had withdrawn from the IB between February 1897 and February 1898, the Scottish Union cancelled their mutual fixtures for these years. It must be said that the Welsh Union found itself in a difficult position for while it remained clear that the player was being financially re-warded for his skill, his Union withdrew their own donation and pointed out that neither had they any control over the testimonial fund nor were they breaking any rules referring to professionalism laid down by the IB. The whole rather unsatisfactory affair was only really settled by the player who retired from the game.

Aikman Smith never halted in his fight against professionalism, for even on the evening of his last journey in 1931 two rather apprehensive young caps were summoned to his compartment and after asking if they had had any contact with rugby league scouts, he firmly warned them to steer clear of such infamous characters.

It was this stern background that was reflected in his committee's opposition to the daily payments made to the 1905 New Zealand tourists, the presentation of goods as prizes for the finalists in Border Sevens, and in 1923 the gift of a £21 watch to each member of a very successful Newport team which included Neil Macpherson, a current Scottish cap.

Even the numbering of the players in an International was frowned upon for he quite openly maintained that the game must be run for the players and not the spectators and so was also dead against any legislation which tended to make play faster thus demanding more in the way of training and preparation from amateur players. We are left to wonder what he would have said about the squad training and tours of today!

Yet it was his careful handling and investing of the Union funds which permitted them to be the first to possess their own field with facilities for the spectators and Press and it is equally clear that he was the instigator of the move from the quite spacious Inverleith to the vast enclosure of Murrayfield which housed over 70,000 spectators for the opening match against England in 1925 but burst at the seams when over 104,000 watched the 1975 Welsh match with several thousand unable to get in – a world record for a rugby attendance.

Incidentally, the late Dr MacMyn and other caps have recalled with relish how he, normally a mild spoken man, had the habit of appearing, wearing his bowler hat, in the dressing room just before the XV went out and there delivering a blistering condemnation of the opposition and a fiercesome exhortation to go out and take them apart!

Needless to say he was one of the permanent Scottish representatives on the IB and he was one of a half dozen who, while remaining loyal to the demands and interests of their own Unions, played significant roles in nursing and developing the IB during its earlier years. These six, with dates and number of attendances, were: R. G. Warren (Ireland): 1887-1938 (68); H. S. Lyne (Wales): 1887-1938 (60); J. A. Smith (Scotland): 1888-1930 (59); E. T. Gurdon (England): 1890-1928 (51); W. Cail (England): 1890-1925 (45); Sir G. Rowland Hill (England): 1890-1928 (39).

WALES 2   SCOTLAND 8
Cardiff
1 February 1890

Wales: W. J. Bancroft (*Swansea*); D. P. M. Lloyd (*Llanelli*), R. M. Garrett (*Penarth*), A. J. Gould (*Newport*), C. J. Thomas (*Newport*); E. James (*Swansea*), W. H. Stadden (*Cardiff*); A. F. Bland (*Cardiff*), W. Brown (*Swansea*), W. R. Evans (*Swansea*), J. Hannan (*Newport*), A. F. Hill* (*Cardiff*), J. Meredith (*Swansea*), S. Thomas (*Llanelli*), W. E. O. Williams (*Cardiff*)
Scotland: G. MacGregor (*Camb. Univ.*); W. E. Maclagan* (*London Scot.*), H. J. Stevenson (*Edin. Acads.*),G. R. Wilson (*RHSFP*); C. E. Orr (*West of Scot.*), D. G. Anderson (*London Scot.*); W. Auld (*West of Scot.*), J. D. Boswell (*West of Scot.*), A. Dalgleish (*Gala*), A. Duke (*RHSFP*), F. W. J. Goodhue (*London Scot.*), M. C. McEwan (*Edin. Acads.*), I. McIntyre (*Edin. Wrs.*), R. G. Macmillan (*West of Scot.*), J. E. Orr (*West of Scot.*)
Referee: A. McAllister (*Ireland*)   **Umpires:** A. R. Don Wauchope, A. Duncan

D. G. Anderson scored; M. C. McEwan failed (2-0); J. D. Boswell scored; M. C. McEwan failed (4-0); W. E. Maclagan scored; M. C. McEwan converted (8-0). (H.T.). A. J. Gould scored; W. J. Bancroft failed (8-2).

The ground was very wet and so not in great condition. Some good play in the first half by the Scottish pack let Anderson score early on and later a forward, believed to be Boswell, also went over. Near half time Maclagan scored after a typical hard dodging run. The four Welsh backs had always been full of running and near full time Gould, who had shown up well, scored in the corner after a great crossfield run.

This match was played using the new International Board scoring rules: Try – 2; drop or mark goal – 3; goal from try – 4.

SCOTLAND 5   IRELAND 0
Raeburn Place
22 February 1890

Scotland: G. MacGregor (*Camb. Univ.*); W. E. Maclagan (*London Scot.*), H. J. Stevenson (*Edin. Acads.*), G. R. Wilson (*RHSFP*); C. E. Orr (*West of Scot.*), D. G. Anderson (*London Scot.*); J. D. Boswell (*West of Scot.*), A. Duke (*RHSFP*), F. W. J. Goodhue (*London Scot.*), H. T. Ker (*Glas. Acads.*), M. C. McEwan* (*Edin. Acads.*), I . MacIntyre (*Edin. Wrs.*), R. G. Macmillan (*West of Scot.*), D. S. Morton (*West of Scot.*), J. E. Orr (*West of Scot.*)
Ireland: H. P. Gifford (*Wanderers*); R. Dunlop (*Dublin Univ.*), R. W. Johnstone (*Dublin Univ.*), T. Edwards (*Lansdowne*); R. G. Warren* (*Lansdowne*), A. C. McDonnell (*Dublin Univ.*); W. J. N. Davis (*Bessbrook*), E. F. Doran (*Lansdowne*), E. G. Forest (*Wanderers*), J. Moffatt (*Albion*), J. H. O'Conor (*Bective Rangers*), H. A. Richey (*Dublin Univ.*), J. Roche (*Wanderers*), R. Stevenson (*Dungannon*), J. Waites (*Bective Rangers*)
Referee: H. L. Ashmore (*England*)   **Umpires:** A. R. Don Wauchope, J. Chambers

J. D. Boswell dropped a goal (3-0); J. E. Orr scored; M. C. McEwan failed (5-0). (H.T.).

Much of the play was confined to the midfield area but a dropped pass was fly-kicked on by Wilson to the Irish posts where Boswell got the ball from the loose and dropped a goal, a move he was much given to doing. Stevenson again was quite outstanding in attack and defence. He also got over the line only to lose the ball after a maul in goal – surely one of the last in International matches. J. E. Orr came out of the pack and stayed out and eventually taking a pass from his brother (which some thought suspiciously forward) used his pace to score far out. He was probably lucky to get a pass for C. E. Orr was considered a very selfish player! Ireland improved in the second half and although they could not score they were able to counter more clever play by Stevenson.

SCOTLAND 0   ENGLAND 6
Raeburn Place
1 March 1890

Scotland: G. MacGregor (*Camb. Univ.*); W. E. Maclagan* (*London Scot.*), H. J. Stevenson (*Edin. Acads.*), G. R. Wilson (*RHSFP*); C. E. Orr (*West of Scot.*), D. G. Anderson (*London Scot.*); J. D. Boswell (*West of Scot.*), A. Dalgleish (*Gala*), F. W. J. Goodhue (*London Scot.*), H. T. Ker (*Glas. Acads.*), M. C. McEwan (*Edin. Acads.*), I. MacIntyre (*Edin. Wrs.*), R. G. Macmillan (*West of Scot.*), D. S. Morton (*West of Scot.*), J. E. Orr (*West of Scot.*).
England: W. G. Mitchell (*Richmond*); P. H. Morrison (*Camb. Univ.*), R. L. Aston (*Camb. Univ.*), J. W. Dyson (*Huddersfield*); F. H. Fox* (*Wellington*), M. T. Scott (*Northern*); H. Bedford (*Morley*), F. Evershed (*Burton*), J. L. Hickson (*Bradford*), E. Holmes (*Manningham*), D. Jowett (*Heckmondwike*), A. Robinson (*Blackheath*), J. H. Rogers (*Moseley*), J. T. Toothill (*Bradford*), S. M. J. Woods (*Camb. Univ.*)
Referee: J. Chamber (*Ireland*)   **Umpires:** A. R. Don Wauchope, G. Rowland Hill

F. Evershed scored; W. G. Mitchell failed (0-2). (H.T.). J. W. Dyson scored; J. Jowett converted (0-6).

This match marked the resumption of fixtures with England following on the settlement of the dispute by arbitration. Conditions were reasonable although some snow fell during play. Maclagan against his wish (he had been suffering from sciatica) was induced to play and was sadly below form; his tackling, previously devastating, let him down especially when Evershed scored. Wilson, who had been on a medical course in Vienna, was not match fit and as a result Stevenson was the only effective back, although once again J. E. Orr was as often with the backs as in the pack. England, on the other hand, had two fast and effective wingers fed by Aston who was in tremendous form. Their pack with a hard core of burly Yorkshire men came in for much praise – none more so than Evershed. One English report noted the presence of the Cameron pipers who 'played what, to a certain proportion of the crowd, was doubtless stirring music'.

SCOTLAND 15   WALES 0
Raeburn Place
7 February 1891

Scotland: H. J. Stevenson (*Edin. Acads.*); W. Neilson (*Merchiston*), G. MacGregor (*Camb. Univ.*), P. R. Clauss (*Oxford Univ.*); C. E. Orr (*West of Scot.*), D. G. Anderson (*London Scot.*); J. D. Boswell (*West of Scot.*), A. Dalgleish (*Gala*), F. W. J. Goodhue (*London Scot.*), H. T. O. Leggatt (*Watsonians*), M. C. McEwan* (*Edin. Acads.*), I. McIntyre (*Edin. Wrs.*) R. G. Macmillan (*London Scot.*), G. T. Neilson (*West of Scot.*), J. E. Orr (*West of Scot.*)
Wales: W. J. Bancroft (*Swansea*); R. M. Garrett (*Penarth*), D. Gwynn (*Swansea*), G. Thomas (*Newport*), W. McCutcheon (*Swansea*); R. B. Sweet-Escott (*Cardiff*), H. M. Ingledew (*Cardiff*); P. Bennett (*Cardiff Harlequins*), W. Bowen (*Swansea*), D. J. Daniell (*Llanelli*), T. C. Graham (*Newport*), S. H. Nicholls (*Cardiff*), W. Rice Evans (*Swansea*), R. L. Thomas (*Llanelli*), W. H. Thomas* (*Llanelli*)
Referee: H. L. Ashmore (*England*)   **Touch judges:** G. Mitchell, A. Duncan

C. E. Orr scored; M. C. McEwan failed (1-0): J. E. Orr scored; M. C. McEwan failed (2-0): F. W. J. Goodhue scored; J. D. Boswell failed (3-0): P. R. Clauss scored; M. C. McEwan failed (4-0). (H.T.). W. Neilson dropped a goal (7-0): H. T. O. Leggatt scored; M. C. McEwan converted (10-0): H. J. Stevenson dropped a goal (13-0): P. R. Clauss scored; M. C. McEwan failed (14-0): J. D. Boswell scored; M. C. McEwan failed (15-0).

Scotland completely dominated this game for Wales had no answer to a pack which scored four of the seven tries while giving their backs plenty of the ball. Scotland were still playing the three back formation and MacGregor, who specialised in feeding his wide set wingers with long accurate passes, struck up a good partnership with Clauss, a small man but fast and aggressive.

Stevenson who had been an automatic and outstanding choice as centre back for four seasons, refused to play this passive type of game, but being too good to omit, was placed at full back. Even here his ability to turn defence into attack was not lost and on several occasions he dashed up field and set the backs off in a passing run. Indeed he could well be classed as the first attacking full back. On the Welsh side, the day of the four back formation was still to come, and only Gwynn and McCutcheon were seen to advantage. Even the famous Bancroft had a bad day. One Welsh writer suggested his team's poor form was the aftermath of a visit earlier in the day to the dissecting rooms of the Royal Infirmary!

IRELAND 0   SCOTLAND 14
Ballynafeigh, Belfast
21 February 1891

Ireland: D. B. Walkington* (*NIFC*); H. G. Wells (*Bective Rangers*), S. Lee (*NIFC*), R. Dunlop (*NIFC*); B. B. Tuke (*Bective Rangers*), E. D. Cameron (*Bective Rangers*); G. Collopy (*Bective Rangers*), W. J. N. Davis (*Bessbrook*), E. F. Fraser (*Bective Rangers*), J. N. Lytle (*NIFC*), J. Moffatt (*Albion*), L. C. Nash (*QC Cork*), J. H. O'Conor (*Bective Rangers*), J. Roche (*Wanderers*), R. D. Stokes (*QC Cork*)
Scotland: H. J. Stevenson (*Edin. Acads.*); P. R. Clauss (*Oxford Univ.*), G. MacGregor (*Camb. Univ.*), G. R. Wilson (*RHSFP*); C. E. Orr (*West of Scot.*), W. Wotherspoon (*Camb. Univ.*); J. D. Boswell (*West of Scot.*), A. Dalgleish (*Gala*), W. R. Gibson (*RHSFP*), F. W. J. Goodhue (*London Scot.*), H. T. O. Leggatt (*Watsonians*), M. C. McEwan* (*Edin. Acads.*), I. McIntyre (*Edin. Wrs.*), G. T. Neilson (*West of Scot.*), J. E. Orr (*West of Scot.*)
Referee: G. Rowland Hill (*England*)   **Touch judges:** G. Mitchell, Kane

W. Wotherspoon scored; J. D. Boswell converted (3-0): P. R. Clauss scored; J. D. Boswell failed (4-0); M. C. McEwan dropped a goal (7-0). (H.T.). W. Wotherspoon scored twice; J. D. Boswell converted the first (11-0): G. MacGregor scored; J. D. Boswell converted (14-0).

Played in fine weather on the Ulster ground at Ballynafeigh. This was a good open game with plenty of action from the Irish forwards and some hard running from their backs but overall Scotland were in control. Wotherspoon and Clauss were outstanding in attack. For Ireland Lee played well and Wells had one run the length of the field and touched down for a score that was disallowed. D. B. Walkington was reported as regularly wearing a monocle when playing, taking it off when making a tackle! Note that touch judges have replaced the umpires on the field.

ENGLAND 3   SCOTLAND 9
Athletic Ground, Richmond
7 March 1891

England: W. G. Mitchell (*Richmond*); P. Christopherson (*Blackheath*), F. H. R. Alderson* (*Hartlepool Rovers*), R. E. Lockwood (*Heckmondwike*); J. Berry (*Tyldesley*), W. R. M. Leake (*Harlequins*); E. Bonham-Carter (*Oxford Univ.*), R. T. D. Budworth (*Blackheath*), D. Jowett (*Heckmondwike*), T. Kent (*Salford*), E. H. G. North (*Oxford Univ.*), J. Richards (*Bradford*), J. H. Rogers (*Moseley*), R. P. Wilson (*Liverpool OB*), S. M. J. Woods (*Camb. Univ.*)
Scotland: H. J. Stevenson (*Edin. Acads.*); P. R. Clauss (*Oxford Univ.*), G. MacGregor (*Camb. Univ.*), W. Neilson (*Merchiston*); C. E. Orr (*West of Scot.*), D. G. Anderson (*London Scot.*); J. D. Boswell (*West of Scot.*), W. R. Gibson (*RHSFP*), F. W. J. Goodhue (*London Scot.*), H. T. O. Leggatt (*Watsonians*), M. C. McEwan* (*Edin. Acads.*), I. McIntyre (*Edin. Wrs.*), R. G. Macmillan (*London Scot.*), G. T. Neilson (*West of Scot.*), J. E. Orr (*West of Scot.*)
Referee: J. Chambers (*Ireland*)   **Touch judges:** D. G. Findlay, E. T. Gurdon

P. R. Clauss dropped a goal (3-0). (H.T.). J. E. Orr scored; G. MacGregor converted (6-0): W. Neilson scored; G. MacGregor converted (9-0): R. E. Lockwood scored; F. H. R. Alderson converted (9-3).

A severe storm and rain did not keep away a crowd of 20,000 who came hoping to see England win the Triple Crown but they had to go away bitterly disappointed. The critics blamed the forwards and halves who were completely outplayed by their opponents. Scotland began well, for within ten minutes C. E. Orr, getting the ball from a scrum, let MacGregor away, and when he passed to Clauss the winger dropped a very good left footed goal. After the restart MacGregor got the ball back from a line out and sent J. E. Orr off on a fast run round the English forwards and backs to score between the posts. Then D. G. Anderson, who had been playing very well, let MacGregor away and a good pass let W. Neilson (who was still at Merchiston) away for another try. The English defence had crumbled badly but Lockwood, who had tackled well, showed his paces and scored just on time. At full back H. J. Stevenson again showed himself to be a player of infinite resource and skill in defence and attack.

The Introduction of the Penalty Kick

Admiral Royd in his comprehensive *History of the Laws of Rugby Football* notes that in the early codes while some acts were classed as 'unlawful' no specific penalty was demanded and usually the offence was followed by a scrummage. Difficulties arose especially following cases of off-side play but the Rugby Football Union was reluctant to introduce further rules, preferring to trust to the sportsmanship of the players. It appears, however, that a judicious 'hack' was often used as an acceptable method of advising an opponent that he should get back 'on his side' or keep within the letter of the law! However, by 1882 a penalty kick was introduced for offside but no goal could be dropped or placed from this. Then in 1888, during the dispute, the RFU decided that a goal could now be scored from such an award but this ruling was not accepted by the new International Board until 1891 after the arbitration settlement.

This of course was a period when the game had spread to areas where most of the players were 'artisans' and 'lacked' the public school or 'Varsity background. This viewpoint is clearly revealed in an article which appeared in the magazine of one Scottish school in May 1893:

Legislation against intentionally handling the ball in a scrummage or wilfully putting the ball unfairly into a scrummage would have been regarded as an insult by the old fashioned football men. The fact that rugby football was hardly played by any except public school men goes a long way to explain such a state of matters. The gradual alteration in the rules and method of play corresponds with the gradual extension of the game to other classes of players. So in the old days penalties were unknown because unnecessary. If a player did make a mistake there was a scrummage and it was not until 1881 [sic] that any free kick penalty was introduced; and then the openly avowed reason for the change was that players, hailing principally from Yorkshire clubs, found it was an advantage under certain circumstances, to play offside. But the Yorkshire players for the most part were not public school men and those who have played against them in later years will, I think, be ready to admit that it is not among them that we must look for the Sir Nigel Lorings of Rugby Football.

It was against such a background that the South clubs in 1889 succeeded in getting one representative on to the Union committee but this did not satisfy them, for in 1891 their representatives, meeting at St Boswells, openly expressed their dissatisfaction with the SFU and even talked of forming a separate South of Scotland RU. Apparently the 1894 decision to double their representation seems to have produced an uneasy peace.

It is equally clear that the selection in 1890 of the first Border cap in the Gala forward, Adam Dalgleish, marked another break through. Dalgleish was an excellent choice for on more than one occasion it was he who was pulled out of the pack as a most successful replacement for an injured back player.

WALES 2   SCOTLAND 7
Swansea
6 February 1892

Wales: W. J. Bancroft (*Swansea*);T. W. Pearson (*Cardiff*). A. J. Gould* (*Newport*), W. M. McCutcheon (*Swansea*), J. C. Rees (*Llanelli*); D. James (*Swansea*), E. James (*Swansea*); P. Bennett (*Cardiff Harlequins*), A. W. Boucher (*Newport*), J. Deacon (*Swansea*), T. C. Graham (*Newport*), J. Hannan (*Newport*), F. Mills (*Swansea*), C. B. Nicholl (*Llanelli*), W. H. Watts (*Newport*)
Scotland: H. J. Stevenson (*Edin. Acads.*); W. Neilson (*Camb. Univ.*), G. T. Campbell (*London Scot.*), P. R. Clauss (*Oxford Univ.*); C. E. Orr* (*West of Scot.*), D. G. Anderson (*London Scot.*); J. D. Boswell (*West of Scot.*), A. Dalgleish (*Gala*), W. R. Gibson (*RHSFP*), F. W. J. Goodhue (*London Scot.*), H. T. O. Leggatt (*Watsonians*), R. G. Macmillan (*London Scot.*), J. N. Millar (*West of Scot.*), G. T. Neilson (*West of Scot.*), J. E. Orr (*West of Scot.*)
Referee: J. R. Hodgson (*England*)

J. Hannen scored; W. J. Bancroft failed (2-0); J. D. Boswell scored; P. R. Clauss failed (2-2); G. T. Campbell scored; J. D. Boswell converted (2-7). (H.T.).

An incessant downpour of rain had left the field so sodden that with a heavier pack the Scots were able to control the scrummages and smother the back play on which Wales depended so much. Yet throughout, the game was quite open and evenly contested and it was good forward play that gave Wales the opening score. Then the Scottish pack livened up and made the game safe. Wales played four backs and J. E. Orr came out of the pack 'to stop the chucking' but this was a frequent move for him. Indeed he must be one of the first winging forwards for he was often slated for doing more work out of the maul than in it. The referee did not please the crowd and he received some rough handling at the end of the match.

SCOTLAND 2   IRELAND 0
Raeburn Place
20 February 1892

Scotland: H. J. Stevenson (*Edin. Acads.*); G. T. Campbell (*London Scot.*), W. Neilson (*Camb. Univ.*), J. C. Woodburn (*Kelvinside Acads.*); C. E. Orr* (*West of Scot.*), W. Wotherspoon (*Camb. Univ.*); J. D. Boswell (*West of Scot.*), W. R. Gibson (*RHSFP*), F. W. J. Goodhue (*London Scot.*), N. F. Henderson (*London Scot.*), H. T. O. Leggatt (*Watsonians*), W. A. Macdonald (*Glas. Univ.*), R. G. Macmillan (*London Scot.*), J. N. Millar (*West of Scot.*), J. E. Orr (*West of Scot.*)
Ireland: T. Peel (*Bective Rangers*); R. Dunlop (*Dublin Univ.*), S. Lee (*NIFC*), W. Gardiner (*NIFC*); T. Thornhill (*Wanderers*), F. E. Davies (*Lansdowne*); A. D. Clinch (*Dublin Univ.*), G. Collopy (*Bective Rangers*). W. J. N. Davis (*Edin. Univ.*), E. F. Frazer (*Bective Rangers*), T. J. Johnston (*QC Belfast*), V. C. Le Fanu* (*Lansdowne*), C. V. Rooke (*Dublin Univ.*), A. K. Wallis (*Wanderers*), E. J. Walsh (*Lansdowne*)
Referee: H. L. Ashmore (*England*)   **Touch judges:** T. Ainslie, A. McAllister

J. N. Millar scored; J. D. Boswell failed (2-0). (H.T.).

There was a slight covering of snow which kept off until the last few minutes, for the game finished in a blinding storm. This was a fine open game with play swaying from end to end. Thornhill was much praised for some dangerous running but the Scottish backs were blamed for too much selfish play. Their defence, however, was very sound, Stevenson at full back being very safe and again he showed his ability to change defence into attack when, near the end, he made a fine solo run through nearly the whole of the opposition. Wotherspoon was very effective behind the scrum. Boswell produced one of his characteristic drop goals which, however, was turned down by the referee.

SCOTLAND 0 ENGLAND 5
Raeburn Place
5 March 1892

Scotland: H. J. Stevenson (*Edin . Acads.*); P. R. Clauss (*Oxford Univ.*), W. Neilson (*Camb. Univ.*), G. T. Campbell (*London Scot.*); C. E. Orr* (*West of Scot.*), D. G. Anderson (*London Scot.*); J. D. Boswell (*West of Scot.*), W. R. Gibson (*RHSFP*), F. W. J. Goodhue (*London Scot.*), W. A. Macdonald (*Glas. Univ.*), M. C. McEwan (*Edin. Acads.*), R. G. Macmillan (*London Scot.*), J. N . Millar (*West of Scot.*), G. T. Neilson (*West of Scot.*), J. E. Orr (*West of Scot.*)
England: T. Coop (*Leigh*); J. W. Dyson (*Huddersfield*), F. H. R. Alderson* (*Hartlepool Rovers*), R. E. Lockwood (*Heckmondwike*); A. Briggs (*Bradford*), H. Varley (*Liversedge*); H. Bradshaw (*Bramley*), W. E. Bromet (*Todcaster*), E. Bullough (*Wigan*), F. Evershed (*Blackheath*), T. Kent (*Salford*), W. Nichol (*Brighouse Rovers*), J. T. Toothill (*Bradford*), S. M. J. Woods (*Wellington*), W. Yiend (*Hartlepool Rovers*)
Referee: Warren (*Ireland*)   **Touch judges:** T. Ainslie, A. Budd.

W. E. Bromet scored; R. E. Lockwood converted (0-5). (H.T.).

After the rout of their pack last year England put eight Yorkshiremen into the team, and this stiffening certainly played its part for all three matches were won without a point being scored against them, but it also introduced an element of toughness into their play. One English report notes, 'Activity and skill were at a discount and very rough play was indulged in by both sides, the brandy bottle having frequently to be requisitioned for the knocked out ones'. The game then, although evenly contested, was mainly a forward battle but Briggs and Varley incensed the spectators by continually arriving too rapidly at the Scottish side of the scrums. As a result they fairly hammered Orr and Anderson and the Scottish backs suffered accordingly. Since the referee failed to penalise this and also disallowed two Scottish touchdowns, he too fell out of favour with the crowd, and some indignant letters appeared later in the local papers. Of the players, Lockwood was praised for his pace and skill, and Stevenson for his defence and willingness to attack from full back.

Before the start of the next season the Union Committee resolved that for the past 1891-92 season and for the future, the trophy caps should be presented by the Union.

Up to this time each player had purchased his own cap locally. Initially the style resembled a plain skullcap but about 1880 the front peak was added.

SCOTLAND 0 WALES 9
Raeburn Place
4 February 1893

Scotland: A. W. Cameron (*Watsonians*); D. D. Robertson (*Camb. Univ.*), G. MacGregor (*London Scot.*), J. J. Gowans (*Camb. Univ.*); R. C. Greig (*Glas. Acads.*), W. Wotherspoon (*West of Scot.*); W. B. Cownie (*Watsonians*), A. Dalgleish (*Gala*), W. R. Gibson (*RHSFP*), T. L. Hendry (*Clydesdale*), H. T. O. Leggatt (*Watsonians*), R. G. Macmillan* (*London Scot.*), H. F. Menzies (*West of Scot.*), J. N. Millar (*West of Scot.*), G. T. Neilson (*West of Scot.*)
Wales: W. J. Bancroft (*Swansea*); W. M. McCutcheon (*Oldham*), A. J. Gould* (*Newport*) G. H. Gould (*Newport*), N. M. Biggs (*Cardiff*); F. C. Parfitt (*Newport*), H. P. Phillips (*Newport*); A. W. Boucher (*Newport*), H. T. Day (*Newport*), T. C. Graham (*Newport*), J. Hannan (*Newport*), A. F. Hill (*Cardiff*), F. Mills (*Swansea*), C. B. Nicholl (*Camb. Univ.*), W. H. Watts (*Newport*)
Referee: Humphrey (*England*) Touch judges: D. S. Morton, W. Wilkins

There was no scoring before half time. G. H. Gould scored (0-2), N. M. Biggs scored (0-4) W. J. Bancroft drop kicked a penalty goal (0-7); W. M. McCutcheon scored (0-9). W. J. Bancroft failed to convert the three tries.

For the first time Scotland was beaten by the 4 back formation and indeed the second half produced such an exhibition of continuous running and passing that the virtues of the system were apparent to all. Yet men of the stature of A. R. Don Wauchope, C. Reid and R. G. Macmillan maintained that it would fail against a team which played the traditional Scottish forward game with wheeling, close dribbling rushes, fast following up and hard tackling, and they predicted that since the ball was needed for the backs these characteristic Scottish skills would in time be lost.

Since this game played a decisive part in establishing the four back formation it is interesting, with hindsight, to note that the win was achieved against a relatively poor side. H. J. Stevenson had not been picked, G. T. Campbell, W. Neilson, J. D. Boswell and J. E. Orr had withdrawn and had these five been present things might have gone differently.

As for the actual play the reports praised the Welsh backs for their spectacular running, A. J. Gould being frequently mentioned. H. F. Menzies got over the line in a forward rush but the score was disallowed. W. J. Bancroft dropped a goal from a penalty awarded for an off-side decision.

IRELAND 0   SCOTLAND 0
Ballynafeigh, Belfast
18 February 1893

Ireland: S. Gardiner (*Albion*); W. Gardiner (*NIFC*), S. Lee* (*NIFC*), L. H. Gwynn (*Dublin Univ.*); W. S. Brown (*Dublin Univ.*), F. E. Davies (*Lansdowne*); E. G. Forrest (*Wanderers*), H. Forrest (*Wanderers*), T. J. Johnston (*Queen's Con.*), J. S. Jameson (*Lansdowne*), H. Lindsay (*Armagh*), B. O'Brien (*Derry*), J. H. O'Conor (*Bective Rangers*), C. V. O'Rooke (*Dublin Univ.*), R. Stevenson (*Dungannon*)
Scotland: H. J. Stevenson (*Edin. Acads.*); G. T. Campbell (*London Scot.*), G. MacGregor (*London Scot.*), W. Neilson (*Camb. Univ.*); J. W. Simpson (*RHSFP*), W. P. Donaldson (*Oxford Univ.*); J. M. Bishop (*Glas. Acads.*), J. D. Boswell* (*West of Scot.*), W. B. Cownie (*Watsonians*), D. Fisher (*West of Scot.*), J. R. Ford (*Gala*), W. R. Gibson (*RHSFP*), T. L. Hendry (*Clydesdale*), H. F. Menzies (*West of Scot.*), J. E. Orr (*West of Scot.*)
Referee: G. Rowland Hill (*England*)   **Touch judges:** J. Stewart, J. Blood

This was played on the Ulster ground which was in poor condition and by half time more resembled a bog than a rugby ground so the game was largely a forward battle, the ball seldom moving out from the half backs. It was recorded that 'J. E. Orr came out of the pack to which he was seldom any more than a hanger on, to stop the rushes of the big Irish forwards.'

ENGLAND 0   SCOTLAND 8
Headingley, Leeds
4 March 1893

England: W. G. Mitchell (*Richmond*); J. W. Dyson (*Huddersfield*), A. E. Stoddart* (*Blackheath*), F. P. Jones (*North Brighton*); H. Duckett (*Bradford*), C. M. Wells (*Camb. Univ.*); H. Bradshaw (*Bramley*), T. Broadley (*Bingley*), W. E. Bromet (*Richmond*), F. Evershed (*Burton*), L. J. Percival (*Rugby*), J. J. Robertson (*Camb. Univ.*), F. Soane (*Bath*), J. T. Toothill (*Bradford*), W. Yiend (*Hartlepool Rovers*)
Scotland: H. J. Stevenson (*Edin. Acads.*); G. T. Campbell (*London Scot.*), G. MacGregor (*London Scot.*), W. Neilson (*Camb. Univ.*); J. W. Simpson (*RHSFP*), W. Wotherspoon (*West of Scot.*); J. D. Boswell* (*West of Scot.*), W. B. Cownie (*Watsonians*), R. S. Davidson (*RHSFP*), W. R. Gibson (*RHSFP*), T. L. Hendry (*Clydesdale*), H. T. O. Leggatt (*Watsonians*), R. G. Macmillan (*London Scot.*), J. E. Orr (*West of Scot.*), T. M. Scott (*Melrose*)
Referee: W. Wilkins (*Wales*)   **Touch judges:** D. S. Morton, W. Gail

J. D. Boswell dropped a goal (0-4). (H.T.). G. T. Campbell dropped a goal (0-8).

This was played on the fairly new Headingley field which was rather bare and also soft after some rain. The strong Scottish pack was quite at home on this and dominated play but the loose slippy surface hampered both sets of backs. Scotland started well; a dash by MacGregor was followed by a pass from Simpson to Neilson whose drop kick hit a post before dropping over, but to their dismay the referee disallowed the score. However he did accept a drop by Boswell, that noted exponent of unexpected drop kicks. The Scottish backs, with Campbell outstanding, did some strong running before half time but were held by good tackling. Shortly after the break Campbell got the ball from a loose scrum and made a good run which finished when Dyson knocked him down with a tackle. In a flash, not having lost the ball, he was back on his feet to drop a fine goal. Dyson and Duckett were praised for their defence but the English backs had too little of the ball to be effective in attack. Wotherspoon was admirable in feeding MacGregor who in turn fed his wing halves effectively. MacGregor, of course, had been selected as centre half for this very purpose. A Test Match wicketkeeper, he was a magnificent handler of the ball, taking all manner of passes and could throw long accurate passes to his wide set wings. The man he had displaced, H. J. Stevenson, was here playing his last game. As a centre half with his club and Scotland he had not been content to

43

be a feeder and tackler but showed an aggression, agility and resource which time and time again allowed him to halt an attack and immediately set up a counter attack. A determined and outspoken man he bluntly refused to change his style when the Union asked him to do so in 1891. He was far too good to drop so they put him at full back and discovered that they now had a full back with a solid defence and a distinct taste for attacking from that position. Undoubtedly he was one of the outstanding backs in the game at this time. Even in cricket his aggression was in evidence for he bowled underhand spin and took many astonishing off-the-bat catches by whipping up the pitch after the delivery. One of his victims commented that this was the first time he had batted against a silly mid on, a silly mid off and a silly bowler.

WALES 7   SCOTLAND 0
Newport
3 February 1894

Wales: W. J. Bancroft (*Swansea*); W. L. Thomas (*Newport*), D. Fizgerald (*Cardiff*), A. J. Gould* (*Newport*), T. W. Pearson (*Cardiff*); F. C. Parfitt (*Newport*), H. P. Phillips (*Newport*); D. J. Daniell (*Llanelli*), H. T. Day (*Newport*), T. C. Graham (*Newport*), J. Hannon (*Newport*), A. F. Hill (*Cardiff*), F. Mills (*Swansea*), C. B. Nicholl (*Camb. Univ.*), W. H. Watts (*Newport*)
Scotland: I. Rogerson (*Kelvinside Acads.*); G. T. Campbell (*London Scot.*), G. MacGregor (*London Scot.*), J. J. Gowans (*Camb. Univ.*), H. T. S. Gedge (*London Scot.*); W. Wotherspoon (*West of Scot.*), J. W. Simpson (*RHSFP*); W. B. Cownie (*Watsonians*), A. Dalgleish (*Gala*), W. R. Gibson (*RHSFP*), W. M. C. McEwan (*Edin. Acad.*), R. G. Macmillan* (*London Scot.*), H. F. Menzies (*West of Scot.*), G. T. Neilson (*West of Scot.*), H. B. Wright (*Watsonians*)
Referee: J. Holmes (*England*)   **Touch judges:** J. A. Smith, W. E. Rees

D. Fitzgerald scored but Bancroft failed (3-0). (H.T.). D. Fitzgerald dropped a goal (7-0).

J. D. Boswell (the elected captain), W. Neilson and H. T. O. Leggatt were replaced by H. B. Wright, J. J. Gowans and W. M. C. McEwan, the last being still at the Academy. He eventually went to Johannesburg and was capped for South Africa in 1903. Wales had to make four changes. For the first time Scotland played four halves and labelled them 'three quarters'. Their pack held its own but the backs were weaker than their opponents who frequently made ground by passing runs, one of which produced the first try.

IRELAND 5   SCOTLAND 0
Lansdowne Road
24 February 1894

Ireland: P. J. Grant (*Bective Rangers*); W. Gardiner (*NIFC*), S. Lee (*NIFC*), L. H . Gwynn (*Dublin Univ.*), H. G. Wells (*Bective Rangers*); W. S. Brown (*Dublin Univ.*), B. B. Tuke (*Bective Rangers*); A. T. W. Bond (*Derry*), T. J. Crean (*Wanderers*), E. G. Forrest* (*Wanderers*), H. Lindsay (*Dublin Univ.*), J. H. Lytle (*NIFC*), J. N. Lytle (*NIFC*), J. H. O'Conor (*Bective Rangers*), C. V. Rooke (*Dublin Uni.*)
Scotland: A. W. Cameron (*Watsonians*); G. T. Campbell (*London Scot.*), G. MacGregor (*London Scot.*), W. Wotherspoon (*West of Scot.*), H. T. S. Gedge (*Edin. Wrs.*); J. W. Simpson (*RHSFP*), W. P. Donaldson (*Oxford Univ.*); A. H. Anderson (*Glas. Acads.*), J. D. Boswell* (*West of Scot.*), W. B. Cownie (*Watsonians*), A. Dalgleish (*Gala*), W. R. Gibson (*RHSFP*), H. T. O. Leggatt (*Watsonians*), R. G. Macmillan (*London Scot.*), G. T. Neilson (*West of Scot.*)
Referee: H. L. Ashmore (*England*)   **Touch judges:** J. A. Smith, Garrett

No scoring at half time. H. G. Wells scored; J. Lytle converted (5-0).

Once again an Irish game was played on a rain sodden ground and play was largely confined to the forwards who were fairly evenly matched. There were one or two near misses with drop kicks, but Ireland won with a late run by the backs which let Wells score. The spectators were not amused at an extra long interval during which the two captains were introduced to the Lord Lieutenant.

SCOTLAND 6   ENGLAND 0
Raeburn Place
17 March 1894

Scotland: G. MacGregor (*London Scot.*); G. T. Campbell (*London Scot.*), W. Neilson (*Camb. Univ.*), H. T. S. Gedge (*Edin. Wrs.*), J. J. Gowans (*Camb. Univ.*); W. Wotherspoon (*West of Scot.*), J. W. Simpson (*RHSFP*), J. D. Boswell* (*West of Scot.*), W. B. Cownie (*Watsonians*), W. R. Gibson (*RHSFP*), H. T. O. Leggatt (*Watsonians*), W. M. C. McEwan (*Edin. Academy*), R. G. Macmillan (*London Scot.*), H. F. Menzies (*West of Scot.*), W. G. Neilson (*Merchiston Castle*)
England: J. F. Byrne (*Moseley*); C. A. Hooper (*Middlesex Wrs.*), W. J. Jackson (*Halifax*), S. Morfitt (*W. Hartlepool*), F. Firth (*Halifax*); E. W. Taylor* (*Rockcliff*), C. M. Wells (*Harlequins*), A. Allport (*Blackheath*), H. Bradshaw (*Bramley*), T. Broadley (*Bingley*), A. E. Elliot (*St Thomas's*), H. Hall (*N. Durham*), F. Sloane (*Bath*), H. Speed (*Castleford*), W. Walton (*Castleford*)
Referee: W. Wilkins (*Wales*)   **Touch judges**: W. E. Maclagan, W. Cail

No scoring at half time. J. D. Boswell scored twice; Wotherspoon and Boswell failed with the kicks (6-0).

Both teams retained the four three quarter formation. Scotland were very much on top throughout. Their forwards played well but the backs indulged in too many speculative drops at goal. Wotherspoon was hurt during the first half but resumed on the wing after the interval. Scotland played two schoolboys in McEwan and W. G. Neilson. The latter joined his brother, Willie, when he replaced another injured brother, George. The XV had played a practice match against Merchiston on 15 March and the committee, after strong representation from the captain and others, decided to nominate young Gordon as first reserve forward.

SCOTLAND 5   WALES 4
Raeburn Place
26 January 1895

Scotland: A. R. Smith (*Oxford Univ.*); J. J. Gowans (*London Scot.*), G. T. Campbell (*London Scot.*), W. Neilson (*London Scot.*), R. Welsh (*Watsonians*); J. W. Simpson (*RHSFP*), M. Elliot (*Hawick*), W. B. Cownie (*Watsonians*), J. H. Dods (*Edin. Acads.*), W. R. Gibson* (*RHSFP*), W. M. C. McEwan (*Edin. Acads.*), R. G. Macmillan (*London Scot.*), G. T. Neilson (*West of Scot.*), T. Scott (*Hawick*), H. O. Smith (*Watsonians*)
Wales: W. J. Bancroft (*Swansea*); E. Lloyd (*Llanelli*), A. J. Gould* (*Newport*), O. Badger (*Llanelli*), T. W. Pearson (*Cardiff*); F. C. Parfitt (*Newport*), S. Biggs (*Cardiff*); A. W. Boucher (*Newport*), E. George (*Pontypridd*), T. C. Graham (*Newport*), J. Hannan (*Newport*), F. Mills (*Cardiff*), C. B. Nicholl (*Llanelli*), H. Packer (*Newport*), T. Pook (*Newport*)
Referee: E. B. Holmes (*England*)

No scoring at half time. J. J. Gowans scored; H. O. Smith converted (5-0); W. J. Bancroft dropped a goal (5-4).

After the protective straw had been removed from the field, the north end was found to be too hard and at the request of the Welsh – who refused to play otherwise – the pitch was shortened by some eighteen yards to eliminate this area. Even so the ground remained unpleasantly hard, and one dangerous run by Gould later on finished when he swerved and slipped. There was a lot of fine play, nevertheless, with the Scottish pack showing up well in the loose. Behind them, Elliot in his first game, did well in attack and defence. In the second half Wales did a fair amount of attacking but Campbell's defence and kicking saved several situations. Ironically, it was a weak drop at goal by him which produced the first score for Bancroft, having fielded the kick, had his own kick charged down and Gowans went over for a try converted by H. O. Smith. Wales fought back but the defence, notably A. R. Smith, was sound. Then McEwan, on his own goal line, marked a dangerous kick ahead and kicked for touch, only to see Bancroft catch the ball, move deliberately infield and drop a fine goal from near half way. This finished the scoring although Gowans had one fine run to be collared on the line in front of the posts.

The Scottish XV had been chosen in two sessions for five places were left vacant until the committee had seen the South v. North game and it is interesting to note that W. R. Gibson the captain, was one of the second batch.

SCOTLAND 6   IRELAND 0
Raeburn Place
2 March 1895

Scotland: A. R. Smith (*Oxford Univ.*); J. J. Gowans (*London Scot.*), G. T. Campbell (*London Scot.*), W. Neilson (*London Scot.*), R. Welsh (*Watsonians*); J. W. Simpson (*RHSFP*), P. R. Clauss (*Birkenhead Park*); W. B. Cownie (*Watsonians*), J. H. Dods (*Edin. Acads.*) W. R. Gibson (*RHSFP*), T. L. Hendry (*Clydesdale*), R. G. Macmillan* (*London Scot.*) J. N. Millar (*West of Scot.*), G. T. Neilson (*West of Scot.*), T. M. Scott (*Hawick*)
Ireland: J. Fulton (*NIFC*); W. Gardiner (*NIFC*), J. T. Magee (*Bective Rangers*), A. Montgomery (*NIFC*), J. O'Conor (*Garryowen*); L. M. Magee (*Bective Rangers*), B. B. Tuke (*Bective Rangers*); A. D. Clinch (*Wanderers*), T. Crean (*Wanderers*), W. J. N. Davis (*Edin. Univ.*), M. S. Egan (*Garryowen*), H. C. McCoull (*Albion*), E. H. McIlwaine (*NIFC*), W. O'Sullivan (*QC Cork*), C. V. Rooke (*Monkstown*)
Referee: H. L. Ashmore (*England*)   **Touch judges:** M. C. McEwan, Macaulay

No scoring at half time. R. Welsh scored; T. M. Scott failed (3-0); G. T. Campbell scored; W. B. Cownie failed (6-0).

This match was postponed twice from January and both team selections were much influenced by influenza. Play was fairly even in the first half, both sides showing good defence but R. Welsh ran dangerously. Ireland started the second half confidently with a fine run by J. T. Magee but Scotland gradually got on top. Cownie had a run, passed to Simpson and the ball went via W. Neilson to Welsh who scored. Shortly afterwards Simpson and Clauss had a good passing run before giving the ball to W. Neilson who sent Campbell off on a grand dodging run through a mass of opponents to score. One reference book shows J. H. Lytle playing with J. T. Magee missing.

ENGLAND 3   SCOTLAND 6
Athletic Ground, Richmond
9 March 1895

England: J. F. Byrne (*Moseley*); J. H. C. Fegan (*Blackheath*), W. B. Thomson (*Blackheath*), E. M. Baker (*Oxford Univ.*), T. H. Dobson (*Bradford*); R. H. B. Cattell (*Moseley*), E. W. Taylor (*Rockcliff*); W. E. Bromet (*Richmond*), G. M. Carey (*Oxford Univ.*), W. H. Finlinson (*Blackheath*), F. Mitchell (*Camb. Univ.*), F. O. Poole (*Oxford Univ.*), C. Thomas (*Barnstaple*), W. E. Tucker (*Camb. Univ.*), S. M. J. Woods* (*Bridgewater*)
Scotland: A. R. Smith (*Oxford Univ.*); R. Welsh (*Watsonians*), W. Neilson (*London Scot.*), J. J. Gowans (*London Scot.*), G. T. Campbell (*London Scot.*); J. W. Simpson (*RHSFP*), W. P. Donaldson (*West of Scot.*); W. B. Cownie (*Watsonians*), J. H. Dods (*Edin. Acads.*), W. R. Gibson (*RHSFP*), W. M. C. McEwan (*Edin. Acads.*), R. G. Macmillan* (*London Scot.*), J. N. Millar (*West of Scot.*), G. T. Neilson (*West of Scot.*), T. M. Scott (*Hawick*)
Referee: W. Wilkins (*Wales*)   **Touch judges:** D. G. Findlay, R. S. Whalley

J. F. Byrne kicked a penalty goal (3-0); G. T. Neilson kicked a penalty goal (3-3); G. T. Neilson scored but failed to convert (3-6). (H.T.).

The Scottish pack controlled the game throughout and tended to keep the ball tight so there was relatively little back play especially as Donaldson, as was his custom, did a lot of kicking to touch. Scotland started well and were startled to find themselves trailing when Byrne kicked England's first ever penalty goal from mid field. However, G. T. Neilson with an equally fine kick from the touchline equalised with Scotland's first penalty goal and it is interesting to note that it took 30 years before another penalty goal was kicked in a Calcutta Cup match. Before half time G. T. Neilson caught Byrne with the ball and securing it was able to run in for a try. A match programme exists for this game and the backs are set out in the formation shown above.

WALES 6   SCOTLAND 0
Cardiff
25 January 1896

Wales: W. J. Bancroft (*Swansea*); F. H. Dauncey (*Newport*), A. J. Gould* (*Newport*), E. G. Nicholls (*Cardiff*), C. Bowen (*Llanelli*); F. C. Parfitt (*Newport*), S. Biggs (*Cardiff*); W. Cope (*Blackheath*), W. Davies (*Cardiff*), D. Evans (*Penygraig*), J. Evans (*Llanelli*), F. Hutchinson (*Neath*), W. Morris (*Llanelli*), C. B. Nicholls (*Llanelli*), H. Packer (*Newport*)
Scotland: A. R. Smith (*Oxford Univ.*); G. T. Campbell (*London Scot.*), A. B . Timms (*Edin. Wrs.*), T. Scott (*Langholm*), R. Welsh (*Watsonians*); J. W. Simpson (*RHSFP*), D. Patterson (*Hawick*), A. Balfour (*Watsonians*), J. H. Couper (*West of Scot.*), J. H. Dods (*London Scot.*), W. M. C. McEwan (*Edin. Acads.*), M. C. Morrison (*RHSFP*), G. T. Neilson* (*West of Scot.*), T. Scott (*Hawick*), H. O. Smith (*Watsonians*)
Referee: G. H. Barnett (*England*)   **Touch judges**: D. G. Findlay, W. Davies

No scoring at half time. C. Bowen and A. J. Gould scored but W. J. Bancroft failed in each case (6-0).

After a week of rain Cardiff Arms Park was a sea of mud and while this suited the Scottish pack in the loose they were beaten in the mauls. The handling of the Scottish backs continually broke down and they were completely outclassed by the Welsh backs who passed, kicked and ran as if the conditions were perfect. Both Welsh scores came from fine passing runs by the backs. So the game became a series of Welsh attacks with intermittent raids by the Scottish forwards who in the last ten minutes strove hard to score, pinning their opponents on their goal line. It is worth recording that two of the game's greatest figures in M. C. Morrison and E. G. Nicholls gained their first caps.

IRELAND 0   SCOTLAND 0
Lansdowne Road
15 February 1896

Ireland: G. H. McAllan (*Dungannon*); W. Gardiner (*NIFC*), S. Lee* (*NIFC*), T. H. Stevenson (*Edin. Univ.*), L. Q. Bulger (*Dublin Univ.*); L. M. Magee (*Bective Rangers*), G. G. Allen (*Derry*), W. G. Byron (*NIFC*), A. D. Clinch (*Wanderers*), T. J. Crean (*Wanderers*), H. Lindsay (*Armagh*), J. H. Lytle (*NIFC*), J. H. O'Conor (*Bective Rangers*), C. V. Rooke (*Monkstown*), J. Sealey (*Dublin Univ.*)
Scotland: A. R. Smith (*Oxford Univ.*); W. Neilson (*London Scot.*), G. T. Campbell (*London Scot.*), J. J. Gowans (*London Scot.*), C. J. N. Fleming (*Edin. Wrs.*); J. W. Simpson (*RHSFP*), W. P. Donaldson (*West of Scot.*); A. Balfour (*Watsonians*), J. H. Couper (*West of Scot.*), J. H. Dods (*London Scot.*), W. M. C. McEwan (*Edin. Acads.*), M. C. Morrison (*RHSFP*), G. T. Neilson* (*West of Scot.*), H. O. Smith (*Watsonians*), G. O. Turnbull (*West of Scot.*)
Referee: E. Holmes (*England*) Touch judges: D. G. Findlay, R. G. Warren

A draw was a fair result for a fast exciting game, full of incident and remarkable for the number of penalties missed by the two recognised goalkickers, H. O. Smith and L. Q. Bulger. Both packs had their spells of domination and the Irish barrage of the last five minutes stretched the defence to its limit. Young McAllan, still at school, had one break through in the second half but passed instead of going on and Gardiner could not get the ball. Later Gowans, who had been handicapped by a damaged finger also had a fine touch line run which was halted just short of the line.

SCOTLAND 11   ENGLAND 0
Old Hampden Park, Glasgow
14 March 1896

Scotland: G. MacGregor (*London Scot.*); H. T. S. Gedge (*London Scot.*), G. T. Campbell (*London Scot.*), C. J. N. Fleming (*Edin. Wrs.*), J. J. Gowans (*London Scot.*); M. Elliot (*Hawick*), W. P. Donaldson (*West of Scot.*), A. Balfour (*Watsonians*), J. H. Dods (*London Scot.*), W. M. C. McEwan (*Edin. Acads.*), M. C. Morrison (*RHSFP*), G. T. Neilson (*West of Scot.*), T. M. Scott (*Hawick*), H. O. Smith (*Watsonians*), G. O. Turnbull (*West of Scot.*)
England: R. W. Poole (*Hartlepool Rovers*); S. Morfitt (*Hull KR*), E. M. Baker (*Oxford Univ.*), J. Valentine (*Swinton*), E. F. Fookes (*Sowerby Bridge*); C. M. Wells (*Harlequins*), R. H. Cattell (*Blackheath*); J. H. Barron (*Bingley*), T. Broadley (*Bingley*),

47

G. E. Hughes (*Barrow*), E. Knowles (*Millom*), F. Mitchell (*Camb. Univ.*), J. Rhodes (*Castleford*), H. Speed (*Castleford*), J. W. Ward (*Castleford*)
Referee: Douglas (*Wales*)   **Touch judges:** D. G. Findlay, R. Walker

H. T. S. Gedge scored; H. O. Smith failed (3-0). (H.T.). J. J. Gowans scored; T. M. Scott failed (6-0); C. J. N. Fleming scored; T. M. Scott converted (11-0).

The Scottish pack dominated the play and although Donaldson kicked too much to touch, Elliot, who replaced J. W. Simpson, played very well and the aggressive Scottish backs had a good supply of the ball. Gedge was fast, Campbell was always a good attacking player and Fleming, weighing some fifteen stones, proved difficult to hold. After some Scottish pressure a good run by Speed and Cattell saw Baker just fail to score. Good touch kicking by Gowans and Gedge took play back and Gedge having made a good run, dropped at goal when he was actually clear. Elliot then broke from a line out and the ball passed from Donaldson and Fleming to Gedge whose pace and swerve let him score at the posts only to see Smith miss the kick. The second half began like the first: Scottish pressure was relieved by some good running by the English backs but they were inclined to run across the field and good tackling halted progress. Then Gedge intercepted a pass and after a strong run a passing movement between himself and Campbell let Fleming score.

SCOTLAND 8   IRELAND 3
Powderhall, Edinburgh
20 February 1897

Scotland: A. R. Smith (*Oxford Univ.*); G. T. Campbell (*London Scot.*), W. Neilson (*London Scot.*), C. J. N. Fleming (*Edin. Wrs.*), T. Scott (*Hawick*); M. Elliot (*Hawick*), R. C. Greig (*Glas. Acads.*); J. H. Dods (*Edin. Acads.*), A. Laidlaw (*Hawick*), W. M. C. McEwan (*Edin. Acads.*), R. G. Macmillan* (*London Scot.*), M. C. Morrison (*RHSFP*), T. M. Scott (*Hawick*), R. C. Stevenson (*London Scot.*), G. O. Turnbull (*London Scot.*)
Ireland: P. E. O'Brien-Butler (*Monkstown*); W. Gardiner (*NIFC*), L. Q. Bulger (*Dublin Univ.*), T. H. Stevenson (*Albion*), L. H. Gwynn (*Dublin Univ.*); L. M. Magee (*Bective Rangers*), G. G. Allen (*Derry*); W. G. Byron (*NIFC*), A. D. Clinch (*Wanderers*), E. F. Forrest* (*Wanderers*), J. H. Lytle (*NIFC*), J. E. McIlwaine (*NIFC*), C. V. Rooke (*Monkstown*), M. Ryan (*Rockwell*), J. Sealey (*Dublin Univ.*)
Referee: A. B. Holmes (*England*)   **Touch judges:** D. G. Findlay, J. E. Dodds

L. Q. Bulger scored but failed (0-3). (H.T.). G. O. Turnbull scored; T. M. Scott converted (5-3); T. M. Scott kicked a penalty (8-3).

Ireland had the benefit of a strong westerly wind but could only score once during the first half and that mainly due to shaky play by Fleming who had a real off-day. M. Elliot showed up well, continually halting the Irish forwards who indulged in their familiar rushing tactics. Scotland got well on top in the second half. Morrison took the ball over the line but was not given the score and T. M. Scott had a penalty goal kick turned down before Turnbull scored the decisive try.

ENGLAND 12   SCOTLAND 3
Fallowfield, Manchester
13 March 1897

England: J. F. Byrne (*Moseley*); E. F. Fookes (*Sowerby Bridge*), W. L. Bunting (*Richmond*), O. G. Mackie (*Camb. Univ.*), G. C. Robinson (*Percy Park*); E. W. Taylor* (*Rockcliff*), C. M. Wells (*Harlequins*); Jas. Davidson (*Aspatria*), H. W. Dudgeon (*Richmond*), L. F. Giblin (*Camb. Univ.*), F. Jacob (*Camb. Univ.*), E. Knowles (*Millom*), R. F. Oakes (*Hartlepool Rovers*), J. Pinch (*Lancaster*), W. B. Stoddart (*Liverpool*)
Scotland: A. R. Smith (*Oxford Univ.*); A. M. Bucher (*Edin. Acads.*), W. Neilson (*London Scot.*), T. Scott (*Hawick*), A. W. Robertson (*Edin. Acads.*); M. Elliot (*Hawick*), J. W. Simpson (*RHSFP*); A. Balfour (*Camb. Univ.*), J. H. Dods (*Edin. Acads.*), W. M. C. McEwan (*Edin. Acads.*), R. G. Macmillan* (*London Scot.*), M. C. Morrison (*RHSFP*), T. M. Scott (*Hawick*), R. C. Stevenson (*London Scot.*), G. O. Turnbull (*London Scot.*)
Referee: J. T. Magee (*Ireland*)   **Touch judges:** D. G. Findlay, R. S. Whalley

No scoring at half time. E. F. Fookes and G. C. Robinson scored; J. F. Byrne converted the first (8-0); A. M. Bucher scored; T. M. Scott failed (8-3); J. F. Byrne dropped a goal (12-3).

48

Scotland came to Manchester as favourites but were outplayed in all departments. The English half backs dominated the game and Robinson on the wing had a great attacking afternoon. R. G. Macmillan often came out of the pack to strengthen the defence although A. R. Smith was very sound at full back. The Scottish score came when Bucher dribbled up to the full back, kicked the ball on and won the race for the touch down.

IRELAND 0 SCOTLAND 8
Balmoral, Belfast
19 February 1898

Ireland: P. E. O'Brien-Butler (*Monkstown*); F. C. Purser (*Dublin Univ.*), F. F. S. Smithwick (*Monkstown*), L. H. Gwynn (*Dublin Univ.*), L. Q. Bulger (*Lansdowne*); G. G. Allen* (*Derry*), L. M. Magee (*Edin. Wrs.*); W. G. Byron (*NIFC*), J. L. Davis (*Monkstown*), J. G. Franks (*Dublin Univ.*), H. Lindsay (*Wanderers*), J. H. Lytle (*NIFC*), J. E. McIlwaine (*NIFC*), J. Ryan (*Rockwell*), M. Ryan (*Rockwell*)
Scotland: J. M. Reid (*Edin. Acads.*); A. R. Smith* (*Oxford Univ.*), E. Spencer (*Clydesdale*), R. T. Neilson (*West of Scot.*), T. Scott (*Hawick*); M. Elliot (*Hawick*), J. T. Mabon (*Jedforest*); J. M. Dykes (*Clydesdale*), G. C. Kerr (*Durham*), W. M. C. McEwan (*Edin. Acads.*), A. Mackinnon (*London Scot.*), M. C. Morrison (*RHSFP*), R. Scott (*Hawick*), T. M. Scott (*Hawick*), H. O. Smith (*Watsonians*)
Referee: E. T. Gurdon (*England*)   **Touch judges**: R. D. Rainie, Rev. R. Huggard

No scoring at half time. T. Scott scored twice and T. M. Scott converted the first only (0-8).

Played on the Show Ground at Balmoral before 12,000 spectators. Smithwick was recorded as a seventeen year old replacement in the Irish backs. Scotland had the benefit of a strong wind in the first half but with eight new caps played a very disjointed game and Ireland were jubilant to be on equal terms at half time. They restarted strongly and only a good tackle by Reid prevented M. Ryan from scoring. Then McEwan was more or less crippled yet Scotland went on the offensive and Tom Scott's pace brought them two winning scores.

SCOTLAND 3 ENGLAND 3
Powderhall, Edinburgh
12 March 1898

Scotland: J. M. Reid (*Edin. Acads.*); A. R. Smith* (*Oxford Univ.*), T. A. Nelson (*Oxford Univ.*), R. T. Neilson (*West of Scot.*), T. Scott (*Hawick*); M. Elliot (*Hawick*), J. T. Mabon (*Jedforest*); J. M. Dykes (*Clydesdale*), G. C. Kerr (*Durham*), W. M. C. McEwan (*Edin. Acads.*), A. MacKinnon (*London Scot.*), M. C. Morrison (*RHSFP*), T. M. Scott (*Hawick*), H. O. Smith (*Watsonians*), R. C. Stevenson (*Northumberland*)
England: J. F. Byrne* (*Moseley*); W. N. Pilkington (*Camb. Univ.*), W. L. Bunting (*Richmond*), P. M. R. Royds (*Blackheath*), P. W. Stout (*Gloucester*); G. T. Unwin (*Blackheath*), A. Rotherham (*Richmond*); W. Ashford (*Exeter*), Jas. Davidson (*Aspatria*), H. W. Dudgeon (*Richmond*), F. Jacob (*Richmond*), R. F. Oakes (*Hartlepool Rovers*), H. E. Ramsden (*Bingley*), J. F. Shaw (*RIEC*), F. M. Stout (*Gloucester*)
Referee: J. Dodds (*Ireland*)   **Touch judges**: R. D. Rainie, R. S. Whalley

No scoring at half time. P. M. R. Royds scored; J. P. Byrne failed (0-3); W. M. C. McEwan scored; T. M. Scott failed (3-3).

Powderhall was used again since the new ground at Inverleith was not ready. Scotland did quite well against the wind in the first half, Tom Scott nearly scoring thrice but their backs were not at their best. In the second half England opened the scoring when Reid's touch kick rebounded off Royds who ran on to score. Fortunately the Scottish pack was in fine fettle and continued pressure saw McEwan burst through for a try that T. M. Scott couldn't convert.

SCOTLAND 3   IRELAND 9
Inverleith
18 February 1899

Scotland: J. M. Reid (*Edin. Acads.*); G. T. Campbell (*London Scot.*), D. B. Monypenny (*London Scot.*), R. T. Neilson (*West of Scot.*), T. Scott (*Langholm*); W. P. Donaldson* (*West of Scot.*), J. T. Mabon (*Jedforest*); J. H. Couper (*West of Scot.*), L. Harvey (*Greenock Wrs.*), G. C. Kerr (*Durham*), W. M. C. McEwan (*Edin. Acads.*), A. Mackinnon (*London Scot.*), M. C. Morrison (*RHSFP*), H. O. Smith (*Watsonians*), R. C. Stevenson (*Northumberland*)
Ireland: P. E. O'Brien-Butler (*Monkstown*); G. P. Doran (*Lansdowne*), J. B. Allison (*Campbell Coll.*), C. Reid (*NIFC*), E. F. Campbell (*Monkstown*); L. M. Magee* (*Bective Rangers*), A. Barr (*Methodist Coll.*); W. G. Byron (*NIFC*), T. J. Little (*Bective Rangers*), J. H. Lytle (*NIFC*), T. M. W. McGown (*NIFC*), A. W. D. Meares (*Dublin Univ.*), J. Ryan (*Rockwell*), M. Ryan (*Rockwell*), J. Sealy (*Dublin Univ.*)
Referee: E. T. Gurdon (*England*)   **Touch judges:** J. D. Boswell

E. F. Campbell and C. Reid scored; J. H. Lytle failed with both (0-6). (H.T.). J. Sealy scored; L. M. Magee failed (0-9); W. P. Donaldson dropped a penalty goal (3-9).

The Welsh match having been postponed this became the opening match on the Union's new field at Inverleith. Ireland had to make six changes to Scotland's three. The match was won by the Irish pack behind which Magee was particularly brilliant for his elusive running, setting up two scores in the first half. Early in the second half a tremendous rush by the Irish forwards put Sealy over for another try and put Reid off the field with a dislocated shoulder. Later Monypenny on his own line kicked the ball clear of the Irish halves, reached it and kicked on again to reach the full back. He put the ball past the full back, over the line and was running on to touch down when he was tackled from behind and brought down. Donaldson dropped a goal from the resultant penalty kick.

SCOTLAND 21   WALES 10
Inverleith
4 March 1899

Scotland: H. Rottenburg (*London Scot.*); H. T. S. Gedge (*London Scot.*), D. B. Monypenny (*London Scot.*), G. A. W. Lamond (*Kelvinside Acads.*), T. Scott (*Langholm*); R. T. Neilson (*West of Scot.*), J. W. Simpson (*RHSFP*); J. M. Dykes (*London Scot.*), G. C. Kerr (*Edin. Wrs.*), W. M. C. McEwan (*Edin. Acads.*), A. Mackinnon (*London Scot.*), M. C. Morrison* (*RHSFP*), H. O. Smith (*Watsonians*), R. C. Stevenson (*London Scot.*), W. J. Thomson (*West of Scot.*)
Wales: W. J. Bancroft* (*Swansea*); W. M. Llewellyn (*Llwynypia*), R. T. Skirmshire (*Newport*), E. G. Nicholls (*Cardiff*), H. V. P. Huzzey (*Cardiff*); G. L. Lloyd (*Newport*), S. Biggs (*Cardiff*); W. H. Alexander (*Llwynypia*), J. Blake (*Cardiff*), A. Brice (*Aberavon*), T. Dobson (*Cardiff*), R. Hellings (*Llwynypia*), J. J. Hodges (*Newport*), W. Parker (*Swansea*), F. Scrimes (*Swansea*)
Referee: M. G. Delaney (*Ireland*)   **Touch judges:** J. D. Boswell, T. D. Schofield

H. T. S. Gedge scored; G. A. W. Lamond failed (3-0); G. L. Lloyd scored; W. J. Bancroft converted (3-5); W. M. Llewellyn scored; W. J. Bancroft converted (3-10). (H.T.). D. B. Monypenny scored; W. J. Thomson failed (6-10); W. J. Thomson kicked a goal from a mark by J. W. Simpson (10-10); G. A. W. Lamond dropped a goal (14-10); H.O. Smith scored; W. J. Thomson failed (17-10); H. T. S. Gedge dropped a goal (21-10).

This was a much postponed match and Wales having thrashed England came as favourites. Scotland however started well when the backs sent Gedge away to score after a fine dodging run but the Welsh backs were equally fast and effective and good running produced two tries before half time. After the restart the home pack got well on top and right away Monypenny scored. Then Neilson had his nose fractured and some of the fluency amongst the backs vanished, the only try coming from a charged down kick. The last score was a surprise for Gedge was given the ball in the clear but decided to drop at goal instead of running.

ENGLAND 0   SCOTLAND 5
Rectory Field, Blackheath
11 March 1899

England: H. T. Gamlin (*Wellington*); E. F. Fookes (*Sowerby Bridge*), W. L. Bunting (*Richmond*), J. C. Matters (*RNEC*), P. W. Stout (*Gloucester*); A. Rotherham* (*Richmond*), R. O. Schwarz (*Richmond*); Jas. Davidson (*Aspatria*), Jos. Davidson (*Aspatria*), A. O. Dowson (*Moseley*), H. W. Dudgeon (*Richmond*), R. F. A. Hobbs (*Blackhealh*), R. F. Oakes (*Hartlepool Rovers*), J. P. Shooter (*Morley*), F. M. Stout (*Gloucester*)
Scotland: H. Rottenburg (*London Scot.*); H. T. S. Gedge (*London Scot.*), D. B. Monypenny (*London Scot.*), G. A. W. Lamond (*Kelvinside Acads.*), T. Scott (*Langholm*); J. I. Gillespie (*Edin. Acads.*), J. W. Simpson (*RHSFP*); J. M. Dykes (*London Scot.*), G. C. Kerr (*Edin. Wrs.*), W. M. C. McEwan (*Edin. Acads.*), A. Mackinnon (*London Scot.*), M. C. Morrison* (*RHSFP*), H. O. Smith (*Watsonians*), R. C. Stevenson (*London Scot.*), W. J. Thomson (*West of Scot.*)
Referee: J. T. Magee (*Ireland*)   **Touch judges:** J. D. Boswell

No scoring at halftime. J. I. Gillespie scored; W. J. Thomson converted (0-5).

Scotland had rather the better of the first half but both sides lost tries by repeatedly knocking on scoring passes. Tom Scott, however, was prominent with much dangerous running. Before half-time J. W. Simpson twisted a knee and although remaining on the field as an extra full back was of no use. H. O. Smith took his place at quarter and played really well there. In spite of this the Scottish pack controlled the game but the English backs, especially Gamlin, defended very well and the only score came from a very long dribbling run by Gillespie who just managed to touch down short of the dead ball line. Gillespie who played well throughout, had replaced the injured Neilson so Scotland for the first time since 1890 were without one of the famous family.

WALES 12   SCOTLAND 3
Swansea
27 January 1900

Wales: W. J. Bancroft (*Swansea*); W. M. Llewellyn (*Llwynypia*), E. G. Nicholls (*Cardiff*), G. Davies (*Swansea*), W. J. Trew (*Swansea*); G. L. Lloyd (*Newport*), L. A. Phillips (*Newport*); J. Blake (*Cardiff*), J. G. Boots (*Newport*), A. Brice (*Aberavon*), G. Dobson (*Cardiff*), J. J. Hodges (*Newport*), F. Miller (*Mountain Ash*), R. Thomas (*Swansea*), W. H. Williams (*Pontyminster*)
Scotland: H. Rottenburg (*London Scot.*); T. Scott (*Langholm*), A. B. Timms (*Edin. Univ.*), W. H. Morrison (*Edin. Acads.*), J. E. Crabbie (*Edin. Acads.*); J . I. Gillespie (*Edin. Acads.*), F. H. Fasson (*London Scon*); D. R. Bedell-Sivright (*Camb. Univ.*), J. M. Dykes (*London Scot.*), F. W. Henderson (*London Scot.*), G. C. Kerr (*Durham*), W. M. C. McEwan (*Edin. Acads.*), M. C. Morrison* (*RHSFP*), T. M. Scott (*Hawick*), W. J. Thomson (*West of Scot.*)
Referee: A. Hartley (*England*)

W. M. Llewellyn scored (3-0); J. M. Dykes scored; T. M. Scott failed (3-3); W. G. Nicholls scored (6-3). (H.T.). W. M. Llewellyn and W. H. Williams scored (12-3); W. J. Bancroft failed with all four conversions.

The Welsh pack was clearly on top and with a plentiful supply of the ball a fine set of backs were continually making brilliant passing runs. Lloyd and Nicholls were especially good and the latter gave Llewellyn many opportunities to utilise his pace on the wing. Play was quite one-sided and the only redeeming feature for Scotland was the determined defence maintained by their backs, Tom Scott in particular. The Scottish try came from a rush in which McEwan and Dykes were prominent and the latter scored when Bancroft made a slip.

IRELAND 0   SCOTLAND 0
Lansdowne Road
24 February 1900

Ireland: C. A. Boyd (*Dublin Univ.*); G. P. Doran (*Lansdowne*), B. R. W. Doran (*Lansdowne*), J. B. Allison (*QC Belfast*), I. G. Davidson (*NIFC*); L. M. Magee* (*Bective Rangers*), J. H. Ferris (*QC Belfast*); C. E. Allen (*Liverpool*) F. Gardiner (*NIFC*), S. T.

Irwin (*QC Belfast*), T. J. Little (*Bective Rangers*), P. C. Nicholson (*Dublin Univ.*), J. Ryan (*Rockwell*), M. Ryan (*Rockwell*), J. Sealey (*Dublin Univ.*)
Scotland: H. Rottenburg (*London Scot.*); T. Scott (*Langholm*), A. R. Smith (*London Scot.*), A. B. Timms (*Edin. Univ.*), W. H. Welsh (*Edin. Univ.*); R. T. Neilson (*West of Scot.*), J. T. Mabon (*Jedforest*); J. A. Campbell (*Camb. Univ.*), J. M. Dykes (*London Scot.*), J. R. C. Greenlees (*Camb. Univ.*), F. W. Henderson (*London Scot.*), G. C. Kerr (*Durham*), R. Scott (*Hawick*), T. M. Scott* (*Hawick*), W. P. Scott (*West of Scot.*)
Referee: Dr Badger (*England*)   **Touch judges:** I. McIntyre, S. Lee

The spell of frosty weather which caused a week's postponement of this match had also left the teams short of match practice so that in spite of the good conditions this was a scrambling game largely confined to the forwards. There were several stops for injuries as rather forcible tactics were indulged in by both teams. Both sides made some good runs but the defences were always sound. W. H. Welsh, however, had a fine debut, his pace being very much in evidence. T. M. Scott was the first from a Border Club to captain the XV.

SCOTLAND 0   ENGLAND 0
Inverleith
10 March 1900

Scotland: H. Rottenburg (*London Scot.*); T. Scott (*Langholm*), G. T. Campbell (*London Scot.*), A. R. Smith (*London Scot.*), W. H. Welsh (*Edin. Univ.*); R. T. Neilson (*West of Scot.*), J. I. Gillespie (*Edin. Acads.*); L. H. I. Bell (*Edin. Acads.*), G. C. Kerr (*Edin. Wrs.*), W. M. C. McEwan (*Edin. Acads.*), A. Mackinnon (*London Scot.*), M. C. Morrison* (*RHSFP*), R. Scott (*Hawick*), W. P. Scott (*West of Scot.*), H. O. Smith (*Watsonians*)
England: H. T. Gamlin (*Blackheath*); R. Forrest (*Blackheath*), W. L. Bunting (*Richmond*), G. W. Gordon-Smith (*Blackheath*), A. C. Robinson (*Percy Park*); J. C. Marquis (*Birkenhead Park*), G. H. Marsden (*Morley*); H. Alexander (*Birkenhead Park*), J. Baxter (*Birkenhead Park*), R. W. Bell (*Northern*), J. Daniell* (*Camb. Univ.*), A. F. C. C. Luxmore (*Richmond*), S. Reynolds (*Richmond*), J. P. Shooter (*Morley*), A. F. Todd (*Blackheath*)
Referee: M. Delaney (*Ireland*)   **Touch judges:** I. McIntyre, J. W. H. Thorpe

A draw was a fair result for a hard struggle largely confined to the forwards where England, good in the scrums, could not match the Scots in the loose. England had the better of the first half where two or three individual efforts nearly brought scores. Both Robinson and Bunting broke clear but in each case the player instead of going on, passed in field to another who was promptly floored, for the Scottish cover defence was fast and effective. The Scottish forwards, with H. O. Smith, McEwan and Morrison prominent, made some telling rushes only to find Gamlin in good form but just on half time he was badly shaken up in tackling Morrison. The restart was held up because Shooter and A. R. Smith were receiving attention and the ball was mislaid! Scotland were clearly on top in the second half, their forwards putting great pressure on the defence. Welsh and Gillespie, who knocked down the corner flag, came near to scoring and later on Gillespie missed a kickable penalty

SCOTLAND 18   WALES 8
Inverleith
9 February 1901

Scotland: A. W. Duncan (*Edin. Univ.*); W. H. Welsh (*Edin. Univ.*), A. B. Timms (*Edin. Univ.*), P. Turnbull (*Edin. Acads.*), A. N. Fell (*Edin. Univ.*); J. I . Gillespie (*Edin. Acads.*), F. H. Fasson (*Edin. Univ.*); D. R. Bedell-Sivright (*Camb. Univ.*), J. A. Bell (*Clydesdale*), J. M. Dykes (*Glas. HSFP*), A. B. Flett (*Edin. Univ.*), A. Frew (*Edin. Univ.*), M. C. Morrison* (*RHSFP*), J. Ross (*London Scot.*), R. S. Stronach (*Glas. Acads.*)
Wales: W. J. Bancroft* (*Swansea*); W. M. Llewellyn (*London Welsh*), E. G. Nicholls (*Cardiff*), G. Davies (*Swansea*), W. J. Trew (*Swansea*); G. L. Lloyd (*Newport*), L. A. Phillips (*Newport*); W. N. Alexander (*Llwynypia*), J. Blake (*Cardiff*), J. G. Boots (*Newport*), A. Brice (*Aberavon*), H. Davies (*Swansea*), R. Hellings (*Llwynypia*), J. J. Hodges (*Swansea*), F. Millar (*Mountain Ash*)
Referee: R. W. Jeffares (*Ireland*)   **Touch judges:** R. G. Macmillan, D. H. Bowen

J. I. Gillespie scored and converted (5-0); A. B. Flett scored; J. I. Gillespie converted (10-0). (H.T.). J. I. Gillespie scored; A. B. Flett converted (15-0); P. Turnbull scored; A. B. Flett failed (18-0); G. L.

Lloyd scored; W. J. Bancroft converted (18-5); J. G. Boots scored; W. J. Bancroft failed (18-8).

This match was postponed because of the death of Queen Victoria and as a mark of respect the spectators were predominently in black.

The Scottish team had eight new caps and contained seven of the outstanding Edinburgh University XV. J. T. Tulloch (Kelvinside Acads.) had been an original selection but after a special practice game he was considered unfit and replaced by Timms.

The heavy Welsh forwards (who were criticised for rough play) played well in the scrums but could not match the Scots in the loose and the Welsh backs were greatly troubled by the speedy and clever Scottish backs. On starting Fell nearly scored, Llewellyn just kicked the ball dead as he dived at it to score. Nicholls and Llewellyn got away with only Duncan to pass but the full back managed to put Llewellyn into touch and shortly after made a saving tackle on Trew. Then came the turning point in the match. From a maul the ball came out on Gillespie's side. He pounced on it, tricked two opponents with a dummy and with a sprint fell over the line with a Welshman hanging on to him. Then Turnbull with his characteristic ability to slip past defenders, wandered through the backs up to Bancroft and gave a scoring pass to Flett. The Scottish backs continued their brilliant running in the second half, Turnbull making several deceptive weaving runs and two more tries were added. A late rally in which Nicholls and Trew were outstanding brought two consolation tries to Wales.

SCOTLAND 9   IRELAND 5
Inverleith
23 February 1901

Scotland: A. W. Duncan (*Edin. Univ.*); W. H. Welsh (*Edin. Univ.*), A. B. Timms (*Edin. Univ.*), P. Turnbull (*Edin. Acads.*), A. N. Fell (*Edin. Univ.*); J. I . Gillespie (*Edin. Acads.*), F. H. Fasson (*Edin. Univ.*); D. R. Bedell-Sivright (*Fet.-Lor.*), J. A. Bell (*Clydesdale*), F. P. Dods (*Edin. Acads.*), J. M. Dykes (*Glas. HSFP*), A. B. Flett (*Edin. Univ.*), A. Frew (*Edin. Univ.*), M. C. Morrison* (*RHSFP*), J. Ross (*London Scot.*)
Ireland: C. A. Boyd (*Wanderers*); A. E. Freear (*Lansdowne*), B. R. W. Doran (*Lansdowne*), J. B. Allison (*Edin. Univ.*), I. G. Davidson (*NIFC*); L. M. Magee* (*Bective Rangers*), A. Barr (*Methodist Coll.*); C. E. Allan (*Derry*), T. A. Harvey (*Dublin Univ.*), P. Healey (*Limerick*), H. A. S. Irvine (*Collegians*), T. J. Little (*Bective Rangers*), T. M. W. McGowan (*NIFC*), J. Ryan (*Rockwell*), M. Ryan (*Rockwell*)
Referee: G. Harnett (*England*)

J. I. Gillespie scored; A. B. Flett failed (3-0); W. H. Welsh scored twice; A. B. Flett failed (9-0); B. R. W. Doran scored; H. A. S. Irvine converted (9-5). (H.T.).

Ireland pressed with good forward rushes checked by Timms. Almost at once Boyd was caught with the ball; the Scottish forwards worked the ball loose and a passing run by Fell and Dykes let Gillespie score. The Scottish backs continued to attack and well timed passing by Turnbull and Timms let Welsh away on a run where his great pace took him round the defenders for a score. From the kick off an almost similar move by the same three gave Welsh a second high speed try-three inside ten minutes. The Irish forwards again came away finely and good play by Magee and Allison put Doran in at the posts. The Scottish backs made several other fine runs but did not break through, Boyd putting in some fine tackles on Welsh.

In the second half there was no scoring but plenty action. Bedell-Sivright broke away and Freear was hurt stopping him. Fell had a hard run halted by a splendid tackle by Magee who was so hurt that he had to go off. Duncan halted the Irish pack several times but eventually was caught with the ball and the game was halted until he recovered. Although badly dazed he managed to halt the two powerful Ryans who threatened trouble with a strong rush. One comment on Mike Ryan ran 'If not over refined is all the same a brilliant forward'. Welsh's great pace was much in evidence. Note with J. B. Allison playing for Ireland, all the Edinburgh University threes and full back were present.

53

ENGLAND 3   SCOTLAND 18
Rectory Field, Blackheath
9 March 1901

England: H. T. Gamlin (*Wellington*); E. W. Elliot (*Sunderland*), N. S. Cox (*Sunderland*), W. L. Bunting* (*Richmond*), G. C. Robinson (*Percy Park*); B. Oughtred (*Hartlepool Rovers*), P. D. Kendall (*Birkenhead Park*); H. Alexander (*Birkenhead Park*), C. S. Edgar (*Birkenhead Park*), N. C. Fletcher (*OMT*), G. R. Gibson (*Northern*), C. Hall (*Gloucester*), B. C. Hartley (*Camb. Univ.*), A. O'Neill (*Torquay A*), H. T. F. Weston (*Northampton*)
Scotland: A. W. Duncan (*Edin. Univ.*); W. H. Welsh (*Edin. Univ.*), A. B. Timms (*Edin. Univ.*), P. Turnbull (*Edin. Acads.*), A. N. Fell (*Edin. Univ.*); J. I . Gillespie (*Edin. Acads.*), R. M. Neill (*Edin. Acads.*); D. R. Bedell-Sivright (*Fet.-Lor.*), J. A. Bell (*Clydesdale*), J. M. Dykes (*Glas. HSFP*), A. B. Flett (*Edin. Univ.*), A. Frew (*Edin. Univ.*), M. C. Morrison* (*RHSFP*), J. Ross (*London Scot.*), R. S. Stronach (*Glas. Acads.*)
Referee: R. W. Jeffares (*Ireland*)   **Touch judges:** R. G. Macmillan, F. H. Fox

J. I. Gillespie scored and converted (0-5); W. H. Welsh and A. B. Timms scored; J. I. Gillespie converted both (0-15). (H.T.). G. C. Robinson scored; H. Alexander failed (3-15); A. N. Fell scored; J. I. Gillespie failed (3-18).

Early on Frew went over but the referee gave Gamlin the benefit of the touch down. England pressed for fifteen minutes, Oughtred and Elliot having a fine run only halted by Fell who came across from the other wing to tackle Elliot. But from here onwards Scotland were clearly on top and scored thrice in ten minutes. Their pack was in good form with dribbling rushes whilst the backs combined beautifully at full pace. Fell and Turnbull combined to put Gillespie in (which meant that he had scored first in every match this season). Bell from the middle of a crowd of forwards flung the ball wide to Welsh whose pace carried him clear to score behind the posts and then Fell and Turnbull made another opening for Timms to score. The second half was less spectacular. Turnbull missed a chance when with Fell outside him, he kicked past Gamlin but lost the touch. Some slack defence let Robinson go through two tackles for the only English score and later from a scrum the ball passed right along the line to Fell who got over for the last score. Gamlin's defence was again splendid especially against a set of Scottish backs whose attacking ability and pace was so great.

WALES   14   SCOTLAND   5
Cardiff
1 February 1902

Wales: J. Strand Jones (*Oxford Univ.*); W. M. Llewellyn (*Llwynypia*), E. G. Nicholls* (*Cardiff*), R. T. Gabe (*Cardiff*), E. T. Morgan (*Guy's*); G. L. Lloyd (*Newport*), R. M. Owen (*Swansea*); J. G. Boots (*Newport*), A. Brice (*Aberavon*), A. F. Harding (*Cardiff*), J. J. Hodges (*Newport*), D. Jones (*Aberdare*), H. Jones (*Penygraig*), W. W. Joseph (*Swansea*), W. T. Osborne (*Mountain Ash*)
Scotland: A. W. Duncan (*Edin. Univ.*); W. H. Welsh (*Edin. Univ.*), A. B. Timms (*Edin. Univ.*), P. Turnbull (*Edin . Acads.*), A. N. Fell (*Edin. Univ.*); J. I . Gillespie (*Edin. Acads.*), F. H. Fasson (*Edin. Univ.*); D. R. Bedell-Sivright (*Camb. Univ.*), J. V. Bedell-Sivright (*Camb. Univ.*), J. A. Bell (*Clydesdale*), A. B. Flett (*Edin. Univ.*), J. R. C. Greenlees (*Camb. Univ.*), W. E. Kyle (*Hawick*), M. C. Morrison* (*RHSFP*), J. Ross (*London Scot.*)
Referee: P. Gilliard (*England*)

W. M. Llewellyn scored twice but A. Brice failed (6-0); R. T. Gabe scored twice; J. Strand Jones converted the second only (14-0). (H.T.). W. H. Welsh scored; J. I. Gillespie converted (14-5).

Scotland were beaten at all quarters, especially forward so that their backs had few chances to attack. Fell was hurt in the first few minutes but returned with a bandage over a cut forehead. Straightway the Welsh backs with a good supply of the ball began fast passing attacks and Llewellyn after dropping one scoring pass, scored twice inside fifteen minutes. After a further 15 minutes Gabe had scored a further two tries, combining well with his winger, Morgan. Right on half time the Scottish backs had one chance to demonstrate their ability and Welsh getting the ball, showed his pace by passing Llewellyn.

Scotland resumed with the wind but although both sets of three-quarters indulged in good combined runs no scores developed. Gillespie made several dribbling runs from the scrums - a well known feature of his play as a half back. The Welsh backs were all good with Lloyd and the very fast Morgan outstanding.

IRELAND 5   SCOTLAND 0
Balmoral, Belfast
22 February 1902

Ireland: J. Fulton* (*NIFC*); I. G. Davidson (*NIFC*), J. B. Allison (*Edin. Univ.*), B. R. W. Doran (*Lansdowne*), G. P. Doran (*Lansdowne*); L. M. Magee (*Bective Rangers*), H. H. Corley (*Dublin Univ.*); J. L. Coffey (*Lansdowne*), F. Gardiner (*NIFC*), G. T. Hamlet (*Old Wesley*), T. A. Harvey (*Dublin Univ.*), P. Healy (*Limerick*), S. T. Irvin (*QC Belfast*), J. C. Pringle (*RIEC*), A. Tedford (*Malone*)
Scotland: A. W. Duncan (*Edin. Univ.*); W. H. Welsh (*Edin. Univ.*), A. S. Drybrough (*Edin. Wrs.*), P. Turnbull (*Edin. Acads.*), J. E. Crabbie (*Oxford Univ.*); J. I. Gillespie (*Edin. Acads.*), R. M. Neill (*Edin. Acads.*); D. R. Bedell-Sivright (*Camb. Univ.*), J. A. Bell (*Clydesdale*), H. H. Bullmore (*Edin. Univ.*), A. B. Flett (*Edin. Univ.*), J. R. C. Greenlees (*Camb. Univ.*), W. E. Kyle (*Hawick*), M. C. Morrison* (*RHSFP*), W. P. Scott (*West of Scot.*)
Referee: A. Hill (*England*)

No scoring at half time. G. P. Doran scored; H. H. Corley converted (5-0).

The Irish pack, helped by some poor defensive kicking against the wind, kept play in the Scottish half. Magee initiated many attacks which failed against a sound defence, Drybrough's tackling being very effective.

The Scottish forwards restarted well, Bell, Morrison and Bedell-Sivright dribbled the ball well into the Irish 25; then Kyle and Bell took it over the line and appeared to touch down before it went over the dead ball line. The referee, however, gave no score. Scotland continued to press and Welsh had two dangerous runs, the first halted by a good tackle and the second finished when Drybrough dropped a scoring pass right on the line. Ireland then improved and from a scrum on the Scottish 25 a passing run put G. B. Doran in for the only score of the game. Again the Scottish pack was mastered but the Irish backs, with the exception of Magee, were not brilliant and so the score was kept down.

SCOTLAND 3   ENGLAND 6
Inverleith
15 March 1902

Scotland: A. W. Duncan (*Edin. Univ.*); A. N. Fell (*Edin. Univ.*), P. Turnbull (*Edin. Acads.*), A. B. Timms (*Edin. Univ.*), W. H. Welsh (*Edin. Univ.*), F. H. Fasson (*Edin. Univ.*), E. D. Simson (*Edin. Univ.*); D. R. Bedell-Sivright (*Camb. Univ.*), J. A. Bell (*Clydesdale*), J. M. Dykes (*Glas. HSFP*), J. R. C. Greenlees (*Camb. Univ.*), W. E. Kyle (*Hawick*), M. C. Morrison* (*RHSFP*), W. P. Scott (*West of Scot.*), H. O. Smith (*Watsonians*)
England: H. T. Gamlin (*Devonport Albion*); T. Simpson (*Rockcliff*), J. T. Taylor (*West Hartlepool*), J . E. Raphael (*Oxford Univ.*), R. Forrest (*Wellington*), B. Oughtred (*Hartlepool Rovers*), E. J . Walton (*Castleford*); J. Daniel* (*Richmond*), D. D. Dobson (*Newton Abbot*), G. Fraser (*Richmond*), P. Hardwick (*Percy Park*), R. C. Hartley (*Blackheath*), J. J. Robinson (*Headingley*), L. R. Tosswill (*Bart's*), S. G. Williams (*Devonport Albion*)
Referee: F. M. Hamilton (*Ireland*)   **Touch judges:** G. T. Neilson, M. Newsome

S. G. Williams scored but J. T. Taylor failed (0-3), J. T. Taylor scored but H. T. Gamlin failed (0-6). (H.T.). A. N. Fell scored but D. R. Bedell-Sivright failed (3-6).

A record crowd of 20,000 watched in brilliant sunshine. There was, however, a strong breeze and the famous 'Inverleith swirl' was in evidence. England played with the wind in the first half and the swirl and sun badly affected Duncan who was sadly off form. A misfield gave Williams a simple score and England were rather fortunate to turn round with two tries advantage. In the second half Scotland attacked for most of the time only to fail against some splendid tackling. Welsh was felled by one vigorous tackle and left the field with an injury which finished his rugby career.

One report notes that Walton was working the scrum, opposed to Fasson, and that Oughtred, receiving the ball, was playing a short punting game.

SCOTLAND 6 WALES 0
Inverleith
7 February 1903

Scotland: W. T. Forrest (*Hawick*); A. N. Fell (*Edin. Univ.*), A. B. Timms (*Edin. Univ.*), H. J . Orr (*London Scot.*), J. E. Crabbie (*Oxford Univ.*); E. D . Simson (*Edin. Univ.*), J. Knox (*Kelvinside Acads.*); D. R. Bedell-Sivright (*Camb. Univ.*), A. G. Cairns (*Watsonians*), J. R. C. Greenless (*Kelvinside Acads.*), N. Kennedy (*West of Scot.*), W. E. Kyle (*Hawick*), M. C. Morrison* (*RHSFP*), W. P. Scott (*West of Scot.*), L. West (*Edin. Univ.*)
Wales: J. Strand-Jones (*Llanelli*); W. R. Arnold (*Llanelli*), R. T. Gabe (*Llanelli*), D. Rees (*Swansea*), W. J. Trew (*Swansea*); G. L. Lloyd* (*Newport*), R. M. Owen (*Swansea*); J. G. Boots (*Newport*), A. Brice (*Aberavon*), A. F. Harding (*Cardiff*), J. J. Hodges (*Newport*), D. Jones (*Treherbert*), W. W. Joseph (*Swansea*), W. T. Osborne (*Mountain Ash*), G. Travers (*Pill Harriers*)
Referee: A. Martelli (*Ireland*)   **Touch judges:** Revd. R. S. Davidson, J. James

A. B. Timms dropped a penalty goal (3-0). (H.T.). W. E. Kyle scored; W. T. Forrest failed (6-0).

Conditions were appalling for the game was played in a fierce gale of wind and blinding rain coming from the south-west. The water-logged pitch was swept clear of pools by workmen just before the start.

Scotland began with the gale behind them but could only score a penalty goal, given for feet up in the scrum and and drop kicked by Timms from just inside halfway. The Welsh pack played to their backs who made one or two sallies only to be halted by stern tackling and the conditions which were really against all handling.

On restarting against the gale the Scottish forwards in a most determined manner gradually took control of the game. Wales did get into the Scottish 25 for a while but firm defence by the forwards and backs, especially Forrest, kept them out. Eventually good play by Orr and Crabbie took play well up field and the momentum was maintained by their forwards, a great surge being crowned by Kyle forcing his way over for a try. It was remarked that the Welsh backs were none too happy about checking the Scottish forwards in their foot rushes.

SCOTLAND 3 IRELAND 0
Inverleith
28 February 1903

Scotland: W. T. Forrest (*Hawick*); C. France (*Kelvinside Acads.*), A. S. Drybrough (*Edin. Wrs.*), J. H. Orr (*London Scot.*); J. E. Crabbie (*Oxford Univ.*); E. D. Simson (*Edin. Univ.*), J. Knox (*Kelvinside Acads.*); D. R. Bedell-Sivright (*Camb. Univ.*), A. G. Cairns (*Watsonians*), J. R. C. Greenlees (*Kelvinside Acads.*), N. Kennedy (*West of Scot.*), W. E. Kyle (*Hawick*), M. C. Morrison* (*RHSFP*), W. P. Scott (*West of Scot.*), L. West (*Edin. Univ.*)
Ireland: J. Fulton (*NIFC*); C. C. Fitzgerald (*Glas. Univ.*), G. A. D. Harvey (*Wanderers*), J. B. Allison (*Edin. Univ.*), H. J. Anderson (*Old Wesley*); L. M. Magee (*Bective Rangers*), H. H. Corley* (*Wanderers*); C. E. Allen (*Derry*), J. J. Coffey (*Lansdowne*), G. T. Hamlet (*Old Wesley*), P. Healy (*Limerick*), S. T. Irwin (*NIFC*), R. S. Smyth (*Dublin Univ.*), A. Tedford (*Malone*), Jos. Wallace (*Wanderers*)
Referee: F. R. Alderson (*England*)

No scoring at half time. J. E. Crabbie scored; W. T. Forrest failed (3-0).

The Irish contingent had a rough crossing and this may have left some effects for apart from Magee their backs were not in form and their pack faded in the second half. They began well enough but could not break a steady defence. Forrest was his usual frightening self – wonderful at times but every now and then making a terrifying mistake only to bring off an astonishing recovery. Corley broke away and when faced with Forrest passed to Magee but Forrest managed to collar Magee and the ball and clear with a run and kick. Magee, Allison and Harvey combined to give Anderson an open field but Simson came across and tackled him.

In the second half the Scottish pack got on top, Morrison and Bedell-Sivright showing up well, and from one rush and scrimmage Simson, Knox and Orr let Crabbie make a sprint for the corner and score.

France came in for Timms who got a bad kick on the mouth at a practice session held on the Tuesday.

ENGLAND 6   SCOTLAND 10
Athletic Ground, Richmond
21 March 1903

England: H. T. Gamlin (*Devonport A*); R. Forrest (*Blackheath*), E. I. M. Barrett (*Lennox*), A. T. Brettargh (*Liwpool OB*), T. Simpson (*Rockcliff*); W. V. Butcher (*Streatham*), P. D. Kendall* (*Birkenhead Park*); V. H. Cartwright (*Oxford Univ.*), D. D. Dobson (*Newton Abbot*), N. C. Fletcher (*OMT*), P. F. Hardwick (*Percy Park*), B. A. Hill (*Blackheath*) R. Pierce (*Liverpool*), F. M. Stout (*Richmond*), S. G. Williams (*Devonport A*)
Scotland: W. T. Forrest (*Hawick*); A. N. Fell (*Edin. Univ.*), H. J. Orr (*London Scot.*), A. B. Timms (*Edin. Univ.*), J. S. Macdonald (*Edin. Univ.*); E. D. Simson (*Edin. Univ.*), J. Knox (*Kelvinside Acads.*); A. G. Cairns (*Watsonians*), J. D. Dallas (*Watsonians*), J. R. C. Greenlees* (*Kelvinside Acads.*), N. Kennedy (*West of Scot.*), W. E. Kyle (*Hawick*), J. Ross (*London Scot.*), W. P. Scott (*West of Scot.*), L. West (*Edin. Univ.*)
Referee: W. N. Douglas (*Wales*)

R. Forrest scored; N. C. Fletcher failed (3-0); A. B. Timms dropped a goal (3-4); J. D. Dallas scored but failed to convert (3-7). (H.T.). D D. Dobson scored; V. H. Cartwright failed (6-7); E. D. Simson scored; J. S. Macdonald failed (6-10).

This was an undistinguished and rather scrambling game. The Scottish pack, although without two of its most powerful members in Morrison and Bedell-Sivright, gave a good account of itself. Early on a sudden English back attack produced a score but soon a fine forward rush followed by a scrimmage saw the ball flung out to Timms who immediately dropped an excellent goal. After another rush Simson started a passing run with the forwards which finished with Dallas scoring. Early in the second half Fell had a good run but could not pass Gamlin and then Brettargh broke clear and although tackled by Fell, got the ball out to Kendall who was stopped short of the line by Simson who actually overhauled him. The score was only delayed, for from a scrummage Dobson went over to reduce the lead to a single point. However, Scotland kept cool and when the forwards caught Gamlin with the ball, it broke to Simson who had a splendid dodging run for a solo try. Forrest again played well. Once with several opponents bearing down on him he failed to gather the ball, fell on it, jumped up with it, dodged the attackers and then put in his clearance. The Scottish threes had a colonial aspect for Timms and Orr were Australians, Fell was from New Zealand and Macdonald had a South African connection.

WALES 21   SCOTLAND 3
Swansea
6 February 1904

Wales: H. B. Winfield (*Cardiff*); W. M. Llewellyn* (*Newport*), C. C. Pritchard (*Newport*), R. T. Gabe (*Cardiff*), E. T. Morgan (*London Welsh*); R. Jones (*Swansea*), R. M. Owen (*Swansea*); A. Brice (*Aberavon*), D. H. Davies (*Neath*), A. F. Harding (*Cardiff*), J. J. Hodges (*Newport*), W. W. Joseph (*Swansea*), W. Neill (*Cardiff*), E. Thomas (*Newport*), H. V. Watkins (*Llanelli*)
Scotland: W. T. Forrest (*Hawick*); H. J. Orr (*London Scot.*), G. E. Crabbie (*Edin. Acads.*), L. M. MacLeod (*Camb. Univ.*), J. S. Macdonald (*Edin. Univ.*); E. D. Simson (*Edin. Univ.*), A. A. Bisset (*RIEC*); D. R. Bedell-Sivright (*West of Scot.*), L. H. I. Bell (*Edin. Acads.*), A. G. Cairns (*Watsonians*), W. E. Kyle (*Hawick*), M. C. Morrison* (*RHSFP*), E. J. Ross (*London Scot.*), W. P. Scott (*West of Scot.*), G. O. Turnbull (*Edin. Wrs.*)
Referee: Nicholls (*England*)   **Touch judges:** R. C. Greig, H. Bowen

H. B. Winfield kicked a penalty goal (3-0); R. T. Gabe and R. Jones scored; H. B. Winfield converted both (13-0). (H.T.). E. T. Morgan scored; H. B. Winfield failed (16-0); H. J. Orr scored; J. S. Macdonald failed (16-3); A. Brice scored; H. B. Winfidd converted (21-3).

Wales always had this game well in hand, their light forwards giving their backs plenty of the ball. Gabe and Morgan were a most effective wing and the score would have been greater but for some splendid tackling of the two by Forrest. Gabe on one occasion tried to jump over a tackle and the game was held up while he recovered after being caught by the ankles and bounced on his head. Winfield opened the scoring with a touch line penalty for 'feet up' and the Welsh backs added two good tries before half time. Scotland restarted well. Simson made an opening for Crabbie who sent Macdonald over the line only to be brought back for a foot in touch a yard out. The Gabe-Morgan wing broke away again and although Forrest got in his tackle he could not stop the scoring pass. Scotland's only score followed a good forward rush from which Simson started a passing movement for Bisset to put Orr clear away and score. Wales replied with a similar effort when Brice after a scrimmage picked up a loose ball and scored. Scotland rallied fiercely in the last ten minutes but could not break through. It was reported that the referee rebuked Bedell-Sivright for roughing up one or two of his opponents.

IRELAND 3 SCOTLAND 19
Lansdowne Road
28 February 1904

Ireland: J. Fulton (*NIFC*); J. E. Moffatt (*Old Wesley*), J. C. Parker (*Dublin Univ.*), H. H. Corley* (*Wanderers*), C. G. Robb (*QC Belfast*); T. T. H. Robinson (*Dublin Univ.*), E. D. Caddell (*Dublin Univ.*); C. E. Allen (*Derry*), F. Gardiner (*NIFC*), G. T. Hamlet (*Old Wesley*), P. Healy (*Limerick*), M. Ryan (*Rockwell*), A. Tedford (*Malone*), Jas. Wallace (*Wanderers*), Jos. Wallace (*Wanderers*)
Scotland: W. T. Forrest (*Hawick*); H. J. Orr (*London Scot.*), A. B. Timms (*Cardiff*), L. M. MacLeod (*Camb. Univ.*), J. S. Macdonald (*Edin. Univ.*), E. D. Simson (*Edin. Univ.*), J. I. Gillespie (*Edin. Acads.*); D. R. Bedell-Sivright (*West of Scot.*), L. H. I. Bell (*Edin. Acads.*), A. G. Cairns (Watsonians), W. E. Kyle (*Hawick*), W. M. Milne (*Glas. Acads.*), M. C. Morrison* (*RHSFP*), W. P. Scott (*West of Scot.*), J. B. Waters (*Camb. Univ.*)
Referee: W. Williams (*England*)

D. R. Bedell-Sivright scored, J. S. Macdonald failed (0-3). (H.T.). A. B. Timms and D. R. Bedell-Sivright scored; J. S. Macdonald converted both (0-13); J. E. Moffatt scored; J. C. Parke failed (3-13); J. S. Macdonald and E. D. Simson scored; J. S. Macdonald failed with both (3-19).

The Irish pack made its usual rousing start and Gardiner appeared to have touched down but the referee gave a drop out. Timms' kick landed play in the Irish 25 and after some scrimmaging the ball was rushed over the line for Bedell-Sivright and Kyle to throw themselves on it for a score. However, the Irish pack were rather on top and made several fierce rushes only halted by some fearless defence by MacLeod, Timms and Forrest. Parke broke away but on meeting Forrest flung out a wretched pass and a scoring chance was lost. Soon after the restart Simson threw out from the scrum to Gillespie who set Macdonald off on a weaving run. A pass to Timms let him break through to score. The Scottish pack livened up after this and put in several foot rushes. In one, Bedell-Sivright kicked the ball too hard but Fulton missed it and Bedell-Sivright with Orr beside him flung himself on the ball for a try. The Irish backs struck back with a nice run which put Moffatt in at the corner and Robb got over only to be brought back for a forward pass. From a scrum in the Irish 25 Gillespie put the ball along the threes from one touch line to the other. Timms made a lot of ground and then Macdonald got in at the corner but ran round behind the posts only to miss the easy kick. Near the close Simson twice dummied opponents and scored a fine solo try. He had been always very deceptive when carrying the ball. Forrest's defence and kicking were again first rate while Morrison and Bedell-Sivright were prominent in the forwards.

SCOTLAND 6 ENGLAND 3
Inverleith
19 March 1904

Scotland: W. T. Forrest (*Hawick*); J. E. Crabbie (*Edin. Acads.*), L. M. MacLeod (*Camb. Univ.*), A. B. Timms (*Cardiff*), J. S. Macdonald (*Edin. Univ.*); J. I. Gillespie (*Edin. Acads.*), E. D. Simson (*Edin. Univ.*); D. R. Bedell-Sivright (*West of Scot.*), A. G. Cairns (*Watsonians*), H. M. Fletcher (*Edin. Univ.*), W. E. Kyle (*Hawick*), W. M. Milne (*Glas. Acads.*), M. C. Morrison* (*RHSFP*), W. P. Scott (*West of Scot.*), J. B. Waters (*Camb. Univ.*)
England: H. T. Gamlin (*Blackheath*); T. Simpson (*Rockcliff*), A. T. Brettargh (*Liverpool OB*), E. W. Dillon (*Harlequins*), E. J. Vivyan (*Devonport Albion*); P. S. Hancock (*Richmond*), W. V. Butcher (*Bristol*); V. H. Cartwright (*Oxford Univ.*), J. Daniel* (*Richmond*), P. F. Hardwick (*Percy Park*), G. H. Keeton (*Richmond*), J. G. Milton (*Bedford GS*), N. J. N. H. Moore (*Bristol*), C. J. Newbold (*Blackheath*), F. M. Stout (*Richmond*)
Referee: S. Lee (*Ireland*)   **Touch judges:** R. C. Greig, M. Newsome

J. E. Crabbie scored but J. S. Macdonald failed (3-0). (H.T.). E. J. Vivyan scored but failed to convert (3-3); J. S. Macdonald scored but failed to convert (6-3).

The first half was fairly evenly contested and both sides missed scores by mishandling. Hancock had a clear run in when Forrest slipped but passed inside and the chance was lost. The Scottish score came from fine passing by Gillespie, MacLeod and Crabbie. In the second half Scotland had rather the better of the play but Vivyan, intercepting a pass, put Brettargh away and was up to take the scoring pass. Intensive pressure on the English line produced a try when Simson lofted a kick that was misfielded and Macdonald got the touch. Both Daniell and Timms were off the field for a while with injuries. One report makes it evident that the old half back style of play was employed.

SCOTLAND 3   WALES 6
Inverleith
4 February 1905

Scotland: W. T. Forrest (*Hawick*); J. S. Macdonald (*Edin. Univ.*), J. L. Forbes (*Watsonians*), L. M. MacLeod (*Camb. Univ.*), J. E. Crabbie (*Oxford Univ.*); P. Munro (*Oxford Univ.*), E. D. Simson (*Edin. Univ.*); A. G. Cairns (*Watsonians*), H. N. Fletcher (*Edin. Univ.*), A. W. Little (*Hawick*), W. M. Milne (*Glas. Acads.*), A. Ross (*RHSFP*), W. P. Scott* (*West of Scot.*), R. S. Stronach (*Glas. Acads.*)
Wales: G. Davies (*Swansea*), W. M. Llewellyn* (*Newport*), D. Rees (*Swansea*), R. T. Gabe (*Cardiff*), E. T. Morgan (*London Welsh*); W. J. Trew (*Swansea*), R. M. Owen (*Swansea*); A. F. Harding (*London Welsh*), J. J. Hodges (*Newport*), D. Jones (*Treherbert*), W. W. Joseph (*Swansea*), W. Neill (*Cardiff*), C. M. Pritchard (*Newport*), G. Travers (*Pill Harriers*), H. V. Watkins (*Llanelli*)
Referee: H. Kennedy (*Ireland*)

A. W. Little scored but J. S . Macdonald failed (3-0); W. M. Llewellyn scored but G. Davies failed (3-3). (H.T.). W. M. Llewellyn scored but G. Davies failed (3-6).

Some 12,000 spectators watched in clear but uncomfortable conditions for a strong stormy wind blew from the north-west. In the first half the Scottish backs, with the wind, did most of the attacking but could only score once. The Welsh backs were equally active, and right on half time a good run by Rees put Llewellyn in at the corner. In the second half the Welsh had most of the play but good defence, particularly by Forrest, prevented any scoring until near the close of play when a fine run by Llewellyn saw him score again. E. D. Simson at half played brilliantly throughout.

SCOTLAND 5   IRELAND 11
Inverleith
25 February 1905

Scotland: W. T. Forrest (*Hawick*); W. T. Ritchie (*Camb. Univ.*), L. M. MacLeod (*Camb. Univ.*), A. B. Timms (*Cardiff*), R. H. McCowat (*Glas. Acads.*); E. D. Simson (*Edin. Univ.*), P. Munro (*Oxford Univ.*); A. G. Cairns (*Watsonians*), M. R. Dickson (*Edin. Univ.*), W. E. Kyle (*Hawick*), W. M. Milne (*Glas. Acads.*), A. Ross (*RHSFP*), W. P. Scott* (*West of Scot.*), R. S. Stronach (*Glas. Acads.*), L. West (*Carlisle*)
Ireland: M. F. Landers (*Cork Const.*); J . E. Moffatt (*Old Wesley*), B. Maclear (*Cork County*), G. A. D. Harvey (*Wanderers*), H. Thrift (*Dublin Univ.*); T. T. H. Robinson (*Dublin Univ.*), E. D. Caddell (*Dublin Univ.*); C. E. Allen* (*Derry*), J. J. Coffey (*Lansdowne*), G. T. Hamlet (*Old Wesley*), H. J. Knox (*Dublin Univ.*), H. J. Millar (*Markstown*), A. Tedford (*Malone*), Jos. Wallace (*Wanderers*); H. G. Wilson (*Glas. Univ.*)
Referee: P. Coles (*England*)

A. Tedford scored; B. Maclear converted (0-5). (H.T.). J. Wallace and J. E. Moffatt scored; B. Maclear failed with both (0-11); A. B. Timms scored; W. T. Forrest converted (5-11).

This might have been a fairly even game had Maclear not been playing, for the big centre was always dangerous. Not only did he create openings but he was extremely difficult to bring down on the move. It was the Irish forwards, however, who took the ball the length of the field for Tedford to score before half time and for Jos. Wallace to score after the restart. Maclear made the opening which let Moffatt score later. In the closing minutes Munro broke away and crosskicked to Timms who scored. The Scottish forwards and halves played quite well but the threes were not up to standard. Forrest, however, was in his best form.

ENGLAND 0 SCOTLAND 8
Athletic Ground, Richmond
18 March 1905

England: J. T. Taylor (*Castleford*); S. F. Cooper (*Blackheath*), J. E. Raphael (*OMT*), A. T. Brettargh (*Liverpool OB*), T. Simpson (*Rockcliff*); A. D. Stoop (*Oxford Univ.*), W. V. Butcher (*Streatham*); V. H. Cartwright (*Nottingham*), T. A. Gibson (*Northern*), C. E. L. Hammond (*Harlequins*), J. L. Mathias (*Bristol*), J. G. Milton (*Camborne*), C. J. Newbold (*Blackheath*), S. H. Osborne (*St Bees*), F. M. Stout (*Richmond*)
Scotland: D. G. Schulze (*London Scot.*); W. T. Ritchie (*Camb. Univ.*), G. A. W. Lamond (*Bristol*), A. B. Timms* (*Cardiff*), T. Elliot (*Gala*); E. D. Simson (*Edin. Univ.*), P. Munro (*Oxford Univ.*); A. G. Cairns (*Watsonians*), W. E. Kyle (*Hawick*), J. C. MacCallum (*Watsonians*), H. G. Monteith (*Camb. Univ.*), A. Ross (*RHSFP*), W. P. Scott (*West of Scot.*), R. S. Stronach (*Glas. Acads.*), L. West (*Carlisle*)
Referee: H. D. Bowen (*Wales*).

No scoring at half time. E. D. Simson and R. S. Stronach scored; W. P. Scott converted the second only (0-8).

England had had a very poor season before this but here they started and finished well. It was only for a while in the second half that the Scottish pack got on top and made the vital scores possible. Play was fairly even during the first half with some individual efforts being made, Simpson being dangerous on the wing. After the restart the Scottish forwards improved greatly and gave their two very active halves chances to open up the game. From one scrum Simson kicked high into the English 25 and followed up so quickly that he caught the ball and was over at the corner before the English defence realised the danger. Later Munro passed to Lamond who gave the ball to Ritchie. He dodged two opponents and then the ball went from Cairns and West before arriving at Stronach who suddenly spurted for the line and just got there as he was tackled. England rallied towards the end without success. This was Stoop's first cap and he played at stand-off half.

SCOTLAND 7 NEW ZEALAND 12
Inverleith
18 November 1905

Scotland: J. G. Scoular (*Camb. Univ.*); J. T. Simson (*Watsonians*), K. G. MacLeod (*Camb. Univ.*), L. M. MacLeod (*Camb. Univ.*), T. Sloan (*Glas. Acads.*); L. L. Greig (*Un. Services*); E. D. Simson (*Edin. Univ.*), P. Munro (*London Scot.*), D. R. Bedell-Sivright* (*Edin. Univ.*), W. E. Kyle (*Hawick*), J. C. MacCallum (*Watsonians*), J. M. Mackenzie (*Edin. Univ.*), W. L. Russell (*Glas. Univ.*), W. P. Scott (*West of Scot.*), L. West (*Carlisle*)
New Zealand: G. A. Gillett (*Canterbury*); G. W. Smith (*Auckland*), R. G. Deans (*Canterbury*), W. J. Wallace (*Wellington*); J. W. Stead (*Southland*), J. Hunter (*Taranaki*); F. Roberts (*Wellington*); S. Casey (*Otago*), W. Cunningham (*Auckland*), D. Gallaher* (*Auckland*), F. T. Glasgow (*Taranaki*), A. McDonald (*Otago*), J. J. O'Sullivan (*Taranaki*), C. E. Seeling (*Auckland*), G. A. Tyler (*Auckland*)
Referee: W. Kennedy (*Ireland*)

E. D. Simson dropped a goal (4-0); F. T. Glasgow scored but W. J. Wallace failed (4-3); G. W. Smith scored but W. J. Wallace failed (4-6); J. C. MacCallum scored but K. G. MacLeod failed (7-6). (H.T.). G. W. Smith scored but G. A. Gillett failed (7-9); W. Cunningham scored but W. J. Wallace failed (7-12).

Much to the annoyance of the Union, Dr Fell called off rather than play against his countrymen. He was replaced by L. L. Greig who was required to play as a third half back outside Simson and Munro – a move designed to counter the formation of seven forwards, one roving forward and seven backs. With hindsight this did not work, for the three half backs were quite unaccustomed to playing this formation and as a result the Scottish back play and defence were disorganised. The New Zealand forwards, packing two-three-two, were very strong and gave their backs much of the ball from the tight and line out, but the ground and ball were slippery after a morning of frost and their handling which was really very poor, lost them several scores. The Scottish pack, however, was formidable in the loose, their dribbling rushes, fierce following up and heavy tackling thoroughly upsetting their opponents. It was from such rushes that both Scottish scores came.

Early in the second half L. M. MacLeod went off with an ankle injury and could only resume with a bad limp, a handicap which played a part during the last five minutes when strong running saw New Zealand score two tries.

E. D. Simson had a good game but K. G. MacLeod, still under eighteen, had a great debut for his great pace and power of kicking were outstanding. On one occasion when the ball was kicked past the full back, he ran back, picked up the ball in the field and 'then cantered off behind the posts and got in a fine kick'.

WALES 9   SCOTLAND 3
Cardiff
3 February 1906

Wales: H. B. Winfield (*Cardiff*); E. T. Morgan (*London Welsh*), C. C. Pritchard (*Pontypool*), E. G. Nicholls* (*Cardiff*), H. T. Maddocks (*London Welsh*); W. J. Trew (*Swansea*), R. A. Gibbs (*Cardiff*); R. M. Owen (*Swansea*); A. F. Harding (*London Welsh*), J. J. Hodges (*Newport*), D. Jones (*Treherbert*), W. W. Joseph (*Swansea*), C. M. Pritchard (*Newport*), G. Travers (*Pill Harriers*), J. F. Williams (*London Welsh*)
Scotland: J. G. Scoular (*Camb. Univ.*); W. C. Church (*Glas. Acads.*), T. Sloan (*Glas. Acads.*), K. G. MacLeod (*Camb. Univ.*), A. B. H. L. Purves (*London Scot.*); E. D. Simson (*Edin. Univ.*), P. Munro (*Oxford Univ.*); D. R. Bedell-Sivright (*Edin. Univ.*), A. G. Cairns (*Watsonians*), W. E. Kyle (*Hawick*), J. C. MacCallum (*Watsonians*), H. G. Monteith (*Camb. Univ.*), W. L. Russell (*Glas. Acads.*), W. P. Scott (*West of Scot.*), L. West* (*Hartlepool Rovers*)
Referee: J. W. Allen (*Ireland*)   **Touch judges:** J. T. Tulloch, J. Garrett

J. J. Hodges scored; H. B. Winfield failed (3-0); C. C. Pritchard scored; R. A. Gibbs failed (6-0) (H.T.). H. T. Maddocks scored; H. B. Winfield failed (9-0); K. G. MacLeod dropped a penalty goal (9-3).

Wales played seven forwards with Travers acting as a recognised hooker but the system was not a success against a good Scottish pack which was again good in the loose with Kyle and Bedell-Sivright outstanding. The latter actually touched down early in the match but as the ball had rebounded off the Chief Constable who was walking about in the in-goal area, the referee gave no score but dead ball. However, the Scottish threes, with the brilliant exception of MacLeod, were not effective although Simson at half was always dangerous. Nor were the Welsh backs much better-all three scores coming from individual efforts rather than team work. A cross kick by Owen was picked up by Morgan who put Hodges over, Nicholls dropped at goal but the ball flew very wide and Pritchard was able to get to it first; while Maddocks only got in because of some poor tackling in the backs. MacLeod who had narrowly missed a drop goal from halfway, converted a penalty kick by a drop.

IRELAND 6   SCOTLAND 13
Lansdowne Road
24 February 1906

Ireland: G. J. Henebrey (*Garryowen*); C. G. Robb (*QC Belfast*), J. C. Parke (*Dublin Univ.*), F. Casement (*Dublin Univ.*), H. J. Anderson (*Old Wesley*); B. Maclear (*Cork County*), E. D. Caddell (*Dublin Univ.*), W. B. Purdon (*QC Belfast*); C. E. Allen* (*Derry*), J. J. Coffey (*Lansdowne*), F. Gardiner (*NIFC*), H. J. Know (*Lansdowne*), A. Tedford (*Malone*), M. White (QC Cork), H. G. Wilson (*Malone*)
Scotland: J. G. Scoular (*Camb. Univ.*); K. G. MacLeod (*Camb. Univ.*), J. L. Forbes (*Watsonians*), M. W. Walter (*London Scot.*), A. B. H. L. Purves (*London Scot.*); E. D. Simson (*Edin. Univ.*), P. Munro (*Oxford Univ.*); D. R. Bedell-Sivright (*Edin. Univ.*), A. G. Cairns(*Watsonians*), W. E. Kyle (*Hawick*), J. C. MacCallum (*Watsonians*), H. G. Monteith (*London Scot.*), W. L. Russell (*Glas. Acads.*), W. P. Scott (*West of Scot.*), L. West* (*London Scot.*)
Referee: V. H. Cartwright (*England*)

D. R. Bedell-Sivright scored; J. C. MacCallum converted (0-5); P. Munro scored; J. C. MacCallum converted (0-10). (H.T.). K. G. MacLeod dropped a goal from a mark (0-13); J. C. Parke scored but failed to convert (3-13); C. G. Robb scored; B. Maclear failed (6-13).

Ireland also tried the seven forward formation but the extra back formation was not a success and was merely a handicap to their best back, Maclear, who apparently at one time went into the pack to help the hard pressed forwards. The Scottish pack was well on top yet the Irish forwards broke quickly and by fine tackling kept the score down. Simson and Munro again played well, each working the scrum in their own side of the field. These two started the game with some persistent attacks which failed against a good defence. Then Russell broke away on a good dribbling run and when the ball went to Bedell-Sivright he crashed over for a try. Ten minutes later Simson from a scrum started a passing run where the ball went from Munro to Forbes to MacLeod and back to Munro for a fine score. Good Irish tackling kept the Scots out during the second half and their only score came when MacLeod marked the ball at midfield and dropped a goal. Then with four minutes to go an Irish passing run saw Parke score and from the kick off the Irish forwards rushed the ball back for Robb to touch down but the final whistle went after the unsuccessful kick. It is of interest to note that M. W. Walter had been invited but declined to play for England v. Ireland on 10 February.

SCOTLAND 3   ENGLAND 9
Inverleith
17 March 1906

Scotland: J. G. Scoular (*Camb. Univ.*); K. G. MacLeod (*Camb. Univ.*), J. L. Forbes (*Watsonians*), M. W. Walter (*London Scot.*),A. B. H. L. Purves (*London Scot.*); E. D. Simson (*Edin. Univ.*), P. Munro (*Oxford Univ.*); D. R. Bedell-Sivright (*Edin. Univ.*), A. G. Cairns (*Watsonians*), W. E. Kyle (*Hawick*), I. C. MacCallum (*Watsonians*), H. G. Monteith (*London Scot.*), W. L. Russell (*Glas. Acads.*), *W. P. Scott (West of Scot.)*, L. West* (*London Scot.*)
England: E. J. Jackett (*Falmouth*); I. E. Raphael (*OMT*), H. E. Shewring (*Bristol*), J. G. G. Birkett (*Harlequins*), T. Simpson (*Rockcliff*); J. Peters (*Plymouth*), A. D. Stoop (*Harlequins*); V. H. Cartwright* (*Nottingham*), R. Dibble (*Bridgewater A*), J. Green (*Skipton*), C. E. L. Hammond (*Harlequins*), T. S. Kelly (*Exeter*), A. L. Kewney (*Rockcliff*), W. A. Mills (*Devonport A*), C. H. Shaw (*Moseley*)
Referee: I. W. Allen (*Ireland*)

J. E. Raphael scored; V. H. Cartwright failed (0-3), A. B. H. L. Purves scored; J. C. MacCallum failed (3-3). (H.T.). T. Simpson and W. A. Mills scored; V. H. Cartwright failed to convert both (3-9).

England, having lost to Wales and Ireland, were not expected to win but did so deservedly. Their pack were much livelier and for once Simson and Munro were well held, Peters and Stoop being definitely the better pair. The English backs were sound while the Scottish defence was poor, but both MacLeod and Bedell-Sivright were injured fairly early on. In the first half Raphael picked up a dropped pass and dashed 40 yards to score. After some Scottish forward pressure Munro went off on his own from a scrum and made an easy opening for Purves to score. Early in the second half a limping MacLeod could not get to a ball; Simpson picked up, cut diagonally across the field, brushed aside two weak tackles and scored. The Scottish pack put in some pressure but the defence, where Raphael showed up well, was too sound and later a good passing run put Mills in for a third try.

SCOTLAND 6   SOUTH AFRICA 0
Hampden Park, Glasgow
17 November 1906

Scotland: J. G. Scoular (*Camb. Univ.*); K. G. MacLeod (*Camb. Univ.*), T. Sloan (*Glas. Acads.*), M. W. Walter (*London Scot.*), A. B. H. L. Purves (*London Scot.*); P. Munro (*Oxford Univ.*), L. L. Greig* (*Un. Services*); D. R. Bedell-Sivright (*Edin. Univ.*), G. M. Frew (*Glas. HSFP*), I. C. Geddes (*London Scot.*), J. C. MacCallum (*Watsonians*), H. G. Monteith (*London Hospital*), W. P. Scott (*West of Scot.*), L. M. Spiers (*Watsonians*), W. H. Thomson (*West of Scot.*)
South Africa: A. F. Marsburg (*GW*); A. C. Stegmann (*WP*), H. A. de Villiers (*WP*), J. D. Krige (*WP*), J. A. Loubser (*WP*); H. W. Carolin* (*WP*), F. J. Dobbin (*GW*); D. J. Brink (*WP*), D. Brookes (*B*), A. F. Burkett (*WP*), W. A. Burger (*B*), H. J. Daneel (*WP*), D. Mare (*T*), W. S. Morkel (*T*), J. W. E. Raaf (*GW*)
Referee: H. H. Chorley (*Ireland*)

There was no scoring at half time. K. G. MacLeod and A. B. H. L. Purves scored but J. C. MacCallum failed to convert either (6-0).

Since this was a third home match for the season it was played at Hampden Park in Glasgow where a record crowd of 32,000 watched a game made memorable by an historic try by K. G. MacLeod. After two days of heavy rain the ground was sodden and heavy, conditions which made running and accurate passing very difficult but which suited a splendid Scottish pack whose fiercesome play in the loose really controlled the game. Behind them P. Munro and K. G. MacLeod were quite outstanding.

In spite of constant pressure there was no scoring at half time although Scotland had the ball twice over the line and MacLeod narrowly missed with a couple of long range drop kicks. Shortly after the resumption Munro broke away to his left from a scrum at the centre and when faced by the cover defence he hoisted a high kick clear across the field to the right wing where MacLeod, running full out, caught the wet ball cleanly and outpaced the defence along the touch line to score at the corner.

A little later, Marsburg who had worked wonders keeping the rampant Scottish pack at bay, had to retire with a head injury sustained by stopping a rush headed by Bedell-Sivright. Morkel took his place but with five minutes to go could not check another forward rush headed by MacCallum and Purves was able to follow up and score. It is fair to note that South Africa had to struggle against injuries for Brink was off for fifteen minutes with a twisted ankle while Mare finished with two broken fingers.

(Many years later I asked Sir Tennant Sloan about Munro's crosskick and he replied 'Oh, I saw it all right and ran for it but couldn't get near it. It was only MacLeod's tremendous pace that allowed him to get under the ball and then he caught it safely at full pace'.)

SCOTLAND 6   WALES 3
Inverleith
2 February 1907

Scotland: T. Sloan (*Glas. Acads.*); K. G. MacLeod (*Camb. Univ.*), D. G. MacGregor (*Pontypridd*), W. M. Walter (*London Scot.*), A. B. H. L. Purves (*London Scot.*); E. D. Simson (*London Scot.*), L. L. Greig* (*Un. Services*); D. R. Bedell-Sivright (*Edin. Univ.*), G. M. Frew (*Glas. HSFP*), I. C. Geddes (*London Scot.*), J. C. MacCallum (*Watsonians*), H. G. Monteith (*London Scot.*), G. A. Sanderson (*RHSFP*), W. P. Scott (*West of Scot.*), L. M. Spiers (*Watsonians*)
Wales: H. B. Winfield (*Cardiff*); H. T. Maddocks (*London Welsh*), J. Evans (*Pontypool*), R. T. Gabe (*Cardiff*), J. L. Williams (*Cardiff*); R. M. Owen (*Swansea*), W. Trew* (*Swansea*); R. A. Gibbs (*Cardiff*), J. Brown (*Cardiff*), W. Dowell (*Newport*), T. Evans (*Llanelli*), C. M. Pritchard (*Newport*), G. Travers (*Pill Harriers*), J. Watts (*Llanelli*), J. Webb (*Abertillary*)
Referee: J. Lefevre (*Ireland*)

H. B. Winfield kicked a penalty (0-3). (H.T.). A. B. H. L. Purves scored but K. G. MacLeod failed (3-3); H. G. Monteith scored but J. C. MacCallum failed (6-3).

Wales, after a good win over England, again adopted the seven forward formation, but this failed against a good defence and a vigorous Scottish pack whose only fault was a tendency to get offside during their dribbling rushes, a fault which cancelled out one touch down. Yet play was fairly even in the first half, the only score being a penalty for offside kicked by Winfield. Early in the second half the Scottish pack took the ball right down to the line and from a lineout swift passing right across the field gave Purves the chance to hand off Maddocks and run in at the corner. Shortly afterwards, Winfield courageously halted another tremendous dribbling rush, but was so injured that he had to leave the field. Near the end Purves had a good run finishing with a cross kick which was picked up by MacGregor and passed to Monteith who scored. Wales put in a great finish; Gibbs touched down after a good run but was brought back for a foot in touch and the Scottish pack cleared the ball from the line out. MacGregor had a fine debut; born in Pontypridd he had a Scottish father and was educated at Watson's College, Edinburgh. He was captain of Pontypridd but played so well for the Watsonians on their Xmas tour at Newport that the Welsh selectors picked him as a reserve for this game only to find him amongst the opposition.

SCOTLAND 15 IRELAND 3
Inverleith
23 February 1907

Scotland: D. G. Schulze (*London Scot.*); A. B. H. L. Purves (*London Scot.*), M. W. Walter (*London Scot.*), D. G. MacGregor (*Pontypridd*), K. G. McLeod (*Camb. Univ.*); E. D. Simson (*London Scot.*), P. Munro* (*London Scot.*); D. R. Bedell-Sivright (*Edin. Univ.*), G. M. Frew (*Glas. HSFP*), I. C. Geddes (*London Scot.*), J. C. MacCallum (*Watsonians*), H. G. Monteith (*London Scot.*), G. A. Sanderson (*RHSFP*), W. P. Scott (*West of Scot.*), L. M. Spiers (*Watsonians*)
Ireland: C. Thompson (*Collegians*); H. Thrift (*Dublin Univ.*), J. C. Parke (*Dublin Univ.*), T. J. Greeves (*NIFC*), B. MacLear (*Cork Const.*); E. D. Cadell (*Wanderers*), T. T. H. Robinson (*Wanderers*); C. E. Allen* (*Derry*), W. St. J. Cogan (*QC Cork*), F. Gardiner (*NIFC*), G. T. Hamlet (*Old Wesley*), H. S. Sugars (*Dublin Univ.*), J. A. Sweeny (*Blackrock Coll.*), A. Tedford (*Malone*), H. G. Wilson (*Malone*)
Referee: A. O. Jones (*England*)

J. C. Parke kicked a penalty (0-3). (H.T.). G. A. Sanderson scored and K. G. MacLeod converted (5-3); A. B. H. L. Purves and G. M. Frew scored for I. C. Geddes to convert both (15-3).

Conditions were good but the usual Inverleith breeze was in evidence. Play in the first half was quite even, both sets of backs making some good runs. MacLear had two fine runs halted by firm tackles and this was the occasion when he handed-off Bedell-Sivright so fiercely that the latter, who was probably the hardest forward ever to play for Scotland, was knocked out and spent quite a while recovering on the straw on the touch line! After the restart the strength of the Scottish pack and the pace of their backs began to tell and Scotland finished good winners.

ENGLAND 3 SCOTLAND 8
Rectory Field, Blackheath
16 March 1907

England: E. J. Jackett (*Falmouth*); W. C. Wilson (*Richmond*), J. G. G. Birkett (*Harlequins*), H. E. Shewring (*Bristol*), A. W. Newton (*Blackheath*); S. P. Start (*Un. Services*), J. Peters (*Plymouth*); J. Green (*Skipton*), T. S. Kelly (*Exeter*), W. A. Mills (*Devonport Albion*), E. Roberts* (*RN*), G. D. Roberts (*Oxford Univ.*), C. H. Shaw (*Moseley*), L. A. N. Slocock (*Liverpool*), S. G. Williams (*Devonport Albion*)
Scotland: D. G. Schulze (*London Scot.*); A. B. H. L. Purves (*London Scot.*), T. Sloan (*Glas. Acads.*), D. G. MacGregor (*Pontypridd*), K. G. MacLeod (*Camb. Univ.*); P. Munro* (*London Scot.*), E. D. Simson (*London Scot.*); D. R. Bedell-Sivright (*Edin. Univ.*), G. M. Frew (Glas. HSFP), I. C. Geddes (*London Scot.*), J. C. MacCallum (*Watsonians*), G. A. Sanderson (*RHSFP*), J. M. B. Scott (*Edin. Acads.*), W. P. Scott (*West of Scot.*), L. M. Spiers (*Watsonians*)
Referee: T. D. Schofield (*Wales*)

No scoring at half time. E. D. Simson and A. B. H. L. Purves scored and I. C. Geddes converted the second (0-8); J. Peters scored but G. D. Roberts failed (3-8).

England started well especially as their pack seemed to be more than holding their own and Scotland were not using the wind sensibly. MacLeod, however, had about six lengthy drops at goal which narrowly missed, one from halfway which rebounded from an upright. In the second half both sets of backs had some exciting thrusts stopped by good tackling but suddenly Simson broke away from midfield to score a magnificent solo try after a long dodging run. It was noted that Bedell-Sivright kept up with him and acted as some form of shield! The Scottish pack finished strongly and from one rush the ball was put over the line for Purves to touch down.

WALES 6 SCOTLAND 5
Swansea
1 February 1908

Wales: H. B. Winfield (*Cardiff*); J. L. Williams (*Cardiff*), R. T. Gabe (*Cardiff*), W. J. Trew (*Swansea*), R. A. Gibbs (*Cardiff*); P. F. Bush (*Cardiff*), T. H. Vile (*Newport*); J. Brown (*Cardiff*), W. H. Dowell (*Pontypool*), A. F. Harding (*London Welsh*), G. Hayward (*Swansea*), W. Neill (*Cardiff*), G. Travers* (*Pill Harriers*), J. Watts (*Llanelli*), J. Webb (*Abertillery*)

Scotland: D. G. Schulze (*Dartmouth RN Coll.*); H. G. Martin (*Oxford Univ.*), T. Sloan (*London Scot.*), M. W. Walter (*London Scot.*), A. B. H. L. Purves (*London Scot.*); L. L. Greig* (*Un. Services*), G. Cunningham (*Oxford Univ.*); D. R. Bedell-Sivright (*Edin. Univ.*),J. A. Brown(*Glas. Acads.*),G. M. Frew(*Glas. HSFP*), I. C. Geddes (*London Scot.*), G. C. Gowlland (*London Scot.*), J. C. MacCallum (*Watsonians*), J. M. B. Scott (*Edin. Acad.*), L. M. Spiers (*Watsonians*)
Referee: W. Williams (*England*)

W. J. Trew scored but H. B. Winfield failed (3-0); A. B. H. L. Purves scored and O. C. Geddes converted (3-5). J. L. Williams scored but H. B. Winfield failed (6-5).

This was a hard slogging game that Scotland were most unlucky to lose. In the first half Purves with a clear run in slipped and was caught, while Walter also clear of the defence was tripped and did not even gain a penalty for the offence. Then in the dying moments Geddes had a winning try disallowed. J. M. B. Scott later recorded that he was up with Geddes who dived and touched down a foot over the line, but, as was claimed by Deans of New Zealand in 1 905, he was pulled back into the field and when the referee arrived and saw the ball short of the line he gave a scrum. It was noted that Purves had scored in six consecutive matches.

IRELAND 16   SCOTLAND 11
Lansdowne Road
29 February 1908

Ireland: W. P. Hinton (*Old Wesley*); H. Thrift* (*Dublin Univ.*), J. C. Parke (*Monkstown*), G. G. P. Beckett (*Dublin Univ.*), C. Thompson (*Collegians*); E. D. Caddell (*Wanderers*), F. N. B. Smartt (*Dublin Univ.*); F. Gardiner (*NIFC*), G. T. Hamlet (*Old Wesley*), T. G. Harper (*Dublin Univ.*), H . J . Knox (*Lansdowne*), T. Smyth (*Malone*), B . Solomans (*Dublin Univ.*), A. Tedford (*Malone*), H. G. Wilson (*Malone*)
Scotland: D. G. Schulze (*London Scot.*); H. Martin (*Oxford Univ.*), K. G. MacLeod (*Camb. Univ.*), M. W. Walter (*London Scot.*), A. B. H. L. Purves (*London Scot.*); L. L. Greig* (*Un. Services*), G. Cunningham (*Oxford Univ.*); D. R. Bedell-Sivright (*Edin. Univ.*), J. A. Brown (*Glas. Acads.*), G. M. Frew (*Glas. HSFP*), J. C. MacCallum (*Watsonians*), G. A. Sanderson (*RHSFP*), J. M. B. Scott (*Edin. Acads.*), L. M. Spiers (*Watsonians*), J. S. Wilson (*London Scot.*)
Referee: W. Williams (*England*)

H. Thrift scored and J. C. Parke converted (5-0); K. G. MacLeod scored but failed to convert (5-3); C. Thompson scored but J. C. Parke failed (8-3); G. Beckett scored and W. P. Hinton converted (13-3). (H.T.). H. Martin scored and K. G. MacLeod converted (13-8); K. G. MacLeod dropped a penalty goal (13-11); H. Thrift scored but J. C. Parke failed (16-11).

Scotland were badly handicapped by injury for M. W. Walter retired with a broken collar bone after five minutes' play and K. G. MacLeod also had to come off towards the end. Lansdowne Road had just been acquired by the Irish Rugby Football Union.

SCOTLAND 16   ENGLAND 10
Inverleith
21 March 1908

Scotland: D. G. Schulze (*London Scot.*); H. Martin (*Oxford Univ.*), K. G. MacLeod (*Camb. Univ.*), C. M. Gilray (*London Scot.*), A. B. H. L. Purves (*London Scot.*), J. Robertson (*Clydesdale*), A. L. Wade (*London Scot.*); G. M. Frew (*Glas. HSFP*), I. C. Geddes* (*London Scot.*), W. E. Kyle (*Hawick*), J. C. MacCallum (*Watsonians*), H. G. Monteith (*London Scot.*), L. Robertson (*London Scot.*), J. M. B. Scott (*Edin. Acads.*), L. M. Spiers (*Watsonians*)
England: G. H. D. Lyon (*Un. Services*); D. Lambert (*Harlequins*), J. G. G. Birkat (*Harlequins*), W. N. Lapage (*Un. Services*), A. Hudson (*Gloucester*); J. Davey (*Redruth*), R. H. Williamson (*Oxford Univ.*); F. Boylen (*Hartlepool Rovers*), R. Dibble (*Bridgwater Albion*), R. Gilbert (*Devonport Albion*), T. S. Kelly (*Exeter*), W. L. Oldham (*Coventry*), L. A. N. Slocock* (*Liverpool*), F. B. Watson (*Un. Services*), T. Woods (*Bridgwater Albion*)
Referee: H. H. Corley (*Ireland*)   **Touch judges:** Dr A. B. Flett, W. Williams

J. G. G. Birkett scored and D. Lambert converted (0-5); K. G. Macleod scored but I. C. Geddes failed (3-5); L. A. N. Slocock scored and D. Lambert converted (3-10); A. B. H. L. Purves dropped a goal (7-10). (H.T.). K. G. MacLeod scored and I. C. Geddes converted (12-10); D. G. Schulze dropped a goal (16-10).

65

A record crowd of 20,000 watched a fast game in excellent conditions. Inside 3 minutes Birkett scored after a brilliant run from near halfway. However, MacLeod, playing in his last International at the age of twenty, was in devastating form. He frequently sent Martin away and being as fast as his winger was up with him twice to accept scoring passes. Many regard these two to be the fastest pair ever to play for Scotland. One report talks of Robertson as 'the stand off-man'.

SCOTLAND 3 WALES 5
Inverleith
6 February 1909

Scotland: D. G. Schulze (*London Scot.*); H. Martin (*Edin. Acads.*), A. W. Angus (*Watsonians*), C. M. Gilray (*London Scot.*), J. T. Simson (*Watsonians*); G. Cunningham (*London Scot.*), J. M. Tennent (*West of Scot.*); G. M. Frew (*Glas. HSFP*), G. C. Gowlland (*London Scot.*), W. E. Kyle (*Hawick*), J. C. MacCallum (*Watsonians*), J. M. Mackenzie (*Edin. Univ.*), A. Ross (*RHSFP*), J. M. B. Scott (*Edin. Acads.*), J. S. Wilson (*London Scot.*)
Wales: J. Bancroft (*Swansea*); A. M. Baker (*Newport*), J. P. Jones (*Newport*), W. J. Trew* (*Swansea*), J. L. Williams (*Cardiff*); R. Jones (*Swansea*), R. M. Owen (*Swansea*); T. H. Evans (*Llanelli*), I. Morgan (*Swansea*), E. Thomas (*Newport*), E. J. R. Thomas (*Mountain Ash*), G. Travers (*Pill Harriers*), P. D. Waller (*Newport*), J. Watts (*Llanelli*), J. Webb (*Abertillery*)
Referee: J. W. Jeffares (*Ireland*)

No scoring at half time, G. Cunningham kicked a penalty (3-0); W. J. Trew scored; J. Bancroft converted (3-5).

This was a poor ragged game; both sets of backs played below standard and the packs were dull, indulging in few rushes, yet the Welsh forwards' tactics continually displeased the referee who awarded many penalties to Scotland. Gilray was badly knocked about early on and only resumed, badly shaken, after half time. Scott was also hurt and the pack, with MacCallum at centre, were two short for a while. Bancroft, who was apt to fall on the ball in defence, took a considerable mauling from the Scottish pack. A poor first half was marked by bad handling and finishing by both sides and after some uneventful to and fro play after restarting Cunningham converted a penalty to put Scotland in the lead. Then with ten minutes to go some Welsh pressure saw Trew score a try converted by Bancroft. There followed a desperate finish by Scotland. Simson was hurled into touch in goal. Then Tennent dribbled away only to be halted by Bancroft getting down on the ball again but, as he was too dazed to get off it, a penalty was awarded to Scotland. Cunningham narrowly missed the kick and the final whistle went at once.

SCOTLAND 9 IRELAND 3
Inverleith
27 February 1909

Scotland: D. G. Schulze (*London Scot.*); R. H. Lindsay-Watson (*Hawick*), T. Sloan (*London Scot.*), J. Pearson (*Watsonians*), J. T. Simson (*Watsonians*); J. R. McGregor (*Edin. Univ.*), J. M. Tennent (*West of Scot.*); G. M. Frew (*Glas. HSFP*), W. E. Kyle (*Hawick*), W. G. Lely (*London Scot.*), J. C. MacCallum (*Watsonians*), J. M. Mackenzie (*Edin. Univ.*), A. Ross (*RHSFP*), J. M. B. Scott* (*Edin. Acads.*), C. D. Stuart (*West of Scot.*)
Ireland: W. P. Hinton (*Old Wesley*); H. Thrift (*Dublin Univ.*), J. C. Parke (*Monkstown*), C. Thompson (*Collegians*), R. M. Magrath (*Cork Const.*); G. Pinion (*Collegians*), F. Gardiner* (*NIFC*); J. C. Blackham (*QC Cork*), M. G. Garry (*Bective Rangers*), T. Halpin (*Garryowen*), G. T. Hamlet (*Old Wesley*), O. J. S. Piper (*Cork Const.*), T. Smyth (*Malone*), B. Solomons (*Dublin Univ.*), H. G. Wilson (*Malone*)
Referee: V. H. Cartwright (*England*)

R. H. Lindsay-Watson scored; J. C. MacCallum failed (3-0). (H.T.). J. C. Parke kicked a penalty (3-3); J. R. McGregor and W. E. Kyle scored; J. C. MacCallum failed with both (9-3).

The Irish pack was on top for most of the first half but their backs made no use of their possession. So Tennent and McGregor had a rough time to begin with and an early arrangement which saw Tennent working the scrum with McGregor standing back was abandoned. As the Scottish pack improved McGregor was able to get the ball out to the threes while Tennent fairly roamed about the field in attack and defence. Gardiner, normally a forward, was not a success in his new role as a half back. Early play then favoured the Irish and most of the game was in the Scottish half. However, near half time, their threes had two good runs from the second of which Pearson made a nice opening for Lindsay-Watson who had to sprint with the greatest determination to get over for a try. In the second half the Scottish pack came on to a game but Simson, lying offside, fielded a kick by Schulze and Parke kicked a fine penalty to level the scores. However, fairly continuous pressure saw McGregor break away from a scrum inside the Irish 25 to score and later Kyle touched down (with MacCallum doing the same to make sure) for the last try. There is evidence that Pearson and Sloan changed places at centre.

ENGLAND 8   SCOTLAND 18
Athletic Ground, Richmond
20 March 1909

England: E. J. Jackett (*Falmouth*); A. C. Palmer (*London Hospitals*), C. C. G. Wright (*Camb . Univ.*), R. W. Poulton (*Oxford Univ.*), E. R. Mobbs (*Northampton*); F. Hutchison (*Headingley*), H. J. H. Sibree (*Harlequins*); R. Dibble* (*Bridgewater A*), F. G. Handford (*Manchester*), H. C. Harrison (*RN*), E. D. Ibbotson (*Headingley*), W. A. Johns (*Gloucester*), A. L. Kewney (*Rockcliff*), H. J. S. Morton (*Camb. Univ.*), F. B. Watson (*RN*)
Scotland: D. G. Schulze (*London Scot.*); H. Martin (*Oxford Univ.*), J. Pearson (*Watsonians*), C. M. Gilray (*Oxford Univ.*), J. T. Simson (*Watsonians*); J. M. Tennent (*West of Scot.*), G. Cunningham* (*Oxford Univ.*), G. M. Frew (*Glas. HSFP*), G. C. Gowlland (*London Scot.*), J. R. Kerr (*Greenock Wrs.*), W. E. Kyle (*Hawick*), J. C. MacCallum (*Watsonians*), J. M. Mackenzie (*Edin. Univ.*), A. R. Moodie (*St Andrews* Univ.), J. M. B. Scott (*Edin. Acads*)
Referee: E. G. Nicholls (*Wales*)   **Touch judges:** Dr A. B. Flett, T. C. Pring

J. T. Simson scored; G. Cunningham failed (0-3); E. R. Mobbs and F. B. Watson scored; A. C. Palmer converted the second (8-3). (H.T.). C. M. Gilray and J. M. Tennent (2) scored; G. Cunningham converted all three (8-18).

This was the last Calcutta Cup match to be played at Richmond and among the 20,000 spectators was HRH, The Prince of Wales. They saw a fine forward battle but the continued aggression of the Scottish halves had much to do with the result. Early on a move by Tennent and Cunningham set Gilray off on a fine run. He passed to Simson who sprinted along the touch line, broke through a tackle at the corner and scored behind the posts only to see the easy kick missed. The English forwards then exerted some considerable pressure and before half time the home team had taken the lead by scoring twice. After half time the Scottish pack began to get on top and saw Gilray dummy and dodge in for a good try. Then Tennent scored twice. The first came from a very fast solo dash and the second when, after following a forward rush, he picked up and although heavily tackled by Jackett, held on and fell over for a try. At this stage Pearson was hurt but carried on, limping, and Scotland had to face up to a terrific onslaught. Wright hit the posts with a drop while Mobbs and Harrison both narrowly failed to get over.

SCOTLAND 27   FRANCE 0
Inverleith
22 January 1910

Scotland: F. G. Buchanan (*Kelvinside Acads.*); I. P. M. Robertson (*Watsonians*), A. W. Angus (*Watsonians*), J. Pearson (*Watsonians*), J. T. Simson (*Watsonians*); G. Cunningham* (*Oxford Univ.*), J. M. Tennent (*West of Scot.*), G. M. Frew (*Glas. HSFP*), G. C. Gowlland (*London Scot.*), J. C. MacCallum (*Watsonians*), A. R. Moodie (*St Andrews Univ.*), J. M. B. Scott (*Edin. Acads.*), L. M. Spiers (*Watsonians*), R. C. Stevenson (*St Andrews Univ.*), C. D. Stuart (*West of Scot.*)
France: J. Combe (*SF*); E. Lesieur (*SF*), J Dedet (*SF*), M. Burgun (*RCF*), C. Vareilles (*SF*); C. Martin (*Lyon*), A. Theuriet (*SCUF*); M. Boudreau (*SCUF*), J. Cadenat (*SCUF*), M. Communeau* (*SF*), P. Guillemin (*RCF*), M. Hourdebaigt (*SBUC*), R. Lafitte (*SCUF*), H. Masse (*SBUC*), P. Mauriat (*Lyon*)
Referee: G. A. Harris (*Ireland*)   **Touch judges:** C. J. N. Fleming, C. F. Rutherford

I. P. M. Robertson, A. W. Angus and J. M. Tennent scored; J. C. MacCallum converted the second only (11-0). (H.T.). J. M. Tennent, I. P. M. Robertson, G. C. Gowlland and J. M. Tennent scored; J. C. MacCallum converted the last two only (27-0).

For this first match against France a full Scottish XV was selected but no caps were awarded, this being a distinction retained for appearances against the home countries. The final selection included the complete Watsonian three-quarter line and indeed so strong was the club side at that time that their two half backs could have been added without weakening the team. The visitors could not match up to this strong opposition: the forwards did not play as a pack and their threes did not combine but were keen and fast as individuals. They were all inclined to get offside and tackle opponents who did not have the ball; one claimed a mark from a kick made behind him but the referee allowed them considerable latitude to keep the game flowing. The Scottish players at first were inclined to halt but eventually got the idea and kept on playing till the whistle went. Scotland played in white jerseys so that France could wear their light blue strip.

The First Contacts with France

The first Scottish contact with French rugby came in April 1896 when a strong Edinburgh XV, which included one Irish and four Scottish caps, travelled to play a Paris XV in that city. In 1898 a French XV made a return visit playing one game at Myreside, Edinburgh and a second at Hamilton Crescent, Glasgow. These trips were organised by J. Welsh (RHSFP) and J. B. Hatt (London Scottish) and both were later suspended by the Union who demanded, and then disapproved of the accounts relating to the second visit. Rugby in France at this time was one of several sports controlled by a composite body formed in 1887, the *Union des Sociétés Françaises des Sports Athlétiques*. This body succeeded in arranging France's first International matches against New Zealand (1906), England (1906), Wales (1908) and Ireland (1909) but although it had first approached the SFU in 1907 it was not until 1910 that the first fixture against Scotland was played in Edinburgh. Scotland in this match played in white, a courtesy which the host nation in this fixture still continues.

The USFSA continued to control the game until 1920 when its function was taken over by a completely separate body, the *Fédération Française de Rugby*.

WALES 14   SCOTLAND 0
Cardiff
5 February 1910

Wales: J. Bancroft (*Swansea*); R. A. Gibbs (*Cardiff*), W. J. Spiller (*Cardiff*), W. J. Trew* (*Swansea*), A. M. Baker (*Newport*); P. F. Bush (*Cardiff*), W. L. Morgan (*Cardiff*); T. H. Evans (*Llanelli*), B. Gronow (*Bridgend*), H. Jarman (*Newport*), E. Jenkins (*Newport*), J. Morgan (*Swansea*), J. Pugsley (*Cardiff*), D. J. Thomas (*Swansea*), J. Webb (*Abertillery*)
Scotland: D. G. Schulze (*London Scot.*); W. R. Sutherland (*Hawick*) A. W. Angus (*Watsonians*), J. Pearson (*Watsonians*), J. T. Simson (*Watsonians*), J. M. Tennent (*West of Scot.*), E. Milroy (*Watsonians*); G. M. Frew*(*Glas. HSFP*), G. C. Gowlland (*London Scot.*), W. E. Kyle (*Hawick*), J. C. MacCallum (*Watsonians*), J. M. Mackenzie (*Edin. Univ.*) J. M. B. Scott (*Edin. Acads.*), L. M. Spiers (*Watsonians*), C. D. Stuart (*West of Scot.*)
Referee: G. H. B. Kennedy (*Ireland*)   **Touch judges:** C. J. N. Fleming, J. Jarrett

J. Pugsley and W. J. Spiller scored; J. Bancroft converted the second, (8-0). (H.T.), A. M. Baker and J. Morgan scored; J. Bancroft failed with both (14-0).

Steady and heavy rain had made the pitch so wet that after ten minutes play it was an utter quagmire. There was little handling by any of the backs but the Welsh forwards with fine footwork were quite irresistible and laid the foundation for all the scores. Tennent had to leave the field before half time with an injured elbow. He came back but almost at once, after the interval, he was badly hurt again and had to retire for good, MacCallum coming out of the pack to replace him. Tennent's injuries were caused by studs and this undoubtedly led to legislation on such matters before the next season. In a team forced on the defensive Schulze was quite outstanding. For the first time special trains were run to Cardiff from Edinburgh and Glasgow.

IRELAND 0   SCOTLAND 14
Balmoral, Belfast
26 February 1910

Ireland: W. P. Hinton (*Old Wesley*); J. P. Quinn (*Dublin Univ.*), C. Thompson (*Collegians*), A. R. Foster (*QU Belfast*), A. S. Taylor (*Queen's*); R. A. Lloyd (*Dublin Univ.*), H. M. Read (*Dublin Univ.*); J. C. Blackham (*Wanderers*), T. Halpin (*Garryowen*), G. T. Hamlet* (*Old Wesley*), G. McIldowie (*Malone*), H. Moore (*QU Belfast*), O. J. S. Piper (*Cork Const.*), T. Smyth (*Newport*), B. Solomans (Wanderers)
Scotland: D. G. Schulze (*Northampton*); D. G. Macpherson (*London Hospital*), M. W. Walter (*London Scot.*), J. Pearson (*Watsonians*), J. D. Dobson (*Glas. Acads.*) G. Cunningham* (Oxford Univ.), A. B. Lindsay (*London Hospitals*); C. H. Abercrombie (*Un. Services*), (G. M. Frew (*Glas. HSFP*), G. C. Gowlland (*London Scot.*), J. C. MacCallum (Watsonians), J . M. Mackenzie (*Edin. Univ.*), J. M. B. Scott (*Edin. Acads.*), R. C. Stevenson (St *Andrews Univ.*), C. D. Stuart (*West of Scot.*)
Referee: V. H. Cartwright (England)

J. D. Dobson scored but C. H. Abercrombie failed (0-3). (H.T.). M. W. Walter scored twice but G. Cunningham failed with both (0-9); C. D. Stuart scored and J. C. MacCallum converted (0-14).

This match was played on the Royal Ulster Agricultural Society's ground in Belfast before 12,000 spectators. Scotland were the better team but the score rather flattered them. The packs were well matched although Scotland finished stronger. The Irish pack tried many foot rushes only to be completely frustrated by some splendid defensive play by Cunningham who was well backed up by Lindsay. The Scottish backs did not combine well in the first half but improved greatly later.

SCOTLAND 5   ENGLAND 14
Inverleith
19 March 1910

Scotland: D. G. Schulze (*London Scot.*); W. R. Sutherland (*Hawick*), J. Pearson (*Watsonians*), A. W. Angus (*Watsonians*), D. G. Macpherson (*London Hospital*); G. Cunningham* (*Oxford Univ.*), J. M. Tennent (*West of Scot.*); C. H. Abercrombie (*Un. Services*), G. C. Gowlland (*London Scot.*), J. C. MacCallum (*Watsonians*), J. M. Mackenzie (*Edin. Univ.*), J. M. B. Scott (*Edin. Acads.*), L. M. Spiers (*Watsonians*), R. C. Stevenson (St *Andrews Univ.*), C. D. Stuart (*West of Scot.*)
England: W. R. Johnston (*Bristol*); P. W. Lawrie (*Leicester*), F. M. Stoop (*Harlequins*), J. G. G. Birkett * (*Harlequins*) F E. Chapman (*Hartlepool Rovers*): A. D. Stoop (*Harlequins*), A. L. H. Gotley (*Oxford Univ.*); L. E. Barrington-Ward (*Edin. Univ.*), H. Berry (*Gloucester*), R. Dibble (*Bridgewater*), R. H. M. Hands (*Oxford Univ.*), L. Haigh (*Manchester*), G. R. Hind (*Guy's*), C. H. Pillman (*Blackheath*), J. A. S. Ritson (*Newcastle N.*)
Referee: G. B. Kennedy (*Ireland*)   **Touch judge:** C. J. N. Fleming

D. G. Macpherson scored, J. C. MacCallum converted (5-0); J. G. G. Birkett scored; F. E. Chapman converted (5-5). (H.T.). J. G. G. Birkett, H. Berry and J. A. S. Ritson scored; F. E. Chapman failed with each (5-14).

A record crowd of 25,000 saw England take complete charge after half time and practically run Scotland off their feet. The Scottish pack began well but hard running by the English backs nearly brought scores. Then a solo effort by Sutherland took play right into the English half and after some sustained pressure, Macpherson scored at the posts. However, a fine run started by A. D. Stoop left Birkett with a clear run in to equalise before half time. In the second half the English pack took command and their backs, enjoying an almost continuous supply of the ball ran in three good tries. A late move by Angus and Pearson set Sutherland away on a magnificent run from the centre to be tackled just short of the line.

England became champions for the first time since 1892 and owed a great deal to the attacking skills of Adrian Stoop not to mention the highly developed wing forward play of Pillman. For Scotland 'Wattie' Sutherland showed that he had real pace allied with football skills.

FRANCE 16   SCOTLAND 15
Colombes
2 January 1911

France: J. Coombe (*SF*); P. Failliot (*RCF*), M. Burgun (*RCF*), A. Francquenelle (*Vangirard*), G. Lane (*RCF*); A. Laterrade (*Tarbes*), M. Peyroutou (*Perigueux*); J. Bavozet (*Lyon*), M. Communeau* (*Beauvais*), P. Decamps (*RCF*), F. Forgues (*Bayonne*), P. Guillemin (*RCF*), M. Legrain (*SF*), P. Mauriat (*Lyon*), P. Mounicq (*Toulouse*)
Scotland: H. B. Tod (*Gala*); W. R. Sutherland (*Hawick*), T. E. B. Young (*Durham*), F. G. Buchanan (*Oxford Univ.*), J. Pearson (*Watsonians*); P. Munro* (*London Scot.*), F. Osler (*Edin. Univ.*); C. H. Abercrombie (*Un. Services*), R. Fraser (*Camb. Univ.*), J. C. MacCallum (*Watsonians*), A. R. Moodie (*St Andrews Univ.*), J. M. B. Scott (*Edin. Acads.*), A. M. Stevenson (*Glas. Univ.*), R. C. Stevenson (St *Andrews Univ.*), F. H . Turner (*Oxford Univ.*)
Referee: M. A. S. Jones (*England*)

J. C. MacCallum scored; H. B. Tod failed (0-3); A. Laterrade scored; P. Decamps converted (5-3); P. Failliot and M. Peyroutou scored; M. Communeau failed to convert (11-3); P. Munro scored; F. H. Turner converted (11-8). (H.T.). J. Pearson dropped a goal (11-12); P. Failliot scored; P. Decamps converted (16-12); C. H. Abercrombie scored; H. B. Tod failed (16-15).

This, France's first win in international rugby, undoubtedly gave the game a boost in that country and a warning to the other nations. One of the established Scottish players had some sour comments to make in his scrapbook: (1) The Scottish Union,still not awarding caps against France, regarded this match as a trial for the home country games still to come and so picked several newcomers as trialists. (2) Pearson, a small light man and normally a centre, was placed on the wing and found himself marking Failliot, who at fourteen stones and six feet tall was probably the fastest amateur sprinter in France. As a result Failliot more or less ran through, rather than round, Pearson. (3) The referee, until the last half hour, held Scotland to the rules while allowing the opposition a fair amount of latitude with offsides, forward passes and knocks-on and only tightened up later when he saw what was happening. (4) In the last minute one of the trialists knocked on a pass which merely needed holding and laying over the line for the winning score.

France had their troubles before the start. M. Garcia in his *Histoire* relates that Vareilles, a centre, had hopped out of his carriage at Melun station to grab a sandwich only to see the train move away at once leaving him stranded on the platform and he only arrived at the field after the game was in progress. Near the time of kick-off the reserve, Francquenelle, was also missing so the committee went out looking for a player and indeed approached two 'Mais, en ces jours de fête, ils ont tous deux fait un trop bon déjeuner et ils se récusent'. Eventually they got someone who had begun to change when Francquenelle (who had missed his train at Saint Lazare station) arrived breathless, stripped and got onto the field some minutes after the start!

SCOTLAND 10   WALES 32
Inverleith
4 February 1911

Scotland: D. G. Schulze (*London Scot,*), D . M . Grant (*Elstow School*), A . W. Angus (*Watsonians*), F. G. Buchanan (*Kelvinside Acads.*); J. M. Macdonald (*Edin. Wrs.*), P. Munro* (*London Scot.*), F. Osler (*Edin. Univ.*); C. H. Abercrombie (*London Scot.*), R. Fraser (*Camb. Univ.*), J. M. Mackenzie (*Edin. Univ.*), L. Robertson (*London Scot.*), A. R. Ross (*Edin. Univ.*), J. M. B. Scott (*Edin. Acads.*), R. C. Stevenson (St *Andrews Univ.*), F. H. Turner (*London Scot.*)
Wales: F. W. Birt (*Newport*); R. A. Gibbs (*Cardiff*), W. J. Spiller (*Cardiff*), L. M. Dyke (*Cardiff*), J. L. Williams (*Cardiff*); W. J . Trew* (*Swansea*), R. M. Owen (*Swansea*); J. Birch (*Neath*), A. P. Coldrich (*Newport*), T. H. Evans (*Llanelli*), J. Pugsley (*Cardiff*) D. J. Thomas (*Swansea*), R. Thomas (*Pontypool*), G. Travers (*Newport*), J. Webb (*Abertillery*)
Referee: J. G. Davidson (*Ireland*)

W. J . Spiller dropped a goal (0-4); J. L. Williams scored; F. W. Birt failed to convert (0-7); P. Munro dropped a goal (4-7). (H.T.). R. Thomas and R. A. Gibbs scored; R. A. Gibbs failed with both kicks (4-13); W. J. Spiller scored; F. W. Birt failed to convert (4-16); W. J. Spiller, J. L. Williams and R. A. Gibbs scored; L. M. Dyke failed with the first but converted the other two (4-29); J. M. B. Scott and F. H. Turner scored; D. M. Grant failed to convert either (10-29); R. A. Gibbs scored; L. M. Dyke failed (10-32).

70

This was Scotland's heaviest defeat to date. They more or less held their own up to half time but then the Welsh pack took control and played to their threes who combined beautifully for their scores. Shortly after half time Macdonald had to go off with a leg injury and Abercrombie (an extraordinary choice) was put out on the wing. This weakness was exploited at once and Wales ran in four tries before he (much to his relief) was replaced by Scott. Almost at once Angus had a good run and passed to Scott who by sheer strength and determination forced his way over for a try. Scotland kept up some pressure and Turner plunged in from a line out but in the last minute Gibbs ran in for the last score. There is evidence that D. M. Grant was still at Elstow School although some reports name his club as East Midlands or London Scottish.

SCOTLAND 10   IRELAND 16
Inverleith
25 February 1911

Scotland: A. Greig (*Glas. HSFP*); J. T. Simson (*Watsonians*), A. W. Angus (*Watsonians*), C. Ogilvy (*Hawick*), D. M. Grant (*Elstow School*); P. Munro* (*London Scot.*), A. B. Lindsay (*London Hospitals*); R. Frazer (*Camb. Univ.*), G. M. Frew (*Glas. HSFP*), J. C . MacCallum (*Watsonians*), J. M. Mackenzie (*Edin. Univ.*), J. M. B. Scott (Edin. Acads.), R. C. Stevenson (*St Andrews Univ.*), C. D . Stuart (*West of Scot.*), F. H. Turner (*Oxford Univ.*)
Ireland: W. P. Hinton (*Old Wesley*); C. T. O'Callaghan (*OMT*), A. R. Foster (*QU Belfast*), A. R. V. Jackson (*Wanderers*), J. P. Quinn (*Dublin Univ.*); R. A. Lloyd (*Dublin Univ.*), H. M. Read (*Dublin Univ.*); C. Adams (*Old Wesley*), S. B. B. Campbell (*Derry*), M. G. Garry (*Bective Rangers*), T. Halpin (*Garryowen*), G. T. Hamlet* (*Old Wesley*), M. R. Heffernan (*Cork Const.*), P. J. Smyth (*Collegians*), T. Smyth (*Malone*)
Referee: V. H. Cartwright (*England*)

C. T. O'Callaghan and A. R. Foster scored; W. P. Hinton converted the first only (0-8); J. T. Simson scored; D. M. Grant failed (3-8). (H.T.). C. Adams scored; R. A. Lloyd converted (3-13); P. Munro dropped a goal (7-13); A. W. Angus scored; D. M. Grant failed (10-13); J. P. Quinn scored; the kick failed (10-16).

Ireland attacked from the beginning and scored twice inside ten minutes, their backs with Lloyd outstanding, running well. There followed some aggression by the Scottish threes and eventually Simson, getting the ball ten yards out, got over by a most determined run although tackled by two defenders. On the restart the Irish pack forced a score by Adams but increasing Scottish pressure saw Munro drop a goal and Angus score. At this stage Campbell came out of the pack to strengthen the defence but had a hand in a fast break by the backs which let Quinn score the last try. Ireland throughout were quicker onto the ball and sounder in defence while Scotland's handling too often let them down. Lindsay was recorded as a 'scrum-half'. This was Pat Munro's last match, and his leave of absence having expired, he left the same evening for London to return to duty in the Sudan as a District Commissioner. Years later a former member of the Sudan Political Service, an Edinburgh Academical, related that Munro, when transferred from the Shilluk Province, gave his Scottish Cap to the tribal chief who was so delighted with it that thereafter he always wore it on state occasions instead of the traditional fez.

ENGLAND   13   SCOTLAND   8
Twickenham
18 March 1911

England: S. H. Williams (*Newport*); P. W. Lawrie (*Leicester*), R. W. Poulton (*Oxford Univ.*), J. G. G. Birkett (*Harlequins*), A. D. Roberts (*Newcastle N.*); A. D. Stoop (*Harlequins*), A. L. H. Gotley* (*Blackheath*), L. G. Brown (*Oxford Univ.*), R. Dibble (*Bridgewater A*), L. Haigh (*Manchester*), A. L. Kewney (*Rockcliff*), J. A. King (*Headingley*), R. O. Lagden (*Oxford Univ.*), C. H. Pillman (*Blackheath*), N. A. Wodehouse (*RN*)
Scotland: C. Ogilvy (*Hawick*); W. R. Sutherland (*Hawick*), G. Cunningham (*London* Scot.), R. F. Simson (London Scot.), S. S. L. Steyn (London Scot.); E. Milroy (Watsonians), J . Y. M. Henderson (*Watsonians*); D. M. Bain (*Oxford Univ.*), J. Dobson (*Glas. Acads.*), R. Fraser (*Camb. Univ.*), G. M. Frew (*Glas. HSFP*), W. R. Hutchison (*Glas. HSFP*), J. C. MacCallum* (*Watsonians*), C. D. Stuart (*West of Scot.*), F. H. Turner (*Oxford Univ.*)
Referee: T. D. Schofield (*Wales*)

71

W. R. Sutherland scored; F. H. Turner failed (3-0); N. A. Wodehouse scored; R. O. Lagden converted (3-5); P. W. Lawrie scored; R. O. Lagden failed (3-8). (H.T.). J. G. G. Birkett scored; R. O. Lagden converted (3-13); R. F. Simson scored, J. C. MacCallum converted (8-13).

The English threes threatened danger early on but were well held. Then Cunningham broke through and when tackled, the ball went to Milroy who passed to Sutherland. The winger beat three men by pace to open the scoring. England struck back at once and a passing run saw Wodehouse up with the backs to score. Sutherland again ran away from the backs but Williams got him on the touch line. Again good passing by the English threes put Lawrie over. Before half time Cunningham broke clear hotly pursued by Birkett and Stoop but looking round for someone to pass to, was tackled. It was reported that modesty dictated the move for he had lost his shorts in the initial burst! In the second half Henderson injured his arm and went to full back. Cunningham moved to half while Ogilvy came into the threes. Another fine run by Stoop and Birkett saw the latter run round the injured Henderson to score. England continued to press but Simson picked up a bad pass, ran clear to Williams, kicked over his head and after nearly colliding with a goalpost, managed to get the touch down. Scotland continued to press but the defence had no trouble in holding out.

SCOTLAND 31 FRANCE 3
Inverleith
20 January 1912

Scotland: W. M. Dickson (*Blackheath*); W. R. Sutherland (*Hawick*), A. W. Angus (*Watsonians*), J. Pearson (*Watsonians*), J. G. Will (*Camb. Univ.*); A. W. Gunn (*RHSFP*), J. Hume. (*RHSFP*); D. M. Bain (*Oxford Univ.*), J. Dobson (*Glas. Acads.*), C. C. P. Hill (*St Andrews Univ.*), D. D. Howie (*Kirkcaldy*), J. C. MacCallum* (*Watsonians*), W. D. C. L. Purves (*Camb. Univ.*), R. D. Robertson (*London Scot.*), F. H. Turner (*Oxford Univ.*)
France: F. Dutour (*Toulouse*); P. Failliot (*RCF*), D. Ihingone (*BEC*), J. Dufau (*Biarritz*), M. Burgun (*RCF*); J. Dedet (*SF*), L. Larribau (*Perigueux*); M. Boyou (*SBUC*), M. Communeau (*Beauvais*), J. Conil De Beyssac (*SBUC*), J. Domercq (*Bayonne*), P. Mauriat (*Lyon*), R. Monnier (*SBUC*), R. Paoli (*SF*), P. Vallot (*SCUF*)
Referee: J. J. Coffey (*Ireland*)   **Touch judges:** J. D. Dallas, C. F. Rutherford

J. Pearson dropped a penalty goal (3-0); A. W. Gunn scored; F. H. Turner converted (8-0); M. Communeau scored; M. Boyou failed (8-3); J. Pearson scored; F. H. Turner converted (13-3). (H.T.). J. G. Will scored; F. H. Turner converted (18-3); F. H. Turner scored but failed to convert (21-3); W. R. Sutherland scored twice and F. H. Turner converted both (31-3) .

France played better than the score suggests, but poor handling not only lost them tries but gave Scotland chances from which they scored. Dutour at full back had a good game, his tackling of Will saving at least three scores. One report places Dedet at centre with Burgun at stand off. For Scotland, who played in white jerseys, Gunn played well while Will proved to be one of the fastest wingers ever picked for Scotland. Gunn was definitely selected to play as stand-off to Hume.

WALES 21 SCOTLAND 6
Swansea
3 February 1912

Wales: J. Bancroft (*Swansea*); G. L. Hirst (*Newport*), W. Davies (*Aberavon*), F. W. Birt (*Newport*,) R. C. S. Plummer (*Newport*); W. J. Trew (*Swansea*), R. M. Owen* (*Swansea*); A. P. Coldrick (*Newport*), H. J. Davies (*Neath*), I. Morgan (*Swansea*), G. Stephens (*Neath*), R. Thomas (*Pontypool*), L. Tramp (*Newport*), H. Uzzell (*Newport*), J. Webb (*Abertillery*)
Scotland: W. M. Dickson (*Blackheath*); W. R. Sutherland (*Hawick*), A. W. Angus (*Watsonians*), J. Pearson (*Watsonians*), J. G. Will (*Camb. Univ.*); A. W. Gunn (*RHSFP*), E. Milroy (*Watsonians*); D. M. Bain (*Oxford Univ.*), J. Dobson (*Glas. Acads.*), D. D. Howie (*Kirkcaldy*), J. C. MacCallum* (*Watsonians*), W. D. C. L. Purves (*London Scot.*), L. Robertson (*London Scot.*), J. M. B. Scott (*Edin. Acads.*), F. H. Turner (*Liverpool*)
Referee: F. C. Potter-Irwin (*England*)   **Touch judge:** J. S. Jones

G. L. Hirst scored; J. Bancroft failed (3-0); W. J. Trew dropped a goal (7-0); J. G. Will scored, F. H. Turner failed (7-3). (H.T.). E. Milroy scored; F. H. Turner failed (7-6);1. Morgan scored; J. Bancroft converted (12-6); F. W. Birt dropped a goal (16-6); R. C. S. Plummer scored; J. Bancroft converted (21-6).

The game was threatened by a heavy fall of snow during the morning but the staff were able to clear the field in time. Scotland made a good fight of it but the excellence of a lively and heavier Welsh pack coupled with the greater individual cleverness of the Swansea halves won the match for Wales. For Scotland Angus was conspicuous in defence and attack.

IRELAND 10   SCOTLAND 8
Lansdowne Road
24 February 1912

Ireland: R. A. Wright (*Monkstown*); J. P. Quinn (*Dublin Univ.*), A. R. Foster (*Derry*), M. Abraham (*Bective Rangers*), C. V. McIvor (*Dublin Univ.*); R. A. Lloyd* (*Dublin Univ.*), H. M. Read (*Dublin Univ.*); C. Adams (*Old Wesley*), G. S. Brown (*Monkstown*), S. B. B. Campbell (*Derry*), T. Halpin (*Garryowen*), R. Hemphill (*Dublin Univ.*), G. V. Killeen (*Garryowen*), H. Moore (QU *Belfast*), R. D. Patterson (*Wanderers*)
Scotland: C. Ogilvy (*Hawick*); S. S. L. Steyn (*Oxford Univ.*), A. W. Angus (*Watsonians*), C. M. Gilray (*London Scot.*), J. G. Will (*Camb. Univ.*); A. W. Gunn (*RHSFP*), E. Milroy (*Watsonians*), J. Dobson (*Glas. Acads.*), C. C. P. Hill (St *Andrews Univ.*), D. D. Howie (*Kirkcaldy*), J. C. MacCallum* (*Watsonians*), W. D. C. L. Purves (*London Scot.*), L. Robertson (*London Scot.*), J. M. B. Scott (*Edin. Acads.*), F. H. Turner (*Liverpool*)
Referee: F. Potter-Irwin (*England*)

R. A. Lloyd kicked a penalty and dropped a goal (7-0); J. G. Will scored; F. H. Turner failed (7-3). (H.T.). F. H. Turner scored; J. C. MacCallum converted (7-8); A. R. Foster scored; R. A. Lloyd failed (10-8).

Although this was a fast and exciting game play did not really reach a high standard. The Scottish forwards were quite effective but the backs had a bad day, their handling being poor. Early on Lloyd kicked a penalty for 'feet up' and then dropped a good goal. Before half time Gilray put up a kick ahead and a good bounce let Will, following up very fast, score. In the second half Will had two good runs, finishing the second off with a cross kick which Turner held and took over. Then Lloyd, who had played well throughout, seized on a bad pass by Milroy, put in a high kick which Angus could not hold and Foster got the ball and went on to score.

SCOTLAND 8   ENGLAND 3
Inverleith
16 March 1912

Scotland: W. M. Dickson (*Blackheath*); W. R. Sutherland (*Hawick*), W. Burnet (*Hawick*), A. W. Angus (*Watsonians*), J. G. Will (*Camb. Univ.*); J. L. Boyd (*Un. Services*), E. Milroy (*Watsonians*); D. M. Bain (*Oxford Univ.*), J. Dobson (*Glas. Acads.*), D. D. Howie (*Kirkcaldy*), J. C. MacCallum* (*Watsonians*), L. Robertson (*London Scot.*), J. M. B. Scott (*Edin. Acads.*), F. H. Turner (*Liverpool*), C. M. Usher (*London Scot.*)
England: W. R. Johnston (*Bristol*); A. D. Roberts (*Northern*), R. W. Poulton (*Harlequins*), J. G. G. Birkett (*Harlequins*), H. Brougham (*Harlequins*); A. D. Stoop (*Harlequins*), J. A. Pym (*Blackheath*); R. Dibble* (*Newport*), J. H. Eddison (*Headingley*), D. Holland (*Devon Albion*), A. L. Kewney (*Rockcliff*), J. A. King (*Headingley*), A. H. MacIlwaine (*Un. Services*), R. C. Stafford (*Bedford*), N. A. Wodehouse (*Un. Services*)
Referee: F. Gardiner (*Ireland*)   **Touch judges:** W. A. Walls, J. Baxter

There was no scoring at half time. W. R. Sutherland scored; J. MacCallum failed (3-0); D. Holland scored; A. H. MacIlwaine failed (3-3); C. M. Usher scored; J. C. MacCallum converted (8-3).

Scotland deserved to win this match but England were badly handicapped by losing King with two broken ribs early in the first half. While this was an accident there is no doubt that the Scottish forwards were in magnificent form in the loose and their tackling fairly upset the opposition including the much lauded Harlequin backs. Johnston, at full back, took a hammering either in tackling Will in full cry or in halting forward rushes. Angus had another good game and Sutherland was always very penetrative.

SCOTLAND 0   SOUTH AFRICA 16
Inverleith
23 November 1912

Scotland: W. M. Dickson (*Oxford Univ.*); W. R. Sutherland (*Hawick*), A. W. Gunn (*RHSFP*), A. W. Angus (*Watsonians*), J. Pearson (*Watsonians*); J. L. Boyd (*Un. Services*), E. Milroy (*Watsonians*); D. M. Bain (*Oxford Univ.*), P. C. B. Blair (*Camb. Univ.*), J. Dobson (*Glas. Acads.*), D. D. Howie (*Kirkcaldy*), W. D. C. L. Purves (*London Scot.*), L. Robertson (*London Scot.*), J. M. B. Scott (*Edin. Acads.*), F. H. Turner* (*Liverpool*)
South Africa: P. G. Morkel (*WP*); J. A. Stegmann (T), R. R. Luyt (*WP*), J. W. H. Morkel (*WP*), E. McHardy (*Orange FS*); F. P. Luyt (*WP*), F. J. Dobbin* (*GW*); J. A. J. Francis (T), A. S. Knight (T), S. H. Ledger (*GW*), J. D. Luyt (*EP*), D. F. T. Morkel (T), W. H. Morkel (*WP*), G. Thompson (*WP*), T. F. Van Vuuren (EP)
Referee: F. C. Potter-Irwin (*England*)   **Touch judges:** J. D. Dallas, M. Honnet

E. E. McHardy scored; P. G. Morkel failed (0-3). (H.T.). J. A. Stegmann scored twice; P. G. Morkel converted the first only (0-11); W. H. Morkel scored; D. T. F. Morkel converted (0-16).

Scotland had an equal share territorially of the game but there was never any real doubt about the outcome for South Africa were both heavier and faster. Sutherland alone had the necessary pace to cope with his opponents and indeed it needed good tackling to prevent him from scoring. In the second half the visitors backs fairly opened out and two of the scores resulted from passing movements which crossed the width of the field at least twice.

FRANCE 3   SCOTLAND 21
Parc des Princes
1 January 1913

France: F. Dutour (*Toulouse*); L. Larribau (*Perigueux*), G. Lane* (*RCF*), J. Sentilles (*Tarbes*), P. Jaureguy (*Toulouse*); M. Burgun (*RCF*), A. Hedembaigt (*Bayonne*); F. Forgues (*Bayonne*), M. Legrain (*SF*), M. Leuvielle (*Bordeaux*), P. Mauriat (*Lyon*), P. Mounicq (*Toulouse*), M. Pascarel (*TOEC*), J. Sebadio (*Tarbes*), P. Thil (*Nantes*)
Scotland: W. M. Dickson (*Oxford Univ.*); W. R. Sutherland (*Hawick*), R. E. Gordon (*Un. Services*), A. W. Angus (*Watsonians*), W. A. Stewart (*London Hospitals*); A. W. Gunn (*RHSFP*), E. Milroy (*Watsonians*); C. H. Abercrombie (*Un. Services*), D. M. Bain (*Oxford Univ.*), P. C. B. Blair (*Camb. Univ.*), D . D. Howie (*Kirkcaldy*), G. A. Ledingham (*Aberdeen GSFP*), J. B. McDougall (*Greenock Wrs.*), F. H. Turner* (*Liverpool*), C. M. Usher (*London* Scot.)
Referee: J. Baxter (*England*)

J. Sebadio scored an unconverted try (3-0); W. A. Stewart scored twice, F. H. Turner converted the first (3-8). (H.T.). R. E. Gordon (2) and W. A. Stewart scored; F. H. Turner converted two (3-21).

Colombes Stadium was rendered unplayable by heavy rain and flooding and Cyril Rutherford, the French secretary, worked a minor miracle by making, within 24 hours, all the necessary arrangements to shift the game to the Parc des Princes.

The teams were much more evenly matched than the score suggests. There was little to choose between the forwards but the Scottish backs were clearly better, especially in combined work. France opened the scoring early on when an unexpected short throw to the front of a line out let Sebadio hurl himself in for a try but eventually some fine play by Gordon and the tremendous pace of Stewart produced five tries for Scotland.

On this occasion the refereeing was from the start firm, even strict, and as a result France was frequently penalised. As the game proceeded the spectators became more and more enraged at Mr Baxter and there were some ugly scenes after the final whistle when the police and many of the players found it necessary to protect and escort the referee from the field. W. M. Dickson, who was quite deaf, completely misinterpreted the crowd scenes at the close and while making his way to the dressing room remarked to Charles Usher how sporting the spectators were in applauding the Scots so enthusiastically.

However, there were repercussions. The Rugby Football Union let it be known that they would not supply any referees for future matches in France but did relent to let an Englishman referee the France-South Africa match in Bordeaux later in the season.

The SFU took a much sterner stand for they refused to renew the 1914 fixture even though it

74

would have been at Inverleith. They made it quite clear that they had no fault to find with the French committee and team but were equally emphatic that they could not accept a situation where the referee's decisions, authority and safety were threatened by the spectators. World War I intervened before further action could be discussed and it may be noted that four of the French XV and nine of the Scots did not survive to see the fixture resumed in 1920.

SCOTLAND 0 WALES 8
Inverleith
1 February 1913

Scotland: W. M. Dickson (*Oxford Univ.*); W. A. Stewart (*London Hospitals*), R. E. Gordon (*Un. Services*), A. W. Angus (*Watsonians*), W. R. Sutherland (*Hawick*), J. H. Bruce Lockhart (London Scot.), E. Milroy (*Watsonians*); C. H. Abercrombie (*Un. Services*), D. M. Bain (Oxford Univ.), P. C. B. Blair (*Camb. Univ.*), D. D. Howie (*Kirkcaldy*), L. Robertson (*London Scot.*), J. M. B. Scott (*Edin. Acads.*), F. H. Turner (*Liverpool*), C. M. Usher (*London Scot.*)
Wales: R. F. Williams (*Cardiff*); H. Lewis (*Swansea*), W. J. Trew* (*Swansea*), T. Jones (*Pontypool*), G. L. Hirst (*Newport*); J. M. C. Lewis (*Cardiff*), R. Lloyd (*Pontypool*), F. Andrews (*Pontypool*), A. Davies (*Swansea*), W. Jenkins (*Cardiff*), P. Jones (*Newport*), F. Perrett (*Neath*), R. Richards (*Aberavon*), G. Stephens (*Neath*), H. Uzzell (*Newport*)
Referee: S. H. Crawford (*Ireland*)   **Touch judges:** J. D. Dallas, W. M. Douglas

J. M. C. Lewis scored but failed to convert (0–3). (H.T.). T. Jones scored; J. M. C. Lewis converted (0–8).

This was rather a dreary game consisting mainly of a series of scrums. The Welsh pack was clearly on top but their backs did not play well. Lewis, the stand off, however, was in excellent form and had the opening score in what was a very even first half. Wales' domination up front saw the second half played mainly in the Scottish half but a good defence prevented any score until late on Lewis dropped at goal, the ball went wide, and a wicked bounce beat two defenders to let Jones get there first to score.

SCOTLAND 29 IRELAND 14
Inverleith
22 February 1913

Scotland: W. M. Dickson (*Oxford Univ.*); W. R. Sutherland (*Hawick*), R. E. Gordon (*Un. Services*), J. Pearson (*Watsonians*), W. A. Stewart (*London Hospitals*); T. C. Bowie (*Watsonians*), E. Milroy (*Watsonians*); D. M. Bain (*Oxford Univ.*), P. C. B. Blair (*Camb. Univ.*), G. H. H. P. Maxwell (*Edin. Univ.*), W. D. C. L. Purves (*London Scot.*), L. Robertson (*London Scot.*), J. M. B. Scott (*Edin. Acads.*), F. H. Turner* (*Liverpool*), C. M. Usher (*London Scot.*).
Ireland: J . W. McConnell (*Lansdowne*), C. V. McIvor (*Dublin Univ.*), G . W. Holmes (*Dublin Univ.*), J. B. Minch (*Bective Rangers*), F. Bennett (*Collegians*); H. M. Read (*Dublin Univ.*), R. A. Lloyd * (*Liverpool*); S. B. B. Campbell (*Edin. Univ.*), J. E. Finlay (*QC Belfast*); E. W. Jeffares (*Wanderers*), A. V. Killeen (*Garyowen*), R. D. Patterson (*Wanderers*), F. G. Schute (*Dublin Univ.*), P. Stokes (*Blackrock*), W. Tyrell (*QU Belfast*).
Referee: J. Baxter (*England*)   **Touch judges:** J. D. Dallas, R. Stevenson

W. A. Stewart scored, F. H. Turner converted (5–0); F. G. Schute scored; R. A. Lloyd converted (5–5); W. A. Stewart (2) and C. M. Usher scored; F. H. Turner converted the first two (18–5). (H.T.). T. C. Bowie and W. A. Stewart scored; F. H. Turner converted one (26–5); P. Stokes scored; C. A. Lloyd converted (26–10); R. A. Lloyd dropped a goal (26–14); W. D. C. L. Purves scored; F. H. Turner failed (29–14).

This was the antithesis of the Welsh match, being full of open play and incidents . In spite of losing Dickson with a shoulder injury during the first half, the Scottish pack with Scott in the backs, more than held their own and good play by the threes produced some fine tries. The Watsonian half backs played well as a pair while Stewart, with four tries, proved much too fast for his opponents, yet for his second score he had to hand off and beat several defenders in a 70 yards run. Later on Campbell came out of the pack as an extra defender. A late Irish rally brought a score by Stokes and an excellent 40 yards drop goal by Lloyd.

ENGLAND 3   SCOTLAND 0
Twickenham
15 March 1913

England: W. R. Johnston (*Bristol*); V. H. M. Coates (*Bath*), R. W. Poulton (*Harlequins*), F. N. Tarr (*Leicester*), C. N. Lowe (*Camb. Univ.*); W. J. A. Davies (*RN*), F. E. Oakeley (*RN*); L. G. Brown (*Blackheath*), J. E. Greenwood (*Camb. Univ.*), J. A. King (*Headingley*) C. H. Pillman (*Blackheath*), J. A. S. Ritson (*Newcastle N*), S. Smart (*Gloucester*), G. Ward (*Leicester*), N. A. Wodehouse* (*RN*)
Scotland: W. M. Wallace (*Camb. Univ.*); J. B. Sweet (*Glas. HSFP*), J. Pearson (*Watsonians*), E. G. Loudoun-Shand (*Oxford Univ.*), W. R. Sutherland (*Hawick*), T. C. Bowie (*Watsonians*), E. Milroy (*Watsonians*); D. M. Bain (*Oxford Univ.*), P. C. B. Blair (*Camb. Univ.*), G. H. H. P. Maxwell (*Edin. Acads.*), W. D. C. L. Purves (*London Scot.*), L. Robertson (*London Scot.*), J. M. B. Scott (*Edin. Acads.*), F. H. Turner* (*Oxford Univ.*), C. M. Usher (*London Scot.*)
Referee: T. D. Schofield (*Wales*)

L. G. Brown scored but J. E. Greenwood failed (3-0). (H.T.).

This was a game made memorable by the play of Sutherland. Always dangerous in attack he achieved wonders in defence after Loudoun-Shand was crippled and changed to the wing. For the rest of the game Sutherland, playing at centre, blotted out single-handedly the potentially great wing pair of Poulton and Coates, and England could only manage a scrambled try scored in the first half. Scott also defended well and had one great run which might have produced a score had Loudoun-Shand been able to keep up with him.

WALES 24   SCOTLAND 5
Cardiff
7 February 1914

Wales: J. Bancroft (*Swansea*); I. T. Davies (*Llanelli*), W. H. Evans (*Llwynypia*), J. Wetter (*Newport*), G. L. Hirst (*Newport*); J. M. C. Lewis (*Cardiff*), R. Lloyd (*Pontypool*); J. A. Davies* (*Llanelli*), J. B. Jones (*Abertillery*), P. Jones (*Pontypool*), T. C. Lloyd (*Neath*), E. Morgan (*Swansea*), H. Uzzell (*Newport*), D. Watts (*Maesteg*), T. Williams (*Swansea*)
Scotland: W. M. Wallace (*Camb. Univ.*): W. S. Stewart (*London Hospital*), R. M Scobie (*RMA*), W. R. Sutherland (*Hawick*), J. G. Will (*Camb. Univ.*); A. T. Sloan (*Edin. Acads.*),A. S. Hamilton (*Headingley*); D. M. Bain* (*Oxford Univ.*), D. G. Donald (*Oxford Univ.*) A. D. Laing (*RHSFP*), G. H. H. P. Maxwell (*Edin. Acads.*), A. R. Ross (*Edin. Univ.*), A. M. Stewart (*Edin. Acads.*), A. W. Symington (*Camb. Univ.*), A. Wemyss (*Gala*)
Referee: V. Drennon (*Ireland*)   **Touch judges:** Dr J. R. C. Greenlees, A. Llewellyn

W. A. Stewart scored; A. D. Laing converted (0-5); G. L. Hirst dropped a goal (4-5); J. Bancroft kicked a penalty (7-5). (H.T.). I. T. Davies and J. Wetter scored; J. Bancroft converted the second (15-5); J. M. C. Lewis dropped a goal (19-5); G. L. Hirst scored; J. Bancroft converted (24-5).

This was a very rough game, one paper commented that there were no drawing-room tactics indulged in. D. M. Bain had six stitches put in a head wound and later commented that the dirtier team won. 'Podger' Laing was one of the first to be felled a challenge that he gladly accepted and returned in full measure. Scotland did relatively well up to half time but Sutherland was lamed and although he stayed on the field on the wing, was practically useless. Wales in the second half exploited this weak wing effectively.

IRELAND 6   SCOTLAND 0
Lansdowne Road
28 February 1914

Ireland: F. P. Montgomery (*Queen's*); J. P. Quinn* (*Dublin Univ.*), A. R. V. Jackson (*Wanderers*), J. B. Minch (*Bective Rangers*), A. R. Foster (*NIFC*); H. W. Jack (UC *Cork*); H. W. Jack (*UC Cork*), V. McNamara (*UC Cork*), C. Adams (*Old Wesley*), W. P. Collopy (*Bective Rangers*), J. C. A. Dowse (*Monkstown*), G. V. Killeen (*Garryowen*), P. O'Connell (*Bective Rangers*) J. S. Parr (*Wanderers*), J. Taylor (*Collegians*), W. Tyrell (*QU Belfast*)
Scotland: W. M. Wallace (*Camb. Univ.*); J. B. Sweet (*Glas. HSFP*), R. M. Scobie (*RMA*), J. R. Warren (*Glas. Acads.*), J. G. Will (*Camb. Univ.*); T. C. Bowie (*Watsonians*), E. Milroy* (*Watsonians*), D. M. Bain (*Oxford Univ.*), D. G. Donald (*Oxford Univ.*),

A. D. Laing (*RHSFP*), J. B. McDougall (*Greenock Wrs.*), G. H. H. P. Maxwell (*Edin. Acads.*), A. R. Ross (*Edin. Univ.*), F. H. Turner (*Liverpool*), A. Wemyss (*Gala*)
Referee: J. Baxter (*England*)

No scoring at half time. J. P. Quinn and V. McNamara scored; H. W. Jack failed to convert (6-0).

In drizzling rain Scotland began well but Ireland developed their characteristic forward rushes which improved as the game went on, the Scottish backs were largely committed to defence. After half time the rain became very heavy and the game developed mainly into a fierce forward battle. Ireland got the ball over the line twice for tries but in spite of great efforts by Will and Sweet Scotland could not score. It was noted that Laing played well and that Turner was useful in 'hooking'.

SCOTLAND 15   ENGLAND 16
Inverleith
21 March 1914

Scotland: W. M. Wallace (*Camb. Univ.*); J. L. Huggan (*London Scot.*), R. M. Scobie (*Un. Services*), A. W. Angus (*Watsonians*), J. G. Will (*Camb. Univ.*); T. C. Bowie (*Watsonians*); E. Milroy* (*Watsonians*); A. D. Laing (*RHSFP*), G. H. H. P. Maxwell (*Edin. Acads.*), I. M. Pender (*London Scot.*), A. R. Ross (*Edin. Univ.*), A. W. Symington (*Camb. Univ.*), F. H. Turner (*Liverpool*), C. M. Usher (*London Scot.*), E. T. Young (*Glas. Acads.*)
England: W. R. Johnston (*Bristol*); C. N. Lowe (*Camb. Univ.*), J. H. D. Watson (*Blackheath*), R. W. Poulton (*Liverpool*), A. J. Dingle (*Hartlepool Rovers*); W. J. A. Davies (*RN*), F. E. Oakeley (*RN*); L. G. Brown (*Blackheath*), J. Brunton (*North Durham*), J. E. Greenwood (*Camb. Univ.*), H. C. Harrison (*Un. Services*), A. F. Maynard (*Camb. Univ.*), C. H. Pillman (*Blackheath*), S. Smart (*Gloucester*), G. Ward (*Leicester*)
Referee: T. D. Schofield (*Wales*)

J. G. Will scored; F. H. Turner failed (3-0); C. N. Lowe scored; J. E. Greenwood failed (3-3). (H.T.). J. L. Huggan scored; F. H. Turner failed (6-3), C. N. Lowe scored twice H. C. Harrison converted both (6-13); R. W. Poulton scored; H. C. Harrison failed (6-16); T. C. Bowie dropped a goal (10-16); J. G. Will scored; F. H. Turner converted (15-16).

This was a great and exciting game. Scotland who completed the season without a win came within a goal kick of beating England who finished as undefeated champions. The match was marked throughout by some splendid attacking rugby by both sides. Milroy got over but was brought back for a forward pass and then Wallace had to touch down in defence but at once Maxwell made ground. Ross and Turner carried the movement on and the ball went to Will who outpaced Lowe to score far out. Turner's long kick just failed. Just before the interval Watson put Lowe over to score with Will hanging on to him. Early in the second half a great forward rush involving most of the Scottish pack finished by Huggan scoring again too far out for Turner to convert. Almost at once a brilliant English run involving their whole back division gave Lowe room to sprint round Wallace and score between the posts. This was the prelude to further fine moves by the English threes and they seemed to have made the game safe by scoring two more sparkling tries. Harrison, having converted two, unaccountably missed the third which was relatively easy. Yet Scotland did not give in for, getting well up field, Bowie dropped a good goal and immediately after, he set Will away at midfield. The winger held off a challenge by Lowe and scored in a position where Turner's conversion brought the scores to 15-16. England then put in a strong attack in which Pillman had to retire with a bad leg injury and Scotland finished with some good running, Will again being prominent, but could not get the vital score.

With the coming of World War I this splendid Calcutta Cup match marked the end of an epoch. Before the close of 1914 three of the players were gone, and by 1918 five of the English and six of the Scottish XV had been killed in action.

FRANCE 0   SCOTLAND 5
Parc des Princes
1 January 1920

France: A. Chilo (*RCF*); A. Jaureguy (*RCF*), R. Lasserre (*Bayonne*), R. Crabos (*RCF*), P. Serre (*Perpignan*); E. Billac (*Bayonne*), P. Struxiano* (*Toulouse*); J. Sebedio (*Beziers*), P. Pons (*Toulouse*), M. F. Lubin-Lebrere (*Toulouse*), A. Cassayet (*Tarbais*), L. Puech (*Toulouse*), R. Thierry (*RCF*), R. Marchand (*Poitiers*), J. Laurent (*Bayonne*)
Scotland: G. L. Pattullo (*Panmure*); A. T. Sloan (*Edin. Acads.*), E. C. Fahmy (*Abertillery*) A. W. Angus (*Watsonians*), G. B. Crole (*Oxford Univ.*); A. S. Hamilton (*Headingley*), J. Hume (*RHSFP*); D. D. Duncan (*Oxford Univ.*), R. A. Gallie (*Glas. Acads.*), F. Kennedy (*Stewart's FP*), A . D. Laing (*RHSFP*), W. A . K. Murray (*London Scot.*), G. Thom (*Kirkcaldy*), C. M. Usher (*London Scot.*), A. Wemyss (*Edin. Wrs.*)
Referee: F. C. Potter-Irwin (*England*)   **Touch judges:** J. R. C. Greenlees, C. F. Rutherford

There was no scoring in the first half. G. B. Crole scored and F. Kennedy converted (0-5).

The game was played in heavy rain on a muddy and slippery ground. The Scottish forwards were much praised especially for their excellent dribbling. The Scottish try came from a fast dribble by Usher and Thom which was carried on by Crole.

SCOTLAND 9   WALES 5
Inverleith
7 February 1920

Scotland: G. L. Patullo (*Panmure*); E. B. Mackay (*Glas. Acads.*), A. W. Angus (*Watsonians*), E. C. Fahmy (*Abertillery*), G. B. Crole (*Oxford Univ.*); A. T. Sloan (*Edin. Acads.*), J A. R. Selby (*Watsonians*); D. D. Duncan (*Oxford Univ.*), R. A. Gallie (*Glas. Acads.*), F. Kennedy (*Stewart's FP*), A. D. Laing (*RHSFP*), N. Macpherson (*Newport*), G. H. H. P. Maxwell (*RAF*), G. Thom (*Kirkcaldy*), C. M. Usher* (*London Scot.*).
Wales: J. Rees (*Swansea*); W. J. Powell (*Cardiff*), J. Shea (*Newport*), A. Jenkins (*Llanelli*), B. Williams (*Llanelli*); B. Beynon (*Swansea*), J. Wetter (*Newport*); C. W. Jones (*Bridgend*) J. Jones (*Aberavon*), S. Morris (*Crosskeys*), G. Oliver (*Pontypool*), T. Parker (*Swansea*), J. Whitfield (*Newport*), J. Williams (*Blaina*), H. Uzzell* (*Newport*)
Referee: J. F. Crawford (*Ireland*)   **Touch judges:** T. Scott, H. Parker

A. Jenkins scored and converted (0-5). (H.T.). F. Kennedy kicked a penalty (3-5); A. T. Sloan scored but Kennedy failed (6-5); F. Kennedy kicked a penalty (9-5).

Wales, having decisively beaten England, came to Inverleith in perfect conditions fully expecting to win. The packs were fairly evenly matched but the Welsh backs were clearly faster. J. Shea was blamed since he continually dropped at goal or tried to go through on his own. A. T. Sloan's try came from a brilliant diagonal solo run from mid field to the corner. F. Kennedy's two penalties were long range efforts; the first was taken from near touch ten yards inside the Welsh half. It was a hard game and both teams had two men hurt or off.

SCOTLAND 19   IRELAND 0
Inverleith
28 February 1920

Scotland: G. L. Pattullo (*Panmure*); A. Browning (*Glas. HSFP*), A. W. Angus (*Watsonians*), A. T. Sloan (*Edin. Acads.*), G. B. Crole (*Oxford Univ.*); E. C. Fahmy (*Abertillery*), J. A. R. Selby (*Watsonians*); D. D. Duncan (*Oxford Univ.*), R. A. Gallie (*Glas. Acads.*), F. Kennedy (*Stewart's FP*), A. D. Laing (*RHSFP*), N. Macpherson (*Newport*), W. A. K. Murray (*London Scot.*), G. Thom (*Kirkcaldy*), C. M. Usher (*London Scot.*).
Ireland: W. E. Crawford (*Lansdowne*); C. H. Bryant (*Cardiff*), T. Wallace (*Cardiff*), P. J. Roddy (*Bective Rangers*), B. A. T. McFarland (*Londonderry*); W. Duggan (UC *Cork*), J. B. O'Neill (QU *Belfast*); H. H. Coulter (QU *Belfast*), A. W. Courtney (UC *Dublin*), R. Y. Crichton (*Dublin Univ.*), W. D. Doherty* (*Guy's*), J. E. Finlay (*Cardiff*), A. H. Price (*Dublin Univ.*), W. J. Roche (UC *Cork*), P. Stokes (*Garryowen*)
Referee: J. Baxter (*England*)   **Touch judges:** T. Scott, A. Tedford

G. B. Crole scored and F. Kennedy converted (5-0); F. Kennedy kicked a penalty (8-0); G. B. Crole scored and Kennedy converted (13-0). (H.T.). A. W. Angus scored (16-0); A. Browning scored but F. Kennedy failed with both (19-0).

The Irish forwards lacked fire while the Scottish pack improved as the match went on. The Irish backs defended well especially as they had to contend with many unexpected moves by their opponents. E. C. Fahmy, moved from centre, had a good match, one dummy and a run followed by a cross kick gave Angus his score. G. B. Crole had a brilliant match. His ability to short punt over an opponent and use his great pace to regain the ball gave him two tries and caused endless trouble to the defence.

ENGLAND 13   SCOTLAND 4
Twickenham
20 March 1920

England: B. S. Cumberlege (*Blackheath*); C. N. Lowe (*Blackheath*), E. Myers (*Bradford*), E. D. G. Hammett (*Newport*), S. W. Harris (*Blackheath*); W. J. A. Davies (*Un. Services*), C. A. Kershaw (*Un. Services*); A. F. Blakiston (*Northampton*), G. S. Conway (*Camb. Univ.*), J. E. Greenwood* (*Camb. Univ.*), F. W. Mellish (*Blackheath*), S. Smart (*Gloucester*), A. T. Voyce (*Gloucester*), W. W. Wakefield (*Harlequins*), T. Woods (*RN*)
Scotland: G. L. Pattullo (*Panmure*); A. T. Sloan (*Edin. Acads.*), A. W. Angus (*Watsonians*), J. H. Bruce Lockhart (London Scot.), G. B. Crole (Oxford Univ.); E. C. Fahmy (Abertillery), C. S. Nimmo (*Watsonians*); D. D. Duncan (*Oxford Univ.*), R. A. Gallie (*Glas. Acads.*), F. Kennedy (*Stewart's FP*), N. Macpherson (*Newport*), G. H. H. P. Maxwell (*RAF*), G. Thom (*Kirkcaldy*), C. M. Usher* (*London Scot.*), A. Wemyss (*Edin. Wrs.*)
Referee: T. D. Schofield (*Wales*)

C. N. Lowe scored and J. E. Greenwood converted (5-0), S. W. Harris scored and Greenwood converted (10-0); J. H. Bruce Lockhart dropped a goal (10-4). (H.T.). C. A. Kershaw scored but Greenwood failed (13-4).

A record crowd of 40,000 saw the teams presented to HM King George V. The Scottish pack showed some aggression in the tight but had no answer to the fine open play by their opponents in the loose. The English backs were obviously better and very ready and quick to capitalise on an error. The new partnership of Fahmy and Nimmo was not a success and it is interesting to note that Nimmo had been selected to replace Selby, his club fellow-half back.

SCOTLAND 0   FRANCE 3
Inverleith
22 January 1921

Scotland: H. H. Forsayth (*Oxford Univ.*); I. J. Kilgour (*RMA*), A. E. Thomson (*Un. Services*), A. L. Gracie (*Harlequins*), J. H. Carmichael (*Watsonians*); A. T. Sloan (*Edin. Acads.*), J. Hume* (*RHSFP*); J. M. Bannerman (*Glas. HSFP*), R. S. Cumming (*Aber. Univ.*), R. A. Gallie (*Glas. Acads.*), A. D. Laing (*RHSFP*), J. B. McDougall (*Wakefield*), N. Macpherson (*Newport*), G. H. H. P. Maxwell (*London Scot.*), W. A. K. Murray (*Kelvinside Acads.*)
France: J. Clement (*RCF*); R. Got (*Perpignan*), R. Crabos* (*RCF*); F. Borde (*RCF*), J. Lobies (*RCF*); E. Billac (*Bayonne*), R. Piteu (*Pau*); M. Biraben (*Dax*), J. Boubee (*Tarbes*), J. Coscoll (*Beziers*), R. Lasserre (*Bayonne*), G. Lubin-Lebrere (*Toulouse*), P. Pons (*Toulouse*), E. Soulie (*CASG*), F. Vaquer (*Perpignan*)
Referee: W. P. Hinton (*Ireland*)   **Touch judges:** J. M. Dykes, C. F. Rutherford

E. Billac scored but Crabos failed (0-3). (H.T.).

This was France's first win in Scotland and was well deserved for their entire XV was faster and more alert. The forwards were fairly evenly matched but the Scottish backs had a bad day. J . Hume was most consistent but got no support. One fumbled pass was smartly seized on by Borde and passed to Billac for the only score. Towards the end the French defence held out against fierce forward pressure.

WALES 8   SCOTLAND 14
Swansea
5 February 1921

Wales: J. Rees (*Swansea*); M. G. Thomas (*Bart's*), A. Jenkins (*Llanelli*), P. E. R. Baker Jones (Army), F. Evans (*Llanelli*), *W.* Bowen (*Swansea*), T. H. Vile* (*Newport*); L. Attewell (*Newport*), W. Hodder (*Pontypool*), J. Jones (*Aberavon*), E. Morgan (*Llanelli*), T. Parker (*Swansea*), T. Roberts (*Risca*), J. Williams (*Blaina*), S. Winmill (*Cross Keys*)
Scotland: H. H. Forsayth (*Oxford Univ.*); A. T. Sloan (*Edin. Acads.*), A. L. Gracie (*Harlequins*), A. E. Thomson (*Un. Services*), J. H. Carmichael (*Watsonians*); R. L. H. Donald (*Glas. HSFP*), J. Hume* (*RHSFP*); J. M. Bannerman (*Glas. HSFP*), J. C. R. Buchanan (*Stewart's FP*), R. S. Cumming (*Aber. Univ.*), G. Douglas (*Jedforest*), R. A. Gallie (*Glas. Acads.*), G. H. H. P. Maxwell (RAF), J. N. Shaw (*Edin. Acads.*),C. M. Usher (*Edin. Wrs.*)
Referee: J. Baxter (*England*)

A. E. Thomson scored but Maxwell failed (0-3); J. C. R. Buchanan scored and Maxwell converted (0-8); G. H. H. P. Maxwell kicked a penalty goal (0-11). (H.T.). A. Jenkins dropped two goals (8-11); A. T. Sloan scored but Maxwell failed (8-14).

This was the first win in Wales since 1892 and the match was remarkable for the unprecedented crowd scenes, for play was held up on several occasions to move spectators from the touch line and goal areas. At one time the referee conferred with the captains about abandoning the game and although Scotland really deserved their win there is no doubt that a crucial break after Jenkins' second drop goal with the score at 11-8 halted the Welsh revival. Wales elected to play against the wind and found themselves 11-0 down at half time. In the second half Jenkins and Vile dropped at goal continually, Jenkins getting two including one from the touchline. Near the end Sloan clinched things with a run down the wing but he only got his try by touching down amongst the spectators who were sitting packed in the Welsh goal area. This was not the end of a hectic day for the Scottish XV who had to grab their clothes, rush into their bus, and catch their train where they washed and changed.

IRELAND 9   SCOTLAND 8
Lansdowne Road
26 February 1921

Ireland: W. E. Crawford (*Lansdowne*); H. S. T. Cormac (*Clontarf*), G. V. Stephenson (*QU Belfast*), A. R. Foster (*Derry*), D. J. Cussen (*Dublin Univ.*), W. Cunningham (*Lansdowne*) T. Mayne (*NIFC*), J. J. Bermingham (*Blackrock*), W. P. Collopy (*Bective Rangers*), A. W. Courtney (UC *Dublin*), W. D. Doherty* (*Camb. Univ.*), C. F. G. T. Hallaran (*RN*), T. A. McClelland (*QU Belfast*), N. M. Purcell (*Lansdowne*), P. Stokes (*Blackrock*)
Scotland: H. H. Forsayth (*Oxford* Univ.), J. W. S. McCrow (*Edin. Acads.*), A. L. Gracie (*Harlequins*), A. T. Sloan (*Edin. Acads.*), J. H. Carmichael (*Watsonians*); R. L. H. Donald (*Glas. HSFP*), J. Hume* (*RHSFP*); J. M. Bannerman (*Glas. HSFP*), J. C. R. Buchanan (*Stewart's FP*), R. A. Gallie (*Glas. Acads.*), J. B. McDougall (*Wakefield*), G. H. H. P. Max*well* (*London Scot.*), G. M. Murray (*Glas. Acads.*), J. N. Shaw (*Edin. Acads.*), J. L. Stewart (*Edin. Acads.*)
Referee: J. Baxter (*England*)

J. Hume scored and Maxwell converted (0-5); D. J. Cussen scored but Crawford failed (3-5); A. T. Sloan scored but Maxwell failed (3-8). (H.T.). G. V. Stephenson scored but Crawford failed (6-8); W. Cunningham scored but Hallaran failed (9-8).

Scotland were beaten forward although the Irish pack was described as robust rather than brilliant. However the Irish backs were poor finishers and faced by some good tackling. Sloan was crippled early on and Scotland were rather fortunate to lead at half time.

SCOTLAND 0 ENGLAND 18
Inverleith
19 March 1921

Scotland: H. H. Forsayth (*Oxford Univ.*); A. T. Sloan (*Edin. Acads.*), A. E. Thomson (*Un. Services*), C. J. G. Mackenzie (*Un. Services*), A. L. Gracie (*Harlequins*), R. H. L. Donald (*Glas. HSFP*), J. Hume* (*RHSFP*); J. M. Bannerman (*Glas. HSFP*), J. C. R. Buchanan (*Stewart's FP*), R. A. Gallie (*Glas. Acads.*), F. Kennedy (*Stewart's FP*), J. B. McDougall (*Wakefield*), N. Macpherson (*Newport*), G. H. H. P. Maxwell (*London Scot.*), C. M. Usher (*Edin. Wrs.*)
England: B. S. Cumberlege (*Blackheath*); C. N. Lowe (*Blackheath*), E. D. G. Hammett (*Newport*), A. M. Smallwood (*Leicester*), Q. E. M. A. King (*Army*), W. J. A. Davies* (*Un. Services*); C. A. Kershaw (*Un. Services*); A. F. Blakiston (*Northampton*), L. G. Brown (*Blackheath*), R. Cove-Smith (*Camb. Univ.*), R. Edwards (*Newport*), E. R. Gardner (*RN*), A. T. Voyce (*Gloucester*), W. W. Wakefield (*Harlequins: RAF*), T. Woods (*Devonport Services*)
Referee: J. C. Crawford (*Ireland*) **Touch judges:** J. M. Dykes, J. Baxter

E. R. Gardner scored but B. S. Cumberlege failed (0-3); T. Woods scored and Hammett converted (0-8). (H.T.). L. G. Brown and Q. E. M. A. King scored for Hammett to convert both (0-18).

The placing of Gracie on the wing was a mistake especially as his centre had a terrible day of mishandling . There was fairly even play for half an hour but the ability of the entire English XV to develop play from Scottish mistakes won the match. The open play and handling of their pack was quite outstanding. Brown's try is often recalled: Davies dropped at goal and the ball rebounded off a post to Brown who instinctively caught it and scored. It was said that he was so far offside that he admitted feeling embarrassed at getting the decision.

FRANCE 3 SCOTLAND 3
Colombes
2 January 1922

France: J. Clement (*Valence*); A. Jaureguy (*Toulouse*), F. Borde (*Toulouse*), R. Crabos* (*St Severs*), R. Got (*Perpignan*), J. Pascot (*Perpignan*), R. Piteu (*Pau*); R. Lasserre (*Cognac*), J. Sebedio (*Carcassone*), F. Cahuc (St *Girons*), P. Moureu (*Beziers*), A. Cassayet (St *Gaudens*), M. Biraben (*Dax*), P. Pons (*Toulouse*), G. Lubin-Lebrere (*Toulouse*)
Scotland: W. C. Johnston (*Glas. HSFP*); A. Browning (*Glas. HSFP*), G. P. S. Macpherson (*Oxford Univ.*), A. L. Gracie (*Harlequins*), E. H. Liddell (*Edin. Univ.*); J. C. Dykes (*Glas. Acads.*), J. Hume (*RHSFP*); A. Wemyss (*Edin. Wrs.*), D. M. Bertram (*Watsonians*), A. K. Stevenson (*Glas. Acads.*), D. S. Davies (*Hawick*), J. M. Bannerman (*Glas. HSFP*), J. R. Lawrie (*Melrose*), C. M. Usher* (*Edin. Wrs.*), G. H. H. P. Maxwell (*London Scot.*)
Referee: H. C. Harrison (*England*) **Touch judges:** J. M. Dykes, C. F. Rutherford

A. Jaureguy scored but Crabos failed: (3-0); A. Browning scored but Maxwell failed (3-3). (H.T.).

The ground was soft after some heavy rain but the dismal conditions did not keep away a record crowd of 37,000. The game was fairly even up to half-time; then rain fell continually so that handling became very difficult. The Scottish pack dominated the second half but no score came from many near things, the French defence being desperate but successful.

SCOTLAND 9 WALES 9
Inverleith
4 February 1922

Scotland: H. H. Forsayth (*Oxford Univ.*); A. Browning (*Glas. HSFP*), R. C. Warren (*Glas. Acads.*), A. L. Gracie (Harlequins), E. H. Liddell (*Edin. Univ.*); G. P. S. Macpherson (*Oxford Univ.*), W. E. Bryce (*Selkirk*); A. Wemyss (*Edin. Wrs.*), D. M. Bertram (*Watsonians*), W. G. Dobson (*Heriot's FP*), D. S. Davies (*Hawick*), J. M. Bannerman (*Glas. HSFP*), J. R. Lawrie (*Melrose*), C. M. Usher* (*Edin. Wrs.*), J. C. R. Buchanan (*Stewart's FP*)
Wales: F. Samuel (*Mountain Ash*); F. Palmer (*Swansea*), I. Evans (*Swansea*), B. E. Evans (*Llanelli*), C. Richards (*Pontypool*); W. Bowen (*Swansea*), W. J. Delahay (*Bridgend*); T. Parker* (*Swansea*), J. Whitfield (*Newport*), S. Morris (*Cross Keys*), D. D. Hiddlestone (*Neath*), T. Roberts (*Risca*), J. G. Stephens (*Llanelli*), W. Cummings (*Treorchy*), T. Jones (*Newport*)
Referee: R. A. Lloyd (*England*) **Touch judges:** J. M. Dykes, W. W. James

There was no scoring at half time. W. Bowen scored and Samuel converted (0-5); A. Browning scored but Bertram failed (3-5); A. Browning kicked a penalty and scored a try which he did not convert (9-5); I. Evans dropped a goal (9-9).

The Scottish forwards played well but their backs did not make good use of a plentiful supply of the ball. Bryce had a fine game making several good breaks one of which gave Browning his first try. The winger also had a good game, scoring all the points. The opening score came when Forsayth, catching a high kick under the posts, had his kick charged down by Bowen who ran on to drop on the rebound. Evans' equaliser came in the last minute and a very disappointed crowd left in stunned silence.

SCOTLAND 6   IRELAND 3
Inverleith
25 February 1922

Scotland: H. H. Forsayth (*Oxford Univ.*); A. Browning (*Glas. HSFP*), R. C. Warren (*Glas. Acads.*), A. L. Gracie (*Harlequins*), E. H. Liddell (*Edin. Univ.*); G. P. S. Macpherson (*Oxford Univ.*), W. E. Bryce (*Selkirk*); A. Wemyss (*Edin. Wrs.*), D. M. Bertram (*Watsonians*), W. G. Dobson (Heriot's *FP*), D. S. Davies (Hawick), J. M. Bannerman (*Glas.* HSFP), J. R. Lawrie (*Melrose*), C. M. Usher* (*Edin. Wrs.*), J. C. R. Buchanan (*Stewart's* FP)
Ireland: W. E. Crawford (*Lansdowne*); H. W. V. Stephenson (*Un. Services*), G. V. Stephenson (QU *Belfast*), D. B. Sullivan (UC *Dublin*), T. G. Wallis (*Wanderers*); J. R. Wheeler (QU *Belfast*), J. B. Clarke (*Bective Rangers*); W. P. Collopy* (*Bective Rangers*), M. J. Bradley (*Dolphin*), I. Popham (*Cork Const.*), F. G. T. Hallaran (*Un. Services*), S. McVicker (QU *Belfast*), R. H. Owens (*Dublin Univ.*), J. K. S. Thompson (*Dublin Univ.*), J. D. Egan (*Bective Rangers*)
Referee: T. D. Schofield (*Wales*)   **Touch judges:** J. M. Dykes, R. M. Mcgrath

J. A. Clarke scored but Wallis failed (0-3). (H.T.). W. E. Bryce and E. H. Liddell scored but Browning failed to convert (6-3).

A strong wind made handling difficult and play often surged from end to end. The Scottish pack, held in the first half, finished strongly to give Bryce, who had another good game and the backs the chances they needed for the Irish defence was fast and effective. G. P. S. Macpherson did not please the critics as a stand-off half.

ENGLAND 11   SCOTLAND 5
Twickenham
18 March 1922

England: J. A. Middleton (*Richmond*); I. J. Pitman (*Oxford Univ.*), A. M. Smallwood (Leicester), E. Myers (Headingley), C. N. Lowe (Camb. Univ.); W. J. A. Davies* (RN), C. A. Kershaw (*RN*); W. W. Wakefield (*Harlequins*), G. S. Conway (*Camb. Univ.*), A. T. Voyce (*Gloucester*), R. Cove-Smith (*Camb. Univ.*), J. E. Maxwell-Hyslop (*Oxford Univ.*), R. F. H. Duncan (*Guy's*), H. L. Price (*Oxford Univ.*), P. B. R. W. Williams-Powlett (*RN*)
Scotland: H. H. Forsayth (*Oxford Univ.*); J. M. Tolmie (*Glas. HSFP*), A. L. Gracie (*Harlequins*), G. P. S. Macpherson (*Oxford Univ.*), E. B. Mackay (*Glas. Acads.*); J. C. Dykes (*Glas. Acads.*), W. E. Bryce (*Selkirk*); J. C. R. Buchanan (*Stewart's FP*), D. M. Bertram (*Watsonians*), W. G. Dobson (*Heriot's FP*), D. S. Davies (Hawick), J. M. Bannerman (*Glas. HSFP*), J. R. Lawrie (*Melrose*), C. M. Usher* (*London Scot.*), G. H. H. P. Maxwell (*Edin. Acads.*)
Referee: R. A. Lloyd (*Ireland*)

J. C. Dykes scored and Bertram converted (0-5). (H.T.). C. N. Lowe scored twice and then W. J. A. Davies once; G. S. Conway converted the second only (11-5).

Another large crowd in fine weather saw the teams presented to HM King George V. Scotland had a good first half but England came away in the end. Again the English pack were splendid in the loose but it was a brilliant display by Davies which, in the second half, brought about their win. G. P. S. Macpherson often showed his skill as an attacker but the wingers were not fast enough to match their opponents.

SCOTLAND 16   FRANCE 3
Inverleith
20 January 1923

Scotland: D. Drysdale (*Heriot's FP*); A . C. Wallace (*Oxford Univ.*), E. McLaren (*RHSFP*), A. L. Gracie* (*Harlequins*), E. H. Liddell (*Edin. Univ.*); S. B. McQueen (*Waterloo*), W. E. Bryce (*Selkirk*); D. S. Kerr (*Heriot's FP*), D. M. Bertram (*Watsonians*), A. K. Stevenson (*Glas. Acads.*), L. M. Stuart (*Glas. HSFP*), J. M. Bannerman (*Glas. HSFP*) J. R. Lawrie (*Melrose*), D. S. Davies (*Hawick*), J. C. R. Buchanan (*Stewart's FP*)
France: J. Clement (*Valance*); M. Lalande (*RCF*), R. Crabos* (St *Sever*), F. Bordes (*Toulouse*), A. Jaureguy (*Toulouse*); J. Pascot (*Toulon*), C. Dupont (*Lourdes*); A. Bernon (*Lourdes*), J. Bayard (*Toulouse*), L. Beguet (*RCF*), P. Moureu (*Beziers*), A. Casseyet (*St Gaudens*), J. Larrieu (*Tarbes*), J. Sebedio (*Carcassone*), A. Guichemerre (*Dax*)
Referee: T. H. Vile (*Wales*)   **Touch judges:** H. S. Dixon, C. F. Rutherford

E. McLaren scored and Drysdale converted (5-0). (H.T.). W. E. Bryce and E. McLaren scored and Drysdale converted the first (13-0); L. Beguet dropped a goal from a mark (13-3); E. H. Liddell scored but Drysdale failed (16-3).

The Scots were not really too impressive; rather that the French proved ineffective. Scotland opened strongly but continually wasted scoring situations and it took a solo dash by McLaren to score. However, against the wind in the second half their forwards kept up the pressure and the backs combined better for their three scores. France were handicapped by injuries to Pascot and Bordes.

WALES 8   SCOTLAND 11
Cardiff
February 1923

Wales: B. O. Male (*Cardiff*), W. R. Harding (*Camb. Univ.*), A. Jenkins (*Llanelli*), R. A. Cornish (*Cardiff*), T. Johnson (*Cardiff*); J. M. C. Lewis* (*Camb. Univ.*), W. J. Delahay (*Cardiff*); A. Baker (*Neath*), S. Morris (*Cross Keys*), D. G. Davies (*Cardiff*), T. Parker (*Swansea*), G. Michael (*Swansea*), G. Thomas (*Llanelli*), L. Jenkins (*Aberavon*), T. Roberts (*Newport*)
Scotland: D. Drysdale (*Heriot's FP*); A. Browning (*Glas. HSFP*), E. McLaren (*RHSFP*), A. L. Gracie* (*Harlequins*), E. H. Liddell (*Edin. Univ.*); S. B. McQueen (*Waterloo*), W. E. Bryce (*Selkirk*), D. S. Kerr (*Heriot's FP*), D. M. Bertram (*Watsonians*), A. K. Stevenson (*Glas. Acads.*), L. M. Stuart (*Glas. HSFP*), J. M. Bannerman (*Glas. HSFP*), J. R. Lawrie (*Melrose*), D. S. Davies (*Hawick*), J. C. R. Buchanan (*Stewart's FP*)
Referee: J. W. Baxter (*England*)

A. Jenkins kicked a penalty (3-0). (H.T.). E. H. Liddell scored but Browning failed (3-3); J. M. C. Lewis scored and Jenkins converted (8-3); L. M. Stuart scored but Browning failed (8-6); A. L. Gracie scored and D. Drysdale converted (8-11).

Although the police closed the gates before the start, a record crowd got in and lined the playing area. They were to witness a hard game which finished with one of the most famous tries in the history of the game. Wales failed to take their chances in the first half and only led by a penalty goal. Straightway Eric Liddell showed his pace by scoring a fine try only for Wales to increase their lead to 8-3 with a converted try. Then with fifteen minutes to go the Scottish pack put in a tremendous finish. Firstly L. M. Stuart scored after a fine forward rush. Then came two scoring attacks by the backs but Liddell and Gracie were both tackled short of the line. With three minutes to go the ball was heeled from a scrum on the 25; Bryce passed to McQueen who went to the left and seeing that McLaren was covered, threw a long pass over his head to Gracie. Now in his own words: 'Running slightly diagonally to the left to go between Arthur Cornish and 'Codger' Johnson I saw in a flash that the latter was in two minds – whether to go for me or run between me and Liddell and prevent me passing to the latter ... as I went on the way opened up for me and the tactics to be adopted were as plain as a pikestaff. Whether I dummied or not I do not remember but I was just able to swerve round my opposite number and in doing so saw I had Male on the wrong foot and all I had to do was to carry on over the line. But here I nearly spoilt everything. The dead ball line at Cardiff was desperately close to the goal line and in trying to touch down near the posts I recklessly ran along the dead ball line, only inches off it, till the close proximity of Cornish and Jenkins made me decide to drop on the ball.' It is recorded that he was so close to the dead ball line that a small boy, sitting there, was struck by Gracie's boot and lost some teeth. One can only add that the disappointed Welsh supporters swarmed onto the field and carried Gracie off the field shoulder high!

IRELAND 3   SCOTLAND 13
Lansdowne Road
24 February 1923

Ireland: W. E. Crawford (*Lansdowne*); D. J. Cussen (*Dublin Univ.*), G. V. Stephenson (*Queen's*), J. B. Gardiner (*NIFC*), R. O. McClenahan (*Instonians*); W. H. Hall (*Instonians*) W. Cunningham (*Lansdowne*); M. Bradley (*Dolphin*), R. Collopy (*Bective Rangers*), W. P. Collopy (*Becttve Rangers*), D. M. Cunningham (*NIFC*), P. E. F. Dunn (*Bective Rangers*) R. D. Gray (*Old Wesley*), T. A. McClelland (*Queen's*), J. K. S. Thompson* (*Dublin Univ.*)
Scotland: D. Drysdale (*Heriot's FP*); A. Browning (*Glas. HSFP*), E. McLaren (*London Scot.*), A. L. Gracie* (*Harlequins*), E. H. Liddell (*Edin. Univ.*); S. B. McQueen (*Waterloo*), W. E. Bryce (*Selkirk*); N. Macpherson (*Newport*), D. M. Bertram (*Watsonians*), J. C. R. Buchanan (*Stewart's FP*), L. M. Stuart (*Glas. HSFP*), J. M. Bannerman (*Glas. HSFP*) J. R. Lawrie (*Melrose*), D. S. Davies (*Hawick*), R. S. Simpson (*Glas. Acads.*)
Referee: T. H. Vile (*Wales*)

D. J. Cusson scored (3-0); E. H. Liddell scored and Browning converted (3-5), A. Browning scored but failed to convert (3-8). (H.T.). S. B. McQueen scored and Browning converted (3-13).

In drizzling rain Ireland played a spoiling game and gave Gracie and McLaren little scope. Nevertheless the two wingers were successes, Liddell showing that he was not only very fast but determined. It was considered that McQueen, given a good supply of the ball from the scrums, did not vary his play enough. Drysdale was praised for his defence.

SCOTLAND 6   ENGLAND 8
Inverleith
17 March 1923

Scotland: D. Drysdale (*Heriot's FP*); A. Browning (*Glas. HSFP*), E. McLaren (*London Scot.*), A. L. Gracie* (*Harlequins*), E. H. Liddell (*Edin . Univ.*); S. B. McQueen (*Waterloo*), W. E. Bryce (*Selkirk*); N. Macpherson (*Newport*), D. M. Bertram (*Watsonians*), A. K. Stevenson (*Glas. Acads.*), L. M. Stuart (*Glas. HSFP*), J. M. Bannerman (*Glas. HSFP*), J. R. Lawrie (*Melrose*), D. S. Davies (*Hawick*), J. C. R. Buchanan (*Stewart's FP*)
England: T. E. Holliday (*Aspatria*); C. N. Lowe (*Blackheath*), E. Myers (*Bradford*), H. M. Locke (*Birkenhead Park*), A. M. Smallwood (*Leicester*); W. J. A. Davies* (*Un. Services*), C. A. Kershaw (Un. *Services*); A. F. Blakiston (*Northampton*), G. S. Conway (*Rugby*), R. Cove-Smith (*OMT*), E. R. Gardner (*Devonport Services*), W. G. E. Luddington (*Devonport Services*), F. W. Sanders (*Plymouth Albion*), A. T. Voyce (*Gloucester*), W. W. Wakefield (*Camb. Univ.*)
Referee: T. H. Vile (*Wales*)   **Touch judges:** H. S. Dixon, J. Baxter

A. M. Smallwood scored but W. G. E. Luddington failed (0-3); E. McLaren scored but A. Browning failed (3-3). (H.T.). A. L. Gracie scored but D. Drysdale failed (6-3); A. T. Voyce scored and W. G. E. Luddington converted (6-8).

The match was played in brilliant weather before a crowd of 30,000 which included the Duke of York. The teams were quite evenly matched but England were expert at seizing chances, their pack being very ready to run with the ball. Smallwood had a good solo try after beating the defenders and this was later matched when Gracie taking the ball on at his feet, kicked it past the full back and only his speed enabled him to fall on the ball just before it went over the dead ball line. The winning score came from an interception by Locke which was carried on by the forwards for Voyce to score.

FRANCE 12   SCOTLAND 10
Stade Pershing
1 January 1924

France: E. Besset (*Grenoble*); A. Jaureguy (*SF*), A. Behoteguy (*Bayonne*), R. Crabos* (*St Sever*), L. Cluchague (*Biarritz*); H. Galau (*Toulouse*), C. Dupont (*Rouen*), L. Lepatey (*Mazamet*), A. Gonnet (*RCF*), L. Beguet (*RCF*), P. Moureu (*Beziers*), A. Cassayet (*St Gaudeas*), R. Lasserre (*Grenoble*), E. Piquaral (*RCF*), J. Etcheberry (*Cognac*)
Scotland: D. Drysdale (*Heriot's FP*), A. C. Wallace (*Oxford Univ.*), A. L. Gracie (*Harlequins*), E. McLaren (*London Scot.*), C. E. W. C. Mackintosh (*London Scot.*); H. Waddell (*Glas. Acads.*), W. E. Bryce (*Selkirk*); D. S. Kerr (*Heriots FP*), A. Ross (*Kilmarnock*), R. A. Howie (*Kirkcaldy*), L. M. Stuart (*Glas. HSFP*), J. M. Bannerman (*Glas. HSFP*), J. C. R. Buchanan* (*Stewart's FP*), D. S. Davies (*Hawick*), K. G. P. Hendrie (*Heriot's FP*)
Referee: E. Roberts (*Wales*)   **Touch judges:** C. F. Rutherford

A. Jaureguy scored (3-0); A. Piquaral scored but Crabos failed (6-0); A. C. Wallace scored but Davies failed (6-3). (H.T.). D. S. Davies kicked a penalty (6-6); H. Waddell dropped a goal (6-10); H. Galau and P. Maureu scored unconverted tries (12-10).

The Colombes pitch was flooded by the Seine but C. F. Rutherford worked a major miracle in transferring the match to the Stade Pershing in 36 hours. It was expected that the heavy conditions would suit the Scottish pack but in fact the French forwards thoroughly outplayed their opponents. The winning try in a scramble following a line out came in the last five minutes.

SCOTLAND 35   WALES 10
Inverleith
2 February 1924

Scotland: D. Drysdale (*Heriot's FP*); I. S. Smith (*Oxford Univ.*), G. P. S. Macpherson (*Oxford Univ.*), G. G. Aitken (*Oxford Univ.*); A. C. Wallace (*Oxford Univ.*); H. Waddell (*Glas. Acads.*), W. E. Bryce (*Selkirk*); A. Ross (*Kilmarnock*), D. M. Bertram (*Watsonians*) R. A. Howie (*Kirkcaldy*), J. C. R. Buchanan* (*Stewart's FP, Exeter*), J. M. Bannerman (*Glas. HSFP*), J. R. Lawrie (*Leicester*), K. G. P. Hendrie (*Heriot's FP*), A. C. Gillies (*Watsonians*)
Wales: B. O. Male (*Cardiff*); H. Davies (*Newport*), M. A. Rosser (*Penarth*), J. E. Evans (*Llanelli*), T. Johnson (*Cardiff*); V. M. Griffiths (*Newport*), E. Watkins (*Neath*); J. Whitfield* (*Newport*), S. Morris (*Cross Keys*), J. I. Morris (*Swansea*), I. Jones (*Llanelli*), T. Jones (*Newport*), C. Pugh (*Maesteg*), W. J. Ould (*Cardiff*), D. G. Francis (*Llanelli*)
Referee: J. B. McGowan (*Ireland*)   **Touch judges:** R. T. Neilson, I. D. Thomas

I. S. Smith scored and Drysdale converted (5-0); Drysdale kicked a penalty (8-0); W. E. Bryce scored and Drysdale converted (13-0); D. M. Bertram scored but Drysdale failed (16-0); I. S. Smith scored but Drysdale failed (19-0); A. C. Wallace scored but Drysdale failed (22-0). (H.T.). H. Waddell scored but Gillies failed (25-0); G. P. S. Macpherson scored and Drysdale converted (30-0); I. S. Smith scored and Drysdale converted (35-0) V. Griffiths and I. Jones scored for Male to convert both (35-10).

A. L. Gracie could not play so Scotland fielded the entire Oxford University backs and this combination proved too fast and clever for the Welshmen. I. S. Smith had a splendid day showing up the opposition by his pace and power. The Scottish pack laid the foundation of the win, being on top in the scrum and loose play. The Welsh tries came during the last six minutes of the game when Scotland, leading 35-0, were easing up.

SCOTLAND 13   IRELAND 8
Inverleith
23 February 1924

Scotland: D. Drysdale (*Heriot's FP*); I. S. Smith (*Oxford Univ.*), G. G. Aitken (*Oxford Univ*), J. C. Dykes (*Glas. Acads.*), R. K . Millar (*London Scot.*); H. Waddell (*Glas. Acads.*), W. E. Bryce (*Selkirk*); R. G. Henderson (*Newcastle N*), D. M. Bertram (*Watsonians*), R. A. Howie (*Kirkcaldy*), J. C. R. Buchanan* (*Stewart's FP*), J. M. Bannerman (*Glas. HSFP*), J. R. Lawrie (*Leicester*), A. C. Gillies (*Watsonians*), K. G. P. Hendrie (*Heriot's FP*)

Ireland: W. J. Stewart (*QU Belfast*); H. W. V. Stephenson (*Un. Services*), G. V. Stephenson (*QU Belfast*), J. B. Gardiner (*NIFC*), A. C. Douglas (*Instonians*); W. H. Hall (*Instonians*), J. A. B. Clarke (*Bective Rangers*); J. D. Clinch (*Dublin Univ.*), W. P. Collopy* (*Bective Rangers*), R. Collopy (*Bective Rangers*), R. Y. Crichton (*Dublin Univ.*), C. F. G. T. Hallaran (*Un. Services*), T. A. McClelland (*QU Belfast*), J. McVicker (*Collegians*), I. M. B. Stuart (*Dublin Univ.*)
Referee: T. H. Vile (*Wales*)　**Touch judges:** R. T. Neilson, H. Thrift

H. Waddell scored and D. Drysdale converted (5-0), D. M. Bertram scored and D. Drysdale converted (10-0); G. V. Stephenson scored and converted (10-5). (H.T.). G. V. Stephenson scored but failed to convert (10-8); H. Waddell scored but D. Drysdale failed (13-8).

This was essentially a robust forward game played mainly in the Scottish half. The Irish backs set out to play a spoiling game which nearly succeeded since two of the Scottish scores came from defensive blunders. For a while in the second half Ireland attacked, the two Stephensons combining well but the Scottish forwards were on top during the last vital quarter. J. D. Clinch was praised as were W. E. Bryce and H. Waddell. The Scottish team changes were puzzling, for R. K. Millar, usually a right wing, was placed on the left while J. C. Dykes and H. Waddell reversed their club positions.

ENGLAND 19　SCOTLAND 0
Twickenham
15 March 1924

England: B. S. Chantrill (*Bristol*); H. C. Catcheside (*Percy Park*), L. J. Corbett (*Bristol*), H. M. Locke (*Birkenhead Park*), H. P. Jacobs (*Oxford Univ.*); E. Myers (*Bradford*), A. T. Young (*Camb. Univ.*); A. F. Blakiston (*Liverpool*), C. S. Conway (*Rugby*), R. Cove-Smith (*OMT*), R. Edwards (*Newport*), W. G. E. Luddington (*Devonport Services*), A. Robson (*Newcastle N*), A. T. Voyce (*Gloucester*), W. W. Wakefield* (*Leicester*)
Scotland: D. Drysdale (*Heriot's FP*); I. S. Smith (*Oxford Univ.*), G. P. S. Macpherson (*Oxford Univ.*), G. G. Aitken (*Oxford Univ.*), A. C. Wallace (*Oxford Univ.*); H. Waddell (*Glas. Acads.*), W. E. Bryce (*Selkirk*); D. S. Davies (*Hawick*), D. M. Bertram (*Watsonians*), R. A. Howie (Kirkcaldy), R. G. Henderson (Newcastle N), J. M. Bannerman (*Glas. HSFP*), J. R. Lawrie (*Leicester*), A. C. Gillies (*Watsonians*), J. C. R. Buchanan* (*Stewart's FP*)
Referee: T. H. Vile (*Wales*)

W. W. Wakefield scored and C. S. Conway converted (5-0). (H.T.). E. Myers dropped a goal and scored for C. S. Conway to convert (14-0); H. C. Catcheside scored and C. S. Conway converted (19-0).

England started very strongly but Scotland eventually rallied and would have scored but for good final tackling. Near half time a fine combined run by the English backs finished with a cross kick which bounced awkwardly to give Wakefield possession and a try between the posts. From the restart Scotland attacked and again came near to scoring. Then came a burst of scoring from Myers who dropped a good goal and scored a fine solo dodging try. The last score came by another solo effort by Catcheside who picked up a fumbled pass in his own half and after rounding Drysdale and handing off Wallace twice, scored a great try. England were the more resourceful but Scotland had chances enough to have scored several times and some praise must go to Chantrill who three times reached Smith in full flight and put in try-saving tackles.

SCOTLAND 25　FRANCE 4
Inverleith
24 January 1925

Scotland: D. Drysdale (*Heriot's FP*); I. S. Smith (*Oxford Univ.*), G. P. S. Macpherson* (*Oxford Univ.*), G. G. Aitken (*Oxford Univ.*), A. C. Wallace (*Oxford Univ.*); J. C. Dykes (*Glas. Acads.*), J. B. Nelson (*Glas. Acads.*); J. C. R. Buchanan (*Exeter*), J. Gilchrist (*Glas. Acads.*), W. H. Stevenson (*Glas. Acads.*), D. J. MacMyn (*Camb. Univ.*), J. M. Bannerman (*Glas HSFP*), J. W. Scott (*Stewart's FP*), A. C. Gillies (*Carlisle*), J. R. Paterson (*Birkenhead*)
France: J. Ducousso (*Tarbes*); F. Raymond (*Toulouse*), J. Ballari (*Toulouse*), M. Baillette (*Perpignan*), J. Halet (*Strasbourg*); Y. du Manoir (*RCF*), C. Dupont (*Havre*) A. Montade (*Perpignan*), C. Marcet (*Albi*), A. Maury (*Toulouse*), A. Cassayet (*Narbonne*), A. Laurent (*Biarritz*), A. Biousa (*Toulouse*), J. Boubee* (*Agen*), E. Ribere (*Perpignan*)
Referee: Dr E. De Courcy Wheeler (*Ireland*)　**Touch judges:** Sir Robert C. Mackenzie, C. F. Rutherford

A. G. Gillies scored and converted (5-0); Y. du Manoir dropped a goal (5-4). (H.T.). A. C. Wallace scored but Gillies failed (8-4); I. S. Smith scored and Drysdale converted (13-4) A. C. Wallace scored but Drysdale failed (16-4); I. S. Smith scored thrice; Dykes failed with the first and Gillies with the other two (25-4).

20,000 turned out to watch the last International to be played at Inverleith, a game marked by a partial eclipse of the sun which reached its maximum during the second half without interrupting play. In spite of the score the critics were unhappy with the display of the Scottish pack which did not dominate play. I. S. Smith, with four tries, and J. B. Nelson both had good games while G. P. S. Macpherson had a hand in practically every score. Y. du Manoir's goal was a really fine one from well out. The French team was numbered and frequently packed down 3–4 with Biousa acting as a rover and even putting the ball into the scrum. The story goes that at the dinner a Frenchman asked I. S. Smith what his time was over 100 yards, and not quite catching the question, he replied 'four' – an answer which fairly astounded the enquirer!

WALES 14   SCOTLAND 24
Swansea
7 February 1925

Wales: T. Johnson (*Cardiff*), C. Thomas (*Bridgend*), E. Williams (*Aberavon*), R. A. Cornish (*Cardiff*), W. P. James (*Aberavon*); W. J. Hopkins (*Aberavon*), W. J. Delahay (*Cardiff*); C. Pugh (*Maesteg*), S. Morris* (*Cross Keys*), B. Phillips (*Aberavon*), S. Herrara (*Cross Keys*), W. I. Jones (*Llanelli*), D. Parker (*Swansea*), I. Richards (*Cardiff*), S. Lawrence (*Bridgend*)
Scotland: D. Drysdale (*Heriot's FP*); I. S. Smith (*Oxford Univ.*), G. P. S. Macpherson* (*Oxford Univ.*), G. G. Aitken (*Oxford Univ.*), A. C. Wallace (*Oxford Univ.*); J. C. Dykes (*Glas. Acads.*), J. B. Nelson (*Glas. Acads.*); D. S. Davies (*Hawick*), J. C. H. Ireland (*Glas. HSFP*), R. A. Howie (*Kirkcaldy*), D. J. MacMyn (*Camb. Univ.*), J. M. Bannerman (*Glas. HSFP*), J. W. Scott (*Stewart's FP*), A. C. Gillies (Carlisle), J. R. Paterson (*Birkenhead Park*)
Referee: J. Baxter (*England*)   **Touch judges:** Sir Robert C. Mackenzie, R. P. Thomas

I. S. Smith scored thrice and Drysdale converted the first only (0-11); D. Drysdale dropped a goal (0-15); A. C. Wallace scored but Gillies failed (0-18). (H.T.). A. C. Wallace scored but Gillies failed (0-21); W. J. Hopkins scored and Parker converted (5-21); I. S. Smith scored but Gillies failed (5-24); I. Jones and R. A. Cornish scored but Parker failed each time (11-24); D. Parker kicked a penalty (14-24).

In the first half the speed and skill of the Scottish backs were quite devastating and once again I. S. Smith scored four tries. However during the last fifteen minutes the Welsh pack lifted its game to put in a storming finish. On occasions in the first half Pugh came out of the pack to help in defence. The Welsh team was numbered.

IRELAND 8   SCOTLAND 14
Lansdowne Road
28 February 1925

Ireland: W. E. Crawford* (*Lansdowne*); H. W. V. Stephenson (*Un. Services*), G. V. Stephenson (*QU Belfast*), J. B. Gardiner (*NIFC*), T. R. Hewitt (*QU Belfast*); F. S. Hewitt (*Instonians*), M. Sugden (*Dublin Univ.*); G. R. Beamish (*Leicester, RAF*), W. F. Browne (*Un. Services*), J. D. Clinch (*Dublin Univ.*), W. R. F. Collis (*Wanderers*), R. Collopy (*Bective Rangers*), R. Y. Crichton (*Dublin Univ.*), J. McVicker (*Collegians*), M. J. Bradley (*Dolphin*)
Scotland: D. Drysdale* (*Heriot's FP*); I. S. Smith (*Oxford Univ.*), J. C. Dykes (*Glas. Acads.*), G. G. Aitken (*Oxford Univ.*), A. C. Wallace (*Oxford Univ.*); H. Waddell (*Glas. Acads.*), J. B. Nelson (*Glas. Acads.*); D. S. Davies (*Hawick*), J. C. H. Ireland (*Glas. HSFP*), R. A. Howie (*Kirkcaldy*), D. J. MacMyn (*Camb. Univ.*), J. M. Bannerman (*Glas. HSFP*), J. W. Scott (*Stewart's FP*), J. C. R. Buchanan (*Exeter*), J. R. Paterson (*Birkenhead Park*)
Referee: A. E. Freethy (*Wales*)

A. C. Wallace scored and Drysdale converted (0-5). (H.T.). W. E. Crawford kicked a penalty (3-5); D. J. MacMyn scored and Dykes converted (3-10), H. W. V. Stephenson scored and Crawford converted (8-10); H. Waddell dropped a goal (8-14).

As against Wales the speed and handling of the Scottish backs was splendid. The absence of

Macpherson had much to do with the comparative quietness of I. S. Smith but the return of Waddell outside to Nelson compensated for this. The second Scottish score was the result of great handling which started in midfield. The ball went from Nelson, Waddell, Dykes, Aitken to Wallace who after a 30-yard run passed the ball back to Dykes and thence via Scott to MacMyn who scored under the posts. The Irish try came from a dodge by H. W. V. Stephenson. Inside the Scottish half he flung the ball in from touch, caught the throw himself and sprinted to score in the corner before a surprised defence could tackle him. As a result of this the touch law was later altered. Ireland was handicapped by an injury to T. Hewitt and W. F. Browne came out of the pack to help the defence.

SCOTLAND 14   ENGLAND 11
Murrayfield
21 March 1925

Scotland: D. Drysdale (*Heriot's FP*); I. S. Smith (*Oxford Univ.*), G. P. S. Macpherson* (*Oxford Univ.*), G. G. Aitken (*Oxford Univ.*), A. C. Wallace (*Oxford Univ.*); H. Waddell (*Glas. Acads.*), J. B. Nelson (*Glas. Acads.*), D. S. Davies (*Hawick*), J. C. H. Ireland (*Glas. HSFP*), R. A. Howie (*Kirkcaldy*), D. J. MacMyn (*London Scot.*), J. M. Bannerman (*Glas. HSFP*), J . W. Scott (*Stewart's FP*), A. C. Gillies (*Carlisle*), J. R. Paterson (*Birkenhead Park*)
England: T. E. Holliday (*Aspatria*); R. H. Hamilton-Wickes (*Harlequins*), L. J. Corbett (*Bristol*), H. M. Locke (*Birkenhead Park*), A. M. Smallwood (*Leicester*); E. Myers (*Bradford*), E. J. Massey (*Leicester*); D. C. Cumming (*Camb. Univ.*), R. R. F. MacLennan (*OMT*), W. G. E. Luddington (*RN*), J. S. Tucker (*Bristol*), A. F. Blakiston (*Liverpool*), A. T. Voyce (*Gloucester*), R. Cove-Smith (*OMT*), W. W. Wakefield* (*Harlequins*)
Referee: A. E. Freethy (*Wales*)   **Touch judges:** R. Welsh, G. C. Robinson.

W. G. E. Luddington kicked a penalty goal (0-3); J. B. Nelson scored and Drysdale converted (5-3); R. H. Hamilton-Wickes scored and Luddington converted (5-8). (H.T.). W. W. Wakefield scored but Luddington failed (5-11); A. C. Wallace scored and Gillies converted (10-11); H. Waddell dropped a goal (14-11).

Beautiful weather for the opening of the new ground at Murrayfield brought out a record crowd of at least 70,000 who watched one of the most exciting matches ever played. The lead changed hands thrice and England's great fight to save the game during the last minutes only failed because of some tremendous tackling by the Scots and the utter exhaustion of the attackers. W. G. E. Luddington had opened the scoring with an early penalty shortly before G. P. S. Macpherson, with a typical dummy and side step, broke through and the ball passed via H. Waddell to J . B. Nelson, who, fending off a tackler with a killing hand-off, scored under the posts. D. Drysdale's conversion put Scotland into the lead but just before half-time. England went ahead when R. H. Hamilton scored after a fine interpassing run with A. T. Voyce.

Shortly after the restart Corbett had a good run, finishing with a cross-kick which H. Waddell, on his line, could not hold and W. W. Wakefield seized the ball to score. W. G. E. Luddington, when about to take the conversion, was startled to find D. J. MacMyn rush out and kick the ball away from the mark – a move accepted by the referee. (Younger readers may be reminded that, at this period, the ball, just before a conversion attempt, was held clear of the ground by a placer. When he put the ball down in the mark for the kick, the defenders were allowed to charge.)

There followed an excellent try in the right-hand corner by A. C. Wallace and a magnificent conversion from the touch-line by A. C. Gillies brought the score to 10-11. At this point I must challenge several statements made about this try in the Calcutta Cup match programme of 1979. Therein it is stated that 'Wakefield and Voyce tackled Ian Smith into touch near the line ... that Smith never got anywhere near the line ... the touch judge was usually the local president, or something, and he was hardly ever within twenty yards ... a photograph ... shows Smith, clearly in touch, still on his feet, with Voyce and Wakefield tackling him and the cumming nowhere near'.

There is, of course, no doubt that the scorer was Johnny Wallace. He had been given an overlap inside the 25 and sprinted for the corner where he dived under Holliday's tackle to touch down just over the line. The photograph on Plate I shows that the corner flag was still upright and the next nearest Englishman still some two yards away. The nearest Scot, G. P. S. Macpherson, was following up in support about five yards away, ready for a possible inside pass and I know that he had no doubts about the try. The touch judge concerned was Robin Welsh, the then Vice President of the SRU, a man whose integrity is beyond question. He was, in 1925, a very active and high grade

88

tennis player and may be seen running five yards back, ideally placed to give a decision on a touch line matter. Later in the evening, when questioned about the score by the late Dr A. C. Gillies, he was quite adamant that the try was good, a point that he made when the referee checked with him at the time.

Scotland now attacked for the next twenty minutes and several times came near to scoring. A. C. Wallace was halted by a forward pass; J. W. Scott beat the fullback only to be felled by A. M. Smallwood cutting across in defence; G. G. Aitken dribbled through only to have the ball rebound wide off a goal post and H. Waddell narrowly missed with a drop goal. Then J. B. Nelson gave H. Waddell a clear pass which let him drop a goal from the 25.

With five minutes left England made desperate efforts to score. A. M. Smallwood broke away but was floored by D. Drysdale; E. Myers was halted on the line by sheer numbers and finally L. J. Corbett broke through only to stumble and fall through sheer exhaustion about a yard short of the line. In the maul that followed the spectators were much incensed at the very unnecessary kick which badly stunned D. Drysdale. There remained a final thrill for Holliday, with practically the last kick of the match, narrowly missed with a very long range drop kick.

It was noted that when the final whistle went, this final desperate burst by England had so exhausted some of their players that they literally staggered off the field.

FRANCE 6 SCOTLAND 20
Colombes
2 January 1926

France: L. Destarac (*Tarbes*); M. Besson (*CASG*), C. Magnanou (*Bayonne*), M. Chapuy (*SF*), A. Jaureguy (*SF*); Y. du Manoir (*RCF*), R. Llary (*Carcassone*); J. Etcheberry (*Vienne*), A. Gonnet (*RCF*), A. Maury (*Toulouse*), A. Puig (*Perpignan*), A. Cassayet* (*Narbonne*), E. Ribere (*Perpignan*), E. Piquiral (*RCF*), A. Bioussa (*Toulouse*)
Scotland: D. Drysdale (*Oxford Univ.*), I. S. Smith (*Edin. Univ.*), R. M. Kinnear (*Heriot's FP*), J. C. Dykes (*Glas. Acads.*), A. C. Wallace (*Oxford Univ.*), H. Waddell (*Gas. Acads.*), J. B. Nelson (*Glas. Acads.*); D. S. Davies (*Hawick*), J. C. H. Ireland (*Glas. HSFP*), W. V. Berkley (*Oxford Univ.*), D. J. MacMyn (*London Scot*), J. M. Bannerman (*Glas. HSFP*), J. W. Scott (*Stewart's FP*), A. C. Gillies (*Watsonians*), J. R. Paterson (*Birkenhead Park*)
Referee: W. M. Llewellyn (*Wales*)   **Touch judge:** R. Welsh

A. C. Gillies kicked a penalty (0-3), A. C. Wallace scored twice but Gillies failed to convert (0-9). (H.T.). D. J. MacMyn scored but Gillies failed (0-12); A. C. Wallace scored but Gillies failed (0-15); A. Gonnet kicked a penalty (3-15); E. Piquiral scored but Gonnet failed (6-15); J. M. Bannerman scored and Drysdale converted (6-20).

The ground was heavy after rain and this suited the Scottish pack who really controlled the game. This was Wallace's last game. He had just graduated in Law and left for Australia after the match. Ribere and Bioussa were both hurt and off for some time in the second half. Bioussa again acted as scrum half to a three-four scrum. A French report tells that the ball often fell into the water-logged ditch around the pitch and that the groundsman had to recover it with a butterfly net – 'Il faut bien rire un peu'.

SCOTLAND 8 WALES 5
Murrayfield
6 February 1926

Scotland: D. Drysdale* (*Oxford Univ.*); I. S. Smith (*Edin. Univ.*), R. M. Kinnear (*Heriots FP*), J. C. Dykes (*Glas. Acads.*), W. M. Simmers (*Glas. Acads.*); H. Waddell (*Glas. Acads.*), J. B. Nelson (*Glas. Acads.*); D. S. Davies (*Hawick*), J. C. H. Ireland (*Glas. HSFP*), G. P. S. Macpherson (*Oxford Univ.*), D. J. MacMyn (*London Scot.*), J. M. Bannerman (*Glas. HSFP*), J. W. Scott (*Stewart's FP*), A. C. Gillies (*Watsonians*), J. R. Paterson (*Birkenhead Park*)
Wales: W. A. Everson (*Newport*); G. E. Andrews (*Newport*), A. R. Stock (*Newport*), R. A. Cornish* (*Cardiff*), W. C. Powell (*London Welsh*); R. Jones (*Northampton*), W. J. Delahay (*Cardiff*); D. M. Jenkins (*Treorchy*), J. H. John (*Swansea*), T. Hopkins (*Swansea*), S. Hinam (*Cardiff*), R. C. Herrera (*Crosskeys*), D. L Jones (*Newport*), S. Lawrence (*Bridgend*); E. Watkins (*Blaina*)
Referee: D. Hallewell (*England*)   **Touch judges:** R. Welsh, E. Thomas

R. C. Herrera scored and Everson converted (0-5). (H.T.). A. C. Gillies kicked a penalty (3-5); H. Waddell scored and Drysdale converted (8-5).

The Welsh captain Rowe Harding called off late and W. C. Powell, a scrum half, took his place on the wing. He was given some credit in that I. S. Smith did not score but the Scottish backs had a thin afternoon being denied much of the ball by a very strong Welsh pack. Fortunately the Welsh backs made little of their chances. Their single score came from a good break by Delahay who was well backed up by his pack. The Scottish scores came within ten minutes of the restart. Gillies kicked a 30-yard penalty and then Waddell with a dummy and cut-back went clean through the defence for a fine solo try. Thereafter some solid tackling kept the Welsh at bay.

SCOTLAND 0   IRELAND 3
Murrayfield
27 February 1926

Scotland: D. Drysdale* (*Oxford Univ.*); I. S. Smith (*Edin. Univ.*), J. C. Dykes (*Glas. Acads.*), R. M. Kinnear (*Heriot's FP*), W. M. Simmers (*Glas. Acads.*); H. Waddell (*Glas. Acads.*), J. B. Nelson (*Glas. Acads.*); D. S. Davies (*Hawick*), J. C. H. Ireland (*Glas. HSFP*), D . S. Kerr (*Heriot's FP*), D. J. MacMyn (*London Scot.*), J. M. Bannerman (*Glas. HSFP*), J. Graham (*Kelso*), J. W. Scott (*Stewart's FP*), J. R. Paterson (*Birkenhead Park*)
Ireland: W. E. Crawford* (*Lansdowne*); D. J. Cussen (*Dublin Univ.*), G. V. Stephenson (*NIFC*), T. R. Hewitt (*Q U Belfast*), J. H. Gage (*QU Belfast*); E. O. Davy (*Univ. Coll*), M. Sugden (*Dublin Univ.*); M. J. Bradley (*Dolphin*), W. F. Browne (*Army*), A. M. Buchanan (*Dublin Univ.*), S. J. Cagney (*London Irish*), J. D. Clinch (*Wanderers*), J. L. Farrell (*Bective Rangers*), C. J. Hanrahan (*Dolphin*), J. McVicker (*Collegians*)
Referee: B. S. Cumberlege (*England*)   **Touch judges:** R. Welsh, F. Strain

No scoring at half-time. J. H. Gage scored but Stephenson failed (0-3).

Heavy rain during the morning left the ground sodden and it cut up heavily during the game. It was a hard and evenly balanced match. Simmers touched down twice only to have the scores cancelled for previous infringements. Ten minutes before full time Waddell had to be carried off concussed so Paterson came out of the pack onto the wing. Then in injury time the Irish backs started a movement which finished with Gage getting in at the corner and the whistle went after the failed conversion kick. Both full backs tackled and kicked well under difficult conditions.

ENGLAND 9   SCOTLAND 17
Twickenham
20 March 1926

Scotland: D. Drysdale* (*Oxford Univ.*); I. S. Smith (*Edin. Univ.*), J. C. Dykes (*Glas. Acads.*), W. M. Simmers (*Glas. Acads.*), G. M. Boyd (*Glas. HSFP*); H. Waddell (*Glas. Acads.*), J. B. Nelson (*Glas. Acads.*); D. S. Davies (*Hawick*), J. C. H. Ireland (*Glas. HSFP*), D. S. Kerr (*Heriot's FP*), D. J. MacMyn (*London Scot.*), J. M. Bannerman (*Glas. HSFP*), J. W. Scott (*Stewart:'s FP*), J. Graham (*Kelso*), J. R. Paterson (*Birkenhead Park*)
England: T. E. Holliday (*Aspatria*); H. L. V. Day (*Leicester*), T. E. S. Francis (*Blackheath*), A. R. Aslett (*Army*), R. H. Hamilton-Wickes (*Harlequins*); H. J. Kittermaster (*Harlequins*), A. T. Young (*Army*); R. Webb (*Northampton*), H. G. Periton (*Waterloo*), R. J. Hanvey (*Aspatria*), C. K. T. Faithful (*Army*), E. Stanbury (*Plymouth Albion*), J. S. Tucker (*Bristol*); A. T. Voyce (*Gloucester*), W. W. Wakefield* (*Harlequins*)
Referee: W. H. Acton (*Ireland*)

J. C. Dykes dropped a goal (0-4); H. Waddell scored and converted (0-9); I. S. Smith scored and H. Waddell converted (0-14); A. T. Voyce scored but H. L. V. Day failed (3-14). (H.T.). J. S. Tucker scored but H. L. V. Day failed (6-14); I. S. Smith scored but D. Drysdale failed (6-17); E. Stanbury scored but T. E. S. Francis failed (9-17).

H. L. V. Day replaced Sir T. G. Devitt at the last minute and the wingers changed over. In dull and cold weather 50,000 people saw the teams presented to HM King George V. The English full back had a bad day for the Scottish tries were scored from errors forced on him by awkward kicks. I. S. Smith was prominent, his pace making two of the scores. The Scottish forwards, although outweighed played well as a pack, making several fine dribbling rushes and giving their backs the chances they needed. The English team was numbered but the Scots were not, in spite of a request for the change from the Rugby Football Union. Comments on this at the dinner nettled the SRU Officials. There is a story that the King had been encouraged to ask J. Aikman Smith about numbering and received the dour reply that 'This was a rugby match and not a cattle sale'. This was the first time England had been defeated by a Home Country at Twickenham since it was opened in 1910.

SCOTLAND 23   FRANCE 6
Murrayfield
22 January 1927

Scotland: D. Drysdale (*Heriot's FP*); I. S. Smith (*Edin. Univ.*), G. P. S. Macpherson* (*Edin. Acads.*), J. C. Dykes (*Glas. Acads.*), W. M. Simmers (*Glas. Acads.*); H. Waddell (*Glas. Acads.*), J. B. Nelson (*Glas. Acads.*); D. S. Davies (*Hawick*), J. C. H. Ireland (*Glas. HSFP*), J. W. Allan (*Melrose*), J. M. Bannerman (*Glas. HSFP*), J. W. Scott (*Stewart's FP*), J. Graham (*Kelso*), A. C. Gillies (*Watsonians*), J. R. Paterson (*Birkenhead Park*)
France: M. Piquemal (*Tarbes*); R. Revillon (*CASG*), R. Graciet (*SBUC*), V. Graule (*Perpignan*), R. Houdet (*SF*); Y du Manoir* (*RCF*), E. Bader (*Primveres*); G. A. Gonnet (*RCF*), R. Hutin (*CASG*), J. Etcheberry (*Vienne*), R. Bousquet (*Albi*), A. Cassayet (*Narbonne*), A. Prevost (*Albi*), E. Ribere (*Quillan*), E. Piquiral (*Lyon*)
Referee: B. S. Cumberlege (*England*)   **Touch judges:** J. M. Mackenzie, C. F. Rutherford

H. Waddell scored and A. C. Gillies converted (5-0); I. S. Smith scored and A. C. Gillies converted (10-0); H. Waddell scored and D. Drysdale converted (15-0), R. Hutin scored but G. Gonnet failed (15-3); I. S. Smith scored and A. C. Gillies converted (20-3). (H.T.). A. C. Gillies kicked a penalty (23-3); E. Piquiral scored but G. Gonnet failed (23-6).

The Scottish pack faded noticeably in the second half but the skill and pace of the backs in the first half produced a winning total. I. S. Smith again used his pace to good effect while G. P. S. Macpherson produced many clever touches. The French XV was numbered.

WALES 0   SCOTLAND 5
Cardiff
5 February 1927

Wales: B. O. Male* (*Cardiff*); J. D. Bartlett (*Llandovery Coll.*), B. R. Turnbull (*Cardiff*), J. Roberts (*Cardiff*), W. R. Harding (*Camb. Univ.*); G. Richards (*Cardiff*), W. J. Delahay (*Cardiff*); I. Jones (*Llanelli*), J. H. John (*Swansea*), T. Arthur (*Neath*), E. M. Jenkins (*Aberavon*), T. Lewis (*Cardiff*), H. Phillips (*Newport*), W. Thomas (*Llanelli*), W. Williams (*Crumlin*)
Scotland: D. Drysdale (*Heriot's FP*); E. G. Taylor (*Oxford Univ.*), G. P. S. Macpherson* (*Edin. Acads.*), J. C. Dykes (*Glas. Acads.*), W. M. Simmers (*Glas. Acads.*); H. Waddell (*Glas. Acads.*), J. B. Nelson (*Glas. Acads.*); D. S. Davies (*Hawick*), J. C. H. Ireland (*Glas. HSFP*), D. S. Kerr (*Heriot's FP*), J. W. Scott (*Stewart's FP*), J. M. Bannerman (*Glas. HSFP*), J. Graham (*Kelso*), A. C. Gillies (*Watsonians*), J. R. Paterson (*Birkenhead Park*)
Referee: W. H. Jackson (*England*)   **Touch judges:** J. McGill, M. Moses

D. S. Kerr scored and A. C. Gillies converted (0-5). (H.T.).

40,000 spectators, including the Prince of Wales, watched a match played on a sodden pitch which turned to a sea of mud and water. Wales looked more dangerous to begin with and missed one chance to score. However the Scottish backs broke through repeatedly only to be kept out by some desperate last minute tackling. Shortly before the interval a high kick was misfielded and in a fine forward rush Davies pushed a foot pass to Kerr who scooped the ball up to score near the corner and Gillies converted the very difficult kick. In the second half the Scottish forwards began to dictate the play with some fine rushes but Wales were handicapped by an injury to T. Arthur. Windsor Lewis was the original choice at stand off and when he called off the Welsh selectors stood down W. C. Powell from scrum half so that the Cardiff pair could play. The Welsh team was numbered from one to sixteen, there being no number thirteen!

IRELAND 6 SCOTLAND 0
Lansdowne Road
26 February 1927

Ireland: W. E. Crawford* (*Lansdowne*); J. B. Ganly (*Monkstown*), F. S. Hewitt (*Instonians*), G. V. Stephenson (*NIFC*), J. H. Gage (*QU Belfast*); E. Davy (*Lansdowne*), M. Sugden (*Wanderers*); A. M. Buchanan (*Dublin Univ.*), W. F. Browne (*Army*), T. O. Pike (*Lansdowne*), H. McVicker (Richmond), J. L. Farrell (*Bective Rangers*), J. McVicker (*Collegians*), C. T. Payne (*NIFC*), C. F. Hanrahan (*Dolphin*)
Scotland: D. Drysdale (*Heriot's FP*); I. S. Smith (*Edin. Univ.*), G. P. S. Macpherson*(*Edin. Acads.*), J. C. Dykes (*Glas. Acads.*), W. M. Simmers (*Glas. Acads.*); H. Waddell (*Glas. Acads.*), J. B. Nelson (*Glas. Acads.*); D. S. Davies (*Hawick*), J. C. H. Ireland (*Glas. HSFP*), D. S. Kerr (*Heriot's FP*), J. W. Scott (*Stewart's FP*), J. M. Bannerman (*Glas. HSFP*), J. Graham (*Kelso*), A. C. Gillies (*Watsonians*), J. R. Paterson (*Birkenhead Park*)
Referee: B. S. Cumberlege (*England*)

T. O. Pike and J. B. Ganly scored but G. V. Stephenson failed to convert (6-0). (H.T.).

The conditions were worse than those in the Welsh match for a continual fierce gale of wind and rain swept down the field. Once again the field became a morass and the players were so caked with mud as to be indistinguishable. A crowd of 40,000, some huddled in the newly erected but unroofed stand, were literally soaked to the skin while reporters had a miserable time trying to write on pulped notebooks.

The Irish team was numbered. Ireland, starting with the gale, got over twice for unconverted tries in the first half. Conditions worsened after the interval but Scotland although getting a fair share of the ball just couldn't score. Before the end G. V. Stephenson had collapsed and was taken off and at no-side some had to be assisted into the dressing rooms. W. F. Browne took half an hour to recover while the referee was also in a poor state, his left hand being lifeless.

SCOTLAND 21 ENGLAND 13
Murrayfield
19 March 1927

Scotland: D. Drysdale* (*Heriot's FP*), I. S. Smith (*Edin. Univ.*), G. P. S. Macpherson (*Edin. Acads.*), J. C. Dykes (*Glas. Acads.*), W. M. Simmers (*Glas. Acads.*), H. Waddell (*Glas. Acads.*), J. B. Nelson (*Glas. Acads.*); J. W. Scott (*Stewart's FP*), J. C. H. Ireland (*Glas. HSFP*), D. S. Kerr (*Heriot's FP*), D. J. MacMyn (*London Scot.*), J. M. Bannerman (*Glas. HSFP*), J. Graham (*Kelso*), A. C. Gillies (*Watsonians*), J. R. Paterson (*Birkenhead Park*)
England: K. A. Sellar (*RN*); J. C. Gibbs (*Harlequins*), L. J. Corbett* (*Bristol*), H. M. Locke (*Birkenhead Park*), H. C. Catcheside (*Percy Park*); H. C. C. Laird (*Harlequins*), A. T. Young (*Army & Blackheath*); K. J. Stark (*Old Alleynians*), J. S. Tucker (*Bristol*), E. Stanbury (*Plymouth Albion*), R. Cove-Smith (*OMT*), W. E. Pratten (*Blackheath*), H. G. Periton (*Waterloo*), W. W. Wakefield (*Harlequins*), J. Hamley (*Plymouth Albion*).
Referee: N. M. Purcell (*Ireland*) **Touch judges:** J. C. Sturrock, G. C. Robinson

G. P. S. Macpherson scored but A. C. Gillies failed (3-0); J. C. Gibbs scored and E. Stanbury converted (3-5); I. S. Smith scored twice but A. C. Gillies failed to convert (9-5); K. J. Stark kicked a penalty (9-8). (H.T.). H. Waddell dropped a goal (13-8); J. C. Dykes scored and A. C. Gillies converted (18-8), H. C. C. Laird scored and K. J. Stark converted (18-13); J. W. Scott scored but D. Drysdale failed (21-13).

Some 70,000 watched a fast game in good conditions which suited the Scottish backs who were in great attacking form. Macpherson was at his elusive best, Smith was fast, Waddell and Nelson made a fine half back pair, whilst Dykes' solo try was the best of the match. Waddell's drop goal was queried by Wakefield who claimed to have touched it but the referee gave the score. For most of the second half England had to play with Hanley on the wing as Catcheside retired with a leg injury. The English team was numbered.

SCOTLAND 10   NEW SOUTH WALES 8
Murrayfield
17 December 1927

Scotland: D. Drysdale* (*London Scot.*); E. G. Taylor (*Oxford Univ.*), R. F. Kelly (*Watsonians*), J. C. Dykes (*Glas. Acads.*), W. M. Simmers (*Glas. Acads.*); H. D. Greenlees (*Leicester*), P. S. Douty (*London Scot.*); J. W. Scott (*Stewart's FP*), W. N. Roughead (*London Scot.*), W. G. Ferguson (*RHSFP*), D. J. MacMyn (*London Scot.*), J. M. Bannerman (*Glas. HSFP*), J. Graham (*Kelso*), W. B. Welsh (*Hawick*), J. R. Paterson (*Birkenhead Park*.)
N.S.W.: A. W. Ross (*University*); E. E. Ford (*Glebe Balmain*), W. B. J. Sheehan (*University*), S. C. King (*Western Suburbs*), A. C. Wallace* (*Glebe Balmain*); T. Lawton (*Western Suburbs*), S. J. Malcolm (*Newcastle*); H. F. Woods (*YMCA*), J. G. Blackwood(*Eastern Suburbs*), B Judd (*Randwick*), A. N. Finlay (*Sydney Univ.*), G. P. Storey (*Western Suburbs*), J. W. Breckonridge (*Glebe Balmain*), J. A. Ford (*Glebe Balmain*), A. J. Tancred (*Glebe Balmain*)
Referee: W. J. Llewellyn (*Wales*)   **Touch judges:** M. M. Duncan, K. Tarleton.

E. E. Ford scored and T. Lawton converted (0-5); J. Graham scored and D. Drysdale converted (5-5). (H.T.). W. B. Welsh scored and D. Drysdale converted (10-5); J. A. Ford scored but T. Lawton failed (10-8).

In a fairly even game the Scottish pack, although outweighted, held its own until the last ten minutes but their backs were better, Simmers in particular playing very well. He was responsible for both scores. In each case he broke away up the wing and crosskicked for Graham and Welsh to run on to the ball and score under the posts. Drysdale also was his usual cool and competent self. The New South Wales team was numbered and played in light blue jerseys.

FRANCE 6   SCOTLAND 15
Colombes
2 January 1928

France: M. Magnol (*Toulouse*); A. Jaureguy* (*SF*), G. Gerald (*RCF*), J. Coulon (*Grenoble*), C. Dulaurens (*Toulouse*); H. Haget (*CASG*), G. Daudignon (*SF*); A. Loury (*RCF*), F. Camicas (*Tarbes*), J. Morere (*Marseilles*), J. Galia (*Quillan*), A. Camel (*Toulouse*), A. Cazenave (*Paloise*), G. Branca (*SF*), E. Ribere (*Quillan*)
Scotland: D. Drysdale* (*Heriot's FP*); G. P. S. Macpherson (*Edin. Acads.*), R. F. Kelly (*Watsonians*), J. C. Dykes (*Glas. HSFP*), W. M. Simmers (*Glas. Acads.*); H. D. Greenlees (*Leicester*), P. S. Douty (*London Scot.*); W. B. Welsh (*Hawick*), W. N. Roughead (*London Scot.*), W. G. Ferguson (*RHSFP*), D. J . MacMyn (*London Scot.*), J. M. Bannerman (*Glas. HSFP*), J. Graham (*Kelso*), J. W. Scott (*Stewart's FP*), J. R. Paterson (*Birkenhead Park*)
Referee: R. McGrath (*Ireland*)   **Touch judges:** R. T. Neilson, M. Muntz

W. M. Simmers scored; D. Drysdale failed (0-3); H. Haget scored but failed to convert (3-3); J. R. Paterson and J. C. Dykes scored unconverted tries (3-9). (H.T.). P. S. Douty and J. W. Scott scored unconverted tries (3-15); A. Camel scored an unconverted try (6-15).

Scotland showed the better team work for the backs played well together and the forwards were good as a pack in the loose. Bad passing by the French backs lost them several chances and certainly one score for Drysdale picked up a loose pass, ran and kicked ahead. Magnol fielded but was caught by the forwards who worked the ball free for Scott to plunge over. The referee did not please the crowd who found him too ready with the whistle and they became especially vocal after he granted Douty a try which they believed had been pushed by a hand over the line. The papers noted that he only blew for 'no side' when he was opposite the tunnel down which he vanished at a fair pace!

SCOTLAND 0   WALES 13
Murrayfield
4 February 1928

Scotland: D. Drysdale (*London Scot.*); J. Goodfellow (*Langholm*), G. P . S. Macpherson (*Edin. Acads.*), R. F. Kelly (*Watsonians*), W. M. Simmers (*Glas. Acads.*), H. D. Greenlees (*Leicester*), P. S. Douty (*London Scot.*); J. H. Ferguson (*Gala*), W. N. Roughead (*London Scot.*), W. G. Ferguson (*RHSFP*), J. W. Scott (*Stewart's FP*), J. M. Bannerman* (*Glas. HSFP*),

J. Graham (*Kelso*), W. B. Welsh (*Hawick*), J. R. Paterson (*Birkenhead Park*)
Wales: B. O. Male* (*Cardiff*); J. D. Bartlett (*London Welsh*), J. Roberts (*Cardiff*), A. Jenkins (*Llanelli*), W. C. Powell (*London Welsh*); A. John (*Llanelli*), D. John (*Llanelli*); F. A. Bowdler (*Cross Keys*), C. Pritchard (*Pontypool*), H. Phillips (*Newport*), E. Jenkins (*Aberavon*), A. Skym (*Llanelli*), Y. Jones (*Llanelli*), T. Hollingdale (*Neath*), I. Jones (*Llanelli*)
Referee: R. W. Harland (*Ireland*)   **Touch judges:** A. A. Lawie, J. Jarrett

A. Jenkins, D. John and J. Roberts scored, B. O. Male converted the first two but failed with the third (0-13). (H.T.).

Wales started with a strong wind and rain at their backs and after fifteen minutes had scored two tries, adding a third later. In the second half, with the ground cutting up they were content to hold on to their lead and did some good defensive kicking. The Scots, however, were a disjointed team. The forwards put in some good dribbling rushes but otherwise were poor and their ragged scrummaging gave the backs few chances. This was Wales' first win in Scotland since 1913.

SCOTLAND 5   IRELAND 13
Murrayfield
25 February 1928

Scotland: D. Drysdale* (*London Scot.*); J. Goodfellow (*Langholm*), J. W. G. Hume (*Oxford Univ.*), J. C. Dykes (*Glas. Acads.*), W. M. Simmers (*Glas. Acads.*); H. Lind (*Dunfermline*), J. B. Nelson (*Glas. Acads.*); J. W. Allan (*Melrose*), W. N. Roughead (*London Scot.*), D. S. Kerr (*Heriot's FP*), W. G. Ferguson (*RHSFP*), J. M. Bannerman (*Glas. HSFP*), J. Graham (*Kelso*), W. B. Welsh (*Hawick*), J. R. Paterson (*Birkenhead Park*)
Ireland: W. J. Stewart (*NIFC*); R. M. Byers (*NIFC*), G. V. Stephenson* (*NIFC*), J. B. Ganly (*Monkstown*), A. C. Douglas (*Instonians*); E. O. Davy (*Lansdowne*), M. Sugden (*Wanderers*); T. O. Pike (*Lansdowne*), S. J. Cagney (*London Irish*),W. F. Browne (*US*), C. T. Payne (*NIFC*), C. J. Hanrahan (*Dolphin*), J. L. Farrell (*Bective Rangers*), J. D. Clinch (*Wanderers*), G. R. Beamish (*RAF*)
Referee: B. S. Cumberlege (*England*)   **Touch judges:** A. W. Angus, Judge Sealey

J. B. Ganly scored an unconverted try (0-3); D. S. Kerr scored: D. Drysdale converted (5-3). (H.T.). E. O. Davy and G. V. Stephenson scored; G. V. Stephenson converted both (5-13).

Some early Scottish attacks failed against fine tackling but the superior resolution and incisiveness of the Irish backs, supported by a robust set of forwards, had the match well won by the close. Scotland certainly did not deserve to be ahead at the interval.

ENGLAND 6   SCOTLAND 0
Twickenham
17 March 1928

England: T. W. Brown (*Bristol*); W. J. Taylor (*Blackheath*), C. D. Aarvold (*Camb. Univ.*), J. V. Richardson (*Birkenhead Park*), G. V. Palmer (*Richmond*); H. C. C. Laird (*Harlequins*) A. T. Young (*Blackheath*); R. H. W. Sparkes (*Plymouth Albion*), J. S. Tucker (*Bristol*), J. Hanley (*Plymouth Albion*), K. J. Stark (*Old Alleynians*), F. D. Prentice (*Leicester*), E. Stanbury (*Plymouth Albion*), H. G. Periton (*Waterloo*), R. Cove-Smith* (*OMT*)
Scotland: D. Drysdale* (*London Scot.*); J. Goodfellow (*Langholm*), G. P. S. Macpherson (*Edin. Acads.*), W. M. Simmers (*Glas. Acads.*), R. F. Kelly (*Watsonians*); A. H. Brown (*Heriot's FP*), J. B. Nelson (*Glas. Acads.*); L. M. Stuart (*Glas. HSFP*), W. N. Roughead (*London Scot.*), D. S. Kerr (*Heriot's FP*), W. G. Ferguson (*RHSFP*), J. M. Bannerman (*Glas. HSFP*), J. Graham (*Kelso*), J. W. Scott (*Stewart's FP*), J. R. Paterson (*Birkenhead Park*)
Referee: T. H. Vile (*Wales*)

H. C. C. Laird scored; J. V. Richardson failed (3-0). (H.T.). J. Hanley scored; F. D. Prentice failed (6-0).

England won all five of their matches this season yet this was one that Scotland, with a little luck, could have drawn. Their backs, with Macpherson in form, came near to scoring on several occasions. A. H. Brown missed a score when after a good break, his kick ahead bounced out of his reach. Defence was the strongest part of the English back play although A. T. Young proved most elusive. The English pack was the better for they handled well, followed up fast and were physically stronger.

SCOTLAND 6 FRANCE 3
Murrayfield
19 January 1929

Scotland: D. Drysdale* (*London Scot.*); I. S. Smith (*Edin. Univ.*), G. G. Aitken (*London Scot.*), J. C. Dykes (*Glas. Acads.*), W. M. Simmers (*Glas. Acads.*); A. H. Brown (*Heriot's FP*), J. B. Nelson (*Glas. Acads.*); J. W. Allan (*Melrose*), H. S. Mackintosh (*West of Scot.*), R. T. Smith (*Kelso*), J. A. Beattie (*Hawick*), J. M. Bannerman (*Glas. HSFP*), K. M. Wright (*London Scot.*), W. V. Berkley (*London Scot.*), J. R. Paterson (*Birkenhead Park*)
France: M. Magnol (*Toulouse*); A. Jaureguy* (*SF*), A. Behoteguy (*Cognac*), G. Gerald (*RCF*), R. Houdet (*SF*); C. Magnanou (*Bayonne*), C. Lacazedieu (*Dax*); J. Hauc (*Toulon*), F. Camicas (*Tarbes*), J. Sayrou (*Perpignan*), A. Camel (*Toulouse*), R. Majerus (*SF*), A. Biousa (*Toulouse*), G. Branca (*SF*), J. Auge (*Dax*).
Referee: B. S. Cumberlege (*England*) **Touch judges:** T. H. H. Warren, C. F. Rutherford

A. H. Brown kicked a penalty (3-0); J. R. Paterson scored and D. Drysdale failed (6-0); A. Behoteguy scored and M. Magnol failed (6-3). (H.T.).

This was anything but a decisive win, for France were full of running especially during the last fifteen minutes when their pack came on to a game and Scotland were lucky to survive several near things. The veteran Jaureguy was in fine form throughout and made the opening for Behoteguy's try. Magnol at full back delighted the crowd with a sound but often acrobatic display. A. H. Brown's penalty was a good 30-yarder. The French were numbered but no numbers appeared in the programme.

WALES 14 SCOTLAND 7
Swansea
2 February 1929

Wales: J. Bassett (*Penarth*); J. C. Morley (*Newport*), H. M. Bowcott (*Camb. Univ.*), W. G. Morgan* (*Camb. Univ.*), J. Roberts (*Camb. Univ.*); F. L. Williams (*Cardiff*), W. C. Powell (*London Welsh*); A. E. Broughton (*Treorchy*), I. Jones (*Llanelli*), H. Peacock (*Newport*), H. Jones (*Neath*), T. Arthur (*Neath*), F. A. Bowdler (*Cross Keys*), C. Pritchard (*Pontypool*), A. Barrel (*Cardiff*)
Scotland: T. G. Aitchison (*Gala*); I. S. Smith (*Edin. Univ.*), J. C. Dykes (*Glas. Acads.*), W. M. Simmers (*Glas. Acads.*), T. G. Brown (*Heriot's FP*), A. H. Brown (*Heriot's FP*), J. B. Nelson (*Glas. Acads.*); J. W. Allan (*Melrose*), H. S. Mackintosh (*Glas. Univ.*), R. T. Smith (*Kelso*), J. A. Beattie (*Hawick*), J. M. Bannerman* (*Glas. HSFP*), K. M. Wright (*London Scot.*), W. V. Berkley (*London Scot.*), J. R. Paterson (*Birkenhead Park*)
Referee: D. Helliwell (*England*) **Touch judge:** E. Thomas

J. Roberts scored but I. Jones failed (3-0); A. H. Brown kicked a penalty, (3-3). (H.T.). A. H. Brown dropped a goal (3-7); H. Peacock scored and I. Jones converted (8-7); J. Roberts scored but I. Jones failed (11-7); W. G. Morgan scored but W. C. Powell failed (14-7)

The Scots, although putting up a hard fight with a late rally in the last quarter, were not good enough. Their pack was outplayed so that the Welsh backs with an ample supply of the ball were constantly on the attack and in spite of a wet ball and treacherous ground handled and ran very well. Scotland, without crossing the line, were fortunate to lead just after the restart but from the kick off the Welsh forwards took the ball right up to the line for a score and Wales continued this domination until the late revival. Right on time Simmers broke through and set Smith off on a sprint which only finished when he was hurled into touch taking the corner flag with him.

IRELAND 7 SCOTLAND 16
Lansdowne Road
23 February 1929

Ireland: W. J. Stewart (*Bolton*); R. M. Byers (*NIFC*), P. F. Murray (*Wanderers*), J. B. Ganly (*Monkstown*), J. E Arigho (*Lansdowne*); E. Davy* (*Lansdowne*), M. Sugden (*Wanderers*); G. R. Beamish (*RAF*), H. C. Browne (*Un. Services*), S. J. Cagney (*London Irish*), J. D. Clinch (*Wanderers*), M. J. Dunne (*Lansdowne*), J. L. Farrell (*Bective Rangers*), C. J. Hanrahan (*Dolphin*), J. S. Synge (*Lansdowne*)

Scotland: T. G. Aitchison (*Gala*); I. S. Smith (*Edin. Univ.*), G. P. S. Macpherson (*Edin. Acads.*), J. C. Dykes (*Glas. Acads.*), W. M. Simmers (*Glas. Acads.*); H. D. Greenlees (*Leicester*), J. B. Nelson (*Glas. Acads.*); R. T. Smith (*Kelso*), H. S. Mackintosh (*Glas. Univ.*), J. W. Allan (*Melrose*), W. V. Berkley (*London Scot.*), J. M. Bannerman* (*Oxford Univ.*), J. R. Paterson (*Birkenhead Park*), K. M. Wright (*London Scot.*), W. B. Welsh (*Hawick*)
Referee: B. S. Cumberlege (*England*)   **Touch judges:** J. Anderson, H. J. Millar

G. P. S. Macpherson scored and J. C. Dykes converted (5-0); E. Davy dropped a goal (5-4); J. E. Arigho scored but P. F. Murray failed (5-7). (H.T.). J. M. Bannerman scored and J. W. Allan converted (10-7); I. S. Smith and W. M. Simmers scored but J. W. Allan failed with both (16-7).

Ireland had already beaten France and England and a fine day brought out a record crowd of 40,000 for their first home match. Unfortunately the spectators encroached on to the field and play had to be halted several times to clear the goal area. Arigho could not run behind the posts when he got over and the referee was forced to refuse a score to Byers who was tackled over the line by Aitchison and flung amongst the crowd.

The Scots started well when Dykes intercepted a pass and gave Macpherson a clear run in but the Irish pack dominated play during the first half. Their backs, apart from the move that gave Arigho his score, were only capable of solo efforts. After half time the Scottish pack took over and fine team work brought three scores. Macpherson had a good game latterly. Dykes was hurt and changed places with Aitchison.

SCOTLAND 12   ENGLAND 6
Murrayfield
16 March 1929

Scotland: T. G. Aitchison (*Gala*); I. S. Smith (*Edin. Univ.*), G. P. S. Macpherson (*Edin. Acads.*), W. M. Simmers (*Glas. Acads.*), C. H. C. Brown (*Dunfermline*); H. D. Greenlees (*Leicester*), J. B. Nelson (*Glas. Acads.*); R. T. Smith (*Kelso*), H. S. Mackintosh (*Glas. Univ.*), J. W. Allan (*Melrose*), J. W. Scott (*Bradford*), J. M. Bannerman* (*Oxford Univ.*), J. R. Paterson (*Birkenhead Park*), K. M. Wright (*London Scot.*), W. B. Welsh (*Hawick*)
England: T. W. Brown (*Bristol*); R. W. Smeddle (*Camb. Univ.*), A. R. Aslett (*Richmond*), G. M. Sladen (*RN*); A. L. Novis (*Army*); S. C. C. Meikle (*Waterloo*), E. E. Richards (*Plymouth Albion*); E. Stanbury (*Plymouth Albion*), R. H. W. Sparks (*Plymouth Albion*), R. Webb (*Northampton*), T. W. Harris (*Northampton*), H. Rew (*Army*), H. Wilkinson (*Halifax*), D. Turquand-Young (*Richmond*), H. G. Periton* (*Waterloo*)
Referee: Dr J. R. Wheeler (*Ireland*)   **Touch judges:** J. Magill, G. C. Robinson

A. L. Novis scored but T. W. Harris failed (0-3). (H.T.). J. B. Nelson scored but J. W. Allan failed (3-3); S. C. C. Meikle scored but A. L. Novis failed (3-6); C. H. Brown and I. S. Smith (2) scored but J. W. Allan failed to convert (12-6).

The conditions were good but cold and dull. After a fairly even first half there was a burst of scoring which left the scores level. Then I. S. Smith, running with great determination scored twice. On each occasion he was firmly tackled by Brown but his impetus carried them both over the line. Neither side was numbered. This was Bannerman's last game.

FRANCE 7   SCOTLAND 3
Colombes
1 January 1930

France: M. Piquemal (*Tarbes*); R. R. Samatan (*Agen*), M. Baillette (*Quillan*), G. Gerald (*RCF*), R. R. Houdet (*SF*); C. Magnanou (*Bayonne*), L. Serin (*Beziers*); A. Ambert (*Toulouse*), C. Bigot (*Quillan*), J. Choy (*Narbonne*), R. Majerus (*SF*), A. Camel (*TOEC*), E. Ribere* (*Quillan*), J. Galia (*Quillan*), A. Biousa (*Toulouse*)
Scotland: R. W. Langrish (*London Scot.*); I. S. Smith(*London Scot.*), G. P. S. Macpherson* (*Edin. Acads.*), J. W. G. Hume (*Edin. Wrs.*), W. M. Simmers (*Glas. Acads.*); W. D. Emslie (*RHSFP*), J. B. Nelson (*Glas. Acads.*); J. W. Allan (*Melrose*), H. S. Mackintosh (*Glas. Univ.*), R. T. Smith (*Kelso*), J. W. Scott (*Waterloo*), J. Stewart (*Glas. HSFP*), W. B. Welsh (*Hawick*), R. Rowand (*Glas. HSFP*), F. H. Waters (*Camb. Univ.*)
Referee: D. Helliwell (*England*)   **Touch judges:** Dr G. W. Simpson

96

A. Biousa scored an unconverted try (3-0) W. M. Simmers scored an unconverted try (3-3). (H.T.). C. Magnanou dropped a goal (7-3).

France thoroughly deserved their win for Scotland, although physically the stronger, were beaten for speed and virility. Magnanou was always dangerous, making the opening for Bioussa's try in the first five minutes and then winning the match in the dying minutes with a splendid 30-yards drop. The French pack, although poor in the set scrums, handled brilliantly in the loose and for once proved to be as fierce and tough as their opponents. The Scottish backs could not penetrate a speedy defence although Macpherson cut through beautifully several times only to find his passes go astray. Both packs were depleted in the second half, Allan having to go off before half time while a collision laid two Frenchmen out for a spell.

SCOTLAND 12   WALES 9
Murrayfield
1 February 1930

Scotland: R. C. Warren (*Glas. Acads.*); I. S. Smith (*London Scot.*), G. P. S. Macpherson* (*Edin. Acads.*), T. M. Hart (*Glas. Univ.*), W. M. Simmers (*Glas. Acads.*); H. Waddell (*Glas. Acads.*), J. B. Nelson (*Glas. Acads.*); R. T. Smith (*Kelso*), H. S. Mackintosh (*Glas. Univ.*), R. Foster (*Hawick*), J. A. Beattie (*Hawick*), F. H. Waters (*London Scot.*), W. C. C. Agnew (*Stewart's FP*), R. Rowand (*Glas. HSFP*), W. B. Welsh (*Hawick*)
Wales: J. Bassett (*Penarth*); G. Davies (*Cheltenham*), B. R. Turnbull (*Cardiff*), G Jones (*Cardiff*), R. Boon (*Carmarthen College*); F. Williams (*Cardiff*), W. C. Powell (*London Welsh*); T. Arthur (*Neath*), H. C. Day (*Newport*), A. Skym (*Cardiff*), E. Jenkins (*Aberavon*), A. Lemon (*Neath*), H. Peacock (*Newport*), D. Thomas (*Swansea*), I . Jones * (*Llanelli*)
Referee: Dr J. R. Wheeler (*Ireland*)   **Touch judges:** Dr G. W. Simpson, A. E. Freethy

W. M. Simmers scored and F. H. Waters converted (5-0); G. Jones scored and I. Jones converted (5-5); G. Jones dropped a goal (5-9); W. M. Simmers scored but F. H. Waters failed (8-9). (H.T.). H. Waddell dropped a goal (12-9).

A drizzle cleared before the start and about 60,000 were present. Scotland had much defending to do in the first half and were indebted to some good backing up by Simmers to be only one point behind at half time. The second half was more equally contested although at one time when Hart was hurt Rowand came out of the pack to act as an extra defender. However the game had a sensational finish when in the last minutes Waddell dropped a goal following a scrum in front of the posts. This was a game that Wales could have won but their backs could not turn a plentiful supply of the ball into scores.

SCOTLAND 11   IRELAND 14
Murrayfield
22 February 1930

Scotland: R. C. Warren (*Glas. Acads.*); I. S. Smith (*London Scot.*), G. P . S. Macpherson* (*Edin. Acads.*), W. M. Simmers (*Glas. Acad.*), D. St. C. Ford (*Un. Services*); T. M. Hart (*Glas. Univ.*), J. B. Nelson (*Glas. Acads.*); H. S. Mackintosh (*Glas. Univ.*), W. N. Roughhead (*London Scot.*), R. T. Smith (*Kelso*), W. C. C. Agnew (*Stewart's FP*), L. M. Stuart (*Glas. HSFP*), W. B. Welsh (*Hawick*), J. Graham (*Kelso*), F. H. Waters (*London Scot.*)
Ireland: F. W. Williamson (*Dolphin*); J. E. Arigho (*Lansdowne*), M. F. Crowe (*Lansdowne*), E. O. Davy (*Lansdowne*), G. V. Stephenson* (*London Hospitals*); P. F. Murray (*Wanderers*), M. Sugden (*Wanderers*); H. O. O'Neill (*QU Belfast*), T. C. Casey (*Young Munsters*), C. J. Hanrahan (*Dolphin*), C. T. Payne (*NIFC*), M. J. Dunne (*Lansdowne*), J. L. Farrell (*Bective Rangers*), J. D. Clinch (*Dublin Univ.*), G. R. Beamish (*RAF*)
Referee: B. S. Cumberlege (*England*)   **Touch judges:** Dr G. W. Simpson, T. I. Greeves

D. St. C. Ford scored but F. H. Waters failed (3-0); E. O. Davy scored but P. F. Murray failed (3-3); E. O. Davy scored and P. F. Murray converted (3-8); E. O. Davy scored but G. V. Stephenson failed (3-11). (H.T.). G. P. S. Macpherson scored and F. H. Waters converted (8-11), M. P. Crowe scored but P. F. Murray failed (8-14); F. H. Waters scored but failed to convert (11-14).

Again the Scottish pack failed to match their opponents, who held their own in the scrums but set a fierce pace in the loose. Scotland were actually on top during the first half hour. Nelson sent

97

Ford away for a good try inside five minutes while two further scores were lost by knocks on. Then Ireland came to life and some good handling put Davy in for three tries in ten minutes' play before half time. Soon after the restart a good run and crosskick by Smith was taken in for a try by Macpherson but this was countered by Crowe scoring after a forward rush. Then the Scottish pack rallied in the last ten minutes but could only manage a single try before time.

ENGLAND 0 SCOTLAND 0
Twickenham
15 March 1930

England: J. C. Hubbard (*Harlequins*); C. C. Tanner (*Richmond*), M. Robson (*Oxford Univ.*), F. W. S. Malir (*Otley*), J. C. R. Reeve (*Harlequins*); R. S. Spong (*Old Millhillians*), W. H. Sobey (*Old Millhillians*); H. Rew (*Army*), J. S. Tucker* (*Bristol*), A. H. Bateson (*Otley*), J. W. Forrest (*Un. Services*), B. H. Black (*Oxford Univ.*), H. G. Periton (*Waterloo*), P. D. Howard (*Oxford Univ.*), P. W. P. Brook (*Camb. Univ.*)
Scotland: R. C. Warren (*Glas. Acads.*); W. M. Simmers (*Glas. Acads.*), G. P. S. Macpherson* (*Edin. Acads.*), J. E. Hutton (*Harlequins*), D. St. C. Ford (*Un. Services*); H. D. Greenlees (*Leicester*), J. B. Nelson (*Glas. Acads.*); H. S. Mackintosh (*West of Scot.*), W. N. Roughead (*London Scot.*), J. W. Allan (*Melrose*), W. B. Welsh (*Hawick*), L. M. Stuart (*Glas. HSFP*), A. H. Polson (*Gala*), J. Graham (*Kelso*), F. H. Waters (*London Scot.*)
Referee: R. W. Jeffares (*Ireland*)

The pointless draw was a fairly accurate reflection of a fiercely contested struggle in which defence triumphed over attack. For England Sobey was a very alert scrum half and had one splendid solo run which narrowly failed to bring a score. For Scotland Macpherson had one typical sidestepping run and his final crosskick found Waters clear but given off-side – a very close decision.

SCOTLAND 6 FRANCE 4
Murrayfield
24 January 1931

Scotland: R. W. Langrish (*London Scot.*); I . S. Smith (*London Scot.*), J. E. Hutton (*Harlequins*), A. W. Wilson (*Dunfermline*), W. M. Simmers (*Glas. Acads.*); H. Lind (*Dunfermline*) J. B. Nelson (*Glas. Acads.*); J. W. Allan (*Melrose*), W. N. Roughead* (*London Scot.*), H. S Mackintosh (*West of Scot.*), J. A. Beattie (*Hawick*), D. A. McLaren (*Durham Co.*), J. S Wilson (*St Andrews Univ.*), A. W. Walker (*Camb. Univ.* , W. B. Welsh (*Hawick*)
France: M. Savy (*Montferrand*); L. Augras (*Agen*), G. Gerald (RCF), M. Baillette (*Toulon*), S. Samatan (*Agen*); M. Servolle (*Toulon*), M. Rousie (*Villeneuve*); R. Scohy (*BEC*), J. Dahan (*SBUC*), A. Duclos (*Lourdes*), A. Clady (*Lezignan*), J. Galia (*Villeneuve*), C. Bigot (*Lezignan*), E. Camo (*Villeneuve*), E. Ribere* (*Quillan*)
Referee: R. W. Jeffares (*Ireland*) **Touch judges:** Dr G. W. Simpson, C. F. Rutherford

J. W. Allan kicked two penalty goals (6-0). (H.T.). L. Servolle dropped a goal (6-4).

The Scottish pack were well on top but the backs could not break through the splendid tackling and covering defence of the speedy French backs. Allan's penalties were both fine long range kicks. Conditions were good and about 50,000 were present. The French team were numbered; Scotland were not and played in white jerseys. Following this match, Scotland and France did not meet again until after the Second World War.

WALES 13 SCOTLAND 8
Cardiff
7 February 1931

Wales: J. Bassett* (*Penarth*); J. C. Morley (*Newport*), E. C. Davey (*Swansea*), T. E. Jones-Davies (*London Welsh*), R. W. Boon (*Cardiff*); H. M. Bowcott (*Cardiff*), W. C. Powell (*London Welsh*); A. Skym (*Cardiff*); H. C. Day (*Newport*), T. Day (*Swansea*), T. Arthur (*Neath*), E. Jenkins (*Aberavon*), N. Fender (*Cardiff*), A. Lemon (*Neath*), W. G. Thomas (*Swansea*)
Scotland: R. W. Langrish (*London Scot.*); I. S. Smith (*London Scot.*), G. P. S. Macpherson (*Edin. Acads.*), W. M. Simmers (*Glas. Acads.*), G. Wood (*Gala*); H. Lind (*Dunfermline*), J. B. Nelson (*Glas. Acads.*); J. W. Allan (*Melrose*), W. M. Roughead* (*London Scot.*), H. S. Mackintosh (*West of Scot.*), A. W. Walker (*Camb. Univ.*), J. A. Beattie (*Hawick*), W. B. Welsh (*Hawick*),

J. S. Wilson (*St Andrews Univ.*), D. Crichton-Miller (*Gloucester*)
Referee: J. E. Bott (*England*)

J. C. Morley scored but J. Bassett failed (3-0); D. Crichton-Miller scored but J. W. Allan failed (3-3). (H.T.). D. Crichton-Miller scored and J. W. Allan converted (3-8); W. Thomas scored and J. Bassett converted (8-8); R. W. Boon scored and J. Bassett converted (13-8).

50,000 spectators were present in fine weather. A minute's silence was observed to mark the passing of J. Aikman Smith who had died on the journey south. It was not a great game, both sides having chances of scoring which were not taken. Boon's try in the last minutes came from a pass that his opponents thought was forward and he was allowed to follow up his kick ahead and touch down unchallenged. Walker was lame for all the first half but Watcyn Thomas played for most of the match with a fractured collar bone and still managed to score. The Welsh team were lettered.

IRELAND 8   SCOTLAND 5
Lansdowne Road
28 February 1931

Scotland: R. W. Langrish (*London Scot.*); I. S. Smith (*London Scot*), W. M. Simmers (*Glas. Acads.*); A. W. Wilson (*Dunfermline*), G. Wood (*Gala*); H. Lind (*Dunfermline*), J. B. Nelson (*Glas. Acads.*); J. W. Allan (*Melrose*), W. N. Roughead* (*London Scot.*), H. S. Mackintosh (*West of Scot.*), A. W. Walker (*Camb. Univ.*), J. A. Beattie (*Hawick*), W. B. Welsh (*Hawick*), J. S. Wilson (*St Andrews Univ.*), D. Crichton-Miller (*Gloucester*)
Ireland: J. C. Entrican (*QU Belfast*); E. J. Lightfoot (*Lansdowne*), E. O. Davy (*Lansdowne*), M. P. Crowe (*Lansdowne*), J. E. Arigho (*Lansdowne*); P. F. Murray (*Wanderers*), M. Sugden* (*Wanderers*); H. C. C. Withers (*Army*), J. A. E. Siggins (*Collegians*), J. Russell (*UC Cork*), N. F. Murphy (*Cork Const.*), V. J. Pike (*Lansdowne*), J. L. Farrell (*Bective Rangers*), J. D. Clinch (*Wanderers*), G. R. Beamish (*RAF*)
Referee: B. S. Cumberlege (*England*)   **Touch judges:** T. H. H. Warren, J. J. Coffey

M. Sugden scored; P. F. Murray failed (3-0); H. S. Mackintosh scored and J. W. Allan converted (3-5). (H.T.). V. J. Pike scored and P. F. Murray converted (8-5).

The conditions played a vital part, for Sugden won the toss and a strong icy wind with several snow showers pinned Scotland down to a persistent and gruelling defence. That it took Ireland half an hour to open the scoring was a tribute to the Scots' tenacity. The first try followed a typical Sugden dart and dummy from a scrum near the line. Pike's try came from a forward rush. The Scottish score followed from a break by Lind who flung a long pass inwards which Mackintosh, amongst a crowd of green jerseys, grabbed and fought his way over. With the wind Scotland had hopes but it seemed that they were too exhausted to beat the defence. I. S. Smith had one good run with a kick ahead, only to see the ball beat Walker down-wind to the dead ball line.

SCOTLAND 28   ENGLAND 19
Murrayfield
21 March 1931

Scotland: A. W. Wilson (*Dunfermline*); I. S. Smith (*London Scot.*), G. P. S. Macpherson* (*Edin. Acads.*), D. St. C. Ford (*RN*), W. M. Simmers (*Glas. Acads.*); H. Lind (*Dunfermline*), W. R. Logan (*Edin. Univ.*); J. W. Allan (*Melrose*), W. N. Roughead (*London Scot.*), H. S. Mackintosh (*West of Scot.*), A. W. Walker (*Camb. Univ.*), J. A. Beattie (*Hawick*), W. B. Welsh (*Hawick*), J. S. Wilson (*St Andrews Univ.*), D. Crichton-Miller (*Gloucester*)
England: E. C. P. Whiteley (*Old Alleynians*); J. S. R. Reeve (*Harlequins*), J. A. Tallent (*Camb. Univ.*), C. D. Aarvold* (*Headingley*); A. C. Harrison (*Hartlepool Rovers*); T. C. Knowles (*Birkenhead Park*), E. B. Pope (*Blackheath*); R. H. W. Sparkes (*Civil Service*), G. G. Gregory (*Taunton*), H. Rew (*Army*), J. W. Forrest (*RN*), B. H. Black (*Blackheath*), P. E. Dunkley (*Harlequin*), P. D. Howard (*Oxford Univ.*), P. C. Hordern (*Blackheath*)
Referee: Dr J. R. Wheeler (*Ireland*)   **Touch judges:** R. B. Waddell, H. A. Haigh-Smith

D. St. C. Ford scored and J. W. Allan converted (5-0); H. S. Mackintosh scored and J. W. Allan converted (10-0); J. A. Tallent scored twice and B. H. Black converted 10-10); W. R. Logan scored and J. W. Allan converted (15-10); J. S. R. Reeve scored but B. H. Black failed (15-13); H. S. Mackintosh scored and J. W. Allan converted (20-13). (H.T.). I. S. Smith scored twice and J. W. Allan converted one (28-13); B. H. Black kicked a penalty (28-16); J. S. R. Reeve scored but B. H. Black failed (28-19).

75,000 watched this most spectacular match which produced some scoring records. The general opinion was that good attacking play faced by some rather moderate tackling was responsible for the flood of scoring. Certainly it was a day where Macpherson did a lot of shadow tackling but engineered many moves which bewildered the opposition and certainly led to two of the scores. Logan had an excellent debut, scoring one try and making another for Smith. There was some splendid goal kicking by Allan and Black. The English players were numbered.

SCOTLAND 3   SOUTH AFRICA 6
Murrayfield
16 January 1932

Scotland: T. H. B. Lawther (*Old Millhillians*); I. S. Smith (*London Scot.*), G. P. S. Macpherson (*Edin. Acads.*), W. M. Simmers* (*Glas. Acads.*), J. E. Forrest (*Glas. Acads.*); H. Lind (*Dunfermline*),W. R. Logan (*Edin. Univ.*); J. W. Allan (*Melrose*), H. S. Mackintosh (*West of Scot.*), R. A. Foster (*Hawick*), M. S. Stewart (*Stewart's FP*), J. A. Beattie (*Hawick*), J. Graham (*Kelso*), F. H. Waters (*London Scot.*), W. B. Welsh (*Hawick*)
South Africa: G. H. Brand (*Hamiltons*); M. Zimmerman (*UCT*), B. G. Gray (*Villagers*), J. H. Van der Westhuizen (*Gardens*), F. D. Venter (*Pretoria*); B. L. Osler* (*Villagers*), D. H. Craven (*Un. Services*); P. J. Mostert (*Somerset*), H. G. Kipling (*Beaconsfield*), M. M. Louw (*Gardens*), G. M. Daneel (*PUC*), W. F. Bergh (*George*), P. J. Nel (*Greytown*), L. C. T. Strachan (*Police*), A. J. McDonald (*Un. Services*)
Referee: B. S. Cumberlege (*England*)   **Touch judges:** Dr G. W. Simpson, Pienaar

H. Lind scored but J. W. Allan failed (3-0). (H.T.). B. L. Osler and D. H. Craven scored but B. L. Osler and G. H. Brand failed (3-6).

65 ,000 attended in a day of very poor conditions. A gale of wind and icy rain blew down the length of the field hampering handling and kicking and testing the endurance of the players. This made it almost entirely a forward game and the South African pack with an obvious weight and height advantage played a major part in the win. Early in the first half Lind broke through and with Welsh running beside him, dummied the full back and ran on to score. Scotland held this lead until shortly after the restart. The South Africans were numbered.

SCOTLAND 0   WALES 6
Murrayfield
6 February 1932

Scotland: T. H. B. Lawther (*Old Millhillians*); I. S. Smith (*London Scot.*), D. St. C. Ford (*US*), W. M. Simmers* (*Glas. Acads.*), G. Wood (*Gala*); H. Lind (*Dunfermline*), W. R. Logan (*Edin. Univ.*); J. W. Allan (*Melrose*), W. N. Roughead (*London Scot.*), H. S. Mackintosh (*West of Scot.*), M. S. Stewart (*Stewart's FP*), J. A. Beattie (*Hawick*), J. Graham (*Kelso*), F. H. Waters (*London Scot.*), W. B. Welsh (*Hawick*)
Wales: J. Bassett* (*Penarth*); J. C. Morley (*Newport*), E. C. Davey (*Swansea*), F. L. Williams (*Cardiff*), R. W. Boon (*Cardiff*); A. R. Ralph (*Newport*), W. C. Powell (*London Welsh*); A. Skym (*Cardiff*), F. A. Bowdler (*Crosskeys*), T. Day (*Swansea*), W. Davies (*Swansea*), D. Thomas (*Swansea*), W. G. Thomas (*Swansea*), A. Lemon (*Neath*), E. M. Jenkins (*Aberavon*)
Referee: T. Bell (*Ireland*)   **Touch judges:** F. J. C. Moffat, Captain J. N. Jones

R. W. Boon scored but J. Bassett failed (0-3). (H.T.). J. Bassett kicked a penalty (0-6).

About 60,000 watched in reasonable conditions. Although it was a fairly even first half Wales finished well on top. There was a bruising game up front but the Welsh backs were too fast for their opponents and only good tackling kept the score to a penalty in the second half. The Welsh team were identified by letters.

SCOTLAND 8 IRELAND 20
Murrayfield
27 February 1932

Scotland: A. H. M. Hutton (*Dunfermline*); I. S. Smith (*London Scot.*), G. Wood (*Gala*), D. St. C. Ford (*Un. Services*), W. M. Simmers* (*Glas. Acads.*); W. D. Emslie (*RHSFP*), W. R. Logan (*Edin. Univ.*); J. W. Allan (*Melrose*), H. S. Mackintosh (*West of Scot.*), R. A. Foster (*Hawick*), M. S. Stewart (*Stewart's FP*), J. A. Beattie (*Hawick*), A. W. Walker (*Birkenhead Park*), F. H. Waters (*London Scot.*), W. B. Welsh (*Hawick*)
Ireland: E. C. Ridgeway (*Wanderers*); S. L. Waide (*NIFC*), E. W. F. de V. Hunt (*Army*), M. P. Crowe (*Lansdowne*), E. J. Lightfoot (*Lansdowne*); E. Davy (*Lansdowne*), P. F. Murray (*Wanderers*); G. R. Beamish* (*RAF*), M. J. Dunne (*Lansdowne*), J. L. Farrell (*Bective Rangers*), N. Murphy (*Cork Const.*), V. J. Pike (*Lansdowne*), W. M. Ross (*QU Belfast*), J. A. E. Siggins (*Collegians*), C. J. Hanrahan (*Dolphin*)
Referee: B. S. Cumberlege (*England*) **Touch judges:** M. A. Allan, W. A. Clarke

E. J. Lightfoot scored and P. F. Murray converted (0-5). (H.T.). G. Wood scored but F. H. Waters failed (3-5); E. W. F. de V. Hunt, E. J. Lightfoot and S. L. Waide scored for P. F. Murray to convert all three (3-20); W. M. Simmers scored and J. W. Allan converted (8-20).

Ridgeway was a very late replacement for D. P. Morris but had a good match. The Scots were disorganised when after twenty minutes Emslie had to leave the field with an ankle injury. Simmers moved to half, not the best choice, and Welsh went out to the wing where he played very well. In one dash down the wing he kicked over Ridgeway's head only to be badly impeded and so missed a touch down.

ENGLAND 16 SCOTLAND 3
Twickenham
19 March 1932

England: T. W. Brown (*Bristol*); C. C. Tanner (*Richmond*), D. W. Burland (*Bristol*), R. A. Gerrard (*Bath*), C. D. Aarvold (*Blackheath*); W. Elliot (*Un. Services*), B. C. Gadney (*Leicester*); A. Vaughan-Jones (*Un. Services*), R. J. Longland (*Northampton*), B. H. Black (*Blackheath*), J. M. Hodgson (*Northern*), G. G. Gregory (*Bristol*), R. G. S. Hobbs (*Richmond*), C. F. H. Wells (*Devonport Services*), N. L. Evans (*Un. Services*)
Scotland: A. S. Dykes (*Glas. Acads.*); I. S. Smith (*London Scot.*), G. P. S. Macpherson* (*Edin. Acads.*), G. Wood (*Gala*), W. M. Simmers (*Glas. Acads.*); H. Lind (*Dunfermline*), J. P. McArthur (*Waterloo*); R. A. Foster (*Hawick*), H. S. Mackintosh (*West of Scot.*), R. Rowand (*Glas. HSFP*), F. A. Wright (*Edin. Acads.*), J. A. Beattie (*Hawick*), W. B. Welsh (*Hawick*), G. F. Ritchie (*Dundee HSFP*), J. S. Wilson (*St Andrews Univ.*)
Referee: Dr J. R. Wheeler (*Ireland*)

I. S. Smith scored but A. S. Dykes failed (0-3), C. C. Tanner and C. D. Aarvold scored but D. W. Burland failed to convert (6-3). (H.T.). C. D. Aarvold and B. H. Black scored for D. W. Burland to convert both (16-3).

65,000 spectators, including the Duke of York, watched in brilliant weather. Although the Scottish backs showed some good touches in attack they were outpaced and the slightly built Wood had an unhappy second half trying to tackle the burly Burland, whose straight running set up two scores.

WALES 3 SCOTLAND 11
Swansea
4 February 1933

Wales: G. Baylis (*Pontypool*); A. Hickman (*Neath*), E. C. Davey (*Swansea*), W. Wooller (*Rydal School*), A. H. Jones (*Cardiff*); R. R. Morris (*Swansea*), B. Evans (*Swansea*); A. Skym (*Cardiff*), B. Evans (*Llanelli*), E. Jones (*Llanelli*), R. B. Jones (*Camb. Univ.*), D. Thomas (*Swansea*), W. G. Thomas* (*Swansea*), T. Arthur (*Neath*), I. Isaacs (*Cardiff*)
Scotland: D. I. Brown (*Camb. Univ.*); I. S. Smith* (*London Scot.*), H. D. B. Lorraine (*Oxford Univ.*), H. Lind (*Dunfermline*), K. C. Fyfe (*Camb. Univ.*); K. L. T. Jackson (*Oxford Univ.*), W. R. Logan (*Edin. Wrs.*); J. A. Waters (*Selkirk*), J. M. Ritchie

101

(*Watsonians*), J. R. Thom (*Watsonians*), J. A. Beattie (*Hawick*), M. S. Stewart (*Stewart's FP*), W. B. Welsh (*Hawick*), R. Rowand (*Glas. HSFP*), J. M. Henderson (*Edin. Acads.*)
Referee: J. G. Bott (*Ireland*)   **Touch judges:** M. A. Allan, J. S. Jones

I. S. Smith scored but K. C. Fyfe failed (0-3); K. C. Fyfe kicked a penalty (0-6). (H.T.). K. L. T. Jackson scored and K. C. Fyfe converted (0-11); T. Arthur scored but W. Wooller failed (3-11).

Wales were forced to make some late changes. M. J. Turnbull called off and it was decided that H. M. Bowcott should stand down to allow the Swansea halves to play together. R. W. Boon and V. G. J. Jenkins were also replaced at the last moment. Scotland had eight new caps including Brown at full back who misfielded the opening kick and thereafter never put a foot wrong. Scotland who held a distinct territorial advantage in the first half, scored twice. Smith scored with a typical run to the corner flag and then Fyfe kicked a good penalty from near the centre. Wales started the second half without D. Thomas who had broken a collar bone and fell further behind when another long run by Smith finished with Jackson scoring. A late revival by the depleted Welsh pack gave Arthur a score after a good forward rush. Lind who defended well was subdued in attack, for Davey tackled viciously and never gave him room to move. Once again the Scots were numbered but this time the decision was not revoked. After the match the SRU selection committee, headed by Dan Drysdale, retired to their hotel room to pick the XV for the next game in Dublin. Although delighted with the result, the committee found points to discuss and after a while deemed it sensible to ring for some further refreshments. When a head was poked round the door Dan said, 'Ah, the same again'. 'Oh, good!', said the face and vanished but nothing arrived and it took another approach before the drinks appeared. Suitably fortified the committee resumed its deliberations and eventually decided to play an unchanged team which was just as well for one morning paper carried the news that 'the same' team had indeed been chosen!

SCOTLAND 3   ENGLAND 0
Murrayfield
18 March 1933

Scotland: D. I. Brown (*Camb. Univ.*); I. S. Smith* (*London Scot.*), H. D. B. Lorraine (*Oxford Univ.*), H. Lind (*Dunfermline*), K. C. Fyfe (*Camb. Univ.*); K. L. T. Jackson (*Oxford Univ.*), W. R. Logan (*Edin. Wrs.*); J. A. Waters (*Selkirk*), J. R. Thom (*Watsonians*), J. M. Ritchie (*Watsonians*), W. B. Welsh (*Hawick*), J. M. Henderson (*Edin. Acads.*), M. S. Stewart (*Stewart's FP*), R. Rowand (*Glas. HSFP*), J. A. Beattie (*Hawick*)
England: T. W. Brown (*Bristol*); L. A. Booth (*Headingley*), D. W. Burland (*Bristol*), R. A. Gerrard (*Bath*), A. L. Novis* (*Army*); W. Elliot (*RN*), B. C. Gadney (*Leicester*); D. A. Kendrew (*Army*), G. G. Gregory (*Bristol*), R. J. Longland (*Northampton*), C. F. H. Webb (*RN*), A. S. Roncoroni (*Richmond*), W. H. Weston (*Northampton*), C. L. Troop (*Army*), E. H. Sadler (*Army*)
Referee: Dr J. R. Wheeler (*Ireland*)   **Touch judges:** F. J. C. Moffat, H. A. Haigh Smith

K. C. Fyfe scored but did not convert (3-0). (H.T.).

It was fortunate for England that they exercised a definite superiority forward, for during the game both their centres went lame and some desperate tackling was needed to keep the score down to a single try.

IRELAND 6   SCOTLAND 8
Lansdowne Road
1 April 1933

Ireland: R. H. Pratt (*Dublin Univ.*); J. J. O'Connor (*UC Cork*), P. B. Coote (*Leicester*), M. P. Crowe (*Lansdowne*), E. J. Lightfoot (*Lansdowne*); E. O. Davy* (*Lansdowne*), P. F. Murray (*Wanderers*); G. R. Beamish (*Leicester*), M. J. Dunne (*Lansdowne*), H. O'Neill (*UC Cork*), J. Russell (*UC Cork*), J. A. E. Siggins (*Collegians*), C. E. St. J. Beamish (*Harlequins*), V. J. Pike (*Lansdowne*), W. M. Ross (*QU Belfast*)
Scotland: D. I. Brown (*Camb. Univ.*); I. S. Smith* (*London Scot.*), H. D. B. Lorraine (*Oxford Univ.*), H. Lind (*Dunfermline*), P. M. S. Gedge (*Edin. Wrs.*); K. L. T. Jackson (*Oxford Univ.*), W. R. Logan (Edin. *Wrs.*); J. A. Waters (*Selkirk*), J. R. Thom (*Watsonians*) J. M. Ritchie (*Watsonians*), J. A. Beattie (*Hawick*), M. S. Stewart (*Stewart's FP*), W. B. Welsh (*Hawick*), R. Rowand (*Glas. HSFP*), J. M. Henderson (*Edin. Acads.*)
Referee: B. S. Cumberlege (*England*)   **Touch judges:** D. Drysdale

M. P. Crowe scored but failed to convert (3-0); K. L. T. Jackson dropped a goal (3-4). (H.T.). P. F. Murray scored but J. A. E. Siggins failed(6-4); H. Lind dropped a goal (6-8).

This game had been postponed from 25 February when an appalling blizzard not only left the ground under inches of slushy snow but also forced the Scottish team's ship to lie off Dublin Bay for sixteen hours and they were in no condition to play when they got ashore on the Saturday morning. For this game Scotland were forced to make the only change during the season when Gedge replaced Fyfe who had been injured in a car accident on the previous day. This was a really bruising match for the ground was very hard and both sides tackled fiercely. Lind suffered a nasty face scrape, Smith was lame for most of the match, Lorraine was tackled so heavily by Coote that he was dazed for the rest of the day, while Gedge broke a bone in his hand attempting a hand off. Scotland, however, led at half time but fell behind immediately after the start. Davy put in a long kick to the corner which, unnoticed by the touch judge and referee, went into touch off the corner post. From the resultant line out and scrum Murray slipped over for a try to put Ireland in the lead. The Scottish pack then set to and controlled play so well that Logan and Jackson, the only fit backs, were able to take play gradually into the Irish 25. With some ten minutes left, Logan, from a scrum, threw a long pass to Lind who just had time to drop a good goal. So in I. S. Smith's last season he had the satisfaction of captaining Scotland to the Triple Crown.

SCOTLAND 6   WALES 13
Murrayfield
3 February 1934

Scotland: K. W. Marshall (*Edin. Acads.*); R. W. Shaw (*Glas. HSFP*), R. C. S. Dick (*Camb.Univ.*), H. Lind* (*Dunfermline*), J. Park (*RHSFP*); K. L. T. Jackson (*Oxford Univ.*), W. R. Logan (*Edin. Wrs.*); W. A. Burnet (*West of cot.*), L. B. Lambie (*Glas. HSFP*), J. M. Ritchie (*Watsonians*), J. D. Lowe (*Heriot's FP*), M. S. Stewart (*Stewart's FP*), D. A. Thom (*London Scot.*), J. A. Waters (*Selkirk*), R. Rowand (*Glas. HSFP*)
Wales: V. G. J. Jenkins (*Bridgend*); B. T. V. Cowey (*Newport*), E. C. Davey* (*Swansea*), J. I. Rees (*Edin. Wrs.*), G. R. R. Jones (*London Welsh*); C. W. Jones (*Camb. Univ.*), B. Jones (*Llanelli*), Y. Evans (*London Welsh*), T. Day (*Swansea*), D. R. Prosser (*Neath*), G. Hughes (*Penarth*), W. Ward (*Cross Keys*), J. Lang (*Llanelli*), G. Prosser (*Neath*), A. Fear (*Newport*)
Referee: H. L. V. Day (*England*)   **Touch judges:** F. J. C. Moffat, A. Wyndham Jones

J. I. Rees scored and V. G. J. Jenkins converted (0-5). (H.T.). B. T. V. Cowey scored and V. G. J. Jenkins converted (0-10); J. M. Ritchie kicked a penalty (3-10); W. R. Logan scored but K. L. T. Jackson failed (6-10); B. T. V. Cowey scored but V. C. J. Jenkins failed (6-13)

Scotland had to find late replacements for D. I. Brown, K. C. Fyfe and J. A. Beattie and so had eight new caps with three in the backs. They understandably were better in defence than in combined play. C. W. Jones played well at half and provided the capable Welsh backs with many opportunities for attack. A. Fear was conspicuous at wing forward, continually harassing Logan but was over-inclined to be offside. Wales seemed comfortably placed with twenty minutes to go when Scotland started to fight back. Dick made a great break and kicked over Jenkins' head. Shaw whipped after the ball to get the touch but it bounced sideways off a post to Cowey who kicked it dead. The rally was sustained for Ritchie kicked a penalty and Logan, following good forward play scored to bring the score to 6-10. But the defence held firm and in the dying minutes Cowey, although knocking down the corner flag, scored in the corner to make the match safe.

SCOTLAND 16   IRELAND 9
Murrayfield
24 February 1934

Scotland: K. W. Marshall (*Edin. Acads.*), R. W. Shaw (*Glas. HSFP*), R. C. S. Dick (*Camb. Univ.*), H. Lind (*Dunfermline*), J. A. Crawford (*Army*); J. L. Cotter (*Hillhead HSFP*), W. R. Logan (*Edin. Wrs.*); J. W. Allan (*Melrose*), G. S. Cottington (*Kelso*), J. M. Ritchie (*Watsonians*), J. A. Beattie (*Hawick*), M. S. Stewart* (*Stewart's FP*), L. B. Lambie (*Glas. HSFP*), J. A. Waters (*Selkirk*), J. G. Watherston (*Edin. Wrs.*)
Ireland: R. H. Pratt (*Dublin Univ.*); D. Lane (*UC Cork*), N. H. Lambert (*Lansdowne*), J. V. Reardon (*Cork Const.*), J. J. O'Connor (*UC Cork*); J. L. Reid (*London Irish*), G. J. Morgan (*Clontarf*); V. J. Pike (*Army*), W. M. Ross (*QU Belfast*),

C. R. Graves (*Wanderers*), S. Walker (*Instonians*), J. A. E. Siggins* (*Collegians*), C. E. St. J. Beamish (*RAF*), M. J. Dunne (*Lansdowne*), J. Russell (*UC Cork*)
Referee: B. S. Cumberlege (*England*)   **Touch judges:** Dr G. W. Simpson, R. D. Gray

J. Russell scored but J. A. E. Siggins failed (0-3); R. C. S. Dick scored and R. W. Shaw converted (5-3); J. W. Allan kicked a penalty (8-3); J. A. Crawford scored but J. W. Allan failed (11-3). (H.T.). R. C. S. Dick scored and R. W. Shaw converted (16-3); J. J. O'Connor and J. Russell scored unconverted tries (16-9).

This was Scotland's first win over Ireland at Murrayfield. The Irish forwards started in their usual bustling style, taking every scrum and it was no surprise when O'Connor gave Russell a chance to force his way over for the opening score. Then Scotland began to win some ball and it became obvious that the Scottish backs were in dangerous form. Cotter made a good break but his final pass to Shaw arrived with a tackler. Then he gave an awkward pass to Lind, who stooped and whipped the ball backwards through his legs to Dick. The defence was baffled and Dick shot off and swerved past the full back to score. After an Allan penalty further good passing set Crawford off along the touch line and a most determined run saw him go in at the corner with two defenders on his back. Shaw also got over but lost the try because of a defective touch down. In the second half Dick had another fine score but then the Irish pack rallied furiously. O'Connor and Russell scored after vigorous rushes. Beamish was only halted by a fierce tackle by Waters, then time ran out.

ENGLAND 6   SCOTLAND 3
Twickenham
17 March 1934

England: H. G. Owen-Smith (*St Mary's*); G. W. C. Meikle (*Waterloo*), R. A. Gerrard (*Bath*), P. Cranmer (*Oxford Univ.*), L. A. Booth (*Headingley*); C. F. Slow (*Leicester*), B. C. Gadney* (*Leicester*); H. Rew (*Blackheath*), G. G. Gregory (*Bristol*), R. J. Longland (*Northampton*) J. W. Forrest (*RN*), J. Dicks (*Northampton*), W. H. Weston (*Northampton*), D. A. Kendrew (*Army*), H. A. Fry (*Liverpool*)
Scotland: K. W. Marshall (*Edin. Acads.*), R. W. Shaw (*Glas. HSFP*), R. C. S. Dick (*Camb. Univ.*), H. Lind (*Dunfermline*), K. C. Fyfe (*Camb. Univ.*); J. L. Cotter (*Hillhead HSFP*), W. R. Logan (*Edin. Wrs.*); J. W. Allan (*Melrose*), G. S. Cottington (*Kelso*), J. M. Ritchie (*Watsonians*), J. A. Beattie (*Hawick*), M. S. Stewart* (*Stewart's FP*), L. B. Lambie (*Glas. HSFP*), J. A. Waters (*Selkirk*), J. G. Watherston (*Edin. Wrs.*)
Referee: F. W. Haslett (*Ireland*)   **Touch judges:** D. Drysdale, H. A. Haigh Smith

R. W. Shaw scored but K. C. Fyfe failed (0-3); G. W. C. Meikle scored but failed to convert (3-3). (H.T.). L. A. Booth scored but D. A. Kendrew failed (6-3).

This was an exciting game played at a tremendous pace. Scotland held the upper hand in the first half but only once got past some fine tackling. Dick had a slashing break through which Lind continued, to send Shaw in at the corner. The first English score came from a penalty kick taken by Forrest near mid-field. The ball hit a Scottish forward on the back and shot sideways to Fry who started a good passing run which gave Meikle a clear run along the touch-line to score. Near the close Lind made three good breaks through the centre but fell to good tackles. On the last break the ball bounced nicely for Booth who was left with a long clear run up to Marshall whose desperate tackle he broke through with a fast swerve.

WALES 10   SCOTLAND 6
Cardiff
2 February 1935

Wales: V. G. J. Jenkins (*Bridgend*); A. Bassett (*Aberavon*), W. Wooller (*Camb. Univ.*), E. C. Davey* (*Swansea*), J. I. Rees (*Edin. Wrs.*); C. W. Jones (*Camb. Univ.*), W. C. Powell (*Northampton*); T. Day (*Swansea*), S. C. Murphy (*Cross Keys*), T. J. Rees (*Newport*), D. Thomas (*Swansea*), T. Williams (*Cross Keys*), A. M. Rees (*Camb. Univ.*), J. Lang (*Llanelli*), A. Fear (*Newport*)
Scotland: K. W. Marshall (*Edin. Acads.*); W. G. S. Johnston (*Camb. Univ.*), R. C. S. Dick (Guy's), R. W. Shaw (*Glas. HSFP*), K. C. Fyfe* (*Camb. Univ.*); C. F. Grieve (*Oxford Univ.*), W. R. Logan (*Edin. Wrs.*); R. O. Murray (*Camb. Univ.*), G. S. Cottington

104

(*Kelso*), R. M. Grieve (*Kelso*), J. A. Beattie (*Hawick*), W. A. Burnet (*West of Scot.*), D. A. Thom (*London Scot.*), J. A. Waters (*Selkirk*), L. B. Lambie (*Glas. HSFP*)
Referees: F. W. Haslett (*Ireland*)   **Touch judges:** D. Drysdale, J. L. Thorn

C. W. Jones scored but V. G. J. Jenkins failed (3-0); W. Wooller scored but V. G. J. Jenkins failed (6-0); D. A. Thom scored but R. W. Shaw failed (6-3). (H.T.). R. W. Shaw scored but K. C. Fyfe failed (6-6); V. G. J. Jenkins dropped a goal (10-6).

This was a match of three phases. At first C. W. Jones was in tremendous form, scoring one fine solo try and sending Wooller in for a second. Then the Scottish pack, with Beattie setting a fine lead, aroused itself; quick dribbling, short passing and keen following up kept the Welsh backs on the defensive but only one score was achieved. However, Jones stopping one such rush had an arm badly wrenched and had to go off, Rees coming to stand off with Fear on the wing. In the second half Wales had the wind which they used most judiciously but late on Shaw moved up to stand off and at once began to run through the Welsh defence. He brought the scores equal only to see Jenkins run back, pick up a kick ahead, turn and drop a magnificent 40 yards goal to win the match.

IRELAND 12   SCOTLAND 5
Lansdowne Road
23 February 1935

Ireland: D. P. Morris (*Bective Rangers*); J. J. O'Connor (*UC Cork*), E. C. Ridgeway (*Wanderers*), A. H. Bailey (*UC Dublin*), D. Lane (*UC Cork*); V. A. Hewitt (*Instonians*), G. J. Morgan (*Clontarf*); S. J. Deering (*Bective Rangers*), J. Russell (*UC Cork*), P. J. Lawlor (*Bective Rangers*), C. R. A. Graves (*Wanderers*), S. Walker (*Instonians*), J. A. E. Siggins* (*Collegians*), C. E. St. J. Beamish (*RAF*), H. J. M. Sayers (*Army*)
Scotland: K. W. Marshall (*Edin. Acads.*); W. G. S. Johnston (*Camb. Univ.*), R. C. S. Dick (*Guy's*), H. Lind (*London Scot.*), K. C. Fyfe (*Camb. Univ.*); R. W. Shaw* (*Glas. HSFP*), W. R. Logan (*Edin. Wrs.*), A. S. B. McNeil (*Watsonians*), G. S. Cottington (*Kelso*), R. M. Grieve (*Kelso*), J. A. Beattie (*Hawick*), W. A. Burnet (*West of Scot.*), D. A. Thom (*London Scot.*), J. A. Waters (*Selkirk*), L. B. Lambie (*Glas. HSFP*)
Referee: J. Hughes (*England*)   **Touch judges:** J. B. Nelson, Dr J. Wallace

J. J. O'Connor scored but E. J. Ridgeway failed (3-0); R. W. Shaw scored and K. C. Fyfe converted (3-5). (H.T.). P. J. Lawlor scored but J. A. E. Siggins failed (6-5); A. H. Bailey scored but E. J. Ridgeway failed (9-5); E. C. Ridgeway scored but H. J. M. Sayers failed (12-5).

In a day of misty rain the much heavier Irish pack ruled the game throughout and eventually an overworked Scottish defence broke down. The Irish backs were not outstanding and a goal kicker was badly needed. The first Irish score came from a bad pass by Morgan which trundled along the ground to O'Connor, who fly kicked it ahead and just beat the defence to the touch. The Scottish score also came from a loose ball. Dick broke through to be tackled inside the Irish half. Lind stabbed the ball forward and Shaw was on to it in a flash, kicking it over the line and getting there first. Then in the second half the continual Irish pressure eventually won the match comfortably. The two Borderers, Waters and Beattie, were the best in the beaten pack.

SCOTLAND 10   ENGLAND 7
Murrayfield
16 March 1935

Scotland: K. W. Marshall (*Edin. Acads.*); J. E. Forrest (*Glas. Acads.*), R. C. S. Dick (*Guy's*), W. C. W. Murdoch (*Hillhead HSFP*), K. C. Fyfe (*Camb. Univ.*); R. W. Shaw* (*Glas. HSFP*), W. R. Logan (*Edin. Wrs.*); R. O. Murray (*Camb. Univ.*), P. W. Tait (*RHSFP*), R. M. Grieve (*Kelso*), J. A. Beattie (*Hawick*), W. A. Burnet (*West of Scot.*), D. A. Thom (*London Scot.*), J. A. Waters (*Selkirk*), L. B. Lambie (*Glas. HSFP*)
England: H. Boughton (*Gloucester*); L. A. Booth (*Headingley*), P. Cranmer (*Richmond*), J. Heaton (*Liverpool Univ.*), R. Leyland (*Waterloo*); J. R. Auty (*Headingley*), B. C. Gadney(*Leicester*); J. Dicks (*Northampton*), E. S. Nicholson (*Oxford Univ.*), R. J. Longland (*Northampton*), A. J. Clark (*Coventry*), C. F. H. Webb (*RN*), W. H. Weston (*Northampton*), A. T. Payne (*Bristol*), A. G. Cridlan (*Blackheath*)
Referee: R. W. Jeffares (*Ireland*)   **Touch judges:** F. J. C. Moffat, H. A. Haigh-Smith

P. Cranmer dropped a goal (0-4); K. C. Fyfe scored and converted (5-4); L. B. Lambie scored and K. C. Fyfe converted (10-4). (H.T.). L. A. Booth scored (10-7).

The English pack with a height and weight advantage had a double share of the ball from the scrum and line out, but were outshone in the loose, a factor which played a part in the only Scottish win of the season. In good conditions there was some fine running by both sets of backs although there was perhaps too much shadow tackling. After Cranmer had dropped a goal Murdoch intercepted a pass and set Shaw away on a move which finished when Fyfe kicked ahead and scored. Then Shaw ran down the touch line and beat two only to be held up over the line, but the ball fell loose for Lambie to touch down. The only score in the second half by Booth came after a run by Cranmer but Leyland had one spectacular run beating man after man only to find his pass to Booth adjudged forward. Right on time Beattie finished a handling run by going over but again the final pass was ruled forward. Logan and Shaw were praised as a partnership.

SCOTLAND 8   NEW ZEALAND 18
Murrayfield
23 November 1935

Scotland: J. M. Kerr (*Heriot's FP*); J. E. Forrest (*Glas. Acads.*), R. C. S. Dick (*Guy's*), W. C. W. Murdoch (*Hillhead HSFP*), K. C. Fyfe (*Camb. Univ.*); R. W. Shaw* (*Glas. HSFP*), W. R. Logan (*Edin. Wrs.*); R. M. Grieve (*Kelso*), G. L. Gray (*Gala*), G. D. Shaw (*Sale*), J. A. Beattie (*Hawick*), W. A. Burnet (*West of Scot.*), L. B. Lambie (*Glas. HSFP*), J. A. Waters (*Selkirk*), D. A. Thom (*London Scot.*)
New Zealand: G. Gilbert (*West Coast*), G. F. Hart (*Canterbury*), C. J. Oliver (*Canterbury*), M. Mitchell (*Southland*); T. H. C. Coughey (*Auckland*); J. L. Griffiths (*Wellington*), B. S. Sadler (*Wellington*); J. Hore (*Otago*), W. E. Hadley (*Auckland*), A. Lambourn (*Wellington*), R. M. McKenzie (*Manawatu*), R. R. King (*West Coast*), S. T. Reid (*Hawke's Bay*), J. E. Manchester* (*Canterbury*), A. Mahoney (*Bush Districts*)
Referee: C. H. Gadney (*England*)   **Touch judges:** F. J. C. Moffat, H. Brown

K. C. Fyfe scored but failed to convert (3-0); T. H. C. Caughey and W. E. Hadley scored and G. Gilbert converted both (3-10); T. H. C. Caughey scored but G. Gilbert failed (3-13). (H.T.). R. C. S. Dick scored and W. C. W. Murdoch converted (8-13); T. H. C. Caughey scored and G. Gilbert converted (8-18).

This was a fine fast game with plenty action from both sets of backs and forwards but New Zealand deserved their win being just that shade faster and more decisive. A good break by Shaw and Dick was finished off by Fyfe beating the defence to the corner, but then Murdoch was injured and eventually came back looking anything but fit. During his absence Caughey scored his first try. After half time Shaw made another good break to send Dick in at the posts and Scotland were back in the game. Indeed Murdoch gave Fyfe a scoring pass which was not taken and in the last minutes Sadler made a good break on the blind side which allowed Caughey to clinch the match.

SCOTLAND 3   WALES 13
Murrayfield
1 February 1936

Scotland: K. W. Marshall (*Edin. Acads.*); W. C. W. Murdoch (*Hillhead HSFP*), R. C. S. Dick* (*Guy's*), H. M. Murray (*Glas. Univ.*), K. C. Fyfe (*Camb. Univ.*); R. W. Shaw (*Glas. HSFP*), W. R. Logan (*Edin. Wrs.*); R. M. Grieve (*Kelso*), W. A. H. Druitt (*London Scot.*), J. A. Waters (*Selkirk*), J. A. Beattie (*Hawick*), W. A. Burnet (*West of Scot.*), M. McG. Cooper (*Oxford Univ.*), P. L. Duff (*Glas. Acads.*), G. D. Shaw (*Sale*)
Wales: V. G. J. Jenkins (*London Welsh*); J. I. Rees (*Edin. Wrs.*), C. Davey*(*Swansea*), W. Wooller (*Camb. Univ.*), B. E. W. McCall (*Welsh Regt.*); C. W. Jones (*Camb. Univ.*), H. Tanner (*Swansea*); T. J. Rees (*Newport*), B. Evans (*Llanelli*), T. Williams (*Cross Keys*), H. Thomas (*Neath*), G. Williams (*Aberavon*), A. M. Ross (*London Welsh*), J. Lang (*Llanelli*), E. Long (*Swansea*)
Referee: C. H. Gadney (*England*)   **Touch judges:** J. B. Nelson, D. Jones

W. Wooller scored but V. J. G. Jenkins failed (0-3), C. Davey scored and V. C. J. Jenkins converted (0-8). (H.T.). H. M. Murray scored but K. C. Fyfe failed (3-8); C. W. Jones scored and V. G. J. Jenkins converted (3-13).

Wales began strongly and eventually a half break by Jones let Wooller race in for the opening score. Near half time a tackle on Murdoch produced a loose ball that was snatched up and Davey scored. Scotland restarted well and picked up a score when Jenkins, in possession, threw out a pass which Murray pounced upon to score at the corner. Shaw and Dick followed with some fine runs which threatened danger but Wales finished strongly and Jones, who had struck up a good partnership with Tanner, rounded off the game with a lovely solo dodging run.

SCOTLAND 4 IRELAND 10
Murrayfield
22 February 1936

Scotland: J. M. Kerr (*Heriot's FP*); W. C. W. Murdoch (*Hillhead HSFP*), R. C. S. Dick* (*Guy's*),H. M. Murray (*Glas. Univ.*), R. J. E. Whitworth (*London Scot.*), R. W. Shaw (*Glas. HSFP*), W. R. Logan (*Edin. Wrs.*); R. M. Grieve (*Kelso*), W. A. H. Druitt (*London Scot.*) J. A. Waters (*Selkirk*), J. A. Beattie (*Hawick*), W. A. Burnet (*West of Scot.*), M. McG. Cooper (*Oxford Univ.*), P. L. Duff (*Glas. Acads.*), V. G. Weston (*Kelvinside Acads.*)
Ireland: G. L. Malcolmson (*NIFC*), J. J. O'Conner (*UC Cork*), A. H. Bailey (*UC Dublin*) L. B. McMahon (*Blackrock Coll.*), C. V. Boyle (*Dublin Univ.*); V. A. Hewitt (*Instonians*), G. J. Morgan (*Clontarf*); R. Alexander (*NIFC*), S. Walker (*Instonians*), C. E. St. J. Beamish (*RAF*), H. J. M. Sayers (*Army*), S. J. Deering (*Bective Rangers*), J. A. E. Siggins* (*Collegians*), C. R. A. Graves (*Wanderers*), J. Russell (*UC Cork*)
Referee: J. W. Faull (*Wales*) **Touch judges:** R. M. Meldrum, S. T. Irwin

S. Walker scored but J. A. E. Siggins failed (0-3); L. B. McMahon scored but A. H. Bailey failed (0-6); V. A. Hewitt dropped a goal (0-10). (H.T.). W. C. W. Murdoch dropped a goal (4-10)

Play was fairly even during the first half but Ireland seized on two loose passes to score. McMahon picked both up and set the Irish forwards away on a good handling run for the first try but ran in on his own for the second. Just on half time Hewitt dropped a goal. Murdoch moved to centre in the second half and although Scotland showed improved form the Irish defence was too sound and all that could be managed was a fine drop goal by Murdoch.

ENGLAND 9 SCOTLAND 8
Twickenham
21 March 1936

England: H. G. Owen-Smith (*St. Mary's*); H. S. Sever (*Sale*), P. Cranmer (*Richmond*), R. A. Gerrard (*Bath*), A. Obolensky (*Oxford Univ.*); P. L. Candler (*St. Bart's*), B. C. Gadney* (*Leicester*); R. J. Longland (*Northampton*), H. B. Toft (*Waterloo*), J. Dicks (*Northampton*), C. F. H. Webb (*RN*), P. E. Dunkley (*Harlequins*), R. Bolton (*Harlequins*), P. W. P. Brook (*Harlequins*), W. H. Weston (*Northampton*)
Scotland: J. M. Kerr (*Heriot's FP*); R. W. Shaw (*Glas. HSFP*), H. Lind (*London Scot.*), R. C. S. Dick (*Guy's*), K. C. Fyfe (*Sale*); C. F. Grieve (*Oxford Univ.*), W. R. Logan (*Edin. Wrs.*); R. M. Grieve (*Kelso*), G. S. Cottington (Headingley), W. A. H. Druitt (*London Scot.*), J. A. Beattie* (*Hawick*), W. A. Burnet (*West of Scot.*), R. W. Barrie (*Hawick*), J. A. Waters (*Selkirk*), V. G. Weston (*Kelvinside Acads.*)
Referee: T. H. Phillips (*Wales*) **Touch judges:** M. A. Allan, H. A. Haigh-Smith

R. Bolton scored but P. Cranmer failed (3-0); K. C. Fyfe kicked a penalty (3-3); P. L. Candler scored but P. Cranmer failed (6-3); H. S. Sever failed (9-3); R. W. Shaw scored and K. C. Fyfe converted (9-8). (H.T.).

In a day of sunshine there was some attractive but not outstanding play. After a fairly even first half, the second spell developed into an English siege, but their backs were well held by a good defence. Fyfe marked the dangerous Obolensky out of the game and Cranmer did some hard running spoiled by poor finishing. It was fortunate that England lacked a kicker for many scoring kicks were missed whereas Fyfe kicked one good 40 yard penalty and a conversion from the touch line. The English pack held an advantage throughout and Logan was handicapped by sluggish heeling and little ball. During the last few minutes one has a memory of England camped on the Scottish line; Gadney kicking to touch at the corner, Scotland taking scrums instead of line-outs, but losing the strike, for the whole process to be repeated for Gadney refused to open the game up.

107

WALES 6 SCOTLAND 13
Swansea
6 February 1937

Wales: T. D. James (*Aberavon*); W. H. Clement (*Llanelli*), W. Wooller (*Cardiff*), J. I. Rees* (*Edin. Wrs.*), W. H. Hopkin (*Chepstow*); R. R. Morris (*Bristol*), H. Tanner (*Swansea*); T. J. Rees (*Newport*), W. H. Travers (*Newport*), T. Williams (*Cross Keys*), H. Thomas (*Neath*) H. Rees (*Cardiff*), E. Long (*Swansea*), E. Watkins (*Cardiff*), A. M. Rees (*London Welsh*)
Scotland: J. M. Kerr (*Heriot's FP*); W. G. S. Johnston (*Richmond*), R. C. S. Dick (*Guy's*), D. J. Macrae (*St Andrews Univ.*), R. W. Shaw(*Glas. HSFP*); W. A. Ross (*Hillhead HSFP*), W. R. Logan* (*Edin. Wrs.*); M. M. Henderson (*Dunfermline*), G. L. Gray (*Gala*), W. M. Inglis (*Camb. Univ.*), G. B. Horsburgh (*London Scot.*), C. L. Melville (*Army*), W. B. Young (*Camb. Univ.*), J. A. Waters (*Selkirk*), G. D. Shaw (*Gala*)
Referee: C. H. Gadney (*England*)   **Touch Judges:** R. M. Meldrum, W. R. Thomas

W. Wooller scored but T. D. James failed (3-0); R. C. S. Dick scored but G. D. Shaw failed (3-3). (H.T.). R. C. S. Dick scored and G. D. Shaw converted (3-8); R. W. Shaw scored and G. D. Shaw converted (3-13); W. Wooller scored but T. D. James failed (6-13).

Scotland after a shaky start settled down and finished in firm control. The Welsh pack had the better of the set scrums, taking a count of 31-16, for Scotland, with five new caps in the pack, had selected four number eights, but by the end of the first half the back row, fast and tackling fiercely, had upset the fluency of the Welsh backs. Wooller, expected to be a match winner, did score both tries but was very firmly contained by Dick. Wales, with the sun and wind began strongly and Wooller, running on to a dropped pass, kicked ahead, got the bounce and ran in for the opening score. Gradually the Scottish loose play began to tell and Macrae with a hard swerving run made an opening for Dick to equalise before half time. Wales restarted strongly but some fine handling by the Scots brought a score. Beginning with Macrae, R. W. Shaw, Inglis and Waters handled before Dick scored again. Then Kerr, fielding an attacking kick ahead, burst up the left wing, drew Hopkins before passing to R. W. Shaw whose pace got him in at the corner. In the last minutes Wooller got into his stride and ran round Johnston to score far out. Logan was praised for his work behind a sluggish tight scrum and it is interesting to note that he and the rival captain were both playing for the same club.

IRELAND 11 SCOTLAND 4
Lansdowne Road
27 February 1937

Ireland: G. L. Malcolmson (*RAF*); C. V. Boyle (*Dublin Univ.*), A. H. Bailey (*UC Dublin*), L. B. McMahon (*Blackrock*), F. G. Moran (*Clontarf*); G. E. Cromey (*QU Belfast*), G. J. Morgan* (*Clontarf*); C. R. A. Graves (*Wanderers*), T. S. Corken (*Collegians*), S. Walker (*Instonians*), S. J. Deering (*Bective Rangers*), J. Russell (*UC Cork*), P. J. Lawlor (*Bective Rangers*), J. A. E. Siggins (*Collegians*), R. Alexander (*NIFC*)
Scotland: J. M. Kerr (*Heriot's FP*); W. G. S. Johnston (*Richmond*), D. J. Macrae (*St Andrews Univ.*), I. Shaw (*Glas. HSFP*), R. W. Shaw (*Glas. HSFP*); R. B. Bruce Lockhart (*Camb. Univ.*), W. R. Logan* (*Edin. Wrs.*); M. M. Henderson (*Dunfermline*), G. L. Gray (*Gala*), W. M. Inglis (*Camb. Univ.*), G. B. Horsburgh (*London Scot.*), C. L. Melville (*Army*), W. B. Young (*Camb. Univ.*), J. A. Waters (*Selkirk*), G. D. Shaw (*Gala*)
Referee: C. H. Gadney (*England*)   **Touch judges:** R. K. Cuthbertson, E. C. Powell

R. Alexander scored but A. H. Bailey failed (3-0). (H.T.). L. B. McMahon and F. G. Moran scored and A. H. Bailey converted the second (11-0); I. Shaw dropped a goal (11-4).

Scotland were perhaps unlucky but Ireland deserved their win for a good first half display against a very strong bitter wind with many flurries of snow. There were some fierce exchanges and many stoppages. R. W. Shaw was concussed early during the first half and had to be taken off mid way through the second half; Waters left the field at half time to return later with three ribs strapped and Russell was also off for a while with a face injury. The Irish scores were snap efforts. Two came from loose passes while the third came after Moran had kicked ahead and the wind carried the ball half the length of the field. R. W. Shaw had to give the Irish sprint champion a yard but passed him with the ball short of the line. He plunged on the ball but only succeeded in knocking it on with the wind. He tried again but stumbled and Moran went past to touch down just short of the dead ball line. The depleted Scottish pack finished strongly but nothing came of it.

SCOTLAND 3   ENGLAND 6
Murrayfield
20 March 1937

Scotland: K. W. Marshall (*Edin. Acads.*); W. G. S. Johnston (*Richmond*), R. W. Shaw (*Glas. HSFP*), D. J. Macrae (*St Andrews Univ.*), R. H. Dryden (*Watsonians*); W. A. Ross (*Hillhead HSFP*), W. R. Logan* (*Edin. Wrs.*); M. M. Henderson (*Dunfermline*), G. L. Gray (*Gala*), W. M. Inglis (*Camb. Univ.*), G. B. Horsburgh (*London Scot.*), C. L. Melville (*Black Watch*), W. B. Young (*Camb. Univ.*), J. A. Waters (*Selkirk*), G. D. Shaw (*Sale*)
England: H. G. Owen-Smith* (*St Mary's*); E. J. Unwin (*Army*), P. L. Candler (*Bart's*), P. Cranmer (*Richmond*), H. S. Sever (*Sale*); F. J. Reynolds (*Army*), B. C. Gadney (*Leicester*); R. J. Longland (*Northampton*), H. B. Toft (*Waterloo*), H. F. Wheatley (*Coventry*), A. A. Wheatley (*Coventry*), T. F. Huskisson (*OMT*), J. G. Cook (*Bedford*), R. Bolton (*Harlequins*), W. H. Weston (*Northampton*)
Referee: S. Donaldson (*Ireland*)   **Touch judges:** F. J. C. Moffat, H. A. Haigh-Smith

E. J. Unwin scored but P. Cranmer failed (0-3). (H.T.). H. S. Sever scored but J. G. Cook failed (0-6); G. D. Shaw kicked a penalty (3-6).

The English forwards were in fine form and their backs should have done better with a good supply of the ball. Some credit must go to the Scottish defence; Shaw and Macrae were too fast for the English centres, Marshall was sound and made at least three try-saving tackles while Logan had a fine game both in defence and attack. Given more ball the Scottish backs would probably have won the match. As it was G. D. Shaw, who had kicked one penalty, just failed to save the game with a last minute kick.

SCOTLAND 8   WALES 6
Murrayfield
5 February 1938

Scotland: G. Roberts (*Watsonians*); A. H. Drummond (*Kelvinside Acads.*), R. C. S. Dick (*Guy's*), D. J. Macrae (*St Andrews Univ.*), J. G. S. Forrest (*Camb. Univ.*); R. W. Shaw* (*Glas. HSFP*), T. F. Dorward (*Gala*); J. B. Borthwick (*Stewart's FP*), J. D. Hastie (*Melrose*), W. M. Inglis (*RE*),G. B. Horsburgh (*London Scot.*), A. Roy (*Waterloo*), W. B. Young (*Camb. Univ.*), P. L. Duff (*Glas. Acads.*), W. H. Crawford (*Un. Services*)
Wales: V. G. J. Jenkins (*London Welsh*); W. H. Clement (*Llanelli*), J. I. Rees (*Edin. Wrs.*), W. Wooller (*Cardiff*), A. Bassett (*Cardiff*); C. W. Jones* (*Cardiff*), H. Tanner (*Swansea*); M. E. Morgan (*Swansea*), W. H. Travers (*Newport*), H. Rees (*Cardiff*), F. L. Morgan (*Llanelli*), E. Watkins (*Cardiff*), A. McCarley (*Neath*), W. Vickery (*Aberavon*), A. M. Rees (*London Welsh*)
Referee: C. H. Gadney (*England*)   **Touch judges:** R. K. Cuthbertson, J. N. Jones

A. McCarley scored twice but V. G. J. Jenkins failed both times (0-6). (H.T.). W. H. Crawford scored and converted (5-6); W. H. Crawford kicked a penalty (8-6).

This match will be remembered for the dramatic penalty goal kicked in the last minutes to give Scotland a win. During the first half Scotland had an equal share of the ball and hardly deserved to be behind at the interval for Shaw was in good form, clearly undisturbed by Jones, and had one saving touch-down which showed that he was the fastest man in the game over 30 yards. Macrae and Dick were thrustful and the latter held Wooller from start to finish. Yet it was a run and good crosskick by Jones that put McCarley in for the first score and the same player seized on an inaccurate pass by Dorward to get his second try. Wales, however, ran into trouble when a rib injury to Morgan forced him to retire just before the interval. In the second half, Scotland with the numerical advantage pressed continuously. Drummond hit the bar with a penalty. He then picked up a pass and went over only to find that the whistle had gone for a Welsh forward pass. Dorward narrowly missed with a drop before Macrae and Forrest had a good run and found Crawford up to take a scoring pass. At this stage Wooller was limping, so McCarley came out of the pack leaving six forwards to contest the scrums. This they did very well although things became rather tousy, Dorward in particular coming in for some hammering. With less than five minutes to go Drummond

109

tried another long range penalty which dropped short but the pressure was sustained. Man after man charged at the line and Dorward seemed to have grounded the ball but the Welsh pack fell on him. There followed a maul on the line in which a Welsh forward was judged to have interfered with the ball and a penalty was awarded. There followed a nerve-racking halt to allow the weary, the maimed and the concussed to get up and get on side whereupon Crawford kicked the goal to win the match.

SCOTLAND 23 IRELAND 14
Murrayfield
26 February 1938

Scotland: G. Roberts (*Watsonians*); A. H. Drummond (*Kelvinside Acads.*), R. C. S. Dick (*Guy's*), D. J. Macrae (*St Andrews Univ.*), J. G. S. Forrest (*Camb. Univ.*); R. W. Shaw* (*Glas. HSFP*), T. F. Dorward (*Gala*); J. B. Borthwick (*Stewart's FP*), J. D. Hastie (*Melrose*), W. M. Inglis (*RE*), G. B. Horsburgh (*London Scot.*), A. Roy (*Waterloo*), W. B. Young (*Camb. Univ.*), P. L. Duff (*Glas. Acads.*), W. H. Crawford (*Un. Services*)
Ireland: R. G. Craig (*QU Belfast*); F. G. Moran (*Clontarf*), A. H. Bailey (*UC Dublin*), L. B. McMahon (*Blackrock*), J. J. O'Connor (*Blackrock*); G. E. Cromey (*QU Belfast*), G. J. Morgan* (*Old Belvedere*); E. Ryan (*Dolphin*), C. R. A. Graves (*Wanderers*), H. Kennedy (*Bradford*), D. B. O'Loughlin (*UC Cork*), D. Tierney (*UC Cork*), R. Alexander (*NIFC*), S. Walker (*Instonians*), J. W. S. Irwin (*NIFC*)
Referee: C. H. Gadney (*England*) **Touch judges:** R. M. Meldrum, R. W. Jeffares

J. G. S. Forrest scored twice and W. H. Crawford converted the second (8-0); G. E. Cromey scored but A. H. Bailey failed (8-3); T. F. Dorward dropped a goal (12-3); A. H. Drummond kicked a penalty (15-3). (H.T.). D. O'Loughlin scored but H. Kennedy failed (15-6); F. Moran scored but A. H. Bailey failed (15-9), D. J. Macrae scored and W. H. Crawford converted (20-9); A. H. Drummond scored but failed (23-9); G. J. Morgan scored and S. Walker converted (23-14).

Scotland were full of brilliant running for Shaw, Macrae and Dick were quite explosive in attack. For Ireland Morgan had many dangerous dodging runs round the blind side but, with the exception of the sprinter Moran, the backs lacked pace and also seemed over-anxious to curb Shaw. The Irish forwards opened with a burst that nearly brought a score but inside fifteen minutes Shaw intercepted a pass, was through at top speed and gave Forrest a clear run in. Shaw continued to worry the defence and found a chance to let Macrae away and give Forrest his second try. After the interval Ireland came back into the game when O'Loughlin charged down a kick and scored and a break by Morgan put Moran in but then a scissors move between Dick and Macrae saw the latter score. There followed a good dribbling run by Duff and Forrest which let Shaw snap up the ball and send Drummond in. With three minutes to go Morgan scored after a fine break.

ENGLAND 16 SCOTLAND 21
Twickenham
19 March 1938

England: G. W. Parker (*Blackheath*); H. S. Sever (*Sale*), P. Cranmer (*Moseley*), P. L. Candler (*St. Bart's*), E. J. Unwin (*Army*); F. J. Reynolds (*Army*), J. L. Giles (*Coventry*); H. F. Wheatley (*Coventry*), H. B. Toft* (*Waterloo*), R. J. Longland (*Northampton*), A. A. Wheatley (*Coventry*), R. M. Marshall (*Oxford Univ.*), A. A. Brown (*Exeter*), D. L. K. Milman (*Bedford*), W. H. Weston (*Northampton*)
Scotland: G. Roberts (*Watsonians*); W. N. Renwick (*London Scot.*), R. C. S. Dick (*Guy's*), D. J. Macrae (*St Andrews Univ.*), J. G. S. Forrest (*Camb. Univ.*); R. W. Shaw* (*Glas. HSFP*), T. F. Dorward (*Gala*); W. F. Blackadder (*West of Scot.*), J. D. Hastie (*Melrose*), W. M. Inglis (*Army*), G. B. Horsburgh (*London Scot.*), A. Roy (*Waterloo*), W. B. Young (*Camb. Univ.*), P. L. Duff (*Glas. Acads.*), W. H. Crawford (*Un. Services*)
Referee: I. David (*Wales*) **Touch judges:** J. C. H. Ireland, H. A. Haigh-Smith

W. N. Renwick scored but W. H. Crawford failed (0-3); G. W. Parker kicked two penalties (6-3); W. N. Renwick scored but W. H. Crawford failed (6-6); R. C. S. Dick scored but W. H. Crawford failed (6-9); E. J. Unwin scored but G. W. Parker failed (9-9); R. W. Shaw scored but W. H. Crawford failed (9-12). (H.T.). F. J. Reynolds dropped a goal (13-12); W. H. Crawford kicked two penalties (13-18); G. W. Parker kicked a penalty (16-18); R. W. Shaw scored but W. H. Crawford failed (16-21).

The King and Queen and 70,000 spectators saw what was probably the most spectacular and exciting Calcutta Cup match ever played and one made memorable by a superb personal performance by R. W. Shaw, who scored two magnificent solo tries, created a third and with the ball in his hands was a source of extreme anxiety to the English defence. Starved of the ball (the scrum count was four-one in England's favour), the Scottish forwards were splendid in the loose and get some credit for the other two tries. As for excitement a glance at the scores show that Scotland took the lead four times, England drew level three times, fluctuations which left the spectators absolutely shattered. England made a good start and it took a touch down and good tackling to keep them out. Then a bad pass missed Reynolds and Shaw like a flash touched it ahead, picked it up and kicked ahead. Renwick ran on to the ball, also kicked ahead, got the bounce and fairly hurled himself in for a good try. Inside ten minutes Parker had kicked England into the lead only to have the Scottish forwards come back and a crashing run by Crawford let Renwick run in again. Then the Scottish forwards on their own 25 lost a scrum but the back row broke so effectively that they got the ball back and shot up field. Duff, Young and Crawford all made ground before the ball was suddenly passed in-field to Dick who sprinted away for a great try. Almost at once a good run by Candler put Irwin in to equalise again. Just before half time, from some loose play at half field the ball was put out to Shaw who dummied Reynolds and cut out to the left touch line, leaving the defenders standing by his acceleration. Faced by Parker he produced a text-book right foot/left foot fast jink which left the full back sprawling in touch and ran in for a wonderful solo try.

On restarting England pressed in spite of another fine dash by Shaw which narrowly failed and from the 25 Reynolds dropped a nice goal to put England into the lead for the last time, for soon Crawford kicked two fairly lengthy penalties for offside. Parker brought the score to 16-18 with another penalty and Sever must have scored had he not collided with the goal post. With some three minutes left the ball, from a scrum near midfield on the right, came out to Shaw who shot diagonally to the left behind the English threes. With his acceleration he was clear and he finished with a five feet dive to score far out. The kick failed but that was the virtual end. Wilson Shaw, who was carried off the field by his team and cheered by all, has two other memories of the afternoon. First the bus driver bringing the Scots to the ground got confused threading his way through the enormous crowd and delivered the players at the wrong gate. Once inside they had to walk a long way round to the dressing room through another dense crowd, who recognising them, offered a range of comments ranging from their chance of winning to the parsimony of the SRU who apparently made their team walk to the match! Later, having showered and dressed, he made his way to the tea room which the players shared with a section of the general public. There he was glad to sink into a vacant chair beside an elderly gentleman and to start the conversation remarked: 'Pretty hard going out there to-day' and got the reply 'Yes, you must be glad you were not a player!'.

Thus Scotland completed their season by winning the Triple Crown, their first since 1933.

WALES 11   SCOTLAND 3
Cardiff
4 February 1939

Wales: C. H. Davies (*Swansea*); S. Williams (*Aberavon*), W. Wooller* (*Cardiff*), M. J. Davies (*Oxford Univ.*), E. L. Jones (*Llanelli*); W. T. H. Davies (*Swansea*), H. Tanner (*Swansea*); W. E. N. Davies (*Cardiff*), W. H. Travers (*Newport*), L. Davies (*Swansea*), E. Watkins (*Cardiff*), R. E. Price (*Weston-super-Mare*), E. Evans (*Llanelli*), L. Manfield (*Otley*), E. Long (*Swansea*)
Scotland: G. Roberts (*Watsonians*); J. B. Craig (*Heriot's FP*), D. J. Macrae (*St Andrews Univ.*), J. R. S. Innes (*Aberdeen Univ.*), W. N. Renwick (*Edin. Wrs.*); R. W. Shaw* (*Glas. HSFP*), W. R. C. Brydon (*Heriot's FP*); G. H. Gallie (*Edin. Acads.*), R. W. F. Sampson (*London Scot.*),W. Purdie (*Jedforest*), G. B. Horsburgh (*London Scot.*), A. Roy (*Waterloo*), W. B. Young (*King's Coll. Hosp.*), P. L. Duff (*Glas. Acads.*),W. H. Crawford (*Un. Services*)
Referee: A. S. Bean (*England*)   **Touch judges:** M. A. Allan, D. Jones

M. J. Davies scored but W. Wooller failed (3-0); W. Wooller kicked a penalty (6-0). (H.T.). W. H. Crawford kicked a penalty (6-3); W. H. Travers scored and W. Wooller converted (11-3).

Both sides had six new caps of whom the most controversial choice was that of Brydon for although he was a fine Sevens player he could not command a place in his Club's 1st XV. In the event Scotland were well beaten by a Welsh side which was workmanlike rather than good. The Scottish pack was weak and steady packing gave Wales a two-one strike count. G. B. Horsburgh played well but the back row were slated for contributing little in the loose and less to the scrums. At the start, Shaw, who had been quite unwell during the journey south, had a typical cut through but his kick ahead was safely touched down. Then before the interval a nice diagonal kick by W. T. H. Davies put M. J. Davies over and Wooller kicked a penalty. In the second half Tanner went off for a while with an arm injury and Crawford kicked a penalty. Shortly before the close Travers broke away from a line out and ran unattended between the right wing pair to score a simple try.

IRELAND 12   SCOTLAND 3
Lansdowne Road
25 February 1939

Ireland: C. J. Murphy (*Lansdowne*); W. J. Lyttle (*Bedford*), J. D. Torrens (*Bohemians*), H. R. McKibbin (*Instonians*), F. G. Morran (*Clontarf*); G. E. Cromey (*QU Belfast*), G. J. Morgan* (*Old Belvedere*); T. A. Headon (*UC Dublin*), C. Teehan (*UC Cork*), H. J. M. Sayers (*Army*), J. G. Ryan (*UC Dublin*), D. B. O'Loughlin (*Garryowen*), R. B. Mayne (*Malone*), J. W. S. Irwin (*NIFC*), R. Alexander (*RUC*)
Scotland: W. M. Penman (*RAF*);J. R. S. Innes (*Aberdeen Univ.*), D. J. Macrae (*St Andrews Univ.*), R. W. Shaw* (*Glas. HSFP*), K. C. Fyfe (*London Scot.*), R. B. Bruce Lockhart (*Camb. Univ.*),T. F. Dorward (*Gala*); I. C. Henderson (*Edin. Acads.*), I. N. Graham (*Edin. Acads.*), W. Purdie (*Jedforest*), G. B. Horsburgh (*London Scot.*), A. Roy (*Waterloo*), G. D. Shaw (*Sale*), D. K. A. Mackenzie (*Edin. Wrs.*), W. B. Young (*King's Coll. Hosp.*)
Referee: C. H. Gadney (*England*)   **Touch judges:** R. M. Meldrum, E. O. Davy

F. G. Moran scored but H. R. McKibbin failed (3-0); H. R. McKibbin kicked a penalty (6-0); H. J. Sayers kicked a mark goal (9-0). (H.T.). J. R. S. Innes scored but D. J. Macrae failed (9-3); J. D. Torrens scored but H. R. McKibbin failed (12-3).

Scotland had to face sudden pelting showers of rain and sleet but by half time the wind had dropped and the field was churned to mud. This suited the Irish tactics for their forwards throughout played well being fiery in the loose. Early on Shaw and Macrae both cut through but the defence held and then the Irish pack really opened out and after some intense pressure Moran followed up a rush to score far out. Before half time Sayers had an unusual score when he marked a poor clearance and kicked a goal. Scotland had some bad luck on restarting for Macrae narrowly missed a penalty from half way. From the scramble Bruce Lockhart dropped at goal only to see a late swirl of wind carry the ball to hit the post high up and fall clear. With fifteen minutes to go Roy sent a ball back which went along the line to Shaw who cut through and passed to Macrae who sent Innes in for a try. However, the Irish forwards continued to press and Torrens was put over for the closing score.

SCOTLAND 6   ENGLAND 9
Murrayfield
18 March 1939

Scotland: G. Roberts (*Watsonians*); J. R. S. Innes (*Aberdeen Univ.*), D. J. Macrae (*St Andrews Univ.*), R. W. Shaw*(*Glas. HSFP*), W. C. W. Murdoch (*Hillhead HSFP*); R. B. Bruce Lockhart (*London Scot.*), T. F. Dorward (*Gala*); I. C. Henderson (*Edin. Acads.*), I. N. Graham (*Edin. Acads.*), W. Purdie (*Jedforest*), G. B. Horsburgh (*London Scot.*), A. Roy (*Waterloo*), W. B. Young (*King's Coll.. Hosp.*), D. K. A. Mackenzie (*Edin. Wrs.*), W. H. Crawford (*Un. Services*)
England: E. J. Parsons (*RAF*); R. H. Guest (*Liverpool Univ.*), J. Heaton (*Waterloo*), G. E. Hancock (*Birkenhead Park*), R. S. L. Carr (*Manchester*); T. A. Kemp (*St Mary's*), J. Ellis (*Wakefield*); D. E. Teden (*Richmond*), H. B. Toft* (*Waterloo*), R. E. Prescott (*Harlequins*), H. F. Wheatley (*Coventry*), T. F. Huskisson (*OMT*), J. K. Watkins (*RN*), R. M. Marshall (*Harlequins*), J. T. W. Berry (*Leicester*)
Referee: I. David (*Wales*)   **Touch judges:** F. J. C. Moffat, H. A. Haigh-Smith

W. C. W. Murdoch and R. W. Shaw scored but W. H. Crawford and W. C. W. Murdoch failed to convert (6-0); J. Heaton kicked two penalties (6-6). (H.T.). J. Heaton kicked a penalty (6-9).

Although it was disappointing to lose because of three penalties the result was fair, for a disciplined English pack dominated the game and a spark of enterprise in their backs would have seen Scotland routed. Yet Scotland began well; a dribble by Crawford and a run by Henderson and Shaw finished in touch only inches short. Then Innes had a run and cross-kicked. The bounce beat Heaton and Murdoch followed up to take the ball over. There followed a fine try from Shaw who had a typical accelerated burst past the defence. He was well covered about twenty yards out so changed pace, sold a dummy which halted the covering backs, and then another acceleration carried him to the line. England, with a lot of the ball (the scrum count was 48–12 in their favour), could not break through, but equalised before half time with two fine 40 yard penalties by Heaton. Immediately after half time he kicked a third which proved to be the winning score. Later in the game Shaw moved to stand off and there was one promising run by Bruce Lockhart which failed when he delayed his pass to Innes. So a year after the Triple Crown brought the Wooden Spoon.

This was the last international match before the Second World War.

SCOTLAND 21   ENGLAND 6
Services Rugby, Inverleith
21 March 1942

Scotland: Captain W. C. W. Murdoch (*Hillhead HSFP*); Lt J. R. S. Innes (*Aberdeen GSFP*), Captain W. H. Munro (*Glas. HSFP*), Ft Lt E. C. Hunter (*Watsonians*), Cadet E. C. K. Douglas (*Edin. Univ.*); Lt T. Gray (*Heriot's FP*), Cadet M. R. Dewar (*Watsonians*); Cpl J. Maltman (*Hawick*), Lt R. M. Grieve (*Kelso*), Lt N. W. Ramsay (*Army*), Lt S. G. A. Harper (*Watsonians*), Major C. L. Melville* (*London Scot.*), Lt A. W. B. Buchanan (*London Scot.*), Captain P. L. Duff (*Glas. Acads.*), Captain G. D. Shaw (*Sale*)
England: Major G. W. Parker (*Blackheath*); Lt E. J. H. Williams (*Camb. Univ.*), Sgt S. Brogden (*Army*), P. Off H. Kenyon (*Coventry*), Lt G. A. Hollis (*Oxford Univ.*); Captain J Ellis (*Wakefield*); Gp Captain G. A. Walker (*Blackheath*); Captain R. E. Prescott* (*Harlequins*), Sq Ldr C. G. Gilthorpe (*Coventry*), Cpl R. J. Lougland (*Northampton*), Captain T. F. Huskisson (*OMT*), Lt Com R. J. L. Hammond (*RN*), Paymaster Lt J. K. Watkins (*RN*), Lt C. L. Newton-Thompson (*Camb. Univ.*), Cpl W. T. Reynolds (*Bristol*)
Referee: A. M. Buchanan (*Ireland*)   **Touch judges:** Lt Col D. J. MacMyn, Captain H. A. Haigh-Smith

G. D. Shaw scored (3-0); M. R. Dewar scored and W. C. W. Murdoch converted (8-0); (H.T.). G. W. Parker kicked a penalty (8-3); W. C. W. Murdoch dropped a goal (12-3); J. Ellis scored (12-6); T. Gray scored and W. C. W. Murdoch converted (17-6); W. C. W. Murdoch dropped a goal (21-6).

This was a good win rather inflated by Murdoch's two drop goals. The Scottish pack was held in the scrum but did well in the loose whilst the backs were much more enterprising than their opponents; Munro in particular showed up well.

ENGLAND 5   SCOTLAND 8
Services Rugby, Wembley, London
11 April 1942

England: PO R. Rankin (*Australia*); Lt G. A. Hollis (*Oxford Univ.*), Sub Lt A. C. Simmonds (*RNEC*), Lt P. R. H. Hastings (*Oxford Univ.*), Lt A. L. Evans (*Rosslyn Park*); Captain J. Ellis (*Wakefield*), PO H. Kenyon (*Coventry*); Captain R. E. Prescott* (*Harlequins*), Sq Ldr C. G. Gilthorpe (*Coventry*), Cpl R. J. Longland (*Northampton*), Captain T. F. Huskisson (*OMT*), Cpl J. Mycock (*Harlequins*), Sgt E. Hodgson (*Broughton Rangers*), PO W. Fallowfield (*Northampton*), Cpl W. T. Reynolds (*Bristol*)
Scotland: Captain W. C. W. Murdoch (*Hillhead HSFP*); Captain J. B. Craig (*Heriot's FP*), Cadet D. A. Roberts (*Edin. Acads.*), FtLt E. C. Hunter (*Watsonians*), Cadet E. C. K. Douglas (*Edin. Univ.*); Lt T Gray (*Heriot's FP*), Cadet M. R. Dewar (*Watsonians*); Cpl J. Maltman (*Hawick*), Lt R. M. Grieve (*Kelso*), Lt N. W. Ramsay (*Army*), Captain J. B. McNeil (*Glas HSFP*), Major C. L. Melville* (*London Scot.*), Lt A. W. B. Buchanan (*London Scot.*), Captain P. L. Duff (*Glas. Acads.*), Captain G. D. Shaw (*Sale*)
Referee: Sq Ldr C. H. Gadney (*England*)   **Touch judges:** Captain T. C. Wilson, Captain H. A. Haigh-Smith

J. Ellis scored and R. Rankin converted (5-0); G. D. Shaw scored and W. C. W. Murdoch converted (5-5). (H.T.). M. R. Dewar scored (5-8).

England rather lost this game by their own shortcomings for they certainly ruled the scrums. The Scottish pack held an advantage in the line out and loose and a nippy pair of halves played well to a set of fast backs.

SCOTLAND 6   ENGLAND 29
Services Rugby, Inverleith
27 February 1943

Scotland: Captain W. C. W. Murdoch (*Hillhead HSFP*); Captain J. R. S. Innes (*Aberdeen GSFP*), Captain W. H. Munro (*Glas. HSFP*), Cadet E. C. K. Douglas (*Edin. Univ.*), Lt T. G. H. Jackson (*Cheltenham*); Lt T. Gray (*Heriot's FP*), Lt J. M. Blair (*Oxford Univ.*); W Cr W. F. Blackadder (*West of Scot.*), Captain I. N. Graham (*Edin. Acads.*), Captain N. W. Ramsay (*Army*), Sgt D. Maltman (*Hawick*), Cpl R. Cowe (*Melrose*), Lt C. McLay (*Edin. Acads.*), Major C. L. Melville* (*London Scot.*), Captain G. D. Shaw (*Sale*)
England: L Cpl E. Ward (*Bradford N.*); Sgt Inst R. L. Francis (*Dewsbury*), Captain M. M. Walford (*Oxford Univ.*), Sgt J. Lawrenson (*Wigan*), Major E. J. Unwin (*Rosslyn Park*); Major F. J. C. Reynolds (*Old Cranleigh*), Captain J. Ellis (*Wakefield*); Cpl R. J. Longland (*Northampton*), F Lt B. J. McMaster (*Bedford*), Captain R. E. Prescott* (*Harlequins*), Cpl J. Mycock (*Harlequins*), Surg Lt R. S. Hall (*Bart's*), Cpl E. H. Sadler (*Castleford*), Captain C. L. Newton-Thompson (*Camb. Univ.*), Cpl G. Hudson (*Gloucester*)
Referee: A. M. Buchanan (*Ireland*)   **Touch judges:** Lt Col D. J. MacMyn, Captain H. A. Haigh-Smith

W. H. Munro scored twice; C. L. Newton-Thompson and M. M. Walford scored and E. Ward converted one (6-8). (H.T.). J. Lawrenson (3), R. L. Francis and E. H. Sadler scored and E. Ward converted all three (6-29).

The first half was evenly contested but thereafter the five Rugby League players in the English threes took full advantage of their pack's superiority.

ENGLAND 24   SCOTLAND 19
Services Rugby, Leicester
10 April 1943

England: Lt R. T. Campbell (*Army*); Sgt Instr R. L. Francis (*Army*), Pte J. Stott (*St Helen's*), AC J. Lawrenson (*RAF*), Lt G. Hollis (*RN*); Captain P. R. Hastings (*Army*), Ft Lt J. Parsons (*RAF*); Sgt G. T. Dancer (*RAF*), Cpl R. J. Longland (*RAF*), Captain R. E. Prescott* (*Army*), Captain G. P. C. Vallence (*Army*), Surg-Lt R. L. Hall (*Bart's*), Cpl E. H. Sadler (*Castleford*), Captain D. L. K. Milman (*Army*), Cpl G. Hudson (*Gloucester*)
Scotland: Captain W. B. Biggart (*Army*); Captain J. R. S. Innes (*Army*), Major C. R. Bruce (*Glas. Acads.*), Cadet E. C. K. Douglas (*Army*), FO E. Grant (*RNZAF*); Lt T. Gray (*Army*), Lt J. M. Blair (*Army*); Sgt J. Maltman (*Army*), Captain I. N. Graham (*Army*), Lt M. D. Kennedy (*Army*), Major C. L. Melville* (*Army*), Captain J. McNeill (*Army*), Captain P. L. Duff (*Army*), Lt J. A. Waters (*Selkirk*), Captain G. D. Shaw (*Army*)
Referee: I. David (*Wales*)   **Touch judges:** Lt Col D. J. MacMyn, Captain H. A. Haigh-Smith

G. Hollis scored (3-0); J. Lawrenson scored and J. Stott converted (8-0); J. R. S. Innes scored and G. D. Shaw converted (8-5); C. R. Bruce scored but G. D. Shaw failed (8-8); P. R. Hastings, J. J. Parsons and J. Stott scored and J. Stott converted one (17-8), J. Stott dropped a goal (21-8); J. R. S. Innes, G. D. Shaw and M. D. Kennedy scored; G. D. Shaw converted one (21-19); R. L. Francis scored (24-19).

Both sides were handicapped by injuries but there was some good open play for even with Sadler out on the wing to replace Lawrenson, the English pack played well to their threes who ran well for their scores. Then Scotland staged a fine recovery to come within two points before Francis scored a good last try to clinch the win.

SCOTLAND 13   ENGLAND 23
Services Rugby, Murrayfield
26 February 1944

Scotland: Captain W. C. W. Murdoch (*Hillhead HSFP*), Cadet A. E. Murray (*Oxford Univ.*), Major C. R. Bruce (*Glas. Acads.*), Captain W. H. Munro (*Glas. HSFP*), Captain J. R. S. Innes (*Aberdeen GSFP*); Lt T. Gray (*Heriot's FP*), Lt J. M. Blair (*Oxford Univ.*); Lt H. H. Campbell (*Camb. Univ.*), LCpl J. D. H. Hastie (*Melrose*), Cpl R. Cowe (*Melrose*) Major C. L. Melville (*London Scot.*), Captain F. H. Coutts (*Melrose*), Captain G. D. Shaw (*Sale*), Captain J. A. Waters* (*Selkirk*), CSM J. E. McClure (*Ayr*)
England: LCpl E. Ward (*Bradford N*); Sgt Instr R. L. Francis (*Dewsbury*), Cfn J. Stott (*St Helen's*), LAC J. Lawrenson (*Wigan*),

114

Lt G. Hollis (*Sale*); Lt P. R. Hastings (*Army*), SqLr J. Parsons (*Leicester*); Captain R. E. Prescott* (*Harlequins*), Cpl R. J. Longland (*Northampton*), FSgt I. Dustin (*RNZAF*), Cpl J. Mycock (*Harlequins*), Schoolmaster J. B. Doherty (*Manchester*), Cpl G. Hudson (*Gloucester*), Sgt G. T. Dancer (*Bedford*), F Lt R. G. H. Weighill (*Waterloo*)
Referee: A. M. Buchanan (*Ireland*)   **Touch judges:** Major A. Wemyss, Captain H. A. Haigh-Smith

T. Gray kicked a penalty (3-0); J. Parsons scored (3-3); G. Hudson scored and J. Lawrenson converted (3-8); J. Stott dropped a goal (3-12); G. Hudson scored (3-15); G. Hudson scored and J. Lawrenson converted (3-20). (H.T.). G. Hudson scored (3-23); T. Gray scored and W. C. W. Murdoch converted (8-23); J. M. Blair scored and W. C. W. Murdoch converted (13-23).

England had a slight advantage in the scrums but G. Hudson showed up well with four tries. The Rugby League players in the backs were outstanding. In the second half C. R. Bruce came to stand off and this set off a spirited rally and a strong finish put a better face on the result.

ENGLAND 27   SCOTLAND 15
Services Rugby, Leicester
18 March 1944

England: L Cpl E. Ward (*Bradford N.*); S Instr R. L. Francis (*Dewsbury*), Cfn J. Stott (*St Helen's*), Cadet LE. Oakley (*Bedford*), Lt G. Hollis (*Sale*); Lt P. R. Hastings (*Welsh Guards*), Sq Lr J. Parsons (*Leicester*); Sgt G. T. Dancer (*Bedford*), Cpl R. J. Longland (*Northampton*), Captain R. E. Prescott* (*Harlequins*), Cpl J. Mycock (*Harlequins*), Schoolmaster J. B. Doherty (*Sale*), Cpl G. Hudson (*Gloucester*), F Lt R. G. H. Weighill (*Waterloo*), Captain F. W. Gilbert (*Coventry*)
Scotland: Captain W. C. W. Murdoch (*Hillhead HSFP*); Captain H. G. Uren (*Glas. Acads.*), F Lt E. Grant (*RNZAF*), Captain W. H. Munro (*Glas. HSFP*), Captain J. R. S. Innes (*Aberdeen GSFP*), Major C. R. Bruce (*Glas. Acads.*), FO E. Anderson (*Camb. Univ*); Lt H. H. Campbell (*Camb. Univ.*), C.S.M. J. R. McClure (*Ayr*), Cpl R. Cowe (*Melrose*), Major C. L. Melville (*London Scot.*), Captain F. H. Coutts (*Melrose*), Pte J. B. Lees (*Gala*), Captain J. A. Waters* (*Selkirk*), Captain G. D. Shaw (*Sale*)
Referee: W Cr C. H. Gadney (*England*)   **Touch judges:** Major A. Wemyss, Captain H. A. Haigh-Smith

Ward kicked a penalty (3-0); G. Hudson scored (6-0); J. R. S. Innes scored (6-3); G. Hollis scored and J. Stott converted (11-3). (H.T.). R. Cowe kicked a penalty (11-6); L. E. Oakley scored and J. Stott converted (16-6); W. C. W. Murdoch dropped a goal (16-10); P. R. Hastings, R. L. Francis (2) scored and J. Stott converted one (27-10); F. H. Coutts scored and R. Cowe converted (27-15).

The English pack get the credit for the success, constantly winning the ball yet good tackling by the Scottish threes and wing forwards really restrained the scoring. Indeed behind a winning pack the Scottish backs would have been dangerous.

ENGLAND 11   SCOTLAND 18
Services Rugby, Leicester
24 February 1945

England: L Cpl E. Ward (*Bradford N.*); Lt G. Hollis* (*Sale*), AB E. Ruston (*RN*), Sgt M. P. Goddard (*RNZAF*), LAC R. J. Forbes (*RAF*); Lt Comr R. E. Bibby (*RN*), Sq Lr J. Parsons (*Leicester*); Cpl R. J. Longland (*Northampton*), Sq Lr C. G. Gilthorpe (*RAF*), Captain F. P. Dunkley (*Army*), Cpl J. Mycock (*Harlequins*), Schoolmaster J. B. Docherty (*Sale*), Sgt E. Bedford (*RAF*), OS J. D. Robins (*RN*), F Lt R. G. H. Weighill (*Waterloo*)
Scotland: Sq Lr K. I. Geddes* (*Wasps*); F Lt E. Grant (*RNZAF*), Surg Lt W. D. MacLennan (*Watsonians*), Captain J. R. Henderson (*Glas. Acads.*), Sq Lr J. B. Nicholls (*NSW*); FO D. D. McKenzie (*Merchistonians*), Cadet A. W. Black (*Edin. Univ.*); SSM J. R. McClure (*Ayr*), Cpl J. D. H. Hastie (*Melrose*), Cadet T. P. L. McGlashan (*RHSFP*), Sub Lt C. Wilhelm (*SA Services*), Pte R. M. McKenzie (*NZ*), PO J. H. Orr (*Heriot's FP*), FO A. L. Barcroft (*Heriot's FP*), Captain J. A. D. Thom (*Hawick*)
Referee: I. Jones (*Wales*)   **Touch judges:** Major A. Wemyss, Captain L. M. Davies

R. M. McKenzie scored and K. I. Geddes converted (0-5); E. Ward kicked a penalty (3-5) E. Grant scored and K. I. Geddes converted (3-10). (H.T.). W. D. MacLennan scored but K. I. Geddes failed (3-13); E. Ward scored (6-13); J. H. Orr scored and K. I. Geddes converted (6-18); M. P. Goddard scored and C. G. Gilthorpe converted (11-18).

There were enforced changes which included playing J. B. Nicholls, a forward, on the wing. A young Scottish pack did well overall and their backs were better with Geddes a good full back. For England, Goddard, the New Zealander, made some capital runs at centre.

115

SCOTLAND 5 ENGLAND 16
Services Rugby, Murrayfield
17 March 1945

Scotland: Sq Lr K. I. Geddes' (*Wasps*); Cadet D. W. C. Smith (*Aberdeen Univ.*), Surg Lt W. D. MacLennan (*Watsonians*), Captain J. R. Henderson (*Glas. Acads.*), Fl Lt. E. Grant (*RNZAF*); FO D. D. McKenzie (*Merchistonians*), Cadet A. W. Black (*Edin. Univ.*); CSM J. R. McClure (*Ayr*), Cpl J. D. H. Hastie (*Melrose*), Cadet T. P. L. McGlashan (*RHSFP*), Lt E. A. Melling (*Sedbergh*), Pte R. M. McKenzie (*NZ*), PO J. H. Orr (*Heriot's FP*), Sq Lr J. B. Nicholls (*NSW*), FO A. L. Barcroft (*Heriot's FP*)
England: Lt M. T. A. Ackermann (*SAAF*); Lt G. Hollis (*RN*), L Cpl E. Ward (*Bradford N.*), Sgt M. P. Goddard (*RNZAF*), LAC R. J. Forbes (*RAF*); AB E. Ruston (*RN*), AC P. W. Sykes (*RAF*); Cpl R. J. Longland (*RAF*), WCom C. G. Gilthorpe (*RAF*), Cpl P. Plumpton (*RAF*), Cpl J. Mycock (*RAF*), Schoolmaster J. B. Doherty (*RN*), Cpl A. G. Hudson (*RAF*), FLt R. G. H. Weighill (*RAF*), Sgt E. Bedford (*RAF*)
Referee: A. M. Buchanan (*Ireland*) **Touch judges:** Major A. Wemyss, Captain A. L. Warr

G. Hollis scored twice and E. Ward converted one (0-8); W. D. MacLennan scored and K. I. Geddes converted (5-8). (H.T.). G. Hollis scored (5-11); A. G. Hudson scored and C. G. Gilthorpe converted (5-16).

The English pack was markedly on top and gave their backs plenty to do, Ward and Hollis being an outstanding pair. K. I. Geddes again shone in defence.

SCOTLAND 11 NEW ZEALAND ARMY 6
Victory International, Murrayfield
19 January 1946

Scotland: K. I. Geddes* (*London Scot.*); J. Anderson (*London Scot.*), W. H. Munro (*Glas. HSFP*), C. R. Bruce (*Glas. Acads.*), D. W. C. Smith (*Aberdeen Univ.*); I. J. M. Lumsden (*Watsonians*), A. W. Black (*Edin. Univ.*); W. I. D. Elliot (*Edin. Acads.-Wrs.*), G. G. Lyall (*Gala*), R. Aitken (*London Scot.*), A. G. M. Watt (*Edin. Acads.-Wrs.*), J. Kirk (*Edin. Acads.-Wrs.*), W. I. D. Elliot (*Edin. Acads.-Wrs.*), D. W. Deas (*Heriot's FP*), J. H. Orr (*Edin. City Police*)
New Zealand Army: H. E. Cooke (*Hawkes Bay*); J. R. Sherratt (*Wellington*), J. B. Smith (*N. Auckland*), W. G. Argus (*Canterbury*), F. R. Allen (*Canterbury*); J. C. Kearney (*Otago*); C. R. Saxton* (*Southland*); N. J. McPhail (*Canterbury*), F. N. Haigh (*Wellington*), J. G. Simpson (*Auckland*), K. D. Arnold (*N. Auckland*), S. W. Woolley (*Marlborough*), S. L. Young (*N. Auckland*), A. W. Blake (*Hawkes Bay*), J. Finlay (*Manawata*)
Referee: C. H. Gadney (*England*) **Touch judges:** F. J. C. Moffat, N. H. Thornton

S. W. Woolley scored but H. E. Cooke failed (0-3). (H.T.). J. Anderson scored but K. I. Geddes failed (3-3); W. H. Munro scored and D. W. C. Smith converted (8-3); H. E. Cooke kicked a penalty (8-6); J. Anderson scored but D. W. C. Smith failed (11-6).

This was the first of six International matches played during the season. These were regarded as 'unofficial' and no caps were awarded. This was a hard exciting game for the Scottish forwards stood up splendidly against a physically stronger pack and their backs more than held their own. The visitors scored first but Scotland might have been level at the interval for their forwards gave the defence a hard time. Half an hour after the interval Bruce had a lovely break through and passed to Anderson who sprinted in at the corner. Then Cooke kicked a penalty and the Kiwis, with their first defeat looming up, stepped up their attack only to find the Scottish pack continually turning defence into offence by fine footwork. Then in the dying minutes Bruce made a break, was knocked down but seemed to drop at goal. The ball went wide to drop over the line at the corner and Anderson's pace let him get there to touch down for a try.

WALES 6 SCOTLAND 25
Victory International, Swansea
2 February 1946

Wales: R. F. Trott (*Penarth*); L. Williams (*Llanelli*), J. Matthews* (*Cardiff*), B. L. Williams (*Cardiff*), W. E. Williams (*Newport*); G. Davies (*Pontypridd CS*), W. Davies (*Cardiff Univ.*); L. Manfield (*Cardiff*), J. R. G. Stephens (*Neath*), D. H. Steer (*Taunton*),

G. Hughes (*Neath*), R. Hughes (*Aberavon*), F. E. Morris (*Pill Harriers*), M. James (*Cardiff*), G. Bevan (*Llanelli*)
Scotland: K. I. Geddes* (*London Scot.*); D. W. C. Smith (*Aberdeen Univ.*), C. R. Bruce (*Glas. Acads.*), W. H. Munro (*Glas. HSFP*), C. W. Drummond (*Melrose*); I. J. M. Lumsden (*Watsonians*), A. W. Black (*Edin. Univ.*); I. C. Henderson (*Edin. Acads.-Wrs.*), G. G. Lyall (*Gala*), R. Aitken (*London Scot.*), A. G. M. Watt (*Edin. Acads.-Wrs.*), J. Kirk (*Edin. Acads.-Wrs.*), W. I. D. Elliot (*Edin. Acads.-Wrs.*), D. W. Deas (*Heriot's FP*), J. H. Orr (*Heriot's FP*)
Referee: H. L. V. Day (*England*)   **Touch judges:** F. J. C. Moffat, I. Jones

W. I. D. Elliot scored but K. I. Geddes failed (0-3); C. R. Bruce scored and K. I. Geddes converted (0-8); C. W. Drummond scored but K. I. Geddes failed (0-11); J. H. Orr scored and K. I. Geddes converted (0-16). (H.T.). G. Davies scored (3-16); W. I. D. Elliot scored but K. I. Geddes failed (3-19); G. Bevan scored (6-19); A. W. Black scored but K. I. Geddes failed (6-22); K. I. Geddes kicked a penalty (6-25).

Scotland were clearly on top in spite of a strong rally by Wales after the interval when Glyn Davies scored after a magnificent solo swerving run of some 50 yards. The Scottish pack were always in command with Elliot outstanding in backing up and defence; he put in a fearsome score-saving tackle on L. Williams.

SCOTLAND 9   IRELAND 0
Victory International, Murrayfield
23 February 1946

Scotland: K. I. Geddes* (*London Scot.*); D. W. C. Smith (*Aberdeen Univ.*), C. R. Bruce (*Glas. Acads.*), W. H. Munro (*Glas. HSFP*), C. W. Drummond (*Melrose*); I. J. M. Lumsden (*Watsonians*), A. W. Black (*Edin. Univ.*); I. C. Henderson (*Edin. Acads.-Wrs.*), G. G. Lyall (*Gala*), R. Aitken (*London Scot.*), J. R. McClure (*Ayr*), J. Kirk (*Edin. Acads.-Wrs.*), W. I. D. Elliott (*Edin. Acads.-Wrs.*), D. W. Deas (*Heriot's FP*), J. H. Orr (*Heriot's FP*)
Ireland: C. J. Murphy (*Lansdowne*); B. T. Quinn (*Old Belvedere*), K. Quinn (*Old Belvedere*), T. Coveney (*St Mary's*), F. G. Moran (*Clontarf*); E. A. Carry (*Old Wesley*), E. Strathdee (*QU Belfast*); D. Hingerty (*Lansdowne*), H. G. Dudgeon (*Collegians*), D. McCourt (*Instonians*), E. Keeffe (*Sunday's Well*), C. P. Callan (*Lansdowne*), M. R. Neely (*RN*), C. Mullen (*Old Belvedere*), J. C. Corcoran (*UC Cork*)
Referee: I. Jones (*Wales*)   **Touch judges:** R. M. Meldrum, R. W. Jeffares

W. H. Munro scored and K. I. Geddes converted (5-0). (H.T.). I. J. M. Lumsden dropped a goal (9-0).

After a strong Irish challenge had been halted, Elliot broke away from his own 25, kicked ahead, regained possession to set the backs moving and Munro cut in for a good try. Ireland, aided by a good pack, continued to press but rather orthodox play was held by a sound defence, the Irish wingers both being put into touch at the corner flags. In the second half Geddes hit the crossbar with a 50 yard penalty before a swift heel by the Scottish pack gave Lumsden a chance to drop a goal.

ENGLAND 12   SCOTLAND 8
Victory International, Twickenham
16 March 1946

England: H. J. M. Uren (*Waterloo*); H. F. Greasley (*Coventry*), E. K. Scott (*St Mary's*), J. Heaton* (*Waterloo*), R. S. L. Carr (*Manchester*); N. M. Hall (*St Mary's*), W. K. T. Moore (*Devonport Services*); J. W. Thornton (*Gloucester*), E. Bole (*Camb. Univ.*), D. B. Vaughan (*RNE Coll.*), H. R. Peel (*Headingley*), J. Mycock (*Sale*), G. A. Kelly (*Bedford*), F. C. H. Hill (*Bristol*), T. W. Price (*Gloucester*)
Scotland: K. I. Geddes* (*London Scot.*); J. R. S. Innes (*Aberdeen GSFP*), C. R. Bruce (*Glas. Acads.*), W. H. Munro (*Glas. HSFP*), C. W. Drummond (*Melrose*); I. J. M. Lumsden (*Watsonians*), K. S. H. Wilson (*London Scot.*); I. C. Henderson (*Edin. Acads.-Wrs.*), G. G. Lyall (*Gala*), R. Aitken (*London Scot.*), A. G. M. Watt (*Edin. Acads.-Wrs.*), J. Kirk (*Edin. Acads.-Wrs.*), W. I. D. Elliot (*Edin. Acads.-Wrs.*), D. W. Deas (*Heriot's FP*), J. H. Orr (*Heriot's FP*)
Referee: I. David (*Wales*)   **Touch judges:** R. K. Cuthbertson, J. A. Haigh-Smith

J. R. S. Innes scored but K. I. Geddes failed (0-3); C. R. Bruce scored and K. I. Geddes converted (0-8). (H.T.). J. Heaton kicked a penalty (3-8); R. S. L. Carr scored and J. Heaton converted (8-8); E. K. Scott dropped a goal (12-8).

The English pack held the whip hand in the loose while their back row harassed Wilson unmercifully on his own heel so that the Scottish back play suffered in consequence. Yet it was a seemingly beaten English team which produced a winning challenge in the last twenty minutes.

SCOTLAND 13   WALES 11
Victory International, Murrayfield
30 March 1946

Scotland: K. I. Geddes (*London Scot.*); J. R. S. Innes (*Aberdeen GSFP*), C. R. Bruce (*Glas. Acads.*), W. H. Munro (*Glas. HSFP*), C. W. Drummond (*Melrose*); I. J. M. Lumsden (*Watsonians*), A. W. Black (*Edin. Univ.*); I. C. Henderson (*Edin. Acads.-Wrs.*), G. G. Lyall (*Gala*), R. Aitken (*London Scot.*), A. G. M. Watt (*Edin. Acads.-Wrs.*), F. H. Coutts (*Melrose*), W. I. D. Elliot (*Edin. Acads.-Wrs.*), D. W. Deas* (*Heriot's FP*), J. H. Orr (*Heriot's FP*)
Wales: T. Griffiths (*Newport*); L. Williams (*Devonport Services*), B. L. Williams (*Cardiff*), J. Matthews (*Cardiff*), W. E. Williams (*Newport*); W. B. Cleaver (*Cardiff*), H. Tanner* (*Swansea*); J. H. Bale (*Newport*), W. J. Evans (*Pontypool*), C. Davies (*Cardiff*), D. J. Davies (*Swansea*), G. Parsons (*Abertillery*), L. Mansfield (*Cardiff*), R. T. Evans (*Newport*), H. Jones (*Cardiff*)
Referee: J. B. G. Whittaker (*England*)   **Touch judges:** W. A. Mackinnon, I. Jones

H. Jones scored and W. B. Cleaver converted (0-5); C. W. Drummond scored and K. I. Geddes converted (5-5). (H.T.). W. E. Williams scored but H. Tanner failed (5-8); K. I. Geddes kicked a penalty (8-8); L. Williams scored but H. Tanner failed (8-11); C. R. Bruce scored and K. I. Geddes converted (13-11).

After being three times in arrears Scotland overhauled a depleted Welsh team and held off a desperate final challenge. T. Griffiths suffered a broken rib after fifteen minutes and Mansfield went to full back until a bruising forward rush knocked him off the ball before Drummond scored, after which Cleaver took over.

SCOTLAND 27   ENGLAND 0
Victory International, Murrayfield
13 April 1946

Scotland: K. I. Geddes (*London Scot.*); W. D. MacLennan (*Watsonians*), C. R. Bruce (*Glas. Acads.*), W. H. Munro (*Glas. HSFP*), T. G. H. Jackson (*Cheltenham*); I. J. M. Lumsden (*Watsonians*), A. W. Black (*Edin. Univ.*); I. C. Henderson (*Edin. Acads.-Wrs.*), G. G. Lyall (*Gala*), R. Aitken (*London Scot.*), A. G. M. Watt (*Edin. Acads.-Wrs.*), F. H. Coutts (*Melrose*), W. I. D. Elliot (*Edin. Acads.-Wrs.*), D. W. Deas* (*Heriot's FP*), J. H. Orr (*Heriot's FP*)
England: H. J. M. Uren (*Waterloo*); R. S. L. Carr (*Manchester*), E. K. Scott (*St Mary's*), J. Heaton* (*Waterloo*), R. H. Guest (*Waterloo*); N. M. Hall (*St Mary's*), W. K. T. Moore (*Devonport Services*); J. W. Thornton (*Gloucester*), D. B. Vaughan (*RNE Coll.*) E. Bole (*Camb. Univ.*), H. R. Peel (*Headingley*), J. Mycock (*Sale*), G. A. Kelly (*Bedford*), F. C. H. Hill (*Bristol*), T. W. Price (*Gloucester*)
Referee: H. Lambert (*Ireland*)   **Touch judges:** R. M. Meldrum, H. A. Haigh-Smith

A. G. M. Watt scored but K. I. Geddes failed (3-0); K. I. Geddes kicked a penalty (6-0); C. R. Bruce scored but K. I. Geddes failed (9-0). (H.T.). I. J. M. Lumsden, A. G. M. Watt, W. H. Munro and W. D. MacLennan scored and K. I. Geddes converted the first three (27-0)

Inside 25 minutes Scotland had scored twice and appeared to have the game well in hand when Uren damaged a knee and had to retire, whereafter the game became quite one sided. The two new Scottish wingers played well; Jackson's pace, physique and determination were noticeable. Geddes again showed up as an attacking full back.

FRANCE 8   SCOTLAND 3
Colombes
1 January 1947

France: A. Alvarez (*Tyrosse*); E. Pebeyre (*Briviste*), L. Junquas* (*Bayonne*), M. Sorrondo (*Montalban*), J. Lassegue (*Toulouse*); M. Terreau (*Bressane*), Y. Bergougnan (*Toulouse*); E. Buzy (*Lourdes*), M. Jol (*Biarritz*), A. Moga (*Beglais*), R. Soro

(*Romanaise*), J. Prat (*Lourdes*), G. Basquet (*Agen*), J. Mathew (*Castres*)
Scotland: K. I. Geddes* (*London Scot.*); T. G. H. Jackson (*Army*), C. R. Bruce (*Glas. Acads.*), C. W. Drummond (*Melrose*), W. D. MacLennan (*Un. Services*); I. J. M. Lumsden (*Bath*), A. W. Black (*Edin. Univ.*); A. G. M. Watt (*Edin. Acads.-Wrs.*), I. C. Henderson (*Edin. Acads.-Wrs.*), T. P. L. McGlashan (*RHSFP*), J. M. Hunter (*London Scot.*), G. L. Cawkwell (*Oxford Univ.*), W. I. D. Elliot (*Edin. Acads.-Wrs.*), D. W. Deas (*Heriot's FP*), J. H. Orr (*Edin. City Police*)
Referee: C. H. Gadney (*England*)   **Touch judges:** D. S. Kerr, L. Carie

K. I. Geddes kicked a penalty (0-3); J. Lassegue scored (3-3); M. Terreau scored and J. Prat converted (8-3). (H.T.).

Scotland started well taking an early lead with a penalty goal but France recovered fairly quickly and persistent attacks put them ahead at the interval. They kept up the pressure in the second half but the Scottish defence held out, Geddes at full back doing much to keep the score down. There was some exciting running in the last quarter, Drummond in particular coming close to a score with a fine solo run which only failed against a crowded defence. France's tackling and speed on and off the ball were deciding factors in their win. For this match caps were awarded for the first time since 1939.

SCOTLAND 8   WALES 22
Murrayfield
1 February 1947

Scotland: K. I. Geddes* (*London Scot.*); T. G. H. Jackson (*Army*), C. W. Drummond (*Melrose*), C. R. Bruce (*Glas. Acads.*), D. D. Mackenzie (*Edin. Univ.*); I. J. M. Lumsden (*Bath*), A. W. Black (*Edin. Univ.*); I. C. Henderson (*Edin. Acads.-Wrs.*), R. W. Sampson (*London Scot.*), R. Aitken (*RN*), F. H. Coutts (*Melrose*), D. W. Deas (*Heriot's FP*), W. I. D. Elliot (*Edin. Acads.-Wrs.*), A. G. M. Watt (*Edin. Acads.-Wrs.*), J. H. Orr (*Edin. City Police*)
Wales: C. H. Davies (*Llanelli*); L. Williams (*Llanelli*), B. L. Williams (*Cardiff*), W. B. Cleaver (*Cardiff*), K. Jones (*Newport*); G. Davies (*Pontypridd*), H. Tanner* (*Cardiff*); C. Davies (*Cardiff*), W. Gore (*Newbridge*), W. J. Evans (*Pontypool*), W. E. Tamplin (*Cardiff*), S. Williams (*Llanelli*), O. Williams (*Llanelli*), R. Stephens (*Neath*), G. Evans (*Cardiff*)
Referee: M. J. Dowling (*Ireland*)   **Touch judges:** D. S. Kerr, R. A. Cornish

B. L. Williams scored but W. E. Tamplin failed (0-3); W. E. Tamplin kicked a penalty (0-6); K. I. Geddes kicked a penalty (3-6); W. I. D. Elliot scored and K. I. Geddes converted (8-6). (H.T.). W. B. Cleaver and K. Jones scored and W. E. Tamplin converted both (8-16); K. Jones and L. Williams scored but W. E. Tamplin failed (8-22).

In arctic conditions Scotland held their own up to half time and then faded badly especially during the last quarter. The Welsh pack were strong in the open and their back row were very hard on Black and Lumsden. Early on B. L. Williams intercepted a pass and a quick swerve put him past the defence for the first score. After two penalties Cleaver fumbled an unexpected pass from the line out and Elliot came up fast to go over for a converted try. The Welsh pack began the second half ominously well and Wales took the lead when B. L. Williams ran straight through to send Cleaver in although well tackled short of the line. Then Scotland faded and a late spate of scoring left Wales clear winners.

SCOTLAND 0   IRELAND 3
Murrayfield
22 February 1947

Scotland: K. I. Geddes (*London Scot.*); W. D. Maclennan (*Un. Services*), C. W. Drummond (*Melrose*), C. R. Bruce (*Glas. Acads.*), D. D. Mackenzie (*Edin. Univ.*); W. H. Munro* (*Glas. HSFP*), E. Anderson (*Stewart's FP*); T. P. L. McGlashan (*RHSFP*), A. T. Fisher (*Waterloo*), H. H. Campbell (*London Scot.*), F. H. Coutts (*Melrose*), A. G. M. Watt (*Edin. Acads.-Wrs.*), D. D. Valentine (*Hawick*), J. B. Lees (*Gala*), D. I. McLean (*RHSFP*)
Ireland: J. A. D. Higgins (*Ulster CS*); B. O'Hanlan (*Dolphin*), J. D. E. Monteith* (*QU Belfast*), J. Harper (*Instonians*), B. Mullan (*Clontarf*); J. W. Kyle (*QU Belfast*), E. Strathdee (*QU Belfast*); M. R. Neely (*Collegians*), K. D. Mullen (*Old Belvedere*), J. C. Daly (*London Irish*), C. P. Callan (*Lansdowne*), E. Keefe (*Sunday's Well*), J. W. McKay (*QU Belfast*), R. D. Agar (*Malone*), D. Hingerty (*UC Dublin*)
Referee: C. H. Gadney (*England*)   **Touch judges:** D. S. Kerr, T. A. Brindley

No scoring at half time. B. Mullan scored but J. A. D. Higgins failed (0-3).

The Irish forwards were on top in the scrums and lineouts but were held in the loose yet put in some ruthless spoiling. Their backs, although the halves combined well, had no real penetration and were easily held by an excellent defence. Then with fifteen minutes to go Strathdee went round the blind side of a scrum, ran up to Geddes and gave B. Mullan a clear run for a try.

ENGLAND 24   SCOTLAND 5
Twickenham
15 March 1947

England: A. Gray (*Otley*); C. B. Holmes (*Manchester*), N. O. Bennett (*St Mary's*), J. Heaton* (*Waterloo*), R. H. Guest (*Waterloo*), N. M. Hall (*St Mary's*), J. O. Newton Thompson (*Oxford Univ.*); H. W. Walker (*Coventry*), A. P. Henderson (*Camb. Univ.*), G. A. Kelly (*Bedford*), J. T. George (*Falmouth*), J. Mycock (*Sale*), M. R. Steele-Bodger (*Camb. Univ.*), R. H. G. Weighill (*RAF*), D. F. White (*Army*).
Scotland: K. I. Geddes (*London Scot.*); T. G. H. Jackson (*London Scot.*), C. W. Drummond (*Melrose*), W. H. Munro (*Glas. HSFP*), D. D. Mackenzie (*Edin. Univ.*), C. R. Bruce* (*Glas. Acads.*), E. Anderson (*Stewart's FP*); T. P. L. McGlashan (*RHSFP*), A. T. Fisher (*Waterloo*), H. H. Campbell (*London Scot.*), F. H. Coutts (*Army*), I. C. Henderson (*Edin. Acads.-Wrs.*), D. D. Valentine (*Hawick*), D. I. McLean (*RHSFP*), W. I. D. Elliot (*Edin. Acads.-Wrs.*)
Referee: I. David (*Wales*)   **Touch judges:** M. A. Allan, H. A. Haigh-Smith

N. M. Hall dropped a goal (4-0); C. B. Holmes and R. H. Guest scored and J. Heaton converted both (14-0). (H.T.). A. P. Henderson and N. O. Bennett scored and J. Heaton converted both (24-0); T. G. H. Jackson scored and K. I. Geddes converted (24-5).

This was a match which was bedevilled by the appalling wintry conditions that had persisted from mid-January. In Scotland clubs had not had a game since that time and the team members who travelled to London on Thursday afternoon had to endure a twenty hours journey. D. I. McLean who travelled later did not join his team mates until six a.m. on the Saturday morning, having spent all day and night on Friday in a train which had neither a restaurant nor sleeping carriage. M. R. Steele-Bodger (who was a student in the RD Vet. College in Edinburgh) had an equally appalling trip. His train had to be dug out of the snow twice before reaching Carlisle and he, too, only arrived in London in the early hours of Saturday morning. The match was played on a hard pitch in bitterly cold weather which deteriorated to a blizzard of snow in the second half. While England were clearly the better team Scotland were badly handicapped by a succession of injuries. Within five minutes Elliot had to hirple off with a leg injury and he later returned limping to play at full back only to see Jackson limp off. Drummond then retired with a broken collar bone but after the restart Jackson returned so giving Scotland fourteen players, two of whom were sadly handicapped. But early in the second half Kelly went off with injured ribs and Holmes had a spell on the touch-line nursing severe cramp so for a while both teams had fourteen on the field. England's first try came from an interception by Holmes who, with Geddes up with his threes, had a 70 yards sprint for a try. Their second try came from a kick ahead by Hall which bounced kindly for Guest who had followed up fast. Then Henderson dribbled in for a try before Holmes and Bennett moved on to a bad pass, kicked the ball ahead and the latter got the touch down. Scotland had a consolation score when a fine run by Munro put Jackson over.

SCOTLAND 7   AUSTRALIA 16
Murrayfield
22 November 1947

Scotland: I. J. M. Lumsden (*Bath*); T. G. H. Jackson (*London Scot.*), J. R. S. Innes* (*Aberdeen GSFP*), T. Wright (*Hawick*), C. McDonald (*Jedforest*); D. P. Hepburn (*Woodford*), W. D. Allardice (*Aberdeen CSFP*); R. M. Bruce (*Gordonians*), G. G. Lyall (*Gala*), I. C. Henderson (*Edin. Acads.*), L. Currie (*Dunfermline*), J. C. Dawson (*Glas. Acads.*), W. I. D. Elliot (*Edin. Acads.*), A. G. M. Watt (*Army*), J. B. Lees (*Gala*)
Australia: B. C. J. Piper (*NSW*); A. E. J. Tonkin (*NSW*), T. Allan* (*NSW*), M. L. Howell (*NSW*), J. W. T. McBride (*NSW*); N. A. Emery (*NSW*), C. T. Burke (*NSW*); C. J. Windon (*NSW*), A. J. Buchan (*NSW*), D. H. Keller (*NSW*), G. M. Cooke (*Queensland*), D. F. Kraefft (*NSW*), E. H. Davis (*Victoria*), K. H. Kearney (*NSW*), E. Tweedale (*NSW*)

Referee: N. H. Lambert (*Ireland*)   **Touch judges:** D. S. Kerr, T. K. Bourke

C. McDonald kicked a penalty (3-0), K. H. Kearney scored but B. J. C. Piper failed (3-3) (H.T.). D. P. Hepburn dropped a goal (7-3); A. E. J. Tonkin, M. L. Howell and G. M. Cooke scored and B. J. C. Piper converted the first two (7-16).

The game was fairly evenly balanced until the last twenty minutes when Wright had to go off with a dislocated shoulder. Up till then the Scottish halves had been combining well while the opposing pair had been troubled by the wet and greasy ball, but now their pack got on top especially at the line out. A nice break by Allan put Tonkin over and the conversion saw Australia leading for the first time. Then Keller broke away from a line out to send Howell in and later a powerful forward rush let Cooke away along the touch line to score. Scotland did not give in and had one spirited counter-attack before the close.

SCOTLAND 9   FRANCE 8
Murrayfield
24 January 1948

Scotland: W. C. W. Murdoch (*Hillhead HSFP*), T. G. H. Jackson (*London Scot.*), J. R. S. Innes* (*Aberdeen GSFP*), C. W. Drummond (*Melrose*), D. D. Mackenzie (*Edin. Univ.*); D. P. Hepburn (*Woodford*), W. D. Allardice (*Aberdeen GSFP*); R. M. Bruce (*Gordonians*), G. G. Lyall (*Gala*), W. P. Black (*Glas. HSFP*), L. R. Currie (*Dunfermline*), J. C. Dawson (*Glas. Acads.*), W. I. D. Elliot (*Edin. Acads.*), A. G. M. Watt (*Army*), J. B. Lees (*Gala*)
France: A. Alvarez (*Tyrosse*); M. Pomathios (*Agen*), L. Junques (*Bayonne*), P. Dizabo (*Tyrosse*), R. Lacaussade (*Beglais*); L. Bordenave (*Toulon*), Y. Bergougnan (*Toulouse*); E. Buzy (*Lourdes*), L. Martin (*Paloise*), L. Aristouy (*Paloise*), R. Soro (*Romans*), A. Moga (*Beglais*), J. Prat (*Lourdes*), G. Basquet* (*Agen*), J. Matheu (*Castres*)
Referee: A. S. Bean (*England*)

R. Lacaussade scored and A. Alvarez converted (0-5); W. C. W. Murdoch kicked a penalty (3-5); J. Prat dropped a penalty goal (3-8). (H.T.). T. G. H. Jackson scored but W. C. W. Murdoch failed (6-8); W. C. W. Murdoch kicked a penalty (9-8).

Scotland showed a welcome stamina and spirit after France had taken a lead at half time and after they had edged in front with some fifteen minutes to go a determined defence saw them through. The game began with an unorthodox tackle on Drummond which laid him out but after a short spell off he returned fit enough. Early on Bergougnan, who was always ready to drop at goal, sent one such kick wide of the posts to pitch over the line. Several defenders did everything but head the ball before Lacaussade nipped in to touch down. There was almost a repeat shortly after but this time Hepburn kicked dead. A break by Mackenzie was halted but, to the obvious disagreement of the French touch judge, a penalty was given and converted by Murdoch. Near half time J. Prat dropped a penalty goal 40 yards out on the touch line to put France in the lead at the interval. Scotland resumed strongly and when Alvarez failed to collect a kick ahead Innes gathered and passed to Jackson who ran some 30 yards closely chased to score. Murdoch failed here but converted a penalty for a blatant offside at a scrum and this one point lead was held for the win, although J. Prat just missed with one huge drop kick penalty. Murdoch, last capped in 1939, came in as a deputy reserve to make a fine come-back and also proved to be a welcome goal kicker. The French style of play was obviously much changed since 1931 both backs and forwards producing some adventurous handling but the pack, although heavy, were too inclined to barge at the line out and get offside in the open.

WALES 14   SCOTLAND 0
Cardiff
7 February 1948

Wales: R. F. Trott (*Cardiff*); K. J. Jones (*Newport*), B. L. Williams (*Cardiff*), W. B. Cleaver (*Cardiff*), J. Matthews (*Cardiff*); G. Davies (*Pontypridd*), H. Tanner* (*Cardiff*); C. Davies (*Cardiff*), M. James (*Cardiff*), L. Anthony (*Neath*), S. Williams (*Llanelli*), W. E. Tamplin (*Cardiff*), O. Williams (*Llanelli*), L. Manfield (*Cardiff*), G. Evans (*Cardiff*)
Scotland: W. C. W. Murdoch (*Hillhead HSFP*); T. G. H. Jackson (*London Scot.*), J. R. S. Innes* (*Aberdeen GSFP*), A. Cameron

121

(*Glas. HSFP*), D. D. Mackenzie (*Edin. Univ.*); D. P. Hepburn (*Woodford*), W. D. Allardice (*Aberdeen GSFP*); R. M. Bruce (*Gordonians*), G. G. Lyall (*Gala*), L. R. Currie (*Dunfermline*), J. C. Dawson (*Glas. Acads.*), W. P. Black (*Glas. HSFP*), W. I. D. Elliot (*Edin. Acads.*), A. G. M. Watt (*Edin. Acads.*), J. B. Lees (*Gala*)
Referee: T. N. Pearce (*England*) **Touch judges:** H. Waddell, A. Cornish

No scoring at half time. B. L. Williams scored and W. E. Tamplin converted (5-0) J. Matthews scored but W. E. Tamplin failed (8-0); W. E. Tamplin kicked a penalty (11-0); K. J. Jones scored but W. E. Tamplin failed (14-0).

Wales were clearly the better team. Their halves were in fine form and gave an active set of backs good possession. This stemmed from a vigorous Welsh pack which controlled the scrums and line outs. As a result Allardice had to do much brave defending round the mauls and his backs saw little of the ball.

Scotland started with the wind and did well enough in the loose to keep play mainly in the Welsh half but could not break through before the interval. Murdoch, too, was unsuccessful with a run of five penalty kicks. After the interval Wales with the wind and a dominating pack were clearly on top and continuous fine play by their backs gave them a clear win.

IRELAND 6   SCOTLAND 0
Lansdowne Road
28 February 1948

Ireland: J. A. D. Higgins (*Civil Service*); B. Mullan (*Clontarf*), M. O'Flanagan (*Lansdowne*), W. D. McKee (*NIFC*), B. O'Hanlon (*Dolphin*); J. W. Kyle (*Queen's*), H. de Lacy (*Harlequins*); A. A. McConnell (*Collegians*), K. D. Mullen* (*Old Belvedere*), J. C. Daly (*London Irish*), C. P. Callan (*Lansdowne*), J. E. Nelson (*Malone*), J. S. McCarthy (*Dolphin*), D. J. O'Brien (*London Irish*), J. W. McKay (*QU Belfast*)
Scotland: W. C. W. Murdoch (*Hillhead HSFP*); T. G. H. Jackson (*London Scot.*), C. W. Drummond (*Melrose*), J. R. S. Innes* (*Aberdeen GSFP*), D. D. Mackenzie (*Edin. Univ.*); D. P. Hepburn (*Woodford*), W. D. Allardice (*Aberdeen GSFP*); I. C. Henderson (*Edin. Acads.*), G. G. Lyall (*Gala*), S. Coltman (*Hawick*), L. R. Currie (*Dunfermline*), H. H. Campbell (*London Scot.*), W. I. D. Elliot (*Edin. Acads.*), W. P. Black (*Glas. HSFP*), R. M. Bruce (*Gordonians*)
Referee: C. H. Gadney (*England*) **Touch judges:** H. Waddell, I. F. Mahoney

No scoring at half time. B. Mullan scored but failed to convert (3-0); J. W. Kyle scored but B. Mullan failed (6-0).

The Irish pack laid the foundation of the win especially after half time when Scotland was continually on the defensive and it was only good tackling by their backs that kept the score down. Kyle, well supplied with the ball in the second half, kept his backs on the move. McKee made the opening for Mullan's try and following a fierce forward rush De Lacy got the ball out to Kyle who cut through to score. One other such forward rush carried the ball and Allardice some 25 yards!

SCOTLAND 6   ENGLAND 3
Murrayfield
20 March 1948

Scotland: W. C. W. Murdoch (*Hillhead HSFP*); T. G. H. Jackson (*London Scot.*), J. R. S. Innes* (*Aberdeen GSFP*), L. Bruce Lockhart (*London Scot.*), C. W. Drummond (*Melrose*); D. P. Hepburn (*Woodford*), A. W. Black (*Edin. Univ.*); I. C. Henderson (*Edin. Acads.*), G. G. Lyall (*Gala*), H. H. Campbell (*London Scot.*), W. P. Black (*Glas. HSFP*), R. Finlay (Watsonians), W. I. D. Elliot (Edin. Acads.), J. B. Lees (Gala), W. B. Young (London Scot.)
England: R. Uren (*Waterloo*); R. H. Guest (*Waterloo*), N. O. Bennett (*Un. Services*), E. K. Scott* (*Redruth*), M. F. Turner (*Blackheath*); I Preece (*Coventry*), R. J. P. Madge (*Exeter*); H. Walker (*Coventry*), A. P. Henderson (*Edin. Wrs.*), T. Price (*Gloucester*), S. V. Perry (*Camb. Univ.*), H. F. Luya (*Headingley*), M. R. Steele-Bodger (*Edin. Univ.*), R. H. G. Weighill (*RAF*), D. B. Vaughan (*Devonport Services*)
Referee: N. H. Lambert (*Ireland*) **Touch judges:** H. Waddell, H. C. Catcheside

R. Uren kicked a penalty (0-3). (H.T.). C. W. Drurnmond scored but L. B. Lockhart failed (3-3); W. B. Young scored but W. C. W. Murdoch failed (6-3).

Play never reached a great standard but England were handicapped by losing Madge after ten minutes play. Steele-Bodger took his place and was quite outstanding even after being badly dazed by a heavy tackle in the second half. Against the wind England actually held the lead at half time although Hepburn did get over with the ball but being smother tackled the referee refused the score. Early in the second half Jackson raced up to a line out and was able to start a movement finished off by Innes, giving Drummond a clear run for a good score at the corner. Later the English pack began to tire and after some slack play at a line out Young was able to grab a loose ball and charge over. After the game it was found that Scott, injured during the second half, had in fact played on with a fractured jaw.

FRANCE 0   SCOTLAND 8
Colombes
15 January 1949

France: N. Baudry (*Montferrand*); M. Pomathios (*Lyon*), M. Terreau (*Bressane*), P. Dizabo (*Tyosse*), M. Siman (*Montferrand*); L. Bordenave (*Toulon*), Y. Bergougnan (*Toulouse*); E. Buzy (*Lourdes*), M. Jol (*Biarritz*), L. Caron (*Lyon*), R. Soro (*Romans*), A. Moga (*Beglais*), J. Prat (*Lourdes*), G. Basquet* (*Agen*), J. Matheu (*Castres*)
Scotland: I. J. M. Lumsden (*Bath*); T. G. H. Jackson (*Army*), L. G. Gloag (*Camb. Univ.*), D. P. Hepburn (*Woodford*), D. W. C. Smith (*Army*); C. R. Bruce (*Glas. Acads.*), W. D. Allardice (*Aberdeen GSFP*); J. C. Dawson (*Glas. Acads.*), J. C. Abercrombie (*Edin. Univ.*), S. Coltman (*Hawick*), L. R. Currie (*Dunfermline*), G. A. Wilson (*Oxford Univ.*), D. H. Keller* (*London Scot.*), P. W. Kininmonth (*Oxford Univ.*), W. I. D. Elliot (*Edin. Acads.*)
Referee: T. N. Pearce (*England*)   **Touch judges:** H. Waddell, M. Gos

W. I. D. Elliot scored (0-3). (H.T.). P. W. Kininmonth scored and W. D. Allardice converted (0-8).

D. H. Keller had played for Australia at Murrayfield during the previous season and his selection as player and captain raised a considerable amount of controversy. France attacked for most of the game for their pack fairly shoved their opponents about, the massive Soro, Moga and Basquet being particularly tough and aggressive. Even after France lost Bergougnan with a broken collar bone after half an hour, their pack continued to dominate the scrums but although J. Prat was an admirable substitute at scrum half the French threes were too prosaic, too often passing without purpose. Scotland were quite effective in the loose and following some good defensive play by Lumsden and Hepburn a fine breakaway by the backs and forwards let Elliot open the scoring after ten minutes' play. In the second half Allardice, who had been defending well, broke away in his own half. Jackson got the ball and kicked inside for Kininmonth to collect and score. France continued to attack but could not break through although they got the ball over the line once. The referee, to the wrath of their supporters, gave the defenders the benefit of a failed touch-down.

SCOTLAND 6   WALES 5
Murrayfield
5 February 1949

Scotland: I. J. M. Lumsden (*Bath*); T. G. H. Jackson (*London Scot.*), L. G. Gloag (*Camb. Univ.*), D. P. Hepburn (*Woodford*), D. W. C. Smith (*London Scot.*); C. R. Bruce (*Glas. Acads.*), W. D. Allardice (*Aberdeen GSFP*); J. C. Dawson (*Glas. Acads.*), J. G. Abercrombie (*Edin. Univ.*), S. Coltman (*Hawick*), L. R. Currie (*Dunfermline*), G. A. Wilson (*Oxford Univ.*), D. H. Keller* (*London Scot.*), P. W. Kininmonth (*Oxford Univ.*), W. I. D. Elliot (*Edin. Acads.*)
Wales: R. F. Trott (*Cardiff*), K. J. Jones (*Newport*), J. Matthews (*Cardiff*), B. L. Williams (*Cardiff*), T. Cook (*Cardiff*); G. Davies (*Camb. Univ.*), H. Tanner* (*Cardiff*); T. G. Jones (*Newport*) E. Colman (*Newport*), W. H. Travers (*Newport*), D. Jones (*Swansea*), J. A. Gwilliam (*Camb. Univ.*), A. Meredith (*Devonport Services*), G. Evans (*Cardiff*), J. R. G. Stephens (*Neath*), W. R. Cole (*Newbridge*).
Referee: N. H. Lambert (*Ireland*)   **Touch judges:** D. A. Thom, J. W. Faull

L. G. Gloag scored but W. D. Allardice failed (3-0). (H.T.). D. W. C. Smith scored but L. R. Currie failed (6-0); B. I. Williams scored and R. F. Trott converted (6-5).

Again the Scottish pack were beaten in the line out and scrums but their fiendishly aggressive back row, with Elliot quite outstanding, fairly demolished the Welsh attacks. Davies took a tremendous hammering and with the Scottish threes also tackling well, a formidable Welsh attack never really got on the move. The Scottish pack, however, were quite effective with their work in the loose

123

yet it was at a line out where Allardice nipped through a gap and good interplay between Hepburn and Elliot finished with Gloag scoring. In the second half Wales continued their fruitless attacking but Smith twice intercepted passes and had one 50 yards dash before the Olympic sprinter, Jones, could catch him. After some loose play Dawson picked up and sent Smith off from midfield. This time he got over before Jones could tackle. With five minutes to go Tanner threw a long pass to B. Williams who jinked his way through a crowded defence to score a great try. The conversion reduced Scotland's lead to a point but a confident defence saw them through. This game was threatened by a thick fog which, however, lifted shortly before the kick off.

SCOTLAND 3　IRELAND 13
Murrayfield
26 February 1949

Scotland: I. J. M. Lumsden (*Bath*); T. G. H. Jackson (*London Scot.*), L. G. Gloag (*Camb. Univ.*), D. P. Hepburn (*Woodford*), D. W. C. Smith (*London Scot.*), C. R. Bruce (*Glas Acads.*), W. D. Allardice (*Aberdeen GSFP*); J. C. Dawson (*Glas. Acads.*), J. G. Abercrombie (*Edin. Univ.*), S. Coltman (*Hawick*), L. R. Currie (*Dunfermline*), A. M. Thomson (St *Andrews Univ.*), D. H. Keller* (*London Scot.*), P. W. Kininmonth (*Oxford Univ.*), W. I. D. Elliot (*Edin. Acads.*)
Ireland: G. W. Norton (*Bective Rangers*); B. O'Hanlan (*Dolphin*), N. J. Henderson (*QU Belfast*), W. D. McKee (*NIFC*), M. F. Lane (*UC Cork*); J. W. Kyle (*Queen's*), E. Strathdee (*Queen's*); T. Clifford (*Young Munster*), K. Mullen* (*Old Belvedere*), L. Griffin (*Wanderers*), J. E. Nelson (*Malone*), R. D. Agar (*Malone*), J. W. McKay (*Queen's*), D. J. O'Brien (*London Irish*), J. S. McCarthy (*Dolphin*)
Referee: A. S. Bean (*England*)　**Touch judges:** D. A. Thom, O. F. Murray

J. S. McCarthy scored and G. W. Norton converted (0-5). (H.T.). G. W. Norton kicked a penalty (0-8); J. S. McCarthy scored and G. W. Norton converted (0-13), W. D. Allardice kicked a penalty (3-13).

The Scottish pack failed to harass the Irish halves. Not only did the Irish pack rather dominate affairs but Kyle made use of good possession by kicking to touch until a winning lead had been established. In contrast the Scottish halves were always under pressure and their backs got little chance to shine. Elliot had one good run in the first half. On reaching the full back he kicked ahead just before he was heavily tackled and laid out but no obstruction was given.

ENGLAND 19　SCOTLAND 3
Twickenham
19 March 1949

England: W. B. Holmes (*Camb. Univ.*); R. D. Kennedy (*Camborne*), C. B. Van Ryneveld (*Oxford Univ.*), L. B. Cannell (*Oxford Univ.*), R. H. Guest (*Waterloo*); I Preece* (*Coventry*), W. K. T. Moore (*Leicester*); B. H. Travers (*Harlequins*), D. B. Vaughan (*Headingley*), V. G. Roberts (*Penryn*), G. R. D. Hosking (*Devonport Services*), J. R. C. Matthews (*Harlequins*), J. M. Kendall-Carpenter (*Oxford Univ.*), J. H. Steeds (*Middlesex Hospital*), T. W. Price (*Cheltenham*)
Scotland: I. J. M. Lumsden (*Bath*); T. G. H. Jackson (*London Scot.*), L. G. Gloag (*Camb. Univ.*), D. P. Hepburn (*Woodford*), W. D. C. Smith (*Army*); C. R. Bruce (*Glas. Acads.*) W. D. Allardice (*Aberdeen GSFP*); S. T. H. Wright (*Stewart's FP*), J. A. R. Macphail (*Edin Acads.*), S. Coltman (*Hawick*), L. R. Currie (*Dunfermline*), G. A. Wilson (*Oxford Univ.*) D H Keller* (*London Scot.*), P. W. Kininmonth (*Oxford Univ.*), W. I. D. Elliot (*Edin. Acads.*)
Referee: N. H. Lambert (*Ireland*)　**Touch judges:** D. A. Thom, H. A. Haigh-Smith

R. D. Kennedy scored but W. B. Holmes failed (3-0). (H.T.). C. B. Van Ryneveld scored and B. H. Travers converted (8-10); G. A. Wilson kicked a penalty (8-3); G. B. Van Rynefeld, G. R. D. Hosking and R. H. Guest scored, B. H. Travers converted the second only (19-3).

The teams were introduced to the Duke of Edinburgh. During the first half the Scottish pack did quite well in the open but their backs could not break through a firm and speedy defence. Later on the English forwards were on top and their backs attacked well. After 25 minutes Jackson, who started with a suspect knee, became very lame and as far as possible took the non-open wing position. Early on Kennedy went past Jackson and got over only to be brought back for a foot in touch. Then Roberts broke away at mid field and Van Ryneveld put Kennedy in. Early in the second

124

half Lumsden fielded a cross kick by Preece but was brought down by two attackers. Van Ryneveld scooped up the ball and scored. After a Wilson penalty England pressed continually and good handling play by both forwards and backs produced two more good tries.

SCOTLAND 8 FRANCE 5
Murrayfield
14 January 1950

Scotland: G. Burrell (*Gala*); D. W. C. Smith (*Army*), R. Macdonald (*Edin. Univ.*), D. A. Sloan (*Edin. Acads.*), C. W. Drummond (*Melrose*); L. Bruce Lockhart (*London Scot.*), A. F. Dorward (*Camb. Univ.*); J. C. Dawson (*Glas. Acads.*), J. G. Abercrombie (*Edin. Univ.*), G. M. Budge (*Edin. Wrs.*), D. E. Muir (*Heriot's FP*), R. Gemmill (*Glas. HSFP*), W. I. D. Elliot* (*Edin. Acads.*), P. W. Kininmonth (*Richmond*), D. H. Keller (*Sheffield*)
France: R. Arcalis (*Brive*); M. Pomathios (*Lyon OU*), J. Merquey (*Toulon*), P. Dizabo (*RCF*), M. Siman (*Castres O*); P Lauga (*Vichy*), G. Dufau (*RCF*); P. Lavergne (*Limoges*), L. Martin (*Paloise*), P. Aristouy (*Paloise*), R. Ferrien (*Tarbais*), F. Bonnus (*Toulon*), J. Prat (*Lourdes*), G. Basquet* (*Agen*), R. Bienes (*Cognac*)
Referee: T. Jones (*Wales*)   **Touch judges:** J. R. S. Innes, R. Lerou

R. Macdonald and G. M. Budge scored and L. B. Lockhart converted the second only (8-0). (H.T.). J. Merquey scored and J. Prat converted (8-5).

Scotland were more emphatic winners than the score suggests although J. Prat in the last minutes nearly saved the match with a drop kick penalty from 50 yards out which narrowly missed. The Scottish pack were on top but the French pack were distinctly fast about the field yet as a team they seemed to have abandoned a running game for a more defensive and destructive style. Budge had a good game and was surprisingly mobile for a prop of his size. After half an hour's play Scotland scored twice; first Budge and Bruce Lockhart combined to put Macdonald over and almost at once Drummond and Dawson put Budge in.

The French pack livened up in the second half and were helped a little when Burrell, Keller and Aristouy were all dazed in the one collision. Burrell went off for a while and Kininmonth deputised at full back. Towards the end Siman broke away, his crosskick beat Smith, and Merquey ran in for a converted try. About this time Arcalis was badly dazed when he halted Elliot who would have scored to make the score more appropriate and Scotland got a fright when J. Prat, 50 yards out, narrowly missed that drop kick from a penalty award.

WALES 12   SCOTLAND 0
Swansea
4 February 1950

Wales: B. J. Jones (*Devonport Services*); K. J. Jones (*Newport*), J. Matthews (*Cardiff*) M. C. Thomas (*Newport*), W. Major (*Maesteg*); W. B. Cleaver (*Cardiff*), W. R. Willis (*Cardiff*), C. Davies (*Cardiff*), D. M. Davies (*Somerset Police*), J. D. Robins (*Birkenhead Park*), R. John (*Neath*), J. D. Hayward (*Newbridge*), W. R. Cole (*Pontypool*), J. A. Gwilliam* (*Edin. Wrs.*), R. T. Evans (*Newport*)
Scotland: G. Burrell (*Gala*); D. W. C. Smith (*Army*), R. Macdonald (*Edin. Univ.*), D. A. Sloan (*Edin. Acads.*), C. W. Drummond (*Melrose*); L. Bruce Lockhart (*London Scot.*), A. W. Black (*Edin. Univ.*); J. C. Dawson (*Glas. Acads.*), J. G. Abercrombie (*Edin. Univ.*) G. M. Budge (*Edin. Wrs.*), D. E. Muir (*Heriot's FP*), R. Gemmill (*Glas. HSFP*), W. I. D. Elliot* (*Edin. Acads.*), P. W. Kininmonth (*Richmond*), D. H. Keller (*Sheffield*)
Referee: M. J. Dowling (*Ireland*)   **Touch judges:** J. R. S. Innes, V. Griffiths

M. C. Thomas scored but B. L. Jones failed (3-0). (H.T.). B. L. Jones kicked a penalty (6-0); K. J. Jones scored but B. L. Jones failed (9-0); W. B. Cleaver dropped a goal (12-0).

Scotland did some early attacking which was held by a solid defence. Then rather against the run of play Matthews (who was always dangerous) had a strong run which finished with Thomas scoring. In the second half Wales were clearly on top but both packs concentrated on spoiling tactics which produced a tiresome stream of penalties for offside and obstruction. Jones had kicked a goal from one before Matthews placed a kick ahead into the corner which Jones got to first for a score, and Cleaver finished the scoring with a drop goal.

125

IRELAND 21   SCOTLAND 0
Lansdowne Road
25 February 1950

Ireland: G. W. Norton (*Bective Rangers*); L. Crowe (*Old Belvedere*), J. Blayney (*Wanderers*), R. J. H. Uprichard (*RAF*), M. F. Lane (*UC Cork*); J. W. Kyle (*Queen's*), R. Carroll (*Lansdowne*); T. Clifford (*Young Munster*), K. D. Mullen* (*Old Belvedere*), D. McKibbin (*Instonians*), J. E. Nelson (*Malone*), J. Maloney (*UC Dublin*), A. B. Curtis (*Oxford Univ.*), D. J. O'Brien (*London Irish*), J. W. McKay (*Queen's*)
Scotland G. Burrell (*Gala*); D. W. C. Smith (*Army*), R. Macdonald (*Edin. Univ.*), C. W. Drummond (*Melrose*), D. M. Scott (*Langholm*); A. Cameron (*Glas. HSFP*), A. W. Black (*Edin. Univ.*); J. C. Dawson (*Glas. Acads.*), J. G. Abercrombie (*Edin. Univ.*), G. M. Budge (*Edin. Wrs.*), D. E. Muir (*Heriot's FP*), R. Gemmill (*Glas. HSFP*), W. I. D. Elliot* (*Edin. Acads.*), P. W. Kininmonth (*Richmond*), D. H. Keller (*Sheffield*)
Referee: T. N. Pearce (*England*)   **Touch judges:** R. W. Shaw. B. V. Fox

G. W. Morton kicked two penalties (6-0). (H.T.). J. Blayney, A. B. Curtis and L. Crowe scored and G. W. Norton converted all three (21-0).

This was Scotland's biggest defeat in Dublin. Nothing went right whereas Ireland picked up everything that was going and Norton was right on target with his kicking. Scotland started brightly enough and produced one spectacular run by Drummond, Cameron, Macdonald and Smith which finished close to the line but they gradually faded. In the second half the Irish forwards were clearly on top. Even with the wind Scotland could not get moving whereas Ireland ran in three good tries.

SCOTLAND 13   ENGLAND 11
Murrayfield
18 March 1950

Scotland: T. Gray (*Northampton*); C. W. Drummond (*Melrose*), R. Macdonald (*Edin. Univ.*), D. A. Sloan (*Edin. Acads.*), D. M. Scott (*Langholm*); A. Cameron (*Glas. HSFP*), A. W. Black (*Edin. Univ.*); J. C. Dawson (*Glas. Acads.*), J. G. Abercrombie (*Edin. Univ.*), G. M. Budge (*Edin. Wrs.*), D. E. Muir (*Heriot's FP*), R. Gemmill (*Glas. HSFP*), W. I. D. Elliot (*Edin. Acads.*), P. W. Kininmonth* (*Richmond*), H. Scott (*St Andrews Univ.*)
England: M. B. Hofmeyr (*Oxford Univ.*); J. P. Hyde (*Army*), B. Boobyer (*Oxford Univ.*), L. B. Cannell (*Oxford Univ.*), J. V. Smith (*Camb. Univ.*); I. Preece* (*Coventry*), W. K. T. Moore (*Leicester*); J. L. Baume (*Army*), J. H. Steeds (*Saracens*), W. A. Holmes (*Nuneaton*) J. R. C. Matthews (*Harlequins*), S. J. Adkins (*Coventry*), H. D. Small (*Oxford Univ.*), J. M. Kendall-Carpenter (*Oxford Univ.*), V. G. Roberts (*Penryn*)
Referee: M. J. Dowling (*Ireland*)   **Touch judges:** J. R. S. Innes, G. Warden

D. A. Sloan scored but T. Gray failed (3-0); J. V. Smith scored but M. B. Hofmeyr failed (3-3); J. G. Abercrombie scored and T. Gray converted (8-3). (H.T.). M. B. Hofmeyr kicked a penalty (8-6); J. V. Smith scored and M. B. Hofmeyr converted (8-11); D. A. Sloan scored and T. Gray converted (13-11).

The Scottish forwards took some credit for the win; beaten in the scrums, they were good in the loose and finished very strongly. Continual rain made handling difficult but Hofmeyr fielded and kicked immaculately. After fifteen minutes an English passing movement broke down near their line; Scott and Sloan dribbled the ball in for the latter to be credited with the score. Within three minutes a rush by the English forwards put the defence in a tangle and when the ball rolled over the line, Smith, a fast and alert winger, got there first to score. Two minutes later Black broke away and, getting the ball again after Cameron was held, passed to Abercrombie who scored near the posts. Straight after the break Hofmeyr kicked a fine long range penalty and within ten minutes England took the lead. Preece placed a fine kick to the corner flag and Smith's pace allowed him to score. Hofmeyr converted with a fine kick. Scotland fought on until right on time some fine foot work by the Scottish forwards let Cameron get the ball and he put in a towering kick which Sloan ran on to and in spite of a mass of defenders got the ball and scored. In pelting rain Gray converted from half way to the touch-line and the whistle went almost immediately after.

126

FRANCE 14   SCOTLAND 12
Colombes
13 January 1951

France: A. J. Alvarez (*Tyrosse*); A. Porthault (*RCF*), M. Terreau (*Bressane*), G. Brun (*Vienne*), M. Pomathios (*Lyon*); J. Carabignac (*Agen*), G. Dufau (*RCF*); R. Bernard (*Bergerac*), P. Pascalin (*Mont-de-Marsan*), R. Bienes (*Cognac*), L. Mias (*Mazamet*), H. Foures (*Toulouse*), J. Prat (*Lourdes*), G. Basquet* (*Agen*), J. Matheu (*Castres*)
Scotland: T. Gray (*Northampton*); A. D. Cameron (*Hillhead HSFP*), I. D. F. Coutts (*Old Alleynians*), F. O. Turnbull (*Kelso*), D. M. Rose (*Jedforest*); A. Cameron (*Glas. HSFP*), I. A. Ross (*Hillhead HSFP*); J. C. Dawson (*Glas. Acads.*) N. G. R. Mair (*Edin. Univ*) R. L. Wilson (*Gala*), H. M. Inglis (*Edin. Acads.*), R. Gemmill (*Glas. HSFP*), W. I. D. Elliot (*Edin. Acads.*), P. W. Kininmonth* (*Richmond*), J. J. Hegarty (*Hawick*)
Referee: T. N. Pearce (*England*)   **Touch judges:** R. W. Shaw, R. Le Roux

J. Prat kicked a penalty (3-0); T. Gray kicked a penalty (3-3); L. Mias scored but A. J. Alvarez failed (6-3); T. Gray kicked a penalty (6-6). (H.T.). D. M. Rose scored twice but T. Gray failed (6-12); A. Porthault scored and J. Prat converted (11-12); J. Prat kicked a penalty (14-12).

Scotland played nine new caps which included a whole new three quarter line while France had five new men. Scotland started well, the backs handling and running whenever possible but could only score by Gray's penalty kicks, two of which counted while a third struck the inside of an upright yet managed to rebound into play. The early French try followed a good touch-line run by Brun and his crosskick fell amongst the mass of the French pack for Mias to score. Prat's kick narrowly missed but the score board registered the full points for the remainder of the game and perhaps it was fortunate that Prat's final kick actually did win the match! After the interval Scotland forged ahead with two tries by Rose stemming from openings made by Coutts and Elliot but with 15 minutes left the French pack rose to the occasion. A fine rush put the ball past the defence over the line and Pomathios, who had been a constant threat, was able to race in to touch down. The try was magnificently converted by Prat but it needed an equally good penalty kick by him in the last minutes to win the match.

SCOTLAND 19   WALES 0
Murrayfield
3 February 1951

Scotland: I. H. M. Thomson (*Heriot's FP*), R. Gordon (*Edin. Wrs.*), D. A. Sloan (*Edin. Acads.*), D. M. Scott (*Langholm*), D. M. Rose (*Jedforest*); A. Cameron (*Glas. HSFP*), I. A. Ross (*Hillhead HSFP*); J. C. Dawson (*Glas. Acads.*), N. G. R. Mair (*Edin. Univ.*), R. L. Wilson (*Gala*), R. Gemmill (*Glas. HSFP*), H. M. Inglis (*Edin. Acads.*), W. I. D. Elliot (*Edin. Acads.*), P. W. Kininmonth* (*Richmond*), R. C. Taylor (*Kelvinside-West*)
Wales: G. Williams (*Llanelli*); M. C. Thomas (*Devonport Services*), B. L. Jones (*Devonport Services*), J. Matthews (*Cardiff*), K. J. Jones (*Newport*); G. Davies (*Camb. Univ.*), W. R. Willis (*Cardiff*); C. Davies (*Cardiff*), D. M. Davies (*Somerset Police*), J. D. Robins (*Birkenhead Park*), E. R. John (*Neath*), D. J. Hayward (*Newbridge*), A. Forward (*Pontypool*), J. A. Gwilliam* (*Edin. Wrs.*), R. T. Evans (*Newport*)
Referee: M. J. Dowling (*Ireland*)   **Touch judges:** D. A. Thom, I. Jones

I. H. M. Thomson kicked a penalty (3-0). (H.T.). P. W. Kininmonth dropped a goal (6-0); R. Gordon scored twice and H. M. Inglis converted the first (14-0); J. C. Dawson scored and I. H. M. Thomson converted (19-0).

In front of a record crowd of some 80,000 (which included about 20,000 Welsh supporters) a young Scottish XV achieved one of the most unexpected results of the season when they demolished a formidable Welsh team which included eleven Lions from the last tour. Wales made a very confident start but found the Scottish pack continually bringing the play back into the Welsh 25 area. The Welsh forwards were well held while their backs were harassed into making mistakes. Scotland actually led at the interval by a Thomson penalty and the twenty-year-old new cap had only come into the side that morning when Gray called off with a cold. On restarting Scotland, full of confidence, stepped up the pace and persistence of their attack and determined efforts by Gordon, Elliot and Rose nearly brought scores. After twenty minutes of this pressure Williams was forced to make a hurried clearance from his own line and his kick was caught cleanly by Kininmonth standing on the touch line at the Welsh 25 flag, whereupon he steadied himself, glanced at the distant posts and then dropped what must rank as one of the historic goals in the history of the game. Badly shaken, Wales moved Lewis Jones up to half and the Welsh pack staged a furious onslaught but achieved no break through. Scotland, however, raised their game in pace and vigour and began an attack which demoralised their opponents. A break away by Scott let Gordon race in for a try and he scored again following up a dribbling run by Elliot and Taylor. The rout was completed when a rush by the Scottish forwards was finished by Dawson scoring. This excellent win was the more remarkable in that it was to be the last until the Welsh match in 1955 for Scotland was now about to enter on an appalling run of seventeen consecutive defeats.

SCOTLAND 5   IRELAND 6
Murrayfield
24 February 1951

Scotland: I. H. M. Thomson (*Heriot's FP*); K. J. Dalgleish (*Edin. Wrs.*), D. A. Sloan (*Edin. Acads.*), D. M. Scott (*Langholm*), D. M. Rose (*Jedforest*); A. Cameron (*Glas. HSFP*), I. A. Ross (*Hillhead HSFP*); J. C. Dawson (*Glas. Acads.*), N. G. R. Mair (*Edin. Univ.*), R. L. Wilson (*Gala*), H. M. Inglis (*Edin. Acads.*), R. Gemmill (*Glas. HSFP*), W. I. D. Elliot (*Edin. Acads.*), P. W. Kininmonth* (*Richmond*), R. C. Taylor (*Kelvinside-West*)
Ireland: A. W. Norton (*Bective Rangers*); M. F. Lane (*UC Cork*), R. C. Chambers (*Instonians*), N. J. Henderson (*QU Belfast*), W. H. J. Millar (*QU Belfast*); J. W. Kyle (*QU Belfast*), J. O'Meara (*UC Cork*); J. H. Smith (*QU Belfast*), K. D. Mullen* (*Old Belvedere*) D. McKibbin (*Instonians*), P. J. Lawlor (*Clontarf*), J. R. Brady (*CIYMS*), J. S. McCarthy (*Dolphin*), D. J. O'Brien (*London Irish*), J. W. McKay (*QU Belfast*)
Referee: T. N. Pearce (*England*)   **Touch judges:** J. R. S. Innes, R. R. Butler

D. A. Sloan scored and I. H. M. Thomson converted (5-0); N. J. Henderson dropped a goal (5-3). (H.T.). D. J. O'Brien scored but D. McKibbin failed (5-6).

Ireland lost Norton after fifteen minutes yet controlled play for the rest of the afternoon. The Scottish pack never gave their halves a decent supply of the ball and they were harried continually by O'Brien and McCarthy. On the other hand Kyle was well served and used the possession to great advantage. For a while Scotland attacked. Thomson missed one penalty and hit the post with another; Cameron had a drop goal disallowed for a previous knock on; from a line out, Scott broke away and Cameron and Sloan backed up for the latter to score. Before half time an Irish quick heel let Henderson drop a goal from the 25. The second half, however, was almost entirely dominated by the short handed Irish pack who maintained a tremendous pace. Lane was nearly in three times before Kyle, who was in fine form, made a diagonal run to send O'Brien over for the winning score. Scotland reacted strongly but all they could achieve were several abortive drops at goal.

ENGLAND 5   SCOTLAND 3
Twickenham
17 March 1951

England: W. G. Hook (*Gloucester*); C. G. Woodruff (*Harlequins*), A. C. Towell (*Bedford*), J. M. Williams (*Penzance-Newlyn*), V. R. Tindall (*Liverpool Univ.*); E. M. P. Hardy (*Army*), D. W. Shuttleworth (*Army*); R. V. Stirling (*RAF*), E. Evans (*Sale*), W. A. Holmes (*Nuneaton*), D. T. Wilkins (*Navy*), B. A. Neale (*Army*), V. G. Roberts (*Penryn*), J. M. Kendall-Carpenter* (*Oxford Univ.*), D. F. White (*Northampton*)
Scotland: T. Gray (*Northampton*); K. J. Dalgleish (*Edin. Wrs.*), D. A. Sloan (*Edin. Acads*), D. M. Scott (*Langholm*), D. M. Rose (*Jedforest*); A. Cameron (*Glas. HSFP*), I. A. Ross (*Hillhead HSFP*); J. C. Dawson (*Glas. Acads.*), N. G. R. Mair (*Edin. Univ.*), R. L. Wilson (*Gala*), W. P. Black (*Glas. HSFP*), H. M. Inglis (*Edin. Acads.*), W. I. D. Elliot (*Edin. Acads.*); P. W. Kininmonth* (*Richmond*), R. C. Taylor (*Kelvinside-West*)
Referee: M. J. Dowling (*Ireland*)

D. F. White scored and W. G. Hook converted (5-0). (H.T.). A. Cameron scored but H. M. Inglis failed (5-3).

This was a desperately hard and fast game on heavy going which got worse when heavy rain

128

fell during the second half. The English forwards began well especially in the loose but some good running by their backs was checked by firm tackling. Cameron, who was always difficult to stop, had a good break but Scott could not hold a difficult, if not forward, pass. England had one run which finished with Hook missing a drop at goal. Cameron broke again with Elliot and Kininmonth in support but Towell got in a saving kick to touch from his own line. Then from a slack Scottish heel White pounced on the ball, sold a dummy and scored. Hook's conversion was to win the match. In heavy rain England started the second half by attacking but the Scottish pack were constantly dangerous with dribbling rushes. England had one counter-attack when Roberts was narrowly beaten to the touch by Gray. With five minutes left some more aggression by the Scottish pack let Cameron score near the corner, too far out for Inglis to overcome the distance and conditions.

SCOTLAND 0   SOUTH AFRICA 44
Murrayfield
24 November 1951

Scotland: G. Burrell (*Gala*); J. G. M. Hart (*London Scot.*), D. M. Scott (*London Scot.*), F. O. Turnbull (*Kelso*), D. M. Rose (*Jedforest*); A. Cameron* (*Glas. HSFP*), A. F. Dorward (*Gala*); J. C. Dawson (*Glas. Acads.*), J. A. R. Macphail (*Edin. Acads.*), R. L. Wilson (*Gala*), H. M. Inglis (*Edin. Acads.*), J. Johnston (*Melrose*), W. I. D. Elliot (*Edin. Acads.*), P. W. Kininmonth (*Richmond*), R. C. Taylor (*Kelvinside Acads.*)
South Africa: J. Buchler (*T*); F. Marais (*Boland*), R. Van Schoor (*Rhodesia*), M. T. Lategan (*WP*), P. Johnstone (*WP*); J. D. Brewis (*NT*), P. W. Du Toit (*NT*); A. Geffin (*T*), W. Delport (*EP*), C. Kock (*Boland*), C. J. Van Wyk (*T*), J. Du Rand (*Rhodesia*), E. Dinkelman (*NT*), S. P. Fry (*WP*), H. Muller* (*T*)
Referee: M. J. Dowling (*Ireland*)   **Touch judges:** R. W. Shaw, S. S. Viviers

J. Du. Rand, R. Van Schoor and C. Koch scored and A. Geffin converted the last two (0-13); J. D. Brewis dropped a goal (0-16); C. Koch scored but A. Geffin failed (0-19). (H.T.). W. Delport, C. J. Van Wyk, H. Muller, M. T. Lategan and E. Dinkelman scored and A. Geffin converted the lot (0-44).

This became known as the Murrayfield Massacre – a defeat so devastating that in retrospect it seemed to inflict a wound on Scottish rugby that took four seasons to heal. In fine conditions Scotland for some fifteen minutes held their opponents and even had one dangerous break headed by Elliot. Then suddenly their weaknesses were piteously exposed and the game exploded into a magnificent exhibition of combined handling and attacking play by the South African backs and forwards, backed up by some accurate goal kicking by A. Geffin who converted seven of the nine tries scored. The South African play was described as seven-a-side rugby played by fifteen men and there is a much-quoted comment made by a dazed Scottish supporter who was asked later what the score was and answered '44-0 and we were bloody lucky to get nothing'.

SCOTLAND 11   FRANCE 13
Murrayfield
12 January 1952

Scotland: I. H. M. Thomson (*Heriot's FP*); R. Gordon (*Edin. Wrs.*), I. F. Cordial (*Edin. Wrs.*), J. L. Allan (*Melrose*), D. M. Scott (*London Scot.*); J. N. G. Davidson (*Edin. Univ.*), A. K. Fulton (*Edin. Univ.*); J. C. Dawson (*Glas. Acads.*), N. M. Munnoch (*Watsonians*), J. Fox (*Gala*), M. Walker (*Oxford Univ.*), J. Johnston (*Melrose*), W. I. D. Elliot (*Edin. Acads.*), P. W. Kininmonth* (*Richmond*), J. T. Greenwood (*Dunfermline*)
France: R. Labarthete (*Pau*); G. Brun (*Vienne*), M. Prat (*Lourdes*), R. Marune (*Lourdes*), F. Cazenave (*Mont-de-Marsan*); R. Furcade (*Perpignan*), P. Lasaosa (*Dax*); R. Brejassou (*Tarbes*), P. Labadie (*A Bayonnais*), R. Bienes (*Cognac*), B. Chevallier (*Montferrand*), F. Varenne (*RCF*), J. Prat (*Lourdes*), G. Basquet* (*Agen*), J. R. Bourdeu (*Lourdes*)
Referee: I. David (*Wales*)   **Touch judges:** J. R. S. Innes, A. Verger

I. H. M. Thomson kicked a penalty (3-0); J. Prat kicked a penalty (3-3); J. Prat scored and converted (3-8). (H.T.). I. H. M. Thomson kicked a penalty (6-8); G. Basquet scored and J. Prat converted (6-13); I. F. Cordial scored and I. H. M. Thomson converted (11-13).

Each side played eight new caps and France won at Murrayfield for the first time. An early penalty by Thomson was matched by a 45 yard kick by J. Prat who, before the interval, supported a break by his brother to score a try which he also converted. After the interval Gordon had one good 40 yards run down the touch line which was halted by J. Prat but the game really came to life in the last ten minutes. Lasaosa went off down the blind side. Again J. Prat was in support and passed to Basquet who knocked two defenders aside before scoring. Scotland came back at once and after a line out a passing run by the Scottish halves was finished by Cordial scoring. Thomson's conversion left Scotland two points behind but time ran out on them. For France J. Prat was outstanding as a breakaway forward and goal kicker while for Scotland Elliot again showed up in attack and cover defence.

WALES 11   SCOTLAND   0
Cardiff
2 February 1952

Wales: G. Williams (*Llanelli*); K. J. Jones (*Newport*), M. C. Thomas (*Newport*), B. L. Williams (*Cardiff*), A. G. Thomas (*Cardiff*); C. I. Morgan (*Cardiff*), W. R. Willis (*Cardiff*); W. O. Williams (*Swansea*), D. M. Davies (*Somerset Police*), D. J. Hayward (*Newbridge*), E. R. John (*Neath*), J. R. G. Stephens (*Neath*), L. Blyth (*Swansea*), J. A. Gwilliam* (*Edin. Wrs.*), A. Forward (*Pontypool*)
Scotland: I. H. M. Thomson (*Heriot's FP*); R. Gordon (*Edin. Wrs.*), I. F. Cordial (*Edin. Wrs.*), J. L. Allan (*Melrose*), D. M. Scott (*London Scot*); J. N. G. Davidson (*Edin. Univ.*), A. F. Dorward (*Gala*); J. C. Dawson (*Glas. Acads.*), N. M. Munnoch (*Watsonians*), J. Fox (*Gala*), J. Johnston (*Melrose*), D. E. Muir (*Heriot's FP*), W. I. D. Elliot (*Edin. Acads.*), H. M. Inglis (*Edin. Acads.*), P. W. Kininmonth* (*Richmond*)
Referee: M. J. Dowling (*Ireland*)   **Touch judges:** D. A. Thom, D. Jones

M. C. Thomas kicked a penalty (3-0); K. J. Jones scored and M. C. Thomas converted (8-0). (H.T.). M. C. Thomas kicked a penalty (11-0).

Although defeated this was actually a most creditable display by Scotland. The Welsh centres seemed handicapped by a soft slippery surface and their scrummaging was not good. It was really M. C. Thomas' place kicking which won the match. The only try stemmed from a strong diagonal run by A. G. Thomas; K. J. Jones moved inside and took a long pass to break clear at full pace. In the second half Scott, Davidson and Kininmonth came close to scoring but the latter was overtaken by Jones short of the line.

IRELAND 12   SCOTLAND   8
Lansdowne Road
23 February 1952

Ireland: J. G. M. W. Murphy (*Dublin Univ.*); W. H. J. Millar (*QU Belfast*), N. J. Henderson (*QU Belfast*), J. R. Notley (*Wanderers*), M. J. Lane (*UC Cork*); J. W. Kyle (*QU Belfast*), J. A. O'Meara (*UC Cork*); T. Clifford (*Young Munster*), K. D. Mullen (*Old Belvedere*), J. H. Smith (*Collegians*), P. J. Lawlor (*Clontarf*), A. O'Leary (*Cork Const.*), M. Dargan (*Old Belvedere*), D. J. O'Brien* (*Cardiff*), J. S. McCarthy (*Dolphin*)
Scotland: I. H. M. Thomson (*Heriot's FP*); R. Gordon (*Edin. Wrs.*), I. F. Cordial (*Edin. Wrs.*), J. L. Allan (*Melrose*), D. M. Scott (*London Scot.*); J. N. G. Davidson (*Edin. Univ.*), A. F. Dorward (*Gala*); J. C. Dawson (*Glas. Acads.*), N. M. Munnoch (*Watsonians*), J. Fox (*Gala*), J. Johnston (*Melrose*), D. E. Muir (*Heriot's FP*), W. I. D. Elliot (*Edin. Acads.*), H. M. Inglis (*Edin. Acads.*), P. W. Kininmonth* (*Richmond*)
Referee: J. Davies (*Wales*)   **Touch judges:** D. A. Thom, R. Mitchell

I. H. M. Thomson kicked a penalty (0-3); N. J. Henderson kicked a penalty (3-3); M. F. Lane and J. W. Kyle scored but N. J. Henderson failed to convert (9-3); J. N. G. Davidson scored and I. H. M. Thomson converted (9-8). (H.T.). N. J. Henderson scored but failed to convert (12-8).

Scotland had an excellent start when right away Thomson kicked a penalty but this was matched almost at once by Henderson. After ten minutes O'Meara went off round the blind side; O'Brien backed up and sent an unmarked Lane in for a try. With Ireland doing well in the scrums, Henderson broke away but was brought down and from the resultant maul Kyle went clean through for a fine solo try. At this stage Lane had to go off with a broken wrist. Just short of half time a good run by Inglis, Kininmonth, Dawson and Fox put Kininmonth clear to give Davidson a try at the posts.

Soon after the interval O'Meara broke away again and sent the ball over the line. A hurried clearance by a defender fell into Millar's hands and a pass to Henderson saw him score at the corner and also get the conversion. The rest of the game was an even struggle with no scoring.

SCOTLAND 3   ENGLAND 19
Murrayfield
15 March 1952

Scotland: N. W. Cameron (*Glas. Univ.*), R. Gordon (*Edin. Wrs.*), I. F. Cordial (*Edin. Wrs.*), I. D. F. Coutts (*Old Alleynians*), T. G. Weatherstone (*Stewart's FP*); J. N. G. Davidson (*Edin. Univ.*), A. F. Dorward* (*Gala*); J. C. Dawson (*Glas. Acads.*), J. Fox (*Gala*), J. M. Inglis (*Selkirk*), J. Johnston (*Melrose*), D. E. Muir (*Heriot's FP*), W. I. D. Elliot (*Edin. Acads.*), J. P. Friebe (*Glas. HSFP*), D. S. Gilbert-Smith (*London Scot.*)
England: P. J. Collins (*Camborne*); C. E. Winn (*Rosslyn Park*), B. Boobyer (*Rosslyn Park*), A. E. Agar (*Harlequins*), J. E. Woodward (*Wasps*); N. M. Hall* (*Richmond*), P. W. Sykes (*Wasps*); W. A. Holmes (*Nuneaton*), E. Evans (*Sale*), R. V. Stirling (*RAF*), J. R. C. Matthews (*Harlequins*), D. T. Wilkins (*RN*), D. F. White (*Northampton*), J. M. Kendall-Carpenter (*Penzance-Newlyn*), A. O. Lewis (*Bath*)
Referee: M. J. Dowling (*Ireland*) **Touch judges:** D. A. Thom, J. B. G. Whittaker

C. E. Winn scored and N. M. Hall converted (0-5). (H.T.). E. Evans, J. E. Woodward and J. M. Kendall-Carpenter scored and N. M. Hall converted the last (0-16); J. Johnston scored but N. W. Cameron failed (3-16); A. E. Agar dropped a goal (3-19).

The Scottish forwards worked hard but not as a pack, whilst the handling of the backs was most uncertain. From one breakdown early on Agar got the ball and broke through the confused defence. A cross kick went to Winn who ran through two tackles to score. Scotland lost further chances by bad handling although Weatherstone was nearly over once. England also had some good runs but there was no further scoring before half time. On restarting the Scottish passing continued to be poor but England improved as a striking force. Twice Boobyer, using the dummy, ran well and Winn nearly scored from the second. From a line out and maul Evans dived over. Further good running brought scores by Woodward and White and then in the closing minute Johnston scored after a forward rush but Agar finished the match with a drop goal.

FRANCE 11   SCOTLAND 5
Colombes
10 January 1953

France: J. Rouan (*Narbonne*); M. Pomathios (*Bressane*), J. Dauger (*Bayonne*), M. Prat (*Lourdes*), A. Porthault (*RCF*); J. Carabignac (*Agen*), G. Dufau (*RCF*); A. Sanac (*Perpignan*), P. Labadie (*Bayonne*), P. Bertrand (*Bressane*), P. Tignol (*Toulouse*), L. Mias (*Mazamet*), J. Prat* (*Lourdes*), R. Bienes (*Cognac*), J. R. Bourdeu (*Lourdes*)
Scotland: N. W. Cameron (*Glas. Univ.*); K. J. Dalgleish (*Camb. Univ.*), D. A. Sloan (*London Scot*), D. M. Scott (*Watsonians*), D. M. Rose (*Jedforest*); J. N. G. Davidson (*Edin. Univ.*), A. F. Dorward* (*Gala*); B. E. Thomson (*Oxford Univ.*), J. H. F. King (*Selkirk*), R. L. Wilson (*Gala*), J. H. Henderson (*Oxford Univ.*), J. J. Hegarty (*Hawick*), A. R. Valentine (*RNAS*), D. C. Macdonald (*Edin. Univ.*), K. H. D. McMillan (*Sale*)
Referee: O. B. Glasgow (*Ireland*)

P. Bertrand kicked a penalty (3-0); J. Carabignac dropped a goal (6-0); D. M. Rose scored and N. W. Cameron converted (6-5). (H.T.). J. R. Bourdeu scored and P. Bertrand converted (11-5).

The pitch was treacherous after frost, snow and sleet. The recast Scottish pack did remarkably well against a heavier and much more experienced set but the Scottish backs were disappointing both in attack and defence. The French were very fast on to the man and the ball but their back play was rather stereotyped. After an early penalty goal Carabignac got the ball from a loose maul and from a long range dropped a rather speculative goal. Before half time a forward rush let Dorward pass to Rose who beat two defenders for a good score. Cameron's conversion kept the game very open. France resumed strongly and missed two chances of scoring before Hegarty, Sloan and

131

MacDonald took play up to the French 25. Then some fine running by France brought play back and a quick heel started another burst of short sharp passing which produced a splendid try by Bourdeu. Scotland fought back; Valentine broke clear, Henderson carried on and passed to Rose who got to the corner flag but could not manage to ground the ball.

SCOTLAND 0   WALES 12
Murrayfield
7 February 1953

Scotland: N. W. Cameron (*Glas. Univ.*); R. Gordon (*Edin. Wrs.*), K. J. Dalgleish (*Camb. Univ.*), J. L. Allan (*Melrose*), D. M. Rose (*Jedforest*); J. N. G. Davidson (*Edin. Univ.*), A. F. Dorward* (*Gala*); B. E. Thomson (*Oxford Univ.*), J. H. F. King (*Selkirk*), R. L. Wilson (*Gala*), J. H. Henderson (*Oxford Univ.*), J. J. Hegarty (*Hawick*), A. R. Valentine (*RNAS*), D. C. Macdonald (*Edin. Univ.*), K. H. D. McMillan (*Sale*).
Wales: T. J. Davies (*Devonport Services*); G. M. Griffiths (*Cardiff*), B. L. Williams* (*Cardiff*), A. G. Thomas (*Cardiff*), K. J. Jones (*Newport*); C. I. Morgan (*Cardiff*), W. R. Willis (*Cardiff*), W. O. G. Williams (*Devonport Services*); G Beckingham (*Cardiff*), C. C. Meredith (*Neath*), J. R. G. Stephens (*Neath*), E. R. John (*Neath*), S. Judd (*Cardiff*), R. J. Robins (*Royal Signals*), R. C. C. Thomas (*Coventry*).
Referee: P. F. Cooper (*England*)   **Touch judges:** J. Graham, D. G. Williams

T. J. Davies kicked a penalty (0-3); K. J. Jones scored but T. J. Davies failed (0-6). (H.T.). B. L. Williams scored twice but T. J. Davies failed (0-12).

Wales were too heavy forward and too alert in the backs yet in what was mainly a forward battle the Scottish pack held its own in the scrums and loose play. Both sets of backs struggled against good defensive play by the forwards.

After a Davies penalty a punt ahead by Morgan fell awkwardly for Cameron. Jones kicked the ball up to the line and had the pace to beat the defence. In the second half Willis hurt his shoulder; went off, came back but again had to retire. Both Welsh tries stemmed from poor Scottish passing. From one loose pass Williams started a passing movement and kept up to get a scoring pass from Jones. Later he snapped up another blind pass and ran some 30 yards to score.

SCOTLAND 8   IRELAND 26
Murrayfield
28 February 1953

Scotland: I. H. M. Thomson (*Army*); T. G. Weatherstone (*Stewart's FP*), A. Cameron* (*Glas. HSFP*), D. Cameron (*Glas. HSFP*), D. W. C. Smith (*London Scot.*); L. Bruce Lockhart (*London Scot.*), K. M. Spence (*London Scot.*); B. E. Thomson (*Oxford Univ.*), G. C. Hoyer-Millar (*Oxford Univ.*), J. H. Wilson (*Watsonians*), J. H. Henderson (*Oxford Univ.*), J. J. Hegarty (*Hawick*), A. R. Valentine (*RNAS*), E. H. Henriksen (*RHSFP*), K. H. D. McMillan (*Sale*)
Ireland: R. J. Gregg (*QU Belfast*); S. J. Byrne (*Lansdowne*), N. J. Henderson (*QU Belfast*), K. Quinn (*Old Belvedere*), M. Mortell (*Bective Rangers*); J. W. Kyle* (*NIFC*), J. A. O'Meara (*UC Cork*), F. E. Anderson (*QU Belfast*), R. Roe (*Dublin Univ.*), W. A. O'Neill (*UC Dublin*), J. R. Brady (*CIYMS*), T. E. Reid (*Garryowen*), W. E. Bell (*Collegians*), J. R. Kavanagh (*UC Dublin*), J. S. McCarthy (*Dolphin*)
Referee: I. David (*Wales*)   **Touch judges:** Dr J. R. S. Innes, C. G. Morton

J. S. McCarthy and S. J. Byrne scored and R. J. Gregg converted both (0-10). (H.T.). S. Byrne scored and R. J. Gregg converted (0-15); I. H. M. Thomson kicked a penalty (3-15); R. Kavanagh scored but R. J. Gregg failed (3-18), J. H. Henderson scored and I. H. M. Thomson converted (8-18); M. Mortell and S. Byrne scored and R. J. Gregg converted the second (8-26).

The Irish forwards were good in the line out and loose play with McCarthy much in evidence and although Kyle was well held his backs were much too fast for their opponents. Bad tackling helped Ireland to score twice before half time although O'Meara's pass to put McCarthy in was suspiciously forward.

Ireland restarted strongly and a dropped pass was picked up by Quinn who sent Byrne in for his second score. Thomson then kicked a penalty before Weatherstone had a fine 40 yards run but when he was tackled Kyle got the ball and started off a fine passing run which let Kavanagh score.

132

A fierce revival by the Scottish pack let Lockhart attempt a drop which was charged down but regaining the ball he started some swift passing that let Henderson score This effort died away and Kyle began a good passing movement which involved half a dozen players before Byrne went over for his third try.

ENGLAND 26   SCOTLAND 8
Twickenham
21 March 1953

England: N. M. Hall* (*Richmond*); R. C. Bazley (*Waterloo*), W. P. C. Davies (*Harlequins*), J. Butterfield (*Northampton*), J. E. Woodward (*Wasps*); M. Regan (*Liverpool*), D. W. Shuttleworth (*Army*); R. V. Stirling (*RAF*), E. Evans (*Sale*), W. A. Holmes (*Nuneaton*), D. T. Wilkins (*RN*), S. J. Adkins (*Coventry*), A. O. Lewis (*Bath*), J. M. K. Kendall-Carpenter (*Bath*), D. F. White (*Northampton*)
Scotland: I. H. M. Thomson (*Army*); T. G. Weatherstone (*Stewart's FP*), A. Cameron* (*Glas. HSFP*), D. Cameron (*Glas. HSFP*), J. S. Swan (*Army*); L. Bruce Lockhart (*London Scot.*), A. F. Dorward (*Gala*); J. C. Dawson (*Glas. Acads.*), J. H. F. King (*Selkirk*), R. L. Wilson (*Gala*), J. H. Henderson (*Oxford Univ.*), J. J. Hegarty (*Hawick*), W. Kerr (*London Scot.*), W. L. K. Cowie (*Edin. Wrs.*), K. H. D. McMillan (*Sale*)
Referee: M. J. Dowling (*Ireland*)   **Touch judges:** J. Graham, Col. G. Warden

R. C. Bazley scored and N. M. Hall converted (5-0); T. G. Weatherstone scored but A. Cameron failed (5-3); R. C. Bazley and S. J. Adkins scored but N. M. Hall failed (11-3). (H.T.). R. V. Stirling and J. Butterfield scored and N. M. Hall converted both (21-3); J. H. Henderson scored and I. H. M. Thomson converted (21-8); J. E. Woodward scored and N. M. Hall converted (26-8).

Again the Scottish centres were guilty of bad marking and tackling. For fifteen minutes Scotland pressed missing two penalties but there was no real attacking power and all that resulted were three wild drops at goal. Then White made a fine break carried on by Regan who was tackled short of the line but the movement was continued and a cross-kick to Bazley saw him beat two defenders to score. After some further English pressure Weatherstone broke away twice down the touch line. On the second run he crosskicked for Dorward to get possession and the ball went via Cameron back to Weatherstone who scored at the corner. However continued forward pressure by England was rewarded by some good passing runs which produced two tries before half time.

On restarting the pressure was maintained and a somewhat demoralised Scottish defence gave away two tries inside ten minutes. A. Cameron then came up to stand-off and one break was carried on by Lockhart supported by Dawson and Henderson who finished by scoring. Before the close Woodward scored a fine try, running from near midfield and handing off a series of defenders.

SCOTLAND 0   FRANCE 3
Murrayfield
9 January 1954

Scotland: J. C. Marshall (*London Scot.*); J. S. Swan (*London Scot.*), A. D. Cameron (*Hillhead HSFP*), D. Cameron (*Glas. HSFP*), T. G. Weatherstone (*Stewart's FP*); J. N. G. Davidson* (*Edin. Univ.*), A. K. Fulton (*Dollar Acads.*); T. P. L. McGlashan (*RHSFP*), R. K. G. MacEwen (*Camb. Univ.*), H. F. McLeod (*Hawick*), E. A. J. Fergusson (*Oxford Univ.*), E. J. S. Michie (*Aberdeen Univ.*), A. Robson (*Hawick*), P. W. Kininmonth (*Richmond*), J. H. Henderson (*Richmond*)
France: M. Vannier (*RCF*); L. Roge (*Beziers*), R. Martine (*Lourdes*), J. Bouquet (*Bourgoin*), M. Pomathios (*Bourg-en-Bresse*); A. Labazuy (*Lourdes*), G. Dufau (*RCF*); R. Bienes (*Cognac*), P. Labadie (*Bayonne*), R. Brejassou (*Tarbes*), B. Chevallier (*Montferrand*), L. Mias (*Mazamet*), H. Domec (*Lourdes*), R. Baulon (*Vienne*), J. Prat* (*Lourdes*)
Referee: I. David (*Wales*)   **Touch judges:** R. W. Shaw, R. Paries

No scoring at half time. R. Brejassou scored (0-3).

Scotland were a shade unlucky to lose but although a new pack showed promise the backs were weak. The halves suffered badly from much destructive tackling by the French forwards so there was much kicking to touch and little combined play. Scotland began briskly, playing some good open rugby and Weatherstone nearly scored. Then France came on to their game with speedy backing up and close passing and but for a forward pass and a knock-on would have scored twice.

Weatherstone had another fine run from midfield and his pace and determination took him past Pomathios only to stumble and lose the ball short of the line. Shortly after the interval Labazuy got the ball from some loose play, broke away and passed to Pomathios who sent Brejasson off on a clear run in for the only score of the game.

SCOTLAND 0   NEW ZEALAND 3
Murrayfield
13 February 1954

Scotland: J. C. Marshall (*London Scot.*), J. S. Swan (*London Scot.*), M. K. Elgie (*London Scot.*), D. Cameron (*Glas. HSFP*), T. G. Weatherstone (*Stewart's FP*); G. T. Ross (*Watsonians*), L. P. MacLachlan (*Oxford Univ.*), T. P. L. McGlashan (*RHSFP*), R. K. G. MacEwen (*Camb. Univ.*), H. F. McLeod (*Hawick*), E. A. J. Fergusson (*Oxford Univ.*), E. J. S. Michie (*Aberdeen Univ.*), W. I. D. Elliot* (*Edin. Acads.*), P. W. Kininmonth (*Richmond*), J. H. Henderson (*Richmond*)
New Zealand: R. W. H. Scott (*Auckland*); R. A. Jarden (*Wellington*), C. J. Loader (*Wellington*), M. J. Dixon (*Canterbury*), D. D. Wilson (*Canterbury*); L. S. Haig (*Otago*), K. Davis (*Auckland*); P. Eastgate (*Canterbury*), R. C. Hemi (*Waikato*), K. L. Skinner (*Otago*), W. H. Clark (*Wellington*), R. A. White (*Poverty Bay*), G. N. Dalzell (*Canterbury*), P. F. H. Jones (*North Auckland*), R. C. Stuart* (*Canterbury*)
Referee: I. David (*Wales*)   **Touch judges:** Dr J. R. S. Innes, J. T. Fitzgerald

No scoring at half time. R. W. H. Scott kicked a penalty (0-3).

This was another game that Scotland did not deserve to lose. Their pack, badly outweighted, was never out-scrummaged in any phase of the play. Elliot made a quite outstanding return to the team. With their pack held in the tight and often outplayed in the open, the New Zealand backs' limitations were exposed. The Scottish tackling was very sound and killed any attempt at running the ball. The Scottish backs, however, were equally well held but did appear smarter at snapping up chances. Before the interval Ross put out a long pass to Weatherstone and a reverse pass to Elgie let Swan away to be held short of the line. After the restart Ross had one cross kick which Weatherstone kicked on over the line only to be narrowly beaten to the touch down. Then Scott took a penalty some 30 yards out and eight yards in from the touch and the kick fairly scraped over the bar for the only score of the game. The Scottish pack still hammered away and one rush did get the ball over the line but again Weatherstone just could not get there first.

IRELAND 6   SCOTLAND 0
Ravenhill, Belfast
27 February 1954

Ireland: R. J. Gregg (*QU Belfast*); M. Mortell (*Bective Rangers*), N. J. Henderson (*NIFC*), R. P. Godfrey (*UC Dublin*), J. T. Gaston (*Dublin Univ.*); S. Kelly (*Lansdowne*), J. A. O'Meara (*Dolphin*); F. E. Anderson (*QU Belfast*), R. Roe (*Dublin Univ.*), B. G. M. Wood (*Garryowen*), R. H. Thompson (*Instonians*), P. J. Lawler (*Clontarf*), G. F. Reidy (*Lansdowne*), J. R. Kavanagh (*Wanderers*), J. S. McCarthy* (*Dolphin*)
Scotland: J. C. Marshall (*London Scot.*); J. S. Swan (*London Scot.*), M. K. Elgie (*London Scot.*), D. Cameron (*Glas HSFP*), T. G. Weatherstone (*Stewart's FP*); G. T. Ross (*Watsonians*), L. P. MacLachlan (*London Scot.*); T. P. L. McGlashan (*RHSFP*), R. K. G. MacEwen (*Camb. Univ.*), H. F. McLeod (*Hawick*), E. A. J. Fergusson (*Oxford Univ.*), E. J. S. Michie (*Aberdeen Univ.*), W. I. D. Elliot* (*Edin. Acads.*), P. W. Kininmonth (*Richmond*), J. H. Henderson (*Richmond*)
Referee: V. Parfitt (*Wales*)

M. Mortell scored, (3-0). (H.T.). M. Mortell scored (6-0).

This was a poor game between two disappointing sides. The only noticeable incidents were the two Irish tries for both sides kicked too much and there was a spate of penalties. In the first half Kavanagh, on his own line, threw a long pass to Gaston who ran some 100 yards before kicking ahead. Three Scots failed to gather the ball and Godfrey picked up, passed to Henderson who sent Mortell in for the try. In the second half Kelly, going off on the blind side, ran 40 yards up to Marshall and a timely pass saw Mortell score again. Scotland lost MacEwen in the second half with a damaged knee. This game was played at Ravenhill in Belfast.

SCOTLAND 3   ENGLAND 13
Murrayfield
20 March 1954

Scotland: J. C. Marshall (*London Scot.*); J. S. Swan (*London Scot.*), M. K. Elgie (*London Scot.*), D. Cameron (*Glas. HSFP*), T. G. Weatherstone (*Stewart's FP*); G. T. Ross (*Watsonians*), L. P. MacLachlan (*Oxford Univ.*); T. P. L. McGlashan (*RHSFP*), J. H. F. King (*Selkirk*), H. F. McLeod (*Hawick*), E. A. J. Fergusson (*Oxford Univ.*), E. J. S. Michie (*Aberdeen Univ.*), W. I. D. Elliot* (*Edin. Acads.*), P. W. Kininmonth (*Richmond*), J. H. Henderson (*Richmond*)
England: N. Gibbs (*Harlequins*); J. E. Woodward (*Wasps*), J. Butterfield (*Northampton*), J. P. Quinn (*New Brighton*), C. E. Winn (*Rosslyn Park*); M. Regan (*Liverpool*), G. Rimmer (*Waterloo*); R. V. Stirling* (*RAF*), E. Robinson (*Coventry*), D. L. Sanders (*Ipswich YMCA*), P. D. Young (*Dublin Wanderers*), J. F. Bance (*Bedford*), D. S. Wilson (*Metropolitan Police*), V. H. Leadbetter (*Edin. Wrs.*), A. R. Higgins (*Army*)
Referee: O. B. Glasgow (*Ireland*)   **Touch judges:** Dr J. R. S. Innes, W. N. Gillmore

P. D. Young scored and N. Gibbs converted (0-5). (H.T.). D. S. Wilson scored and N. Gibbs converted (0-10); M. K. Elgie scored but J. C. Marshall failed (3-l0); D. S. Wilson scored but N. Gibbs failed (3-13).

The English backs were clearly superior whilst their pack slowly improved as the game progressed; D. S. Wilson in particular showed speed and initiative to score twice. For fifteen minutes the Scots held their own and better goal kicking could have given them the lead, for the English passing was shaky and one interception by Cameron nearly produced a score. Then Marshall was stranded by an awkward bounce during a forward rush and Robinson threw a pass to Young who ran twenty yards to score. Cameron had one break through to put Weatherstone away down the touch only to be well tackled by Young short of the corner flag. On the restart Elliot broke away from the loose and his final kick ahead found touch at the corner but nothing came of it. A counter attack saw Butterfield cover 40 yards to cross the line only to be bundled into touch in goal. Then a fast run by Quinn and Regan found Wilson up to score his first try. Cameron caught Quinn in possession and Elgie successfully chased a long boot ahead to score. In the last minutes a slow heel and pass back let Wilson dash in, intercept and be over the line before the defence could come alive.

WALES 15   SCOTLAND 3
Swansea
10 April 1954

Wales: V. Evans (*Neath*); K. J. Jones* (*Newport*), G. M. Griffiths (*Cardiff*), B. L. Williams (*Cardiff*), R. Williams (*Llanelli*); C. I. Morgan (*Cardiff*), W. R. Willis (*Cardiff*); C. C. Meredith (*Neath*), B. V. Meredith (*St. Lukes*), W. O. G. Williams (*Swansea*), R. H. Williams (*Llanelli*), R. J. Robins (*Pontypridd*), R. C. C. Thomas (*Swansea*), S. Judd (*Cardiff*), L. Davies (*Llanelli*)
Scotland: J. C. Marshall (*London Scot.*); J. S. Swan (*London Scot.*), M. K. Elgie (*London Scot.*), A. D. Cameron (*Hillhead HSFP*), T. G. Weatherstone (*Stewart's FP*); G. T. Ross (*Watsonians*), L. P. MacLachan (*Oxford Univ.*); T. P. L. McGlashan (*RHSFP*), R. K. G. MacEwen (*Camb. Univ.*), H. F. McLeod (*Hawick*), E. A. J. Fergusson (*Oxford Univ.*) J. W. Y. Kemp (*Glas. HSFP*), W. I. D. Elliot* (*Edin. Acads.*), P. W. Kininmonth (*Richmond*), J. H. Henderson (*Richmond*)
Referee: P. F. Cooper (*England*)   **Touch judges:** R. W. Shaw, I. Jones

R. H. Williams and B. V. Meredith scored but V. Evans failed to convert (6-0). (H.T.). R. Williams scored but V. Evans failed (9-0); V. Evans kicked a penalty (12-0); C. I. Morgan scored but S. Judd failed (15-0); J. H. Henderson scored but M. K. Elgie failed (15-3).

This match had been postponed from January because of frost and was the last to be played on the historic St Helen's ground. Although four tries were scored the Welsh attack was not too convincing. They attacked continually during the first half but took 35 minutes to open the scoring and then it was a forward who went over from a short line out at the corner. Just before half time another forward, B. V. Meredith, took a pass from Robins to score. The Scottish pack, not so good at the line out, were doing well enough otherwise. In the second half Elliot had one burst, catching Evans who fumbled his kick ahead into the sun, but Morgan managed to clear. For once a good passing run put Ray Williams in at the corner and after an Evans penalty, Morgan kicked hard along the ground past Marshall and just beat Weatherstone to the touch down. With ten minutes to go Kininmonth and Fergusson got the ball across the line but missed the touch. Then Ross nearly put Henderson over. Evans managed to get a kick in but Marshall fielded and gave an inside pass to Elgie who sent Henderson in for the final score.

FRANCE 15   SCOTLAND 0
Colombes
8 January 1955

France: M. Vannier (*RCF*); J. Lepatey (*Mazamet*), L. Roge (*Beziers*), M. Prat (*Lourdes*), A. Boniface (*Montois*); R. Martine (*Lourdes*), G. Dufau (*RCF*), A. Domenech (*Vichy*), J. Labadie (*Bayonne*), R. Brejassou (*Tarbes*), B. Chevallier (*Montferrand*), J. Barthe (*Lourdes*), J. Prat* (*Lourdes*), M. Celaya (*Biarritz*), H. Domec (*Lourdes*)
Scotland: A. Cameron (*Glas. HSFP*); J. S. Swan (*London Scot.*), M. K. Elgie (*London Scot.*), M. L. Grant (*Harlequins*), T. G. Weatherstone (*Stewart's FP*); J. T. Docherty (*Glas. HSFP*), A. F. Dorward (*Gala*); H. F. McLeod (*Hawick*), W. K. L. Relph (*Stewart's FP*), I. R. Hastie (*Kelso*), J. J. Hegarty (*Hawick*), J. W. Y. Kemp (*Glas. HSFP*), H. Duffy (*Jedforest*), J. T. Greenwood* (*Dunfermline*), A. Robson (*Hawick*)
Referee: H. B. Elliot (*England*)

A. Boniface scored (3-0); M. Vannier kicked a penalty (6-0); J. Prat scored (9-0). (H.T.). A. Domenech and G. Dufau scored (15-0).

The French team was in tremendous form, continually indulging in brilliant and bewildering movements in which the speed and handling even of their heavier forwards was noticeable. Scotland never really looked like scoring and on the odd occasions when they got into an attacking position they were met by a most merciless defence. Only Kemp, especially at the line out, with McLeod and Robson came in for any commendation. The French pack was so much in control that Dufau could vary his tactics as he pleased and J. Prat, hardly needing to push, had a happy afternoon joining in all the handling moves.

SCOTLAND 14   WALES 8
Murrayfield
5 February 1955

Scotland: A. Cameron* (*Glas. HSFP*); A. R. Smith (*Camb. Univ.*), M. K. Elgie (*London Scot.*), R. G. Charters (*Hawick*), J. S. Swan (*London Scot.*); J. T. Docherty (*Glas. HSFP*), J. A. Nichol (*RHSFP*), H. F. McLeod (*Hawick*), W. K. L. Relph (*Stewart's FP*), T. Elliot (*Gala*), E. J. S. Michie (*Aberdeen Univ.*), J. W. Y. Kemp (*Glas. HSFP*), W. S. Glen (*Edin. Wrs.*), J. T. Greenwood (*Dunfermline*), A. Robson (*Hawick*)
Wales: A. B. Edwards (*London Welsh*), K. J. Jones (*Newport*), G. T. Wells (*Cardiff*), A. G. Thomas (*Llanelli*), T. J. Brewer (*London Welsh*); C. I. Morgan (*Bective Rangers*), W. R. Willis* (*Cardiff*); W. O. Williams (*Swansea*), B. V. Meredith (*Newport*), C. C. Meredith (*Neath*), R. J. Robins (*Pontypridd*), R. H. Williams (*Llanelli*), S. Judd (*Cardiff*), J. R. G. Stephens (*Neath*), R. C. C. Thomas (*Swansea*)
Referee: M. J. Dowling (*Ireland*)   **Touch judges:** C. W. Drummond, I. Jones

T. J. Brewer scored (0-3). (H.T.). A. R. Smith scored but M. K. Elgie failed (3-3); J. T. Docherty dropped a goal (6-3); M. K. Elgie kicked a penalty (9-3); T. J. Brewer scored and J. R. G. Stephens converted (9-8); J. A. Nichol scored and M. K. Elgie converted (14-8).

At last Scotland broke the disheartening run of defeats with another unexpected win over Wales at Murrayfield. Wales began ominously well, for inside five minutes a well placed diagonal kick by Morgan laid the line wide open for Brewer to score. The success of this manoeuvre seemed to influence Morgan since he repeated it rather too often without success although passing movements just failed to put Brewer and K. J. Jones over before half time. On restarting the Scottish pack began a vigorous recovery showing a welcome mood of aggression especially in the loose. Suddenly Robson threw a pass to A. R. Smith hemmed in on the right touch line. The winger ran some 30 yards, shaking off a couple of tackles, punted the ball over Edward's head, tapped the ball on by foot and then picked it up to go in at the corner for one of the finest solo tries ever seen at Murrayfield. This fairly lifted the Scots and inside fifteen minutes they increased their lead by Docherty's drop and Elgie's penalty. Wales struck back when Morgan set his backs away and Stephen's conversion of a

136

try by Brewer put them back in the game. However, the Scottish pack battled on and from a scrum near the Welsh line Willis was forced to throw back a bad pass which missed Morgan. Like a flash Nichol went past him to score the clinching try.

SCOTLAND 12   IRELAND 3
Murrayfield
26 February 1955

Scotland: R. W. T. Chisholm (*Melrose*); A. R. Smith (*Camb. Univ.*), M. K. Elgie (*London Scot.*), R. G. Charters (*Hawick*), J. S. Swan (*Coventry*), A Cameron* (*Glas HSFP*), J. A. Nichol (*RHSFP*); H. F. McLeod (*Hawick*), W. K. L. Relph (*Stewart's FP*), T. Elliot (*Gala*), E. J. S. Michie (*Aberdeen Univ.*), J. W. Y. Kemp (*Glas. HSFP*), I. A. A. MacGregor (*Hillhead HSFP*), J. T. Greenwood (*Dunfermline*), A. Robson (*Hawick*)
Ireland: W. R. Tector (*Wanderers*); A. C. Pedlow (*QU Belfast*), A. J. F. O'Reilly (*Old Belvedere*), N. J. Henderson (*NIFC*), R. E. Roche (*UC Galway*); S. Kelly (*Lansdowne*) S. J. McDermott (*London Irish*); P. J. O'Donoghue (*Bective Rangers*), R. Roe (*Lansdowne*), F. E. Anderson (*NIFC*), T. E. Reid (*London Irish*), M. N. Madden (*Sunday's Well*), D. A. McSweeney (*Blackrock*), R. H. Thompson* (*London Irish*), M. J. Cunningham (*UC Cork*)
Referee: L. M. Boundy (*England*)   **Touch judges:** G. G. Crerar, A. Archer

S. Kelly kicked a penalty (0-3); M. K. Elgie kicked a penalty (3-3); J. S. Swan scored but M. K. Elgie failed (6-3). (H.T.). A. Cameron dropped a goal (9-3); M. K. Elgie kicked a penalty (12-3).

Scotland thoroughly deserved to win and indeed the margin would have been greater had Elgie not been off form with his place kicking. Docherty having called off, Cameron moved up to half and, more or less ignoring his threes, concentrated on some tactical kicking which sadly troubled the Irish defence. He was helped in this by the power of the pack, McLeod in the scrums, Kemp in the line out and Robson in the loose all being particularly effective. The backs not seen in attack nevertheless defended well – one report noted that young O'Reilly had the makings of a good player! Near the interval, with the score level Swan intercepted a pass and sprinted about 40 yards diagonally away from everyone for his try. During the second half, Scotland remained clearly on top and after Cameron had fielded a drop out and replied with a drop goal, Elgie added a penalty to finish the scoring.

ENGLAND 9   SCOTLAND 6
Twickenham
19 March 1955

England: N. S. D. Estcourt (*Blackheath*); F. D. Sykes (*Northampton*), J. Butterfield (*Northampton*), W. P. C Davies (*Harlequins*), R. C. Bazley (*Waterloo*); D. G. S. Baker (*OMT*), J. E. Williams (*Old Millhillians*); G. W D. Hastings (*Gloucester*), N. A. Labuschagne (*Guy's*), D. St. G. Hazell (*Leicester*), P. D. Young* (*Wanderers*), P. G. Yarranton (*Wasps*), D. S. Wilson (*Metropolitan Police*), I. D. S. Beer (*Harlequins*), R. Higgins (*Liverpool*)
Scotland: R. W. T. Chisholm (*Melrose*); A. R. Smith (*Camb. Univ.*), M. K. Elgie (*London Scot.*), R. G. Charters (*Hawick*), J. S. Swan (*Coventry*), A. Cameron* (*Glas. HSFP*), J. A. Nichol (*RHSFP*); H. F. McLeod (*Hawick*), W. K. L. Relph (*Stewart's FP*), T. Elliot (*Gala*), E. J. S. Michie (*Aberdeen Univ.*), J. W. Y. Kemp (*Glas. HSFP*), I. A. A. MacGregor (*Hillhead HSFP*), J. T. Greenwood (*Dunfermline*), A. Robson (*Hawick*)
Referee: D. C. Joynson (*Wales*)   **Touch judges:** C. W. Drummond, E. V. Barnes

D S. Hazell kicked a penalty (3-0); F. D. Sykes scored but D. S. Hazell failed (6-0); A. Cameron dropped a penalty (6-3); I. D. S. Beer scored but D. S. Hazell failed (9-3). (H.T.). A. Cameron scored but M. K. Elgie failed (9-6).

Once again Scotland came to Twickenham and failed to lift the Triple Crown. A heavy English pack started well and their backs ran in two tries before the interval. Yet Scotland had some bad luck for an awkward bounce robbed Swan of a try and Elgie had several narrow misses with penalties. Cameron's penalty came from a majestic drop kick taken some 45 yards out. The Scottish pack greatly improved after the break but the only score started with Chisholm, who took a kick ahead and shot through a startled mass of attackers to pass to Cameron. He set Elgie off on a dummying run right up to the right hand corner and from some loose play Cameron got the ball again. This time he lifted a high kick to the posts and from the ensuing loose play Nichol broke on the blind side and passed to Cameron whose momentum sent him through a mass of defenders.

SCOTLAND 12   FRANCE 0
Murrayfield
14 January 1956

Scotland: R. W. T. Chisholm (*Melrose*); A. R. Smith (*Camb. Univ.*), A. Cameron* (*Glas. HSFP*), K. R. Macdonald (*Stewart's FP*), J. S. Swan (*Coventry*); M. L. Grant (*Harlequins*), N. M. Campbell (*London Scot.*); H. F. McLeod (*Hawick*), R. K. G. MacEwen (*London Scot.*), T. Elliot (*Gala*), E. J. S. Michie (*Aberdeen GSFP*), J. W. Y. Kemp (*Glas. HSFP*), I. A. A. MacGregor (*Llanelli*), J. T. Greenwood (*Dunfermline*), A. Robson (*Hawick*)
France: M. Vannier (*RCF*); J. Dupuy (*Tarbes*), A. Boniface (*Mont-de- Marsan*), G. Stener (*Paris Univ.*), S. Torreilles (*Perpignan*); J. Bouquet (*Vienne*), G. Dufaur (*RCF*); A. Domenech (*Brive*), R. Vigier (*Montferrand*), R. Bienes (*Cognac*), B. Chevallier (*Montferrand*), G. Roncaries (*Perpignan*), J. Carrere (*Vichy*), M. Celaya (*Biarritz*), R. Baulon (*Bayonne*)
Referee: M. J. Dowling (*Ireland*)   **Touch judges:** R. F. Kelly, S. Saulnier

A. R. Smith kicked a penalty (3-0); A. Cameron kicked a penalty (6-0). (H.T.). J. W. Y. Kemp scored twice but A. Cameron failed to convert (12-0).

On a wet murky day some traditional Scottish forward play was most effective, many fierce well controlled rushes greatly upsetting the French defence, yet Scotland could only manage two penalties before half time. In the second half, however, Kemp scored twice, once after a tremendous heave by the pack on the French line and later when Campbell broke to give him a scoring pass. During this half a great run by the French pack only finished when Bienes was heaved into touch at the corner flag.

WALES 9   SCOTLAND 3
Cardiff
4 February 1956

Wales: G. D. Owen (*Newport*); K. J. Jones (*Newport*), H. P. Morgan (*Newport*), M. C. Thomas (*Newport*), C. L. Davies (*Cardiff*); C. I. Morgan* (*Cardiff*), D. O. Brace (*Newport*); W. O. G. Williams (*Swansea*), B. V. Meredith (*Newport*), R. Prosser (*Pontypool*), R. H. Williams (*Llanelli*), J. R. G. Stephens (*Neath*), R. C. C. Thomas (*Swansea*), L. H. Jenkins (*Newport*), B. Sparks (*Neath*)
Scotland: R. W. T. Chisholm (*Melrose*), A. R. Smith (*Camb. Univ.*), A. Cameron* (*Glas. HSFP*), K. R. Macdonald (*Stewart's FP*), J. S. Swan (*Coventry*); M. L. Grant (*Harlequins*), N. M. Campbell (*London Scot.*); H. F. McLeod (*Hawick*), R. K. G. MacEwen (*London Scot.*), T. Elliot (*Gala*), E. J. S. Michie (*Aberdeen GSFP*), J. W. Y. Kemp (*Glas. HSFP*) I. A. A. MacGregor (*Llanelli*), J. T. Greenwood (*Dunfermline*), A. Robson (*Hawick*)
Referee: L. M. Boundy (*England*)   **Touch judges:** C. W. Drummond, J. Jones

H. P. Morgan scored but G. D. Owen failed (3-0); A. Cameron kicked a penalty (3-3); C. L. Davies scored but G. D. Owen failed (6-3). (H.T.). C. I. Morgan scored but G. D. Owen failed (9-3).

The ground was only made playable by the use of dozens of braziers kept burning throughout the night and it looked a sorry mess when play began on a surface made treacherous by a misty rain. These conditions greatly troubled the Scottish halves and centres but in contrast Morgan fairly sparkled at half and continually set his backs attacking. The Scottish pack and the neglected wingers could be absolved for the defeat.

IRELAND 14   SCOTLAND 10
Lansdowne Road
25 February 1956

Ireland: P. J. Berkery (*Lansdowne*); A. C. Pedlow (*QU Belfast*), A. J. F. O'Reilly (*Old Belvedere*), N. J. Henderson* (*NIFC*), W. J. Hewitt (*Instonians*); J. W. Kyle (*NIFC*), J. A. O'Meara (*Dolphin*); W. B. Fagan (*Moseley*), R. Roe (*London Irish*), B. G. M. Wood (*Garryowen*), B. M. Guerin (*Galwegians*), L. M. Lynch (*Lansdowne*), C. T. J. Lydon (*Galwegians*), J. R. Kavanagh

(*Wanderers*), M. J. Cunningham (*Cork Const.*)
Scotland: R. W. T. Chisholm (*Melrose*); A. R. Smith (*Camb. Univ.*), T. McClung (*Edin. Acads.*), K. R. Macdonald (*Stewart's FP*), J. S. Swan (*Coventry*), A. Cameron* (*Glas. HSFP*), A. F. Dorward (*Gala*); H. F. McLeod (*Hawick*), R. K. G. MacEwen (*London Scot.*), T. Elliot (*Gala*), E. J. S. Michie (*Aberdeen GSFP*), J. W. Y. Kemp (*Glas. HSFP*) I. A. A. McGregor (*Llanelli*), J. T. Greenwood (*Dunfermline*), A. Robson (*Hawick*)
Referee: H. B. Elliott (*England*)   **Touch judges:** G. G. Crerar, J. A. Deacy

N. J. Henderson and A. J. O'Reilly scored but A. C. Pedlow failed (6-0); E. J. S. Michie scored and T. McClung converted (6-5). (H.T.). J. A. O'Meara scored and A. C. Pedlow converted (10-5); A. R. Smith scored and T. McClung converted (11-10); J. W. Kyle scored but A. C. Pedlow failed (14-10).

Almost at once Hewitt was over but called back for a forward pass and then Cameron, concussed in a tackle, went off and a reshuffle brought McClung to half, Swan to centre with MacGregor on the wing. Kyle was able to make use of some greater freedom and Henderson had one fine solo try while making another for O'Reilly. Before the interval Smith had a good run and his kick ahead was kicked on by Kemp for Michie to get the touch. After half time Macdonald made an opening for a Smith score but the Irish halves each engineered a good solo try. The short handed Scottish pack did not fade but the cover defence was weakened.

SCOTLAND 6   ENGLAND 11
Murrayfield
17 March 1956

Scotland: R. W. T. Chisholm (*Melrose*); A. R. Smith (*Camb. Univ.*), J. T. Docherty (*Glas. HSFP*), G. D. Stevenson (*Hawick*), J. S. Swan (*Coventry*); T. McClung (*Edin. Acads.*), A. F. Dorward (*Gala*); H. F. McLeod (*Hawick*), R. K. G. MacEwen (*London Scot.*), T. Elliot (*Gala*), E. J. S. Michie (*Aberdeen GSFP*), J. W. Y. Kemp (*Glas. HSFP*), I. A. A. MacGregor (*Llanelli*), J. T. Greenwood* (*Dunfermline*), A. Robson (*Hawick*)
England: D. F. Allison (*Coventry*); J. E. Woodward (*Wasps*), J. Butterfield (*Northampton*), L. B. Cannell (*St Mary's*), P. H. Thompson (*Headingley*); M. Regan (*Liverpool*), J. E. Williams (*Old Millhillians*); D. L. Sanders (*Harlequins*), E. Evans* (*Sale*), C. R. Jacobs (*Northampton*), R. W. D. Marques (*Camb. Univ.*), J. D. Currie (*Oxford Univ.*), P. G. D. Robbins (*Oxford Univ.*), A. Ashcroft (*Waterloo*), V. G. Roberts (*Harlequins*)
Referee: M. J. Dowling (*Ireland*)   **Touch judges:** A. W. Wilson, B. S. Mills

J. D. Currie kicked a penalty (0-3); J. E. Williams scored and J. D. Currie converted (0-8); A. R. Smith kicked a penalty (3-8); J. D. Currie kicked a penalty (3-11); G. D. Stevenson scored but T. McClung failed (6-11). (H.T.).

In perfect conditions England deserved their success but were not too convincing for if Scotland had carried a goal kicker they could have won – at least five penalties were missed in a disappointing and scoreless second half. Again the Scottish pack did well in the first half and were noticeably dangerous as the game went on. However although the backs defended well they were not much seen in attack.

FRANCE 0   SCOTLAND 6
Colombes
12 January 1957

France: M. Vannier (*RCF*); J. Dupuy (*Tarbes*), L. Roge (*Beziers*), M. Prat (*Lourdes*), A. Boniface (*Montois*); J. Bouquet (*Vienne*), G. Dufau (*RCF*); A. Domenech (*Brive*), R. Vigier (*Montferrand*), H. Lazies (*Toulouse*), B. Chevallier (*Montferrand*), A. Sanac (*Perpignan*), R. Baulon (*Bayonne*), M. Celaya* (*Biarritz*), J. Barthe (*Lourdes*)
Scotland: K. J. F. Scotland (*Royal Signals*); A. R. Smith (*Camb. Univ.*), E. McKeating (*Heriot's FP*), G. D. Stevenson (*Hawick*), J. S. Swan (*Coventry*); M. L. Grant (*Harlequins*), A. F. Dorward (*Gala*); H. F. McLeod (*Hawick*), R. K. G. MacEwan (*London Scot.*), T. Elliot (*Gala*), E. J. S. Michie (*London Scot.*), J. W. Y. Kemp (*Glas. HSFP*), I. A. A. MacGregor (*Llanelli*), J. T. Greenwood* (*Perthshire Acads.*), A. Robson (*Hawick*)
Referee: L. M. Boundy (*England*)   **Touch judges:** W. C. W. Murdoch, R. B. Marie

No scoring at half time. K. J. F. Scotland dropped a goal and kicked a penalty (0-6).

France made a belligerent start but even after losing MacEwen after two minutes play the depleted Scottish pack held their own without him and was clearly on top after he returned some fifteen minutes later. About this time heavy rain began and continued to the end of the game. Barthe and Baulon, when not conducting a private feud with MacGregor, gave the Scottish halves a hard time and Grant, under the conditions, closed up the game. The backs defended solidly as did the new full back, Scotland. In the second half he dropped a calculated goal from 30 yards out and completed the scoring with an equally lengthy penalty.

SCOTLAND 9   WALES 6
Murrayfield
2 February 1957

Scotland: K. J. F. Scotland (*Royal Signals*); A. R. Smith (*Camb. Univ.*), E. McKeating (*Heriot's FP*), K. R. Macdonald (*Stewart's FP*), J. S. Swan (*Coventry*), T. McClung (*Edin. Acads.*), A. F. Dorward (*Gala*); H. F. McLeod (*Hawick*), R. K. G. MacEwen (*London Scot.*), T. Elliot (*Gala*), E. J. S. Michie (*London Scot.*), J. W. Y. Kemp (*Glas. HSFP*), I. A. A. MacGregor (*Hillhead HSFP*), J. T. Greenwood* (*Perthshire Acads.*), A. Robson (*Hawick*)
Wales: T. J. Davies (*Llanelli*); K. J. Jones (*Newport*), G. M. Griffiths (*Cardiff*), M. C. Thomas* (*Newport*), G. Howells (*Llanelli*); C. I. Morgan (*Cardiff*), L. H. Williams (*Cardiff*); C. C. Meredith (*Neath*), B. V. Meredith (*London Welsh*), R. Prosser (*Pontypool*), R. H. Williams (*Llanelli*), J. R. G. Stephens (*Neath*), R. H. Davies (*Oxford Univ.*), R. J. Robins (*Ponypridd*), B. Sparks (*Neath*)
Referee: R. C. Williams (*Ireland*) **Touch judges:** R. F. Kelly; I. Jones

T. J. Davies kicked a penalty (0-3); K. J. F. Scotland kicked a penalty (3-3); R. H. Davies scored but T. J. Davies failed (3-6); A. R. Smith scored but K. J. F. Scotland failed (6-6). (H.T.). A. F. Dorward dropped a goal (9-6).

In fine conditions a capacity crowd watched a most exciting game. This was a most ferocious forward battle, well controlled by the referee, and the issue was in doubt until the close. Scoring started with splendid long range penalty kicks by each full back before R. H. Davies scored in a forward rush. Near half time Michie and MacGregor had a good clearance dribble to mid field where McClung placed a lovely kick into the left corner. From the maul he got the ball again and put an equally fine kick into the other corner for Smith to race up and score. Play was even after the interval and although Morgan always looked dangerous he could not break past good defence by the Scottish back row and backs. After twenty minutes T. J. Davies was forced to halt a rush by a mark but his kick was caught by Dorward who, standing 40 yards out and 10 yards from the touch, dropped a prodigious goal for a lead that was not lost.

SCOTLAND 3   IRELAND 5
Murrayfield
23 February 1957

Scotland: K. J. F. Scotland (*Royal Signals*); A. R. Smith* (*Camb. Univ.*), T. McClung (*Edin. Acads.*), K. R. Macdonald (*Stewart's FP*), J. L. F. Allan (*Camb. Univ.*); J. M. Maxwell (*Langholm*), A. F. Dorward (*Gala*); H. F. McLeod (*Hawick*), R. K. G. MacEwen (*London Scot.*), T. Elliot (*Gala*), E. J. S. Michie (*London Scot.*), J. W. Y. Kemp (*Glas. HSFP*), I. A. A. MacGregor (*Hillhead HSFP*), G. K. Smith (*Kelso*), A. Robson (*Hawick*)
Ireland: P. J. Berkery (*Lansdowne*); A. C. Pedlow (*QU Belfast*), N. J. Henderson* (*NIFC*), A. J. F. O'Reilly (*Old Belvedere*), R. E. Roche (*Galwegians*); J. W. Kyle (*NIFC*), A. A. Mulligan (*Camb. Univ.*)¡ B. G. M. Wood (*Garryowen*), R. Roe (*London Irish*), J. I. Brennan (*CIYMS*), T. E. Reid (*London Irish*), J. R. Brady (*CIYMS*), J. R. Kavanagh (*Wanderers*), P. J. A. O'Sullivan (*Galwegians*), H. S. O'Connor (*Dublin Univ.*)
Referee: L. M. Boundy (*England*) **Touch judges:** R. Tod, M. E. Holland

P. J. A. O'Sullivan scored and P. J. Berkery converted (0-5). (H.T.). K. J. F. Scotland kicked a penalty (3-5).

A heavy snowstorm which continued throughout the afternoon affected the pitch and ruined any hopes of a handling game for the players skidded and mishandled a slippery ball. The Irish pack adapted well to the conditions and dictated much of the play and it was from a diagonal kick by Kyle that the forwards rushed the ball over for a try by O'Sullivan. The pack maintained their control during the second half and all Scotland could manage was a good penalty by Scotland. Maxwell took a heavy tackle early on and later changed places with McClung.

ENGLAND 16   SCOTLAND 3
Twickenham
16 March 1957

England: R. Challis (*Bristol*); P. B. Jackson (*Coventry*), J. Butterfield (*Northampton*), W. P. C. Davies (*Harlequins*), P. H. Thompson (*Headingley*); R. M. Bartlett (*Harlequins*), R. E. G. Jeeps (*Northampton*); C. R. Jacobs (*Northampton*), E. Evans* (*Sale*), G. W. D. Hastings (*Gloucester*), R. W. D. Marques (*Camb. Univ.*), J. D. Currie (*Oxford Univ.*), P. G. D. Robbins (*Oxford Univ.*), A. Ashcroft (*Waterloo*), R. Higgins (*Liverpool*)
Scotland: K. J. F. Scotland (*Royal Signals*); A. R. Smith (*Camb. Univ.*), T. McClung (*Edin. Acads.*), K. R. Macdonald (*Stewart's FP*), J. L. F. Allan (*Camb. Univ.*); G. H. Waddell (*London Scot.*), A. F. Dorward (*Gala*); H. F. McLeod (*Hawick*), R. K. G. MacEwen (*London Scot.*), T. Elliot (*Gala*), E. J. S. Michie (*London Scot.*), J. W. Y. Kemp (*Glas. HSFP*), G. K. Smith (*Kelso*), J. T. Greenwood* (*Perthshire Acads.*), A. Robson (*Hawick*)
Referee: R. Mitchell (*Ireland*)   **Touch judges:** C. W. Drummond, S. C. Dwyer

J. Butterfield scored but R. Challis failed (3-0). (H.T.). R. Challis kicked a penalty (6-0); K. J. F. Scotland kicked a penalty (6-3); P. H. Thompson and R. Higgins scored and R. Challis converted both (16-3).

The Queen and Prince Philip joined with a crowd of 70,000 who saw England finish the season undefeated. Scotland were quite outclassed by the best team of the year. Their backs had pace and skill while their pack was always clearly on top. Even so a grim defence kept the lead to 3-6 until the last fifteen minutes when the English backs began to throw the ball about freely and soon put the issue beyond doubt. Scotland got so little of the ball that there was really no danger and their only score came from a penalty by K. J. F. Scotland who therefore had scored in every game during the year.

SCOTLAND 11   FRANCE 9
Murrayfield
11 January 1958

Scotland: R. W. T. Chisholm (*Melrose*); A. R. Smith* (*Camb. Univ.*), G. D. Stevenson (*Hawick*), J. T. Docherty (*Glas. HSFP*), J. S. Swan (*Leicester*); G. H. Waddell (*Devonport Services*), J. A. T. Rodd (*Un. Services*); H. F. McLeod (*Hawick*), N. S. Bruce (*Blackheath*), I. R. Hastie (*Kelso*), M. W. Swan (*Oxford Univ.*), J. W. Y. Kemp (*Glas. HSFP*), G. K. Smith (*Kelso*), J. T. Greenwood (*Perthshire Acads.*), M. A. Robertson (*Gala*)
France: M. Vannier (*RCF*); G. Mauduy (*Perigueux*), A. Boniface (*Mont-de-Marsan*), J. Bouguet (*Vienne*), J. Dupuy (*Tarbes*); C. Vignes (*RCF*), P. Danos (*Beziers*); A. Domenech (*Brive*), R. Vigier (*Montferrand*), A. Quaglio (*Mazamet*), L. Mias (*Mazamet*), M. Celaya* (*Biarritz*), M. Crauste (*RCF*), J. Barthe (*Lourdes*), J. Carrere (*Toulon*)
Referee: L. M. Boundy (*England*)   **Touch judges:** A. M. Nicol, M. Lavrent

R. W. T. Chisholm kicked a penalty (3-0); M. Vannier kicked a penalty (3-3); G. D. Stevenson scored and R. W. T. Chisholm converted (8-3); J. Dupuy scored but M. Vannier failed (8-6). (H.T.). M. Vannier kicked a penalty (8-9); I. R. Hastie scored but R. W. T. Chisholm failed (11-9).

This was a hard punishing game where Scotland played orthodox rugby and by good defence countered the ornate French attacks. Certainly France had two speedy centres and a tricky stand off but all were inclined to be too individualistic. The Scottish pack controlled the set scrums and line-out but Waddell used the touch line so much that the threes were more seen in defence than attack, yet, after a penalty by each full back, it was he who made the opening for Stevenson's score. Before the interval Dupuy's pace allowed him to score from a kick ahead which bounced unkindly for the defence. After the interval a Vannier penalty put France ahead but the Scottish pack stepped up their game: G. K. Smith and Stevenson came near to scoring before Hastie from a short line out caught an astute throw in by Smith and bullocked his way over for the winning score.

WALES 8   SCOTLAND 3
Cardiff
1 February 1958

Wales: T. J. Davies (*Llanelli*); J. R. Collins (*Aberavon*), M. C. Thomas (*Newport*), C. A. H. Davies (*Llanelli*), G. T. Wells (*Cardiff*); C. I. Morgan (*Cardiff*), L. H. Williams (*Cardiff*); R. Prosser (*Pontypool*), B. V. Meredith (*Newport*), D. Devereux (*Neath*), R. H. Williams (*Llanelli*), W. R. Evans (*Cardiff*), R. C. C. Thomas* (*Swansea*), J. Faull (*Swansea*), H. J. Morgan (*Abertillery*)
Scotland: R. W. T. Chisholm (*Melrose*); A. R. Smith* (*Camb. Univ.*), G. D. Stevenson (*Hawick*), J. T. Docherty (*Glas. HSFP*), T. G. Weatherstone (*Stewart's FP*); G. H. Waddell (*Devonport Services*), J. A. T. Rodd (*Un. Services*); H. F. McLeod (*Hawick*), R. K. G. MacEwen (*Lansdowne*), T. Elliot (*Gala*), M. W. Swan (*Oxford Univ.*), J. W. Y. Kemp (*Glas. HSFP*), G. K. Smith (*Kelso*), J. T. Greenwood (*Perthshire Acads.*), A. Robson (*Hawick*)
Referee: N. M. Parkes (*England*)   **Touch judges:** G. Burrell, D. Pritchard

G. T. Wells scored and T. J. Davies converted (5-0). (H.T.). A. R. Smith kicked a penalty (5-3); J. R. Collins scored but T. J. Davies failed (8-3).

The strength of the Welsh pack was eventually a deciding factor and the Scottish halves, much harassed by the back row, were not seen in attack. As a result their centres had little useful ball whilst the wingers had to fend for themselves but at least their defence was sound. Play was mainly in the Welsh half before the interval and Scotland missed two hard but kickable penalties before Wells ran onto a kick ahead by C. Davies and beat Smith for the touch. In the second half Wales came more into the game and after a Smith penalty L. H. Williams and Collins had an interpassing run (which many thought had started with a forward pass) which finished with the latter scoring a vital try.

SCOTLAND 12   AUSTRALIA 8
Murrayfield
15 February 1958

Scotland: R. W. T. Chisholm (*Melrose*); A. R. Smith* (*Gosforth*), G. D. Stevenson (*Hawick*), J. T. Docherty (*Glas. HSFP*), T. G. Weatherstone (*Stewart's FP*); G. H. Waddell (*Devonport Services*), J. A. T. Rodd (*Un. Services*); H. F. McLeod (*Hawick*), N. S. Bruce (*Blackheath*), T. Elliot (*Gala*), M. W. Swan (*Oxford Univ.*), J. W. Y. Kemp (*Glas. HSFP*), G. K. Smith (*Kelso*), J. T. Greenwood (*Perthshire Acads.*), A. Robson (*Hawick*)
Australia: T. G. P. Curley (*NSW*); K. J. Donald (*Queensland*), J. K. Lenehan (*NSW*), S. W. White (*NSW*), R. Phelps (*NSW*); A. J. Summons (*NSW*), D. M. Connor (*Queensland*); G. N. Vaughan (*Victoria*), J. V. Brown (*NSW*), R. A. L. Davidson* (*NSW*), A. R. Miller (*NSW*), D. M. Emanuel (*NSW*), E. M. Purkiss (*NSW*), N. M. Hughes (*NSW*), J. E. Thornett (*NSW*)
Referee: R. C. Williams (*Ireland*)   **Touch judges:** R. P. Burrell, R. M. Harvey

K. J. Donald scored and J. K. Lenehan converted (0-5); T. G. Weatherstone scored but A. R. Smith failed (3-5); J. E. Thornett scored (3-8); A. R. Smith kicked a penalty (6-8). (H.T.). A. R. Smith kicked a penalty (9-8), G. D. Stevenson scored but A. R. Smith failed (12-8).

Australia were perhaps unlucky to lose for, a point behind with ten minutes left, they lost White injured and concussed checking a fine forward rush. Up till then they had shown themselves to be the better running and attacking team with a pack that had an edge in the scrums and line out. From this point the Scottish pack took command, Waddell became more prominent and a run in which Chisholm took part saw Stevenson score-although some thought the move included a forward pass. Australia took an early lead when Curley came into the threes and after a 30 yards run, kicked the ball over Chisholm's head. Donald, credited with 9.8 seconds for 100 yards, caught the ball and was not overtaken. However, ten minutes later a fast Scottish heel let Waddell make a break for Docherty to crosskick, Weatherstone gathered the ball and scored at the corner. Within minutes Summons made a break and Thornett was in support to score. Two penalties by Smith, the second after the interval being from near half field, put Scotland in the lead then Australia lost White and the initiative.

142

IRELAND 12   SCOTLAND 6
Lansdowne Road
1 March 1958

Ireland: P. J. Berkery (*London Irish*); A. C. Pedlow (*CIYMS*), D. Hewitt (*QU Belfast*), N. J. Henderson* (*NIFC*), A. J. F. O'Reilly (*Old Belvedere*); J. W. Kyle (*NIFC*), A. A. Mulligan (*Wanderers*); P. J. O'Donoghue (*Bective Rangers*), A. R. Dawson (*Wanderers*), B. G. M. Wood (*Garryowen*), J. B. Stevenson (*Instonians*), W. A. Mulcahy (*UC Dublin*), J. A. Donaldson (*Collegians*), J. R. Kavanagh (*Wanderers*), N. A. A. Murphy (*Cork Const.*)
Scotland: R. W. T. Chisholm (*Melrose*), A. R. Smith* (*Gosforth*), G. D. Stevenson (*Hawick*), J. T. Docherty (*Glas. HSFP*), T. G. Weatherstone (*Stewart's FP*); G. H. Waddell (*Devonport Services*), J. A. T. Rodd (*Un. Services*); H. F. McLeod (*Hawick*), N. S. Bruce (*Blackheath*), T. Elliot (*Gala*), M. W. Swan (*Oxford Univ.*), J. W. Y. Kemp (*Glas. HSFP*) D. C. Macdonald (*Edin. Univ.*), J. T. Greenwood (*Perthshire Acads.*), A. Robson (*Hawick*)
Referee: W. N. Gillmore (*England*)   **Touch judges:** J. I. Morrison, S. V. Crawford

A. R. Smith scored but failed to convert (0-3), T. G. Weatherstone scored but A. R. Smith failed (0-6). (H.T.). N. J. Henderson kicked a penalty (3-6); A. C. Pedlow scored but P. J. Berkery failed (6-6); P. J. Berkery kicked a penalty (9-6); A. C. Pedlow scored but P. J. Berkery failed (12-6).

Rather against the run of play Scotland scored first when Stevenson picked up a missed pass and set Smith off on a spectacular 65 yards run for the first try. A few minutes later Rodd broke from a scrum and put Weatherstone in at the corner. Just on half time Chisholm was hurt checking a forward rush and was taken off. Smith went to full back with Robson on the wing but Ireland held the advantage during the second half and finished clear winners.

SCOTLAND 3   ENGLAND 3
Murrayfield
15 March 1958

Scotland: K. J. F. Scotland (*Heriot's FP*); C. Elliot (*Langholm*), G. D. Stevenson (*Hawick*), J. T. Docherty (*Glas. HSFP*), T. G. Weatherstone (*Stewart's FP*); G. H. Waddell (*Devonport Services*), J. A. T. Rodd (*Un. Services*); H. F. McLeod (*Hawick*), N. S. Bruce (*Blackheath*), I. R. Hastie (*Kelso*), M. W. Swan (*London Scot.*), J. W. Y. Kemp (*Glas. HSFP*), D. C. Macdonald (*Edin. Univ.*), J. T. Greenwood* (*Perthshire Acads.*), A. Robson (*Hawick*)
England: D. F. Allison (*Coventry*); P. B. Jackson (*Coventry*), J. Butterfield (*Northampton*), M. S. Phillips (*Oxford Univ.*), P. H. Thompson (*Headingley*); R. M. Bartlett (*Harlequins*), R. E. G. Jeeps (*Northampton*); C. R. Jacobs (*Northampton*), E. Evans* (*Sale*), G. W. D. Hastings (*Gloucester*), R. W. D. Marques (*Camb. Univ.*), J. D. Currie (*Oxford Univ.*), A. J. Herbert (*Wasps*), A. Ashcroft (*Waterloo*), P. G. D. Robbins (*Oxford Univ.*)
Referee: R. C. Williams (*Ireland*)   **Touch judges:** J. A. Cessford, D. A. Brown

No scoring at half time. C. Elliot kicked a penalty (3-0); G. W. D. Hastings kicked a penalty (3-3).

Scotland showed such improved form that they really deserved to win for they set a fierce pace from the start and never eased up. The much-vaunted English threes never really got moving and only near half time did they show their class when Jackson ran the ball from his own line across field for five others to handle in a movement brought to a halt by a good tackle by K. J. F. Scotland. Their defence, however, was sound and the giants, Marques and Currie, were prominent at the line-outs. Scotland attacked frequently; Waddell came close with a drop kick whilst Bruce and Weatherstone were both nearly over. Just before the close Jeeps was laid out when he tackled Elliot and so saved a certain score. The winger was a late replacement for A. R. Smith and raised a tremendous cheer when, after others had failed, he kicked a penalty shortly after the interval to give Scotland a rather short lived lead.

FRANCE 9   SCOTLAND 0
Colombes
10 January 1959

France: P. Lacaze (*Lourdes*); J. Dupuy (*Tarbes*), A. Marquesuzaa (*RCF*), J. Bouquet (*Vienne*), H. Rancoule (*Lourdes*); A. Labazuy (*Lourdes*), P. Danos (*Beziers*); A. Qualio (*Mazamet*), R. Vigier (*Monteferrand*), A. Roques (*Cahors*), L. Mias (*Mazamet*), B. Mommejat (*Cahors*), F. Moncla (*RCF*), J. Barthe (*Lourdes*), M. Celaya (*Biarritz*)
Scotland: K. J. F. Scotland (*Camb. Univ.*); A. R. Smith (*Gosforth*), T. McClung (*Edin. Acads.*), I. H. P. Laughland (*London Scot.*), C. Elliot (*Langholm*); G. H. Waddell (*Camb. Univ.*), S. Coughtrie (*Edin. Acads.*); H. F. McLeod (*Hawick*), N. S. Bruce (*Blackheath*), I. R. Hastie (*Kelso*), M. W. Swan (*London Scot.*), J. W. Y. Kemp (*Glas. HSFP*), G. K. Smith (*Kelso*), J. T. Greenwood* (*Perthshire Acads.*), A. Robson (*Hawick*)
Referee: G. Walters (*Wales*)   **Touch judges:** J. A. Cessford, R. B. Marie

P. Lacaze dropped a goal (3-0); F. Moncla scored (6-0). (H.T.). P. Lacaze dropped a goal (9-0)

The score barely reflected France's superiority *'grâce à sa ligne d'avants et l'étonnant Pierre Danos'* and indeed the home pack were outstanding in a game that was fast from beginning to end. Coughtrie did well behind a beaten pack but the backs spent a busy afternoon in defence and never at any time looked like winning. The only try came from a movement started by Danos from a loose scrum and Moncla was involved twice before he crashed in for his try. Danos was also involved in getting the ball away to Lacaze when he dropped his second goal. Later at the official dinner Dr D. J. MacMyn, then President of the SRU, greatly pleased and moved his hosts of the FFR when he presented them with the jersey of the late Y. du Manoir, which he had kept since the game in 1926.

SCOTLAND 6   WALES 5
Murrayfield
7 February 1959

Scotland: K. J. F. Scotland (*Camb. Univ.*); A. R. Smith (*Gosforth*), T. McClung (*Edin. Acads.*), G. D. Stevenson (*Hawick*), T. G. Weatherstone (*Stewart's FP*); G. H. Waddell (*Camb. Univ.*), S. Coughtrie (*Edin. Acads.*); H. F. McLeod (*Hawick*), N. S. Bruce (*Blackheath*), I. R. Hastie (*Kelso*), M. W. Swan (*London Scot.*), J. W. Y. Kemp (*Glas. HSFP*), G. K. Smith (*Kelso*), J. T. Greenwood* (*Perthshire Acads.*), A. Robson (*Hawick*)
Wales: T. E. Davies (*Llanelli*); J. R. Collins (*Aberavon*), H. J. Davies (*Camb. Univ.*), M. J. Price (*Pontypool*), D. I. Bebb (*Carmarthen TC*); C. Ashton (*Aberavon*), L. H. Williams (*Cardiff*); R. Prosser (*Pontypool*), B. V. Meredith (*Newport*), D. R. Main (*London Welsh*), R. H. Williams (*Llanelli*), I. Ford (*Newport*), R. C. C. Thomas* (*Swansea*), J. Faull (*Swansea*), J. Leleu (*London Welsh*)
Referee: R. C. Williams (*Ireland*)   **Touch judges:** R. P. Burrell, G. Thomas

M. J. Price scored and T. E. Davies converted (0-5); K. J. F. Scotland kicked a penalty (3-5); N. S. Bruce scored but K. J. F. Scotland failed (6-5). (H.T.).

The Scottish pack held their own in the scrums and line outs but were clearly on top in the loose, being very fast in following up. Waddell benefited from Coughtrie's good and lengthy service and had one fine 60 yard run that narrowly failed to bring a score. Nevertheless Wales were first to score within five minutes when Price burst away from a line out and ran some 40 yards to score. 30 minutes later K. J. F. Scotland kicked a penalty. Then, just on the interval, the Welsh pack in a rush nearly scored, only to see the Scottish pack headed by G. K. Smith, take the ball 80 yards downfield in a dribbling rush, which finished with Waddell picking up and passing to Bruce who went for the corner to score. In the second half Scotland missed two penalties and only the sternest defence denied them at least two scores. Yet they nearly lost the match in the closing minutes when a long drop by Ashton dropped just short of the bar.

SCOTLAND 3   IRELAND 8
Murrayfield
28 February 1959

Scotland: K. J. F. Scotland (*Camb. Univ.*); A. R. Smith (*Ebbw Vale*), T. McClung (*Edin. Univ.*), G. D. Stevenson (*Hawick*), T. G. Weatherstone (*Stewart's FP*); G. H. Waddell (*Camb. Univ.*), S. Coughtrie (*Edin. Acads.*), H. F. McLeod (*Hawick*), N. S. Bruce (*Blackheath*), I. R. Hastie (*Kelso*), M. W. Swan (*London Scot.*), J. W. Y. Kemp (*Glas. HSFP*), G. K. Smith (*Kelso*), J. T. Greenwood* (*Perthshire Acads.*), A. Robson (*Hawick*)
Ireland: N. J. Henderson (*NIFC*); N. H. Brophy (*UC Dublin*), D. Hewitt (*QU Belfast*), J. F. Dooley (*Galwegians*), A. F. O'Reilly (*Old Belvedere*); M. A. F. English (*Bohemians*), A. A. Mulligan (*London Irish*); B. G. M. Wood (*Garryowen*), A. R. Dawson* (*Wanderers*), S. Mlllar (*Ballymena*), W. A. Mulcahy (*UC Dublin*), M. G. Culliton (*Wanderers*), N. A. A. Murphy (*Cork Const.*), P. J. A. O'Sullivan (*Galwegians*), J. R. Kavanagh (*Wanderers*)
Referee: L. M. Boundy (*England*)   **Touch judges:** J. I. Morrison, P. J. Lavery

D. Hewitt kicked a penalty (0-3); J. F. Dooley scored and D. Hewitt converted (0-8). (H.T.) K. J. F. Scotland kicked a penalty (3-8).

After ten minutes Greenwood came off with a dislocated shoulder and before he came back to play as a complete passenger Hewitt had kicked a fine 40 yard penalty from a difficult angle. Just before the interval O'Reilly cut in from the wing to join a handling movement and smart handling saw Hewitt go through a gap and send Dooley in. Scotland never managed to produce the dash that they showed against Wales but their halves and backs were harried and spent most of the time in defence. In fact K. J. F. Scotland was probably their most penetrating runner at full back.

ENGLAND 3   SCOTLAND 3
Twickenham
21 March 1959

England: J. G. G. Hetherington (*Northampton*); P. B. Jackson (*Coventry*), M. S. Phillips (*Oxford Univ.*), J. Butterfield* (*Northampton*), P. H. Thompson (*Waterloo*); A. B. W. Risman (*Manchester Univ.*), S. R. Smith (*Camb. Univ.*); St. L. H. Webb (*Bedford*), H. O. Godwin (*Coventry*), G. J. Bendon (*Wasps*), R. W. D. Marques (*Harlequins*), J. D. Currie (*Harlequins*), A. J. Herbert (*Wasps*), A. Ashcroft (*Waterloo*), J. W. Clements (*Old Cranleighans*)
Scotland: K. J. F. Scotland (*Camb. Univ.*); A. R. Smith (*Ebbw Vale*), J. A. P. Shackleton (*London Scot.*), G. D. Stevenson (*Hawick*), T. G. Weatherstone (*Stewart's FP*); G. H. Waddell* (*Camb. Univ.*), S. Coughtrie (*Edin. Acads.*); D. M. D. Rollo (*Howe of Fife*), N. S. Bruce (*Blackheath*), H. F. McLeod (*Hawick*), F. H. ten Bos (*Oxford Univ.*), J. W. Y. Kemp (*Glas. HSFP*), G. K. Smith (*Kelso*), J. A. Davidson (*London Scot.*), A. Robson (*Hawick*)
Referee: G. Walters (*Wales*)   **Touch judges:** H. B. Laidlaw, J. V. Pollard

K. J. F. Scotland kicked a penalty (3-0); A. B. W. Risman kicked a penalty (3-3). (H.T.).

A heavy English pack were better in the scrums while Scotland showed up well in the open, Robson being particularly noticeable. The newcomer Rollo, in spite of a knock on the face, was a solid but active prop. Both stand-offs lay deep yet never really escaped the attention of the back row forwards. Waddell depended mainly on lofty punts but Hetherington was quite untroubled by this form of attack. In the first half a dangerous run by Phillips was halted by a fine tackle by Scotland who again showed his flair for attacking from the back position. The Scottish pack made a very vigorous start to the second half and nearly forced a score against a very good defence. The four very talented wingers were hardly brought into the play.

SCOTLAND 11   FRANCE 13
Murrayfield
9 January 1960

Scotland: K. J. F. Scotland (*Camb. Univ.*); A. R. Smith* (*Ebbw Vale*), J. J. McPartlin (*Harlequins*), I. H. P. Laughland (*London Scot.*), C. Elliot (*Langholm*), G. Sharp (*Stewart's FP*), J. A. T. Rodd (*Un. Services*); H. F. McLeod (*Hawick*), N. S. Bruce (*London Scot.*) D. M. D. Rollo (*Howe of Fife*), F. H. ten Bos (*Oxford Univ.*), J. W. Y. Kemp (*Glas. HSFP*), G. K. Smith (*Kelso*), K. R. F. Bearne (*Camb. Univ.*), A. Robson (*Hawick*)

France: M. Vannier (*RCF*); L. Roge (*Besiers*), J. Bouquet (*Vienne*), A. Marquesuzaa (*Lourdes*), S. Mericq (*Agen*); R. Martine (*Lourdes*), P. Danos (*Beziers*); A. Domenech (*Brive*), J. de Gregorio (*Grenoble*), A. Roques (*Cahors*), B. Mommejat (*Cahors*), M. Celaya (*Bordeaux*), F. Moncla* (*Pau*), M. Crauste (*Lourdes*), S. Meyer (*Perigueux*)
Referee: G. Walters (*Wales*)   **Touch judges:** G. Burrell, M. Laurent

S. Meyer scored and M. Vannier converted (0-5). (H.T.). S. Mericq and F. Moncla scored and M. Vannier converted the second (0-13); A. R. Smith scored and C. Elliot converted (5-13); C. Elliot kicked a penalty (8-13); A. R. Smith scored but C. Elliot failed (11-13).

This was an exciting match which Scotland might have won had they changed their tactics early on. After some ten minutes Roge fractured his hand tackling Smith but remained on the field as an extra back and Meyer came out of the pack onto the wing. This arrangement worked because the depleted French pack held their own everywhere except in the set scrums and their ferocious tackling and speed onto the man and ball stifled all the Scottish attacks. Near half time Bouquet intercepted a pass at half field and, when Smith ran him down, a pass to Meyer produced a score at the posts. France restarted in tremendous fashion scoring two tries inside three minutes for a 13 points lead. Then Scotland began to play on the injured Roge. He was forced to fly kick at a high bouncing ball and a miss let Smith pick up and score for Elliot to convert this and almost at once kick a penalty for off-side. After a scrum Sharp kicked ahead and when two defenders collided Smith again picked up to streak round Vannier and score too far out for Elliot to convert – and then time ran out for Scotland.

WALES 8   SCOTLAND 0
Cardiff
6 February 1960

Wales: N. Morgan (*Newport*); F. C. Coles (*Pontypool*), M. J. Price (*RAF*), G. W. Lewis (*Richmond*), D. I. Bebb (*Carmarthen TC*); C. Ashton (*Aberavon*), D. O. Brace (*Llanelli*); R. Prosser (*Pontypool*), B. V. Meredith* (*Newport*), L. J. Cunningham (*Aberavon*), G. W. Payne (*Army*), D. J. E. Harris (*Cardiff*), B. Cresswell (*Newport*), G. D. Davidge (*Newport*), G. Whitson (*Newport*)
Scotland: K. J. F. Scotland (*Camb. Univ.*); A. R. Smith* (*Ebbw Vale*), J. J. McPartlin (*Harlequins*), I. H. P. Laughland (*London Scot.*), G. D. Stevenson (*Hawick*); T. McClung (*Edin. Acads.*), J. A. T. Rodd (*Un. Services*); H. F. McLeod (*Hawick*), N. S. Bruce (*London Scot.*), D. M. D. Rollo (*Howe of Fife*), F. H. ten Bos (*Oxford Univ.*), J. W. Y. Kemp (*Glas. HSFP*), G. K. Smith (*Kelso*), K. R. F. Bearne (*Camb. Univ.*), C. E. B. Stewart (*Kelso*)
Referee: K. Kelleher (*Ireland*)   **Touch judges:** J. Imrie, A. Williams

No scoring at half time. D. I. Bebb scored and N. Morgan converted (5-0); N. Morgan kicked a penalty (8-0).

There was a disappointing display by both sets of backs. Behind beaten forwards and receiving a poor service McClung had to rely mainly on placing diagonal kicks, especially as A. R. Smith was clearly the best back on the field. One long run by the latter would have given G. K. Smith a score had the final pass not been so wide. Brace did relatively well behind a strong pack but it was lucky for Scotland that his backs were so off form with their handling. The only try came early in the second half when a kick ahead by Brace was fumbled and Bebb nipped in to score.

IRELAND 5   SCOTLAND 6
Lansdowne Road
27 February 1960

Ireland: T. J. Kiernan (*UC Cork*); A. C. Pedlow (*CIYMS*), D. Hewitt (*QU Belfast*), J. C. Walsh (*UC Cork*), W. W. Bornemann (*Wanderers*); M. A. F. English (*Bohemians*), A. A. Mulligan* (*London Irish*); B. G. M. Wood (*Lansdowne*), B. McCallan (*Ballymena*), S. Millar (*Ballymena*), W. A. Mulcahy (*UC Dublin*), M. G. Culliton (*Wanderers*), N. A. A. Murphy (*Cork Const.*), T. McGrath (*Garryowen*), J. R. Kavanagh (*Wanderers*)
Scotland: K. J. F. Scotland (*Camb. Univ.*); A. R. Smith (*Ebbw Vale*), G. D. Stevenson (*Hawick*), I. H. P. Laughland (*London Scot.*), R. H. Thomson (*London Scot.*); G. H. Waddell* (*Camb. Univ.*), R. B. Shillinglaw (*KOSB*); D. M. D. Rollo (*Howe of Fife*), N. S. Bruce (*London Scot.*), H. F. McLeod (*Hawick*), T. O. Grant (*Hawick*), J. W. Y. Kemp (*Glas. HSFP*), G. K. Smith (*Kelso*), J. A. Davidson (*Edin. Wrs.*), D. B. Edwards (*Heriot's FP*)
Referee: D. G. Walters (*Wales*)   **Touch judges:** D. McIntyre, A. B. Robertson

146

B. G. M. Wood scored and D. Hewitt converted (5-0); R. H. Thomson scored but K. J. F. Scotland failed (5-3); K. J. F. Scotland dropped a goal (5-6). (H.T.).

This was Scotland's first win in Dublin since 1933 and while Ireland had chances that they did not take, there were welcome signs of improvement in an altered Scottish team. Shillinglaw at scrum half had an excellent debut and Waddell, benefiting from a good long service, was much more able to dictate play, especially towards the close when Ireland fought hard to save the game. Then his ability to place lengthy but accurate kicks to touch was invaluable. During this period the threes, not great in attack, were immense in defence especially as both centres had earlier been injured. After an early Irish score K. J. F. Scotland, who fielded beautifully all afternoon, came up to join a movement and put Thomson over for his try. He failed with the conversion but shortly afterwards he dropped a goal after a set scrum in front of the posts – having come up deliberately to take the pass from the scrum.

SCOTLAND 12   ENGLAND 21
Murrayfield
19 March 1960

Scotland: K. J. F. Scotland (*Camb. Univ.*); A. R. Smith (*Ebbw Vale*), G. D. Stevenson (*Hawick*), I. H. P. Laughland (*London Scot.*), R. H. Thomson (*London Scot.*); G. H. Waddell* (*Camb. Univ.*),R. B. Shillinglaw (*KOSB*); D. M. D. Rollo (*Howe of Fife*), N. S. Bruce (*London Scot.*), H. F. McLeod (*Hawick*), T. O. Grant (*Hawick*), J. W. Y. Kemp (*Glas. HSFP*), G. K. Smith (*Kelso*), J. A. Davidson (*Edin. Wrs.*), D. B. Edwards (*Heriot's FP*)
England: D. Rutherford (*Percy Park*); J. R. C. Young (*Harlequins*), M. S. Phillips (*Oxford Univ.*), M. P. Weston (*Richmond*), J. Roberts (*Old Millhillians*); R. A. W. Sharp (*Oxford Univ.*), R. E. G. Jeeps* (*Northampton*); C. R. Jacobs (*Northampton*), S. A. M. Hodgson (*Durham City*), T. P. Wright (*Blackheath*), R. W. D. Marques (*Harlequins*), J. D. Currie (*Harlequins*), P. G. D. Robbins (*Moseley*), W. G. D. Morgan (*Medicals*), R. E. Syrett (*Wasps*)
Referee: R. C. Williams (*Ireland*)   **Touch judges:** J. A. S. Taylor, W. Howarth

R. A. W. Sharp dropped a goal (0-3); R. E. Syrett and J. Roberts scored and D. Rutherford converted both (0-13); D. Rutherford kicked a penalty (0-16); K. J. F. Scotland kicked two penalties (6-16). (H.T.). K. J. F. Scotland kicked a penalty (9-16); J. R. C. Young scored and D. Rutherford converted (9-21); A. R. Smith scored but K. J. F. Scotland failed (12-21).

This was a spectacular game, full of exciting action. England were particularly well served by Sharp at half and Phillips at centre. For Scotland Shillinglaw did well under constant pressure from Jeeps and the English back row but there was no penetration further back and the wingers saw little of the ball. Inside five minutes Sharp dropped a 35 yard goal and then England rattled on two tries converted by Rutherford who followed with a penalty for a 16 points lead. Before half time K. J. F. Scotland had reduced the deficit by kicking two long range penalties and ten minutes after the interval added another from 40 yards. Scotland had one chance of scoring spoiled by a dropped pass before Phillips made a fine opening to send Young in. Late on K. J. F. Scotland showed the threes what could be done when he came upfield and made an opening for A. R. Smith to show his pace and score.

SOUTH AFRICA 18   SCOTLAND 10
Port Elizabeth
30 April 1960

South Africa: M. C. Gerber (*EP*); J. P. Engelbrecht (*WP*), I. A. Kirkpatrick (*GW*), J. L. Gainford (*WP*), R. J. Twigge (*NT*); D. A. Stewart (*WP*), F. W. Gerike (*T*); D. N. Holton (*EP*), A. J. Van der Merwe (*Boland*), M. J. Bekker (*NT*), J. T. Claassen (*WT*), P. B. Allen (*EP*), D. C. Van Jaarsveldt* (*Rhodesia*), D. J. Hopwood (*WP*), G. H. Van Zyl (*WP*)
Scotland: R. W. T. Chisholm (*Melrose*); A. R. Smith (*Ebbw Vale*), P. J. Burnet (*London Scot.*), G. D. Stevenson (*Hawick*), R. H. Thomson (*London Scot.*); G. H. Waddell* (*Camb. Univ.*), R. B. Shillinglaw (*Gala*); H. F. McLeod (*Hawick*), N. S. Bruce (*London Scot.*), D. M. D. Rollo (*Howe of Fife*), F. H. ten Bos (*Oxford Univ.*), J. W. Y. Kemp (*Glas. HSFP*), D. B. Edwards (*Heriot's FP*), T. O. Grant (*Hawick*), W. Hart (*Melrose*)
Referee: Dr E. A. Strasheim

N. S. Bruce scored and A. R. Smith converted (0-5); G. H. Van Zyl scored and M. C. Gerber converted (5-5). (H.T.). G. H. Van Zyl scored but M. C. Gerber failed (8-5); F. W. Gerike scored and M. C. Gerber converted (13-5); D. C. Van Jaarsveldt scored and M. C. Gerber converted (18-5); A. R. Smith scored and converted (18-10).

This, the first short tour by any country, was a distinct success and clearly set a pattern for others in the future. Since it was the start of the South African season they were hoping that their physical advantages in the pack would compensate for a lack of match fitness. As it turned out the lighter Scottish forwards held their own in the scrums, were faster in the loose and did well at the line outs but their back row failed to subdue Gerike who engineered three vital tries by breaking fast round the scrum. The Scottish halves were the better pair, making some good breaks but while the centres tackled soundly they handled indifferently and the dangerous A. R. Smith had more or less to fend for himself. Stevenson, however, was throughout badly affected by a nasty knock he got after five minutes' play. The best score of the game was a try by Jaarsveldt who picked up a loose ball near mid field and outstripped everyone in a 50 yard dash.

FRANCE 11   SCOTLAND 0
Colombes
7 January 1961

France: R. Martine (*Lourdes*); J. Dupuy (*Tarbes*), J. Bouquet (*Vienne*), G. Boniface (*Mont-de-Marsan*), J. Gachassin (*Lourdes*); P. Albaladejo (*Dax*), P. Lacroix (*Agen*); A. Domenech (*Brive*), J. de Gregoria (*Grenoble*), A. Roques (*Cahors*), L. Echave (*Agen*), M. Celaya (*Biarritz*), F. Moncla (*Pau*), R. Crancee (*Lourdes*), M. Crauste (*Lourdes*)
Scotland: K. J. F. Scotland (*London Scot.*); A. R. Smith (*Edin. Wrs.*), R. C. Cowan (*Selkirk*), G. D. Stevenson (*Hawick*), R. H. Thomson (*London Scot.*), G. H. Waddell* (*Camb. Univ.*), R. B. Shillinglaw (*KOSB*); H. F. McLeod (*Hawick*), N. S. Bruce (*London Scot.*), D. M. D. Rollo (*Howe of Fife*), F. H. ten Bos (*Oxford Univ.*), M. J. Campbell-Lamerton (*Blackheath*), G. K. Smith (*Kelso*), C. E. B. Stewart (*Kelso*), J. Douglas (*Stewart's FP*)
Referee: R. C. Williams (*Ireland*)   **Touch judges:** D. C. J. McMahon, B. Marie

No scoring at half time. P. Albaladejo dropped a goal and kicked a penalty (6-0); G. Boniface scored and P. Albaladejo converted (11-0).

C. E. B. Stewart suffered a leg injury in the first minute and although he returned he was merely a passenger for the rest of the afternoon. In spite of this the Scottish pack played so well that there was no scoring during the first half although the French forwards showed their customary flair for handling. It was well on in the second half before Boniface scored the only try and meantime Scotland came near to scoring; Waddell was held under the posts and Thomson got over only to be recalled for a previous infringement.

SCOTLAND 5   SOUTH AFRICA 12
Murrayfield
21 January 1961

Scotland: K. J. F. Scotland (*London Scot.*); A. R. Smith* (*Edin. Wrs.*), E McKeating (*Heriot's FP*), G. D. Stevenson (*Hawick*), R. H. Thomson (*London Scot.*); I. H. P. Laughland (*London Scot.*), R. B. Shillinglaw (*Gala*); H. F. McLeod (*Hawick*), N. S. Bruce (*London Scot.*), D. M. D. Rollo (*Howe of Fife*), F. H. ten Bos (*Oxford Univ.*), M J. Campbell-Lamerton (*Blackheath*), G. K. Smith (*Kelso*), J. Douglas (*Stewart's FP*), K. I. Ross (*Boroughmuir FP*)
South Africa: D. A. Stewart (*WP*), J. P. Englebrecht (*WP*), J. L. Gainsford (*WP*), A. I. Kirkpatrick (*Orange FS*), H. J. Van Zyl (*T*); K. Oxlee (*Natal*), P. de W. Vys (*NT*); S. P. Kuhn (*T*), G. F. Malan (*WP*), P. S. du Toit (*Boland*), G. H. Van Zyl (*WP*), A. S. Malan* (*T*), J. T. Claassen (*WT*), F. C. Du Preez (*NT*), D. J. Hopwood (*WP*)
Referee: L. M. Boundy (*England*)   **Touch judges:** G. Burrell, P. J. Van Zyl

D. J. Hopwood scored but F. C. Du Preez failed (0-3), J. T. Claassen scored but F. C. Du Preez failed (0-6). (H.T.). A. R. Smith scored and K. J. F. Scotland converted (5-6), F. C. Du Preez kicked 2 penalties (5-12).

Both sides played open rugby in a most exhilarating game. The heavier and faster South African forwards produced some great handling and backing up movements, but an improved Scottish pack, beaten in the scrums and line outs, were by no means outshone in the loose and the splendid tackling of the whole team did much to counter the great combined play of the visitors. K. J. F. Scotland was again at his best, his positioning and long accurate touch kicking being first rate. It was 25 minutes before Hopwood broke from a scrum to score and shortly afterwards he made an opening for another forward to score. Scotland's score came after a long run by Shillinglaw, Laughland, McKeating and Thomson. From a line out Laughland's drop at goal went wide but A. R. Smith raced in to touch down just short of the dead ball line and the conversion left Scotland one point behind. It is a measure of Scotland's resistance that South Africa could only manage two penalty kicks after that.

SCOTLAND 3   WALES 0
Murrayfield
11 February 1961

Scotland: K. J. F. Scotland (*London Scot.*); A. R. Smith* (*Edin. Wrs.*), E. McKeating (*Heriot's FP*), G. D. Stevenson (*Hawick*), R. H. Thomson (*London Scot.*); I. H. P. Laughland (*London Scot.*), A. J. Hastie (*Melrose*); H. F. McLeod (*Hawick*), N. S. Bruce (*London Scot.*), D. M. D. Rollo (*Howe of Fife*), F. H. ten Bos (*London Scot.*), M. J. Campbell-Lamerton (*Halifax*), K. I. Ross (*Boroughmuir FP*), J. Douglas (*Stewart's FP*), G. K. Smith (*Kelso*)
Wales: T. J. Davies* (*Llanelli*); P. M. Rees (*Newport*), G. Britton (*Newport*), H. M. Roberts (*Cardiff*), D. I. Bebb (*Swansea*); K. Richards (*Bridgend*), A. O'Connor (*Aberavon*); P. E. J. Morgan (*Aberavon*), B. V. Meredith (*Newport*), K. D. Jones (*Cardiff*), W. R. Evans (*Bridgend*), D. J. E. Harris (*Cardiff*), G. D. Davidge (*Newport*), D. Nash (*Ebbw Vale*), H. J. Morgan (*Abertillery*)
Referee: R. C. Williams (*Ireland*)   **Touch judges:** G. K. Rome, E. M. Lewis

A. R. Smith scored but K. J. F. Scotland failed (3-0). (H.T.).

This was mainly a hard forward battle played in wind and rain. The Scottish pack held their own in the scrums and were clearly on top in the open and with their backs tackling accurately, the Welsh threes had a profitless afternoon. After half an hour Hastie set his backs away and Scotland came into the line to make a break and send A. R. Smith in far out. Scotland failed with the long conversion and had an off-day with his place kicking, missing some penalties also, but in the second half he saved a certain score when at the corner he felled Bebb after a great 50 yards run. Bebb at once threw the ball in and getting it back went over only to have the score refused by the referee who ruled that the throw-in was short.

SCOTLAND 16   IRELAND 8
Murrayfield
25 February 1961

Scotland: K. J. F. Scotland (*London Scoi.*); A. R. Smith* (*Edin. Wrs.*), E. McKeating (*Heriot's FP*), G. D. Stevenson (*Hawick*), R. H. Thomson (*London Scot.*); I. H. P. Laughland (*London Scot.*), A. J. Hastie (*Melrose*); H. F. McLeod (*Hawick*), N. S. Bruce (*London Scot.*), D. M. D. Rollo (*Howe of Fife*), F. H. ten Bos (*London Scot.*), M. J. Campbell-Lamerton (*Halifax*), K. I. Ross (*Boroughmuir FP*), J. Douglas (*Stewart's FP*), G. K. Smith (*Kelso*)
Ireland: T. J. Kiernan (*UC Cork*); A. C. Pedlow (*CIYMS*), D. Hewitt (*QU Belfast*), J. C. Walsh (*UC Cork*), N. H. Brophy (*Blackrock*); M. A. F. English (*Bohemians*), J. W. Moffett (*Ballymena*); B. G. M. Wood (*Lansdowne*), A. R. Dawson* (*Wanderers*), S. Millar (*Ballymena*), W. A. Mulcahy (*UC Dublin*), M. G. Culliton (*Wanderers*), J. R. Kavanagh (*Wanderers*), P. J. A. O'Sullivan (*Galwegians*), N. A. A. Murphy (*Garryowen*)
Referee: M. H. R. King (*England*)   **Touch judges:** G. W. D. Hastie, J. Bell

J. R. Kavanagh scored and J. W. Moffett converted (0-5); K. J. F. Scotland kicked a penalty (3-5); J. Douglas scored and K. J. F. Scotland converted (8-5). (H.T.). K. I. Ross scored and K. J. F. Scotland converted (13-5); D. Hewitt scored but J. W. Moffett failed (13-8); K. I. Ross scored but K. J. F. Scotland failed (16-8).

This was a fast spectacular game with a great exhibition of forward play by two splendid packs, the Scottish back row in particular showing excellent form both in attack and defence. In spite of a greasy ball and slippery surface, Ireland played well to their wingers, who only failed against some firm tackling. They began, however, by keeping the ball amongst the forwards and it was Kavanagh

149

who scored inside ten minutes. Good play by the pack regained the lead for Scotland and in the second half a sally into the line by K. J. F. Scotland saw him finish a touch line run by putting Ross over for a good try. Ireland retaliated with a tremendous passing movement which flowed to and fro across the field before Hewitt held on to a doubtful pass and scored what was really a lovely try. Ross, however, capped a fine afternoon's work with another score in the last ten minutes.

ENGLAND 6   SCOTLAND 0
Twickenham
18 March 1961

England: J. G. Willcox (*Oxford Univ.*); P. B. Jackson (*Coventry*), W. M. Patterson (*Sale*), M. P. Weston (*Richmond*), J. Roberts (*Sale*); J. P. Horrocks-Taylor (*Leicester*), R. E. G. Jeeps* (*Northampton*); C. R. Jacobs (*Northampton*), E. Robinson (*Coventry*), T. P. Wright (*Blackheath*), R. J. French (*St Helen's*), V. S. J. Harding (*Saracens*), D. P. Rogers (*Bedford*), W. G. D. Morgan (*Medicals*), L. I. Rimmer (*Bath*)
Scotland: K. J. F. Scotland (*Heriot's FP*); A. R. Smith* (*Edin. Wrs.*) E. McKeating (*Heriot's FP*), G. D. Stevenson (*Hawick*), R. H. Thomson (*London Scot.*); I. H. P. Laughland (*London Scot.*), A. J. Hastie (*Melrose*); H. F. McLeod (*Hawick*), N. S. Bruce (*London Scot.*), D. M. D. Rollo (*Howe of Fife*), F. H. ten Bos (*London Scot.*), J. Douglas (*Stewart's FP*), K. I. Ross (*Boroughmuir FP*), G. K. Smith (*Kelso*), J. C. Brash (*Camb. Univ.*)
Referee: K. D. Kelleher (*Ireland*)   **Touch judges:** J. R. Hunter, L. M. Boundy

J. Roberts scored but J. G. Willcox failed (3-0). (H.T.). J. P. Horrocks-Taylor kicked a penalty (6-0).
    Once again at Twickenham Scotland failed to lift the Triple Crown for the whole team turned in a lack-lustre performance. Undoubtedly the enforced rearrangement of their pack was not a success; the backs never got going and even K. J. F. Scotland could not raise his game and missed several penalties normally within his range. In contrast J. P. Horrocks-Taylor (coming in at half for Sharp) played brilliantly, exhibiting a vast range of attacking moves and he certainly made life utterly miserable for one Scottish back row man of whom a disgruntled critic later said that not only did he fail to tackle Horrocks and Taylor but never once even caught the bloody hyphen. There was one flurry of excitement near the close when Douglas close to the line tried to pick up the slippy ball, but knocked on when a tap over would surely have produced a touch down.

SCOTLAND 3   FRANCE 11
Murrayfield
13 January 1962

Scotland: K. J. F. Scotland (*Leicester*); A. R. Smith* (*Edin. Wrs.*), J. J. McPartlin (*Oxford Univ.*), I. H. P. Laughland (*London Scot.*), R. C. Cowan (*Selkirk*); G. H. Waddell (*London Scot.*), J. A. T. Rodd (*London Scot.*); H. F. McLeod (*Hawick*), N. S. Bruce (*London Scot.*), D. M. D. Rollo (*Howe of Fife*), F. H. ten Bos (*London Scot.*), M. J. Campbell-Lamerton (*Halifax*), R. J. C. Glasgow (*Dunfermline*), J. Douglas (*Stewart's FP*), K. I. Ross (*Boroughmuir FP*)
France: L. Casaux (*Tarbes*); J. Dupuy (*Tarbes*), J. Pique (*Pau*), J. Bouquet (*Vienne*), H. Rancoule (*Tarbes*); P. Albaladejo (*Dax*), P. Lacroix* (*Agen*); A. Domenech (*Brive*), J. de Gregorio (*Grenoble*), A. Roques (*Cahors*), B. Mommejat (*Albi*), J. P. Saux (*Pau*), M. Crauste (*Lourdes*), H. Romero (*Montauban*), R. Gensane (*Beziers*)
Referee: R. C. Williams (*Ireland*)   **Touch judges:** H. W. Leach, M. J. Meynard

A. R. Smith kicked a penalty (3-0); P. Albaladejo kicked a penalty (3-3). (H.T.). P. Albaladejo kicked a penalty (3-6); H. Rancoule scored and P. Albaladejo converted (3-11).
    The Scottish pack showed up well but their great efforts were wasted by a lack of initiative behind. Waddell, seemingly slower, was worried by the cover defence and concentrated on gaining territorial advantage by some powerful kicking. As a result the backs were never given a chance. Laughland managed to engineer one good break which failed when his winger knocked on a vital pass. Then Scotland only converted one of five reasonably easy penalty kicks. In the second half the match swung as the result of one incident. Defending grimly France kicked a penalty given against Campbell-Lamerton for his treatment of an opponent. If justice had been done France should have been penalised for the offence which stung the Scot into an open but understandable retaliation. France gained heart from their lead and Crauste and Gensane broke away from a line out in a dribbling run which put the ball over the line. Rancoule outpaced the

defence to touch down just short of the dead ball line. Before the whistle Albaladejo narrowly missed with two drop kicks.

WALES 3   SCOTLAND 8
Cardiff
3 February 1962

Wales: K. Coslett (*Aberavon*); D. R. R. Morgan (*Llanelli*), D. K. Jones (*Llanelli*), H. M. Roberts (*Cardiff*), D. I. Bell (*Swansea*); A. Rees (*Maesteg*), L. H. Williams* (*Cardiff*); D. Greenslade (*Newport*), B. V. Meredith (*Newport*), L. J. Cunningham (*Aberavon*), W. R. Evans (*Bridgend*), B. E. V. Price (*Newport*), R. H. Davies (*London Welsh*), A. Pask (*Abertillery*), H. J. Morgan (*Abertillery*)
Scotland: K. J. F. Scotland (*Leicester*); A. R. Smith* (*Edin. Wrs.*), J. J. McPartlin (*Oxford Univ.*), I. H. P. Laughland (*London Scot.*), R. C. Cowan (*Selkirk*); G. H. Waddell (*London Scot.*), S. Coughtrie (*Edin. Acads.*); H. F. McLeod (*Hawick*), N. S. Bruce (*London Scot.*) D. M. D. Rollo (*Howe of Fife*), F. H. ten Bos (*London Scot.*), M. J. Campbell-Lamerton (*Halifax*), R. J. C. Glasgow (*Dunfermline*), J. Douglas (*Stewart's FP*), K. I. Ross (*Boroughmuir*)
Referee: N. M. Parkes (*England*)   **Touch judges:** R. P. Burrell, J. P. Evans

R. J. C. Glasgow and F. ten Bos scored and K. J. F. Scotland converted the second (0-8). (H.T.). A. Rees dropped a goal (3-8).

In wretched conditions a storming display by the pack brought Scotland its first win at Cardiff since 1927 and although they started with the wind and rain behind them there was no weakening of effort in the second half when some Welsh pressure could only manage a drop goal. The massive Scottish second row, totalling $34^1/_2$ stones, was most effective but there was little back play for under the conditions Coughtrie concentrated mainly on some accurate and lengthy kicking to touch. After fifteen minutes the pack held the ball in the scrum and then Douglas with ten Bos broke away and sent Glasgow over for the first score. Five minutes later Waddell put up a high kick which was misfielded, ten Bos picked up the rebound and his momentum did the rest.

IRELAND 6   SCOTLAND 20
Lansdowne Road
24 February 1962

Ireland: F. G. Gilpin (*QU Belfast*); W. R. H. Hunter (*CIYMS*), M. K. Flynn (*Wanderers*) D. Hewitt (*Instonians*), N. H. Brophy (*Blackrock*); G. G. Hardy (*Bective Rangers*), J. T. M. Quirke (*Blackrock*); S. Millar (*Ballymena*), A. R. Dawson (*Wanderers*), R. J. McLoughlin (*UC Dublin*), W. A. Mulcahy* (*Bohemians*), D. Scott (*Malone*), M. L. Hipwell (*Terenure*) M. G. Culliton (*Wanderers*)
Scotland: K. J. F. Scotland (*Leicester*); A. R. Smith* (*Edin. Wrs.*), J. J. McPartlin (*Oxford Univ.*), I. H. P. Laughland (*London Scot.*), R. C. Cowan (*Selkirk*); G. H. Waddell (*London Scot.*), S. Coughtrie (*Edin. Acads.*); H. F. McLeod (*Hawick*), N. S. Bruce (*London Scot.*) R. Steven (*Edin. Wrs.*), F. H. ten Bos (*London Scot.*), M. J. Campbell-Lamerton (*Halifax*) R. J. C. Glasgow (*Dunfermline*), J. Douglas (*Stewart's FP*), K. I. Ross (*Boroughmuir FP*)
Referee: N. M. Parkes (*England*)   **Touch judges:** G. K. Rome, J. Griffin

K. J. F. Scotland kicked a penalty (0-3); A. R. Smith and R. C. Cowan scored but K. J. F. Scotland failed to convert (0-9). (H.T.). W. R. Hunter kicked a penalty (3-9); W. R. Hunter scored but failed (6-9); K. J. F. Scotland kicked a penalty (6-12); A. R. Smith scored and K. J. F. Scotland converted (6-17); S. Coughtrie dropped a goal (6-20).

Scotland, while deserving to win, were rather flattered by the margin. The pack were rather beaten in the scrums but did rally strongly in the latter stages when Ireland with the wind staged a revival. The Scottish backs were very sound. Again Waddell, greatly helped by the fine form shown by Coughtrie, made good use of the touch line but did set his threes moving more than usual. Ireland started well against the wind and Hunter just failed to beat Cowan to the touch following a missed drop kick by Hardy. Then after a Scotland penalty Waddell burst through and when his long pass went to ground McPartlin snapped up the bouncing ball and sent Smith in at the corner. Shortly before half-time Waddell began another movement which finished with Cowan scoring. Soon after the interval Hunter got a penalty and a try, and Ireland looked dangerous. Flynn also touched down but he was brought back for offside. At this stage the Scottish pack held the challenge off. Then Scotland kicked a penalty before Smith scored after a good run by Coughtrie, Waddell and McLeod, and near full time Coughtrie dropped a goal from a wide angle.

SCOTLAND 3   ENGLAND 3
Murrayfield
17 March 1962

Scotland: K. J. F. Scotland (*Leicester*); A. R. Smith* (*Edin. Wrs.*), J. J. McPartlin (*Oxford Univ.*), I. H. P. Laughland (*London Scot.*), R. C. Cowan (*Selkirk*); G. H. Waddell (*London Scot.*), S. Coughtrie (*Edin. Acads.*); H. F. McLeod (*Hawick*), N. S. Bruce (*London Scot.*), D. M. D. Rollo (*Howe of Fife*), F. H. ten Bos (*London Scot.*), M. J. Campbell-Lamerton (*Halifax*), R. J. C. Glasgow (*Dunfermline*), J. Douglas (*Stewart's FP*), K. I. Ross (*Boroughmuir FP*)
England: J. G. Willcox (*Oxford Univ.*); A. C. B. Hurst (*Wasps*), A. M. Underwood (*Northampton*), J. M. Dee (*Hartlepool Rovers*), J. Roberts (*Sale*); J. P. Horrocks-Taylor (*Leicester*), R. E. G. Jeeps* (*Northampton*); P. E. Judd (*Coventry*), S. A. M. Hodgson (*Durham City*), T. P. Wright (*Blackheath*), T. A. Pargetter (*Coventry*), V. S. J. Harding (*Sale*), P. G. D. Robbins (*Coventry*), P. J. Taylor (*Northampton*), S. J. Purdy (*Rugby*)
Referee: K. D. Kelleher (*Ireland*)   **Touch judges:** D. C. J. McMahon, A. E. R. Cotterill

J. G. Willcox kicked a penalty (0-3); K. J. F. Scotland kicked a penalty (3-3). (H.T.).

Once again England prevented Scotland from lifting the Triple Crown with the third penalty draw in five seasons. Scotland had their chances but let them slip for they held a definite territorial advantage especially during the last twenty minutes. Neither of two heavy packs could claim dominance and both sides made great use of the kick ahead as a form of attack so that back play was restricted. England were never really in a position to dictate the run of play yet were always capable of holding any Scottish attack and always ready to set up a counterattack; indeed Hurst nearly scored in the dying moments. Near half time Willcox kicked a good 50 yard penalty cancelled out almost at once by K. J. F. Scotland who had failed with three previous attempts.

FRANCE 6   SCOTLAND 11
Colombes
12 January 1963

France: J. P. Razat (*Agen*); P. Besson (*Brive*), A. Boniface (*Mont-de-Marsan*), G. Boniface (*Mont-de-Marsan*), C. Darrouy (*Mont-de-Marsan*); P. Albaledejo (*Dax*), P. Lacroix* (*Agen*); F. Mas (*Beziers*), J de Gregorio (*Grenoble*), A. Roques (*Cahors*), B. Mommejat (*Albi*), J. P. Saux (*Pau*), R. Gensane (*Beziers*), J. Fabre (*Toulouse*), M. Crauste (*Lourdes*)
Scotland: K. J. F. Scotland* (*Leicester*); R. H. Thomson (*London Scot.*), J. A. P. Shackleton (*London Scot.*), D. M. White (*Kelvinside Acads.*), G. D. Stevenson (*Hawick*), I. H. P. Laughland (*London Scot.*), S. Coughtrie (*Edin. Acads.*); A. C. W. Boyle (*London Scot.*), N. S. Bruce (*London Scot.*), D. M. D. Rollo (*Howe of Fife*), F. H. ten Bos (*London Scot.*), M. J. Campbell-Lamerton (*Halifax*), K. I. Ross (*Boroughmuir*), J. Douglas (*Stewart's FP*), W. R. A. Watherston (*London Scot.*)
Referee: R. C. Williams (*Ireland*)   **Touch judges:** J. R. Hunter, B. Marie

A Boniface dropped a goal (3-0); P. Albaladejo kicked a penalty (6-0). (H.T.). K. J. F. Scotland dropped a goal and kicked a penalty (6-6); R. H. Thomson scored and K. J. F. Scotland converted (6-11).

Because of the severe frost the pitch, in spite of the protective straw, had remained uncomfortably hard so the ground staff left an inch or so of the straw lying, set fire to it and then swept the ashes off so that the game was played on a brownish grassless pitch. France started with the wind but their pack was so outweighted and outplayed that all they could manage by half time was a drop goal from A. Boniface (who halted in the middle of a passing movement to make his successful pot at goal) and a penalty by Albaladejo. In the second half Scotland took a firm grip on the game but it was twenty minutes before K. J. F. Scotland caught a faulty kick to touch and dropped a superb goal from near the line and fifteen minutes later equalised with a penalty yielded by a desperate defender handling the ball on the ground. Then right on 'no side' from a line out Campbell-Lamerton got possession and the ball went via Rollo to Laughland who from 45 yards out dropped at goal. The ball dropped short of the left hand post only to bounce wickedly high over

Besson's head and Thomson, the right winger, appeared, seemingly from nowhere, gathered the ball in full cry to score in the left corner one of the most sensational tries on record, for the whistle went after the conversion.

SCOTLAND 0   WALES 6
Murrayfield
2 February 1963

Scotland: K. J. F. Scotland* (*Heriot's FP*); R. H. Thomson (*London Scot.*), J. A. P. Shackleton (*London Scot.*), D. M. White (*Kelvinside Acads.*), G. D. Stevenson (*Hawick*); I. H. P. Laughland (*London Scot.*), S. Coughtrie (*Edin. Acads.*); A. C. W. Boyle (*London Scot.*), N. S. Bruce (*London Scot.*), D. M. D. Rollo (*Howe of Fife*), F. H. ten Bos (*London Scot.*) M. J. Campbell-Lamerton (*Halifax*), K. I. Ross (*Boroughmuir*), J. Douglas (*Stewart's FP*), W. R. A. Watherston (*London Scot.*)
Wales: G. T. R. Hodgson (*Neath*); D. R. R. Morgan (*Llanelli*), R. Evans (*Bridgend*), D. B. Davies (*Llanelli*), W. J. Morris (*Pontypool*); D. Watkins (*Newport*), D. C. T. Rowlands(*Pontypool*); D. Williams (*Ebbw Vale*), N. R. Gale (*Llanelli*), K. D. Jones (*Cardiff*), B. E. V. Price (*Newport*), B. E. Thomas (*Camb. Univ.*), G. Jones (*Ebbw Vale*), A. E. I. Pask (*Abertillery*), H. J. Morgan (*Abertillery*)
Referee: R. C. Williams (*Ireland*)   **Touch judges:** J. G. R. Howie, T. Pritchard

G. T. R. Hodgson kicked a penalty (0-3). (H.T.). D. C. T. Rowlands dropped a goal (0-6).

This must rank as the dreariest match ever played. The Welsh pack gave Rowlands a major share of the ball but the Welsh captain embarked on a rigid policy of kicking to touch and it was recorded later that there were 111 line outs during the afternoon. At least he could claim that his tactics broke a run of four defeats at Murrayfield. Unfortunately the Scottish halves with less of the ball also tended to kick and it was not until far on in the second half that their backs were set moving. Then, too late, it was obvious that they had the ability to worry the opposition. In the first half Hodgson kicked a good penalty against the wind and after the interval Rowlands, from the line, dropped a very good angled goal.

SCOTLAND 3   IRELAND 0
Murrayfield
23 February 1963

Scotland: C. F. Blaikie (*Heriot's FP*); R. H. Thomson (*London Scot.*), I. H. P. Laughland (*London Scot.*), D. M. White (*Kelvinside Acads.*), G. D. Stevenson (*Hawick*); K. J. F. Scotland* (*Heriot's FP*), S. Coughtrie (*Edin. Acads.*); A. C. W. Boyle (*London Scot.*), N. S. Bruce (*London Scot.*), D. M. D. Rollo (*Howe of Fife*), F. H. ten Bos (*London Scot.*), M. J. Campbell-Lamerton (*Halifax*), R. J. C. Glasgow (*Dunfermline*), J. Douglas (*Stewart's FP*), W. R. A. Watherston (*London Scot.*)
Ireland: T. J. Kiernan (*UC Cork*); W. R. Hunter (*CIYMC*), J. C. Walsh (*UC Cork*), P. J. Casey (*UC Dublin*), A. J. F. O'Reilly (*Old Belvedere*); M. A. F. English (*Lansdowne*), J. C. Kelly (*UC Dublin*); S. Millar (*Ballymena*), A. R. Dawson (*Wanderers*), R. J. McLoughlin (*Gosforth*), W. A. Mulcahy* (*Bective Rangers*), W. J. McBride (*Ballymena*), E. P. McGuire (*UC Galway*), C. J. Dick (*Ballymena*), M. D. Kiely (*Lansdowne*)
Referee: G. J. Trehavre (*Wales*)   **Touch judges:** P. A. Macdonald, G. A. Jamieson

S. Coughtrie kicked a penalty (3-0). (H.T.).

Ireland could be regarded as unlucky for they ran the ball frequently and indeed came near to scoring more than once, but the intrusion of the penalty goal into the modern game was marked. Coughtrie missed three long range kicks before kicking a penalty after 36 minutes. Scotland played a forward game but the pack, already suspect after the Welsh game, never got on top – they were, however, handicapped by an injury to Boyle. He changed places with ten Bos who was clearly not suited to the prop position. Glasgow, the oldest man on the field, again shone in the open, his fiercesome tackling being much in evidence. K. J. F. Scotland, handicapped by slow heeling, was much troubled by the Irish back row and had to kick more often than pass.

ENGLAND 10 SCOTLAND 8
Twickenham
16 March 1963

England: J. G. Willcox (*Harlequins*); P. B. Jackson (*Coventry*), M. S. Phillips (*Fylde*), M. P. Weston (*Durham City*), J. Roberts (*Sale*); R. A. W. Sharp* (*Wasps*), S. J. S. Clarke (*Camb. Univ.*); P. E. Judd (*Coventry*), H. O. Godwin (*Coventry*), N. J. Drake-Lee (*Camb. Univ.*), A. M. Davis (*Torquay A.*), J. E. Owen (*Coventry*), D. P. Rogers (*Bedford*), D. G. Perry (*Bedford*), D. C. Manley (*Exeter*)
Scotland: C. F. Blaikie (*Heriot's FP*); C. Elliot (*Langholm*), B. C. Henderson (*Edin. Wrs.*) D. M. White (*Kelvinside Acads.*), R. H. Thomson (*London Scot.*); K. J. F. Scotland* (*Heriot's FP*), S. Coughtrie (*Edin. Acads.*), J. B. Neill (*Edin. Acads.*), N. S. Bruce (*London Scot.*), D. M. D. Rollo (*Howe of Fife*), F. H. ten Bos (*London Scot.*), M. J. Campbell-Lamerton (*Halifax*), R. J. C. Glasgow (*Dunfermline*), J. P. Fisher (*RHSFP*), K. I. Ross (*Boroughmuir*)
Referee: G. Walters (*Wales*)   **Touch judges:** T. F. E. Grierson, W. J. Willeard

R. J. C. Glasgow scored and S. Coughtrie converted (0-5); K. J. F. Scotland dropped a goal (0-8); N. J. Drake-Lee scored and J. G. Willcox converted (5-8). (H.T.). R. A. W. Sharp scored and J. G. Wilcox converted (10-8).

Both teams showed changes. England having a new front row while Scotland made alterations to the threes and brought two new caps into the pack. Scotland with the wind made an impressive start and after some strong forward play Glasgow broke from a long line out to score. Later Willcox was caught with the ball and a quick heel let K. J. F. Scotland drop a goal. Before half time Sharp started a movement and passed to Jackson whose kick ahead was taken on by his forwards for Drake-Lee to go over. Early in the second half from a scrum close to the right touch line Clarke put out a good pass to Sharp who feinted to pass out to Weston but cutting back into the gap ran some 40 yards to score a classic try. Scotland fought back desperately but a stern defence kept them out.

SCOTLAND 10 FRANCE 0
Murrayfield
4 January 1964

Scotland: S. Wilson (*Oxford Univ.*), C. Elliot (*Langholm*), B. C. Henderson (*Edin. Wrs.*), I. H. P. Laughland (*London Scot.*), R. H. Thomson (*London Scot.*); G. Sharp (*Stewart's FP*), J. A. T. Rodd (*London Scot.*); J. B. Neill* (*Edin. Acads.*), N. S. Bruce (*London Scot.*) D. M. D. Rollo (*Howe of Fife*), W. J. Hunter (*Hawick*), P. C. Brown (*West of Scot.*), J. W. Telfer (*Melrose*), T. O. Grant (*Hawick*), J. P. Fisher (*RHSFP*)
France: C. Lacaze (*Angouleme*); J. Gachassin (*Lourdes*), G. Boniface (*Mont-de-Marsan*), A. Boniface (*Mont-de-Marsan*), J. Dupuy (*Tarbes*); P. Albaladejo (*Dax*), J. C. Lasserre (*Dax*), J. C. Berejnoi (*Tulle*), J. M. Cabanier (*Montauban*), J. Bayardon (*Chalon*), D. Dauga (*Mont-de-Marsan*), J. le Droff (*Auch*), J. J. Rupert (*Tyrosse*), J. Fabre* (*Toulouse*), M. Crauste (*Lourdes*)
Referee: R. C. Williams (*Ireland*)   **Touch judges:** D. Hill, M. Laurent

I. H. P. Laughland scored and S. Wilson converted (5-0). (H.T.). R. H. Thomson scored and S. Wilson converted (10-0).

Conditions were unpleasant for a heavy rain left surface water on the pitch. Nevertheless France handled often and well especially in the second half when both backs and forwards indulged in some spectacular interpassing with sudden changes in direction and they only failed against a very strong defence. Wilson was sound at full back, Henderson's tackling was as murderous as ever and the back row of Telfer, Grant and Fisher were good in the line out and cover defence. Midway through the first half Fisher and Henderson moved on to a loose pass and started a rush which ended in Laughland scoring. The second try came just before full time. A. Boniface, caught in possession parted with the ball but Thomson intercepted and ran from the 25 to score.

154

SCOTLAND 0   NEW ZEALAND 0
Murrayfield
18 January 1964

Scotland: S. Wilson (*Oxford Univ.*); C. Elliot (*Langholm*), J. A. P. Shackleton (*London Scot.*), I. H. P. Laughland (*London Scot.*), R. H. Thomson (*London Scot.*); G. Sharp (*Stewart's FP*), J. A. T. Rodd (*London Scot.*); J. B. Neill* (*Edin. Acads.*), N. S. Bruce (*London Scot.*), D. M. D. Rollo (*Howe of Fife*), W. J. Hunter (*Hawick*), P. C. Brown (*West of Scot.*), J. W. Telfer (*Melrose*), T. O. Grant (*Hawick*), J. P. Fisher (*RHSFP*)
New Zealand: D. B. Clarke (*Waikato*); R. W. Coulton (*Wellington*), P. F. Little (*Auckland*), M. J. Dick (*Auckland*); M. A. Herewini (*Auckland*); B. A. Watt (*Canterbury*), K. C. Briscoe (*Taranaki*); K. F. Gray (*Wellington*), D. Young (*Canterbury*), W. J. Whineray* (*Auckland*), B. J. Lochore (*Wairarapa*), A. J. Stewart (*Canterbury*), C. E. Meads (*King Country*), D. J. Graham (*Canterbury*), K. R. Tremain (*Hawkes Bay*)
Referee: R. C. Williams (*Ireland*)   **Touch judges:** A. S. R. Davidson, E. W. Kirton

This was a splendid performance by Scotland for the tourists finished by beating all the other Home Countries and France. Indeed with a bit of luck Scotland might have won, for at least three times they seriously threatened the New Zealand line whereas only once did the visitors look like scoring. For the first fifteen minutes the powerful New Zealand pack set about softening up the opposition only to meet with a completely successful resistance. The lighter Scottish pack beaten in the scrums, were quicker on to the ball in the loose and their backing-up and cover defence were first rate. In view of the poor conditions Sharp preferred to kick and this reduced the chances for New Zealand who had shown themselves masters at attacking from their opponents' mistakes. All the wingers had a lean time. In a final bid to win New Zealand made much use of high speculative kicks only to find that Wilson was not only dead safe but also capable and willing to come forward with the ball in attack.

WALES 11   SCOTLAND 3
Cardiff
1 February 1964

Wales: G. T. R. Hodgson (*Neath*); S. J. Watkins (*Newport*), D. K. Jones (*Llanelli*), K. Bradshaw (*Bridgend*), D. I. Bebb (*Swansea*); D. Watkins (*Newport*), D. C. T. Rowlands* (*Pontypool*); D. Williams (*Ebbw Vale*), N. R. Gale (*Llanelli*), L. J. Cunningham (*Aberavon*), B. Price (*Neath*), B. E. Thomas (*Neath*), G. J. Prothero (*Bridgend*), A. I. E. Pask (*Abertillery*), D. J. Hayward (*Cardiff*)
Scotland: S. Wilson (*Oxford Univ.*); C. Elliot (*Langholm*), J. A. P. Shackleton (*London Scot.*), I. H. P. Laughland (*London Scot.*), R. H. Thomson (*London Scot.*); G. Sharp (*Stewart's FP*), J. A. T. Rodd (*London Scot.*); J. B. Neill* (*Edin. Acads.*), N. S. Bruce (*London Scot.*), D. M. D. Rollo (*Howe of Fife*), W. J. Hunter (*Hawick*), P. C. Brown (*West of Scot.*), J. W. Telfer (*Melrose*), T. O. Grant (*Hawick*), J. P. Fisher (*RHSFP*)
Referee: P. G. Brook (*England*)   **Touch judges:** J. Dun, A. I. Griffiths

I. H. P. Laughland scored but S. Wilson failed (0-3). (H.T.). K. Bradshaw scored and converted (5-3); K. Bradshaw kicked a penalty (8-3); B. E. Thomas scored but K. Bradshaw failed (11-3).

Scotland played far below their standard of the New Zealand game and the score did not exaggerate the Welsh supremacy but at least there was no cracking up under the continual pressure of the latter stages. Rowlands this year changed his tactics and used high attacking kicks rather than aiming at touch. Scotland, starting with the sun and wind at their backs made a good start. Sharp hoisted an up and under, and when the clearance was missed Laughland came up fast enough to dive on the ball and score. Early in the second half Rowlands broke away and sent Bradshaw in. The scorer converted the try and a penalty soon afterwards. Continual pressure saw Thomas plunge over but although Scotland fought on their pack could not beat a strong Welsh eight.

IRELAND 3   SCOTLAND 6
Lansdowne Road
22 February 1964

Ireland: T. J. Kiernan (*Cork Const.*); P. J. Casey (*UC Dublin*), M. K. Flynn (*Wanderers*), J. C. Walsh (*UC Cork*), K. J. Houston (*QU Belfast*); C. M. H. Gibson (*Camb. Univ.*), J. C. Kelly (*UC Dublin*); P. J. Dwyer (*UC Dublin*), A. R. Dawson (*Wanderers*), R. J. McLoughlin (*Gosforth*), W. A. Mulcahy (*Bective Rangers*), W. J. McBride (*Ballymena*), E. P. McGuire (*UC Galway*), M. G. Culliton (*Wanderers*), N. A. A. Murphy (*Cork Const.*)
Scotland: S. Wilson (*Oxford Univ.*); C. Elliot (*Langholm*), B. C. Henderson (*Edin. Wrs.*) I. H. P. Laughland (*London Scot.*), W. D. Jackson (*Hawick*); D. H. Chisholm (*Melrose*), A. J. Hastie (*Melrose*); J. B. Neill* (*Edin. Acads.*), N. S. Bruce (*London Scot.*), D. M. D. Rollo (*Howe of Fife*), P. C. Brown (*West of Scot.*), M. J. Campbell-Lamerton (*London Scot.*), J. W. Telfer (*Melrose*), J. P. Fisher (*RHSFP*), R. J. C. Glasgow (*Dunfermline*)
Referee: A. C. Luff (*England*)   **Touch judges:** C. R. G. Reid, M. Barry

S. Wilson kicked two penalties (0-6). (H.T.). T. J. Kiernan kicked a penalty (3-6).

Scotland started with the rain and wind in their favour but could only manage two 40 yard penalties by Wilson before the interval. Early in the second half Kiernan, who was timed to take a deliberate 105 seconds to place the ball, also kicked a penalty but against the elements Scotland, with their pack clearly in control, closed the game up – a style of play at which the Melrose halves excelled. The young and gifted Gibson got little chance against a vigorous defence by Glasgow but it must be noted that McLoughlin was sadly handicapped by a leg injury sustained during the first half.

SCOTLAND 15   ENGLAND 6
Murrayfield
21 March 1964

Scotland: S. Wilson (*Oxford Univ.*); C. Elliot (*Langholm*), B. C. Henderson (*Edin. Wrs.*), I. H. P. Laughland (*London Scot.*), G. D. Stevenson (*Hawick*); D. H. Chisholm (*Melrose*), A. J. Hastie (*Melrose*); J. B. Neill* (*Edin. Acads.*), N. S. Bruce (*London Scot.*), D. M. D. Rollo (*Howe of Fife*), P. C. Brown (*West of Scot.*), M. J. Campbell-Lamerton (*London Scot.*), J. P. Fisher (*RHSFP*), J. W. Telfer (*Melrose*), R. J. C. Glasgow (*Dunfermline*)
England: J. G. Willcox (*Harlequins*); R. W. Hosen (*Northampton*), M. S. Phillips (*Fylde*), M. P. Weston (*Durham City*), J. M. Ranson (*Rosslyn Park*); T. J. Brophy (*Liverpool*), S. R. Smith (*Blackheath*); C. R. Jacobs* (*Northampton*), H. O. Godwin (*Coventry*), D. F. B. Wrench (*Harlequins*), C. M. Payne (*Harlequins*), A. M. Davis (*Torquay A*), P. J. Ford (*Gloucester*), T. G. A. H. Peart (*Hartlepool Rovers*), D. P. Rogers (*Bedford*)
Referee: R. C. Williams (*Ireland*)   **Touch judges:** D. McIntyre, J. Burgum

R. J. C. Glasgow and N. S. Bruce scored and S. Wilson converted both (10-0). (H.T.). R. W. Hosen kicked a penalty (10-3); J. W. Telfer scored and S. Wilson converted (15-3); D. P. Rogers scored but R. W. Hosen failed (15-6).

This was a very convincing win with much of the credit going to the Scottish forwards. They were solid in the scrums and well on top in the loose, being faster on to the ball and showing an ability to handle. Their aggressive back row was again in evidence; Fisher exhibiting his basket ball skills at the tail of the line out. The backs too played well Henderson being especially effective with his hearty tackling while Wilson again played an attacking game from full back. After half an hour Telfer picked up and passed to Glasgow who fairly crashed over for the opening score and near the interval further passing between Brown and Telfer put Bruce over. Early in the second half Hosen kicked a good 45 yard penalty but Scotland were not disturbed and Stevenson was nearly in at the corner before a break by Hastie was finished off by a spectacular try by Telfer. In spite of this the English pack fought back and near the close succeeded in scoring a pushover try credited to Rogers.

During the summer of 1964 Scotland toured Canada but no international match was played.

FRANCE 16 SCOTLAND 8
Colombes
9 January 1965

France: P. Dedieu (*Beziers*); J. Gachassin (*Lourdes*), G. Boniface (*Mont-de-Marsan*), J. Pique (*Pau*), C. Darrouy (*Mont-de-Marsan*); J. P. Capdouze (*Pau*), L. Camberabero, (*La Voulte*); A. Gruarin (*Toulon*), J. M. Cabonier (*Montauban*), J. C. Berejnoi (*Tulle*), W. Spanghero (*Narbonne*), D. Dauga (*Mont-de-Marsan*), M. Lira (*La Voulte*), A. Herrero (*Toulon*), M. Crauste (*Lourdes*)
Scotland: K. J. F. Scotland (*Aberdeenshire*); C. Elliot (*Langholm*), B. C. Henderson (*Edin. Wrs.*), I. H. P. Laughland (*London Scot.*), G. D. Stevenson (*Hawick*); B. M. Simmers (*Glas. Acads.*), J. A. T. Rodd (*London Scot.*); J. B. Neill* (*Edin. Acads.*), F. A. L. Laidlaw (*Melrose*), D. M. D. Rollo (*Howe of Fife*), P. K. Stagg (*Sale*), M. J. Campbell-Lamerton (*London Scot.*), D. Grant (*Hawick*), J. W. Telfer (*Melrose*), J. P. Fisher (*London Scot.*)
Referee: K. D. Kelleher (*Ireland*) **Touch judges:** J. Young, B. Marie

J. Gachassin scored and P. Dedieu converted (5-0); B. C. Henderson scored and K. J. F. Scotland converted (5-5). (H.T.). C. Darrouy and J. Pique scored but P. Dedieu failed (11-5); B. C. Henderson scored but K. J. F. Scotland failed (11-8); C. Darrouy scored and P. Dedieu converted (16-8).

With the new hooker doing well Scotland tried to play an open game but France with a clear edge in pace and teamwork fully deserved their win. Almost at once a well placed kick ahead bounced kindly for Pique who gave Gachassin a clear run in. Following some broken play Laughland made a break and the ball went via Fisher to Henderson who ran in his most aggressive style for 40 yards past and through several opponents to bring the scores level at half time. Soon after restarting a clearance kick was blocked by Darroux who went on to score and then Pique with a neat switch of direction beat the defence. Simmers broke from well inside his own half; the ball went along the line to Elliot and back to Simmers who sent Henderson over. Finally a bad pass by Rodd to Laughland arrived with Crauste who unceremoniously upended the centre and the ball was quickly worked clear to Darrouy for his second score.

SCOTLAND 12 WALES 14
Murrayfield
6 February 1965

Scotland: S. Wilson (*London Scot.*); C. Elliot (*Langholm*), B. C. Henderson (*Edin. Wrs.*) I. H. P. Laughland (*London Scot.*), D. J. Whyte (*Edin. Wrs.*); B. M. Simmers (*Glas. Acads.*), J. A. T. Rodd (*London Scot.*); N. Suddon (*Hawick*), F. A. L. Laidlaw (*Melrose*), D. M. D. Rollo (*Howe of Fife*), P. K. Stagg (*Sale*), M. J. Campbell-Lamerton* (*London Scot.*), J. P. Fisher (*London Scot.*), J. W. Telfer (*Melrose*), R. J. C. Glasgow (*Dunfermline*)
Wales: T. G. Price (*Llanelli*); S. J. Watkins (*Newport*), J. R. Uzzell (*Newport*) S. J. Dawes (*London Welsh*), D. I. Bebb (*Swansea*); D. Watkins (*Newport*), D. C. T. Rowlands* (*Pontypool*); D. Williams (*Ebbw Vale*), N. R. Gale (*Llanelli*), R. Waldron (*Neath*), B. Price (*Newport*), W. J. Morris (*Newport*), G. J. Prothero (*Bridgend*), A. I. E. Pask (*Abertillery*) H. J. Morgan (*Abertillery*)
Referee: R. W. Gilliland (*Ireland*) **Touch judges:** G. G. Murray, O. P. Bevan

B. M. Simmers dropped a goal (3-0); T. G. Price kicked a penalty (3-3); S. Wilson kicked a penalty (6-3); S. J. Watkins scored and T. G. Price converted (6-8). (H.T.). T. G. Price kicked a penalty (6-11), S. Wilson kicked a penalty (9-11), B. M. Simmers dropped a goal (12-11); N. R. Gale scored but T. G. Price failed (12-14).

This was a most exciting game won by Wales in the dying minutes. The forward exchanges were always vigorous but one gave as good as the other. Again Fisher's skill at the tail of the line was evident and Glasgow's tackling worried Watkins at half. Simmers started well and dropped a nice long goal after a pass from a set scrum but his knee gave way so that his play and that of the backs was unsettled. After an exchange of penalties Watkins went away on the blind side and stabbed the ball on. A lame Simmers failed to get the ball into touch and Watkins was able to collect and go on to score. After half time and another exchange of penalties Scotland took the lead with another drop by Simmers after a set scrum in front of the posts. Then in the last minutes a Scottish throw in was badly deflected and Gale grabbed the ball and crashed over for the winning score.

157

SCOTLAND 6   IRELAND 16
Murrayfield
27 February 1965

Scotland: S. Wilson (*London Scot.*); C. Elliot (*Langholm*), B. C. Henderson (*Edin. Wrs*) J. A. P. Shackleton (*London Scot.*), D. J. Whyte (*Edin. Wrs.*). I. H. P. Laughland (*London Scot.*), J. A. T. Rodd (*London Scot.*); N. Suddon (*Hawick*), F. A. L. Laidlaw (*Melrose*), D. M. D. Rollo (*Howe of Fyfe*), P. C. Brown (*West of Scot.*), M. J. Campbell-Lamerton* (*London Scot.*), J. P. Fisher (*London Scot.*), J. W. Telfer (*Melrose*), R. J. C. Glasgow (*Dunfermline*)
Ireland: T. J. Kiernan (*Cork Const.*); P. J. Casey (*Lansdowne*), J. C. Walsh (*UC Cork*), M. K. Flynn (*Wanderers*), P. J. McGrath (*UC Cork*), C. M. H. Gibson (*Camb. Univ.*), R M Young (*QU Belfast*); S. MacHale (*Lansdowne*), K. W. Kennedy (*QU Belfast*), R. J. McLoughlin* (*Gosforth*), W. J. McBride (*Ballymena*), W. A. Mulcahy (*Bective Rangers*) M. G. Doyle (*UC Dublin*), H. Wall (*Dolphin*), N. A. A. Murphy (*Cork Const.*)
Referee: D. G. Walters (*Wales*)   **Touch judges:** C. E. Allardyce, M. S. Smyth

I. H. P. Laughland dropped a goal (3-0); P. J. McGarth and R. M. Young scored and T. J. Kiernan converted the second (3-8). (H.T.). C. M. H. Gibson dropped a goal (3-11); N. A. A. Murphy scored and T. J. Kiernan converted (3-16); S. Wilson kicked a penalty (6-16).

Ireland, greatly helped by defensive weaknesses, were clear winners. Neither pack could claim domination in the line outs or scrums but the swift heeling from the set scrums gave Gibson a freedom which let him dictate the run of play. Scotland scored from the first scrum in front of the Irish posts but a swift passing run amongst the Irish threes put McGrath in and then a dummy scissors move by Flynn let Young clear away. In the second half Gibson dropped a goal before Murphy, peeling off on the blind side of a scrum, took Young's pass and found himself clear away for a score.

ENGLAND 3   SCOTLAND 3
Twickenham
20 March 1965

England: D. Rutherford (*Gloucester*); E. L. Rudd (*Oxford Univ.*), D. W. A. Rosser (*Camb. Univ.*), G. P. Frankcom (*Camb. Univ.*), A. W. Hancock (*Northampton*); M. P. Weston (*Durham City*), S. J. S. Clarke (*Blackheath*); A. L. Horton (*Blackheath*), S. B. Richards (*Richmond*), P. E. Judd (*Coventry*), J. E. Owen (*Coventry*), C. M. Payne (*Harlequins*), N. Silk (*Harlequins*), D. G. Perry* (*Bedford*), D. P. Rogers (*Bedford*)
Scotland: S. Wilson* (*London Scot.*); D. J. Whyte (*Edin. Wrs.*), B. C. Henderson (*Edin. Wrs.*), I. H. P. Laughland (*London Scot.*), W. D. Jackson (*Hawick*); D. H. Chisholm (*Melrose*), A. J. Hastie (*Melrose*), N. Suddon (*Hawick*), F. A. L. Laidlaw (*Melrose*), D. M. D. Rollo (*Howe of Fife*), P. K. Stagg (*Sale*), M. J. Campbell-Lamerton (*London Scot.*), J. P. Fisher (*London Scot.*), P. C. Brown (*West of Scot.*), D. Grant (*Hawick*)
Referee: D. G. Walters (*Wales*)   **Touch judges:** D. Haultain, D. L. Head

There was no scoring before half time. D. H. Chisholm dropped a goal (0-3); A. W. Hancock scored a try but D. Rutherford failed (3-3).

This was Hancock's match, for it was his extraordinary last minute try which denied Scotland a much desired win at Twickenham. After an early thrust by England, Scotland held the advantage during the first half and had such an obvious grip on the game later that the single score made shortly after half time seemed adequate especially as Chisholm and Hastie came near to scoring. Then in injury time Whyte got the ball inside the English 25. Had he kicked the ball dead the whistle may well have gone for no side but he, being relatively clear, ran for the line and was tackled. From the ensuing rush Weston got the ball, moved to the blind side and still inside the 25 passed to Hancock who set off along the left touch line. At least three defenders came across at him but a hand off and change of pace kept him free and with Laughland at his heels he crossed the line and was content to touch down at once. Rutherford failed with the kick from the touch line and the whistle went.

158

SCOTLAND 8   SOUTH AFRICA 5
Murrayfield
17 April 1965

Scotland: S. Wilson* (*London Scot.*); D. J. Whyte (*Edin. Wrs.*), J. A. P. Shackleton (*London Scot.*), I. H. P. Laughland (*London Scot.*), W. D. Jackson (*Hawick*); D. H. Chisholm (*Melrose*), A. J. Hastie (*Melrose*); N. Suddon (*Hawick*), F. A. L. Laidlaw (*Melrose*), D. M. D. Rollo (*Howe of Fife*), P. K. Stagg (*Sale*), M. J. Campbell-Lamerton (*London Scot.*), J. P. Fisher (*London Scot.*), P. C. Brown (*West of Scot.*), D. Grant (*Hawick*)
South Africa: L. G. Wilson (*WP*); J. P. Englebrecht (*WP*), W J. Mans (*WP*), J L Gainsford (*WP*), C. W. Dirksen (*EN Transvaal*); J. H. Barnard (*T*), D. J. De Vos (*WP*); S. P. Kuhn (*T*), D. C. Walton (*Natal*), J. F. K. Marais (*WP*), A. S. Malan* (*T*), G. Carelse (*EP*), J. Schoeman (*WP*), D. J. Hopwood (*WP*), M. R. Suter (*Natal*)
Referee: D. G. Walters (*Wales*)   **Touch judges:** J. A. H. Blake

J. A. P. Shackleton scored and S. Wilson converted (5-0). (H.T.). J. P. Englebrecht scored and W. J. Mans converted (5-5); D. H. Chisholm dropped a goal (8-5).

South Africa had undertaken a short tour of Ireland and Scotland at the beginning of their season and were obviously short of match practice. This was a narrow but sound win for Scotland for the visitors clearly tired before the finish and there was no doubt that the Scottish pack did well at the line out and in the loose. Again the Melrose halves had a good game, Chisholm making many fine breaks but was not so well supported as usual by the back row. After ten minutes Chisholm hoisted a high kick to the posts and when the full back failed to hold a swinging ball Shackleton was up to pick and score. Soon after the interval De Vos made a good break from a ruck and the ball went via Gainsford to Engelbrecht who beat the full back with alarming ease. Tremendous Scottish pressure followed but all that was achieved was a good drop goal from a wide angle by Chisholm after a quick heel. South Africa had one last attack: De Vos put Engelbrecht away but this time Wilson tackled him firmly and an inside pass was intercepted by Shackleton whose kick to touch finished the match.

SCOTLAND 3   FRANCE 3
Murrayfield
15 January 1966

Scotland: S. Wilson* (*London Scot.*); A. J. W. Hinshelwood (*London Scot.*), B. C. Henderson (*Edin. Wrs.*), I. H. P. Laughland (*London Scot.*), D. J. Whyte (*Edin. Wrs.*); D. H. Chisholm (*Melrose*), A. J. Hastie (*Melrose*); J. D. Macdonald (*London Scot.*), F. A. L. Laidlaw (*Melrose*), D. M. D. Rollo (*Howe of Fife*), P. K. Stagg (*Sale*), M. J. Campbell-Lamerton (*London Scot.*), J. P. Fisher (*London Scot.*), J. W. Telfer (*Melrose*), D. Grant (*Hawick*)
France: C. Lacaze (*Angouleme*); J. Gachassin (*Lourdes*), G. Boniface (*Mont-de-Marsan*), A. Boniface (*Mont-de-Marsan*), C. Darrouy (*Mont-de-Marsan*); J. C. Roques (*Brive*), M. Puget (*Brive*); A. Gruarin (*Toulon*), J. M. Cabanier (*Montauban*), J. C. Berejnoi (*Tulle*), W. Spanghero (*Narbonne*), E. Cester (*TOEC*), J. J. Rupert (*Tyrosse*), D. Dauga (*Mont-de-Marsan*), M. Crauste* (*Lourdes*)
Referee: D. M. Hughes (*Wales*)   **Touch judges:** G. V. Cooper, M. Laurent

C. Lacaze kicked a penalty (0-3); D. J. Whyte scored but S. Wilson failed (3-3). (H.T.).

Scotland played well but failed to turn their territorial and tactical advantages into points. Their pack was well on top. As Garcia puts it, *'c'est encore l'enfer pour les avants français'*. Laidlaw hooked very well, Stagg, Campbell-Lamerton and Fisher shone at the line out and the famous French peel at the tail never got going. As a result the French halves had an unhappy afternoon. In contrast the Scottish pair were very sound giving no loose chances for the French back row to snap up. Yet France scored first after fifteen minutes – admittedly by a penalty kick – before Chisholm sparked off a great handling movement. He moved inside G. Boniface and the ball went from Henderson and Laughland to Whyte who made a good run. When hemmed in by the cover defence the attack swung infield and a pass by Fisher reached Campbell-Lamerton before Hastie with a long pass set Whyte diving in at the corner. After half time Scotland missed three kickable penalties and Chisholm failed with two drops. On one occasion near the posts he kicked neatly on and was blatantly obstructed but the referee, understandably, was watching the ball and missed the incident.

WALES 8   SCOTLAND 3
Cardiff
5 February 1966

Wales: T. G. R. Hodgson (*Neath*); S. J. Watkins (*Newport*), D. K. Jones (*Cardiff*), K. Bradshaw (*Bridgend*), L. Davies (*Bridgend*); D. Watkins (*Newport*), A. R. Lewis (*Abertillery*), D. Williams (*Ebbw Vale*), N. R. Gale (*Llanelli*), D. J. Lloyd (*Bridgend*), B. Price (*Newport*), B. E. Thomas (*Neath*), G. J. Prothero (*Bridgend*), A. I. E. Pask* (*Abertillery*), H. J. Morgan (*Abertillery*)
Scotland: S. Wilson* (*London Scot.*); A. J. W. Hinshelwood (*London Scot.*), B. C. Henderson (*Edin. Wrs.*), I. H. P. Laughland (*London Scot.*), D. J. Whyte (*Edin. Wrs.*); J. W. C. Turner (*Gala*), A. J. Hastie (*Melrose*); J. D. Macdonald (*London Scot.*), F. A. L. Laidlaw (*Melrose*), D. M. D. Rollo (*Howe of Fife*), P. K. Stagg (*Sale*), M. J. Campbell-Lamerton (*London Scot.*), J. P. Fisher (*London Scot.*), J. W. Telfer (*Melrose*), D. Grant (*Hawick*)
Referee: M. H. Titcomb (*England*)   **Touch judges:** T. Pearson, I. Davies

D. K. Jones scored but K. Bradshaw failed (3-0). (H.T.). D. K. Jones scored and K. Bradshaw converted (8-0); S. Wilson kicked a penalty (8-3).

This game was played on a sodden, sticky muddy field swept by driving rain and Scotland did well to hold the score down in the first half. After some 15 minutes Watkins, at a scrum, ran left but Lewis fed Jones on the right. The ball went out to Watkins who passed back to Jones for his try. After the interval a typical bruising tackle by Henderson produced a loose ball which Hinshelwood picked up and hurled himself at the line. Instead of mauling the ball on over the line the pack heeled and nothing came of the move. Now against the wind Wales rallied and from a scrum Watkins, who had all through been most elusive, made a lovely break which finished with a try by Jones. Scotland were by no means overwhelmed but their pack lacked speed and cohesion and all that could be achieved was a penalty goal.

IRELAND 3   SCOTLAND 11
Lansdowne Road
26 February 1966

Ireland: T. J. Kiernan (*Cork Const.*); W. R. Hunter (*CIYMS*), M. K. Flynn (*Wanderers*), J. C. Walsh (*Sunday's Well*), P. J. McGrath (*UC Cork*); C. M. H. Gibson (*Camb. Univ.*) R. M. Young (*QU Belfast*); S. MacHale (*Lansdowne*), A. M. Brady (*Dublin Univ.*), R. J. McLaughlin* (*Gosforth*), W. J. McBride (*Ballymena*), O. C. Waldron (*Oxford Univ.*), N. A. A. Murphy (*Cork Const.*), R. A. Lamont (*Instonians*), M. G. Doyle (*Camb. Univ.*)
Scotland: S. Wilson (*London Scot.*); A. J. W. Hinshelwood (*London Scot.*), B. C. Henderson (*Edin. Wrs.*), I. H. P. Laughland* (*London Scot.*), D. J. Whyte (*Edin. Wrs.*); D. H. Chisholm (*Melrose*), A. J. Hastie (*Melrose*); J. D. Macdonald (*London Scot.*), F. A. L. Laidlaw (*Melrose*), D. M. D. Rollo (*Howe of Fife*), P. K. Stagg (*Sale*), M. J. Campbell-Lamerton (*London Scot.*), J. P. Fisher (*London Scot.*), J. W. Telfer (*Melrose*), D. Grant (*Hawick*)
Referee: D. M. Hughes (*Wales*)   **Touch judges:** J. K. Hunter, T. B. Kearns

A. J. W. Hinshelwood scored and S. Wilson converted (0-5); T. J. Kiernan kicked a penalty (3-5). (H.T.). A. J. W. Hinshelwood and D. Grant scored but S. Wilson failed (3-11).

Chisholm's return to half brought an obvious improvement; even the pack seemed to benefit with the back row outstanding. Henderson as usual tackled ferociously. The Scottish pack dominated the scrums especially as the referee and the Irish hooker could not see eye to eye over Law Fifteen! Gibson, in spite of the scrum worries and a perturbed Young, was a constant threat. Scotland began with a blustery wind and saw Hunter go off injured early on. Hastie after a sustained shove and quick heel worked a dummy scissors with Henderson before putting Hinshelwood in at the corner. Before half time Kiernan kicked a penalty. In the second half Scotland often used a shortened line out with Fisher operating successfully at the tail. One throw he touched down to Campbell-Lamerton who was tackled but Telfer and Grant moved the ball on and it went from Stagg, Fisher and Hastie to Hinshelwood who scored at the corner. Towards the close another delayed but controlled heel let Hastie break sharply and send Grant over.

160

SCOTLAND 6   ENGLAND 3
Murrayfield
19 March 1966

Scotland: C. F. Blaikie (*Heriot's FP*); A. J. W. Hinshelwood (*London Scot.*), B. C. Henderson (*Edin. Wrs.*), I. H. P. Laughland* (*London Scot.*), D. J. Whyte (*Edin. Wrs.*); D. H. Chisholm (*Melrose*), A. J. Hastie (*Melrose*); J. D. Macdonald (*London Scot.*), F. A. L. Laidlaw (*Melrose*), D. M. D. Rollo (*Howe of Fife*), P. K. Stagg (*Sale*), M. J. Campbell-Lamerton (*London Scot.*), J. P. Fisher (*London Scot.*), J. W. Telfer (*Melrose*), D. Grant (*Hawick*)
England: D. Rutherford (*Gloucester*); E. L. Rudd (*Liverpool*), R. D. Hearn (*Bedford*), C. W. McFadyean (*Moseley*), K. F. Savage (*Northampton*); M. P. Weston (*Durham City*), T. C. Wintle (*Northampton*); A. L. Horton (*Blackheath*), W. T. Treadwell (*Wasps*), P. E. Judd (*Coventry*), J. E. Owen (*Coventry*), C. M. Payne (*Harlequins*), J. R. H. Greenwood (*Waterloo*), G. A. Sherriff (*Saracens*), D. P. Rogers* (*Bedford*)
Referee: K. D. Kelleher (*Ireland*)   **Touch judges:** I. Stirling, D. L. Head

C. F. Blaikie kicked a penalty (3-0). (H.T.). C. W. McFadyean dropped a goal (3-3); D. J. Whyte scored but C. F. Blaikie failed (6-3).

The English pack held a slight advantage in the scrums and indulged in a fair amount of obstructive play in the line out, none suffering more from this than Fisher at the tail. The Melrose pair exhibited their own brand of half back play, mixing sound defence with sudden attacking bursts. The Scottish defence also benefited from some uncompromising tackles by both centres and by Grant from the back of the scrums. Early in the second half McFadyean equalised with a drop kick. Then from a line out Hastie flung a grand long pass to Chisholm who cut through. The ball travelled from Henderson to Laughland who was half checked but got a pass away to Grant who came up on the outside. A further pass sent Whyte off at full pace to score far out.

SCOTLAND 11   AUSTRALIA 5
Murrayfield
17 December 1966

Scotland: S. Wilson (*London Scot.*); A. J. W. Hinshelwood (*London Scot.*), J. W. C. Turner (*Gala*), B. M. Simmers (*Glas. Acads.*), D. J. Whyte (*Edin. Wrs.*); D. H. Chisholm (*Melrose*), A. J. Hastie (*Melrose*); N. Suddon (*Hawick*), F. A. L. Laidlaw (*Melrose*), D. M. D. Rollo (*Howe of Fife*), P. K. Stagg (*Sale*), P. C. Brown (*West of Scot.*), J. P. Fisher* (*London Scot.*), A. H. W. Boyle (*St Thomas's*), D. Grant (*Hawick*)
Australia: J. K. Lenehan (*NSW*); A. M. Cardy (*NSW*), J. E. Brass (*NSW*), R. J. Marks (*Queensland*), S. Boyce (*NSW*); P. R. Gibbs (*Victoria*), K. W. Catchpole* (*NSW*); J. M. Miller (*NSW*), P. G. Johnson (*NSW*), A. R. Miller (*NSW*), R. G. Teitzel (*Queensland*), P. C. Crittle (*NSW*), M. P. Purcell (*Queensland*), J. F. O'Gorman (*NSW*), G. V. Davis (*NSW*)
Referee: M. Joseph (*Wales*)   **Touch judges:** A. J. K. Monro, D. J. S. Spink

S. Wilson kicked a penalty (3-0); J. E. Brass scored and J. K. Leneham converted (3-5); D. H. Chisholm scored and S. Wilson converted (8-5). (H.T.). A. H. W. Boyle scored but S. Wilson failed (11-5).

Australia, having just beaten Wales for the first time, were fairly confident and, although forced to replace the injured Hawthorne at stand-off, might well have won this game had his replacement, Gibbs, not been injured in the last ten minutes. Scotland, playing with the wind, had a tremendous start for Wilson kicked a 35 yard penalty for an offence at the first scrum, but after twenty minutes Australia went into the lead when Brass charged down a clearance and scored. Ten minutes before half time and after some good work by Fisher and Brown, Chisholm wrong-footed the defence to score a fine solo try. In the second half Australia with the wind did a lot of attacking but their backs, rather inclined to run across the field, could not break a good defence and it was their forwards who looked more dangerous. With ten minutes to go Gibbs suffered a leg injury but stayed on the field as an extra full back and O'Gorman came out of the pack. This undoubtedly helped Scotland for the forwards made some tremendous rushes and Boyle got over for the last score.

161

FRANCE 8   SCOTLAND 9
Colombes
14 January 1967

France: C. Lacaze (*Angouleme*); B. Duprat (*Bayonne*), C. Dourthe (*Dax*), J. Maso (*Perpignan*), C. Darrout* (*Mont-de-Marsan*); J. Gachassin (*Lourdes*), J. C. Lasserre (*Dax*); A. Gruarin (*Toulon*), J. M. Cabanier (*Montauban*), J. C. Berejnoi (*Tulle*), W. Spanghero (*Narbonne*), D. Dauga (*Mont-de-Marsan*), J. P. Salut (*Toulouse*), A. Herrero (*Toulon*), C. Carrere (*Toulon*)
Scotland: S. Wilson (*London Scot.*); A. J. W. Hinshelwood (*London Scot.*), J. W. C. Turner (*Gala*), B. M. Simmers (*Glas. Acads.*), D. J. Whyte (*Edin. Wrs.*); D. H. Chisholm (*Melrose*), A. J. Hastie (*Melrose*); J. D. MacDonald (*London Scot.*), F. A. L. Laidlaw (*Melrose*), D. M. D. Rollo (*Howe of Fife*), P. K. Stagg (*Sale*), W. J. Hunter (*Hawick*), J. P. Fisher* (*London Scot.*), A. H. W. Boyle (*St Thomas's*), D. Grant (*Hawick*)
Referee: K. D. Kelleher (*Ireland*)   **Touch judges:** J. W. A. Ireland, B. Marie

S. Wilson kicked a penalty (0-3): B. Duprat scored but J. Gachassin failed (3-3); S. Wilson kicked a penalty (3-6). (H.T.). B. M. Simmers dropped a goal (3-9); C. Carrere scored and J. Gachassin converted (8-9).

Within two minutes a 40 yard penalty kick by Wilson put Scotland into the lead but the French backs were moving the ball beautifully and a half break by Gachassin, carried on by Dourthe, put Duprat over for a fine try. The lead was short lived for after five minutes Wilson kicked another penalty. Both sets of backs, with their fullbacks coming into the line, were running well but grim defence prevented any further score. Just before the interval Maso hurt a leg and Salut came out to act as an extra threequarter. France returned fiercely but fell further behind when Simmers dropped a goal after a line out at the 25. However, the seven French forwards came away with some fine rushes and Carrere got over for what proved to be the last score.

SCOTLAND 11   WALES 5
Murrayfield
4 February 1967

Scotland: S. Wilson (*London Scot.*); A. J. W. Hinshelwood (*London Scot.*), J. W. C. Turner (*Gala*), B. M. Simmers (*Glas. Acads.*), D. J. Whyte (*Edin. Wrs.*); D. H. Chisholm (*Melrose*), A. J. Hastie (*Melrose*); J. D. MacDonald (*London Scot.*), F. A. L. Laidlaw (*Melrose*), D. M. D. Rollo (*Howe of Fife*), P. K. Stagg (*Sale*), W. J. Hunter (*Hawick*), J. P. Fisher* (*London Scot.*), J. W. Telfer (*Melrose*), D. Grant (*Hawick*)
Wales: T. G. Price (*Leicester Univ.*); D. I. Bebb (*Swansea*), T. G. R. Davies (*Cardiff*), W. H. Raybould (*Camb. Univ.*), S. J. Watkins (*Newport*); B. John (*Llanelli*), W. Hullin (*Cardiff*); J. O'Shea (*Cardiff*), B. Rees (*London Welsh*), D. J. Lloyd (*Bridgend*), B. Price (*Newport*), W. Mainwaring (*Aberavon*), K. Braddock (*Newbridge*), A. E. I. Pask* (*Abertillery*), J. Taylor (*London Welsh*)
Referee: K. D. Kelleher (*Ireland*)   **Touch judges:** T. F. E. Grierson, A. H. D. North

S. J. Watkins scored and T. G. Price converted (0-5). (H.T.). A. J. W. Hinshelwood scored but S. Wilson failed (3-5); D. H. Chisholm dropped a goal (6-5); J. W. Telfer scored and S. Wilson converted (11-5).

Wales held some territorial advantage early on but there was little back play, only grim mauling between the two packs. Whyte had to go off with an injured hand and Grant was taken out of the pack. At a lineout the ball shot back off a Scottish hand and Watkins caught it and ran fifteen yards unopposed to score at the corner. Whyte returned just after the interval to find Scotland defending but a good clearance put them into Welsh territory and from a scrum the ball was whipped along the line to Hinshelwood who had a fine sprint to throw himself in at the corner. Hereabout the Scottish pack began to improve and the ball coming to Chisholm he dropped a neat goal on the run. Near the close the Scottish forwards took the ball upfield and from a scrum near the line Hastie sold a dummy and passed to Telfer who crashed his way over.

SCOTLAND 3 IRELAND 5
Murrayfield
25 February 1967

Scotland: S. Wilson (*London Scot.*); A. J. W. Hinshelwood (*London Scot.*), J. W. C. Turner (*Gala*), R. B. Welsh (*Hawick*), D. J. Whyte (*Edin. Wrs.*); B. M. Simmers (*Glas. Acads.*), A. J. Hastie (*Melrose*); J. D. MacDonald (*London Scot.*), F. A. L. Laidlaw (*Melrose*), A. B. Carmichael (*West of Scot.*), P. K. Stagg (*Sale*), W. J. Hunter (*Hawick*), J. P. Fisher* (*London Scot.*), J. W. Telfer (*Melrose*), D. Grant (*Hawick*)

Ireland: T. J. Kiernan (*Cork Const.*); N. H. Brophy (*Blackrock*), J. C. Walsh (*Sunday's Well*), F. P. K. Bresnihan (*UC Dublin*), A. T. A. Duggan (*Lansdowne*), C. M. H. Gibson (*NIFC*), B. F. Sherry (*Terenure Coll.*); S. MacHale (*Lansdowne*), K. W Kennedy (*CIYMS*), S. A. Hutton (*Malone*), W. J. McBride (*Ballymena*), M. G. Molloy (*UC Calway*) N. A. A. Murphy* (*Cork Const.*), K. G. Goodhall (*Newcastle Univ.*), M. G. Doyle (*Edin.* Wrs.)

Referee: D. M. Hughes (*Wales*)   **Touch judges:** J. A. S. Taylor, M. Barry

No scoring at half time. N. A. A. Murphy scored and T. J. Kiernan converted (0-5). S. Wilson kicked a penalty (3-5).

Ireland ran the ball from the beginning and it was soon obvious that Gibson was going to be a real danger for he continually stretched the defence with well placed kicks or attacking runs. The Irish score, half way through the second half, came from a fierce burst away from a lineout by Kiernan and all that Scotland could manage in reply was a 45 yard penalty by Wilson. Once again Fisher at the tail of the lineout showed his skill at catching and distributing the ball.

ENGLAND 27 SCOTLAND 14
Twickenham
18 March 1967

England: R. W. Hosen (*Bristol*); K. F. Savage (*Northampton*), R. D. Hearn (*Bedford*), C. W. McFadyean (*Moseley*), R. C. Webb (*Coventry*); J. F. Finlan (*Moseley*), R. D. A. Pickering (*Bradford*); P. E. Judd* (*Coventry*), S. B. Richards (*Richmond*), M. J. Coulman (*Moseley*), J. N. Pallant (*Notts*), D. E. J. Watt (*Bristol*), D. P. Rogers (*Bedford*), D. M. Rollitt (*Bristol*), R. B. Taylor (*Northampton*)

Scotland: S. Wilson (*London Scot.*); A. J. W. Hinshelwood (*London Scot.*), J. W. C. Turner (*Gala*), R. B. Welsh (*Hawick*), D. J. Whyte (*Edin. Wrs.*); I. H. P. Laughland (*London Scot.*), I. G. McCrae (*Cordonians*); J. D. MacDonald (*London Scot.*), F. A. L. Laidlaw (*Melrose*), D. M. D. Rollo (*Howe of Fife*), P. K. Stagg (*Sale*), W. J. Hunter (*Hawick*), J. P. Fisher* (*London Scot.*), J. W. Telfer (*Melrose*), D. Grant (*Hawick*)

Referee: D. P. D'Arcy (*Ireland*)   **Touch judges:** R. S. Waddell, R. F. Johnson

R. W. Hosen kicked a penalty (3-0); J. W. C. Turner scored but S. Wilson failed (3-3); A. J. W. Hinshelwood scored and S. Wilson converted (3-8), C. W. McFadyean scored and R. W. Hosen converted (8-8); S. Wilson kicked a penalty (8-11). (H.T.). R. B. Taylor scored and R. W. Hosen converted (13-11); S. Wilson kicked a penalty (13-14); R. W. Hosen kicked a penalty (16-14); R. E. Webb scored but R. W. Hosen failed (19-14); C. W. McFadyean scored and R. W. Hosen converted (24-14); J. F. Finlan dropped a goal (27-14).

Scotland held their own in the first half but crumbled during the last half hour, when the English forwards took a firm grip in the scrums and loose mauls.

SCOTLAND 3 NEW ZEALAND 14
Murrayfield
2 December 1967

Scotland: S. Wilson (*London Scot.*); A. J. W. Hinshelwood (*London Scot.*), J. W. C. Turner (*Gala*), J. N. M. Frame (*Edin. Univ.*), R. R. Keddie (*Watsonions*); D. H. Chisholm (*Melrose*), A. J. Hastie (*Melrose*); A. B. Carmichael (*West of Scot.*), F. A. L. Laidlaw (*Melrose*), D. M. D. Rollo (*Howe of Fife*), P. K. Stagg (*Sale*), G. W. E. Mitchell (*Edin. Wrs.*), J. P. Fisher* (*London Scot.*), A. H. W. Boyle (*London Scot.*), D. Grant (*Hawick*)

New Zealand: W. F. McCormick (*Canterbury*); A. G. Steel (*Canterbury*), I. R. MacRae, (*Hawkes Bay*), W. L. Davis (*Hawkes Bay*), W. M. Birtwhistle (*Waikato*); E. W. Kirton (*Otago*), C. R. Laidlaw (*Otago*); K. F. Gray (*Wellington*), B. E. McLeod

163

(*Counties*), A. E. Hopkinson (*Canterbury*), S. C. Strahan (*Manawata*), C. E. Meads (*King County*), K. R. Tremain (*Hawkes Bay*), B. J. Lochore (*Wairarapa*), G. C. Williams (*Wellington*)
Referee: K. D. Kelleher (*Ireland*)   **Touch judges:** R. P. Burrell, J. G. Dow

D. H. Chisholm dropped a goal (3-0); W. F. McCormick kicked a penalty (3-3); I. R. MacRae scored but W. F. McCormick failed (3-6); W. F. McCormick kicked a penalty (3-9). (H.T.). W. L. Davis scored and W. F. McCormick converted (3-14).

Scotland did remarkably well against their very powerful opponents who were held in check by some determined tackling. The forwards, although beaten in the loose, had some success at the lineouts where Fisher at the tail did a lot of fine catching and cover tackling. It was unpleasant to note that before Davis scored the only try in the second half, Fisher could not cover Kirton from the lineout for he was quite clearly put out of the game by a nudge that laid him flat. It was a hard vigorous game yet not dirty in spite of the incident at the end of play. Chisholm stopped to pick up a rolling ball only to recoil to avoid a swinging kick aimed by Meads in the direction of the ball. The referee (and many others) regarded this as dangerous play and since he had already warned the player for dangerous foot work in the ruck, had no option but to send him off; a sad ending to an exciting game which the visitors deserved to win.

SCOTLAND 6   FRANCE 8
Murrayfield
13 January 1968

Scotland: S. Wilson (*London Scot.*); A. J. W. Hinshelwood (*London Scot.*), J. W. C. Turner (*Gala*), J. N. M. Frame (*Edin. Univ.*), G. J. Keith (*Wasps*); D. H. Chisholm (*Melrose*), A. J. Hastie (*Melrose*); A. B. Carmichael (*West of Scot.*), F. A. L. Laidlaw (*Melrose*), D. M. D. Rollo (*Howe of Fife*), P. K. Stagg (*Sale*), G. W. E. Mitchell (*Edin. Wrs.*), J. P. Fisher* (*London Scot.*), A. H. W. Boyle (*London Scot.*), D. Grant (*Hawick*)
France: C. Lacaze (*Angouleme*); A. Campaes (*Lourdes*), J. Trillo (*Begles*), J. Maso (*Perpignan*), B. Duprat (*Bayonne*); G. Camberabero (*La Voulte*), L. Camberabero (*La Voulte*); A. Abadie (*Graulhet*), J. M. Cabanier (*Montauban*), A. Gruarin (*Toulon*), D. Dauga (*Mont-de-Marsan*), E. Cester (*TOEC*), J. J. Rupert (*Tyrosse*), W. Spanghero (*Narbonne*), C. Carrere* (*Toulon*)
Referee: K. D. Kelleher (*Ireland*)   **Touch judges:** H. B. Laidlaw, R. Calmet

B. Duprat scored but G. Camberabero failed (0-3); G. J. Keith scored but S. Wilson failed (3-3). (H.T.). S. Wilson kicked a penalty (6-3); A. Campaes scored and G. Camberabero converted (6-8).

Inside five minutes France took the lead. From a line out G. Camberabero dropped for goal. The ball flew wide but Duprat had followed up so fast that he just beat Wilson to the touch down. Play thereafter tended to be in the French half although their backs handled well and even attacked from behind their own line. Right on the half hour the ball came from a line out to Chisholm who made a good burst, handed on to Turner who ripped through the defence and then the ball went via Frame to Keith who scored in the corner. Soon after the interval Wilson put Scotland into the lead with a penalty but after fifteen minutes France snatched a try when Dauga picked up a bad pass, crashed through the forwards and passed to Trillo who put Campaes in at the corner for Camberabero to convert. Scotland pressed but could not break down a fast covering defence.

WALES 5   SCOTLAND 0
Cardiff
3 February 1968

Wales: D. Rees (*Swansea*); S. J. Watkins (*Newport*), K. S. Jarrett (*Newport*), T. G. R. Davies (*Cardiff*), W. K. Jones (*Cardiff*); B. John (*Cardiff*), G. O. Edwards* (*Cardiff*); J. O'Shea (*Cardiff*), J. Young (*Harrogate*), D. J. Lloyd (*Bridgend*), M. Wiltshire (*Aberavon*), W. D. Thomas (*Llanelli*), W. D. Morris (*Neath*), R. E. Jones (*Coventry*), A. J. Gray (*London Welsh*)
Scotland: S. Wilson (*London Scot.*); A. J. W. Hinshelwood (*London Scot.*), J. W. C. Turner(*Gala*), J. N. M. Frame (*Edin. Univ.*), G. J. Keith (*Wasps*); D. H. Chisholm (*Melrose*), A. J. Hastie (*Melrose*); A. B. Carmichael (*West of Scot.*), F. A. L. Laidlaw (*Melrose*), D. M. D. Rollo (*Howe of Fife*), P. K. Stagg (*Sale*), G. W. E. Mitchell (*Edin. Wrs.*), J. P. Fisher*(*London Scot.*), A. H. W. Boyle (*London Scot.*), T. G. Elliot (*Langholm*)
Referee: G. C. Lamb (*England*)   **Touch judges:** R. F. King, G. D. Francis

W. K. Jones scored and K. S. Jarrett converted (5-0). (H.T.).

The opening exchanges were mainly confined to the forwards with the halves kicking to touch and it was early seen that the new Welsh pack were faster on the ball and holding their own at the lineouts. After twenty minutes following a scrum on the Scottish 25 Jarrett made a half break and gave a pass (which seemed well forward) to Davies who put Jones in at the corner for the only score of the match. There were many exciting runs from both sides which produced near misses. Edwards had one lovely break up the left touchline but his kick over Wilson's head beat him to the dead ball line. Fisher who had a good game at the line out and in the loose was held up more than once on the line. Jarrett, although kicking a good conversion, had an off-day with penalty kicks.

IRELAND 14   SCOTLAND 6
Lansdowne Road
24 February 1968

Ireland: T. J. Kiernan (*Cork Const.*); A. T. A. Duggan (*Lansdowne*), B. A. P. O'Brien (*Shannon*), F. P. K. Bresnihan (*UC Dublin*), R. D. Scott (*QU Belfast*); C. M. H. Gibson (*NIFC*), J. Quirke (*Blackrock*); S. Millar (*Ballymena*), A. M. Brady (*Malone*), P. O'Callaghan (*Dolphin*), M. G. Malloy (*UC Galway*), W. J. McBride (*Ballymena*), M. G. Doyle (*Blackrock*), T. J. Doyle (*Wanderers*), K. G. Goodall (*Derry*)
Scotland: S. Wilson (*London Scot.*); A. J. W. Hinshelwood (*London Scot.*), J. W. C. Turner (*Gala*), J. N. M. Frame (*Edin. Univ.*), C. G. Hodgson (*London Scot.*); D. H. Chisholm (*Melrose*), I. G. McCrae (*Gordonians*); A. B. Carmichael (*West of Scot.*), F. A. L. Laidlaw (*Melrose*), D. M. D. Rollo (*Howe of Fife*), P. K. Stagg (*Sale*), A. F. McHarg (*West of Scot.*), J. P. Fisher* (*London Scot.*), A. H. W. Boyle (*London Scot.*), R. J. Arneil (*Edin. Acads.*)
Referee: M. Joseph (*Wales*)   **Touch judges:** K. A. G. Boxer, J. E. Leslie

T. J. Kiernan kicked a penalty (3-0); A. T. A. Duggan scored but T. J. Kiernan failed (6-0). (H.T.). S. Wilson kicked a penalty (6-3); F. P. K. Bresnihan scored but T. J. Kiernan failed (9-3); S. Wilson kicked a penalty (9-6); A. T. A. Duggan scored and T. J. Kiernan converted (14-6).

Again the Scottish pack did not come up to expectations; the new half back combination was not a success and although there was some bad luck there was too much mishandling by the backs. Ireland, on the other hand, took their chances when scoring their tries. The first came from an O'Brien run and crosskick which Duggan caught and although well tackled managed to fall over the line for the score. The second followed a charged down clearance kick which broke to Bresnihan for a gift try. Towards the close, three points behind, Scotland put in a fighting finish and Chisholm had a short run and pass inside to Boyle who charged into a ruck. Suddenly from this Quirke emerged with the ball and had a clear run up to Wilson. He collected his kick ahead and set up a passing run by O'Brien which gave Duggan his second score.

SCOTLAND 6   ENGLAND 8
Murrayfield
16 March 1968

Scotland: S. Wilson (*London Scot.*); A. J. W. Hinshelwood (*London Scot.*), J. W. C. Turner (*Gala*), J. N. M. Frame (*Edin. Univ.*), C. G. Hodgson (*London Scot.*); I. Robertson (*London Scot.*), G. C. Connell (*Trinity Acads.*); N. Suddon (*Hawick*), D. T. Deans (*Hawick*), A. B. Carmichael (*West of Scot.*), P. K. Stagg (*Sale*), A. F. McHarg (*West of Scot.*), J. P. Fisher (*London Scot.*), J. W. Telfer* (*Melrose*), R. J. Arneil (*Edin. Acads.*)
England: R. B. Hiller (*Harlequins*); R. E. Webb (*Coventry*), R. H. Lloyd (*Harlequins*), T. J. Brooke (*Richmond*), K. F. Savage (*Northampton*); M. P. Weston* (*Durham City*), R. D. A. Pickering (*Bradford*); B. W. Keen (*Newcastle Univ.*), J. V. Pullin (*Bristol*), M. J. Coulman (*Moseley*), P. J. Larter (*Northampton*), M. J. Parsons (*Northampton*), P. J. Bell (*Blackheath*), D. J. Gay (*Bath*), B. R. West (*Loughborough*)
Referee: D. P. d'Arcy (*Ireland*)   **Touch judges:** D. C. J. McMahon, Dr C. R. Narkham

S. Wilson kicked a penalty (3-0); G. C. Connell dropped a goal (6-0). (H.T.). M. J. Coulman scored and R. B. Miller converted (6-5); R. B. Hiller kicked a penalty (6-8).

Scotland began with a strong wind behind them and after fifteen minutes Wilson kicked a penalty. The new pair of half backs started well, Robertson placing some dangerous diagonal kicks and then after half an hour Connell, almost under the posts, stopped a rolling ball, whipped round and dropped a neat goal. Against the wind England had barely been over the Scottish 25 line but immediately on restarting one kick from Weston found touch far upfield. Fortunately the Scottish back row was giving both Pickering and him a harassing time. Then from a four man line out Coulman ran on to the throw and had a 35 yard run through a flat defence for a splendid try. With ten minutes to go Hiller kicked a lovely penalty from the right touchline, a kick which emphasised Scotland's continual failures with penalties, not only in this game but throughout the whole season.

SCOTLAND 9   AUSTRALIA 3
Murrayfield
2 November 1968

Scotland: C. F. Blaikie (*Heriot's FP*); A. J. W. Hinshelwood (*London Scot*), J. W. C. Turner (*Gala*), C. W. W. Rea (*West of Scot.*), W. D. Jackson (*Hawick*); C. M. Telfer (*Hawick*), G. C. Connell (*Trinity Acads.*); N. Suddon (*Hawick*), F. A. L. Laidlaw (*Melrose*), A. B. Carmichael (*West of Scot.*), P. K. Stagg (*Sale*), A. F. McHarg (*London Scot.*), T. G. Elliot (*Langholm*), J. W. Telfer* (*Melrose*), R. J. Arneil (*Edin. Acads.*)
Australia: B. D. Honan (*Queensland*); J. W. Cole (*NSW*), J. E. Brass (*NSW*), P. V. Smith (*NSW*), T. R. Forman (*NSW*); J. P. Ballesty (*NSW*), J. N. B. Hipwell (*NSW*); K. R. Bell (*Queensland*), P. G. Johnson* (*NSW*), R. B. Prosser (*NSW*), P. N. P. Reilly (*Queensland*), S. C. Gregory (*Queensland*), H. A. Rose (*NSW*), D. A. Taylor (*Queensland*), G. V. Davis (*NSW*)
Referee: M. H. Titcomb (*England*)   **Touch judges:** R. P. Burrell, F. Parker

C. F. Blaikie kicked a penalty (3-0); A. J. W. Hinshelwood scored but C. F. Blaikie failed (6-0); J. E. Brass kicked a penalty (6-3); C. F. Blaikie kicked a penalty (9-3). (H.T.).

The Scottish pack held the whip hand throughout and Colin Telfer with a good share of the ball, played well in his first game. The solitary try came from a short penalty taken by Connell. The ball went from Colin Telfer to Rea who made a nice break and a further passing run by Jim Telfer and Arneil saw Hinshelwood score far out. The Australian attack was not much seen but in the second half the Scottish threes produced a lot of fine constructive play and were unlucky not to score although they did have the ball over the line twice but were recalled for infringements.

FRANCE 3   SCOTLAND 6
Colombes
11 January 1969

France: P. Villepreux (*Toulouse*); J. M. Bonal (*Toulouse*), J.-P. Lux (*Tyrosse*), J. Maso (*Narbonne*), A. Campaes (*Lourdes*); J. Gachassin (*Lourdes*), J. L. Berot (*Toulouse*), M. Lasse, M. Yachvili (*Tulle*), J. M. Esponda (*Perpignan*), E. Cester (*TOEC*), B. Dauga (*Mont-de-Marsan*), J. Iracabal (*Bayonne*), W. Spanghero (*Narbonne*), C. Carrere* (*Toulon*)
Scotland: C. F. Blaikie (*Heriot's FP*), A. J. W. Hinshelwood (*London Scot.*), J. W. C. Turner (*Gala*), C. W. W. Rea (*West of Scot.*), W. D. Jackson (*Hawick*); C. M. Telfer (*Hawick*), G. C. Connell (*London Scot.*); N. Suddon (*Hawick*), F. A. L. Laidlaw (*Melrose*), A. B. Carmichael (*West of Scot.*), P. K. Stagg (*Sale*), A. F. McHarg (*London Scot.*), T. G. Elliot (*Langholm*), J. W. Telfer* (*Melrose*), R. J. Arneil (*Edin. Acads.*) Repl.: I. G. McCrae (*Gordonians*)
Referee: G. C. Lamb (*England*)

C. F. Blaikie kicked a penalty (0-3). (H.T.). P. Villepreux kicked a penalty (3-3); J. W. Telfer scored but C. F. Blaikie failed (3-6).

Even before the game began Salut twisted his ankle running on to the pitch and was replaced by Iracabal so causing a shuffle in the pack. Then after Blaikie had kicked a penalty Connell had to retire hurt and McCrae came on as a replacement as allowed under the new law. For the remainder of the half France were very active and dangerous for Dauga and Carrere were nearly over while Maso came near with a drop. Early in the second half Villepreux, who had not been kicking well, equalised with a tremendous penalty from midfield and there followed some fine French handling, one move sweeping the length of the field. Then towards the close Scotland grabbed a try when a French heel on their 25 let McCrae pounce on a loose ball and pass to Jim Telfer who fairly crashed over for the winning score.

SCOTLAND 3   WALES 17
Murrayfield
1 February 1969

Scotland: C. F. Blaikie (*Heriot's FP*); A. J. W. Hinshelwood (*London Scot.*), J. N. M. Frame (*Gala*), C. W. W. Rea (*West of Scot.*), W. D. Jackson (*Hawick*); C. M. Telfer (*Hawick*), I. G. McCrae (*Gordonians*); N. Suddon (*Hawick*), F. A. L. Laidlaw (*Melrose*), A. B. Carmichael (*West of Scot.*), P. K. Stagg (*Sale*), A. F. McHarg (*London Scot.*), T. G. Elliot (*Langholm*), J. W. Telfer* (*Melrose*), R. J. Arneil (*Edin. Acads.*)
Wales: J. P. R. Williams (*London Welsh*); M. C. R. Richards (*Cardiff*), T. G. R. Davies (*Cardiff*), K. S. Jarrett (*Newport*), S. J. Watkins (*Newport*); B. John (*Cardiff*), G. O. Edwards (*Cardiff*); D. Williams (*Ebbw Vale*), J. Young (*Harrogate*), D. J. Lloyd (*Bridgend*), B. Price* (*Newport*), B. E. Thomas (*Neath*), W. D. Morris (*Neath*), T. M. Davies (*London Welsh*), J. Taylor (*London Welsh*)
Referee: K. D. Kelleher (*Ireland*)   **Touch judge:** D. C. J. McMahon, E. R. Morgan

K. S. Jarrett kicked two penalty goals (0-6). (H.T.). G. O. Edwards scored but K. S. Jarrett failed (0-9); C. F. Blaikie kicked a penalty (3-9); M. C. R. Richards scored but K. S. Jarrett failed (3-12); B. John scored and K. S. Jarrett converted (3-17).

The Welsh team, with a trip to the Antipodes coming off, had taken to squad training under a national coach but they won this match not so much by team work as by capitalising on blunders by their opponents. In the first half Jarrett kicked two fine penalties awarded for simple offences. In the second half Edwards scored by pouncing on a bad Scottish heel on their line. Richards was given a clear run in along the line from a ball knocked back to him at a line out and then John having half charged down a kick, picked up and got over as he was tackled. Scotland, however, could not break through a good defence but Blaikie, who eventually kicked a 45 yard penalty, had hard lines in the first half when each of three long range kicks went narrowly past – kicks that could have given Scotland a 9-6 lead at half time.

SCOTLAND 0   IRELAND 16
Murrayfield
22 February 1969

Scotland: C. F. Blaikie (*Heriot's FP*); A. J. W. Hinshelwood (*London Scot.*), J. N. M. Frame (*Gala*), C. W. W. Rea (*West of Scot.*), W. D. Jackson (*Hawick*); C. M. Telfer (*Hawick*), R. C. Allan (*Hutchesons' GSFP*); N. Suddon (*Hawick*), F. A. L. Laidlaw (*Melrose*), A. B. Carmichael (*West of Scot.*), P. C. Brown (*Gala*), A. F. McHarg (*London Scot.*), W. Lauder (*Neath*),J. W. Telfer* (*Melrose*), R. J. Arneil (*Edin. Acads.*) Repl.: P. K. Stagg (*Sale*), W. G. Macdonald (*London Scot.*)
Ireland: T. J. Kiernan* (*Cork Const.*), A. T. A. Duggan (*Lansdowne*), F. P. K. Bresnihan (*UC Dublin*), C. M. H. Gibson (*NIFC*), J. C. M. Moroney (*London Irish*); B. J. McGann (*Lansdowne*), R. M. Young (*QU Belfast*); S. Millar (*Ballymena*), K. W. Kennedy (*London Irish*), P. O'Callaghan (*Dolphin*), W. J. McBride (*Ballymena*), M. G. Molloy (*London Irish*), J. C. Davidson (*Dungannon*), K. G. Goodall (*Derry*), N. A. A. Murphy (*Cork Const.*) Repl.: M. L. Hipwell (*Terenure*)
Referee: M. Joseph (*Wales*)   **Touch judges:** H. B. Laidlaw, F. I. Howard

A. T. A. Duggan scored but J. C. N. Moroney failed (0-3). (H.T.). B. J. McGann, C. M. H. Gibson and F. P. K. Bresnihan scored and J. C. M. Moroney converted the last two (0-16).

After some wintry weather, conditions were harsh and there were many stoppages for injury with three replacements coming on during the match. W. G. Macdonald, incidentally must hold some kind of record for he only played during the final two minutes of the game. Scotland lost their captain after fifteen minutes but frankly could not match a very experienced Irish team which mustered a fantastic total of 287 caps. McGann had a good game, placing the ball over the line to give Duggan a simple try and scoring a fine solo try himself. The other two scores came after strong running by the Irish backs.

ENGLAND 8   SCOTLAND 3
Twickenham
15 March 1969

England: R. B. Hiller (*Harlequins*); K. J. Fielding (*Moseley*), J. S. Spencer (*Camb. Univ.*), D. J. Duckham (*Coventry*), R. E. Webb (*Coventry*); J. F. Finlan (*Moseley*), T. C. Wintle (*Northampton*); D. L. Powell (*Northampton*), J. V. Pullin (*Bristol*), K. E. Fairbrother (*Coventry*), N. E. Horton (*Moseley*), P. J. Larter (*Northampton*), R. B. Taylor (*Northampton*), D. M. Rollitt (*Bristol*), D. P. Rogers* (*Bedford*) Repl.: T. J. Dalton (*Coventry*)
Scotland: C. F. Blaikie (*Heriot's FP*); W. C. C. Steele (*Langholm: RAF*), J. N. M. Frame (*Gala*), I. Robertson (*Watsonians*), W. D. Jackson (*Hawick*); C. M. Telfer (*Hawick*), G. C. Connell (*London Scot.*); J. McLauchlan (*Jordanhill Coll.*), F. A. L. Laidlaw (*Melrose*), A. B. Carmichael (*West of Scot.*), P. C. Brown (*Gala*), A. F. McHarg (*London Scot.*), W. Lauder (*Neath*), J. W. Telfer* (*Melrose*), R. J. Arneil (*Edin. Acads.*)
Referee: C. Durand (*France*)   **Touch judges:** D. H. Collier, Major C. Tyler

D. J. Duckham scored and R. B. Hiller converted (5-0). (H.T.). D. J. Duckham scored but R. B. Hiller failed (8-0); P. C. Brown kicked a penalty (8-3).

Although Scotland had the better of the first half they found themselves trailing at half time when Duckham snatched a score after Blaikie failed to hold a very high attacking kick. Duckham also finished off a fine handling run by the English backs in the second half. The Scottish pack although heavily outweighted showed considerable improvement and were well supported by their halves but no break-through was achieved. Again many penalty kicks were not converted and Brown was the third to be tried when he scored at the end of the match.

ARGENTINA 20   SCOTLAND XV 3
Buenos Aires
13 September 1969

Argentina: D. Morgan (*Old Georgian*); M. Pascual (*Pucara*), A. Travaglini (*CASI*), A. R. Jurado (*San Isidro*), M. Walther (*San Isidro*); T. Harris-Smith (*Old Georgian*), A. Etchegaray (*CASI*); M. Farina (*CASI*), R. Handley (*Old Georgian*), L. G. Yanez (*San Fernando*), B. Otano (*Pucara*), A. Anthony (*San Isidro*), R. Loyola (*Belgrano*), H. Silva* (*Los Tilos*), H. Miguens (*CUBA*)
Scotland: C. F. Blaikie (*Heriot's FP*); M. A. Smith (*London Scot.*), I. R. Murchie (*West of Scot.*), A. V. Orr (*London Scot.*), A. D. Gill (*Gala*); I. Robertson (*Watsonians*), D. S. Paterson (*Gala*); J. McLauchlan (*Jordanhill Coll.*), F. A. L. Laidlaw (*Melrose*), A. B. Carmichael (*West of Scot.*), P. K. Stagg (*Sale*), A. F. McHarg (*London Scot.*), R. J. Arneil (*Edin. Acads.*), J. W. Telfer* (*Melrose*), W. Lauder (*Neath*)
Referee: R. Colombo

A. Travaglini scored and T. Harris-Smith converted (5-0); M. Walther scored but T. Harris-Smith failed (8-0). (H.T.). T. Harris-Smith kicked a penalty and dropped a goal (14-0); M. A. Smith scored but C. F. Blaikie failed (14-3); A. Travaglini scored but T. Harris-Smith failed (17-3); T. Harris-Smith dropped a goal (20-3).

Scotland were early handicapped for I. R. Murchie took a bad blow on his shoulder in the opening minutes and, after A. Travaglini had scored, had to leave the field with a broken collar bone. W. Lauder came out of the pack to play at centre. Thereafter in a scorching heat and on a hard pitch they gradually wilted and tired visibly later in the second half. Nevertheless, the Scottish pack took a major share of the ball in the line-outs and scrums and it took firm tackling by a lively Puma team to keep control during the first half.

ARGENTINA 3   SCOTLAND XV 6
Buenos Aires
27 September 1969

Argentina: D. Morgan (*Old Georgian*); M. Pascual (*Pucara*), A. Travaglini (*CASI*), D. Benzi (*Duendez*), M. Walther (*San Isidro*); T. Harris-Smith (*Old Georgian*), A. Etchegaray (*CASI*); M. Farini (CASI), R. Handley (*Old Georgian*), L. G. Yanez (*San Fernando*), B. Stano (*Pucara*), A. Anthony (*San Isidro*), R. Loyola (*Belgrano*), H. Silva* (*Los Tilos*), H. Miguens (*CUBA*)

Scotland: C. F. Blaikie (*Heriot's FP*); M. A. Smith (*London Scot.*), B. Laidlaw (*RHSFP*), C. W. W. Rea (*West of Scot.*), W. C. C. Steele (*Langholm*); I. Robertson (*Watsonians*), D. S. Paterson (*Gala*); J. McLauchlan (*Jordanhill Coll.*), F. A. L. Laidlaw (*Melrose*), A. B. Carmichael (*West of Scot.*), P. K. Stagg (*Sale*), A. F. McHarg (*London Scot.*), R. J. Arneil (*Edin. Acads.*), J. W. Telfer* (*Melrose*), W. Lauder (*Neath*)
Referee: C. A. Pozzi

B. Stano scored but T. Harris-Smith failed (3-0); A. B. Carmichael scored but C. F. Blaikie failed (3-3); C. F. Blaikie kicked a penalty (3-6). (H.T.).

A more settled Scottish team, playing on a softer pitch, shrugged off an early score and gradually asserted their authority in all departments during the remainder of a fast but distinctly rugged match. Extremely close and hard marking by the Scots upset the fluency of the Puma's fast backs, especially as the forwards gave Harris-Smith a hard time.

Right away Blaikie grabbed a bouncing ball five yards out and when tackled passed back to Smith but the ball went wide and Stano got to it first. Ten minutes later Telfer broke from a loose maul at midfield and started a fine run in which at least half of the team handled before Carmichael went over at the corner. Just before half time Blaikie kicked a fine penalty from midfield for a lead which was safely held during the second half.

SCOTLAND 6   SOUTH AFRICA 3
Murrayfield
6 December 1969

Scotland: I. S. G. Smith (*London Scot.*); A. G. Biggar (*London Scot.*), J. N. M. Frame (*Gala*) C. W. W. Rea (*West of Scot.*), A. J. W. Hinshelwood (*London Scot.*); I. Robertson (*Watsonians*), D. S. Paterson (*Gala*); J. McLauchlan (*Jordanhill Coll.*), F. A. L. Laidlaw (*Melrose*) A. B. Carmichael (*West of Scot.*), P. K. Stagg (*Sale*), G. L. Brown (*West of Scot.*), W. Lauder (*Neath*), J. W. Telfer* (*Melrose*), R. J. Arneil (*Leicester*)
South Africa: H. O. de Villiers (*WP*); S. H. Nomis (*T*), O. A. Roux (*NT*), E. Olivier (*WP*), G. H. Muller (*WP*); P. J. Visagie (*GW*), D. J. J. de Vos (*WT*); J. B. Neethling (*WP*), C. H. Cockrell (*WP*), J. F. K. Marais (*NE*), F. C. H. du Preez (*NT*), G. Carelse (*EP*), P. J. F. Greyling (*T*), T. P. Bedford* (*Natal*), J. H. Ellis (*SWA*). Repl.: A. E. Van der Watt (*WP*)
Referee: M. Joseph (*Wales*)   **Touch judges:** R. P. Burrell, G. O. McInnes

P. J. Visagie kicked a penalty (0-3). (H.T.). I. S. G. Smith kicked a penalty, then scored a try which he failed to convert (6-3).

Straight away mention must be made of the almost intolerable strain placed on the tourists throughout the entire tour by the actions of those who professed to oppose the apartheid policy of the South African Government. For this match some 25,000 spectators were contained in the stand or in one section of the terracing directly opposite where a highly efficient group of policemen assisted by Stewards saw to it that the game was never interrupted by those militants who did come inside. The tourists were further handicapped by the late withdrawal of their captain, Dawie de Villiers but really Scotland deserved their narrow win. They dominated the lineout where the South African throw in was completely disrupted by placing the 6 feet 10 inch Stagg at Number Two and they more than held their own in the tight and loose scrums. But again they lacked a goal kicker for Smith could only convert one of the six penalties. However, he did make a well-timed entry into the line when five minutes from the end Frame, fed by Robertson, made a powerful break through and then left Smith with a clear run in for the winning try.

SCOTLAND 9   FRANCE 11
Murrayfield
10 January 1970

Scotland: I. S. G. Smith (*London Scot.*); A. G. Biggar (*London Scot.*), J. N. M. Frame (*Gala*), C. W. W. Rea (*West of Scot.*), A. J. W. Hinshelwood (*London Scot.*); I. Robertson (*Watsonians*), G. C. Connell (*London Scot*); J. McLauchlan (*Jordanhill Coll.*), F. A. L. Laidlaw (*Melrose*),A. B. Carmichael (*West of Scot.*), P. K. Stagg (*Sale*), G. L. Brown (*West of Scot.*), W. Lauder (*Neath*), J. W. Telfer* (*Melrose*), R. J. Arneil (*Leicester*)
France: P. Villepreux (*Toulouse*); J. Sillieres (*Tarbes*), J.-P. Lux (*Tyrosse*), A. Marot (*Brive*), R. Bougarel (*Toulouse*); L.

Paries (*Biarritz*), G. Sutra (*Narbonne*); J. Iracabal (*Bayonne*), R. Benesis (*Narbonne*), J.-L. Azarne (*Dax*), J.-P. Bastiat (*Dax*), E. Cester (*TOEC*), C. Carrere* (*Toulon*), G. Viard (*Narbonne*), B. Dauga (*Mont-de-Marsan*)
Referee: G. C. Lamb (*England*)   **Touch judges:** J. Young, C. Durand

B. Dauga scored and L. Paries converted (0-5), I. S. G. Smith scored but W. Lauder failed (3-5); L. Paries dropped a goal (3-8); W. Lauder kicked a penalty (6-8); J. P. Lux scored but P. Villepreux failed (6-11). (H.T.). W. Lauder kicked a penalty (9-11).

Scotland started well but after eighteen minutes Dauga picked the ball up from a scrum fifteen yards out and literally bulldozed his way in for a score. Scotland struck back with a try from Smith who made a well timed entry into a handling run. Then Paries failed to kick a penalty only to find a bad return kick come into his hands whereupon he dropped a good goal. Lauder then kicked a 35 yard penalty before Lux receiving from Sillieres crashed past three defenders for a spectacular try right on half time. Play was fairly even after restarting, but with twenty minutes to go Lauder kicked a penalty and then Scotland fairly put the pressure on a somewhat rattled French side, but several chances and one penalty were missed and the match lost.

WALES 18   SCOTLAND 9
Cardiff
7 February 1970

Wales: J. P. R. Williams (*London Welsh*); L. C. T. Daniel (*Newport*), S. J. Davies (*London Welsh*), P. Bennett (*Llanelli*), I. Hall (*Aberavon*); B. John (*Cardiff*), G. O. Edwards* (*Cardiff*); D. B. Llewelyn (*Newport*), V. C. Perrins (*Newport*), D. Williams (*Ebbw Vale*), W. D. Thomas (*Llanelli*), T. G. Evans (*London Welsh*), W. D. Morris (*Neath*), T. M. Davies (*London Welsh*), D. Hughes (*Newbridge*)
Scotland: I. S. G. Smith (*London Scot.*); M. A. Smith (*London Scot.*), J. N. M. Frame (*Gala*), C. W. W. Rea (*West of Scot.*), A. J. W. Hinshelwood (*London Scot.*); I. Robertson (*Watsonians*), R. G. Young (*Watsonians*); J. McLaughlan (*Jordanhill Coll.*), F. A. L. Laidlaw (*Melrose*), A. B. Carmichael (*West of Scot.*), P. K. Stagg (*Sale*), P. C. Brown (*Gala*), W. Lauder (*Neath*), J. W. Telfer* (*Melrose*), R. J. Arneil (*Leicester*). Repl.: G. L. Brown (*West of Scot.*)
Referee: D. P. D'Arcy (*Ireland*)   **Touch judges:** P. A. Macdonald, E. M. Lewis

I. Robertson dropped a goal (0-3); W. Lauder kicked a penalty (0-6), I. Robertson scored but I. S. G. Smith failed (0-9); L. C. T. Daniel scored and converted (5-9). (H.T.). D. B. Llewelyn, S. J. Davies and W. D. Morris scored and G. O. Edwards converted the last two (18-9).

For the first twenty minutes the Scottish pack provided some good ball and, with the wind, their backs responded well. Robertson dropped a neat goal and Lauder kicked a penalty before Robertson, fielding a weak kick, set P. C. Brown and Young away and he was up to get the final pass to beat two defenders and score a good try. But just before the interval a short penalty move put Daniel in at the corner for a try which he converted. Just after restarting P. C. Brown limped off to be replaced by his brother (one wit suggested that the family could collect a good few caps if they pursued this act further!) but with the wind the Welsh pack really began to dominate play. Another short penalty move using the forwards saw Llewelyn crash over. Davies collected a charged down kick and scored, and later Morris scored when the pack shoved the scrum over the Scottish line.

IRELAND 16   SCOTLAND 11
Lansdowne Road
28 February 1970

Ireland: T. J. Kiernan* (*Cork Const.*); A. T. A. Duggan (*Lansdowne*), F. P. K. Bresnihan (*London Irish*), C. M. H. Gibson (*NIFC*), W. J. Brown (*Malone*); B. J. McGann (*Cork Const.*), R. M. Young (*Collegians*); S. Millar (*Ballymena*), K. W. Kennedy (*London Irish*), P. O'Callaghan (*Dolphin*), W. J. McBride (*Ballymena*), M. G. Malloy (*London Irish*), R. A. Lamont (*Instonians*), K. G. Goodall (*Derry*), J. F. Slattery (*UC Dublin*)
Scotland: I. S. G. Smith (*London Scot.*); M. A. Smith (*London Scot.*), J. N. M. Frame (*Gala*), C. W. W. Rea (*West of Scot.*), A. G. Biggar (*London Scot.*); I. Robertson (*Watsonians*), D. S. Paterson (*Gala*); N. Suddon (*Hawick*), F. A. L. Laidlaw (*Melrose*), A. B. Carmichael (*West of Scot.*), P. K. Stagg (*Sale*), G. L. Brown (*West of Scot.*), W. Lauder (*Neath*), J. W. Telfer* (*Melrose*), R. J. Arneil (*Leicester*)
Referee: C. Durand (*France*)   **Touch judges:** E. J. Mentiplay, G. A. Jamieson

M. G. Malloy scored but C. M. H. Gibson failed (3-0); I. Robertson dropped a goal (3-3); K. G. Goodall and C. M. H. Gibson scored and T. J. Kiernan converted both (13-3). (H.T.). W. J. Brown scored but R. M. Young failed (16-3); W. Lauder and M. A. Smith scored and I. S. G. Smith converted the first only (16-11).

Ireland dominated this game until the last fifteen minutes when Scotland staged a tremendous rally to score twice and come close a few times, Biggar in particular running robustly. The first Irish score was a solo effort by Malloy who grabbed a loose ball at a line out ten yards out and crashed his way over for the try. The other three scores were the result of some fine running and passing by the Irish backs. The Irish team raised its total of caps to a new level of 315!

SCOTLAND 14   ENGLAND 5
Murrayfield
21 March 1970

Scotland: I. S. G. Smith (*London Scot.*); M. A. Smith (*London Scot.*), J. N. M. Frame (*Gala*), J. W. C. Turner (*Gala*), A. G. Biggar (*London Scot.*); I. Robertson (*Watsonians*), D. S. Paterson (*Gala*); N. Suddon (*Hawick*), F. A. L. Laidlaw* (*Melrose*), A. B. Carmichael (*West of Scot.*), P. K. Stagg (*Sale*), G. L. Brown (*West of Scot.*), T. G. Elliot (*Langholm*), P. C. Brown (*Gala*), R. J. Arneil (*Leicester*)
England: R. B. Hiller* (*Harlequins*); M. J. Novak (*Harlequins*), J. S. Spencer (*Camb. Univ.*), D. J. Duckham (*Coventry*), M. P. Bullpitt (*Blackheath*); I. R. Shackleton (*Camb. Univ.*), N. C. Starmer-Smith (*Harlequins*); C. B. Stevens (*Penzance-Newlyn*), J. V. Pullin (*Bristol*), K. E. Fairbrother (*Coventry*), A. M. Davis (*Harlequins*), P. J. Larter (*Northampton*), A. L. Bucknall (*Richmond*), R. B. Taylor (*Northampton*), B. R. West (*Northampton*) Repl.: B. S. Jackson (*Broughton Park*)
Referee: M. Joseph (*Wales*)   **Touch judges:** T. F. E. Grierson, R. A. B. Crowe

P. C. Brown kicked a penalty (3-0); A. G. Biggar scored but P. C. Brown failed (6-0). (H.T.). P. C. Brown kicked a penalty (9-0); J. S. Spencer scored and R. B. Hiller converted (9-5); J. W. C. Turner scored and P. C. Brown converted (14-5).

Scotland, who had dropped two of their back row including their ex-captain, started briskly for within ten minutes Brown had kicked a long range penalty followed by a good run by Robertson and Frame which finished with Biggar racing in at the corner. There was no further scoring before half time although Hiller had hard luck with four mammoth kicks at goal. Another good penalty by Brown seemed to make things safe but with seven minutes left England took a swift short penalty which set Spencer off on a magnificent 75 yard run to score at the corner; Hiller's great conversion put England back in the game.

At this point West went off with a leg injury and was replaced by Jackson but Turner clinched the match in the last minutes by scoring after taking a well-timed reverse pass from Robertson.

For the Scotland v. Barbarians, match, 9 May 1970, see page 254

AUSTRALIA 23   SCOTLAND 3
Sydney
6 June 1970

Australia: A. N. McGill (*NSW*); J. W. Cole (*NSW*), S. O. Knight (*NSW*), G. A. Shaw (*NSW*), R. P. Batterham (*NSW*); R. G. Rosenblum (*NSW*), J. N. B. Hipwell (*NSW*); J. L. Howard (*NSW*), P. G. Johnson (*NSW*), J. R. Roxburgh (*NSW*), A. J. Skinner (*NSW*), O. F. Butler (*NSW*), G. V. Davis* (*NSW*), H. A. Rose (*NSW*), B. S. McDonald (*NSW*)
Scotland: J. W. C. Turner (*Gala*); M. A. Smith (*London Scot.*), J. N. M. Frame (*Gala*), C. W. W. Rea (*West of Scot.*), A. G. Biggar (*London Scot.*); I. Robertson (*Watsonians*), D. S. Paterson (*Gala*); N. Suddon (*Hawick*), F. A. L. Laidlaw* (*Melrose*), A. B. Carmichael (*West of Scot.*), P. K. Stagg (Sale), G. L. Brown (*West of Scot.*), W. Lauder (*Neath*), G. K. Oliver (*Gala*), R. J. Arneil (*Leicester*)
Referee: I. R. Vanderfield

J. N. B. Hipwell and R. P. Batterham scored and A. N. McGill converted the first (8-0); W. Lauder kicked a penalty (8-3). (H.T.). R. G. Rosenblum scored but A. N. McGill failed (11-3); A. N. McGill kicked a penalty (14-3); J. W. Cole, R. P. Batterham and J. W. Cole scored but A. McGill failed to convert (23-3).

Scotland finished off a short tour to Australia by being completely overrun in the one International played. They started well but mishandling let them down and Australia soon took command of the play. With the wind in the second half their backs made good use of a plentiful supply of the ball and ran in four unconverted tries to finish convincing winners.

FRANCE 13   SCOTLAND 8
Colombes
16 January 1971

France: P. Villepreux (*Toulouse*); J. Sillieres (*Tarbes*), J. Trillo (*Begles*), J.-P. Lux (*Tyrosse*), J. Cantoni (*Beziers*); J.-L. Berot (*Toulouse*), M. Barrau (*Beaumont*); M. Etchevery (*Pau*), R. Benesis (*Narbonne*), J.-L. Azarne (*St Jean de Lux*), J.-P. Bastiat (*Dax*), Y. le Droff (*Auch*), G. Viard (*Narbonne*), B. Dauga* (*Mont-de-Marsan*), D. Dubois (*Begles*)
Scotland: I. S. G. Smith (*London Scot.*); A. G. Biggar (*London Scot.*), J. N. M. Frame (*Gala*) C. W. W. Rea (*Headingley*), W. C. C. Steele (*Bedford*); J. W. C. Turner (*Gala*), D. S. Paterson (*Gala*); J. McLauchlan (*Jordanhill Coll.*), F. A. L. Laidlaw (*Melrose*), A. B. Carmichael (*West of Scot.*), A. F. McHarg (*London Scot.*), G. L. Brown (*West of Scot.*), N. A. MacEwan (*Gala*), P. C. Brown* (*Gala*), R. J. Arneil (*Leicester*) Repl.: B. M. Simmers (*Glas. Acads.*)
Referee: K. D. Kellehar (*Ireland*)   **Touch judges:** D. C. J. McMahon, R. Calmet

P. Villepreux kicked a penalty (3-0); I. S. G. Smith kicked a penalty (3-3). (H.T.). W. C. C. Steele scored and P. C. Brown converted (3-8); J. Sillieres scored and P. Villepreux converted (8-8); P. Villepreux scored and converted (13-8).

At the end of a fairly even first half Smith had to leave the field injured by a hard late tackle. He was replaced in the second half by Simmers who, however, was placed at stand off and Turner who had been playing well there, went to full back. This move was not really a success and came in for much criticism later. The Scottish try started when Rea, inside his own 25, pounced on a loose pass and the ball went via Frame to Steele who chipped ahead, gathered and scored in the corner. The French backs kept running the ball and inside the last ten minutes ran in two fine tries to win.

SCOTLAND 18   WALES 19
Murrayfield
6 February 1971

Scotland: I. S. G. Smith (*London Scot.*); W. C. C. Steele (*Bedford*), J. N. M. Frame (*Gala*), C. W. W. Rea (*Headingley*), A. G. Biggar (*London Scot.*); J. W. C. Turner (*Gala*), D. S. Paterson (*Gala*); J. McLauchlan (*Jordanhill Coll.*), F. A. L. Laidlaw (*Melrose*), A. B. Carmichael (*West of Scot.*), A. F. McHarg (*London Scot.*), G. L. Brown (*West of Scot.*), N. A. MacEwan (*Gala*), P. C. Brown* (*Gala*), R. J. Arneil (*Leicester*)
Wales: J. P. R. Williams (*London Welsh*); T. G. R. Davies (*Camb. Univ.*), S. J. Dawes* (*London Welsh*), A. J. Lewis (*Ebbw Vale*), J. C. Bevan (*Cardiff CE*); B. John (*Cardiff*), G. O. Edwards (*Cardiff*); D. B. Llewelyn (*Llanelli*), J. Young (*Harrogate*), D. Williams (*Ebbw Vale*), W. D. Thomas (*Llanelli*), M. G. Roberts (*London Welsh*), W. D. Norris (*Neath*), T. M. Davies (*London Welsh*), J. Taylor (*London Welsh*)
Referee: M. H. Titcomb (*England*)   **Touch judges:** J. Young, D. L. Daniels

P. C. Brown kicked a penalty (3-0); B. John kicked a penalty (3-3); P. C. Brown kicked a penalty (6-3); J. Taylor scored and B. John converted (6-8). (H.T.). G. O. Edwards scored but J. Taylor failed (6-11); A. B. Carmichael scored but P. C. Brown failed (9-11); P. C. Brown kicked a penalty (12-11); B. John scored but failed (12-14); P. C. Brown kicked a penalty (15-14); C. W. W. Rea scored but P. C. Brown failed (18-14); T. G. R. Davies scored and J. Taylor converted (18-19).

This must rank as one of the most exciting matches ever played. Scotland, very much the underdogs, held the lead four times and only lost by what was virtually the last kick of the game. The Welsh team whose half backs were outstanding was undoubtedly good and with a try tally of 4-2 could not really be grudged their win, but credit must be given to a Scottish XV which never gave in. The Scottish tries came from powerful and determined solo efforts by Carmichael and Rea while the Welsh scores savoured more of team work superbly finished off by the gifted individuals concerned. In the last minutes Wales won a line out inside the 25 and the ball went across the line to the right. The inside centre was missed out and Williams came into the line to put Davies over

172

at the corner. Taylor won the match with a left-footed kick which has been described elsewhere as 'the greatest conversion since St Paul's!

SCOTLAND 5   IRELAND   17
Murrayfield
27 February 1971

Scotland: I. S. G. Smith (*London Scot.*); W. C. C. Steele (*Bedford*), J. N. M. Frame (*Gala*) A. G. Biggar (*London Scot.*), R. S. M. Hannah (*West of Scot.*); J. W. C. Turner (*Gala*), D. S. Paterson (*Gala*); J. McLauchlan (*Jordanhill Coll.*), F. A. L. Laidlaw (*Melrose*), A. B. Carmichael (*West of Scot.*), A. F. McHarg (*London Scot.*), G. L. Brown (*West of Scot.*), N. A. MacEwan (*Gala*), P. C. Brown* (*Gala*), R. J. Arneil (*Leicester*)
Ireland: B. J. O'Driscoll (*Manchester*); A. T. A. Duggan (*Lansdowne*), F. P. K. Bresnihan (*London Irish*), C. M. H. Gibson* (*NIFC*), E. L. Grant (*CIYMS*); B. J. McGann (*Cork Const.*), R. M. Young (*Collegians*); R. J. McLoughlin (*Blackrock*), K. W. Kennedy (*London Irish*), J. F. Lynch (*St Mary's*), W. J. McBride (*Ballymena*), M. G. Molloy (*London Irish*), M. L. Hipwell (*Terenure*), D. J. Hickie (*St Mary's*), J. F. Slattery (*UC Dublin*)
Referee: W. K. M. Jones (*Wales*)   **Touch judges:** T. F. E. Grierson, P. Beatty

C. H. M. Gibson kicked a penalty (0-3), A. T. A. Duggan scored but B. J. O'Driscoll failed (0-6); C. M. H. Gibson kicked a penalty (0-9). (H.T.); J. N. M. Frame scored and P. C. Brown converted (5-9); E. L. Grant scored but C. M. H. Gibson failed (5-12); A. T. A. Duggan scored and C. M. H. Gibson converted (5-17).

The first half belonged to Ireland who, with an advantage in the scrums, continually ran the ball and a blind side run by Young and McGann put Duggan in for a try. Gibson also kicked two fine long range penalties before the interval. Scotland improved a little in the second half and several individual bursts narrowly failed before Frame crashed over to score. Heartened by this Scotland fought hard only to hand Ireland two gift tries in injury time. The first came when Young picked up a wretched Scottish heel from a scrum and gave Grant a clear run in. A minute later an interception near half field gave Duggan another try to finish the match.

ENGLAND 15   SCOTLAND 16
Twickenham
20 March 1971

England: R. Hiller (*Harlequins*); J. P. Janion (*Bedford*), C. S. Wardlow (*Northampton*), J. S. Spencer* (*Headingley*), D. J. Duckham (*Coventry*); A. R. Cowman (*Loughborough*), J. J. Page (*Bedford*); D. L. Powell (*Northampton*), J. V. Pullin (*Bristol*), F. E. Cotton (*Loughborough*), P. J. Larter (*Northampton*), N. E. Horton (*Moseley*), A. L. Bucknall (*Richmond*), R. B. Taylor (*Northampton*), A. Neary (*Broughton Park*) Repl.: I. D. Wright (*Northampton*)
Scotland: A. R. Brown (*Gala*); W. C. C. Steele (*Bedford*), J. N. M. Frame (*Gala*), C. W. W. Rea (*Headingley*), A. G. Biggar (*London Scot.*); J. W. C. Turner (*Gala*), D. S. Paterson (*Gala*); J. McLauchlan (*Jordanhill Coll.*), Q. Dunlop (*West of Scot.*), A. B. Carmichael (*West of Scot.*), A. F. McHarg (*London Scot.*), G. L. Brown(*West of Scot.*), N. A. MacEwan (*Gala*), P. C. Brown* (*Gala*), R. J. Arneil (*Leicester*) Repl.: A. S. Turk (*Langholm*)
Referee: C. Durand (*France*)   **Touch judges:** H. B. Laidlaw, G. C. Lamb

R. Hiller scored but failed (3-0); P. C. Brown scored and converted (3-5); R. Hiller kicked two penalties (9-5). (H.T.). D. S. Paterson dropped a goal (9-8); A. Neary scored but R. Hiller failed (12-8); R. Hiller kicked a penalty (15-8); D. S. Paterson scored but P. C. Brown failed (15-11); C. W. W. Rea scored and P. C. Brown converted (15-16).

For the second time in the season Scotland were involved in a match won by the last kick of the game but this time Brown's conversion gave them their first win at Twickenham since 1938. England opened the scoring when Janion fielded a kick ahead and beat several men before the ball passed from Cowman, Taylor and Spencer to Hiller who scored at the corner. Frame had previously gone off with an injured thigh and Turk now came on as a replacement. Soon P. C. Brown followed a break by Rea and finished a handling run by Biggar and MacEwan to score a try which he converted to give Scotland the lead. However two penalties by Hiller put England in front at the interval. At this stage Wardlow was replaced by Wright who went on to the wing with Duckham at centre. Paterson soon had a smart drop goal but once again poor Scottish heeling gave Page a chance to pick up and send Neary in for a try and England looked very safe when Hiller kicked his third penalty with eight minutes to go. Then Paterson took advantage of a defensive fumble to score and in the last minute Rea, who had been the sharpest centre all afternoon, whipped through a gap to score a try which Brown converted to win the match.

SCOTLAND 26   ENGLAND 6
Murrayfield
27 March 1971

Scotland: A. R. Brown (*Gala*); W. C. C. Steele (*Bedford*), J. N. M. Frame (*Gala*), C. W. W. Rea (*Headingley*), A. G. Biggar (*London Scot.*); J. W. C. Turner (*Gala*), D. S. Paterson (*Gala*); J. McLauchlan (*Jordanhill Coll.*), Q. Dunlop (*West of Scot.*), A. B. Carmichael (*West of Scot.*), A. F. McHarg (*London Scot.*), G. L. Brown (*West of Scot.*), N. A. MacEwan (*Gala*), P. C. Brown* (*Gala*), R. J. Arneil (*Leicester*) Repl.: G. M. Strachan (*Jordanhill Coll.*)
England: R. Hiller (*Harlequins*); J. P. Janion (*Bedford*), C. S. Wardlow (*Northampton*), J. S. Spencer* (*Headingley*), D. J. Duckham (*Coventry*); A. R. Cowman (*Loughborough*), N. C. Starmer-Smith (*Harlequins*); D. L. Powell (*Northampton*), J. V. Pullin (*Bristol*), F. E. Cotton (*Loughborough*), P. J. Larter (*Northampton*), C. W. Ralston (*Richmond*), A. L. Bucknall (*Richmond*), R. B. Taylor (*Northampton*), A. Neary (*Broughton Park*)
Referee: M. Joseph (*Wales*)   **Touch judges:** R. P. Burrell, T. F. E. Grierson

J. N. M. Frame scored and A. R. Brown converted (5-0); P. C. Brown kicked a penalty (8-0); A. R. Cowman dropped a goal (8-3); P. C. Brown scored but did not convert (11-3). (H.T.). J. N. M. Frame scored and A. R. Brown converted (16-3); R. Hiller kicked a penalty (16-6); W. C. C. Steele and C. W. W. Rea scored and A. R. Brown converted both (26-6).

This was an extra game played in Edinburgh to mark the Centenary of the first International at Raeburn Place on the same date in 1871. It was attended by the Prince of Wales and the Prime Minister. There was an extraordinary start to the match. Turner kicked off and Hiller fielded the ball near his right hand corner flag. He passed inside and left to Janion who at once handed on to Cowman. His pass to Spencer was dropped and Frame, moving up for the tackle, took the ball over the line to score in what was estimated to be 10-12 seconds after the kick-off – surely the quickest try ever scored in an International match! By half time a penalty and a try by P. C. Brown against a drop goal by Cowman made the score 11-3. In the second half some fine combined play by the Scots produced three good tries and England could only reply with a penalty by Hiller to make the score 26-6. Just after Steele's try an injured G. L. Brown was replaced by Strachan.

SCOTLAND 20   FRANCE 9
Murrayfield
15 January 1972

Scotland: A. R. Brown (*Gala*); W. C. C. Steele (*Bedford*), J. N. M. Frame (*Gala*), J. M. Renwick (*Hawick*), A. G. Biggar (*London Scot.*); C. M. Telfer (*Hawick*), I. G. MacCrae (*Gordonians*); J. McLauchlan (*Jordanhill Coll.*), R. L. Clark (*Edin. Wrs.*), A. B. Carmichael (*West of Scot.*), A. F. McHarg (*London Scot.*), G. L. Brown (*West of Scot.*), N. A. MacEwan (*Gala*), P. C. Brown* (*Gala*), R. J. Arneil (*Northampton*). Repl.: A. J. M. Lawson (*Edin. Wrs.*)
France: P. Villepreux (*Toulouse*); R. Bertranne (*Bagneres*), J. Trillo (*Begles*), J.-P. Lux (*Dax*), J. Cantoni (*Beziers*); J.-L. Berot (*Toulouse*), J.-M. Aguirre (*Bagneres*); A. Vacquerin (*Beziers*), R. Benesis (*Agen*), J.-L. Martin (*Beziers*), J.-P. Bestiat (*Dax*), B. Dauga* (*Mont-de-Marsan*), O. Saisset (*Beziers*), C. Spanghero (*Narbonne*), V. Boffelli (*Aurillac*)
Referee: M. Joseph (*Wales*)   **Touch judges:** T. F. E. Grierson, J. Saint-Guilhem

C. M. Telfer scored but P. C. Brown failed (4-0) C. M. Telfer dropped a goal (7-0), P. C. Brown kicked a penalty (10-0). (H.T.). P. Villepreux kicked a penalty (10-3); J. M. Renwick scored but P. C. Brown failed (14-3); B. Dauga scored and P. Villepreux converted (14-9); J. N. M. Frame scored and A. R. Brown converted (20-9).

The French backs were full of running but the defence was solid and overall the Scottish pack were splendid in the loose and line out. Their first try came from a rush that was halted; MacEwan pounced on a bad heel and got the ball out to Biggar who sent Telfer in. Then a Telfer drop goal came from fine possession at a line out on the 25 yard line. McCrae had to go off with rib trouble after ten minutes of the second half. Villepreux kicked a penalty just before Lawson came on as a replacement. Then Arthur Brown picked up a French kick through, ran the ball out to link with Biggar who put Renwick over near the left corner. The French replied with a fierce rush by their forwards finished off by the powerful Dauga crashing over. Right on time Telfer got good possession from a line out and slipped a reverse pass to Frame who smashed his way through four or five tackles to score at the posts. After the whistle for the conversion the delighted crowd erupted onto the field and had to be sent back for another minute of injury time.

WALES 35   SCOTLAND 12
Cardiff
5 February 1972

Wales: J. P. R. Williams (*London Welsh*); T. G. R. Davies (*London Welsh*), R. T. E. Bergiers (*Cardiff*), A. J. Lewis (*Ebbw Vale*), J. C. Bevan (*Cardiff*); B. John (*Cardiff*), G. O. Edwards (*Cardiff*); D. J. Lloyd* (*Bridgend*), J. Young (*RAF*), D. B. Llewelyn (*Llanelli*), W. D. Thomas (*Llanelli*), T. G. Evans (*London Welsh*), W. D. Morris (*Neath*), T. M. Davies (*London Welsh*), J. Taylor (*London Welsh*). Repl.: P. Bennett (*Llanelli*)
Scotland: A. R. Brown (*Gala*); W. C. C. Steele (*Bedford*), J. N. M. Frame (*Gala*), J. M. Renwick (*Hawick*), A. G. Biggar (*London Scot.*); C. M. Telfer (*Hawick*), D. S. Paterson (*Gala*); J. McLauchlan (*Jordanhill Coll.*), R. L. Clark (*Edin. Wrs.*), A. B. Carmichael (*West of Scot.*), I. R. Barnes (*Hawick*), G. L. Brown (*West of Scot.*), N. A. MacEwan (*Gala*), P. C. Brown* (*Gala*), R. J. Arneil (*Northampton*). Repl.: L. G. Dick (*Loughborough*)
Referee: G. A. Jamieson (*Ireland*)   **Touch judges:** F. Parker, E. M. Lewis

J. M. Renwick kicked a penalty (0-3); B. John kicked a penalty (3-3); T. G. R. Davies scored but B. John failed (7-3); P. C. Brown kicked a penalty (7-6); B. John kicked a penalty (10-6). (H.T.). R. L. Clark scored and P. C. Brown converted (10-12); G. O. Edwards scored twice and B. John converted the first only (20-12); B. John kicked a penalty (23-12); R. T. E. Bergiers and J. Taylor scored and B. John converted both (35-12).

In spite of some hard running by the Welsh backs who were given good possession by their pack, Scotland held grimly onto a narrow lead until fifteen minutes after the restart when Edwards scored a somewhat suspect try following a peel from a line out on the Scottish line. Then the Welsh pack, with Davies prominent in the lineout, dominated the game with the result that their threes smashed through the Scottish defence for three fierce tries, Edwards and T. G. R. Davies being particularly dangerous. J. P. R. Williams was replaced by P. Bennett after twenty minutes of the first half whilst Dick came on for Biggar after six minutes of the second half.

SCOTLAND 23   ENGLAND 9
Murrayfield
18 March 1972

Scotland: A. R. Brown (*Gala*); W. C. C. Steele (*Bedford*), J. N. M. Frame (*Gala*), J. M. Renwick (*Hawick*), L. G. Dick (*Loughborough*); C. M. Telfer (*Hawick*), A. J. M. Lawson (*Edin. Wrs.*); J. McLauchlan (*Jordanhill Coll.*), R. L. Clark (*Edin. Wrs.*), A. B. Carmichael (*West of Scot.*), A. F. McHarg (*London Scot.*), G. L. Brown (*West of Scot.*), N. A. MacEwan (*Gala*), P. C. Brown* (*Gala*), R. J. Arneil (*Northampton*)
England: P. M. Knight (*Bristol*); K. J. Fielding (*Moseley*), J. P. A. G. Janion (Bedford), G. W. Evans (*Coventry*), D. J. Duckham (*Coventry*); A. G. B. Old (*Middlesbrough*), L. E. Weston (*West of Scot.*); C. B. Stevens (*Harlequins*), J. V. Pullin (*Bristol*), M. A. Burton (*Gloucester*), A. Brinn (*Gloucester*), C. W. Ralston (*Richmond*), P. J. Dixon* (*Harlequins*), A. G. Ripley (*Rosslyn Park*), A. Neary (*Broughton Park*)
Referee: M. Joseph (*Wales*)   **Touch judges:** J. Young, A. Welsby

N. A. MacEwan scored but A. R. Brown failed (4-0); A. G. B. Old kicked a penalty (4-3); P. C. Brown kicked a penalty (7-3); P. C. Brown scored but A. R. Brown failed (11-3), C. M. Telfer dropped a goal (14-3). (H.T.). A. G. B. Old kicked two penalties (14-9); A. R. Brown kicked a penalty (17-9); P. C. Brown kicked two penalties (23-9).

This was not a great exhibition of open rugby yet Scotland could be moderately satisfied with a try tally of 2-0. The first came from a bad pass to Old which Telfer tapped on to catch Knight with the ball and MacEwan was there to snap up the ball and score. Well through the first half P. C. Brown took a clean catch at the tail of the lineout and charged over from three yards out. Right on the interval another clean catch by Brown let Telfer drop a nice goal. The second half was marked by five penalty goals although Steele and Janion each had exciting solo runs.

SCOTLAND 9   NEW ZEALAND 14
Murrayfield
16 December 1972

Scotland: A. R. Irvine (*Heriot's FP*); W. C. C. Steele (*Bedford*), I. W. Forsyth (*Stewart's FP*), J. M. Renwick (*Hawick*), D. Shedden (*West of Scot.*); I. R. McGeechan (*Headingley*) I. G. McCrae (*Gordonians*); J. McLauchlan (*Jordanhill Coll.*), R. L. Clark (*Edin. Wrs.*), A. B. Carmichael (*West of Scot.*), A. F. McHarg (*London Scot.*), G. L. Brown (*West of Scot.*), N. A. MacEwan (*Gala*), P. C. Brown* (*Gala*), R. J. Arneil (*Northampton*)
New Zealand: J. F. Karam (*Wellington*); B. G. Williams (*Auckland*), B. Robertson (*Counties*), R. M. Parkinson (*Poverty Bay*), G. B. Batty (*Wellington*); I. N. Stevens (*Wellington*), S. M. Going (*North Auckland*); J. D. Matheson (*Otago*), R. W. Norton (*Canterbury*), G. J. Whiting (*King Country*), P. J. Whiting (*Auckland*), H. H. McDonald (*Canterbury*), I. A. Kirkpatrick* (*Poverty Bay*), A. I. Scown (*Taranaki*), A. J. Wyllie (*Canterbury*) Repl.b: K. K. Lambert (*Manawata*)
Referee: G. Domercq (*France*)   **Touch judges:** A. M. Hosie, J. G. Dow

A. J. Wyllie scored and J. F. Karam converted (0-6). (H.T.). A. R. Irvine kicked a penalty (3-6); G. B. Batty scored but J. F. Karam failed (3-10); I. R. McGeechan dropped a goal (6-10); A. R. Irvine kicked a penalty (9-10); S. M. Going scored but J. F. Karam failed (9-14)

Play was mainly confined to the Scottish half for the powerful and active New Zealand forwards dominated play in the loose although Scotland did quite well in the set scrums and line out. Behind his fine pack Going was a constant menace, setting up the first try for Wyllie and scoring the vital try in the last minute by intercepting a dangerous pass at midfield and running on to score. The second New Zealand try came when Robertson, after a wandering run in the Scottish 25 area, placed a lovely kick to the corner which allowed Batty to run on to the ball and score. For Scotland, the new caps defended well, Irvine making a particularly impressive debut, but really the whole team raised their game and were making a tremendous fight to score in injury time when Going clinched the match with his runaway score.

FRANCE 16   SCOTLAND 13
Parc des Princes
13 January 1973

France: J. Cantoni (*Beziers*); J.-P. Lux (*Dax*), C. Dourthe (*Dax*), J. Trillo (*Begles*), R. Bougarel (*Toulouse*); J.-P. Romeu (*Montferrand*), M. Barrau (*Toulouse*); A. Vaquerin (*Beziers*), A. Lubrano (*Beziers*), J. J. Iracabal (*Bayonne*), E. Cester (*Valence*), A. Esteve (*Beziers*), O. Saisset (*Beziers*), W. Spanghero* (*Narbonne*), P. Biemouret (*Agen*)
Scotland: A. R. Irvine (*Heriot's FP*); W. C. C. Steele (*Bedford*), I. W. Forsyth (*Stewarts FP*), J. M. Renwick (*Hawick*), D. Shedden (*West of Scot.*); I. R. McGeechan (*Headingley*), A. J. M. Lawson (*Edin. Wrs.*); J. McLauchlan (*Jordanhill Coll.*), R. L. Clark (*Edin. Wrs.*), A. B. Carmichael (*West of Scot.*), A. F. McHarg (*London Scot.*), R. W. J. Wright (*Edin. Wrs.*), N. A. MacEwan (*Gala*), P. C. Brown* (*Gala*), W. Lauder (*Neath*)
Referee: K. A. Pattinson (*England*), F. Palmade (*France*)   **Touch judges:** J. Dun, F. Palmade

J.-P. Romeu kicked two penalties (6-0); P. C. Brown kicked a penalty (6-3); C. Dourthe scored but J. -P. Romeu failed (10-3); I. R. McGeechan dropped a goal (10-6). (H.T.). A. J. M. Lawson scored but P. C. Brown failed (10-10); J.-P. Romeu kicked two penalties (16-10); P. C. Brown kicked a penalty (16-13).

This was the first match in the new stadium at Parc des Princes. Although there was only a penalty difference between the scores France deserved to win because of their extra sharpness in the broken play. Back play was dominated by too much kicking. The French try came from a loose ball picked up by Cester and passed through several hands to Dourthe who went through a Scotland defence. The Scottish try started from a high kick by McGeechan; Renwick flattened the catcher and

Clark got the loose ball away to Lawson who scored. After thirteen minutes Mr Pattinson had to retire with a leg injury and was replaced by the French touchjudge who proved to be a most impartial and strict referee.

SCOTLAND 10   WALES 9
Murrayfield
3 February 1973

Scotland: A. R. Irvine (*Heriot's FP*); W. C. C. Steele (*Bedford*), I. R. McGeechan (*Headingley*), I. W. Forsyth (*Stewart's FP*), D. Shedden (*West of Scot.*); C. M. Telfer (*Hawick*), D. W. Morgan (*Melville Coll. FP*); J. McLauchlan* (*Jordanhill*), R. L. Clark (*Edin. Wrs.*), A. B. Carmichael (*West of Scot.*), A. F. McHarg (*London Scot.*), P. C. Brown (*Gala*), N. A. MacEwan (*Gala*), G. M. Strachan (*Jordanhill*), J. G. Millican (*Edin. Univ.*)
Wales: J. P. R. Williams (*London Welsh*); T. G. R. Davies (*London Welsh*), R. T. E. Bergiers (*Llanelli*), A. J. L. Lewis* (*Ebbw Vale*), J. C. Bevan (*Cardiff*); P. Bennet (*Llanelli*), G. O. Edwards (*Cardiff*); G. Shaw (*Neath*), J. Young (*London Welsh*), D. J. Lloyd (*Bridgend*), W. D. Thomas (*Llanelli*), D. L. Quinnell (*Llanelli*). W. D. Morris (*Neath*), T. M. Davies (*Swansea*), J. Taylor (*London Welsh*)
Referee: F. Palmade (*France*)   **Touch judges:** J. Young, J. Mescall

C. M. Telfer and W. C. C. Steele scored and D. W. Morgan converted the first only (10-0) P. Bennett and J. Taylor kicked penalties (10-6). (H.T.). P. Bennett kicked a penalty (10-9).

Wales with nine Lions in their team and five successive wins against Scotland arrived as favourites but found themselves up against a pack which held them, especially at the lineouts, nor could their backs break through a defence which covered their every move and tackled ruthlessly.

Wales attacked from the start but a fine follow-up tackle by McGeechan on Williams resulted in a scrum won by Scotland and Telfer, with Forsyth running outside him, dummied, and broke inside for a fine try. Some more strong Welsh running broke against a solid defence and then a fast run from defence by Irvine ended by Wales having to carry over and touch down. Scotland won the strike; Telfer went off on a decoy run and the ball was passed instead to Steele who shot through a scattered defence to score. For the rest of the match Scotland fairly held their own, putting in strong attacks while halting every Welsh move. All that Wales could manage were three good penalties which closed the scoring but Irvine came close with a drop at goal while a late penalty attempt by Morgan went so close that the touch judges hesitated before deciding against it.

SCOTLAND 19   IRELAND 14
Murrayfield
24 February 1973

Scotland: A. R. Irvine (*Heriot's FP*); W. C. C. Steele (*Bedford*), I. R. McGeechan (*Headingley*), I. W. Forsyth (*Stewart's FP*), D. Shedden (*West of Scot.*); C. M. Telfer (*Hawick*), D. W. Morgan (*Melville Coll. FP*), J. McLauchlan* (*Jordanhill Coll.*), R. L. Clark (*Edin. Wrs.*), A. B. Carmichael (*West of Scot.*), A. F. McHarg (*London Scot.*), P. C. Brown (*Gala*), N. A. MacEwan (*Gala*), G. M. Strachan (*Jordanhill Coll.*), J. G. Millican (*Edin. Univ.*)
Ireland: T. J. Kiernan* (*Cork Const.*); T. O. Grace (*St Mary's*), R. A. Milliken (*Bangor*), C. M. H. Gibson (*NIFC*), A. W. McMaster (*Ballymena*); B. J. McGann (*Cork Const.*), J. J. Maloney (*St Mary's*); R. J. McLoughlin (*Blackrock*), K. W. Kennedy (*London Irish*), J. F. Lynch (*St Mary's*), K. M. A. Mays (*UC Dublin*), W. J. McBride (*Ballymena*), J. F. Slattery (*Blackrock*), T. A. P. Moore (*Highfield*), J. H. Buckley (*Sunday's Well*) Repl.: R. D. H. Bryce (*West of Scot.*)
Referee: R. Lewis (*Wales*)   **Touch judges:** T. F. E. Grierson, J. R. West

D. W. Morgan kicked a penalty (3-0); B. J. McGann kicked two penalties (3-6); D. W. Morgan dropped a goal and kicked a penalty (9-6). A. W. McMaster scored but B. J. McGann failed (9-10). (H.T.). I. R. McGeechan dropped a goal (12-10); T. J. Kiernan scored but B. J. McGann failed (12-14); I. W. Forsyth scored but D. W. Morgan failed (16-14); D. W. Morgan dropped a goal (19-14).

Ireland, who had not lost at Murrayfield since 1963, came with a very experienced team captained by Kiernan whose 54th and last cap this was to be. However, the Scottish pack gave as good as they got in a hard uncompromising forward battle while their backs were probably more dangerous than their opponents especially as McGann tended to overkick at half. The play opened

177

with a series of penalties and a drop goal for Morgan who managed to hold on to a desperate clearance by Kiernan and get in his kick. Just before half time McLauchlan had to go off with a cracked fibula and from a scrum McGann went blind and put McMaster in at the corner to regain the lead. Bryce came on for the second half and a nice drop by McGeechan put Scotland back in the lead. Then Gibson made a nice break and the ball went from McMaster to Kiernan who crossed at the corner only to be crashed into touch in goal. To the dismay of all Scots he was adjudged to have scored and so Ireland took the lead for the third time. With some ten minutes to go Scotland fairly raised their game. Steele was halted by a firm tackle and then just lost the touch down to Grace, but in the last minutes Irvine came up with the ball, was supported by a galloping McHarg who passed to Forsyth and the burly centre crashed over in the left corner. Morgan missed the long conversion but right on time dropped a fine goal from near the left touch line to finish the game.

ENGLAND 20   SCOTLAND 13
Twickenham
17 March 1973

England: A. M. Jorden (*Blackheath*); P. J. Squires (*Harrogate*), G. W. Evans (*Coventry*), P. S. Preece (*Coventry*), D. J. Duckham (*Coventry*); M. J. Cooper (*Moseley*), S. J. Smith (*Sale*); C. B. Stevens (*Penzance-Newlyn*), J. V. Pullin* (*Bristol*), F. E. Cotton (*Loughborough*), R. M. Uttley (*Gosforth*), C. W. Ralston (*Richmond*), P. J. Dixon (*Gosforth*), A. Neary (Broughton Park), A. G. Ripley (*Rosslyn Park*)
Scotland: A. R. Irvine (*Heriot's FP*); W. C. C. Steele (*Bedford*), I. R. McGeechan (*Headingley*), I. W. Forsyth (*Stewart's FP*), D. Shedden (*West of Scot.*); C. M. Telfer (*Hawick*), D. W. Morgan (*Melville Coll. FP*); J. McLauchlan* (*Jordanhill Coll.*), R. L. Clark (*Edin. Wrs.*), A. B. Carmichael (*West of Scot.*), A. F. McHarg (*London Scot.*), P. C. Brown (*Gala*), N. A. MacEwan (*Gala*), G. M. Strachan (*Jordanhill Coll.*), J. G. Millican (*Edin. Univ.*) Repl.: G. L. Brown (*West of Scot.*)
Referee: J. C. Kelleher (*Ireland*)   **Touch judges:** Dr K. B. Slawson, M. H. Titcomb

P. J. Squires and P. J. Dixon scored but A. M. Jorden failed to convert (8-0). (H.T.). P. J. Dixon scored and A. M. Jorden converted (14-0); D. W. Morgan kicked a penalty (14-3); W. C. C. Steele scored twice but D. W. Morgan failed with the first and A. R. Irvine converted the second (14-13); G. W. Evans scored and A. M. Jorden converted (20-13).

Scotland went to Twickenham with high hopes of lifting the Triple Crown but foundered against an English pack which was on top in all phases of forward play. J. McLauchlan, who had had no match play since his injury against Ireland, was quite determined to play, a decision that many both before and after the game considered to be most unwise. However, Cooper, with an ample supply of the ball, tended to kick rather than release an obviously active set of backs and it was some twenty minutes before a run saw Squires score. Almost from the kick-off Evans set Duckham off on a run halted by McHarg on the line, but Dixon was up to score. Soon after the interval a peel from a lineout finished with Dixon scoring again. With ten minutes to go Scotland came right back into the game. Morgan kicked a 50 yard penalty and then Steele, hemmed in on the touch line, kicked ahead, charged down Smith's attempted clearance and was first to the ball for a score. Here a concussed Millican was replaced by G. L. Brown. Duckham was again halted on the line and then from a sluggish English heel Morgan hacked the ball on and it reached McGeechan who fed P. C. Brown. The latter threw a long pass to Steele who got in with three men hanging on to him. Irvine's conversion from the touch line brought the score to 14-13 but almost at once a punt over the line by Preece bounced awkwardly and Evans was able to beat the defence for the last score.

SCOTLAND 27   S.R.U. PRESIDENT'S XV 16
Murrayfield
31 March 1973

Scotland: A. R. Irvine (*Heriot's FP*); A. D. Gill (*Gala*), I. R. McGeechan (*Headingley*), I. W. Forsyth (*Stewart's FP*), D. Shedden (*West of Scot.*); C. M. Telfer (*Hawick*), D. M. Morgan (*Melville Coll. FP*); J. McLauchlan* (*Jordanhill Coll.*), R. L. Clark (*Edin. Wrs.*), A. B. Carmichael (*West of Scot.*), A. F. McHarg (*London Scot.*), G. L. Brown (*West of Scot.*), N. A. MacEwan (*Gala*), P. C. Brown (*Gala*), G. M. Strachan (*Jordanhill Coll.*) Repl.: J. N. M. Frame (*Gala*)
S.R.U. President's XV: R. A. Carlson (*South Africa*); J. J. McLean (*Australia*), D. R. Burnet (*Australia*), D. A. Hales (*New*

178

Zealand), G. B. Batty (*New Zealand*); I. N. Stevens (*New Zealand*), G. L. Colling (*New Zealand*); J. Iracabal (*France*), R. Benesis (*France*), D. A. Dunworth (*Australia*), B. Dauga (*France*), A. R. Sutherland (*New Zealand*), J. H. Ellis (*South Africa*), A. J. Wyllie* (*New Zealand*), P. J. F. Greyling (*South Africa*)
Referee: M. Joseph (*Wales*)   **Touch judges:** T. F. E. Grierson (*Hawick*), A. M. Hosie (*Hillhead HSFP*)

D. Shedden scored but P. C. Brown failed (4-0); J. J. McLean scored and converted (4-6); A. D. Gill scored and A. R. Irvine converted (10-6). (H.T.). A. D. Gill scored but A. R. Irvine failed (14-6); A. F. McHarg scored but D. W. Morgan failed (18-6); D. A. Hales and D. R. Burnet scored and J. J. McLean converted the second only (18-16); A. R. Irvine kicked a penalty (21-16); C. M. Telfer scored and A. R. Irvine converted (27-16).

Caps were awarded for this fixture arranged as part of the Centenary celebrations and the XVs were presented to Sir Alec Douglas Home before the kick off. This overseas XV did remarkably well for a group which had only a few day's preparation and it was not surprising that Scotland finished the stronger, especially on a blustery, rain-swept day. Gill, a last minute substitute for an injured Steele, had a fine debut. McHarg, as he had done all season, showed up well in the loose but Irvine was particularly prominent, making many searing runs from full back, two of which produced the first two tries. McGeechan hurt his neck after thirteen minutes play and was replaced by Frame.

SCOTLAND XV 12   ARGENTINA 11
Murrayfield
24 November 1973

Scotland: A. R. Irvine (*Heriot's FP*); W. C. C. Steele (*Bedford*), J. M. Renwick (*Hawick*), M. D. Hunter (*Glas. HSFP*), A. D. Gill (*Gala*); C. M. Telfer (*Hawick*), D. W. Morgan (*Stewart's FP*); J. McLauchlan* (*Jordanhill Coll.*), D. F. Madsen (*Gosforth*), A. B Carmichael (*West of Scot.*), A. F. McHarg (*London Scot.*), G. L. Brown (*West of Scot.*), N. A. MacEwan (*Highland*), W. S. Watson (*Boroughmuir*), G. M. Strachan (*Jordanhill Coll.*)
Argentina: M. F. Alonzo (*San Isidro*), R. Matarazzo (*San Isidro*), A. Travaglini (*San Isidro*), A. R. Jurado (*San Isidro*), E. R. Morgan (*Old Georgians*); H. Porta (*Banco Nacion*), L. Gradin (*Belgrano*); F. G. Insua (*San Isidro*), J. E. Dumas (*Universitario*), R. Fariello (*Mendoza*), J. A. Virasoro (*San Martin*), J. J. Fernandez (*Deportiva Francesa*), N. Carbone (*Puchara*), H. R. Miguens* (*Universitario*), J. Carracedo (*San Isidro*)
Referee: J. S. P. Evans (*Wales*)   **Touch judges:** T. F. E. Grierson, J. M. Buchan

H. Porta scored but E. R. Morgan failed (0-4); A. Travaglini scored but E. R. Morgan failed (0-8); D. W. Morgan kicked two penalties (6-8); H. Porta dropped a goal (6-11). (H.T.). D. W. Morgan kicked a penalty (9-11); C. M. Telfer dropped a goal (12-11).

This Scottish XV, practically a fully capped team, were most fortunate to finish as winners. They had to yield two good tries and could not penetrate an excellent defence to score themselves. Porta was an excellent half while Travaglini proved a powerful centre both in attack and defence. The Argentine forwards, however, although splendid in the loose, were overshadowed in the scrums and line outs. The game finished sourly. The referee had continually to penalise the visitors for an assortment of offences which included a stiff-arm tackle on Irvine, and Morgan eventually placed three good goals to keep Scotland in contention. Inside the last seven minutes Telfer dropped a goal to put Scotland in the lead and almost at once an ugly brawl developed which left Madsen with a head wound that required stitching. The visitors then put in a great finish, running the ball continually from all positions but narrowly failed to save the game. Then as they left the field one of their forwards felled Gordon Brown standing in the tunnel and later their manager complained that the Welsh referee was not neutral – in fact, could not be neutral since he came from the British Isles – a comment where the logic was as false as the initial statement.

WALES 6   SCOTLAND 0
Cardiff
19 January 1974

Wales: J. P. R. Williams (*London Welsh*); T. G. R. Davies (*London Welsh*), K. Hughes (*London Welsh*), I. Hall (*Aberavon*), J. J. Williams (*Llanelli*); P. Bennett (*Llanelli*), G. O. Edwards* (*Cardiff*); G. Shaw (*Neath*), R. Windsor (*Pontypool*),

P. D. Llewellyn (*Swansea*), A. J. Martin (*Aberavon*), D. L. Quinnell (*Llanelli*), W. D. Morris (*Neath*), T. M. Davies (*Swansea*), T. Cobner (*Pontypool*)
Scotland: A. R. Irvine (*Heriot's FP*); A. D. Gill (*Gala*), J. M. Renwick (*Hawick*), I. R. McGeechan (*Headingley*), L. G. Dick (*Jordanhill Coll.*); C. M. Telfer (*Hawick*), A. J. M. Lawson (*Edin. Wrs.*); J. McLauchlan* (*Jordanhill Coll.*), D. F. Madsen (*Gosforth*), A. B. Carmichael (*West of Scot*); A F McHarg (*London Scot*), G. L. Brown (*West of Scot.*), N. A. MacEwan (*Highland*), W. S. Watson (*Boroughmuir*), W. Lauder (*Neath*)
Referee: R. F. Johnson (*England*) **Touch judges:** W. B. Watt, J. C. Kelleher

T. Cobner scored and P. Bennett converted (6-0). (H.T.).

After some early pressure by Scotland, during which Irvine came close with a penalty, Wales with the wind, came into the game. After 22 minutes they heeled against the head and a lovely side stepping run by T. G. R. Davies put Cobner in for the only score of the match. Both sides attacked throughout the second half but the defences were sound. The Scottish pack played much better especially in the loose where the back five of the pack were often in evidence. J. P. R. Williams, however, was in fine form and like Irvine frequently joined his threes in attack.

SCOTLAND 16 ENGLAND 14
Murrayfield
2 February 1974

Scotland: A. R. Irvine (*Heriot's FP*); A. D. Gill (*Gala*), J. M. Renwick (*Hawick*), I. R. McGeechan (*Headingley*), L. G. Dick (*Jordanhill Coll.*); C. M. Telfer (*Hawick*), A. J. M. Lawson (*Edin. Wrs.*); J. McLauchlan* (*Jordanhill Coll.*), D. F. Madsen (*Gosforth*), A. B. Carmichael (*West of Scot.*), A. F. McHarg (*London Scot.*), G. L. Brown (*West of Scot.*), N. A. MacEwan (*Highland*), W. S. Watson (*Boroughmuir*), W. Lauder (*Neath*)
England: P. A. Rossborough (*Coventry*); P. J. Squires (*Harrogate*), D. Roughley (*Liverpool*), G. W. Evans (*Coventry*), D. J. Duckham (*Coventry*); A. G. B. Old (*Leicester*), J. G. Webster (*Moseley*); C. B. Stevens (*Penzance-Newlyn*), J. V. Pullin* (*Bristol*), F. E. Cotton (*Coventry*), C. W. Ralston (*Richmond*), N. E. Horton (*Moseley*), P. J. Dixon (*Gosforth*), A. G. Ripley (*Rosslyn Park*), A. Neary (*Broughton Park*)
Referee: M. J. Saint Guilhem (*France*) **Touch judges:** N. R. Sanson, J. Straughan

A. R. Irvine kicked a penalty (3-0); W. Lauder scored and A. R. Irvine converted (9-0); F. E. Cotton scored but P. A. Rossborough failed (9-4); A. G. B. Old kicked a penalty (9-7). (H.T.). A. Neary scored but P. A. Rossborough failed (9-11); A. R. Irvine scored but failed to convert (13-11); P. A. Rossborough dropped a goal (13-14); A. R. Irvine kicked a penalty (16-14).

For the first time since 1880 the Calcutta Cup match, because of a new system of cycling International games, lost its traditional placing as the last game of the season in March. This proved to be a fast hard game with a story book finish. Scotland began well scoring nine points within twelve minutes. Irvine took three long range penalties and converted one from about 45 yards out. Then Madsen pounced on a loose ball from a line out and a pass to Lauder left him with an easy score far out but beautifully converted by Irvine. England rallied strongly and a run by Squires was carried on by Ripley, Neary and Cotton who crashed over for a try. Just short of half time Old kicked a penalty. After restarting England attacked continuously but were halted by some great tackling, especially by McGeechan. In the last 20 minutes the lead changed four times. Firstly a short penalty manoeuvre by Webster and Ripley put Neary over. There followed a fine dodging run by Irvine who scored a try he could not convert. With some three minutes left Rossborough caught a bad clearance and dropped a good 35-yard goal to put England ahead 11-14. Then in the third minute of injury time Irvine kicked a magnificent penalty from 40 yards out on the touch line – and the final whistle went.

IRELAND 9 SCOTLAND 6
Lansdowne Road
2 March 1974

Ireland: A. H. Ensor (*Lansdowne*); T. O. Grace (*UC Dublin*), R. A. Milliken (*Bangor*), C. M. H. Gibson (*NIFC*), A. W. McMaster (*Ballymena*); M. A. Quinn (*Lansdowne*), J. J. Moloney (*St Mary's*); R. J. McLoughlin (*Blackrock*), K. W. Kennedy (*London*

Irish), J. F. Lynch (*St Mary's*), M. I. Keane (*Lansdowne*), W. J. McBride* (*Ballymena*), S. A. McKinney (*Dungannon*), T. A. P. Moore (*Highfield*), J. F. Slattery (*Blackrock*)
Scotland: A. R. Irvine (*Heriot's FP*); A. D. Gill (*Gala*), J. M. Renwick (*Hawick*), I. R. McGeechan (*Headingley*), L. G. Dick (*Jordanhill Coll.*); C. M. Telfer (*Hawick*), D. W. Morgan (*Stewart's FP*); J. McLauchlan* (*Jordanhill Coll.*), D. F. Madsen (*Gosforth*), A. B. Carmichael (*West of Scot.*), A. F. McHarg (*London Scot.*), G. L. Brown (*West of Scot.*), N. A. MacEwan (*Highland*), W. S. Watson (*Boroughmuir*), W. Lauder (*Neath*)
Referee: F. Palmade (*France*) **Touch judges:** J. W. McLeod, D. P. D'Arcy

S. A. McKinney kicked a penalty (3-0); R. A. Milliken scored and C. M. H. Gibson converted (9-0). (H.T.). A. R. Irvine kicked two penalties (9-6).

Scotland had a poor first half but eventually their pack began to take control and play was mainly inside the Irish half for the last twenty minutes. The only try came from a long throw-in taken by Slattery who after a nice run gave the ball to Milliken. The centre went for the line and when tackled was bundled over the line by his own forwards. After the restart Ireland began strongly and twice they came near to scoring but then came the final rally by Scotland who failed, however, to get the ball over the line and Irvine's two penalties were not enough to win the match.

SCOTLAND 19   FRANCE 6
Murrayfield
16 March 1974

Scotland: A. R. Irvine (*Heriot's FP*); A. D. Gill (*Gala*), J. M. Renwick (*Hawick*), M. D. Hunter (*Glas. HSFP*), L. G. Dick (*Jordanhill Coll.*); I. R. McGeechan (*Headingley*), D. W. Morgan (*Stewart's FP*); J. McLauchlan* (*Jordanhill Coll.*) D. F. Madsen (*Gosforth*); A. B. Carmichael (*West of Scot.*), A. F. McHarg (*London Scot.*), G. L. Brown (*West of Scot.*), N. A. MacEwan (*Highland*), W. S. Watson (*Boroughmuir*), W. Lauder (*Neath*) Repl.: I. A. Barnes (*Hawick*)
France: M. Droitecourt (*Montferrand*); J.-F. Gourdon (*RCF*), J.-P. Lux (*Dax*), J. Pecune (*Tarbes*), R. Bertranne (*Bagneres*); J.-P. Romeu (*Montferrand*), M. Barrau (*Agen*); J. Iracabal (*Bayonne*), C. Benesis (*Agen*), A. Vaquerin (*Besiers*), E. Cester* (*Valence*), A. Esteve (*Beziers*), J.-C. Skrela (*Toulouse*), C. Spanghero (*Narbonne*), V. Boffelli (*Aurillac*)
Referee: K. H. Clark (*Ireland*) **Touch judges:** A. M. Hosie, F. Flingou

J. -P. Romeu kicked a penalty (0-3); D. W. Morgan kicked a penalty (3-3); A. F. McHarg scored and A. R. Irvine converted (9-3). (H.T.). J.-P. Romeu dropped a goal (9-6); A. R. Irvine kicked two penalties (15-6); L. G. Dick scored but A. R. Irvine failed (19-6).

France came needing a win to head the International table but met a Scottish team which played well to win comfortably. The visitors began with some brisk handling amongst their forwards before Romeu put them in the lead with a penalty but it was not long before Morgan levelled the scores. A succession of penalties were missed by Irvine and Morgan but right on half time a magnificent handling run involving ten pairs of hands criss-crossed the field three times before Irvine came into the line and his pass saw McHarg crash over for a wonderful try. Scotland restarted briskly only to see Romeu seize a chance to drop a neat goal. Irvine restored the lead with a penalty and saw an injured MacEwan replaced by Barnes before he repeated the feat. For the last fifteen minutes a confident Scotland attacked and inside the final ten minutes Irvine ran from inside his own half and yet another fine passing run which involved McHarg, Carmichael, Lauder, McGeechan and Renwick put Dick in for a great try. The Scottish pack were very good: the front three were solid, Brown and McHarg were good in the lineouts and the back row sound in defence and attack. Yet McHarg deserved extra notice for his ability to get out and about in the open.

SCOTLAND XV 44   TONGA 8
Murrayfield
28 September 1974

Scotland: A. R. Irvine (*Heriot's FP*); W. C. C. Steele (*London Scot.*), J. M. Renwick (*Hawick*), I. R. McGeechan (*Headingley*), L. G. Dick (*Jordanhill Coll.*); C. M. Telfer (*Hawick*), D. W. Morgan (*Stewart's FP*); J. McLauchlan* (*Jordanhill Coll.*) D. F. Madsen (*Gosforth*), A. B. Carmichael (*West of Scot.*), A. F. McHarg (*London Scot.*), G. L. Brown (*West of Scot.*), N. A. MacEwan (*Highland*), W. S. Watson (*Boroughmuir*), W. Lauder (*Neath*)
Tonga: Valita Ma'ake; Isikeli Vave, Samuiela Lata, Sitafoti 'Aho, Talilotu Ngaluafe; Malakai 'Alatini, Ha'unga Fonua; Siosaia

181

Fifita, Tevita Pulumufila, Lialeni Pahulu, Fa'aleo Tupi, Polutele Tu'ihalamaka, Saimone Vaea, Sione Mafi*, Fakahau Valu
Referee: G. Domercq (*France*)   **Touch judges:** A. M. Hosie, E. N. Sheret

A. R. Irvine kicked two penalties (6-0). (H.T.). W. C. C. Steele (2) and L. G. Dick scored and A. R. Irvine converted two (22-0); S. Fifita scored but V. Ma'ake failed (22-4); W. C. C. Steele (2), D. W. Morgan and J. McLauchlan scored and A. R. Irvine converted three (44-4); I. Vave scored but V. Ma'ake failed (44-8).

No caps were awarded for this match although a full Scottish XV was put out. Throughout the game Scotland maintained control of the scrums and line outs but in the first half all their attacks failed against a stout defence and they could only manage two penalties. In the second half the Tongan defence tired and some fine passing runs saw Scotland's wingers run in five of the seven tries scored. Yet the visitors never ceased to play their own style of adventurous running rugby and one such move brought them their first score. In the last minutes Vave intercepted a pass near his own line and the winger ran some 90 yards, throwing off tackles by Irvine and Gill, to score a great solo try.

SCOTLAND 20   IRELAND 13
Murrayfield
1 February 1975

Scotland: A. R. Irvine (*Heriot's FP*); W. C. C. Steele (*London Scot.*), J. M. Renwick (*Hawick*), D. L. Bell (*Watsonians*), L. G. Dick (*Jordanhill Coll.*); I. R. McGeechan (*Headingley*), D. W. Morgan (*Stewart's FP*); J. McLauchlan* (*Jordanhill Coll.*), D. F. Madsen (*Gosforth*), A. B. Carmichael (*West of Scot.*), A. F. McHarg (*London Scot.*), G. L. Brown (*West of Scot.*), M. A. Biggar (*London Scot.*), D. G. Leslie (*Dundee HSFP*), W. Lauder (*Neath*)
Ireland: A. H. Ensor (*Wanderers*); T. O. Grace (*St Mary's*), R. A. Milliken (*Bangor*), C. M. H. Gibson (*NIFC*), J. P. Dennison (*Garryowen*); W. M. McCombe (*Bangor*), J. J. Maloney (*St Mary's*); R. J. McLoughlin (*Blackrock*), P. C. Whelan (*Garryowen*), R. J. Clegg (*Bangor*), W. J. McBride* (*Ballymena*), M. I. Keane (*Lansdowne*), J. F. Slattery (*Blackrock*), W. P. Duggan (*Blackrock*), S. A. McKinney (*Dungannon*)
Referee: R. F. Johnson (*England*)   **Touch judges:** A. M. Hosie, S. A. Causland

D. W. Morgan dropped a goal (3-0); J. Dennison scored and W. M. McCombe converted (3-6); I. R. McGeechan dropped a goal (6-6); J. M. Renwick and W. C. C. Steele scored but A. R. Irvine failed to convert (14-6). (H.T.). W. M. McCombe kicked a penalty (14-9); A. R. Irvine kicked a penalty (17-9); T. O. Grace scored but W. M. McCombe failed (17-13); A. R. Irvine kicked a penalty (20-13).

Last season's champions, Ireland, came to their happy hunting ground at Murrayfield in their Centenary season with a win over England behind them but met a Scottish team whose pack more than held its own and whose backs ran and defended well. Scotland had a great start for within a minute Dick went down the left wing, was halted but from the ruck Biggar got the ball out to Morgan who dropped a goal. Another fine run saw Steele nearly in but then Ireland began to run the ball and a fine handling movement by their forwards got the ball out to Gibson who gave Dennison a clear run in. Scotland, however, struck back before half time. McGeechan dropped a goal from a Scottish heel; Bell with a dummy scissors move put Renwick through and right on half time a splendid dash by Steele brought a second score. After restarting Ireland came back into the game with a McCombe penalty which, however, was cancelled out by another from Irvine. Both sides kept on attacking without success until inside the last ten minutes poor lineout play let the Irish backs whip the ball along the line fast enough to allow Grace to get round the defence and score far out but just short of time Irvine made the win safe by kicking another penalty.

FRANCE 10   SCOTLAND 9
Parc des Princes
15 February 1975

France: M. M. Taffary (*RCF*); J.-F. Gourdon (*RCF*), C. Dourthe* (*Dax*), R. Bertranne (*Bagneres*), J. L. Averous (*La Voulte*); L. Paries (*Narbonne*), R. Asure (*Beziers*); A. Vaquerin (*Beziers*), J. P. Ugartemendia (*St. Jean de Luz*), G. Cholly (*Castres*), A. Guilbert (*Toulon*), C. Spanghero (*Narbonne*), J.-P. Rives (*Toulouse*), V. Boffelli (*Aurillac*), J. C. Skrela (*Toulouse*)

Scotland: A. R. Irvine (*Heriot's FP*); W. C. C. Steele (*London Scot.*), J. M. Renwick (*Hawick*), D. L. Bell (*Watsonians*), L. G. Dick (*Jordanhill Coll.*); I. R. McGeechan (*Headingley*), D. W. Morgan (*Stewart's FP*); J. McLauchlan* (*Jordanhill Coll.*), D. F. Madsen (*Gosforth*), A. B. Carmichael (*West of Scot.*), A. F. McHarg (*London Scot.*), G. L. Brown (West of Scot.), M. A. Biggar (London Scot.), D. G. Leslie (Dundee HSFP), W. Lauder (Neath)
Referee: S. M. Lewis (*Wales*) **Touch judges:** R. E. W. Thomas, N. J. Saint Guilhem

A. R. Irvine kicked a penalty (0-3); R. Asure dropped a goal (3-3). (H.T.). C. Dourthe scored but L. Paries failed (7-3); A. R. Irvine kicked a penalty (7-6); L. Paries kicked a penalty (10-6); A. R. Irvine kicked a penalty (10-9).

This was a scrappy, bad-tempered match which Scotland could well have won if one or two of them had kept cool throughout. Straight away there was scrapping amongst the forwards and the mood persisted, but another factor was the tactics of the halves who were prone to kick rather than get their backs going. This of course left Irvine out as an attacking force. In addition the full back had an off-day with his kicking, converting three out of nine penalties, one of the last at short range. The single try came from a line out from which Skrela and Rives, two fast and skilful flankers, broke away to let Dourthe cut through. Scotland did have bad luck on two occasions when a final pass did not go to hand. Following one of the near misses the Scottish pack went for a push over score only to find Rives diving in amongst Scottish feet. The scrum collapsed and France got a penalty!

SCOTLAND 12   WALES 10
Murrayfield
1 March 1975

Scotland: A. R. Irvine (*Heriot's FP*); W. C. C. Steele (*London Scot.*), J. M. Renwick (*Hawick*), D. L. Bell (*Watsonians*), L. G. Dick (*Jordanhill Coll.*); I. R. McGeechan (*Headingley*), D. W. Morgan (*Stewart's FP*); J. McLauchlan* (*Jordanhill Coll.*), D. F. Madsen (*Gosforth*), A. B. Carrnichael (*West of Scot.*), A. F. McHarg (*London Scot.*), G. L. Brown (*West of Scot.*), M. A. Biggar (*London Scot.*), D. G. Leslie (*Dundee HSFP*), N. A. MacEwan (*Highland*)
Wales: J. P. R. Williams (*London Welsh*); T. G. R. Davis (*Cardiff*), S. P. Fenwick (*Bridgend*), R. W. R. Gravell (*Llanelli*), J. J. Williams (*Llanelli*); J. D. Bevan (*Aberavon*), G. O. Edwards (*Cardiff*); A. G. Faulkner (*Pontypool*), R. W. Windsor (*Pontypool*), G. Price (*Pontypool*), A. J. Martin (*Aberavon*), M. G. Roberts (*London Welsh*), T. J. Cobner (*Pontypool*), T. M. Davies* (*Swansea*), T. P. Evans (*Swansea*) Repl.: P. Bennett (*Llanelli*), W. R. Blyth (*Swansea*)
Referee: J. R. West (*Ireland*) **Touch judges:** N. R. Sanson, A. B. Daniel

D. W. Morgan kicked a penalty (3-0); S. P. Fenwick kicked a penalty (3-3); D. W. Morgan kicked a penalty (6-3); S. P. Fenwick kicked a penalty (6-6); D. W. Morgan kicked a penalty (9-6). (H.T.). I. R. McGeechan dropped a goal (12-6); T. P. Evans scored but A. J. Martin failed (12-10).

Wales who had already had comfortable wins against France and England brought an enormous following to Edinburgh. Two hours before the kick off Murrayfield and its approaches were jammed solid and it was later revealed that the game was watched by a world record crowd of 104,000 plus with several thousands eventually locked out.

The match proved to be a hard, bruising and exciting one but the standard of rugby was really not very high. The first half was mainly a tale of brief runs and kicks at goal – five successful penalties, three misses by Wales and a near-drop by McGeechan, but Wales had to replace both Bevan and Fenwick by Bennett and Blyth, the latter normally a full back. The second half produced two more missed penalties but also a neat successful and valuable drop by McGeechan but again there was little running till in the fourth minute of injury time J. P. R. Williams burst into the line and Gerald Davies put Evans over far out for a good try. To Scotland's relief Martin's long range kick just failed and the whistle went.

ENGLAND 7   SCOTLAND 6
Twickenham
15 March 1975

England: A. M. Jorden (*Bedford*); P. J. Squires (*Harrogate*), P. J. Warfield (*Camb. Univ.*), K. Smith (*Roundhay*), A. J. Morley (*Bristol*); W. N. Bennat (*Bedford*), J. J. Page (*Northampton*); C. B. Stevens (*Penzance-Newlyn*), J. V. Pullin (*Bristol*),

F. E. Cotton* (*Coventry*), R. M. Uttley (*Gosforth*), C. W. Ralston (*Richmond*), D. M. Rollitt (*Bristol*), A. Neary (*Broughton Park*), A. G. Ripley (*Rosslyn Park*)
Scotland: A. R. Irvine (*Heriot's FP*); W. C. C. Steele (*London Scot.*), J. M. Renwick (*Hawick*), D. L. Bell (*Watsonians*), L. G. Dick (*Jordanhill Coll.*); I. R. McGeechan (*Headingley*), D. W. Morgan (*Stewart's FP*); J. McLauchlan* (*Jordanhill Coll.*), D. F. Madsen (*Gosforth*), A. B. Carmichael (*West of Scot.*), A. F. McHarg (*London Scot.*), G. L. Brown (*West of Scot.*), M. A. Biggar (*London Scot.*), D. G. Leslie (*Dundee HSFP*), N. A. MacEwan (*Highland*) Repl.: I. A. Barnes (*Hawick*)
Referee: D. P. D'Arcy (*Ireland*)   **Touch judges:** W. K. Burrell, R. F. Johnson

D. W. Morgan kicked a penalty (0-3); W. N. Bennett kicked a penalty (3-3). (H.T.). D. W. Morgan kicked a penalty (3-6); A. J. Morley scored but W. W. Bennett failed (7-6).

For the fourth time since the War, Scotland's attempt to win the Triple Crown failed at Twickenham. This was a game that they could have won but once again this season they could not score except by penalties. They had much the better of play in the first half but finished poorly. They played equally well during the second half and were shocked when Morley chased an awkward kick ahead and beat Irvine to the rolling ball for a try. They continued to press for the last fifteen minutes but a heartened English pack gave nothing away and when two late penalties by Morgan and a snap at goal by McGeechan failed the match was lost. MacEwan came off after two minutes of play and was replaced by Barnes.

NEW ZEALAND 24   SCOTLAND 0
Auckland
14 June 1975

New Zealand: J. F. Karam (*Horowhenua*); B. G. Williams (*Auckland*), W. N. Osborne (*Wanganui*), L. L. Jaffray (*Otago*), G. B. Batty (*Wellington*); D. J. Robertson (*Otago*), S. M. Going (*N Auckland*); K. E. R. Tanner (*Canterbury*), T. E. Norton (*Canterbury*), W. K. Bush (*Canterbury*), J. A. Callesen (*Manawata*), H. H. Macdonald (*N. Auckland*), K. W. Stewart (*Southland*), A. N. Leslie* (*Wellington*), I. A. Kirkpatrick (*Poverty Bay*)
Scotland: B. H. Hay (*Boroughmuir*); A. R. Irvine (*Heriot's FP*), G. A. Birkett (*Harlequins*), J. M. Renwick (*Hawick*), L. G. Dick (*Jordanhill Coll.*); I. R. McGeechan (*Headingley*) D. W. Morgan (*Stewart's FP*); J. McLauchlan* (*Jordanhill Coll.*), C. D. Fisher (*Waterloo*), A. B. Carmichael (*West of Scot.*), I. R. Barnes (*Hawick*), A. F. McHarg (*London Scot.*), D. G. Leslie (*Dundee HSFP*), W. S. Watson (*Boroughmuir*), W. Lauder (*Neath*) Repl.: W. C. C. Steele (*London Scot.*)
Referee: P. McDavitt (*Wellington*)   **Touch judges:** R. F. McMullen, M. G. Farnworth

H. McDonald scored and J. F. Karam converted (6-0). (H.T.). B. G. Williams (2) and D. J. Robertson scored and J. F. Karam converted all three (24-0).

This was a match which should never have been played, for something like four inches of rain had fallen in less then twelve hours and large areas of the field lay under pools of water. But the Scots were flying home the next day; no alternative date was possible; 45,000 spectators had braved the conditions and so the decision to play was taken. Scotland started facing into a gale of torrential rain only to find after half time that the wind had veered right round and once again they had to face into icy lashing rain. Having found that excuse, one must admit that the New Zealand pack was, in the conditions, much superior. Then there were some vital fielding errors by the Scottish backs which yielded scores but it is difficult to be too critical considering the circumstances.

Within fifteen minutes Scotland lost Hay who had an arm broken when he stood his ground claiming a fair catch which was not granted and the forward rush that followed let Macdonald in for the first score. Irvine then went to full back and Steele came out to play on the wing. In the second half Steele having taken a difficult high kick slipped and the ball which rolled back over the line was touched down by Williams. Then in their own in-goal Irvine and Dick collided going for a high kick and Robertson was left to touch down. Finally Dick flykicked the ball for touch only to see it land and stop dead in a pool of water. Williams was at hand to pick it out and charge past a surprised defence for a try.

Three after-match comments may be quoted. Leslie, the New Zealand captain remarked that 'this was one of the greatest moments in New Zealand swimming'. McLauchlan congratulated Leslie on the win but said that 'it is just sheer luck that nobody was drowned!' while Carmichael actually said that he had played in worse conditions, 'I once played in four inches of snow and that was worse, but I was worried because I can't swim very well'.

SCOTLAND 10   AUSTRALIA 3
Murrayfield
6 December 1975

Scotland: B. H. Hay (*Boroughmuir*); A. R. Irvine (*Heriot's FP*), J. M. Renwick (*Hawick*), I. R. McGeechan (*Headingley*), L. G. Dick (*Jordanhill Coll.*); C. M. Telfer (*Hawick*), D. W. Morgan (*Stewart's FP*); J. McLauchlan* (*Jordanhill Coll.*), C. D. Fisher (*Waterloo*), A. B. Carmichael (*West of Scot.*), A. F. McHarg (*West of Scot.*), G. L. Brown (*West of Scot.*), W. Lauder (*Neath*), G. Y. Mackie (*Highland*), D. G. Leslie (*West of Scot.*)
Australia: P. E. McLean (*Queensland*); P. G. Batch (*Queensland*), R. D. L'Estrange (*Queensland*), J. Berne (*NSW*), L. E. Monaghan (*NSW*); J. C. Hindmarsh (*NSW*), J. N. B. Hipwell* (*NSW*); J. E. C. Meadows (*Victoria*), P. A. Horton (*NSW*), R. Graham (*NSW*), G. Fay (*NSW*), R. A. Smith (*NSW*), G. Cornelsen (*NSW*), D. W. Hillhouse (*Queensland*), A. A. Shaw (*Queensland*) Sub: L. T. Weatherstone (*Capital Territory*)
Referee: R. F. Johnson (*England*)   **Touch judges:** A. M. Hosie, A. Bryce

L. G. Dick scored but D. W. Morgan failed (4-0); J. M. Renwick scored and D. W. Morgan converted (10-0). (H.T.). P. E. McLean kicked a penalty (10-3).

Sandy Carmichael was given the honour of leading the team onto the field, this being his record 41st full cap. Scotland started well but soon found that the tourists were very fast in their counter attacking and Hay in particular had to tackle well to prevent possible scores. However, a break away by Morgan and Mackie set up a ruck from which Morgan put McGeechan and Hay away to finish with Dick scoring. Right on half time McGeechan intercepted a pass and set Renwick away on a 35 yard scoring run.

In the second half the Scottish pack was well in command and halted many Australian moves by winning loose mauls, but their backs although having some good runs, could not score. Midway through the half McLean kicked a fine angled penalty, all of 50 yards.

One writer, noting Irvine's appearance as a winger, commented that it was many years ago since Scotland fielded three full backs, this being a humorous reference to McHarg's habit of appearing, both in defence and attack, anywhere amongst the backs – but it must be remembered that the same character was always a more than useful performer at the line outs.

SCOTLAND 6   FRANCE 13
Murrayfield
10 January 1976

Scotland: B. H. Hay (*Boroughmuir*); A. R. Irvine (*Heriot's FP*), J. M. Renwick (*Hawick*), I. R. McGeechan (*Headingley*), L. G. Dick (*Jordanhill Coll.*); C. M. Telfer (*Hawick*), D. W. Morgan (*Stewart's FP*); J. McLauchlan* (*Jordanhill Coll.*), D. F. Madsen (*Gosforth*), A. B. Carmichael (*West of Scot.*), A. F. McHarg (*London Scot.*), G. L. Brown (*West of Scot.*),W. Lauder (*Neath*), G. Y. Mackie (*Highland*), D. G. Leslie (*West of Scot.*)
France: M. Droitecourt (*Montferrand*); J.-F. Gourdon (*RCF*), R. Bertranne (*Bagneres*), F. Sangali (*Narbonne*), A. Dubertrand (*Montferrand*); J. P. Romeu (*Montferrand*), J. Fouroux* (*La Voulte*); G. Cholley (*Castres*), A. Paco (*Beziers*), R. Paparemborde (*Pau*), F. Haget (*Agen*), M. Palmie (*Besiers*), J. P. Rives (*Toulouse*), J. P. Bastiat (*Dax*), J. C. Skrela (*Toulouse*)
Referee: K. A. Pattinson (*England*)   **Touch judges:** N. R. Sanson, Dr A. Cuny

D. W. Morgan dropped a goal (3-0); J. P. Romeu kicked a penalty (3-3); A. Dubertrand scored but J. P. Romeu failed (3-7). (H.T.). J. Romeu kicked a penalty (3-10); J. M. Renwick kicked a penalty (6-10); J. P. Romeu kicked a penalty (6-13).

Scotland's run of ten home wins was halted by a side which was competent enough but gradually took heart as they saw their opponents fail with their goal kicking and handling. The game, however, seldom got moving, play being continually halted by unsuccessful shots at goal. Morgan missed four and Irvine five before Renwick, who was as competent a club kicker as the other two, put one over. In fairness it must be said some of the misses were long range efforts taken under very windy conditions and Irvine's second attempt went over only to be cancelled by the referee who decided that it was a fault for McLauchlan to lie in front of the ball while holding it in place – an erroneous and sad decision – for another Scottish score at that stage might have lifted their game. As it happened a neat drop by Morgan was cancelled out by a touch line penalty by

185

Romeu before Gourdon snatched up a loose pass and crosskicked to set off a handling run that put Dubertrand over at the other wing. It could be noted that Romeu who tied the win up with three penalties, missed the conversion and two other penalties.

WALES 28   SCOTLAND 6
Cardiff
7 February 1976

Wales: J. P. R. Williams (*London Welsh*); T. G. R. Davies (*Cardiff*), R. W. R. Gravell (*Llanelli*), S. P. Fenwick (*Bridgend*), J. J. Williams (*Llanelli*); P. Bennett (*Llanelli*), G. O. Edwards (*Cardiff*); A. G. Faulkner (*Pontypool*), R. W. Windsor (*Pontypool*), G. Price (*Pontypool*), A. J. Martin (*Aberavon*), G. A. D. Wheel (*Swansea*), T. J. Cobner (*Pontypool*), T. M. Davies* (*Swansea*), T. P. Evans (*Swansea*)
Scotland: A. R. Irvine (*Heriot's FP*); W. C. C. Steele (*London Scot.*), J. M. Renwick (*Hawick*), A. G. Cranston (*Hawick*), D. Shedden (*West of Scot.*); I. R. McGeechan (*Headingley*), D. W. Morgan (*Stewart's FP*); J. McLauchlan* (*Jordanhill Coll.*), C. D. Fisher (*Waterloo*), A. B. Carmichael (*West of Scot.*), A. F. McHarg (*London Scot.*), G. L. Brown (*West of Scot.*), M. A. Biggar (*London Scot.*), G. Y. Mackie (*Highland*), D. G. Leslie (*West of Scot.*)
Referee: Dr A. Cuny (*France*)   **Touch judges:** A. Bryce, M. Joseph

J. J. Williams scored and P. Bennett converted (6-0); A. R. Irvine scored and D. W. Morgan converted (6-6); P. Bennett kicked 2 penalties (12-6). (H.T.). P. Bennett kicked a penalty (15-6); S. P. Fenwick dropped a goal (19-6); T. P. Evans and G. O. Edwards scored and P. Bennett converted the second only (28-6).

Wales made a great start; a lovely diagonal kick beat the defence and J. J. Williams dived in to score inside two minutes. However, good possession from a maul saw McHarg make a run and put Irvine in at the corner but before half time the accurate Bennett had added two penalties. In the second half Wales were clearly on top but met with some stern defending and it was well on before some fine handling gave them two good tries. This latter stage was clearly affected by the refusal of the referee to leave the field after he had injured a leg muscle and during the last half hour he limped along well behind play, often missing offences with a resultant exasperation among the players.

SCOTLAND 22   ENGLAND 12
Murrayfield
21 February 1976

Scotland: A. R. Irvine (*Heriot's FP*); W. C. C. Steele (*London Scot.*), A. G. Cranston (*Hawick*), I. R. McGeechan (*Headingley*), D. Shedden (West *of Scot.*); R. Wilson (*London Scot.*), A. J. M. Lawson (*London Scot.*); J. McLauchlan* (*Jordanhill Coll.*), C. D. Fisher (*Waterloo*), A. B. Carmichael (*West of Scot.*), A. J. Tomes (*Hawick*), G. L. Brown (*West of Scot.*), M. A. Biggar (*London Scot.*), A. F. McHarg (*London Scot.*), D. G. Leslie (*West of Scot.*) Repl.: J. M. Renwick (*Hawick*)
England: A. J. Hignell (*Camb. Univ.*); K. C. Plummer (*Bristol*), A. W. Maxwell (*Headingley*), D. A. Cooke (*Harlequins*), D. J. Duckham (*Coventry*); A. G. B. Old (*Middlesbrough*), M. S. Lampkowski (*Headingley*); F. E. Cotton (*Sale*), P. J. Wheeler (*Leicester*), M. A. Burton (*Gloucester*), W. B. Beaumont (*Fylde*), R. M. Wilkinson (*Bedford*), M. Keyworth (*Swansea*), A. G. Ripley (*Rosslyn Park*), A. Neary* (*Broughton Park*) Repl.: D. M. Wyatt (*Bedford*), W. N. Bennet (*Bedford*)
Referee: D. M. Lloyd (*Wales*)   **Touch judges:** T. F. E. Grierson, Reverend R. N Newell

A. W. Maxwell scored and A. G. B. Old converted (0-6); A. R. Irvine kicked a penalty (3-6); A. G. B. Old kicked a penalty (3-9); A. J. M. Lawson scored and A. R. Irvine converted (9-9); A. G. B. Old kicked a penalty (9-12). (H.T.). A. R. Irvine kicked a penalty (12-12); D. G. Leslie and A. J. M. Lawson scored and A. R. Irvine converted the second only (22-12).

Her Majesty the Queen attended and the XV's were presented to her before the start. With Prince Philip, she and a capacity all-ticket crowd of 70,000 watched a match full of incident. The English pack dominated for long periods especially in the set scrums but the Scottish forwards rallied well in the lineouts and the loose mauls and gave their backs some good possession. England had a fine start for within six minutes some broken play finished with Old putting Maxwell over for a converted try. Half way through Shedden caught an attacking kick ahead and sparked off a splendid handling run by Biggar, Carmichael and Tomes which put Lawson over but Old, by kicking two penalties to Irvine's one, put England in the lead at the interval. During this half Duckham and Shedden, both injured in tackles, were replaced by Wyatt and Renwick. England restarted strongly winning a string of rucks to set their backs running well only to be firmly held, Cranston in particular putting in some bruising tackles. Irvine had levelled the scores with a penalty when Leslie charged down a hurried defensive kick by Old, picked up the bounce and ran 25 yards to score. More Scottish pressure gave Lawson a chance to whip through a gap for his second try. England counter attacked for the last ten minutes but uncompromising tackling held them out. During this second half Bennet replaced Maxwell.

IRELAND 6   SCOTLAND 15
Lansdowne Road
20 March 1976

Ireland: L. A. Moloney (*Garryowen*); T. O. Grace* (*St Mary's*), J. A. Brady (*Wanderers*), C. M. H. Gibson (*NIFC*), S. E. F. Blake-Knox (*NIFC*); B. J. McGann (*Cork Const.*), J. J. Moloney (*St Mary's*); P. A. Orr (*Old Wesley*), J. Cantrell (*UC Dublin*), P. O'Callaghan (*Dolphin*), M. I. Keane (*Lansdowne*), R. F. Hakin (*CIYMS*), S. M. Deering (*Garryowen*), W. P. Duggan (*Blackrock*), S. A. McKinney (*Dungannon*) Repl.: C. H. McKibbin (*Instonians*)
Scotland: A. R. Irvine (*Heriot's FP*); W. C. C. Steele (*London Scot.*), A. G. Cranston (*Hawick*), I. R. McGeechan (*Headingley*), D. Shedden (*West of Scot.*); R. Wilson (*London Scot.*), A. J. M. Lawson (*London Scot.*); J. McLauchlan* (*Jordanhill Coll.*), C. D. Fisher (*Waterloo*), A. B. Carmichael (*West of Scot.*), A. J. Tomes (*Hawick*), G. L. Brown (*West of Scot.*), M. A. Biggar (*London Scot.*), A. F. McHarg (*London Scot.*), D. G. Leslie (*West of Scot.*)
Referee: M. S. Lewis (*Wales*)   **Touch judges:** J. A. Short, J. R. West

B. J. McGann kicked a penalty (3-0); A. R. Irvine kicked two penalties (3-6); B. J. McGann kicked a penalty (6-6). (H.T.). A. R. Irvine kicked two penalties (6-12); R. Wilson dropped a goal (6-15).

This was Scotland's first away win since Twickenham in 1971 and their first at Lansdowne Road since 1966, but it was achieved without a try being scored. True, continuous rain and a heavy pitch was against handling but the game was continually halted by a succession of penalty kicks and here Irvine converted four out of eight attempts while McGann succeeded with two out of six. The Scottish pack more than held their own while their backs, seldom seen in attack, were solid in defence. Near the close Gibson went off with a pulled muscle and was replaced by McKibbin.

SCOTLAND XV 34   JAPAN 9
Murrayfield
25 September 1976

Scotland: A. R. Irvine (*Heriot's FP*); W. B. B. Gammell (*Edin. Wrs.*), K. W. Robertson (*Melrose*), I. R. McGeechan* (*Headingley*), D. M. Ashton (*Ayr*); R. Wilson (*London Scot.*), A. J. M. Lawson (*London Scot.*); J. Aitken (*Gala*), C. D. Fisher (*Waterloo*), N. E. K. Pender (*Hawick*), A. J. Tomes (*Hawick*), J. G. Carswell (*Jordanhill Coll.*), M. A. Biggar (*London Scot.*), W. S. Watson (*Boroughmuir*), D. G. Leslie (*West of Scot.*) Repl.: G. Y. Mackie (*Highland*)
Japan: N. Tanaka; M. Fujiwara, S. Mori, M. Yoshida, K. Aruga; S. Hoshino, R. Imazato; T. Takata, T. Wada, T. Yasui, K. Shibata, T. Terai, Y. Izawa, I. Kobayashi, H. Akama Repl.: K. Muraguchi
Referee: K. H. Clark (*Ireland*)   **Touch judges:** A. M. Hosie, F. Parker

N. Tanaka kicked a penalty (0-3); W. B. B. Gammell, I. R. McGeechan and A. R. Irvine scored but A. R. Irvine converted the first only (14-3). (H.T.). C. D. Fisher and W. B. B. Gammell scored and A. R. Irvine converted the second (24-3); M. Fujiwara scored and N. Tanaka converted (24-9); A. J. M. Lawson and D. M. Ashton scored and A. R. Irvine converted the first (34-9).

The visitors whose forwards were giving away an average of two stones and three inches per man, were obviously handicapped in the set scrums and line outs. They were, however, very fast in the loose, ran the ball whenever possible and tackled firmly until they tired a bit towards the end. Their try was the reward for a succession of good handling moves which set up a scrum from which their halves gave Fujiwara a chance to run hard and force his way over. Tanaka, a small ten stone full back, not only defended well but was always ready and able to run out of defence. Mackie replaced Leslie in the second half and Aruga also came off near the end.

187

International Rugby Union

ENGLAND 26   SCOTLAND 6
Twickenham
15 January 1977

England: A. J. Hignell (*Camb. Univ.*); P. J. Squires (*Harrogate*), B. J. Corless (*Moseley*) C. P. Kent (*Rosslyn Park*), M. A. C. Slemen (*Liverpool*); M. J. Cooper (*Moseley*), M. Young (*Gosforth*); R. J. Cowling (*Leicester*), P. J. Wheeler (*Leicester*), F. E. Cotton (*Sale*), W. B. Beaumont (*Fylde*), N. E. Horton (*Moseley*), P. J. Dixon (*Gosforth*), R. M. Uttley* (*Gosforth*), M. Rafter (*Bristol*)
Scotland: A. R. Irvine (*Heriot's FP*); W. C. C. Steele (*London Scot.*), I. R. McGeechan* (*Headingley*), A. G. Cranston (*Hawick*), L. G. Dick (*Swansea*); R. Wilson (*London Scot.*), A. J. M. Lawson (*London Scot.*); J. Aitken (*Gala*), D. F. Madsen (*Gosforth*), A. B. Carmichael (*West of Scot.*), A. J. Tomes (*Hawick*), A. F. McHarg (*London Scot.*), W. Lauder (*Neath*), D. S. M. Macdonald (*Oxford Univ.*), A. K. Brewster (*Stewart's FP*)
Referee: M. Joseph (*Wales*)   **Touch judges:** R. C. Quittenton (*England*), K. Kelleher (*Wales*)

A. R. Irvine kicked a penalty (0-3); M. A. C. Slemen scored but A. J. Hignell failed (4-3); A. J. Hignell kicked a penalty (7-3); A. R. Irvine kicked a penalty (7-6), M. Young scored and A. J. Hignell converted (13-6). (H.T.). A. J. Hignell kicked a penalty (16-6); C. P. Kent scored but A. J. Hignell failed (20-6); R. M. Uttley scored and A. J. Hignell converted (26-6).

Scotland's recast team was badly shown up; the English forwards dictated play all afternoon and took full advantage of a very shaky back row defence. As a result the Scottish backs were barely seen as an attacking force and again our only scores came from penalties by Irvine, his second being a colossal effort from inside his own half. Fortunately his opposite number only converted two out of seven penalty attempts.

SCOTLAND 21   IRELAND 18
Murrayfield
19 February 1977

Scotland: A. R. Irvine (*Heriot's FP*); W. B. B. Gammell (*Edin. Wrs.*), I. R. McGeechan* (*Headingley*), J. M. Renwick (*Hawick*), D. Shedden (*West of Scot.*); R. Wilson (*London Scot.*), D. W. Morgan (*Stewart's FP*); J. Aitken (*Gala*), D. F. Madsen (*Gosforth*), N. E. K. Pender (*Hawick*), I. A. Barnes (*Hawick*), A. F. McHarg (*London Scot.*), M. A. Biggar (*London Scot.*), D. S. M. McDonald (*London Scot.*), W. S. Watson (*Boroughmuir*) Repl.: A . B. Carmichael (*West of Scot.*)
Ireland: F. Wilson (*CIYMS*); T. O. Grace* (*St Mary's*), A. R. McKibbin (*Instonians*), C. M. H. Gibson (*NIFC*), D. St. J. Brown (*Cork Const.*), M. A. Quinn (*Lansdowne*), J. C. Robbie (*Dublin Univ.*); P. A. Orr (*Old Wesley*), P. C. Whelan (*Garryowen*), E. M. J. Byrne (*Blackrock*), M. I. Keane (*Lansdowne*), C. W. Murtagh (*Portadown*), S. A. McKinney (*Dungannon*), W. P. Duggan (*Blackrock*), J. F. Slattery (*Blackrock*)
Referee: M. Joseph (*Wales*)   **Touch judges:** P. J. Wilmshurst, C. A. P. Thomas (Wales)

A. R. Irvine kicked a penalty (3-0); C. M. H. Gibson kicked a penalty (3-3); W. B. B. Gammell scored but A. R. Irvine failed (7-3); M. A. Quinn dropped a goal (7-6); C. M. H. Gibson kicked a penalty (7-9). (H.T.)W. B. B. Gammell scored but A. R. Irvine failed (11-9); A. R. Irvine kicked a penalty (14-9); D. F. Madsen scored but A. R. Irvine failed (18-9); M. A. Quinn kicked a penalty (18-12); D. W. Morgan dropped a goal (21-12); C. M. H. Gibson scored and converted (21-18).

Scotland made eight changes to Ireland's five, each including two new caps. The pitch was soft after heavy rain and was soon cutting up, and both sides opened their scoring with penalties, Irvine's being a 45 yard effort. After fifteen minutes Pender went off with a rib injury and was replaced by a warmly welcomed Carmichael. Soon after McGeechan had a fine run and his blocked pass went to Gammell who crashed over for a good try. Almost at once Quinn caught a poor drop out and dropped a neat goal and with a Gibson penalty Ireland led at the interval. Ireland attacked on the restart but in one run Wilson missed a pass which Gammell seized and ran 30 yards to score. The Irish pack reacted vigorously but the defence held and in fact the Scottish backs were often quick to counter attack. However, it was Madsen who scored next from an Irish error at a line out and then Barnes gave Morgan the chance to drop a neat goal. In the last minute the score was made to look respectable for Ireland when an attacking kick by Grace bounced wickedly for the defence and Gibson scored a try which he converted.

188

FRANCE 23   SCOTLAND 3
Parc des Princes
5 March 1977

France: J. M. Aguirre (*Bagneres*); D. Harize (*Toulouse*), R. Bertranne (*Bagneres*), F. Sangalli (*Narbonne*), J. L. Averous (*La Voulte*); J. P. Romeu (*Montferrand*), J. Fouroux* (*Auch*); G. Cholley (*Castres*), A. Paco (*Beziers*), R. Paperemborde (*Pau*), M. Palmie (*Beziers*), J. F. Imbernon (*Perpignan*), J. P. Rives (*Toulouse*), J. P. Basiat (*Dax*), J. C. Skrela (*Toulouse*)
Scotland: A. R. Irvine (*Heriot's FP*); W. B. B. Gammell (*Edin. Wrs.*), I. R. McGeechan* (*Headingley*), J. M. Renwick (*Hawick*), D. Shedden (*West of Scot.*); R. Wilson (*London Scot.*), D. W. Morgan (*Stewart's FP*); J. Aitken (*Gala*), D. F. Madsen (*Gosforth*), A. B. Carmichael (*West of Scot.*), I. A. Barnes (*Hawick*), A. F. McHarg (*London Scot.*), M. A. Biggar (*London Scot.*), D. S. M. Macdonald (*London Scot.*), W. S. Watson (*Boroughmuir*)
Referee: M. Joseph (*Wales*)   **Touch judges:** M. Thomas (*Wales*), J.-P. Bonnet (*France*)

A. R. Irvine kicked a penalty (0-3); A. Paco scored and J. P. Romeu converted (6-3); J. P. Romeu kicked a penalty (9-3). (H.T.). D. Harize, R. Bertranne and R. Paperemborde scored and J. P. Romeu converted the last (23-3).

The game opened with a magnificent punch by Cholley which felled Macdonald and since he was penalised later for his equally rough treatment of Renwick and Wilson he was lucky to be left on the field. Not that he was alone in this for a good few of the Scots had to halt for recovery, which was a pity for this French team was very much on top and perfectly capable of scoring by fine handling. Scotland never came into the game. They held their own at the lineout but the ball seldom got out to the threes and the French pack was well on top in the loose play.

SCOTLAND 9   WALES 18
Murrayfield
19 March 1977

Scotland: A. R. Irvine (*Heriot's F. P*); W. B. B. Gammell (*Edin. Wrs.*), J. M. Renwick (*Hawick*), A. G. Cranston (*Hawick*), D. Shedden (*West of Scot.*); I. R. McGeechan* (*Headingley*), D. W. Morgan (*Stewart's FP*); J. McLauchlan (*Jordanhill Coll.*), D. F. Madsen (*Gosforth*), A. B. Carmichael (*West of Scot.*), I. A. Barnes (*Hawick*), A. F. McHarg (*London Scot.*), M. A. Biggar (*London Scot.*), D. S. M. Macdonald (*London Scot.*), W. S. Watson (*Boroughmuir*)
Wales: J. P. R. Williams (*Bridgend*); T. G. R. Davies (*Cardiff*), S. P. Fenwick (*Bridgend*), D. H. Burcher (*Newport*), J. J. Williams (*Llanelli*); P. Bennett* (*Llanelli*), G. O. Edwards (*Cardiff*); C. Williams (*Aberavon*), R. W. Windsor (*Pontypool*), G. Price (*Pontypool*), A. J. Martin (*Aberavon*), G. A. D. Wheel (*Swansea*), T. J. Cobner (*Pontypool*), D. L. Quinnell (*Llanelli*), R. C. Burgess (*Ebbw Vale*)
Referee: G. Domercq (*France*)   **Touch judges:** P. C. Robertson, F. Palmade (*France*)

I. R. McGeechan dropped a goal (3-0); P. Bennett kicked a penalty (3-3). (H.T.). A. R. Irvine scored and converted (9-3); T. G. R. Davies scored and P. Bennett converted (9-9); P. Bennett kicked a penalty (9-12); P. Bennett scored and converted (9-18).

Scotland made a sensational start for inside the first minute Biggar got the ball away from a ruck to Morgan whose pass let McGeechan drop a goal. There followed two near penalty misses, Bennett hitting the post from near the touch line and Irvine narrowly missing from five yards inside his own half. Then Bennett, after a foul on Quinnell, levelled the scores with a fine 40 yard penalty. There was no further scoring before half time although both sides produced some good handling runs. Scotland restarted well for early on Morgan, breaking from a scrum, set Renwick off on a fine run which ended with Irvine joining in to score a try which he converted. Within five minutes Wales drew level when Edwards and J. P. R. Williams combined to put J. J. Williams over and Bennett converted from the touch line. Another Bennett penalty put them into the lead before Fenwick, taking the ball in his own 25, started an attack which set Davies off on a great run up the touch line continued by Burcher with Edwards and Bennett in support. A final pass to Bennett saw him make a clear run to score between the posts and convert. The fact that many Scots were certain that the final pass was forward could not detract from the qualify of such a fine attacking run from defence.

JAPAN 9 SCOTLAND XV 74
Tokyo
18 September 1977

Japan: S. Tanaka; H. Ujino, M. Yoshida, S. Mori, M. Fujiwara; Y. Matsuo, J. Matsumoto; T. Yasui, T. Takada*, T. Hatakeyama, N. Kumagai, K. Segawa, H. Akama, H. Ogasawara, I. Kobayashi
Scotland: C. D. R. Mair (*West of Scot.*); W. B. B. Gammell (*Edin. Wrs.*), J. M. Renwick (*Hawick*), A. G. Cranston (*Hawick*), L. G. Dick (*Swansea*); R. Wilson (*London Scot.*), R. J. Laidlaw (*Jedforest*); J. McLauchlan (*Jordanhill Coll.*), C. T. Deans (*Hawick*), R. F. Cunningham (*Gala*), A. J. Tomes (*Hawick*), I. A. Barnes (*Hawick*), M. A. Biggar* (*London Scot.*), D. S. M. Macdonald (*London Scot.*), G. Dickson (*Gala*). Repls.: R. A. Moffat (*Melrose*), G. M. McGuinness (*West of Scot.*)
Referee: P. E. Hughes (*England*)

W. B. B. Gammell (4), R. J. Laidlaw (2), A. G. Cranston, G. Dickson, R. A. Moffat, G. M. McGuinness and R. Wilson scored . C. D. R. Mair kicked nine goals and four penalties. For Japan, H. Ujino scored and S. Tanaka converted. Y. Matsuo kicked a penalty.

Japan resisted well up to half-time when the score was only 3-15 but thereafter the taller and heavier Scottish forwards wore down their opponents and some penetrative running by the Scottish backs, Laidlaw, Renwick and Gammell in particular, put Scotland in complete command. This was the final match in a short tour to Thailand, Hong Kong and Japan.

IRELAND 12 SCOTLAND 9
Lansdowne Road
21 January 1978

Ireland: A. H. Ensor (*Wanderers*); T. O. Grace (*St Mary's*), A. R. McKibben (*London Irish*), P. P. McNaughton (*Greystones*), A. C. McLennan (*Wanderers*); A. J. P. Ward (*Garryowen*), J. J. Moloney* (*St Mary's*); P. A. Orr (*Old Wesley*), P. C. Whelan (*Garryowen*), M. P. Fitzpatrick (*Wanderers*), M. I. Keane (*Lansdowne*), D. Spring (*Dublin Univ.*), J. B. O'Driscoll (*London Irish*), W. P. Duggan (*Blackrock*), J. F. Slattery (*Blackrock*) Repl.: S. A. McKinney (*Dungannon*), L. A. Moloney (*Garryowen*)
Scotland: B. H. Hay (*Boroughmuir*); A. R. Irvine (*Heriot's FP*), J. M. Renwick (*Hawick*), I. R. McGeechan (*Headingley*), D. Shedden (*West of Scot.*); R. Wilson (*London Scot.*), D. W. Morgan* (*Stewart's FP*); J. McLauchlan (*Jordanhill Coll.*), D. F. Madsen (*Gosforth*), A. B. Carmichael (*West of Scot.*), A. J. Tomes (*Hawick*), A. F. McHarg (*London Scot.*), M. A. Biggar (*London Scot.*), D. S. M. Macdonald (*West of Scot.*), C. B. Hegarty (*Hawick*)
Referee: P. E. Hughes (*England*)   **Touch judges:** A. Welsby (*England*), O. E. Doyle (*Ireland*)

D. W. Morgan kicked a penalty (0-3); A. J. P. Ward kicked a penalty (3-3); D. W. Morgan kicked a penalty (3-6); A. J. P. Ward kicked a penalty (6-6); S. A. McKinney scored and A. J. P. Ward converted (12-6). (H.T.). D. W. Morgan kicked a penalty (12-9).

Ireland started strongly and it was ten minutes before Scotland got to the Irish 25 whereupon the new Scottish captain promptly kicked a penalty. Scrappy play followed with Ireland having the better of the loose play and at the end of 40 minutes the scores were level at two penalties each. Here O'Driscoll retired hurt and was replaced by McKinney who at once took part in a fierce forward rush and then from the resulting scrum took a pass from Slattery and scored. The second half was slightly more open with the Irish backs being more in evidence mainly because their forwards were clearly better in the lineout and loose play. Irvine, clearly isolated on the wing, was allowed to take one shot at goal and narrowly missed with a tremendously long kick. Later Morgan kicked another penalty but missed another in the 44th minute. Hegarty then nearly got in at the corner. From the line out Scotland got a penalty, obviously kickable, but Morgan elected to run the ball for a winning try. The Irish defence killed the move and the whistle went. This was a long match for the first half lasted 47 minutes and the second one 48 minutes. Ensor, badly concussed in a collision, was replaced by L. A. Moloney half way through the second half.

SCOTLAND 16 FRANCE 19
Murrayfield
4 February 1978

Scotland: A. R. Irvine (*Heriot's FP*); B. H. Hay (*Boroughmuir*), J. M. Renwick (*Hawick*), I. R. McGeechan (*Headingley*), D. Shedden (*West of Scot.*), R. Wilson (*London Scot.*), D. W. Morgan* (*Stewart's FP*); J. McLauchlan (*Jordanhill Coll.*), C. T. Deans (*Hawick*), N. E. K. Pender (*Hawick*), A. J. Tomes (*Hawick*), A. F. McHarg (*London Scot.*), M. A. Biggar (*London Scot.*), G. Y. Mackie (*Highland*), C. B. Hegarty (*Hawick*) Repl.: A. G. Cranston (*Hawick*), C. G. Hogg (*Boroughmuir*)
France: J. M. Aguirre (*Bagneres*); J. F. Gourdon (*Bagneres*), R. Bertranne (*Bagneres*), C. Belascain (*Bayonne*), J.-L. Averous (*La Voulte*); B. Vives (*Agen*), J. Gallion (*Toulon*); G. Cholley (*Castres*), A. Paco (*Beziers*), R. Paparemborde (*Pau*), M. Palmie (*Beziers*), F. Haget (*Agen*), J. P. Rives (*Toulouse*), J.-P. Bestiat* (*Dax*), J.-C. Skrela (*Toulouse*)
Referee: C. P. G. Thomas (*Wales*) **Touch judges:** A. Bryce, C. Norling (*Wales*)

D. W. Morgan kicked a penalty (3-0); D. Shedden scored but D. W. Morgan failed (7-0); A. R. Irvine scored and D. W. Morgan converted (13-0); J. Gallion scored but J. M. Aguirre failed (13-4). (H.T.). J. M. Aguirre kicked a penalty (13-7); F. Haget scored and J. M. Aguirre converted (13-13); J. M. Aguirre kicked a penalty (13-16); D. W. Morgan dropped a goal (16-16); J. M. Aguirre kicked a penalty (16-19).

During the first half in wet conditions Scotland harried the French by being fast on to the loose ball. Shedden came through after a diagonal kick by Morgan, charged down Gourdon's kick and scored. Then Irvine followed up a long kick ahead by Morgan, kicked the ball over the line and although blatantly impeded, got to the ball first. Unfortunately he landed awkwardly and hurt his shoulder. While he was off, Gallion made a break and kicked a high ball into the ingoal area where Hegarty (playing on the wing with Hay at full back) could not hold the wet ball and a kindly bounce gave Gallion a try. Irvine returned but early in the second half both he and Shedden had to retire to be replaced by Cranston and Hogg. France, even in the rain, kept up the attack and a good handling run by Belascun, Skrela and Averous put Haget in at the corner but Aguirre made a fine conversion and then kicked a penalty to put France ahead. Morgan levelled the scores with a drop goal taken after a non-scoring penalty award and certainly some of the French team protested that he had omitted the tap kick before making the drop! Minutes later Aguirre kicked another penalty and although Scotland put in a great attacking finish they could not get the vital score.

WALES 22 SCOTLAND 14
Cardiff
18 February 1978

Wales: J. P. R. Williams (*Bridgend*); T. G. R. Davies (*Cardiff*), R. W. R. Gravell (*Llanelli*), S. P. Fenwick (*Bridgend*), J. J. Williams (*Llanelli*); P. Bennett* (*Llanelli*), G. O. Edwards (*Cardiff*); A. G. Faulkner (*Pontypool*), R. W. Windsor (*Pontypool*), G. Price (*Pontypool*), A. J. Martin (*Aberavon*), G. A. D. Wheel (*Swansea*), T. J. Cobner (*Pontypool*), D. L. Quinnell (*Llanelli*), J. Squire (*Newport*)
Scotland: B. H. Hay (*Boroughmuir*); W. B. B. Gammell (*Edin. Wrs.*), J. M. Renwick (*Hawick*), A. G. Cranston (*Hawick*), D. Shedden (*West of Scot.*); I. R. McGeechan (*Headingley*), D. W. Morgan* (*Stewart's FP*); J. McLauchlan (*Jordanhill Coll.*), C. T. Deans (*Hawick*), N. E. K. Pender (*Hawick*), A. J. Tomes (*Hawick*), A. F. McHarg (*London Scot.*), M. A. Biggar (*London Scot.*), D. S. M. Macdonald (*West of Scot.*), C. B. Hegarty (*Hawick*) Repl.: C. G. Hogg (*Boroughmuir*)
Referee: J. R. West (*Ireland*) **Touch judges:** D. M. D. Rea (*Ireland*), A. W. Bevan (*Wales*)

D. W. Morgan kicked a penalty (0-3); G. O. Edwards scored but P. Bennett failed (4-3); J. M. Renwick scored but D. W. Morgan failed (4-7); R. W. R. Gravell scored but P. Bennett failed (8-7). (H.T.). P. Bennett dropped a goal (11-7); S. P. Fenwick scored but P. Bennett failed (15-7); P. Bennett kicked a penalty (18-7); D. L. Quinnell scored but P. Bennett failed (22-7); D. W. Morgan kicked a penalty (22-10); A. J. Tomes scored but D. W. Morgan failed (22-14).

Wales chose to play against the wind in the first half and were content with their narrow half-time lead for although the Scottish pack were on top in the line out Wales were controlling the scrums and loose play. Inside three minutes Scotland lost Shedden and once again he was replaced by Hogg. After a 40 yard penalty by Morgan, Edwards from a ten yards scrum dummied and crashed his way through for a score. After Morgan had missed two penalties, he sent McGeechan away and with Hay coming into the line Renwick was given a scoring pass. Almost at once Edwards took a short penalty which led to Gravell barging through the defence for a determined try. Restarting with the wind Wales scored fourteen points in as many minutes and appeared to have the match won, yet for the last twenty minutes Scotland fought back most determinedly but could not make up the deficit.

SCOTLAND 0   ENGLAND 15
Murrayfield
4 March 1978

Scotland: A. R. Irvine (*Heriot's FP*); W. B. B. Gammell (*Edin. Wrs.*), J. M. Renwick (*Hawick*), A. G. Cranston (*Hawick*), B. H. Hay (*Boroughmuir*); R. W. Breakey (*Gosforth*) D. W. Morgan* (*Stewart's FP*); J. McLauchlan (*Jordanhill Coll.*), C. T. Deans (*Hawick*), N. E. K. Pender (*Hawick*), A. J. Tomes (*Hawick*), D. Gray (*West of Scot.*), M. A. Biggar (*London Scot.*), D. S. M. Macdonald (*West of Scot.*), C. B. Hegarty (*Hawick*)
England: D. Caplan (*Headingley*); P. J. Squires (*Harrogate*), B. J. Corless (*Moseley*), P. A. Dodge (*Leicester*), M. A. C. Slemen (*Liverpool*); J. P. Horton (*Bath*), M. Young (*Gosforth*); B. G. Nelmes (*Cardiff*), P. J. Wheeler (*Leicester*), F. E. Cotton (*Sale*), W. B. Beaumont* (*Fylde*), M. Colclough (*Angouleme*), P. J. Dixon (*Gosforth*), J. P. Scott (*Rosslyn Park*), M. J. Rafter (*Bristol*)
Referee: J. R. West (*Ireland*)   **Touch judges:** J. A. Short, D. I. H. Burnett (*Ireland*)

P. J. Squires scored and M. Young converted (0-6); P. A. Dodge kicked a penalty (0-9). (H.T.). B. G. Nelmes scored and M. Young converted (0-15).

Both countries came to Murrayfield without a win but it was England who returned with the Calcutta Cup leaving Scotland with the wooden spoon. Again the Scottish pack did well at the line out only to be outplayed in the scrums and loose mauls. England started with the wind and their new full back nearly scored in the first minutes. It was a full twenty minutes before Scotland got into their opponents' half but poor finishing ruined their attacks. After 30 minutes Slemen broke away to initiate a splendid handling run which ended by Squires on the opposite wing scoring a fine try. Just on half time Dodge kicked a massive 55 yard penalty. With the wind Scotland did some attacking, Gammell and Renwick both being caught at the corner but again poor finishing let them down and with 10 minutes to go England clinched the win when a scissors movement by their centres was completed by Nelmes who fairly smashed his way over.

SCOTLAND 9   NEW ZEALAND 18
Murrayfield
9 December 1978

Scotland: A . R. Irvine (*Heriot's FP*); K. W. Robertson (*Melrose*), J. M. Renwick (*Hawick*), A. G. Cranston (*Hawick*), B. H. Hay (*Boroughmuir*); I. R. McGeechan* (*Headingley*), A. J. M. Lawson (*London Scot.*); J . McLauchlan (*Jordanhill Coll.*), C. T. Deans (*Hawick*), R. F. Cunningham (*Gala*), A. J. Tomes (*Hawick*), A. F. McHarg (*London Scot.*), M. A. Biggar (*London Scot.*), D. G. Leslie (*Gala*), G. Dickson (*Gala*) Repl.: I. K. Lambie (*Watsonians*)
New Zealand: B. J. McKechnie (*Southland*); S. S. Wilson (*Wellington*), B. J. Robertson (*Counties*), W. M. Osborne (*Wanganui*), B. G. Williams (*Auckland*); D. D. Bruce (*Canterbury*), M. W. Donaldson (*Manawata*); B. R. Johnstone (*Auckland*), A. G. Dalton (*Counties*), G. A. Knight (*Manawata*), A. M. Haden (*Auckland*), F. J. Oliver (*Otaga*), L. M. Rutledge (*Southland*), G. A. Seear (*Otago*), G. N. K. Mourie* (*Taranaki*)
Referee: J. R. West (*Ireland*)   **Touch judges:** P. C. Robertson, D. I. H. Burnett (*Ireland*)

B. H. Hay scored and A. R. Irvine converted (6-0); B. J. McKechnie kicked a penalty (6-3); G. A. Seear scored and B. J. McKechnie converted (6-9). (H.T.). B. J. McKechnie kicked a penalty (6-12); I. R. McGeechan dropped a goal (9-12); B. J. Robertson scored and B. J. McKechnie converted (9-18).

In a day of rain visibility became so poor that the kick off was actually advanced by five minutes but the game finished in a very dim light. The wet conditions caused many handling errors and the opening score came when Bruce slithered past a loose ball which Hay kicked on and gathered to dive over for a try converted from the touch line by Irvine. Strong New Zealand forward play followed and after McKechnie had kicked a penalty Seear drove over for a try. Early in the second half Leslie limped off to be replaced by Lambie. Scotland came away strongly and a McKechnie penalty was cancelled out by a drop goal by McGeechan. The Scots continued to attack only to give away a most unlucky score. McGeechan, with his threes up in attack, dropped at goal only to find the ball bouncing off Bruce. Robertson shot on to the rebound and with two long hacks ahead was able to put the ball the length of the field and keep ahead of a shocked defence to score under the posts.

SCOTLAND 13   WALES 19
Murrayfield
20 January 1979

Scotland: A. R. Irvine (*Heriot's FP*); K. W. Robertson (*Melrose*), J. M. Renwick (*Hawick*), I. R. McGeechan* (*Headingley*), B. H. Hay (*Boroughmuir*); J. Y. Rutherford (*Selkirk*), A. J. M. Lawson (*London Scot.*); J. McLauchlan (*Jordanhill Coll.*), C. T. Deans (*Hawick*), R. F. Cunningham (*Gala*), A. J. Tomes (*Hawick*), A. F. McHarg (*London Scot.*), M. A. Biggar (*London Scot.*), I. K. Lambie (*Watsonians*), G. Dickson (*Gala*)
Wales: J. P. R. Williams* (*Bridgend*); H. E. Rees (*Neath*), R. W. R. Gravell (*Llanelli*), S. P. Fenwick (*Bridgend*), J. J. Williams (*Llanelli*); W. G. Davies (*Cardiff*), T. D. Holmes (*Cardiff*); A. G. Faulkner (*Pontypool*), R. W. Windsor (*Pontypool*), G. Price (*Pontypool*), A. J. Martin (*Aberavon*), G. A. D. Wheel (*Swansea*), P. Ringer (*Llanelli*), D. L. Quinnell (*Llanelli*), J. Squire (*Pontypool*)
Referee: F. Palmade (*France*)   **Touch judges:** J. W. Dinsmore, G. Chevrier (*France*)

S. P. Fenwick kicked a penalty (0-3); A. R. Irvine kicked two penalties (6-3), A. R. Irvine scored but failed to convert (10-3); S. P. Fenwick kicked a penalty (10-6); A. R. Irvine kicked a penalty (13-6). (H.T.). S. P. Fenwick kicked a penalty (13-9); H. E. Rees and T. D. Holmes scored and S. P. Fenwick converted the second (13-19).

In spite of the very wintry conditions the electric blanket had kept the pitch in beautiful condition. For the first half Scotland had the benefit of a bitterly cold wind blowing down the pitch from the clock end, but a heavy and active Welsh pack dominated the line out and scrums. The Scottish backs had always to work with a limited supply of good ball, yet their try was as fine a combined effort as one could wish to see. Irvine, having fielded a kick ahead, side stepped and ran on to link with Hay. The ball went loose but Lawson pounced on it and set Rutherford racing through a gap to link up with McGeechan and Tomes. The big lock then flung out an overhead pass which Irvine took up and side stepped over for a great score.

With the wind in the second half Wales attacked continually. Fenwick, who had kicked a third penalty, combined with Gravell to set J. P. R. Williams away. A nice chip ahead let Rees go in for the equalising score. Scotland held on grimly but in the dying minutes a powerful surge by the Welsh pack put Holmes over for the winning score.

ENGLAND 7   SCOTLAND 7
Twickenham
3 February 1979

England: A. J. Hignell (*Bristol*); P. J. Squires (*Harrogate*), A. M. Bond (*Sale*), P. W. Dodge (*Leicester*), M. A. C. Slemen (*Liverpool*); W. N. Bennett (*London Welsh*), M. Young (*Gosforth*); R. J. Cowling (*Leicester*), P. J. Wheeler (*Leicester*), G. S. Pearce (*Northampton*), W. B. Beaumont (*Fylde*), N. E. Horton (*Toulouse*), A. Neary (*Broughton Park*), R. M. Uttley* (*Gosforth*), M. Rafter (*Bristol*) Repl.: J. P. Scott (*Cardiff*)
Scotland: A. R. Irvine (*Heriot's FP*); K. W. Robertson (*Melrose*), J. M. Renwick (*Hawick*), I. R. McGeechan* (*Headingley*), B. H. Hay (*Boroughmuir*); J. Y. Rutherford (*Selkirk*), A. J. M. Lawson (*London Scot.*); J. McLauchlan (*Jordanhill Coll.*), C. T. Deans (*Hawick*), R. F. Cunningham (*Gala*), A. J. Tomes (*Hawick*), A. F. McHarg (*London Scot.*), M. A. Biggar (*London Scot.*), I. K. Lambie (*Watsonians*), G. Dickson (*Gala*)
Referee: C. Norling (*Wales*)   **Touch judges:** C. Thomas (*Wales*), A. Welsby (*England*)

M. A. C. Slemen scored but W. N. Bennett failed (4-0); W. N. Bennett kicked a penalty (7-0); J. Y. Rutherford scored but A. R. Irvine failed (7-4). (H.T.). A. R. Irvine kicked a penalty (7-7).

A capacity crowd which included Prince Philip saw England make a great start, for after a straightforward threequarter run, Slemen went over at the corner inside five minutes play. The home pack was dominating both the line out and second phase play but their backs did not make effective use of the possession. The Scottish backs looked good but were given few real chances to attack. Bennett had kicked a long range penalty before Renwick seized a loose ball and Irvine in the line kicked ahead only to be rather obviously tripped. Rutherford, however, followed up for the score which was not converted. The second half followed much the same pattern with the English backs failing to make use of a plentiful supply of the ball and eventually an Irvine penalty levelled the scores. Near the close Uttley was hurt and replaced by Scott.

SCOTLAND 11   IRELAND 11
Murrayfield
3 March 1979

Scotland: A. R. Irvine (*Heriot's FP*); K. W. Robertson (*Melrose*), J. M. Renwick (*Hawick*), I. R. McGeechan* (*Headingley*), B. H. Hay (*Boroughmuir*); J. Y. Rutherford (*Selkirk*), A. J. M. Lawson (*London Scot.*); J. McLauchlan (*Jordanhill Coll.*), C. T. Deans (*Hawick*), I. G. Milne (*Heriot's FP*), A. J. Tomes (*Hawick*), D. Gray (*West of Scot.*), M. A. Biggar (*London Scot.*), W. S. Watson (*Boroughmuir*), G. Dickson (*Gala*)
Ireland: W. R. J. Elliott (*Bangor*); C. M. H. Gibson (*NIFC*), A. R. McKibbin (*London Irish*), P. P. McNaughton (*Greystones*), A. C. McLennan (*Wanderers*); A. J. P. Ward (*Garryowen*), C. S. Patterson (*Instonians*); P. A. Orr (Old Wesley), P. C. Whelan (Garryowen), G. A. J. McLoughlin (*Shannon*), M. I. Keane (*Lansdowne*), D. E. Spring (*Dublin Univ.*), W. P. Duggan (*Blackrock*), M. E. Gibson (*Lansdowne*), J. F. Slattery* (*Blackrock*)
Referee: C. Thomas (*Wales*)   **Touch judges:** J. R. Colquhoun, K. Rowlands (*Wales*)

J. Y. Rutherford scored but A. R. Irvine failed (4-0); C. S. Patterson scored but A. J. P. Ward failed (4-4); A . R. Irvine kicked a penalty (7-4). (H.T.). A . R. Irvine scored but failed to convert (11-4). A. J. P. Ward kicked a penalty (11-7); C. S. Patterson scored but A. J. P. Ward failed (11-11).

There was a strong swirling wind which baffled the kicks at goal but made attacking kicks doubly dangerous, Ward in particular hoisting some wicked ones. Yet there were some fine runs especially by the Scottish threes. Both Irish tries followed good work by their forwards and Patterson scored with typical scrum half's fast breaks near the line. Ireland were unlucky that Ward's last conversion effort swung to strike a post. The first Scottish score followed an interception by Lawson who covered at least 50 yards before failing to reach Renwick with a pass. From a line out thereafter nice running by Milne, Deans and Lawson put Rutherford in at the corner. Their second score came from a neat kick ahead by Renwick which Robertson took on the run and then put Irvine in.

FRANCE 21   SCOTLAND 17
Parc des Princes
17 March 1979

France: J. M. Aguirre (*Bagneres*); J. F. Gourdon (*Bagneres*), R. Bertranne (*Bagneres*), C. Belascain (*Bayonne*), F. Costes (*Montferrand*); R. R. Aguerre (*Biarritz*), J. Gallion (*Toulon*); G. Cholley (*Castres*), A. Paco (*Besiers*), R. Paparemborde (*Pau*), F. Haget (*Biarritz*), J. F. Marchal (*Lourdes*), J. P. Rives* (*Toulouse*), J. L. Joinel (*Brive*), Y. Malquier (*Narbonne*)
Scotland: A. R. Irvine (*Heriot's FP*); K. W. Robertson (*Melrose*), J. M. Renwick (*Hawick*), I. R. McGeechan* (*Headingley*), B. H. Hay (*Boroughmuir*); J. Y. Rutherford (*Selkirk*), A. J. M. Lawson (*London Scot.*); J. McLauchlan (*Jordanhill Coll.*), C. T. Deans (*Hawick*), I. G. Milne (*Heriot's FP*), A. J. Tomes (*Hawick*), D. Gray (*West of Scot.*), M. A. Biggar (*London Scot.*), G. Dickson (*Gala*), W. S. Watson (*Boroughmuir*)
Referee: R. C. Quittenton (*England*)   **Touch judges:** A. Welsby (*England*), N. J. St Guilhem (*France*)

C. Belascain scored but Aguerre failed (4-0); K. W. Robertson scored but Irvine failed (4-4); R. Aguerre kicked a penalty and dropped a goal (10-4); G. Dickson scored and Irvine converted(10-10). (H.T.). A. R. Irvine kicked a penalty(10-13); Y. Malquier scored but Aguerre failed (14-13); A. R. Irvine scored but failed (14-17); Y. Malquier scored but Aguerre failed (18-17); R. Aguerre kicked a penalty (21-17).

This was a game which could have gone either way yet France with a strong pack always looked the more dangerous. R. Aguerre, although scoring nine points, had an off day with his place kicking but clinched the match in the last four minutes by kicking a penalty from beyond the centre line.

SCOTLAND 6   NEW ZEALAND 20
Murrayfield
10 November 1979

Scotland: A. R. Irvine (*Heriot's FP*); K. W. Robertson (*Melrose*), J. M. Renwick (*Hawick*), D. I. Johnston (*Watsonians*), B. H. Hay (*Boroughmuir*); J. Y. Rutherford (*Selkirk*), A. J. M. Lawson (*Heriot's FP*); J. McLauchlan* (*Jordanhill Coll.*), C. T. Deans (*Hawick*), I. G. Milne (*Heriot's FP*), A. J. Tomes (*Hawick*), D. Gray (*West of Scot.*), M. A. Biggar (*London Scot.*), I. K. Lambie (*Watsonians*), G. Dickson (*Gala*)
New Zealand: R. G. Wilson (*Canterbury*); S. S. Wilson (*Wellington*), G. Cunningham (*Auckland*), M. Taylor (*Waikato*), B. F. Fraser (*Wellington*); E. Dun (*North Auckland*), D. S. Loveridge (*Taranaki*); B. R. Johnstone (*Auckland*), A. G. Dalton (*Counties*), J. E. Spiers (*Counties*), A. M. Haden (*Auckland*), J. K. Fleming (*Wellington*), K. W. Stewart (*Southland*), M. G. Mexted (*Wellington*), G. N. K. Mourie* (*Taranaki*) Repl.: M. Donaldson (*Manawatu*)
Referee: R. C. Quittenton (*England*)   **Touch judges:** J. M. Prideaux, C. J. High (*England*)

D. S. Loveridge scored: R. G. Wilson failed (0-4). (H.T.). M. G. Mexted scored: R. G. Wilson converted (0-10); A. R. Irvine kicked two penalties (6-10); S. S. Wilson and E. Dunn scored: R. G. Wilson converted the second (6-20).

The Scottish pack held its own in the line out and scrums but was no match for the New Zealand pack in loose play. The Scottish backs did little handling and against a solid defence never really looked like scoring. In contrast some of the Scottish tackling was poor; Mexted scored his try by a solo breakaway from a two man line out on the Scottish 22 metre line.

IRELAND 22   SCOTLAND 15
Lansdowne Road
2 February 1980

Ireland: R. C. O'Donnell (*St Mary's*); T. J . Kennedy (*St Mary's*), A . R. McKibbin (*London Irish*), P. P. McNaughton (*Greystones*), A. C. McLennan (*Wanderers*); S. O. Campbell (*Old Belvedere*), C. S. Patterson (*Instonians*); P. A. Orr (*Old Wesley*), C. F. Fitzgerald (*St Mary's*), M. P. Fitzpatrick (*Wanderers*), J. J. Glennon (*Skerries*), M. I. Keane (*Lansdowne*), J. B. O'Driscoll (*London Irish*), D. E. Spring (*Dublin Univ.*), J. R. Slattery* (*Blackrock*)
Scotland: A. R. Irvine (*Heriot's FP*); S. Munro (*Ayr*), J. M. Renwick (*Hawick*), D. I. Johnston (*Watsonians*), B. H. Hay (*Boroughmuir*); J. Y. Rutherford (*Selkirk*), R. J. Laidlaw (*Jedforest*); J. N. Burnett (*Heriot's FP*), C. T. Deans (*Hawick*), I. G. Milne (*Heriot's FP*), W. Cuthbertson (*Kilmarnock*), D. Gray (*West of Scot.*), M. A. Biggar* (*London Scot.*), J. R. Beattie (*Glas. Acads.*), A. K. Brewster (*Stewart's FP*)
Referee: G. Chevrier (*France*)   **Touch judges:** F. Palmade, J. P. Bonnet (*France*)

A. R. Irvine kicked a penalty (0-3); D. I. Johnston scored and A. R. Irvine converted (0-9); S. O. Campbell kicked 2 penalties (6-9); M. I. Keane scored but S. O. Campbell failed (10-9). (H.T.). T. J. Kennedy scored and S. O. Campbell converted (16-9); S. O. Campbell kicked a penalty and dropped a goal (22-9); D. I. Johnston scored and A. R. Irvine converted (22-15).

Yet again the Scottish pack held their own in the line out and scrums only to be beaten in the loose and show weaknesses in their cover defence. Their backs looked sharp enough, but never really got good possession and it was disheartening to find their early lead being frittered away. Campbell had missed three penalties before kicking his first but here Irvine was most unlucky to be penalised in front of the posts . Having called for a mark he stood his ground only to be penalised for not releasing the ball on being tackled.

SCOTLAND 22   FRANCE 14
Murrayfield
16 February 1980

Scotland: A. R. Irvine (*Heriot's FP*); S. Munro (*Ayr*), J. M. Renwick (*Hawick*), D. I. Johnston (*Watsonians*), B. H. Hay (*Boroughmuir*); J. Y. Rutherford (*Selkirk*), R. J. Laidlaw (*Jedforest*); J. N. Burnett (*Heriot's FP*), C. T. Deans (*Hawick*), I. G. Milne (*Heriot's FP*), A. J. Tomes (*Hawick*) D. Gray (*West of Scot.*), M. A. Biggar* (*London Scot./*), J. R. Beattie (*Glas. Acads.*), A. K. Brewster (*Stewart's FP*)
France: S. Gabernet (*Toulouse*); D. Bustaffa (*Carcassonne*), R. Bertranne (*Bagneres*), D. Cordorniou (*Narbonne*), J. L. Averous (*La Voulte*); A. Caussade (*Lourdes*), J. Gallion (*Toulon*); A. Vaquerin (*Beziers*), P. Dintrans (*Tarbes*), R. Paparemborde (*Pau*), F. Haga (*Biarritz*), J. F. Marchal (*Lourdes*), J. P. Rives* (*Toulouse*), M. Clement (*Oloron*), J. L. Joinel (*Brive*)
Referee: J. R. West (*Ireland*)   **Touch judges:** A. O'Sullivan, M. Reddan (*Ireland*)

J. Gallion scored but A. Caussade failed (0-4); J. Y. Rutherford scored but A. R. Irvine failed (4-4); S. Gabernet kicked a penalty (4-7). (H.T.). S. Gaberna scored but A. Caussade failed (4-11); A. Caussade dropped a goal (4-14); A. R. Irvine scored and converted (10-14); A. R. Irvine scored and J. M. Renwick converted (16-14); A. R. Irvine kicked 2 penalties (22-14).

After thirteen games without a win it was an extraordinary and very late revival by Scotland that broke the sequence. Initially France got much reasonable possession from the loose play but did not make good use of it. Their first try was a typical scrum half's move following a fine rush by the pack while the second followed a long defensive kick which Gabernet fielded and then made a very fast break up the touch line. Interpassing with Averous gave the full back a fine score. A. R. Irvine took a series of penalty kicks which were so off target that the crowd began to shout for a change of kicker. Then with some fifteen minutes to go the Scottish backs began to handle and run and after some eight players had taken part in a movement, Irvine was right up to get in at the corner—and this time he kicked a goal. Inside five minutes backs and forwards combined beautifully at pace and again Irvine was right up to take a scoring pass. Renwick converted this and in the closing minutes Irvine completely re-established himself as the hero of the crowd by kicking two penalty goals. So Scotland pulled off an amazing win by scoring 18 points inside 12 minutes to change the score from 4-14 to 22-14!

WALES 17   SCOTLAND 6
Cardiff
1 March 1980

Wales: W. R. Blyth (*Swansea*); H. E. Rees (*Neath*), D. S. Richards (*Swansea*), S. P. Fenwick (*Bridgend*), D. Keen (*Aberavon*); W. G. Davies (*Cardiff*), T. D. Holmes (*Cardiff*); C. Williams (*Swansea*), A. J. Phillips (*Cardiff*), G. Price (*Pontypool*), A. J. Martin (*Aberavon*), G. A. D. Wheel (*Swansea*), J. M. Lane (*Cardiff*), E. T. Butler (*Pontypool*), J. Squire* (*Pontypool*) Repl.: P. Morgan (*Llanelli*)
Scotland: A. R. Irvine (*Heriot's FP*), K. W. Robertson (*Melrose*), J. M. Renwick (*Hawick*), D. I. Johnston (*Watsonians*), B. H. Hay (*Boroughmuir*); B. M. Gossman (*West of Scot.*), R. J. Laidlaw (*Jedforest*); J. N. Burnett (*Heriot's FP*), K. G. Lawrie (*Gala*) N. A. Rowan (Boroughmuir), A. J. Tomes (*Hawick*), D. Gray (*West of Scot.*), M. A. Biggar* (*London Scot.*), J. R. Beattie (*Glas. Acads.*), G. Dickson (*Gala*) Repl.: A. J. M. Lawson (*Heriot's FP*)
Referee: L. M. Prideaux (*England*)   **Touch judges:** R. C. Quittenton, C. J. High (*England*)

S. P. Fenwick kicked a penalty (3-0); T. D. Holmes scored but S. P. Fenwick failed (7-0). (H.T.). D. Keen scored but S. P. Fenwick failed (11-0); D. S. Richards scored and W. R. Blyth converted (17-0); J. M. Renwick scored and A. R. Irvine converted (17-6).

The teams were presented to the Prince of Wales. The Scots were forced to make three changes and in fact Gossman was a third choice at half. The forwards did well enough in the scrums and line out but Laidlaw (who retired hurt after twenty minutes) had always to put up with some very untidy ball. The Welsh pack, however, were clearly superior in the loose, giving their backs much clean possession and aided by some rather weak tackling they ran in three tries. Yet the Scottish defence held out twice when the Welsh pack were literally encamped on their line. Just before half

196

time one five minute siege finished when the Scottish backs ran the ball from behind the line to gain touch near midfield. Just before the end these backs again showed their potential when a dropped pass by Fenwick went via Gossman, Beattie and Irvine to Robertson who after a mazy run gave Renwick a pass to complete a fine handling movement. Shortly before half time P. Morgan replaced an injured G. Davies.

SCOTLAND 18   ENGLAND 30
Murrayfield
15 March 1980

Scotland: A. R. Irvine* (*Heriot's FP*), K. W. Robertson (*Melrose*), J. M. Renwick (*Hawick*), D. I. Johnston (*Watsonians*), B. H. Hay (*Boroughmuir*); J. Y. Rutherford (*Selkirk*), R. J. Laidlaw (*Jedforest*); J. N. Burnett (*Heriot's FP*), K. G. Lawrie (*Gala*), N. A. Rowan (*Boroughmuir*), A. J. Tomes (*Hawick*), D. Gray (*West of Scot.*), D. G. Leslie (*Gala*), J. R. Beattie (*Glas. Acads.*), M. A. Biggar (*London Scot.*)Sub: J. S. Gossman (*West of Scot.*)
England: W. H. Hare (*Leicester*); J. Carleton (*Orrell*), C. R. Woodward (*Leicester*), P. W. Dodge (*Leicester*), M. A. C. Slemen (*Liverpool*); J. P. Horton (*Bath*), S. J. Smith (*Sale*); F. E. Cotton (*Sale*), P. J. Wheeler (*Leicester*), P. J. Blakeway (*Gloucester*), W. B. Beaumont* (*Fylde*), M. J. Colclough (*Angouleme*), R. M. Uttley (*Wasps*), J. P. Scott (*Cardiff*), A. Neary (*Broughton Park*)
Referee: J. P. Bonnet (*France*)   **Touch judges:** F. Palmade and G. Chevrier (*France*)

J. Carleton (2) and M. A. C. Slemen scored; W. H. Hare converted the first two (0-16); A. R. Irvine kicked a penalty (3-16); W. H. Hare kicked a penalty (3-19). (H.T.). A. R. lrvine kicked a penalty (6-19); S. J. Smith scored but W. H. Hare failed (6-23); A. J. Tomes scored and A. R. Irvine converted (12-23); W. H. Hare kicked a penalty (12-26); J. Carleton scored but W. H. Hare failed (12-30); J. Y. Rutherford scored and A. R. Irvine converted (18-30).

The foundation of a good English win was laid during the first half during which period their pack was clearly on top in all phases of play. The English backs enjoyed plenty clear possession and aided by some poor cover defence ran in three tries before half time and another soon after the restart. Yet the Scots never ceased to attack whenever they got the ball in their hands and indeed looked most dangerous running in two excellent tries and narrowly failing at least twice. As a result the second half was a most exhilarating exhibition of attacking rugby.

Scotland toured France in April and May 1980. Of the 3 matches played, a Scotland XV lost 2 and drew 1: French Select 20 Scotland XV 6; French Barbarians 26 Scotland XV 22; French Select 6 Scotland XV 6. No Test matches were played.

FRANCE 16   SCOTLAND 9
Parc des Princes, Paris
17 January 1981

France: S. Gabernet (*Toulouse*); S. Blanco (*Biarritz*), R. Bertranne (*Bagnères*), D. Codorniou (*Narbonne*), L. Pardo (*Bayonne*); B. Viviès (*Agen*), P. Berbizier (*Lourdes*); R. Paparemborde (*Pau*), P. Dintranes (*Tarbes*), P. Salas (*Narbonne*), J-L Joinel (*Brives*), J-F Imbernon (*Perpignan*), D. Revallier (*Graulhet*), J-P Rives* (*Toulouse*), M. Carpentier. (*Lourdes*). Replacement: A. Caussade (*Lourdes*) for B. Vivies (30 min.).
Scotland: A. R. Irvine* (*Heriot's FP*); S. Munro (*Ayr*), J. M. Renwick (*Hawick*), K. W. Robertson (*Melrose*), B. H. Hay (*Boroughmuir*); J. Y. Rutherford (*Selkirk*), R. J. Laidlaw (*Jedforest*); N. A. Rowan (*Boroughmuir*), C. T. Deans (*Hawick*), J. Aitken (*Gala*), J. H. Calder (*Stewart's-Melville*), A. J. Tomes (*Hawick*), D. Gray (*W. of Scot.*), G. Dickson (*Gala*), J. R. Beattie (*Heriot's FP*).
Referee: K. Rowlands (*Wales*).

Try by S. Blanco (4-0); penalty goal by B. Viviès (7-0); penalty goal by A. Irvine (7-3); penalty goal by S. Gabernet (10-3); try by R. Bertranne, conv. by A. Caussade (16-3). (H.T.). Try by J. Rutherford, conv. by J. Renwick (16-9).

197

In the opening half of this match the Scots put on an abysmal show. Poor tackling and circumspect forward play led to their trailing 3-16 at half-time. They tightened things up in the second half and prevented any further French scores. Scotland's second half converted try made the score more respectable but they never looked like winning the match and, overall, gave a very disappointing display.

Upon scoring Scotland's penalty, Andrew Irvine raised his total number of points scored in internationals to 213 – a new world record. He had previously shared the record of 210 points with Phil Bennett of Wales.

SCOTLAND 15 WALES 6
Murrayfield
7 February 1981

Scotland: A. R. Irvine* (*Heriot's FP*); S. Munro (*Ayr*), J. M. Renwick (*Hawick*), K. W. Robertson (*Melrose*), B. H. Hay (*Boroughmuir*); J. Y. Rutherford (*Selkirk*), R. J. Laidlaw (*Jedforest*); N. A. Rowan (*Boroughmuir*), C. T. Deans (*Hawick*), J. Aitken (*Gala*), D. G. Leslie (*Gala*), A. J. Tomes (*Hawick*), W. Cuthbertson (*Kilmarnock*), J. H. Calder (*Stewart's-Melville*), J. R. Beattie (*Heriot's FP*).
Wales: J. P. R. Williams (*Bridgend*); R. Ackerman (*Newport*), S. P. Fenwick* (*Bridgend*), D. S. Richards (*Swansea*), D. L. Nicholas (*Llanelli*); W. G. Davies (*Cardiff*), D. B. Williams (*Swansea*); G. Price (*Pontypool*), A. J. Phillips (*Cardiff*), I. Stephens (*Bridgend*), J. Squire (*Pontypool*), C. E. Davies (*Newbridge*), G. A. D. Wheel (*Swansea*), J. R. Lewis (*S. Glamorgan Inst.*), G. P. Williams (*Bridgend*).
Replacement: G. Evans (*Maesteg*) for D. L. Nicholas (half-time).
Referee: D. I. H. Burnett (*Ireland*)

Penalty goal by J. Renwick (3-0); penalty goal by S. Fenwick (3-3); try by A. Tomes, conv. by J. Renwick (9-3); penalty goal by S. Fenwick (9-6). (H.T.) Penalty try, conv. by J. Renwick (15-6).

The Scottish team performance was unrecognisable compared with that in Paris in the previous international. They convincingly defeated a rather lack-lustre Welsh side. The Scottish pack was a revelation: they had been expected to play second fiddle to their Welsh counterparts but finished well on top.

Scotland's 9-6 half-time lead stood until 8 minutes from no-side when Ackerman, the recipient of a 'hospital pass', was caught in possession. The resulting loose ball was hacked on by Hay. A desperate chase between Irvine and Gareth Davies resulted. The Scot seemed to be winning the race when the Welshman rashly pulled at his opponents shirt. Irvine's plunge over the line was also obstructed by Davies, causing the Scot to miss the touch-down. Referee David Burnett duly awarded a penalty try which was converted by Jim Renwick to reinforce a well-deserved Scotland victory

ENGLAND 23 SCOTLAND 17
Twickenham
21 February 1981

England: W. H. Hare (*Leicester*); J. Carleton (*Orrell*), C. R. Woodward (*Leicester*), P. W. Dodge (*Leicester*), M. A. C. Slemen (*Liverpool*); G. H. Davies (*Coventry*), S. J. Smith (*Sale*); P. J. Blakeway (*Gloucester*), P. J. Wheeler (*Leicester*), C. E. Smart (*Newport*), D. H. Cooke (*Harlequins*), M. J. Colclough (*Augoulême*), W. B. Beaumont* (*Fylde*), N. C. Jeavons (*Moseley*), J. P. Scott (*Cardiff*).
Replacement: R. Hesford (*Bristol*) for N. Jeavons (14 min.).
Scotland: A. R. Irvine* (*Heriot's FP*); S. Munro (*Ayr*), J. M. Renwick (*Hawick*), K. W. Robertson (*Melrose*), B. H. Hay (*Boroughmuir*); J. Y. Rutherford (*Selkirk*), R. J. Laidlaw (*Jedforest*); N. A. Rowan (*Boroughmuir*), C. T. Deans (*Hawick*), J. Aitken (*Gala*), J. H. Calder (*Stewart's-Melville*), A. J. Tomes (*Hawick*), W. Cuthbertson (*Kilmarnock*), D. G. Leslie (*Gala*), J. R. Beattie (*Heriot's FP*).
Referee: D. I. H. Burnett (*Ireland*).

Penalty goal by A. Irvine (0-3); penalty goal by W. Hare (3-3); try by S. Munro (3-7); try by C. Woodward, conv. by W. Hare (9-7). (H.T.). Try by S. Munro, conv. by A. Irvine (9-13); penalty goal

198

by W. Hare (12-13); try by M. Slemen (16-13); try by J. Calder (16-17); try by G. Davies (20-17); penalty goal by W. Hare (23-17).

This was an exciting game, full of sparkling rugby. Six tries were scored – three by each side. The lead changed hands five times. Scotland led by 17-16 with but six minutes of the match remaining but a dramatic try by Huw Davies, when he jinked his way through the Scottish defence, and a late penalty goal by Dusty Hare saw England triumph. Earlier, Clive Woodward scored the try of the match when he side-stepped several would-be Scottish tacklers before crossing the line. The game had been one of the most spectacular seen at Twickenham for years.

SCOTLAND 10   IRELAND 9
Murrayfield
21 March 1981

Scotland: A. R. Irvine* (*Heriot's FP*); S. Munro (*Ayr*), J. M. Renwick (*Hawick*), K. W. Robertson (*Melrose*), B. H. Hay (*Boroughmuir*); J. Y. Rutherford (*Selkirk*), R. J. Laidlaw (*Jedforest*); N. A. Rowan (*Boroughmuir*), C. T. Deans (*Hawick*), J. Aitken (*Gala*), J. H. Calder (*Stewart's-Melville*), A. J. Tomes (*Hawick*), W. Cuthbertson (*Kilmarnock*), D. G. Leslie (*W. of Scot.*), J. R. Beattie (*Heriot's FP*).
Ireland: H. P. MacNeill (*Dublin Univ.*); K. J. Hooks (*Queen's Univ., Belfast*), D. G. Irwin (*Queen's Univ., Belfast*), S. O. Campbell (*Old Belvedere*), A. C. McLennan (*Wanderers*); A. J. P. Ward (*Garryowen*), J. C. Robbie (*Greystones*); M. P. Fitzpatrick (*Wanderers*), J. L. Cantrell (*Blackrock Coll.*), P. A. Orr (*Old Wesley*), J. F. Slattery* (*Blackrock Coll.*), M. I. Keane (*Lansdowne*), B. O. Foley (*Shannon*), J. B. O'Driscoll (*Lond. Irish*), W. P. Duggan (*Blackrock Coll.*).
Referee: L. M. Prideaux (*England*)

Dropped goal by J. Rutherford (3-0); try by B. Hay (7-0); penalty goal by A. Irvine (10-0). (H.T.). Penalty goal by S. Campbell (10-3); try by D. Irwin, conv. by S. Campbell (10-9).

Continuous driving rain spoiled this match as a spectacle. The disappointing play reflected the gloomy weather. Kick-and-rush tactics from both sides meant few opportunities for the backs.

In the second half, the Scots held on to their 10-0 interval lead and only just managed to thwart strenuous efforts by the Irish to win the match. This defeat completed Ireland's 'white-wash' in the season's Five Nations series.

Five Nations Championship 1980-81

	P	W	L	D	F	A	Pts
France	4	4	0	0	70	49	8
England	4	2	2	0	64	60	4
Scotland	4	2	2	0	51	54	4
Wales	4	2	2	0	51	61	4
Ireland	4	0	4	0	36	48	0

NEW ZEALAND 11   SCOTLAND 4
Carisbrook, Dunedin
13 June 1981

New Zealand: A. R. Hewson (*Wellington*); S. S. Wilson (*Wellington*), B. J. Robertson (*Counties*), A. C. R. Jefferd (*E. Coast*), B. G. Fraser (*Wellington*); E. Dunn (*N. Auckland*), D. S. Loveridge (*Taranaki*); G. A. Knight (*Manawatu*), A. G. Dalton (*Counties*), R. C. Ketels (*Counties*), G. N. K. Mourie* (*Taranaki*), G. Higginson (*Canterbury*), H. Rickit (*Waikato*), M. W. Shaw (*Manawatu*), M. G. Mexted (*Wellington*).
Scotland: A. R. Irvine* (*Heriot's FP*); S. Munro (*Ayr*), A. G. Cranston (*Hawick*), J. M. Renwick (*Hawick*), B. H. Hay (*Boroughmuir*); J. Y. Rutherford (*Selkirk*), R. J. Laidlaw (*Jedforest*); I. G. Milne (*Heriot's FP*), C. T. Deans (*Hawick*), J. Aitken (*Gala*), D. G. Leslie (*Gala*), A. J. Tomes (*Hawick*), W. Cuthbertson (*Kilmarnock*), J. H. Calder (*Stewart's-Melville*), I. A. M. Paxton (*Selkirk*).
Referee: R. G. Byres (*Australia*).

Penalty goal by A. Hewson (3-0). (H.T.). Try by D. Loveridge (7-0); try by S. Wilson (11-0); try by C. Deans (11-4).

This was a particularly low-key international. The All Blacks led at half-time by a solitary penalty goal. New Zealand pressure early in the second half produced a try when, following a scrummage near the Scottish line, Colin Deans' successful hook caught Roy Laidlaw wrong-footed. Loveridge threw himself into a mass of legs and successfully touched down.

The Scots stepped up the pace in the last ten minutes and scored a try when Colin Deans successfully followed up a kick-ahead. Andy Irvine's attempted conversion scraped past a post.

NEW ZEALAND 40   SCOTLAND 15
Eden Park, Auckland
20 June 1981

New Zealand: A. R. Hewson (*Wellington*); S. S. Wilson (*Wellington*), A. C. R. Jefferd (*E. Coast*), B. J. Robertson (*Counties*), B. G. Fraser (*Wellington*); D. L. Rollerson (*Manawatu*), D. S. Loveridge (*Taranaki*); G. A. Knight (*Manawatu*), A. G. Dalton (*Counties*), R. C. Ketels (*Counties*), G. N. K. Mourie* (*Taranaki*), A. M. Haden (*Auckland*), H. Rickit (*Waikato*), M. W. Shaw (*Manawatu*), M. G. Mexted (*Wellington*).
Scotland: A. R. Irvine* (*Heriot's FP*); S. Munro (*Ayr*), A. G. Cranston (*Hawick*), J. M. Renwick (*Hawick*), B. H. Hay (*Boroughmuir*); J. Y. Rutherford (*Selkirk*), R. J. Laidlaw (*Jedforest*); I. G. Milne (*Heriot's FP*), C. T. Deans (*Hawick*), J. Aitken (*Gala*), J. H. Calder (*Stewart's-Melville*), W. Cuthbertson (*Kilmarnock*), A. J. Tomes (*Hawick*), D. G. Leslie (*Gala*), I. A. M. Paxton (*Selkirk*).
Referee: C. K. Collett (*Australia*).

Try by S. Wilson, converted by A. Hewson (6-0); penalty goal by A. Irvine (6-3); dropped goal by J. Renwick (6-6); try by A. Hewson (10-6). (H.T.). Try by G. Mourie, converted by A. Hewson (16-6); try by S. Wilson, converted by A. Hewson (22-6); try by B. Hay, converted by A. Irvine (22-12); penalty goal by A. Irvine (22-15); try and conversion by A. Hewson (28-15); try by S. Wilson, converted by A. Hewson (34-15); try by B. Robertson, converted by A. Hewson (40-15).

In marked contrast with the First Test, this one had skill, excitement and plenty of points scored – things mostly missing in the previous Test.

Despite losing by 15-40, Scotland were not on the receiving end of a drubbing. In fact, with the score at 22-15 in the second half, the Scots looked as if poised to make a winning thrust but they scorned at least two opportunities to score and the chance was gone. The All Blacks scored 18 points in the final seven minutes.

Scotland surprised the All Blacks by dominating the second phase and thus forced their hosts to change from their traditional methods. Jim Calder crossed the New Zealand line but the final pass was adjudged to have been forward.

This was the first time that the All Blacks had scored 40 points in an international.

SCOTLAND 12   ROMANIA 6
Murrayfield
26 September 1981

Scotland: A. R. Irvine* (*Heriot's FP*); S. Munro (*W. of S.*), J. M. Renwick (*Hawick*), D. I. Johnston (*Watsonians*), K. W. Robertson (*Melrose*); R. Wilson (*Lond. Scot.*), R. J. Laidlaw (*Jedforest*); I. G. Milne (*Heriot's FP*), J. Aitken (*Gala*), D. G. Leslie (*Gala*), A. J. Tomes (*Hawick*), W.Cuthbertson (*Kilmarnock*), J. H. Calder (*Stewart's Melville*), I. A. M. Paxton (*Selkirk*).
Romania: G. Floria; S. Fuicu, A. Lungu, I. Constantin, M. Aldea; D. Alexandru, M. Parachiv*; O. Corneliu, M. Munteanu, I. Bucan, E. Stoica, E. Caragea, J. Dumitru, A. Radulescu, P. Bors.
Referee: M. D. M. Rea (Ireland).

Two penalty goals, by A. Irvine (6-0); penalty goal by I. Constantin (6-3); penalty goal by A. Irvine (9-3); penalty goal by I. Constantin (9-6). (H.T.). Penalty goal by A. Irvine (12-6).

The weather conditions during this match were atrocious, stong wind and driving rain prevailing throughout. The elements were not conducive to safe handling and this was probably largely responsible for there being no tries scored. By scoring four penalty goals to the visitors's two,

200

Scotland won comfortably enough. Andy Irvine excelled for the Scots. His handling and fielding of high balls, under difficult conditions, was superb. By scoring all twelve points for Scotland the full back brought his personal tally to 217 in international matches – surpassing All Black Don Clarke's world record of 207.

The Scottish forwards dominated and controlled the game throughout. Brought in as a replacement, stand-off Ron Wilson had a splendid match in winning his eighth cap for Scotland.

SCOTLAND 24 AUSTRALIA 15
Murrayfield
19 December 1981

Scotland: A. R. Irvine* (*Heriot's FP*); K. W. Robertson (*Melrose*), J. M. Renwick (*Hawick*), D. I. Johnston (*Watsonians*), G. R. T. Baird (*Kelso*); J. Y. Rutherford (*Selkirk*), R. J. Laidlaw (*Jedforest*); I. G. Milne (*Heriot's FP*), C. T. Deans (*Hawick*), J. Aitken (*Gala*), J. H. Calder (*Stewart's-Melville*), A. J. Tomes (*Hawick*), W. Cuthbertson (*Kilmarnock*), D. G. Leslie (*Gala*), I. A. M. Paxton (*Selkirk*).
Australia: R. G. Gould; M. Cox, A. G. Slack, P. E. McLean, B. J. Moon; M. Ella, P. Cox; A. M. D'Arcy, C. M. Carberry, J. E. C. Meadows, S. P. Poidevin, A. A. Shaw*, P. W. McLean, G. Cornelsen, M. E. Loane.
Referee: R. C. Quittenon (*England*).

Three penalty goals by A. Irvine (9-0); try by S. Poidevin (9-4); try by B. Moon (9-8); try by A. Slack (9-12); penalty goal by Paul McLean (9-15); penalty goal by A. Irvine (12-15). (H.T.). Penalty goal by A. Irvine (15-15); dropped goal by J. Rutherford (18-15); try by J. Renwick, conv. by A. Irvine (24-15).

In this exciting match, Australia won the try count by 3-1 but some devastatingly accurate kicking by Scotland's captain, Andrew Irvine, gave the home side an advantage which the visitors could not match.

Play was marred by one controversial incident which resulted in Bill Cuthbertson, the Scotland lock, being punched to the ground. The Australian culprit was lucky to be allowed to stay on the field of play.

SCOTLAND 9 ENGLAND 9
Murrayfield
15 January 1982

Scotland: A. R. Irvine* (*Heriot's FP*); K. W. Robertson (*Melrose*), J. M. Renwick (*Hawick*), D. I. Johnston (*Watsonians*), G. R. T. Baird (*Kelso*); J. Y. Rutherford (*Selkirk*), R. J. Laidlaw (*Jedforest*); I. G. Milne (*Heriot's FP*), C. T. Deans (*Hawick*), J. Aitken (*Gala*), D. G. Leslie (*Gala*), A. J. Tomes (*Hawick*), W. Cuthbertson (*Kilmarnock*), J. H. Calder (*Stewart's-Melville*), I. A. M. Paxton (*Selkirk*).
England: W. M. H. Rose (*Camb. Univ.*); J. Carleton (*Orrell*), C. R. Woodward (*Leicester*), P. W. Dodge (*Leicester*), M. A. C. Slemen (*Liverpool*); G. H. Davies (*Camb. Univ.*), S. J. Smith (*Sale*); G. S. Pearce (*Northampton*), P. J. Wheeler (*Leicester*), C. E. Smart (*Newport*), N. C. Jeavons (*Moseley*), W. B. Beaumont* (*Fylde*), M. J. Colclough (*Angoulème*), P. J. Winterbottom (*Headingley*), R. Hesford (*Bristol*).
Referee: K. Rowlands (*Wales*).

Dropped goal by J. Rutherford (3-0); penalty goal by P. Dodge (3-3); penalty goal by A. Irvine (6-3); penalty goal by P. Dodge (6-6); penalty goal by M. Rose (6-9). (H.T.). Penalty goal by A. Irvine (9-9).

Despite the lack of tries, this match was a thriller. Although England led 9-6 from half-time, the final result was always in doubt. With no-side fast approaching, the Scots mounted one last desperate attack. Their endeavour seemed to have been thwarted when, with a minute left, play was taken back to just inside their own half. It was then that Smart, the England prop, barged into Iain Paxton the Scottish no. 8 when the Scot was not in possession of the ball. The penalty was awarded two metres inside the Scottish half, almost in the centre of the field. Andy Irvine, the Scottish captain, had no choice – he had to 'have a go' at kicking the goal. The wind was behind him but, with everything hanging on the result of the kick, the pressure on the player was phenomenal. When the touch judges flags went up the roar of the crowd must have been heard for miles. Scotland had drawn the match: England had had victory snatched from them in the fourth minute of added-on time.

IRELAND 21   SCOTLAND 12
Lansdowne Road
20 February 1982

Ireland: H. P. MacNeill (*Dublin Univ.*); M. C. Finn (*Cork Inst.*), M. J. Kiernan (*Dolphin*), P. M. Dean (*St Mary's Coll.*), K. D. Crossan (*Instonians*); S. O. Campbell (*Old Belvedere*), R. J. M. McGrath (*Wanderers*); G. A. J. McLoughlin (*Shannon*), C. J. Fitzgerald* (*St Mary's Coll.*), P. A. Orr (*Old Wesley*), J. B. O'Driscoll (*Lond. Irish*), M. I. Keane (*Lansdowne*), D. G. Lenihan (*U. C. Cork*), J. F. Slattery (*Blackrock Coll.*), W. P. Duggan (*Blackrock Coll.*).
Scotland: A. R. Irvine* (*Heriot's FP*); K. W. Robertson (*Melrose*), J. M. Renwick (*Hawick*), D. I. Johnston (*Watsonians*), G. R. T. Baird (*Kelso*); J. Y. Rutherford (*Selkirk*), R. J. Laidlaw (*Jedforest*); I. G. Milne (*Heriot's FP*), C. T. Deans (*Hawick*) J. Aitken (*Gala*), R. E. Paxton (*Kelso*), W. Cuthbertson (*Kilmarnock*), A. J. Tomes (*Hawick*), J. H. Calder (*Stewart's-Melville*), I. A. M. Paxton (*Selkirk*).
Referee: C. Norling (*Wales*)

Two penalty goals by S. Campbell (6-0); try by J. Rutherford, conv. by A. Irvine (6-6); penalty goal by S. Campbell (9-6); dropped goal by S. Campbell (12-6); penalty goal by S. Campbell (15-6). (H.T.). Penalty goal by S. Campbell (18-6); penalty goal by J. Renwick (18-9); penalty goal by S. Campbell (21-9); penalty goal by J. Renwick (21-12).

Ollie Campbell's 21 points for Ireland superceded his own previously-held Irish record of 19 points in an international match. This win gave Ireland their first Triple Crown for 33 years and their supporters celebrated in fine style after no-side. Campbell's kicking had been decisive but the rest of the Irish team deserve credit for a first-class all-round performance. Andy Irvine, the Scottish fullback missed four successive penalty kick attempts before handing over to Jim Renwick.

SCOTLAND 16   FRANCE 7
Murrayfield
6 March 1982

Scotland: A. R. Irvine* (*Heriot's FP*); K. W. Robertson (*Melrose*), J. M. Renwick (*Hawick*), D. I. Johnston (*Watsonians*), G. R. T. Baird (*Kelso*); J. Y. Rutherford (*Selkirk*), R. J. Laidlaw (*Jedforest*); I. G. Milne (*Heriot's FP*), C. T. Deans (*Hawick*), J. Aitken (*Gala*), D. B. White (*Gala*), W. Cuthbertson (*Kilmarnock*), A. J. Tomes (*Hawick*), J. H. Calder (*Stewart's-Melville*), I. A. M. Paxton (*Selkirk*).
France: M. Sallefranque (*Dax*); S. Blanco (*Biarritz*), P. Perrier (*Bayonne*), C. Belascain (*Bayonne*), L. Pardo (*Bayonne*); J-P Lescaboura (*Dax*), G. Martinez (*Toulouse*); D. Dubroca (*Agen*), P Dintrans (*Tarbes*), M. Crémaschi (*Lourdes*), J-L Joinel (*Brive*), D. Revallier (*Graulher*), L. Rodriguez (*Mont-de-Marsan*), J-P Rives* (*Toulouse*), M. Carpentier (*Lourdes*).
Referee: J. A. F. Trigg (*England*).

Penalty goal by A. Irvine (3-0); try by J-P Rives (3-4); penalty goal by M. Sallafranque (3-7). (H.T.). Penalty goal by A. Irvine (6-7); dropped goal by J. Renwick (9-7); try by J. Rutherford (13-7); penalty goal by A. Irvine (16-7).

Despite being behind at half-time, Scotland were in control for most of this match. The Scottish forwards gave a rousing all-round display whilst their French counterparts lacked organisation and became progressively ineffective.

Following Jim Renwick's dropped goal which put them in the lead again, the Scots never looked back. The pack took command of the game and scrum half Roy Laidlaw took full advantage and gave a scintillating display. French misery was completed when their players disputed a refereeing decision and forfeited 10 metres. The penalty kick was still from half-way but Andy Irvine made no mistake in capping a good all-round display by Scotland.

WALES 18 SCOTLAND 34
Cardiff Arms Park
20 March 1982

Wales: G. Evans (*Maesteg*); R. A. Ackerman (*Newport*), R. W. R. Gravell (*Llanelli*), A. J. Donovan (*Swansea*), C. F. W. Rees (*Lond. Welsh*); W. G. Davies* (*Cardiff*), G. W. Williams (*Bridgend*); G. Price (*Pontypool*), A. J. Phillips (*Cardiff*), I. Stephens (*Bridgend*), R. C. Burgess (*Ebbw Vale*), R. L. Norster (*Cardiff*), R. D. Moriarty (*Swansea*), J. R. Lewis (*Cardiff*), E. T. Butler (*Pontypool*).
Scotland: A. R. Irvine* (*Heriot's FP*); J. Pollock (*Gosforth*), J. M. Renwick (*Hawick*), D. I. Johnston (*Watsonians*), G. R. T. Baird (*Kelso*); J. Y. Rutherford (*Selkirk*), R. J. Laidlaw (*Jedforest*); I. G. Milne (*Heriot's FP*), C. T. Deans (*Hawick*), J. Aitken (*Gala*), D. B. White (*Gala*), W. Cuthbertson (*Kilmarnock*), A. J. Tomes (*Hawick*), J. H. Calder (*Stewart's-Melville*), I. A. M. Paxton (*Selkirk*).
Replacement: G. Dickson (*Gala*) for I. Paxton (11 min.).
Referee: J-P Bonnet (*France*).

Penalty goal by G. Evans (3-0); try by J. Calder (3-4); dropped goal by J. Renwick (3-7); try by J. Renwick, conv. by A. Irvine (3-13); two penalty goals by G. Evans (9-13). (H.T.). Try by J. Pollock, conv. by A. Irvine (9-19); try by D. White, conv. by A. Irvine (9-25); try by D. Johnston, conv. by A. Irvine (9-31); dropped goal by J. Rutherford (9-34); try by E. Butler, conv. by G. Evans (15-34); penalty goal by G. Evans (18-34).

Prior to this match, Scotland's last win in Wales had been in 1962. The memories of the unsuccessful intervening years vanished with this display of superb and exciting rugby. The Scots scored five tries to the one by Wales. It was a great tribute to the Scots that, long before no-side, the Welsh supporters, thrilled by what they were witnessing, were cheering the visiting side.

Wales had not lost an international at the Arms Park since 1968 when France defeated them 14-9. This match also ended a remarkable run of 27 unbeaten championship matches for the home side, at the Arms Park. To further Wales' indignity, 34 points was the most they had ever previously surrendered in an international match at Cardiff Arms Park.

Wales opened the scoring with a penalty goal by fullback Evans. A promising Welsh attack came to nought when Gareth Davies, with a two-to-one overlap near the Scotland 22, elected to kick instead of passing. Roger Baird pounced on the ball and set up a counter-attack, ably supported by Iain Paxton, Alan Tomes and Jim Calder – who raced over for the try. In giving the pass, Iain Paxton was injured and was replaced by Gordon Dickson. Jim Pollock, making his international debut, scored a try in the second half.

The sporting scribes reported this match as being 'the game of the championship'.

Five Nations Championship 1981-82

	P	W	L	D	F	A	Pts
Ireland	4	3	1	0	66	61	6
England	4	2	1	1	68	47	5
Scotland	4	2	1	1	71	55	5
France	4	1	3	0	56	74	2
Wales	4	1	3	0	59	83	2

AUSTRALIA 7 SCOTLAND 12
Ballymore, Brisbane
4 July 1982

Australia: G. J. Ella; M. J. Hawker, A. G. Slack, M. D. O'Connor, B. J. Moon; M. G. Ella, P. A. Cox; S. Pilecki, W. S. Ross, A. M. D'Arcy, A. A. Shaw, P. W. McLean, D. Hall, C. Roche, M. A. Loane*.
Scotland: A. R. Irvine* (*Heriot's FP*); K. W. Robertson (*Melrose*), R. J. Gordon (*Lond. Scot.*), D. I. Johnston (*Watsonians*), G. R. T. Baird (*Kelso*); J. Y. Rutherford (*Selkirk*), R. J. Laidlaw (*Jedforest*); I. G. Milne (*Heriot's FP*), C. T. Deans (*Hawick*), G. M. McGuinness (*W. of Scot.*), J. H. Calder (*Stewart's-Melville*), A. J. Tomes (*Hawick*), W. Cuthbertson (*Kilmarnock*),

D. B. White (*Gala*), I. A. M. Paxton (*Selkirk*).
Referee: R. G. Byres (*Australia*).

Dropped goal by J. Rutherford (0-3); penalty goal by M. Hawker (3-3). (H.T.). Try by K. Robertson, conv. by A. Irvine (3-9); try by M. Hawker (7-9); penalty goal by A. Irvine (7-12).

The rugby played by these two evenly-matched teams was far from inspiring. Scotland won because they made fewer errors. However, from a Scottish point of view the game was memorable for two reasons: (1) Andy Irvine won his 50th Scotland cap thus equalling Sandy Carmichael's record and (2) it was Scotland's first victory in a full international in the Southern Hemisphere (previously, they had lost three times to New Zealand, and once each to South Africa and Australia). Australia started the match without either of their recognised goal-kickers, Roger Gould and Paul McLean. Michael Hawker was deputed to take any kicks but was successful with only one from five attempts.

AUSTRALIA 33 SCOTLAND 9
Cricket Ground, Sydney
10 July 1982

Australia: R. G. Gould; P. C. Grigg, M. D. O'Connor, M. J. Hawker, B. J. Moon; P. E. McLean, P. A. Cox; S. Pilecki, W. S. Ross, A. M. D'Arcy, A. A. Shaw, P. W. McLean, D. Hall, C. Roche, M. A. Loane*.
Scotland: A. R- Irvine* (*Heriot's FP*); K. W. Robertson (*Melrose*), R. J. Gordon (*Lond. Scot.*), D. I. Johnston (*Watsonians*), G. R. T. Baird (*Kelso*); J. Y. Rutherford (*Selkirk*), R. J. Laidlaw (*Jedforest*); I. G. Milne (*Heriot's FP*), C. T. Deans (*Hawick*), G. M. McGuinness (*W. of Scot.*), D. B. White (*Gala*), A. J. Tomes (*Hawick*), W. Cuthbertson (*Kilmarnock*), J. H. Calder (*Stewart's-Melville*), I. A. M. Paxton (*Selkirk*).
Replacement: R. E. Paxton (*Kelso*) for I. Paxton (47 min.).
Referee: R. G. Byres (*Australia*).

Two penalty goals by P. McLean (6-0); penalty goal by A. Irvine (6-3); try by R. Gould, conv. by P. McLean (12-3); penalty goal by P. McLean (15-3); try by R. Gould, conv. by P. McLean (21-3); penalty goal by A. Irvine (21-6). (H.T.). Penalty goal by P. McLean (24-6); penalty goal by P. McLean (27-6); penalty goal by A. Irvine (27-9); try by M. O'Connor, conv. by P. McLean (33-9). Australia avenged their defeat in the first Test by beating Scotland comprehensively, recording their highest number of points scored in an international in the process. Paul McLean's individual haul of 21 points set a new Australian record (he kicked eight goals from nine attempts).

Andy Irvine's nine points for Scotland made him the first player to score over 300 points in international rugby: 273 for Scotland, 18 for the British Isles.

The second half was played in torrential rain.

SCOTLAND XV 32 FIJI 12
Murrayfield
25 September 1982

Scotland: P. W. Dods (*Gala*); K. W. Robertson (*Melrose*), J. M. Renwick (*Hawick*); D. I. Johnston (*Watsonians*), G. R. T. Baird (*Kelso*); J. Y. Rutherford (*Selkirk*), R. J. Laidlaw* (*Jedforest*); I. G. Milne (*Heriot's FP*), C. T. Deans (*Hawick*), G. M. McGuinness (*W. of Scot.*), D. B. White (*Gala*), A. J. Tomes (*Hawick*), W. Cuthbertson (*Harlequins*), J. H. Calder (*Stewart's-Melville*), J. R. Beattie (*Glas. Acad.*).
Fiji: Severo; Komeli, Salusalu, Nacaka, Isileli; Elia, Viriviri; Tulmasi, Tamata, Namoro, Emasi, Taoba, Vilikesa, Nadruka, Felini.
Replacement: Ratu for Kamali (40 min.); Naikidi for Taoba (79 min.).
Referee: C. Norling (*Wales*).

Penalty goal by P. Dods (3-0); dropped goal by J. Rutherford (6-0); penalty goal by Severo (6-3); try by J. Calder (10-3); try by Nadruka, conv. by Severo (10-9). (H.T.). Try by D. Johnston (14-9); try and conv. by P. Dods (20-9); penalty goal by Severo (20-12); try by J. Beattie, conv. by P. Dods (26-12); try and conv. by P. Dods (32-12).

This was Fiji's fourth match of their UK Tour and they came to Murrayfield following a thrashing from Edinburgh (12-47) and, although improved performances, defeats at the hands of South of Scotland (17-23) and the Anglo-Scots (19-29). This made it unlikely that the tourists would cause an upset in the First International of the tour. Scotland had decided not to award caps for this match but they did select the best players available. In the absence of Andy Irvine (injured), the captaincy was entrusted to Roy Laidlaw. The only uncapped player was fullback Peter Dods who, by scoring 17 points, including two tries, justified his selection.

Although fairly conclusive, Scotland's victory was unsatisfactory. The forwards won plenty of ball but, mostly, chances were squandered. The Scots forward dominance should have brought a lot more points than the 32 actually scored. Not a game to remember.

SCOTLAND 13   IRELAND 15
Murrayfield
15 January 1983

Scotland: P. W. Dods (*Gala*); K. W. Robertson (*Melrose*), J. M. Renwick (*Hawick*), D. I. Johnston (*Watsonians*), G. R. T. Baird (*Kelso*); R. Wilson (*Lond. Scot.*), R. J. Laidlaw* (*Jedforest*); I. G. Milne (*Heriot's FP*), C. T. Deans (*Hawick*), G. M. McGuinness (*W. of Scot.*), D. G. Leslie (*Gala*), W. Cuthbertson (*Harlequins*), A. J. Tomes (*Hawick*), J. H. Calder (*Stewart's-Melville*), I. A. M. Paxton (*Selkirk*).
Ireland: H. P. MacNeill (*Oxford Univ.*); T. M. Ringland (*Ballymena*), D. G. Irwin (*Instonians*), M. J. Kiernan (*Dolphin*), M. Finn (*Constitution*); S. O. Campbell (*Old Belvedere*), R. J. McGrath (*Wanderers*); G. A. McLoughlin (*Shannon*), C. F. Fitzgerald* (*St Mary's Coll.*), P. A. Orr (*Old Wesley*), J. F. Slattery (*Blackrock Coll.*), M. I. Keane (*Lansdowne*), D. G. Lenihan (*Constitution*), J. B. O'Driscoll (*Manchester*), W. P. Duggan (*Blackrock Coll.*).
Referee: J-C Yche (*France*).

Penalty goal by S. Campbell (0-3); try by R. Laidlaw (4-3); penalty goal by S. Campbell (4-6); try by M. Kiernan, conv. by S. Campbell (4-12); penalty goal by S. Campbell (4-15). (H.T.). Dropped goal by J. Renwick (7-15); two penalty goals by P. Dods (13-15).

This was the first international match played before the new East Stand. The Irish played with the wind in the first half and made full use of that advantage. Their experienced and committed pack were too strong for the disappointing Scots.

In the second half, the Scots gradually chipped away at Ireland's lead and, in the end, were but one score away from reversing the result. The final score did not do justice to the Irish efforts – and it required a prodigious leap by Fergus Slattery to prevent a second dropped goal by Jim Renwick which looked as if it was going to be successful.

FRANCE 19   SCOTLAND 15
Parc des Princes, Paris
5 February 1983

France: S. Blanco (*Biarritz*); P. Sella (*Agen*), C. Belascain (*Bayonne*), D. Cordornion (*Narbonne*), P. Estève (*Narbonne*); C. Delage (*Agen*), P. Berbizier (*Lourdes*); R. Paparemborde (*Pau*), J-L Dupont (*Agen*), P. Dospital (*Bayonne*), L. Rodriguez (*Mont-de-Marson*), J-C Orso (*Nice*), J. Condom (*Boucau*), J-P Rives* (*Racing Club*), J-L Joinel (*Brive*).
Replacement: D. Erbarri (*Agen*) for L. Rodriguez (65 min.).
Scotland: P. W. Dods (*Gala*); K. W. Robertson (*Melrose*), J. M. Renwick (*Hawick*), D. I. Johnston (*Watsonians*), G. R. T. Baird (*Kelso*); B. M. Gossman (*W. of Scot.*), R. J. Laidlaw* (*Jedforest*); I. G. Milne (*Heriot's FP*), C. T. Deans (*Hawick*), J. Aitken (*Gala*), J. H. Calder (*Stewart's-Melville*), A. J. Tomes (*Hawick*), W. Cuthbertson (*Harlequins*), D. G. Leslie (*Gala*), J. R. Beattie (*Glas. Acad.*).
Referee: A. Richards (*Wales*).

Penalty goal by P. Dods (0-3); penalty goal by S. Blanco (3-3); try by K. Robertson, conv. by P. Dods (3-9); dropped goal by B. Gossman (3-12); penalty goal by S. Blanco (6-12); try by P Esteve, conv. by S. Blanco (12-12); dropped goal by B. Gossman (12-15); penalty goal by S. Blanco (15-15). (H.T.). Try by P. Estève (19-15).

Scotland could not be faulted for lack of courage and effort in this match. They came to Paris as underdogs but fought superbly throughout to equal the French efforts. The Scots led 12-3 at one stage but the French side rallied and fought back to level the scores at 15-15 by half-time.

With no-side nearing, Peter Dods missed what, for him, would normally have been an easy penalty attempt. This would have given Scotland an 18-15-lead. However, P. Esteve scored a second and decisive try for France.

SCOTLAND 15   WALES 19
Murrayfield
19 February 1983

Scotland: P. W. Dods (*Gala*); K. W. Robertson (*Melrose*), J. M. Renwick (*Hawick*), D. I. Johnston (*Watsonians*), G. R. T. Baird (*Kelso*); B. M. Gossman (*W. of Scot.*), R. J. Laidlaw* (*Jedforest*); I. G. Milne (*Heriot's FP*), C. T. Deans (*Hawick*), J. Aitken (*Gala*), J. H. Calder (*Stewart's-Melville*), A. J. Tomes (*Hawick*), W. Cuthbertson (*Harlequins*), D. G. Leslie (*Gala*), J. R. Beattie (*Glas. Acad.*).
Wales: M. Wyatt (*Swansea*); H. E. Rees (*Neath*), R. A. Ackerman (*Lond. Welsh*), D. S. Richards (*Swansea*), C. F. W. Rees (*Lond. Welsh*); M. Dacey (*Swansea*), T. D. Holmes (*Cardiff*); I. Eidman (*Cardiff*), W. Jones (*Aberavon*), S. T. Jones (*Pontypool*), J. Squire (*Pontypool*), J. Perkins (*Pontypool*), R. Norster (*Cardiff*), D. Pickering (*Llanelli*), E. T. Butler* (*Pontypool*).
Referee: R. C. Quittenton (*England*).

Penalty goal by M. Wyatt (0-3); try by S. Jones, conv. by M. Wyatt (0-9); penalty goal by P. Dods (3-9); penalty goal by M. Wyatt (3-12); penalty goal by P. Dods (6-12); penalty goal by M. Wyatt (6-15). (H.T.). Penalty goal by P. Dods (9-15); try by E. Rees (9-19); try by J. Renwick, conv. by P. Dods (15-19).

It was an angry Welsh team that ran out on to the Murrayfield turf: the selection had been heavily criticised back home and they were out to prove themselves. A determined and inspired performance saw Wales ahead for the entire match. Near the end, including seven minutes of injury time, with the score at 15-19, they had to mount desperate defence to keep the Scots out but no-side saw Wales worthy winners of this encounter, the 87th between the two countries.

In this game, Jim Renwick won his 50th Scotland cap.

ENGLAND 12   SCOTLAND 22
Twickenham
5 March 1983

England: W. H. Hare (*Leicester*); J. Carleton (*Orrell*),G. H. Davies (*Coventry*), P. W. Dodge (*Leicester*), A. H. Swift (*Swansea*); J. P. Horton (*Bath*), S. J. Smith (*Sale*); G. S. Pearce (*Northampton*), P. J. Wheeler (*Leicester*), C. E. Smart (*Newport*), P. J. Winterbottom (*Headingley*), S. Bainbridge (*Gosforth*), S. B. Boyle (*Gloucester*), N. C. Jeavons (*Moseley*), J. P. Scott* (*Cardiff*).
Scotland: P. W. Dods (*Gala*); J. Pollock (*Gosforth*), J. M. Renwick (*Hawick*), K. W. Robertson (*Melrose*), G. R. T. Baird (*Kelso*); J. Y. Rutherford (*Selkirk*), R. J. Laidlaw (*Jedforest*); I. G. Milne (*Heriot's FP*), C. T. Deans (*Hawick*), J. Aitken* (*Gala*), D. G. Leslie (*W. of Scot.*), I. A. M. Paxton (*Selkirk*), T. Smith (*Gala*), J. H. Calder (*Stewart's-Melville*), J. R. Beattie (*Glas. Acad.*).
Referee: T. F. Doocey (*New Zealand*).

Dropped goal by J. Horton (3-0); penalty goal by P. Dods (3-3); penalty goal by W. Hare (6-3); penalty goal by P. Dods (6-6); penalty goal by W. Hare (9-6); penalty goal by P. Dods (9-9). (H.T.). Try by R. Laidlaw, conv. by P. Dods (9-15); penalty goal by W. Hare (12-15); dropped goal by K. Robertson (12-18); try by T. Smith (12-22).

England started this match with only one championship point – from their drawn game with Wales at Cardiff. Scotland came to Twickenham, where they had last won in 1971, facing a whitewash.

Roy Laidlaw, relieved of the captaincy in favour Jim Aitken, and renewing his partnership with John Rutherford, gave his best display of the international season. The restoration of the half-back partnership brought stability and assurance to the backs.

Jim Renwick looked certain to score a try for Scotland in the first half when Keith Robertson's final pass looked to put him in the clear. Before he could gather the ball, Renwick was unceremoniously dumped from behind. Denied what seemed to be a certain score, the indignant Scots were further irritated with the referee's award of a penalty. Peter Dods successfully kicked the points – but 3 instead of a possible 6 was hard to bear.

Tom Smith completed his debut international in style when, near the end, he took the ball cleanly at a lineout near the English line and went over for the try.

Five Nations Championship 1982-83

	P	W	L	D	F	A	Pts
France	4	3	1	0	70	61	6
Ireland	4	3	1	0	71	67	6
Wales	4	2	1	1	64	53	5
Scotland	4	1	3	0	65	65	2
England	4	0	3	1	55	79	1

SCOTLAND 13   BARBARIANS 26
Murrayfield
26 March 1983

Scotland: P. W. Dods (*Gala*); J. A. Pollock (*Gosforth*), J. M. Renwick (*Hawick*), K. W. Robertson (*Melrose*), G. R. T. Baird (*Kelso*); J. Y. Rutherford (*Selkirk*), R. J. Laidlaw (*Jedforest*); J. Aitken* (*Gala*), C. T. Deans (*Hawick*), N. A. Rowan (*Boroughmuir*), T. J. Smith (*Gala*), I. A. M. Paxton (*Selkirk*), J. H. Calder (*Stewart's-Melville*), J. R. Beattie (*Glas. Acad.*), D. G. Leslie (*Gala*).
Replacement: D. I. Johnston (Watsonians) for K. Robertson (7 min.).
Barbarians: J-B Lafond (*France*); J. Carleton (*England*), D. Gerber (*S. Africa*), E. G. Tobias (*S. Africa*), C. F. W. Rees (*Wales*); W. G. Davies (*Wales*), T. D. Holmes (*Wales*); P. A. G. Rendall (*England*), P. Dintrans (*France*), R. Paperemborde (*France*), J. H. Bekker (*S. Africa*), R. J. Norster (*Wales*), P. J. Winterbottom (*England*), J. P. Scott (*England*), J. F. Slattery (*Ireland*).
Referee: R. Hourquet (*France*).

Penalty goal by P. Dods (3-0); try by J. Bekker (3-4); try by J-P Lafond (3-8); try by J. Rutherford (7-8). (H.T.). Try by J. Carleton, converted by G. Davies (7-14); try by D. Gerber, converted by G. Davies (7-20); try by J. Rutherford, converted by P. Dods (13-20); try by D. Gerber, converted by G. Davies (13-26).

This match celebrated the official opening of Murrayfield's new East Stand by H. R. H. The Princess Anne. It would have been preferable to have recorded a Scotland victory – but it was a fine match despite the defeat. Scotland were unfortunate to lose Keith Robertson early in the game (he suffered a severely dislocated collar bone, the result of a hefty tackle). Three Barbarians players who excelled were Danie Gerber (South Africa), Jean-Baptiste Lafond (France) and Terry Holmes (Wales).

SCOTLAND 25   NEW ZEALAND 25
Murrayfield
12 November 1983

Scotland: P. W. Dods (*Gala*); J. Pollock (*Gosforth*), A. E. Kennedy (*Watsonians*), D. I. Johnston (*Watsonians*), G. R. T. Baird (*Kelso*); J. Y. Rutherford (*Selkirk*), R. J. Laidlaw (*Jedforest*); J. Aitken* (*Gala*), C. T. Deans (*Hawick*), I. J. Milne (*Heriot's FP*), W. Cuthbertson (*Harlequins*), T. J. Smith (*Gala*), J. H. Calder (*Stewart's-Melville*), I. A. M. Paxton (*Selkirk*), J. Beattie (*Glas. Acad.*).
New Zealand: R. Deans; S. Wilson*, S. Pokere, W. Taylor, B. Fraser; W. Smith, A. Donald; B. McGrattan, H. Reid, B. Crichton, G. Braid, A. Anderson, J. Hobbs, M. Maxted, M. Shaw.
Replacement: C. Green for W. Taylor (Half-time).
Referee: R. Hourquet (*France*).

Dropped goal by J. Rutherford (3-0); penalty goal by R. Deans (3-3); dropped goal by J. Rutherford (6-3); try by M. Hobbs (6-7); try by B. Fraser, converted by R. Deans (6-13); penalty goal by P. Dods

(9-13); penalty goal by R. Deans (9-16); penalty goal by P. Dods (12-16); penalty goal by P. Dods (15-16). (H.T.). Try by B. Fraser, converted by R. Deans (15-22); penalty goal by P. Dods (18-22); penalty goal by P. Dods (21-22); penalty goal by R. Deans (21-25); try by J. Pollock (25-25).

This drawn match was the nearest Scotland had ever been to defeating the All Blacks: the New Zealanders had won 10 of the 11 previous encounters, the 1964 match at Murrayfield having ended in a scoreless draw. The reason for this particular game having been Scotland's 'nearest' to a win was because, with the score at 25-21 in New Zealand's favour, Jim Pollock scored a try in the very last minute. The crowd waited with baited breath as Peter Dods attempted the conversion which would surely have won the match for Scotland – but the kick missed the target by a whisker. Thus did Scotland fail to register their first win over New Zealand – but it was a glorious failure. No blame could be attached to Peter Dods: he had given a flawless display at fullback, scoring 15 points (5 penalty goals from 6 attempts). Nor should be forgotten John Rutherford's two dropped goals. The Scottish pack had been immense throughout.

Scotland opened the scoring, New Zealand drew level, the Scots went ahead again, then the All Blacks went ahead and, at one point, stretched their lead to 16-9, before two penalty goals by Peter Dods brought the Scots to within one point of the visitors, at 15-16. Immediately after the interval, the All Blacks went further ahead with a converted try, to 22-16. Again, successive penalties by Peter Dods brought the scores to 22-21 in New Zealand's favour. A penalty goal by fullback R. Deans put the New Zealander's four points ahead but, with no-side looming, Jim Pollock scored a dramatic try which levelled the scores. Peter Dods just failed to convert.

Even then the drama and excitement were not over. Just on the final whistle the referee awarded a penalty to the All Blacks, one which looked to be kickable. However, touch judge Brian Anderson drew the referee's attention to some other infringement which resulted in that official reversing his decision and awarding the penalty to Scotland – which allowed them to clear the danger.

WALES 9   SCOTLAND 15
Cardiff Arms Park
21 January 1984

Wales: H. Davies (*Bridgend*); M. H. Titley (*Bridgend*), H. A. Ackerman (*Lond. Welsh*), B. Bowen (*S. Wales Police*), A. M. Hadley (*Cardiff*); M. Dacey (*Swansea*), M. Douglas (*Llanelli*); S. Jones (*Pontypool*), W. J. James (*Aberavon*), R. Morgan (*Newport*), S. J. Perkins (*Pontypool*), R. L. Norster (*Cardiff*), R. D. Moriarty (*Swansea*), E. T. Butler* (*Pontypool*), D. F. Pickering (*Llanelli*).
Scotland: P. W. Dods (*Gala*); S. Munro (*Ayr*), A. E. Kennedy (*Watsonians*), D. I. Johnston (*Watsonians*), G. R. T. Baird (*Kelso*); J. Y. Rutherford (*Selkirk*), R. J. Laidlaw (*Jedforest*); J. Aitken* (*Gala*), C. T. Deans (*Hawick*), I. G. Milne (*Heriot's FP*), W. Cuthbertson (*Harlequins*), A. J. Tomes (*Hawick*), J. H. Calder (*Stewart's-Melville*), I. A. M. Paxton (*Selkirk*), D. G. Leslie (*Gala*).
Referee: O. E. Doyle (*Ireland*).

Penalty goal by H. Davies (3-0); try by I. Paxton, conv. by P. Dods (3-6). (H.T.). Try by M. Titley, conv. by H. Davies (9-6); penalty goal by P. Dods (9-9); try by J. Aitken, conv. by P. Dods (9-15).

This win, away from home in the first match of the series, was important and acted as a confidence-boost for the Scots. The Scottish forwards were a revelation: they exploited Welsh weaknesses to the full with David Leslie and Jim Calder plundering most of the loose possession. Scotland had purple patches – especially in the second quarter during which, with some better judgement and a bit of luck, they could well have put the match beyond Wales' reach.

Jim Aitken, besides scoring his first international try, played a captain's part throughout. This win was Scotland's second in succession at Cardiff: a workmanlike performance – but the selectors and coaches were left to wonder how to inspire the backs to make better use of so much possession provided by the forwards.

SCOTLAND 18   ENGLAND 6
Murrayfield
4 February 1984

Scotland: P. W. Dods (*Gala*); K. W. Robertson (*Melrose*), D. I. Johnston (*Watsonians*), A. E. Kennedy (*Watsonians*), G. R. T. Baird (*Kelso*); J. Y. Rutherford (*Selkirk*), R. J. Laidlaw (*Jedforest*); J. Aitken* (*Gala*), C. T. Deans (*Hawick*), I. G. Milne (*Heriot's FP*), W. Cuthbertson (*Harlequins*), A. J. Tomes (*Hawick*), J. H. Calder (*Stewart's-Melville*), I. A. M. Paxton (*Selkirk*), D. G. Leslie (*Gala*).
Replacements: J. R. Beattie (*Glas. Acad.*) for W. Cuthbertson. J. A. Pollock (*Gosforth*) for A. Kennedy.
England: W. H. Hare (*Leicester*); J. Carleton (*Orrell*), C. R. Woodward (*Leicester*), G. H. Davies (*Wasps*), M. A. C. Slemen (*Liverpool*); L. Cusworth (*Leicester*), M. G. Youngs (*Leicester*); G. S. Pearce (*Northampton*), P. J. Wheeler* (*Leicester*), C. White (*Gosforth*), M. J. Colclough (*Wasps*), S. J. Bainbridge (*Gosforth*), P. D. Simpson (*Bath*), J. P. Scott (*Cardiff*), P. J. Winterbottom (*Headingley*).
Replacement: J. Hall (*Bath*) for P. Winterbottom.
Referee: D. I. H. Burnett (*Ireland*).

Try by D. Johnston, conv. by P. Dods (6-0); penalty goal by W. Hare (6-3). (H.T.). Try by A. Kennedy, conv. by P. Dods (12-3); penalty goal by W. Hare (12-6); two penalty goals by P. Dods (18-6).

The first-ever international rugby match was contested between these two countries in Edinburgh in 1871, the result being a win for the Scots. This, the 100th match between Scotland and England, again saw Scotland triumph.

England's plodding attempts to impose themselves at forward came to nil and, after that, they had nothing to offer and were thoroughly outplayed by the Scots. The Scottish pack proved themselves to be superior to their English counterparts with David Leslie having an outstanding game.

England's tactics of concentrating on the set pieces were fatally flawed. The Scots positively buzzed in the loose, always alert to picking up and exploiting the bits and pieces. They forced England back time and again with some driving rucks but their commitment and enthusiasm were not allowed to deteriorate into frenzied disorder: the halfback pairing of Rutherford and Laidlaw saw to that. These two experienced troopers proved themselves to be generals in directing and conducting the play: they created order from what might have deteriorated into chaos.

Dusty Hare's failures at goal-kicking (two successes from eight attempts) proved particularly expensive for England but it would have been a travesty of justice had England won on penalties.

This victory put Scotland on course for the Triple Crown when they were due to play Ireland in Dublin in their next match. Who could criticise the optimism and confidence in a side which had already done the hard work?

IRELAND 9   SCOTLAND 32
Lansdowne Road
3 March 1984

Ireland: J. Murphy (*Greystones*); T. Ringland (*Ballymena*), M. Kiernan (*Lansdowne*), M. Finn (*Constitution*), K. Crossan (*Instonians*); T. Ward (*St Mary's Coll.*), T. Doyle (*Greystones*); P. Orr (*Old Wesley*), H. Harbison (*Bective Rangers*), D. Fitzgerald (*Lansdowne*), D. McGrath (*UCD*), D. Lenihan (*Constitution*), M. Keane (*Lansdowne*), J. O'Driscoll (*Lond. Irish*), W. Duggan* (*Blackrock Coll.*)
Replacement: H. C. Condon (*Lond. Irish*) for D.G. McGrath.
Scotland: P. W. Dods (*Gala*); J. M. Pollock (*Gosforth*), K. W. Robertson (*Melrose*), D. I. Johnston (*Watsonians*), G. R. T. Baird (*Kelso*); J. Y. Rutherford (*Selkirk*), R. J. Laidlaw (*Jedforest*); I. G. Milne (*Heriot's FP*), C. T. Deans (*Hawick*), J. Aitken* (*Gala*), J. H. Calder (*Stewart's-Melville*), A. J. Tomes (*Hawick*), A. J. Campbell (*Hawick*), D. G. Leslie (*Gala*), I. A. M. Paxton (*Selkirk*).
Replacement : I. G. Hunter (*Selkirk*) for R. Laidlaw.
Referee: F. A. Howard (*England*).

Try by R. Laidlaw, conv. by P. Dods (0-6); two penalty goals by P. Dods (0-12); penalty try, conv. by P. Dods (0-18); try by R. Laidlaw (0-22). (H.T.). Penalty goal by J. Murphy (3-22); try by M.

209

Kiernan, conv. by J. Murphy (9-22); try by K. Robertson, conv. by P. Dods (9-28); try by P. Dods (9-32).

Ireland, having won the toss, surprisingly elected to play against the wind. The Scots took full advantage of this Irish aberration and promptly scored 12 early points in the first fourteen minutes: a goal and two penalty goals. The Scots thoroughly deserved their 22-0 half-time lead, having outplayed the Irish XV in nearly all departments. Ireland raised their game in the second half and scored a peach of a try through Michael Kiernan but it was not enough to hold back the tartan tide and the Scottish victory saw the Scots achieve their first Triple Crown for 46 years (their previous success had been in 1938).

The only cloud over the Scots were the injuries sustained by scrum-half Roy Laidlaw (a type of migraine), and his replacement, Gordon Hunter (fractured cheekbone). Hunter's injury was particularly unfortunate: after no-side, in a freak accident, he collided with a young spectator who had invaded the pitch.

This victory put Scotland on course for the Grand Slam when France were due at Murrayfield in their next match. Both countries were on 6 championship points after three victories from three matches played.

SCOTLAND 21   FRANCE 12
Murrayfield
17 March 1984

Scotland: P. W. Dods (*Gala*); J. A. Pollock (*Gosforth*), K. W. Robertson (*Melrose*), D. I. Johnston (*Watsonians*), G. R. T. Baird (*Kelso*); J. Y. Rutherford (*Selkirk*) R. J. Laidlaw (*Jedforest*); J. Aitken* (*Gala*), C. T. Deans (*Hawick*), I. G. Milne (*Heriot's FP*), A. J. Campbell (*Hawick*), A. J. Tomes (*Hawick*), J. H. Calder (*Stewart's-Melville*), I. A. M. Paxton (*Selkirk*), D. G. Leslie (*Gala*).
France: S. Blanco (*Biarritz*); J. Begu (*Dax*), P. Sella (*Agen*),D. Codorniou (*Narbonne*), P. Esteve (*Narbonne*); J-P Lescarboura (*Dax*), J. Gallion (*Toulon*); P. Dospital (*Bayonne*), P. Dintrans (*Tarbes*), D. Dubroca (*Agen*), F. Haget (*Biarritz*), J. Condom (*Boucau*), J-P Rives* (*Racing Club*), J-L Joinel (*Brive*), J-C Orso (*Nice*).
Replacement: P. Berbizier (*Lourdes*) for J. Gallion.
Referee: W. Jones (*Wales*).

Penalty goal by P. Dods (3-0); try by J. Gallion, conv. by J-P Lescarboura (3-6). (H.T.). Penalty goal by J-P Lescarboura (3-9); two penalty goals by P. Dods (9-9); dropped goal by J-P Lescarboura (9-12); penalty goal by P. Dods (12-12); try by J. Calder, conv. by P. Dods (18-12); penalty goal by P. Dods (21-12).

The Scots withstood intense French pressure in the first quarter of the game. They weathered the storm and, in the second half, turned the game around and pressurised the French to breaking point. Late on it was still anybody's game but the French began to crack and indiscipline played a part in their undoing. With the score at 9-12 in favour of France, Gallic temperament saw them concede a penalty 50 metres from their own goal. Their indiscipline spilled over into argument with the referee who promptly marched them back a further 10 metres. A missable 50-metre kick was turned into a kickable 40 metres – and Peter Dods made no mistake to level at 12-12.

Following that incident, France really began to reel. Serge Blanco made a complete hash of attempting to field and clear a high ball. From the resulting lineout, almost on the French line, Jim Calder caught the ball cleanly and plunged over for the try. Peter Dods kicked the conversion and then was successful with another penalty kick when he himself was late-tackled. The Scots had scored 18 points in the last 14 minutes of the game to secure a well-earned victory.

Peter Dods suffered an eye injury in the first quarter of the match and played the remainder with one eye practically closed. He overcame that handicap and kicked 17 points, setting a new Scottish record for points in a championship season with 50. His 17 points equalled Andy Irvine's record of 17 in an international, and broke Irvine's record of 35 in a championship season.

The final whistle saw hordes of Scottish supporters invade the pitch and completely swamp their heroes. A 59-year gap between Grand Slams – and the joy of the Scots knew no bounds. The players had to be rescued by the police and escorted to the tunnel leading to the dressing rooms. The players disappeared from view, waving happily to the delirious supporters.

210

Five Nations Championship 1983-84

	P	W	L	D	F	A	Pts
Scotland	4	4	0	0	86	36	8
France	4	3	1	0	90	66	6
Wales	4	2	2	0	67	60	4
England	4	1	3	0	51	83	2
Ireland	4	0	4	0	39	87	0

ROMANIA 28   SCOTLAND 22
Bucharest
20 May 1984

Romania: I. Vasile; A. Lungu, G. Varzaru, M. Margescu, M. Aidea; D. Alexandru, M. Paraschiv; S. Constantin, A. Radulescu, L. Constantin, D. Gheorghe, F. Murariu, V. Padcu, M. Munteanu, I. Bucan.
Scotland: P. W. Dods (*Gala*); G. A. Pollock (*Gosforth*), J. M. Renwick (*Hawick*), D. I. Johnston (*Watsonians*), K. W. Robertson (*Melrose*); J. Y. Rutherford (*Selkirk*), R. J. Laidlaw (*Jedforest*); J. Aitken* (*Gala*), G. J. Callander (*Kelso*), N. A. Rowan (*Boroughmuir*), A. J. Campbell (*Hawick*), A. J. Tomes (*Hawick*), S. McGaughey (*Hawick*), D. G. Leslie (*Gala*), J. R. Beattie (*Glas. Acad.*).
Referee: O. E. Doyle (*Ireland*).

Try by D. Leslie, conv. by P. Dods (0-6); try and conv. by D. Alexandru (6-6); penalty goal by D. Alexandru (9-6); dropped goal by K. Robertson (9-9); penalty goal by P. Dods (9-12); try by P. Dods (9-16). (H.T.). Penalty goal by D. Alexandru (12-16); penalty goal by P. Dods (12-19); dropped goal by D. Alexandru (15-19); try by M. Paraschiv (19-19); penalty goal by P. Dods (19-22); try by A. Radulescu conv. by D. Alexandru (25-22); penalty goal by D. Alexandru (28-22).

The match was played in sweltering conditions with temperatures reaching the 90s. It was no surprise the Scots' stamina flagged in the second half. The Romanian pack proved to be stronger than expected and that plus a head injury to the Scottish captain, Jim Aitken, proved to be real handicaps to Scotland.

With the score at 19-22 in Scotland's favour, D. Alexandru punted high toward the Scottish posts. Peter Dods, standing his ground waiting for the ball, was crash tackled by several opponents – illegally and before the ball arrived, stated some reports – but the referee was in no doubt and allowed play to continue. In the resulting scramble, Radulescu crashed through to touch down for the score. The result was disappointing but the Scots were not disgraced and the final score in no way tarnished what had been a vintage season for Scottish rugby.

SCOTLAND 12   AUSTRALIA 37
Murrayfield
8 December 1984

Scotland: P. W. Dods (*Gala*); P. D. Steven (*Heriot's FP*), A. E. Kennedy (*Watsonians*), K. W. Robertson (*Melrose*), G. R. T. Baird (*Kelso*); D. S. Wyllie (*Stewart's-Melville*), R. J. Laidlaw* (*Jedforest*); A. D. G. Mackenzie (*Selkirk*), C. T. Deans (*Hawick*), I. G. Milne (*Harlequins*), A. J. Tomes (*Hawick*), W. Cuthbertson (*Harlequins*), J. H. Calder (*Stewart's-Melville*), J. R. Beattie (*Glas. Acad.*). J. Jeffrey (*Kelso*).
Australia: R. Gould; F. Grigg, A. Slack*, M. Lynagh, D. Campese; M. Ella, N. Farr-Jones; E. Rodriguez, T. Lawton, A. McIntyre, S. Cutler, S. Williams, D. Codey, S. Tuynman, S. Poidevin.
Referee: S. R. Hilditch (*Ireland*).

Penalty goal by M. Lynagh (0-3); penalty goal by P. Dods (3-3); try by D. Campese, conv. by M. Lynagh (3-9); penalty goal by M. Lynagh (3-12); penalty goal by P. Dods (6-12); penalty goal by P. Dods (9-12). (H.T.). Two penalty goals by M. Lynagh (9-18); penalty goal by P. Dods (12-18); try by M. Ella, conv. by M. Lynagh (12-24); try by N. Farr-Jones (12-28); penalty goal by M. Lynagh (12-31); try by D. Campese, conv. by M. Lynagh (12-37).

Normally there is no fun in watching one's country on the receiving end of a thrashing but the quality of rugby displayed by this Australian team left true rugby followers enthralled. They could not help but admire the manual dexterity, athletic running and all-round intelligent play of the visitors. Mark Ella was an exceptional player and David Campese's side-stepping was a delight to see.

Out-thought and out-manoeuvred for much of the game, the Scots stuck manfully to their task but, on the day, they were simply out-played.

SCOTLAND 15   IRELAND 18
Murrayfield
2 February 1985

Scotland: P. W. Dods (*Gala*); G. R. T. Baird (*Kelso*), K. T. Murray (*Hawick*), K. W. Robertson (*Melrose*), I. Tukalo (*Selkirk*); J. Y. Rutherford (*Selkirk*), R. J. Laidlaw* (*Jedforest*); G. McGuiness (*W. of Scot.*), C. T. Deans (*Hawick*), N. S. Rowan (*Boroughmuir*), T. J. Smith (*Gala*), S. Campbell (*Hawick*), J. H. Calder (*Stewart's-Melville*), J. R. Beattie (*Glas. Acad.*), J. Jeffrey (*Kelso*).
Replacement: I. A. M. Paxton (*Selkirk*), for J. Beattie.
Ireland: H. P. MacNeill (*Oxford Univ.*); T. Ringland (*Ballymena*), B. J. Mullin (*Dublin Univ.*), M. J. Kiernan (*Lansdowne*), K. D. Crossan (*Instonians*); P. M. Dean (*St Mary's Coll.*), M. T. Bradley (*Cork Const.*); P. A. Orr (*Old Wesley*), C. F. Fitzgerald* (*St. Mary's Coll.*), J. J. McCoy (*Dungannon*), D. G. Lenihan (*Cork Const.*), W. A. Anderson (*Dungannon*), P. M. Matthews (*Ards*), B. Spillane (*Bohemians*), N. Carr (*Ards*).
Referee: S. Strydom (*South Africa*).

Penalty goal by P. Dods (3-0); dropped goal by J. Rutherford (6-0); dropped goal by M. Kiernan (6-3). (H.T.). Try by T. Ringland, conv. by M. Kiernan (6-9); two penalty goals by P. Dods (12-9); penalty goal by M. Kiernan (12-12); penalty goal by P. Dods (15-12); try by T. Ringland, conv. by M. Kiernan (15-18).

This was rather a flat international. The lead changed hands four times but real, pulsating excitement was missing. The Scotland team had chances to score tries: early in the second half when the ball went into touch-in-goal, tantalisingly inches ahead of the diving Roger Baird, and later when John Rutherford drove over the Irish line in a huddle of players, but the referee decided that the ball had not been properly grounded.

In truth, Ireland were the better of two very ordinary international teams but Scotland looked to have won the match with Peter Dods' fourth penalty goal with but three minutes of play remaining. The Irish had other ideas, however, and, on the stroke of no-side, they scored a try fit to win any match – Trevor Ringland scoring his second try of the game.

Peter Dods' 12 points in the match brought his total in internationals to 137 in 12 matches – a phenomenally successful ratio by any standard.

FRANCE 11   SCOTLAND 3
Parc des Princes
16 February 1985

France: S. Blanco (*Biarritz*); L. Pardo (*Monteferrand*), P. Sella (*Agen*), J. Codorniou (*Narbonne*), P. Estève (*Narbonne*); J-P Lescarboura (*Dax*), J. Gallion (*Toulon*); P. Dospital (*Bayonne*), P. Dintrans* (*Tarbes*), J-P Garuet (*Lourdes*), F. Haget (*Biarritz*), J. Condom (*Boucau*), J. Gratton (*Agen*), J-L Joinel (*Brive*), L. Rodriguez (*Mont-de-Marsan*).
Scotland: P. W. Dods (*Gala*); P. Steven (*Heriot's FP*), K. T. Murray (*Hawick*), K. W. Robertson (*Melrose*), J. A. Pollock (*Gosforth*); J. Y. Rutherford (*Selkirk*), R. J. Laidlaw (*Jedforest*); G. M. McGuinness (*W. of Scot.*), C. T. Deans (*Hawick*), I. G. Milne (*Harlequins*), A. J. Campbell (*Hawick*), T. J. Smith (*Gala*), J. H. Calder (*Stewart's-Melville*), I. A. M. Paxton (*Selkirk*), D. G. Leslie* (*Gala*).
Replacement: I. G. Hunter (*Selkirk*) for R. Laidlaw.
Referee: L. M. Prideaux (*England*).

Penalty goal by P. Dods (0-3); try by S. Blanco (4-3); penalty goal by J-P Lescarboura (7-3); try by S. Blanco (11-3). (H.T.).

All points were scored in the first half. Overall, the Scots were outclassed by their French opponents. The Scots lacked nothing in courage and managed to keep the points scored against them to a mere 11 – but courage alone was not enough against a cleverer team.

A worrying feature for Scotland was the lack of form of the half-back pairing. Before departing the field, injured, at half-time, Roy Laidlaw had been experiencing difficulties in dealing with bad ball at lineouts and John Rutherford's kicking was short of the high standards he had set himself.

SCOTLAND 21   WALES 25
Murrayfield
2 March 1985

Scotland: P. W. Dods (*Gala*); P. D. Steven (*Heriot's FP*), K. T. Murray (*Hawick*), K. W. Robertson (*Melrose*), G. R. T. Baird (*Kelso*); J. Y. Rutherford (*Selkirk*), I. G. Hunter (*Selkirk*); G. M. McGuinness (*W. of Scot.*), C. T. Deans (*Hawick*), I. G. Milne (*Harlequins*), A. J. Campbell (*Hawick*), A. J. Tomes (*Hawick*), J. H. Calder (*Stewart's-Melville*), I. A. M. Paxton (*Selkirk*), D. G. Leslie* (*Gala*).
Replacement: D. S. Wyllie (*Stewart's-Melville*) for K. Murray.
Wales: M. A. Wyatt (*Swansea*); M. H. Titley (*Bridgend*), R. A. Ackerman (*Lond. Welsh*), M. G. Ring (*Cardiff*), P. I. Lewis (*Llanelli*); W. G. Davies (*Cardiff*), T. D. Holmes* (*Cardiff*); J. Whitefoot (*Cardiff*), W. J. James (*Aberavon*), I. H. Eidman (*Cardiff*), S. J. Perkins (*Pontypool*), R. L. Norster (*Cardiff*), M. Morris (*S. Wales Police*), R. D. Moriarty (*Swansea*), D. F. Pickering (*Llanelli*).
Referee: R. Hourquet (*France*).

Dropped goal by W. Davies (0-3); try by I. Paxton, conv. by P. Dods (6-3); two penalty goals by M. Wyatt (6-9); penalty goal by P. Dods (9-9). (H.T.). Try by I. Paxton, conv. by P. Dods (15-9); penalty goal by M. Wyatt (15-12); dropped goal by J. Rutherford (18-12); try by D. Pickering, conv. by M. Wyatt (18-18); dropped goal by J. Rutherford (21-18); try by D. Pickering (21-22); penalty goal by M. Wyatt (21-25).

This match saw an improved performance from Scotland, compared with the previous games against Australia, Ireland and France – but it was still not good enough. There was no suggestion that Scotland should have won: Wales were the better side – just!

Scotland's scrummage was one of the better points – the pack having a good 'shove', as was acknowledge by the Welsh after the game. John Rutherford's two dropped goals brought his total to nine in internationals – two better than the record of seven previously held by Ian McGeechan.

Scotland were next due to face England at Twickenham, a match in which, if they were to lose, would mean a 'whitewash' for this series.

ENGLAND 10   SCOTLAND 7
Twickenham
16 March 1985

England: C. R. Martin (*Bath*); S. T. Smith (*Wasps*), K. G. Simms (*Camb. Univ.*), P. W. Dodge* (*Leicester*), R. Underwood (*Leicester*); C R. Andrew (*Camb. Univ.*), R. M. Harding (*Bristol*); P. J. Blakeway (*Gloucester*), S. E. Brain (*Coventry*), G. S. Pearce (*Northampton*), J. Orwin (*Gloucester*), W. A. Dooley (*Preston Grasshoppers*), J. P. Hall (*Bath*), P. Hesford (*Bristol*), D. H. Cooke (*Harlequins*).
Scotland: P. W. Dods (*Gala*); P. D. Steven (*Heriot's FP*), D. S. Wyllie (*Stewart's-Melville*), K. W. Robertson (*Melrose*), G. R. T. Baird (*Kelso*); J. Y. Rutherford (*Selkirk*), I. G. Hunter (*Selkirk*); G. M. McGuinness (*W. of Scot.*), C. T. Deans (*Hawick*), I. G. Milne (*Harlequins*), A. J. Campbell (*Hawick*), A. J. Tomes (*Hawick*), J. Jeffrey (*Kelso*), I. A. M. Paxton (*Selkirk*), D. G. Leslie* (*Gala*).
Referee: C. Norling (*Wales*).

Penalty goal by R. Andrew (3-0); try by K. Robertson (3-4); penalty goal by R. Andrew (6-4). (H.T.). Penalty goal by P. Dods (6-7); try by S. Smith (10-7).

Scotland's shortcomings at lineouts were cruelly exposed by England – but the Scots were still adjudged to have the best rucking pack in the Five Nations. The England pack had a decidedly leaden-footed look about it. The best forward afield was John Jeffrey: his mobility and general indefatigability were a bonus beyond price for Scotland.

Scotland ended this Five Nations series with the wooden spoon and a 'whitewash'.

Five Nations Championship 1984-85

	P	W	L	D	F	A	Pts
Ireland	4	3	0	1	67	49	7
France	4	2	0	2	49	30	6
Wales	4	2	2	0	61	71	4
England	4	1	2	1	44	53	3
Scotland	4	0	4	0	46	64	0

Scotland toured North America in May 1985, playing five matches of which the Scotland XV lost one game 13-22 to British Columbia but won the other four. The final match of the tour saw Scotland record a massive 79-0 victory over Alberta. No Test matches were played.

SCOTLAND 18   FRANCE 17
Murrayfield
18 January 1986

Scotland: A. G. Hastings (*Camb. Univ.*); M. D. F. Duncan (*W. of Scot.*), D. I. Johnston (*Watsonians*), S. Hastings (*Watsonians*), G. R. T. Baird (*Kelso*); J. Y. Rutherford (*Selkirk*), R. J. Laidlaw (*Jedforest*); D. M. B. Sole (*Bath*), C. T. Deans* (*Hawick*), I. G. Milne (*Harlequins*), A. J. Campbell (*Hawick*), A. J. Campbell-Lamerton (*Lond. Scot.*), J. Jeffrey (*Kelso*), J. R. Beattie (*Glas. Acad.*), F. Calder (*Stewart's-Melville*).
France: S. Blanco (*Biarritz*); J-P Lafond (*Racing Club*), P. Sella (*Agen*), P. Chadebach (*Brive*), P. Esteve (*Narbonne*); J. Laporte (*Graulhet*), P. Berbizier (*Agen*); P. Marocco (*Montferrand*), D. Dubroca* (*Agen*), J-P Garuet (*Lourdes*), F. Haget (*Biarritz*), J. Condom (*La Boucan*), J. Gratton (*Agen*), J-L Joinel (*Brive*), D. Erbani (*Agen*).
Referee: D. I. H. Burnett (*Ireland*)

Try by P. Berbizier (0-4); two penalty goals by A. G. Hastings (6-4); penalty goal by J. Laporte (6-7); two penalty goals by A. G. Hastings (12-7). (H.T.). Dropped goal by J. Laporte (12-10); penalty goal by A. G. Hastings (15-10); try by P. Sella (15-14); penalty goal by A. G. Hastings (18-14); penalty goal by J. Laporte (18-17).

Scotland fielded no less than six new caps in this match: the Hastings brothers (Gavin and Scott), Matt Duncan, David Sole, Jeremy Campbell-Lamerton and Finlay Calder. Gavin Hastings scored all of Scotland's points, setting a new personal match record for a Scot, beating that previously held jointly by A. R. Irvine (17 points against Australia in 1981) and P. Dods (17 against France in 1984). The Hastings' were the first brothers, this century, to make simultaneous international debuts for Scotland.

France's first try, scored 20 seconds from the start, provided the game with a talking point for years to come. A. G. Hastings put the kick-off straight into touch. The Scots were retreating towards the middle of the pitch, expecting a restart. P. Berbizier had other ideas: he took up position on half-way, took a quick throw-in to himself, then sprinted 70 yards to touch down in the corner. The new-look Scots team, although shaken, rallied and gave a spirited display. A. G. Hastings had an opportunity late on to set a world points-scoring record with a seventh penalty, but he hooked wide from just outside the French 22 metres.

It is worthy of attention that had today's 5-point valuation of a try been in practice, France, with two tries to Scotland's one, would have won the match 19-18.

WALES 22   SCOTLAND 15
Cardiff Arms Park
1 February 1986

Wales: P. H. Thorburn (*Neath*); P. I. Lewis (*Llanelli*), J. A. Devereux (*S. Glamorgan Inst.*), B. Bowen (*S. Wales Police*), A. M. Hadley (*Cardiff*); J. Davies (*Neath*), R. J. Jones (*Swansea*); J. Whitefoot (*Cardiff*), W. J. James (*Aberavon*), I. H. Eidman (*Cardiff*), S. J. Perkins (*Pontypool*), D. R. Waters (*Newport*), M. Brown (*Pontypool*), P. T. Davies (*Llanelli*), D. F. Pickering* (*Llanelli*).

Scotland: A. G. Hastings (*Camb. Univ.*); M. D. F. Duncan (*W. of Scot.*), D. I. Johnston (*Watsonians*), S. Hastings (*Watsonians*), G. R. T. Baird (*Kelso*); J. Y. Rutherford (*Selkirk*), R. J. Laidlaw (*Jedforest*); D. M. B. Sole (*Bath*), C. T. Deans* (*Hawick*), I. G. Milne (*Harlequins*), A. J. Campbell (*Hawick*), I. A. M. Paxton (*Selkirk*), J. Jeffrey (*Kelso*), J. R. Beattie (*Glas. Acad.*), F. Calder (*Stewart's-Melville*).
Referee: R. C. Francis (*New Zealand*).

Two penalty goals by P. Thorburn (6-0); try by M. Duncan (6-4); try by J. Jeffrey (6-8); penalty goal by P. Thorburn (9-8); try by A. G. Hastings (9-12). (H.T.). Try by A. M. Hadley (13-12); penalty goal by A. G. Hastings (13-15); dropped goal by J. Davies (16-15); two penalty goals by P. Thorburn (22-15).

Following Wales' two opening penalties, Scott Hastings crossed the Welsh line for what seemed to be a good try in a good position for conversion – only for the Scots to discover that the referee had blown for a scrum, the ball having been judged to have come back from a collapsed second phase. Matt Duncan scored his first international try. At 6-4, Scotland had a let-off when Paul Thorburn hit a post with a penalty kick. A neat passing movement, involving six Scots, put Scotland in the lead with a try from John Jeffrey.

Wales snatched the lead again with another Thorburn penalty. Persistent support play was rewarded when Scotland scored a second try through Gavin Hastings – and the Scots had regained the lead before half-time.

The lead changed hands again early in the second half when A. Hadley scored a try for Wales. Intense pressure by the Scots saw them encamped on the Welsh line. Wales escaped from an attempted push-over try and two close-in tap penalties, the referee twice thwarting Scottish claims that David Sole had scored. A Gavin Hastings penalty restored the lead to Scotland – but the lead changed hands for the sixth time when J. Davies dropped a goal for Wales. Paul Thorburn kicked two more penalties for Wales, the first of which was one of the longest in living memory. The Welsh fullback kicked the goal from fully 12 metres inside his own half, thus giving the perfect answer to shouts about time-wasting as he carefully placed and positioned the ball prior to giving it a memorable and history-making punt.

SCOTLAND 33   ENGLAND 6
Murrayfield
15 February 1986

Scotland: A. G. Hastings (*Watsonians*); M. D. F. Duncan (*W. of Scot.*), D. I. Johnston (*Watsonians*), S. Hastings (*Watsonians*), G. R. T. Baird (*Kelso*); J. Y. Rutherford (*Selkirk*), R. J. Laidlaw (*Jedforest*); A. K. Brewster (*Stewart's-Melville*), C. T. Deans* (*Hawick*), I. G. Milne (*Harlequins*), A. J. Campbell (*Hawick*), I. A. M. Paxton (*Selkirk*), J. Jeffrey (*Kelso*), J. R. Beattie (*Glas. Acad.*), F. Calder (*Stewart's-Melville*).
England: G. H. Davies (*Wasps*); S. T. Smith (*Wasps*), S. J. Halliday (*Bath*), J. L. B. Salmon (*Harlequins*), M. E. Harrison (*Wakefield*); C. R. Andrew (*Nottingham*), N. D. Melville* (*Wasps*); P. A. G. Rendall (*Wasps*), S. E. Brain (*Coventry*), G. S. Pearce (*Northampton*), W. A. Dooley (*Preston Grasshoppers*), M. J. Colclough (*Swansea*), J. F. Hall (*Bath*), G. L. Robbins (*Coventry*), P. J. Winterbottom (*Headingley*).
Referee: R. C. Francis (*New Zealand*).

Penalty goal by A. G. Hastings (3-0); penalty goal by C. R. Andrew (3-3); two penalty goals by A. G. Hastings (9-3); penalty goal by C. R. Andrew (9-6); penalty goal by A. G. Hastings (12-6). (H.T.). Try by M. Duncan, conv. by A. G. Hastings (18-6); penalty goal by A. G. Hastings (21-6); try by J. Rutherford, conv. by A. G. Hastings (27-6); try by S. Hastings, conv. by A. G. Hastings (33-6).

A flurry of successful penalty kicks (4 to Scotland, 2 to England) gave the Scots a 12-6 lead at the interval – but there was no hint of the drama that was to follow in the second half. The Scottish forwards won good ball for Laidlaw who passed to Gavin Hastings whose pass to Duncan sent the wing over for his second international try. The fullback kicked the conversion from the touchline. This he followed with another penalty goal. Then Calder plundered a ball from near the feet of Andrew and gave to Beattie. The Scots No. 8 lobbed to Laidlaw who passed on to Rutherford. The stand-off jinked his way to the English line for his seventh international try. Impressive handling by the Scots saw Scott Hastings race over for a third Scottish try which was converted by his brother on the very stroke of no-side. The Scots had recaptured the Calcutta Cup.

215

IRELAND 9   SCOTLAND 10
Lansdowne Road
15 March 1986

Ireland: H. P. MacNeill (*Lond. Irish*); T. M. Ringland (*Ballymena*), B. J. Mullin (*Dublin Univ.*), M. J. Kiernan (*Dolphins*), K. D. Crossan (*Instonians*); A. J. P. Ward (*Greystones*), M. T. Bradley (*Cork Inst.*); P. A. Orr (*Old Wesley*), C. F. Fitzgerald* (*St Mary's Coll.*), D. C. Fitzgerald (*Lansdowne*), D. G. Lenihan (*Cork Const.*), B. W. McCall (*Lond. Irish*), R. D. Morrow (*Bangor*), N. J. Carr (*Ards*), W. A. Anderson (*Dungannon*).
Scotland: A. G. Hastings (*Watsonians*); K. W. Robertson (*Melrose*), D. I. Johnston (*Watsonians*), S. Hastings (*Watsonians*), G. R. T. Baird (*Kelso*); J. Y. Rutherford (*Selkirk*), R. J. Laidlaw (*Jedforest*); A. K. Brewster (*Stewart's-Melville*), C. T. Deans* (*Hawick*), I. G. Milne (*Harlequins*), A. J. Campbell (*Hawick*), I. A. M. Paxton (*Selkirk*), J. Jeffrey (*Kelso*), F. Calder (*Stewart's-Melville*), J. R. Beattie (*Glas. Acad.*).
Referee: F. Palmade (*France*).

Penalty goal by M. Kiernan (3-0); try by T. Ringland, conv. by M. Kiernan (9-0). (H.T.). Two penalty goals by A. G. Hastings 9-6; try by R. Laidlaw (9-10).

A penalty goal by M. Kiernan, and his conversion of Ringland's try gave Ireland a 9-0 interval lead. Scotland, playing downwind in the second half, quickly got points on the board from two Gavin Hastings penalty goals, the second of which was a prodigious effort from inside his own half. Laidlaw sold Morrow a dummy and ran through the Irish defence to score his fifth international try. Scotland escaped what seemed to be a penalty offence in front of their own posts when the referee spotted his touch judge signalling foul play by the Irish. Ireland missed with another penalty award which would have given them the lead. Afterwards, the Scottish captain was to observe that '... it's not three points till it's between the posts ...'

Five Nations Championship 1985-86

	P	W	L	D	F	A	Pts
France	4	3	1	0	98	52	6
Scotland	4	3	1	0	76	54	6
Wales	4	2	2	0	74	71	4
England	4	2	2	0	62	100	4
Ireland	4	0	4	0	50	83	0

ROMANIA 18   SCOTLAND 33
23 August Stadium, Bucharest
29 March 1986

Romania: L. Hodorca; R. Vionov, A. Lungu, V. David, M. Toader; G. Ignat, M. Parachiv*; I. Bacan, M. Munteanu, V. Pascu, G. Caragea, L. Constantin, F. Murariu, S. Constantin, V. Giuglea.
Scotland: A. G. Hastings (*Watsonians*); M. D. F. Duncan (*W. of Scot.*), D. I. Johnston (*Watsonians*), S. Hastings (*Watsonians*), G. R. T. Baird (*Kelso*); J. Y. Rutherford (*Selkirk*), R. J. Laidlaw (*Jedforest*); A. K. Brewster (*Stewart's-Melville*), C. T. Deans* (*Hawick*), I. G. Milne (*Harlequins*), A. J. Campbell (*Hawick*), I. A. M. Paxton (*Selkirk*), J. Jeffrey (*Kelso*), J. R. Beattie (*Glas. Acad.*), F. Calder (*Stewart's-Melville*).
Referee: R. C. Quittenton (*England*).

Penalty goal by A. G. Hastings (0-3); dropped goal by G. Ignat (3-3); penalty goal by A. G. Hastings (3-6); penalty goal by G. Ignat (6-6); two penalty goals by A. G. Hastings (6-12); penalty goal by G. Ignat (9-12); penalty goal by .A. G. Hastings (9-15); penalty goal by G. Ignat (12-15). (H.T.). Try by J. Jeffrey, conv. by A. G. Hastings (12-21); penalty goal by G. Ignat (15-21); try by S. Hastings, conv. by A. G. Hastings (15-27); penalty goal by G. Ignat (18-27); try by C. Deans, conv. by A. G. Hastings (18-33).

Five penalty goals by the Scots and three plus a dropped goal by the Romanians gave a half-time scoreline of 12-15. One feature of the match was the kicking by Gavin Hastings of 21 points (5 penalty goals and 3 conversions), making eight successful kicks from ten attempts. In this, his first season as a full international, he had recorded 73 points which, incredibly, placed him third on the list of scorers for Scotland – behind Andy Irvine and Peter Dods. Another element of the match were

216

the two near-miss try attempts by Roger Baird. In this, his twenty-fifth international for his country, but never having scored a try, he almost did the trick twice within a minute. Midway through the first half, with Scotland leading 12-6, he was firstly held up just short of the Romanian line. From the resulting scrummage, Roy Laidlaw swung the ball out to Baird who went over the line, in the corner. The Scots, players officials and supporters alike, were on their feet cheering at the wing-threequarter's breaking his 'duck'. Their joy quickly turned to disappointment and chagrin when it was observed that the touch judge had flagged for 'foot-in-touch' – and, besides, the player had snapped the corner flagpost when he dived for the line. The player was to play a total of 27 full internationals for Scotland but that first, elusive try was to be forever denied him.

Scotland toured Spain and France in April and May 1986. Of the five matches played, a Scotland XV won 2, lost 2 and drew 1. No Test matches were played.

SCOTLAND XV 33 JAPAN 18
Murrayfield
27 September 1986

Scotland: P. W. Dods (*Gala*); M. D. F. Duncan (*W. of Scot.*), D. I. Johnston (*Watsonians*), S. Hastings (*Watsonians*), I. Tukalo (*Selkirk*); D. S. Wyllie (*Stewart's-Melville*), R. J. Laidlaw (*Jedforest*); D. M. B. Sole (*Bath*), C. T. Deans*(*Hawick*), N. Rowan (*Boroughmuir*), A. Campbell (*Hawick*), I. A. M. Paxton (*Selkirk*), J. Jeffrey (*Kelso*), J. R. Beattie (*Glas. Acad.*), F. Calder (*Stewart's-Melville*).
Replacement: A. B. M. Ker (*Kelso*) for D. Wyllie
Japan: K. Ishil; N. Taumoefolau, S. Hirao, E. Kutsuki, S. Onuki; K. Matsuo, Y. Konishi; O. Ohta, T. Fujita, M. Alzawa, S. Kurthara, Y. Sakuraba, H. Talona, M. Chida, T. Hayashi*.
Replacement: Mlyamoto for H. Talona.
Referee: L. M. Prideaux (England)

Try by I. Tukalo, conv. by P. Dods (6-0); penalty goal by K. Matsuo (6-3); dropped goal by K. Matsuo (6-6); penalty goal by P. Dods (9-6); try by I. Tukalo (13-6). (H.T.). Try by I. Tukalo (17-6); try by M. Duncan, conv. by P. Dods (23-6); try by I. Tukalo, conv. by P. Dods (29-6); try by A. Campbell (33-6); try by S. Onuki (33-10); try by M. Chida (33-14); try by E. Kutsuki (33-18).

Scotland looked to be cruising toward a comfortable victory of cricket-score proportions when they led Japan by 33-6 going into the last quarter of the match. However, with the Scots tiring visibly, Japan stepped up the pace and scored three tries to put a more respectable complexion on the scoreline. One of the outstanding performances of the game was by Iwan Tukalo who came into the Scottish side as a replacement for the injured Roger Baird. The winger scored four tries, the third being a splendid piece of strong, fast and aggressive wing play. Receiving the ball with little room to manoeuvre, he came crisply off his right foot to leave his marker for dead and scorched to the line to score. Scoring opportunities were scorned by both sides missing conversions and penalty attempts. The Japanese players lacked nothing in flair and guts – but they simply do not have the physical attributes necessary to compete at international level. To state simply that the Scots missed players of the calibre of Gavin Hastings, John Rutherford and Iain Milne is to be euphemistic.

SCOTLAND 16 IRELAND 12
Murrayfield
21 February 1987

Scotland: A. G. Hastings (*Watsonians*); M. D. F. Duncan (*W. of Scot.*), D. S. Wyllie (*Stewart's-Melville*), S. Hastings (*Watsonians*), I. Tukalo (*Selkirk*); J. Y. Rutherford (*Selkirk*), R. J. Laidlaw (*Jedforest*); D. M. B. Sole (*Bath*), C. T. Deans* (*Hawick*), A. J. Tomes (*Hawick*), I. G. Milne (*Heriot's FP*), I. A. M. Paxton (*Selkirk*), J. Jeffrey (*Kelso*), J. R. Beattie (*Glas. Acad.*), F. Calder (*Stewart's-Melville*).
Ireland: H. T. MacNeill (*Lond. Irish*); T. M. Ringland (*Ballymena*), B. J. Mullin (*Oxford Univ.*), M. J. Kiernan (*Dolphin*), K. D. Crossan (*Instonians*); P. M. Dean (*St Mary's Coll.*), M. T. Bradley (*Cork Const.*), P. A. Orr (*Old Wesley*), H. T. Harbiston

217

(*Bective Rangers*), D. T. C Fitzgerald (*Lansdowne*), D. G Lenihan* (*Cork Const.*), J. J. Glennon (*Skerries*), P. M. Matthews (*Wanderers*), W. A. Anderson (*Dungannon*), N. J. Carr (*Ards*).
Referee: R. C. Quittenton (*England*).

J. Y. Rutherford dropped two goals (6-0); try by D Lenihan, conv. by M. Kiernan (6-6); dropped goal by M. Kiernan (6-9); try by R. Laidlaw (10-9). (H.T.). Try by I. Tukalo, conv. by A. G. Hastings (16-9); penalty goal by M. Kiernan(16-12)

Following two dropped goals by John Rutherford, the Irish hit back with a try by Donal Lenihan which was converted by Michael Kiernan to level the scores. Kiernan put Ireland ahead with a dropped goal but, on the stroke of half-time, Scotland regained the lead through a Roy Laidlaw try. Gavin Hastings failed to convert.

The second half was fairly evenly contested. In the last quarter Rutherford flicked a ball with his boot out to Tukalo who went over the Irish line. Gavin Hastings, who had had a poor afternoon with his kicking, made the important conversion, leaving Ireland requiring at least two scores to level or win. A late penalty goal by Kiernan was all they could manage.

One of the talking points was that, in eight full internationals against Ireland, Roy Laidlaw had now scored five tries, plus two more in a B international.

FRANCE 28 SCOTLAND 22
Parc des Princes, Paris
7 March 1987

France: S. Blanco (*Biarritz*); P. Berot (*Agen*), P. Sella (*Agen*), D. Charvet (*Toulouse*), E. Bonneval (*Toulouse*); F. Mesnel (*Racing Club*), P. Berbizier (*Agen*), P. Ordarts (*Biarritz*), D. Dubroca* (*Agen*), J-P Garnet (*Lourdes*), E. Champ (*Toulon*), F. Haget (*Biarritz*), J. Condom (*Biarritz*), D. Erbani (*Agen*).
Scotland: A. G. Hastings (*Watsonians*); M. D. F. Duncan (*W. of Scot.*), D. S. Wyllie (*Stewart's-Melville*), S. Hastings (*Watsonians*), I. Tukalo (*Selkirk*); J. Y. Rutherford (*Selkirk*), R. Laidlaw (*Jedforest*); D. M. B. Sole (*Bath*), C. T. Deans* (*Hawick*), I. G. Milne (*Heriot's FP*), J. Jeffrey (*Kelso*), A. J. Tomes (*Hawick*), I. A. M. Paxton (*Selkirk*), F. Calder (*Stewart's-Melville*), J. R. Beattie (*Glas. Acad.*).
Replacement: K. W. Robertson (*Melrose*) for D. Wyllie (55 min.).
Referee: K. H. Lawrence (*New Zealand*).

Try by E. Bonneval (4-0); try by J. Beattie (4-4); dropped goal by F. Mesnel (7-4); try by E. Bonneval (11-4); try by P. Berot (15-4); penalty goal by A. G. Hastings (15-7); penalty goal by P. Berot (18-7). (H.T.) . Try by E. Bonneval (22-7); penalty goal by A. G. Hastings (22-10); penalty goal by P. Berot (25-10); penalty goal by A. G. Hastings (25-13); try by S. Hastings, conv. by A. G. Hastings (25-19); penalty goal by P. Berot (28-19); penalty goal by A. G. Hastings (28-22).

This match turned out to be a rugby classic and will be recorded as one of the most memorable at international level. An early French try by Bonneval (the first of a hat-trick by the player) was levelled by one from John Beattie who kept his eye on the ball and charged down an attempted clearance by Blanco (following a Rutherford up-and-under). The French had built a lead of 18-7 by half-time and had increased that to 22-7 in the second half when the Scots started a memorable fight-back. A try by Scott Hastings was converted by brother Gavin – whose two successful penalty kicks, bridging the try, brought the score to 25-19. However, a Berot penalty goal stretched the French lead again.

The Hastings brothers had combined to give Scotland the second try. Gavin, following up a John Rutherford chip ahead, plucked the ball out of the air whilst moving at speed and passed to brother Scott who crossed for the score. Gavin's conversion proved to be an extraordinary affair: the ball started to topple over as he ran up to kick – but, despite this, the conversion was successful. The scoring was completed by an exchange of penalty goals by each side. The Scots had given their all in a great fight-back but, following no-side, were quick to congratulate the French team on a magnificent display of fast, running rugby. In truth, the French had deserved to win.

Some newspaper headlines following the match:
'Scots play part in a memorable match'. Scotsman.
'The finest game I have seen at this level'. The Times.
'A classic game at the Parc'. Sunday Times.

SCOTLAND 21   WALES 15
Murrayfield
21 March 1987

Scotland: A. G. Hastings (*Watsonians*); M. D. F. Duncan (*W. of Scot.*), K. W. Robertson (*Melrose*), S. Hastings (*Watsonians*), I. Tukalo (*Selkirk*); J. Y. Rutherford (*Selkirk*) R. J. Laidlaw (*Jedforest*); D. M. B. Sole (*Bath*),C. T. Deans* (*Hawick*), I. G. Milne (*Heriot's FP*), D. B. White (*Gala*), I. A. M. Paxton (*Selkirk*), J. Jeffrey (*Kelso*), J. R. Beattie (*Glas. Acad.*), F. Calder (*Stewart's-Melville*).
Wales: M. A. Wyatt (*Swansea*); G. M. Webbe (*Bridgend*), J. A. Deveraux (*S. Glamorgan Inst.*), K. Hopkins (*Swansea*), I. C. Evans (*Llanelli*); J. Davies (*Neath*), R. N. Jones (*Swansea*); J. Whitefoot (*Cardiff*), W. J. James (*Aberavon*), P. Francis (*Maesteg*), R. L. Norster (*Cardiff*), S. Sutton (*S. Wales Police*), W. P. Moriarty (*Swansea*), M. A. Jones (*Neath*), D. F. Pickering* (*Llanelli*).
Replacement: A. Hadley (*Cardiff*) for I. Evans (28 min.).
Referee: K. Lawrence (*New Zealand*).

Try by J. Beattie, conv. by A. G. Hastings (6-0); penalty goal by A. G. Hastings (9-0); dropped goal by J. Davies (9-3); penalty goal by A. G. Hastings (12-3). (H.T.). Two penalty goals by M. Wyatt (12-9); dropped goal by J. Rutherford (15-9); try by J. Jeffrey, conv. by A. G. Hastings (21-9); try by M. Jones conv. by M. Wyatt (21-15).

During the first half, Scotland dominated most of the play except the lineouts. A half-time lead of 12-3 was not an accurate reflection of the flow of play. The Scots forwards, driving at speed, had the Welsh in ragged disarray at times.

That the Scots did not put more points on the scoreboard was due entirely to some unfortunate handling errors – knocking on or dropping the ball when tries seemed imminent. In the lineouts, the Welsh team dominated. Colin Deans, the Scotland captain, afterwards remarked that the Scottish finishing was not on a par with the build-up.

ENGLAND 21   SCOTLAND 12
Twickenham
4 April 1987

England: W. M. H. Rose (*Harlequins*); M. E. Harrison* (*Wakefield*), S. J. Halliday (*Bath*), J. L. B. Salmon (*Harlequins*), R. Underwood (*Leicester*); P. N. Williams (*Orrell*), R. M. Harding (*Bristol*); P. A. G. Rendall (*Wasps*), B. C. Moore (*Nottingham*), G. S. Pearce (*Northampton*), J. P. Hall (*Bath*), S. Bainbridge (*Fylde*), G. W. Rees (*Nottingham*), D. Richards (*Leicester*).
Scotland: A. G. Hastings (*Watsonians*); M. D. F. Duncan (*W. of Scot.*), K. W. Robertson (*Melrose*), G. R. T. Baird (*Kelso*), I. Tukalo (*Selkirk*); J. Y. Rutherford (*Selkirk*), R. J. Laidlaw (*Jedforest*); D. M. B. Sole (*Bath*), C. T. Deans* (*Hawick*), I. G. Milne (*Heriot's FP*), J. Jeffrey (*Kelso*), D. B. White (*Gala*), I. A. M. Paxton (*Selkirk*), F. Calder (*Stewart's-Melville*), J. R. Beattie (*Glas. Acad.*).
Replacement: A. J. Tomes (*Hawick*) for J. Beattie.
Referee: O. E. Doyle (*Ireland*).

Penalty goal by A. G. Hastings (0-3); penalty goal by M. Rose(3-3); penalty try. conv. by M. Rose (9-3). (H.T.). Penalty goal by M. Rose (12-3); try and conv. by M. Rose (18-3); penalty goal by A. G. Hastings (18-6); penalty goal by M. Rose (21-6); try by K. Robertson, conv. by A. G. Hastings (21-12).

A soft pitch, a slippery ball and incessant rain throughout made conditions poor for this match. Lineouts were mostly dominated by England. A penalty try apart, all of England's points were scored by fullback Marcus Rose.

The Scots gifted both English tries. Ironically, the first originated from a rare piece of Scottish possession from a lineout. The ball went to Roger Baird whose attempted pass to John Rutherford went astray. The Scottish stand-off attempted to fly-hack the ball but succeeded only in giving possession to Mike Harrison who kicked through and over the Scottish line. Matt Duncan tackled the English wing without the ball and Marcus Rose easily converted the awarded penalty try. Up to that point, despite all their possession, England had been working hard, though unsuccessfully, to find a way through the Scottish defence. The last thing the Scots wanted to do was the hard work for their opponents as when they gave possession of a loose ball to the English, behind their own threequarter line. The second England try was tragedy for the Scots. Gavin Hastings failed to find touch with a kick and Rose hoisted a high ball toward the Scottish posts. In the wind, three Scots failed to field the ball and it popped up into the arms of the following Rose who ran over for the try. This game should have been played on 17 January but was postponed due to heavy snow

Five Nations Championship 1986-87

	P	W	L	D	F	A	Pts
France	4	4	0	0	82	59	8
Ireland	4	2	2	0	57	46	4
Scotland	4	2	2	0	71	76	4
Wales	4	1	3	0	54	64	2
England	4	1	3	0	48	67	2

SCOTLAND XV 25 SPAIN 7
Murrayfield
19 April 1987

Scotland: A. G. Hastings (*Watsonians*); M. D. F. Duncan (*W. of Scot.*), K. W. Robertson (*Melrose*), D. S. Wyllie (*Stewart's-Melville*), I. Tukalo (*Selkirk*); A. B. M. Ker (*Kelso*), R. J. Laidlaw (*Jedforest*); D. M. B. Sole (*Bath*), C. T. Deans* (*Hawick*), N. A. Rowan (*Boroughmuir*), D. B. White (*Gala*), A. J. Tomes (*Hawick*), J. Jeffrey (*Kelso*), I. A. M. Paxton (*Selkirk*), F. Calder (*Stewart's-Melville*).
Spain: G. Rivero; J. Torino, S. Torres, J. Azkargorta, E. Uzquiano; F. Puertas, J. Diaz; J. Alvarezl A. Trenzano, J. Moral, B. Abascal, F. Mendez, S. Noriega, J. Ruiz, A. Malo.
Referee: W. D. Bevan (*Wales*)

Penalty goal by A. G. Hastings (3-0); penalty goal by F. Puertas (3-3); try by I. Tukalo (7-3). (H.T.). Try by I. Paxton, conv. by A. G. Hastings (13-3); try by C. Deans, conv. by A. G. Hastings (19-3); try by M. Duncan, conv. by A. G. Hastings (25-3); try by J. Moral (25-7).

This match was intended as a dress rehearsal for the forthcoming Rugby World Cup competition in Australia and New Zealand. It turned out to be a frustrating disappointment for the Scots.The Scottish players may have been, unconsciously, trying to avoid injury and this could explain some features of this lack-lustre display. The Scots found Spain to be a difficult side to play. The Spanish tackling was first-rate and they made general nuisances of themselves in broken play following set pieces. The Scots never reached a level of dominance which had been expected of them. Perhaps the players had one eye on the ball and the other on southern horizons.

RUGBY WORLD CUP – POOL 4
The inaugural competition for the Webb Ellis Trophy
In Australia and New Zealand

FRANCE 20 SCOTLAND 20
Lancaster Park, Christchurch, New Zealand
23 May 1987

France: S. Blanco (*Biarritz*); P. Lagisquet (*Bayonne*), P. Sella (*Agen*); D. Clarvet (*Toulouse*), P. Esteve (*Lavelanet*); F. Mesnel (*Racing Club*), P. Berbizier (*Agen*); P. Ordarts (*Biarritz*), D. Dubroca (*Agen*), J-P Garnet (*Lourdes*) A. Lorieux (*Aix-les-Bains*), J. Condom (*Biarritz*), E. Champ (*Toulon*), L. Rodriguez (*Montferrand*), D. Erbani (*Agen*).
Scotland: A. G. Hastings (*Watsonians*); M. D. F. Duncan (*W. of Scot.*), K. W. Robertson (*Melrose*), D. S. Wyllie (*Stewart's-Melville*), I. Tukalo (*Selkirk*); J. Y. Rutherford (*Selkirk*), R. J. Laidlaw (*Jedforest*); D. M. B. Sole (*Bath*), C. T. Deans* (*Hawick*), I. G. Milne (*Heriot's FP*), D. B. White (*Gala*), A. J. Tomes (*Hawick*), J. Jeffrey (*Kelso*), I. A. M. Paxton (*Selkirk*), F. Calder (*Stewart's-Melville*)
Replacement: A. V. Tait (*Kelso*) for J. Rutherford (7 min.).
Referee: F. A. Howard (*England*).

220

Try by D. White (0-4); penalty goal by S. Blanco (3-4); penalty goal by A. G. Hastings (3-7); penalty goal by A. G. Hastings (3-10); penalty goal by S. Blanco (6-10); penalty goal by A. G. Hastings (6-13). (H.T.). Penalty goal by A. G. Hastings (6-16); try by P. Sella (10-16); try by P. Berbizier (14-16); try and conv. by S. Blanco (20-16); try by M. Duncan (20-20).

Following on from their epic encounter in Paris a few weeks previously, the rugby teams representing these two countries contrived to give another show of all that is best in the game: exciting play, drama and controversy.

The Scots got off to a wonderful start in this, their first, World Cup match, Derek White scoring a try within minutes of the kick-off. Drama was to follow in the seventh minute when John Rutherford, in attempting to field the ball, fell awkwardly and damaged a knee so severely that he had to be stretchered off. As things turned out, the player was to take no further part in the tournament.

Controversy came in the second half when Scotland had a slender lead of 16-14. France had been awarded a penalty. Berbizier, the French scrum half, had been injured and needed attention. Colin Deans, the Scots captain, called to the referee that Matt Duncan, too, required attention to a head cut. The referee was making sure that Berbizier went off the pitch for attention and did not hear Deans' shout. Meanwhile, Blanco took a tap penalty to himself and sprinted off past the bemused Scots to touch down between the posts. The resulting conversion put France ahead for the first time in the match (20-16). By the letter of the law, Blanco was correct but, by the spirit of the game, he had seriously erred.

The drama continued right through to no-side. Matt Duncan, his face streaming blood from a head cut, dived over the French line to level the scores at 20-20. Gavin Hastings' attempted conversion, from almost the touchline, drifted wide thus denying Scotland what would have been a historic win.

Afterwards, to their great credit, the Scots did not complain about the manner of Blanco's try. Scotland's coach, Derrick Grant, summed up their acceptance of the incident and the outcome when he said: 'We were dreaming, we should have been alert'.

RUGBY WORLD CUP

SCOTLAND 60   ZIMBABWE 21
Athletic Park, Wellington, New Zealand
20 May 1987

Scotland: A. G. Hastings (*Watsonians*); M. D. F. Duncan (*W. of Scot.*), A. V. Tait (*Kelso*), K. W. Robertson (Melrose), I. Tukalo (*Selkirk*); D. S. Wyllie (*Stewart's-Melville*), G. H. Oliver (*Hawick*); D. M. B. Sole (*Bath*), C. T. Deans* (*Hawick*), I. G. Milne (*Heriot's FP*), J. R. E. Campbell-Lamerton (*Lond. Scot.*), A. J. Tomes (*Hawick*), F. Calder (*Stewart's-Melville*), I. A. M. Paxton (*Selkirk*), J. Jeffrey (*Kelso*).
Zimbabwe: A. Ferreira; E. Barratt, K. Graham, A. Buitendag, S. Graham; M. Grobler, M. Jellicoe; A. Nicholls, L. Bray, A. Tucker, M. Sawyer, M. Martin, R. Gray, D. Buitendag, M. Neill.
Referee: D. I. H. Burnett (Ireland).

Try by A. Tait, conv. by A. G. Hastings (6-0); try by M. Duncan, conv. by A. G. Hastings (12-0); penalty goal by M. Grobler (12-3); try by G. Oliver (16-3); try by I. Tukalo, conv. by A. G. Hastings (22-3); try and conv. by A. G. Hastings (28-3); try by I. Paxton, conv. by A. G. Hastings (34-3); penalty goal by M. Grobler (34-6); try by A. Tait, conv. by A. G. Hastings (40-6). (H.T.). Try by I. Paxton, conv. by A. G. Hastings (46-6); try by D. Buitendag, conv. by M Grobler (46-12); penalty goal by M. Grobler (46-15); try by M. Duncan (50-15); two penalty goals by M. Grobler (50-21); try by J. Jeffrey, conv. by A. G. Hastings (56-21); try by I. Tukalo (60-21).

This match proved to be the most one-sided international in which Scotland had been engaged. Scotland's captain, Colin Deans, playing his 50th international (a world record for a hooker), saw several previously-held records go by the board. Scotland's best score, prior to this match, had been 35 points against Wales at Inverleith in 1924. Gavin Hastings raised most conversions in an international from 5 to 8. Ian Paxton's first try, his fourth in international rugby, made him the first Scottish forward to lay claim to such a distinction.

Leading 40-6 at half-time, the Scots went off the boil in the second half. Zimbabwe, with the wind behind them, started to make things awkward for the Scots who started to give away penalties with careless profligacy. With the scores at 50-21, Zimbabwe had scored more second half points than the Scots but a late rally saw Scotland score two tries, one being converted.

RUGBY WORLD CUP

ROMANIA 28   SCOTLAND 55
Carisbrook, Dunedin, New Zealand
2 June 1987

Romania: V. Ion; M. Toader, S. Tofan, A. Lungu, A. Pilotschi; D. Alexandru, M. Paraschiv*; I. Bucan, E. Grigore, G. Leonte, L. Constantin, S. Constantin, F. Murariu, C. Raducanu, H. Dumitras.
Replacement: G. Dumitru for C. Raducanu.
Scotland: A. G. Hastings (*Watsonians*); M. D. F. Duncan (*W. of Scot.*), A. V. Tait (*Kelso*), S. Hastings (*Watsonians*), I. Tukalo (*Selkirk*); D. S. Wyllie (*Stewart's-Melville*), R. J. Laidlaw (*Jedforest*); N. Rowan (*Boroughmuir*), C. T. Deans* (*Hawick*), D. M. B. Sole (*Bath*), F. Calder (*Stewart's-Melville*), D. B. White (*Gala*), A. J. Tomes (*Hawick*), J. Jeffrey (*Kelso*), I. A. M. Paxton (*Selkirk*).
Replacements: R. I. Cramb (*Harlequins*) for S. Hastings. J. R. E. Campbell-Lamerton (*Lond. Scot.*) for A. Tomes.
Referee: S. R. Hilditch (*Ireland*).

Try by A. Tait, conv. by A. G. Hastings (0-6); penalty goal by A. G. Hastings (0-9); try by J. Jeffrey, conv. by A. G. Hastings (0-15); try by M. Duncan, conv. by A. G. Hastings (0-21); try by A. Tait, conv. by A. G. Hastings (0-27); penalty goal by D. Alexandru (3-27); try by J. Jeffrey, conv. by A. G. Hastings (3-33); try by F. Murariu (7-33). (H.T.). Try by J. Jeffrey, conv. by A. G. Hastings (7-39); try by M. Toader, conv. by D. Alexandru (13-39); two penalty goals by D. Alexandru (19-39); try by A. G. Hastings (19-43); penalty goal by V. Ion (22-43); try by I. Tukalo, conv. by A. G. Hastings (22-49); try and conv. by A. G. Hastings (22-55); try by F. Murariu, conv. by V. Ion (28-55).

Scotland were never in trouble in their third World Cup tie. Scores came regularly and Scotland had 27 points on the board before Romania opened their account with a penalty goal. When Gavin Hastings converted Iwan Tukalo's try to put the Scots ahead 49-22, he had equalled his own record of 21 points in an international match (he had previously scored the same number against England, and also against Romania in 1986). He then capped the afternoon by scoring a spectacular try when he made an interception in his own half and then romped through to cross the Romanian line. He converted the try himself, thus setting a new world record of 27 points in an international. That record, however, stood for only 1½ hours, after which time Didier Camberabero, playing for France against Zimbabwe, scored 30 points. Gavin shrugged off the incident with a comment that '... Records are there to be broken ...'.

This win ensured Scotland's qualifying for the quarter-finals of the Rugby World Cup. They were now destined to play the New Zealand All Blacks.

RUGBY WORLD CUP – Quarter Final

NEW ZEALAND 30   SCOTLAND 3
Lancaster Park, Christchurch, New Zealand
6 June 1987

New Zealand: J. Gallacher; J. Kirwan, J. Stanley, W. Taylor, C. Green; G. Fox, D. Kirk*; S. McDowell, S. Fitzpatrick, J. Drake, M. Pierce, G. Whetton, A. Whetton, M. Jones, W. Shelford.
Replacement: B. J. Cahill for W. Taylor (20 min.).
Scotland: A. G. Hastings (*Watsonians*); M. D. F. Duncan (*W. of Scot.*), A. V. Tait (*Kelso*), K. W. Robertson (*Melrose*), I. Tukalo (*Selkirk*); D. S. Wyllie (*Stewart's-Melville*), R. J. Laidlaw (*Jedforest*); D. M. B. Sole (*Bath*), C. T. Deans* (*Hawick*), I. G. Milne (*Heriot's FP*), D. B. White (*Gala*), A. J. Tomes (*Hawick*), D. J. Turnbull (*Hawick*), F. Calder (*Stewart's-Melville*), I. A. M. Paxton (*Selkirk*).
Referee: D. I. H. Burnett (*Ireland*).

Two penalty goals by G. Fox (6-0); penalty goal by A. G. Hastings (6-3); penalty goal by G. Fox (9-3). (H.T.). Try by A. Whetton, conv. by G. Fox (15-3); three penalty goals by G. Fox (24-3); try by J. Gallacher, conv. by G. Fox (30-3).

This match turned out to be unsatisfactory for rugby purists. Twenty-nine penalty awards did much to contribute to a plethora of broken play. Grant Fox successfully kicked six penalty goals for the All Blacks, and Gavin Hastings one for Scotlannd. It was a thoroughly deserved New Zealand victory, the final score being the widest margin between these two countries who had met on twelve previous occasions, stretching back to 1905.

This result ended Scotland's participation in the inaugural competition for the Rugby World Cup. They had played 4 matches, won 2, drawn 1, lost 1. Scotland scored 138 points and conceded 99, scoring 22 tries, 16 conversions and 6 penalty goals.

New Zealand went on to win the Webb Ellis Trophy by defeating Wales in the semi-final (49-6) and France in the final (29-9).

SCOTLAND XV 15 FRANCE XV 12
Netherdale, Galashiels
26 September 1987

Scotland XV: I. J. Ramsay (*Melrose*); M. D. F. Duncan (*W. of Scot.*), T. J. Exeter (*Moseley*), A. E. Kennedy (*Watsonians*), I. Tukalo (*Selkirk*); R. I. Cramb (*Harlequins*), G. H. Oliver (*Hawick*); D. M. B. Sole (*Bath*), G. J. Callander* (*Kelso*), N. A. Rowan (*Boroughmuir*), C. A. Gray (*Nottingham*), D. F. Cronin (*Bath*), G. R. Marshall (*Wakefield*), A. J. Macklin (*Lond. Scot.*), D. J. Turnbull (*Hawick*).
France XV: J. Bianchi (*Toulon*); J-B Lafond (*Racing Club*), M. Andrieu (*Nimes*), A. Gely (*Grenoble*), P. Peytavin (*Bayonne*); F. Mesnel (*Racing Club*), B. Berbizier (*Agen*); L. Armary (*Lourdes*), P. Dintrans* (*Tarbes*), J-P Garnet (*Lourdes*), J. Gratton (*Agen*), A. Carminati (*Beziers*), J. Condom (*Biarritz*), K. Janik (*Toulouse*), H. Chaffardon (*Grenoble*) .
Referee: B. Anderson (*Currie*)

Two penalty goals by I. Ramsay (6-0); penalty goal by J. Bianchi (6-3); try by F. Mesnel, conv. by J. Bianchi (6-9); penalty goal by J. Bianchi (6-12). (H.T.). Three penalty goals by I. Ramsay (15-12).

The Scots could be satisfied with their victory in this non-cap match but, perhaps, not the manner of it. French indiscipline cost them dear as Ian Ramsay kicked five successful penalty goals. The Scots had a lot of possession but kicked much of it away.

IRELAND 22 SCOTLAND 18
Lansdowne Road
16 January 1988

Ireland: P. P. Danaher (*Lansdowne*); T. M. Ringland (*Ballymena*), B. J. Mullin (*Blackrock Coll.*), M. J. Kiernan (*Dolphin*), K. D. Crossan (*Instonians*); P. M. Dean (*St Mary's Coll.*), M. T. Bradley (*Constitution*); J. J. Fitzgerald (*Young Munster*), T. J. Kingston (*Dolphin*), D. G. Fitzgerald (*Lansdowne*), D. G. Lenihan* (*Constitution*), W. A. Anderson (*Dungannon*), M. E. Gibson (*Lond. Irish*).
Replacement: H. T. MacNeill (*Lond. Irish*) for T. Ringland (5 min.).
Scotland: A. G. Hastings (*Watsonians*); M. D. F. Duncan (*W. of Scot.*), A. V. Tait (*Kelso*), S. Hastings (*Watsonians*), G. R. T. Baird (*Kelso*); R. I. Cramb (*Harlequins*) R. J. Laidlaw (*Jedforest*); D. M. B. Sole (*Edin. Acad.*), G. J. Callander* (*Kelso*), N. A. Rowan (*Boroughmuir*), D. B. White (*Gala*), D. F. Cronin (*Bath*), J. Jeffrey (*Kelso*), F. Calder (*Stewart's-Melville*), I. A. M. Paxton (*Selkirk*).
Referee: R. C. Quittenton (*England*).

Try by B. Mullin (4-0); try by H. MacNeill, conv. by M. Kiernan (10-0); try by R. Laidlaw, conv. by A. G. Hastings (10-6). (H.T.). Penalty by M. Kiernan (13-6); dropped goal by M. Kiernan (16-6); penalty goal by A. G. Hastings (16-9); try by M. Bradley, conv. by M. Kiernan (22-9); penalty goal by A. G. Hastings (22-12); try by S. Hastings, conv. by A. G. Hastings (22-18).

Gavin Hastings missed a crucial penalty kick in the opening minutes, in front of the Irish posts. The let-off saw Ireland swarm to the other end and score the opening try. Unfortunately, T. J. Ringland, in the build-up to the try, suffered what, at the time, seemed to be a serious neck injury

223

and had to be stretchered off. The teamwork of the Irish was superior to that of the Scots: they won most of the lineouts with something to spare and scored three sparkling tries.

SCOTLAND 23   FRANCE 12
Murrayfield
6 February 1988

Scotland: A. G. Hastings (*Watsonians*); M. D. F. Duncan (*W. of Scot.*), A. V. Tait (*Kelso*), S. Hastings (*Watsonians*), I. Tukalo (*Selkirk*); R. I. Cramb (*Harlequins*), R. J. Laidlaw (*Jedforest*); D. M. B. Sole (*Edin. Acad.*), G. J. Callander* (*Kelso*), N. A. Rowan (*Boroughmuir*), D. J. Turnbull (*Hawick*), A. J. Campbell (*Hawick*), D. F. Cronin (*Bath*), F. Calder (*Stewart's-Melville*), D. B. White (*Gala*).
France: S. Blanco (*Biarritz*); P. Bèrot (*Agen*), P. Sella (*Agen*), M. Andrieu (*Nimes*) P. Lagisquet (*Bayonne*); J-P Lescarboura (*Dax*), P. Berbizier (*Agen*); L. Armary (*Lourdes*), D. Dubroca* (*Agen*), J-P Garuet (*Lourdes*), E. Champ (*Toulon*), A. Lorieux (*Aix-les-Bains*), J. Condom (*Biarritz*), D. Erbani (*Agen*), L. Rodriguez (*Montferrand*).
Referee: F. Muller (*South Africa*).

Dropped goal by J-P Lescarboura (0-3); dropped goal by R. Cramb (3-3); penalty goal by P. Bèrot (3-6); try by A. G. Hastings (7-6); try by I. Tukalo (11-6). (H.T.). Four penalty goals by A. G. Hastings (23-6); try by P. Lagisquet, conv. by P. Bèrot (23-12).

Following the defeat by Ireland in Dublin, this was a match that Scotland had to win. An early French dropped goal by J-P Lescarboura was answered by one from Richard Cramb. France went ahead again through a penalty goal by F. Berot but Gavin Hastings then scored a glorious individual try to put the Scots ahead for the first time. France won a lineout and fast accurate passing saw the ball go out to Lagisquet who found himself with space. Running at speed, he tried to chip ahead when confronted by Gavin Hastings. The Scotland fullback blocked the chip (saving what would almost certainly have been a French try) and, gathering the ball, raced into the French half. The French cover closed in and he kicked ahead. Berbizier made a soccer-like challenge but only succeeded in slithering the ball into the Scotsman's path. Hastings kicked over the French line and dived on the ball to claim the try. The Scots were never behind again in the match and ran out deserved winners.

WALES 25   SCOTLAND 20
Cardiff Arms Park
20 February 1988

Wales: P. H. Thorburn (*Neath*); I. C. Evans (*Llanelli*), M. G. Ring (*Pontypool*), P. Bowen* (*S. Wales Police*), A. M. Hadley (*Cardiff*); J. Davies (*Llanelli*), R. N. Jones (*Swansea*); S. T. Jones (*Pontypool*), I. Watkins (*Ebbw Vale*), D. Young (*Swansea*), P. May (*Llanelli*), R. L. Norster (*Cardiff*), R. Phillips (*Neath*), W. P. Moriarty (*Swansea*), R. G. Collins (*S. Wales Police*) Replacement: J. Pugh (*Neath*) for S. Jones (13 min.).
Scotland: A. G. Hastings (*Watsonians*); M. D. F. Duncan (*W. of Scot.*), A. V. Tait (*Kelso*), S. Hastings (*Watsonians*), I. Tukalo (*Selkirk*); A. B. M. Ker (*Kelso*), R. J. Laidlaw (*Jedforest*); D. M. B. Sole (*Edin. Acad.*), G. J. Callander* (*Kelso*), N. A. Rowan (*Boroughmuir*), A. J. Campbell (*Hawick*), D. F. Cronin (*Bath*), J. Jeffrey (*Kelso*), D. B. White (*Gala*), F. Calder (*Stewart's-Melville*).
Referee: Y. Bressy (*France*).

Try by F. Calder (0-4); penalty goal by A. G. Hastings (0-7); try by J. Davies (4-7); try by I. Evans, conv. by P. Thorburn (10-7); try by M. Duncan (10-11); two penalty goals by A. G. Hastings (10-17). (H.T.). Penalty goal by A. G. Hastings (10-20); try by I. Watkins, conv. by P. Thorburn (16-20); penalty goal by P. Thorburn (19-20); two dropped goals by J. Davies (25-20).

The lead changed hands three times in this exciting encounter. The Scots drew first blood by crossing the Welsh line twice within the first 90 seconds but only the second crossing counted. Firstly, Scott Hastings beat Mark Ring and looked to have scored in the corner but the referee ruled that the Scot had been in touch. From the resulting lineout the Welsh diverted the ball over their own line and Finlay Calder pounced on it to score. This was followed by a successful penalty kick by Gavin Hastings and Scotland were 7 points ahead after 5 minutes play. The Welsh replied by way of a try and a goal to take the lead 10-7.

The Scots fought back and points came by way of a Matt Duncan try and two penalty goals by Gavin Hastings – 17-10 in Scotland's favour at half-time. Scotland went further ahead early in the second half by way of a Gavin Hastings penalty. Wales scored a spectacular try which they goaled and this was followed by two Jonathan Davies dropped goals to give Wales a win that, over the piece, they just deserved. So ended what, by any standard, had been a marvellous match.

SCOTLAND 6 ENGLAND 9
Murrayfield
5 March 1988

Scotland: A. G. Hastings (*Watsonians*); M. D. F. Duncan (*W. of Scot.*), A. V. Tait (*Kelso*), K. W. Robertson (*Melrose*), I. Tukalo (*Selkirk*); A. B. M. Ker (*Kelso*), R. J. Laidlaw (*Jedforest*); D. M. B. Sole (*Edin. Acad.*), G. J. Callander* (*Kelso*), N. A. Rowan (*Boroughmuir*), D. J. Turnbull (*Hawick*), D. B. White (*Gala*), D. F. Cronin (*Bath*), F. Calder (*Stewart's-Melville*), I. A. M. Paxton (*Selkirk*).
England: J. M. Webb (*Bristol*); R. Underwood (*Leicester*), W. D. C. Carling (*Harlequins*), S. J. Halliday (*Bath*), C. Oti (*Nottingham*); C. R. Andrew (*Wasps*), N. D. Melville* (*Wasps*); P. A. G. Rendall (*Wasps*), B. C. Moore (*Nottingham*), J. A. Probyn (*Wasps*), M. G. Skinner (*Harlequins*), J. Orwin (*Bedford*), W. A. Dooley (*Fylde*), P. J. Winterbottom (*Headingley*), D. Richards (*Leicester*).
Replacement: G. W. Rees (*Nottingham*) for P. Winterbottom (4 min.).
Referee: W. Jones (*Wales*).

No score at half-time. Second half: penalty goal by A. G. Hastings (3-0); dropped goal by R. Andrew (3-3); penalty goal by J. Webb (3-6); penalty goal by. G. Hastings (6-6); penalty goal by J. Webb (6-9).

This was one of the poorest international matches witnessed for many a long day. Dull and unexciting for much of the time, the game looked to be played at funereal pace. The first half was a chapter of missed penalty kicks and collapsed scrummages. The resulting tedium spawned stodgy and colourless rugby which bored the spectators. A match to forget.

Five Nations Championship 1987-8

	P	W	L	D	F	A	Pts
Wales	4	3	1	0	57	42	6
France	4	3	1	0	57	47	6
England	4	2	2	0	56	30	4
Scotland	4	1	3	0	67	68	2
Ireland	4	1	3	0	40	90	2

ZIMBABWE 10 SCOTLAND XV 31
Bulawayo
21 May 1988

Zimbabwe: M. Grobler; P. Kaulback, M. Letcher, R. Khun, W. Schultz; C. Brown, A. Ferreira*; D. Watson, P. Albasini, N. Valdal, A. McIntosh, G. Davidson, D. Buitendag, M. Carrabott, B. Dawson.
Scotland: P. W. Dods* (*Gala*); M. D. F. Duncan (*W. of Scot.*), R. R. W. Maclean (*Gloucester*), D. S. Wyllie (*Stewart's-Melville*), A. Moore (*Edin. Acad.*); C. M. Chalmers (*Melrose*), G. H. Oliver (*Hawick*); D. J. D. Butcher (*Harlequins*), J. A. Hay (*Hawick*), A. P. Burnell (*Lond. Scot.*), C. A. Gray (*Nottingham*), D. F. Cronin (*Edin. Acad.*), K. P. Rafferty (*Heriot's FP*), H. M. Parker (*Kilmarnock*), D. J. Turnbull (*Hawick*).
Replacement: S. W. McAslan (*Heriot's FP*) for R. Maclean (66 min.).
Referee: S. Turnock (*Zimbabwe*).

Try by M. Duncan (0-4); penalty goal by M. Grobler (3-4); try by G. Oliver, conv. by P. Dods (3-10); try by D. Butcher, conv. by P. Dods (3-16); try by G. Oliver, conv. by P. Dods (3-22). (H.T.). Penalty goal by P. Dods (3-25); penalty goal by M. Grobler (6-25); try by G. Oliver, conv. by P. Dods (6-31); try by R. Khun (10-31)

Playing in stiffling heat (in the 80s) the Scottish players struggled for breath. It was no surprise,

225

therefore, in the strength-sapping conditions the Scots rather lost their way a bit when leading 25-3, eleven minutes into the second half. The forwards dominated for most of the match – a dramatic transformation from the provincial match, a week previously against Mashonaland, when they had struggled.

The Scots notched up five tries, Greig Oliver scoring a hat-trick and finishing the game as top scorer with 12 points. The Zimbabweans must have viewed his presence with some trepidation – he scored two tries against them in the 1987 Rugby World Cup. Apart from the five tries which counted, Hugh Parker was denied a score when he crossed the line from a scrum pick-up, and Douglas Wyllie seemed certain to score when he was tackled into touch-in-goal.

The Scottish coaches opined that, had they eliminated a plethora of small errors, the score could have been stretched to at least 50 points.

ZIMBABWE 7   SCOTLAND XV 34
Harare
28 May 1988

Zimbabwe: M. Grobler; W. Schultz, M. Letcher, R. Kuhn, J. Kanda; C. Brown, M. Jellicoe*; D. Watson, P. Albasini, N. Valdal, G. Davidson, A. McIntosh, D. Bultendag, M. Carrabott, B. Dawson.
Scotland: P. W. Dods* (*Gala*); M. D. F. Duncan (*W. of Scot.*), R. R. W. Maclean (*Gloucester*), D. S. Wyllie (*Stewart's-Melville*), A. Moore (*Edin. Acad.*); C. M. Chalmers (*Melrose*), G. H. Oliver (*Hawick*); D. J. D. Butcher (*Harlequins*), J. A. Hay (*Hawick*), A. P. Burnell (*Lond. Scot.*), C. A. Gray (*Nottingham*), J. F. Richardson (*Edin. Acad.*), D. J. Turnbull (*Hawick*), H. M. Parker (*Kilmarnock*), K. P. Rafferty (*Heriot's FP*).
Referee: K. Went (*Zimbabwe*).
Dropped goal by C. Chalmers (0-3); penalty goal by P. Dods (0-6); try by H. Parker, conv. by P. Dods (0-12); penalty goal by M. Grobler (3-12); penalty goal by P. Dods (3-15). (H.T.). Penalty goal by P. Dods (3-18); try by K. Rafferty, conv. by P. Dods (3-24); try and conversion by P. Dods (3-30); try by T. Kanda (7-30); try by A. Moore (7-34).

In this, the final match of the tour, the Scottish backs enjoyed good possession from their pack. Peter Dods, the Scots captain, had an outstanding game, scoring 19 points in the match (44 on the tour), his contribution culminating with the try-of-the-match. From a lineout on halfway the ball went from Jeremy Richardson to Paul Burnell to Jim Hay to Craig Chalmers. The stand-off missed out both his centres, his pass being taken by Peter Dods who had come into the line at speed. The fullback cut inside the Zimbabwean left wing and ran on to score a great and memorable try which he duly converted himself.

At the post-match function, Mr W. L. Connon, President of the SRU, stressed the importance that Scotland had placed on the tour: 'The SRU regard this tour as an integral part of our forward planning for the next World Cup in 1991'.

The Scots finished the five-match tour with a one hundred per cent success record.

SCOTLAND 13   AUSTRALIA 32
Murrayfield
19 November 1988

Scotland: A. G. Hastings (*Lond. Scot.*); M. D. F. Duncan (*W. of Scot.*), S. Hastings (*Watsonians*), K. W. Robertson (*Melrose*), I. Tukalo (*Selkirk*); R. I. Cramb (*Harlequins*), G. Armstrong (*Jedforest*); D. M. B. Sole (*Edin. Acad.*), G. J. Callender* (*Kelso*), I. G. Milne (*Heriot's FP*), A. J. Campbell (*Hawick*), D. F. Cronin (*Bath*), D. B. White (*Gala*), I. A. M. Paxton (*Selkirk*), J. Jeffrey (*Kelso*).
Replacement: G. R. Marshall (*Selkirk*) for D. White.
Australia: A. J. Leeds; A. S. Niuqila, M. T. Cook, L. Walker, D. I. Campese; M. P. Lynagh, N. C. Farr-Jones*; R. Lawton, T. A. Lawton, A. J. McIntyre, S. A. G. Cutler, D. Frawley, J. S. Miller, T. Gavin, S. R. Gourlay.
Referee: D. J. Bishop (*New Zealand*).

Try by D. Campese, conv. by M. Lynagh (0-6); penalty goal by M. Lynagh (0-9); penalty goal by A. G. Hastings (3-9); try by T. Lawton, conv. by M. Lynagh (3-15). (H.T.). Try by D. Campese, conv. by M. Lynagh (3-21); try by K. Robertson (7-21); try by S. Gourlay (7-25); penalty goal by M.

Lynagh (7-28); try and conv. by A. G. Hastings (13-28); try by T. Lawton (13-32).

Nothing should be allowed to detract from a win by a very good Australian side but Scotland contributed to their own downfall with some very loose play. In particular, the Scots kicking to touch was very bad and was deservedly punished by the Australians. One plus for Scotland was the international debut of scrumhalf Gary Armstrong who had a fine game. A crowd of 50,000 saw some scintillating rugby, especially from the Wallabies, and with seven tries being scored, the spectators went on their way, happy to have witnessed a lively and exciting match.

SCOTLAND 23   WALES 7
Murrayfield
21 January 1989

Scotland: P. W. Dods (*Gala*); M. D. F. Duncan (*W. of Scot.*), S. Hastings (*Watsonians*) S. R. Lineen (*Boroughmuir*), I. Tukalo (*Selkirk*); C. M. Chalmers (*Melrose*), G. Armstrong (*Jedforest*); D. M. B. Sole (*Edin. Acad.*), K. S. Milne (*Heriot's FP*), I. G. Milne (*Heriot's FP*), J. Jeffrey (*Kelso*), C. A. Gray (*Nottingham*), D. F. Cronin (*Bath*), F. Calder* (*Stewart's-Melville*), D. B. White (*Gala*).
Wales: P. H. Thorburn* (*Neath*); M. R. Hall (*Bridgend*), N. G. Davies (*Llanelli*), J. A. Devereux (*Bridgend*), C. Davies (*Llanelli*); B. Bowen (*Swansea*), J. Griffiths (*Llanelli*); J. Griffiths (*Bridgend*), I. J. Watkins (*Ebbw Vale*); D. Young (*Cardiff*), R. Phillips (*Neath*), K. Moseley (*Pontypool*), P. T. Davies (*Llanelli*), D. Bryant (*Bridgend*), M. Jones (*Neath*).
Replacement: H. Williams-Jones (*S. Wales Police*) for D. Young (51 min.).
Referee: J-C Doulcet (*France*).

Two penalty goals by P. Dods (6-0); try by G. Armstrong (10-0); try by D. White, conv. by P. Dods (16-0); dropped goal by C. Chalmers (19-0). (H.T.). Try by M. Hall (19-4); penalty goal by B. Bowen (19-7); try by C. Chalmers (23-7).

After an absence of four years, Peter Dods was recalled to the full Scotland International side. Craig Chalmers made his debut at stand-off half, and there were first full caps for Sean Lineen, Kenny Milne and Chris Gray, and Finlay Calder captained the Scots for the first time.

The lineouts were dominated by the Scots in the first half but Wales came out on top after the interval. This match saw the half-back pairing of Gary Armstrong and Craig Chalmers for the first time, both players giving a polished performance.

The final scoreline of 23-7 in no way flattered the Scots: they had dominated in most phases of the game, except for the lineouts in the second half, and thoroughly merited their victory.

ENGLAND 12   SCOTLAND 12
Twickenham
4 February 1989

England: J. M. Webb (*Bristol*); R. Underwood (*Leicester*), W. D. C. Carling* (*Harlequins*), S. J. Halliday (*Bath*), C. Oti (*Wasps*); C. R. Andrew (*Wasps*), C. D. Morris (*Liverpool St Helens*); P. A. G. Rendall (*Wasps*), B. C. Moore (*Nottingham*), J. A. Probyn (*Wasps*), W. A. Dooley (*Preston Grasshoppers*), P. J. Ackford (*Harlequins*), M. C. Teague (*Gloucester*), D. Richards (*Leicester*), R. A. Robinson (*Bath*).
Scotland: P. W. Dods (*Gala*); K. W. Robertson (*Melrose*), S. Hastings (*Watsonians*), S. R. P. Lineen (*Boroughmuir*), I. Tukalo (*Selkirk*); C. M. Chalmers (*Melrose*), G. Armstrong (*Jedforest*); D. M. B. Sole (*Edin. Acad.*), K. S. Milne (*Heriot's FP*), A. P. Burnell (*Lond. Scot.*), C. A. Gray (*Nottingham*), D. F. Cronin (*Bath*), J. Jeffrey (*Kelso*), D. B. White (*Gala*), F. Calder* (*Stewart's-Melville*).
Referee: G. Maurette (*France*).

Penalty goal by R. Andrew (3-0); penalty goal by P. Dods (3-3); penalty goal by R. Andrew (6-3); try by J. Jeffrey, conv. by P. Dods (6-9). (H.T.). Penalty goal by P. Dods (6-12); two penalty goals by J. Webb (12-12).

Paul Burnell made his cap debut at prop for Scotland.

England had enough possession to have won several matches but their woeful place-kicking let them down badly. Neither Rob Andrew nor Jonathan Webb was 'on song' with his kicking.

For all their possession and territorial advantage, England could not make progress against the terrier-like tackling of the Scots. The tactical kicking of Scotland's youthful half-backs was an object lesson for the English – and they did far more off limited possession than did Rob Andrew or Dewi Morris from a stream of ball won by the English forwards. English media pundits were afterwards to depict the Scottish breakaway forwards as 'scavengers' – '... piling over the top, coming in on the wrong side and scrabbling about on the floor ... to the very limit of the law ...'. Scavengers or not, the tactics proved to be very effective against this England team. At the after-match press conference, one Irish journalist remarked: 'If England think Scotland are good scavengers, just wait until they meet Ireland in Dublin in a fortnight's time!'

SCOTLAND 37   IRELAND 21
Murrayfield
4 March 1989

Scotland: P. W. Dods (*Gala*); K. W. Robertson (*Melrose*), S. Hastings (*Watsonians*), S. R. P. Lineen (*Boroughmuir*), I. Tukalo (*Selkirk*); C. M. Chalmers (*Melrose*), G. Armstrong (*Jedforest*); D. M. B. Sole (*Edin. Acad.*), K. S. Milne (*Heriot's FP*), A. P. Burnell (*Lond. Scot.*), C. A. Gray (*Nottingham*), D. F. Cronin (*Bath*), J. Jeffrey (*Kelso*), D. B. White (*Gala*), F. Calder* (*Stewart's-Melville*).
Ireland: F. J. Dunlea (*Lansdowne*); M J. Kiernan (*Dolphin*), B. J. Mullin (*Lond. Irish*), D. G. Irwin (*Instonians*), K. D. Crossan (*Instonians*); P. M. Dean (*St Mary's Coll.*), L. F. P. Aherne (*Lansdowne*); T. P. J. Clancy (*Lansdowne*), S. J. Smith (*Ballymena*), J. J. McCoy (*Bangor*), D. G. Lenihan (*Cork Const.*), N. P. Francis (*Lond. Irish*), P. M. Matthews* (*Wanderers*), N. F. Mannion (*Corinthians*), W. D. McBride (*Malone*).
Referee: K. V. J. Fitzgerald (*Australia*).

Penalty goal by P. Dods (3-0); try by I. Tukalo (7-4); try by B. Mullin, conv. by M. Kiernan (7-6); try by J. Jeffrey, conv. by P. Dods (13-6); try by I. Tukalo, conv. by P. Dods (19-6); penalty goal by M. Kiernan (19-9); try by F. Dunlea, conv. by M. Kiernan (19-15); try by K. Crossan, conv. by M. Kiernan (19-21). (H.T.). Two penalty goals by P. Dods (25-21); try by D. Cronin, conv. by P. Dods (31-21); try by I. Tukalo, conv. by P. Dods (37-21).

This, the 100th match between these two nations (including an abandoned fixture in 1885), turned out to be a glorious celebration of rugby – a sort of Hogmanay-cum-Burns Night-cum-St Patrick's Day rolled into one. The players treated the crowd to eight tries – five for Scotland (including an Iwan Tukalo hat-trick) and three for Ireland. Iwan Tukalo's three tries were the first by a Scot, in the championship, since A. C. Wallace against France in 1926.

With the Five Nations international season nearing its rather undistinguished end, this match brought it to belated life with breathtaking exuberance. The Scots and Irish had been labelled as 'scavengers' by the southern rugby scribes and, following this match, the Chairman of the Scotland selectors, Bob Munro, was heard to quip, 'Not bad for a pair of scavengers, eh?'.

Scotland saw their lead of 19-6 turned into a 19-21 deficit by half-time. However, two converted tries and two penalty goals in the second half saw them seal victory over worthy opponents. The Scots may have won the match but the real winners were the game of rugby and the 60,000 spectators who witnessed a match full of free running, excellent handling, good support play and rapport between both sets of forwards and backs.

FRANCE 19   SCOTLAND 3
Parc des Princes, Paris
18 March 1989

France: S. Blanco (*Biarritz*); P. Berot (*Agen*), P. Sella (*Agen*), I. Andrieu (*Nimes*), P. Lagisquet (*Bayonne*); F. Mesnel (*Racing Club*), P. Berbizier* (*Agen*); L. Armary (*Lourdes*), P. Dintrans (*Tarbes*), J-P Garuet (*Lourdes*), D. Erbani (*Agen*), J. Condom (*Biarritz*), A. Carminati (*Beziers*), L. Rodriguez (*Dax*), E. Champ (*Toulon*).
Scotland: P. W. Dods (*Gala*); K. W. Robertson (*Melrose*), S. Hastings (*Watsonians*), S. R. P. Lineen (*Boroughmuir*), I. Tukalo (*Selkirk*); C. M. Chalmers (Melrose), G. Armstrong (*Jedforest*); D. M. B. Sole (*Edin. Acad.*), K. S. Milne (*Heriot's FP*), A. P. Burnell (*Lond. Scot.*), C. A. Gray (*Nottingham*), D. F. Cronin (*Bath*), J. Jeffrey (*Kelso*), F. Calder* (*Stewart's-Melville*), D. B. White (*Gala*).
Referee: O. E. Doyle (*Ireland*).

Penalty goal by P. Dods (0-3); try by P. Berbizier, conv. by P. Berot (6-3); try by S. Blanco (10-3). (H.T.). Penalty goal by P. Berot (13-3); try by F. Lagisquet, conv. by P. Berot (19-3).

The French forwards, using weight advantage to full effect, forced the Scottish pack on the back foot throughout this match. That physical advantage apart, the French had obviously done their homework on the Scottish team and, as Finlay Calder the Scots captain acknowledged afterwards, France had them thoroughly sussed before the game began. The Scottish forwards efforts to drive as they had done against Ireland, were thwarted and nullified by French ambushing and robbing. The French had done their homework on Gary Armstrong, too. The Scottish scrum-half's kicking from the base of the scrum had wreaked havoc against the Irish but Blanco altered his usual line of patrol to snaffle up the kicks in this match.

This game marked the end of a mixed season for Scotland.

Five Nations Table 1988-89

	P	W	D	L	F	A	Fts
France	4	3	0	1	76	47	6
England	4	2	1	1	48	27	5
Scotland	4	2	1	1	75	59	5
Ireland	4	1	0	3	64	92	2
Wales	4	1	0	3	44	82	2

The series try-count makes interesting reading. France scored 11, Scotland 9, Ireland 6, England 4 and Wales 3.

JAPAN 28   SCOTLAND XV 24
Chichibu Stadium, Tokyo
28 May 1989

Japan: T. Yamamoto; T. Nohomuri, E. Kutsuki, S. Hirao*, Y. Yoshida; S. Aoki, M. Horikoshi; O. Ota, T. Fujita, S. Takura, T. Hyashi, A. Oyagi, H. Kajiwara, T. Latu, S. Nakashima.
Scotland XV: C. Glasgow (*Camb. Univ.*); M. D. F. Duncan (*W. of Scot.*), R. R. W. Maclean (*Gloucester*), S. R. P. Lineen (*Boroughmuir*), I. Tukalo (*Selkirk*); D. S. Wyllie (*Stewart's-Melville*), G. H. Oliver (*Hawick*); A. Brewster* (*Stewart's-Melville*), J. A. Hay (*Hawick*), G. D. Wilson (*Boroughmuir*), C. A. Gray (*Nottingham*), D. F. Cronin (*Bath*), D. J. Turnbull (*Hawick*), I. A. M. Paxton (*Selkirk*), G. R. Marshall (*Selkirk*).
Referee: L. J. Peart (*Wales*).

Two penalty goals by T. Yamamoto (6-0); try by Y. Yoshida (10-0); penalty goal by G. Oliver (10-3); try by T. Hyashi (14-3); try by E. Kutsuki, conv. by T. Yamamoto (20-3); penalty goal by G. Oliver (20-6). (H.T.). Try by J. Hay, conv. by G. Oliver (20-12); two penalty goals by G. Oliver (20-18); try by T. Yamamoto (24-18); penalty goal by G. Oliver (24-21); try by T. Nohomuri (28-21); dropped goal by D. Wyllie (28-24).

The Scots were always behind in this poor non-cap Test. It made a disappointing end to what had been, prior to this game, a successful tour, the Scots having won all four of the earlier matches. For the most part, Scotland had taken a young and inexperienced squad of players on the tour and, despite having lost the Test, were pleased at the promise shown. For their part, the Japanese had, unusually, fielded 75 different players in the five games, keeping their best fifteen till last. During the Test, the Japanese had conceded 25 penalties to the Scots 8. Most of the penalties awarded to the Scots were for ruck infringements by their opponents.

SCOTLAND 38   FIJI 17
Murrayfield
28 October 1989

Scotland: A. G. Hastings (*Lond. Scot.*); A. G. Stanger (*Hawick*), S. Hastings (*Watsonians*), S. R. P. Lineen (*Boroughmuir*), I. Tukalo (*Selkirk*); C. M. Chalmers (*Melrose*), C. Armstrong (*Jedforest*); D. M. B. Sole* (*Edin. Acad.*), K. S. Milne (*Heriot's FP*), A. P Burnell (*Lond. Scot.*), C. A. Gray (*Nottingham*), D. F. Cronin (*Bath*), J. Jeffrey (*Kelso*), D. B. White (*Lond. Scot.*),

G. Marshall (*Selkirk*).
Fiji: S. Koroduadua; T. Lovo, L. Erenavula, N. Nadruku, I Waqavatu; W. Serevi, L. Vasuvulagi, M. Tage, S. Naivilawasa, S. Naituku, I. Savai, M Rasari, P. Naruma, A Dere, E. Teleni*.
Referee: P. Robin (France).

Penalty goal by A. G. Hastings (3-0); penalty goal by S. Koroduadua (3-3); penalty goal by A. G. Hastings (6-3); try by K. Milne, conv. by A. G. Hastings (12-3); try by A. Stanger, conv. by A. G. Hastings (18-3); penalty goal by S. Koroduadua (18-6). (H.T.). Try by A. Stanger (22-6); penalty goal by W. Serevi (22-9); try by C. Gray, conv. by A. G. Hastings (28-9); try and conv. by A. G. Hastings (34-9); try by T. Lovo (34-13); try by M. Rosari (34-17); try by I. Tukalo (38-17).

Tony Stanger won his first cap for Scotland and celebrated by scoring two tries. The Scots ran in six tries to two by the visitors.

The Fijians seemed strangely reluctant to play in their usual exuberant style. The luscious Murrayfield turf looked to be tailor-made for the Fijians running game but, in this match, they elected to kick a good deal more than is usual for them. Despite this, they displayed some wonderful handling skills. David Sole, playing his first game as Scotland's captain, led by example: the Fijians found him to be quite a handful. The visitors had a massive weight advantage in the scrum but that proved to be no match against Scottish technique and know-how. It was only in the last quarter that the visitors started to play with something approaching their usual flowing game and, in this period, they scored two tries.

For the first time at Murrayfield, 'The Flower of Scotland' was played and sung instead of the traditional national anthem. David Sole was to comment afterwards that '... it was nice to have an anthem which the players could sing and to which the crowd reacted'.

SCOTLAND 32   ROMANIA 0
Murrayfield
9 December 1989

Scotland: A G. Hastings (*Lond. Scot.*); A. G. Stanger (*Hawick*), S. Hastings (*Watsonians*), S. R. P. Lineen (*Boroughmuir*), W. L. Renwick (*Lond. Scot.*); D. S. Wyllie (*Stewart's-Melville*), G. Armstrong (*Jedforest*); D. M. B. Sole* (*Edin. Acad.*), K. S. Milne (*Heriot's FP*), A. P. Burnell (*Lond. Scot.*), J. Jeffrey (*Kelso*), C. A. Gray (*Nottingham*), D. F. Cronin (*Bath*), F. Calder (*Stewart's-Melville*), D. B. White (*Lond. Scot.*).
Romania: M. Toader (*Dinamo Bucharest*); S. Chirila (*Politechnica Iasi*), A. Lungu (*Dinamo Bucharest*), G. Sava (*Baia Mare*), B. Serban (*Steaua Bucharest*); G. Ignat (*Steaua Bucharest*); D. Neage (*Dinamo Bucharest*); G. Leonte (*Steaua Bucharest*), G. Ion (*Dinamo Bucharest*), G. Dumitrescu (*Steaua Bucharest*), O. Sugar (*Baia Mare*), S. Ciorascu (*Baia Mare*), C. Raducanu (*Dinamo Bucharest*), I. Doja (*Dinamo Bucharest*); H. Dumitras* (*Contactoare Buzau*),
Replacemant: M. Motoi (*Steaua Bucharest*) for O. Sugar.
Referee: S. R. Hilditch (*Ireland*).

Penalty goal by A. G. Hastings (3-0); try by A. Stanger, conv. by A. G. Hastings (9-0). (H.T.). Try by D. White conv. by A. G. Hastings (15-0); try by A. Stanger, conv. by A. G. Hastings (21-0); try by A. Stanger (25-0); penalty goal by A. G. Hastings (28-0); try by D. Sole (32-0).

Despite the margin of victory and the good, overall, display of the Scottish team, the side posed questions for the selectors and coaches about their lineout and midfield work. The defence was solid enough as was the scrummage. The Romanians looked to be a dispirited team and played a dated, old-fashioned style of rugby: they were no match for the Scots. The political and economic state of their country meant that the Romanians had to travel by bus from Heathrow Airport in London to Edinburgh for the game, then start the return journey at 2 a.m. on the morning following the match. The players and officials must have been completely shattered.

Plusses for Scotland were the three tries scored by Tony Stanger who had now scored scored five tries in two internationals.

Following the match, one of the Romanian players, Cristian Reducanu, defected and sought political asylum.

IRELAND 10   SCOTLAND 13
Lansdowne Road
3 February 1990

Ireland: K. Murphy (*Constitution*); M. J. Kiernan (*Dolphin*), B. J. Mullin (*Blackrock Coll.*), D. G. Irwin (*Instonians*), K. D. Crossan (*Instonians*); L. F. P. Aherne (*Lansdowne*), J. J. Fitzgerald (*Young Munster*); J. P. McDonald (*Malone*), D. C. Fitzgerald (*Lansdowne*), P. J. O'Hara (*Sunday's Well*), D. G. Lenihan (*Constitution*), W. A. Anderson* (*Dungannon*), P. M. Matthews (*Wanderers*), N. P. Mannion (*Corinthians*).
Replacement: P. C. Collins (*Lond. Irish*) for P. J. O'Hara.
Scotland: A. G. Hastings (*Lond. Scot.*); A. G. Stanger (*Hawick*), S. Hastings (*Watsonians*), S. R. P. Lineen (*Boroughmuir*), I. Tukalo (*Selkirk*); C. M. Chalmers (*Melrose*), G. Armstrong (*Jedforest*); D. M. B. Sole* (*Edin. Acad.*), K. S. Milne (*Heriot's FP*), Burnell (*Lond. Scot.*), J. Jeffrey (*Kelso*), C. A. Gray (*Nottingham*), D. F. Cronin (*Bath*), F. Calder (*Stewart's-Melville*), D. B. White (*Lond. Scot.*).
Referee: C. Norling (*Wales*).

Penalty goal by M. Kiernan (3-0); try by J. Fitzgerald (7-0). (H.T.). Try by D. White, conv. by C. Chalmers (7-6), penalty goal by M. Kiernan (10-6); pen goal by C. Chalmers (10-9); try by D. White (10-13).

This was an untidy error-strewn match. The wonder is that Scotland won despite missing goal-kicks and try-scoring opportunities, kicking badly and coming out second-best at the lineouts – although they did do better in the second half (14-11 compared with 6-14 before the interval). The things they did do well were to ruck and maul, to drive, and to put in some great tackles. Their support play, too, was exemplary.

SCOTLAND 21   FRANCE 0
Murrayfield
17 February 1990

Scotland: A. G. Hastings (*Lond. Scot.*); A. G. Stanger (*Hawick*), S. Hastings (*Watsonians*), S. R. P. Lineen (*Boroughmuir*), I. Tukalo (*Selkirk*); C. M. Chalmers (*Melrose*), G. Armstrong (*Jedforest*); D. M. B. Sole* (*Edin. Acad.*), K. S. Milne (*Heriot's FP*), A. P. Burnell (*Lond. Scot.*), J. Jeffrey (*Kelso*), C. A. Gray (*Nottingham*), D. F. Cronin (*Bath*), F. Calder (*Stewart's-Melville*), D. B. White (*Lond. Scot.*).
France: S. Blanco (*Biarritz*); P. Hontas (*Biarritz*), P. Sella (*Agen*), F. Mesnel (*Racing Club*), P. Lagisquet (*Bayonne*); D. Camberabero (*Beziers*), H. Sanz (*Narbonne*); M. Pujolle (*Nice*), L. Almary (*Lourdes*), P. Ondarts (*Biarritz*), J-M Lhermet (*Montferrand*), T. Devergie (*Nimes*), O. Roumat (*Dax*), A. Carminati (*Beziers*), L. Rodriguez* (*Dax*).
Referee: F. A. Howard (*England*).

Penalty goal by A. G. Hastings (3-0). (H.T.). Penalty goal by C. Chalmers (6-0); try by F. Calder, conv. by C. Chalmers (12-0); try by I. Tukalo, conv. by C. Chalmers (18-0); penalty goal by C. Chalmers (21-0).

This was France's sixth succesive defeat at Murryafield: they had last won there in 1978. That they were beaten again came about in no small measure because of the unscheduled departure of back-row forward A. Carminati who committed one indiscretion too many. The referee had every right and no option but to send the player off for persistent stamping.

The Scots had the advantage of a strong wind in the first half. Unfortunately for France it subsided considerably following the interval. That, plus the fact that they were 0-3 down when Carminati made his departure, thus leaving their pack a man light, did nothing to help their cause. It was a game the French will want to forget – none more so than their illustrious fullback Serge Blanco who had a nightmare of a match with a series of ball-fumbles and wrong-option taking.

With New Zealander Colin Meads having been dismissed from the field of play when the All Blacks played Scotland in 1967, Carminati became only the second player to have been sent off at Murrayfield. Not an incident to be proud of.

International Rugby Union

WALES 9   SCOTLAND 13
Cardiff Arms Park
3 March 1990

Wales: P. H. Thorburn (*Neath*); M. R. Hall (*Cardiff*), M. G. Ring (*Cardiff*), A. G. Bateman (*Neath*), A. Emyr (*Swansea*); D. W. Evans (*Cardiff*), R. N. Jones* (*Swansea*); B. R. Williams (*Neath*), K. H. Phillips (*Neath*), J. D. Pugh (*Neath*), M. A. Perego (*Llanelli*), G. O. Llewellyn (*Neath*), R. G. Collins (*Cardiff*), M. A. Jones (*Neath*).
Replacement: A. Clement (*Swansea*) for D. Evans.
Scotland: A. G. Hastings (*Lond. Scot.*); A. G. Stanger (*Hawick*), S. Hastings (*Watsonians*), S. R. P. Lineen (*Boroughmuir*), I. Tukalo (*Selkirk*); C. M. Chalmers (*Melrose*), G. Armstrong (*Jedforest*); D. M. B. Sole* (*Edin. Acad.*), K. S. Milne (*Heriot's FP*), A. P. Burnell (*Lond. Scot.*), J. Jeffrey (*Kelso*), C. A. Gray (*Nottingham*), D. F. Cronin (*Bath*), F. Calder (*Stewart's-Melville*), D. B. White (*Lond. Scot.*).
Referee: R. Hourquet (*France*).

Try by D. Cronin (0-4); penalty goal by P. Thorburn (3-4); two penalty goals by C. Chalmers (3-10). (H.T.). Try by A. Emyr, conv. by P. Thorburn (9-10); penalty goal by C. Chalmers (9-13).

The Neath club provided seven players plus the coach for the Welsh XV. The Scots had more of the ball than the Welsh and this should have resulted in far greater control than was evident in this match. This was a poor Welsh team by the standards that nation had set themselves in seasons past.

Persistent Welsh hammering at the Scottish defence brought absolutely no dividend whatsoever: the hard steely defenders that the Scots are, stood firm. This Welsh team lacked sparkle, invention and class: they were completely devoid of ideas.

Following this result, Murrayfield beckoned the Scots where they were due to meet England a fortnight later when the Calcutta Cup, the Triple Crown, the Grand Slam, and the Five Nations Championship would all be at stake.

SCOTLAND 13   ENGLAND 7
Murrayfield
17 March 1990

Scotland: A. G. Hastings (*Lond. Scot.*); A. G. Stanger (*Hawick*), S. Hastings (*Watsonians*), S. R. P. Lineen (*Boroughmuir*), I. Tukalo (*Selkirk*); C. M. Chalmers (*Melrose*), G. Armstrong (*Jedforest*); D. M. B. Sole* (*Edin. Acad.*), K. S. Milne (*Heriot's FP*), A. P. Burnell (*Lond. Scot.*), C. A. Gray (*Nottingham*), J. Jeffrey (*Kelso*), D. B. White (*Lond. Scot.*), F. Calder (*Stewart's-Melville*).
Replacement: D. J. Turnbull (*Hawick*) for D. White (13 min.).
England: S. D. Hodgkinson (*Nottingham*); S. J. Halliday (*Bath*), W. D. C. Carling* (*Harlequins*), J. C. Guscott (*Bath*), R. Underwood (*Leicester*); C. R. Andrew (*Wasps*), R. J. Hill (*Bath*); P. A. G. Rendall (*Wasps*), B. C. Moore (*Nottingham*), J. A. Probyn (*Wasps*), W. A. Dooley (*Preston Grasshoppers*), E. J. Ackford (*Harlequins*), M. G. Skinner (*Harlequins*), M. C. Teague (*Gloucester*), P. J. Winterbottom (*Harlequins*).
Replacement: M. Bailey (*Wasps*) for J. Guscott.
Referee: D. J. Bishop (*New Zealand*).

Two penalty goals by C. Chalmers (6-0); try by J. Guscott (6-4); penalty goal by C. Chalmers (9-4). (H-T). Try by A. Stanger (13-4); penalty goal by S. Hodgkinson (13-7).

With the Calcutta Cup, the mythical Triple Crown and Grand Slam and the championship of the Five Nations tournament all hinging on the outcome of this game, it was not surprising that the pre-match hype reached previously unknown levels. Some of the newspaper headlines which appeared during the build-up to the game seemed as if they were trying to stretch public credulity beyond the bounds of reasonable belief:

'Tally Ho' The Shark plans to fox England' (Edinburgh Evening News).

'Scots space invaders hold the key in close encounter' (The Observer).

By all reports the England side turned up for the game with what was to be proved ill-advised and extravagant cockiness. The eighty minutes of play served to verify the folly of their attitude.

One television pundit (a former Scottish international) opined, on the eve of the match, that the Scots would charge out of the Murrayfield tunnel and on to the pitch at '100 miles per hour'. In the event, the Scottish team walked on to the pitch with slow determined steps. Measured and dignified,

232

it perhaps presaged what was to follow. The singing of 'The Flower of Scotland' by the Scots in the packed stadium steeled further the players determination and sent the adrenaline coursing through their veins. The game started with the Scots knowing that only a win would secure the championship and all else that was at stake. A draw would see England crowned as champions because of their superior points differential.

Two early penalty goals by Craig Chalmers settled the Scots but Jeremy Guscott scored a wonderful try to make the score 6-4 – this being England's first try at Murrayfield in 10 years. Another Chalmers penalty goal before half-time stretched the lead to 9-4.

That the English were rattled was plain for all to see. Scotland's opening onslaught had their opponents reeling and it was not until after Guscott's try that the England team began to inflict sustained pressure on the Scots. A series of scrummages close to the home line saw England try all they knew to break down the Scots defence but they found the dark blue line to be impenetrable.

In the first minute of the second half the Scots scored a superb try. Gary Armstrong gave to Gavin Hastings who, just before being bundled into touch, chipped a high ball ahead. The English defence was shredded as Tony Stanger and Finlay Calder steamed through in pursuit of the ball, the winger using his height to stretch for it and touch down in the corner (13-4). This psychological blow proved to be fatal for the English cause, a second half penalty being their only consolation. The England team tried everything they knew, pressurising the Scots, forcing them to defend like demons. Rob Andrew's precision kicking kept the home side on the defensive for long spells but the dark blue line held firm: the spoils of the conflict were Scotland's.

Following the match, some of the newspaper headlines were as entertaining as the match itself:

'Sole's decision to take wind quickly justified' (The Scotsman).

'A grand slamming from the Scots' The Independent).

'Scotland slam those of little faith' (Daily Telegraph). 'Scotland play their tune of glory' (Independent on Sunday).

'Scotland find crowning glory to leave England slammed' (Sunday Telegraph).

'Savouring the Sassenach surrender' (Sunday Telegraph).

'England weren't playing a team, they were playing an entire nation' (Edinburgh Evening News).

Perhaps the last headline is nearer the truth than one might suspect.

Five Nations Championship 1989-90

	P	W	L	D	F	A	Pts
Scotland	4	4	0	0	60	26	8
England	4	3	1	0	90	26	6
France	4	2	2	0	67	78	4
Ireland	4	1	3	0	36	75	2
Wales	4	0	4	0	42	90	0

NEW ZEALAND 31   SCOTLAND 16
Carisbrook, Dunedin
16 June 1990

New Zealand: K. Crowley; J. Kirwan, J. Stanley, W. Little, T. Wright; G. Fox, G. Bachop; S. McDowell, S. Fitzpatrick, R. Loe, I. Jones, G. Whetton, A. Whetton, M. Brewer, W. Shelford*.

Scotland: A. G. Hastings (*Lond. Scot.*); A. G. Stanger (*Hawick*), S. Hastings (*Watsonians*), S. R. P. Lineen (*Boroughmuir*), I. Tukalo (*Selkirk*); C. M. Chalmers (*Melrose*), G. Armstrong (*Jedforest*); D. M. B. Sole* (*Edin. Acad.*), J. Allan (*Edin. Acad.*), I. G. Milne (*Heriot's FP*), C. A. Gray (*Nottingham*), D. F. Cronin (*Bath*), J. Jeffrey (*Kelso*), D. B. White (*Lond. Scot.*), F. Calder (*Stewart's-Melville*).

Referee: C. J. High (*England*).

Penalty goal by G. Fox (3-0); try by S. Lineen, conv. by A. G. Hastings (3-6); try by K. Crowley, conv. by G. Fox (9-6); try by C. Gray (9-10); try and conv. by G. Fox (15-10). (H.T.). Try by I. Jones, conv. by G. Fox (21-10); try by J. Kirwan (25-10); try by J. Kirwan, conv. by G. Fox (31-10); try by

D. Sole, conv. by A. G. Hastings (31-16).

Prior to this encounter, the All Blacks had played 19 successive tests without being defeated. Despite Scotland's promising start, this match was to give the New Zealanders their twentieth victory on the trot. Scotland's brave and committed performance, especially in the first half, was not enough, despite their ferocious tackling and sterling defence. The All Blacks rugby machine rumbled on. Two Scottish errors cost them dear: the first gifted to Grant Fox his first try for his country, and the second saw Ian Jones punish a misfield to the full.

The Scots gave of their best but it was not enough to secure a victory over the All Blacks – despite more errors than usual from the latter.

NEW ZEALAND 21   SCOTLAND 18
Eden Park, Auckland
23 June 1990

New Zealand: K. Crowley; J. Kirwan, J. Stanley, W. Little, T. Wright; G. Fox, G. Bachop; S. McDowell, S. Fitzpatrick, R. Loe, I. Jones, G. Whetton, A. Whetton, W. Shelford*, R. Brewer.
Scotland: A. G. Hastings (*Lond. Scot.*); A. G. Stanger (*Hawick*), S. Hastings (*Watsonians*), S. R. P. Lineen (*Boroughmuir*), A. Moore (*Edin. Acad.*); C. M. Chalmers (*Melrose*), G. Armstrong (*Jedforest*); D. M. B. Sole* (*Edin. Acad.*), K. S. Milne (*Heriot's FP*), I. G. Milne (*Heriot's FP*), C. A. Gray (*Nottingham*), D. F. Cronin (*Bath*), J. Jeffrey (*Kelso*), D. B. White (*Lond. Scot.*), F. Calder (*Stewart's-Melville*)
Replacement: G. H. Oliver (*Hawick*) for G. Armstrong (73 min.).
Referee: W. D. Bevan (*Wales*).

Two penalty goals by A. G. Hastings (0-6); penalty goal by G. Fox (3-6); try by A. G. Stanger, conv. by A. G. Hastings (3-12); try by R. Loe, conv. by G. Fox (9-12); try by A. Moore, conv. by A. G. Hastings (9-18); penalty goal by G. Fox (12-18). (H.T.). Three penalty goals by G. Fox (21-18).

In this second Test Match, Scotland more than held their own against the All Blacks and won the try-count by 2-1 – all to no avail. Grant Fox, the New Zealand stand-off was in deadly kicking form. He kicked six goals from six attempts – five penalty goals and a conversion. Scotland's coach Ian McGeechan, remarked: 'With Grant Fox among the opposition, give away a penalty within range of your posts and you give away three points, give away a try and it's six.

A controversial point in the game, one which was to provide discussion long after no-side, came when the Scots were leading 18-15. Gavin Hastings fielded a huge punt from K. Crowley, the New Zealand fullback. In trying to change direction, the Scot slipped and was tackled by All Black Mike Brewer. The referee penalised the Scot for not releasing the ball. The controversial question was: 'was Brewer onside when he made the tackle?' Brewer was well in front of Crowley when the latter kicked the ball and, to be onside, Brewer should have been not within ten metres of Gavin Hastings or else the place where the ball had pitched. Had his position met either requirement? The second point was: had the ball-carrying opponent (Gavin Hastings) run five metres?

Controversy or not, Grant Fox kicked the equalising three points and went on to kick the winning three – and those points put the All Blacks ahead for the first time in the match with but ten minutes left for play. So near and yet ... the Scots had come ever so close to defeating New Zealand for the first time in 15 tests stretching back to 1905. The Scots were really beaten by the boot of one Grant Fox who kicked 17 points. The headline in *The Guardian* which read 'Scots hounded by Fox' was more of a truth than hyperbolic rhetoric.

SCOTLAND 49   ARGENTINA 3
Murrayfield
10 November 1990

Scotland: A. G. Hastings (*Watsonians*); A. G. Stanger (*Hawick*), S. Hastings (*Watsonians*), S. R. P. Lineen (*Boroughmuir*), A. Moore (*Edin. Acad.*); C. M. Chalmers (*Melrose*), G. Armstrong (*Jedforest*); D. M. B. Sole* (*Edin. Acad.*), K. S. Milne (*Heriot's FP*), A. P. Burnell (*Lond. Scot.*), J. Jeffrey (*Kelso*), C. A. Gray (*Nottingham*), G. W. Weir (*Melrose*), G. A. E. Buchanan-Smith (*Heriot's FP*), G. R. Marshall (*Selkirk*).
Argentina: G. P. Angaut (*La Plata*); D. Cuesta Silva (*SIC*), L. Arbizu (*Belgrano Ath.*) S. Meson (*Tucuman*), M. Allen (*CASI*); H. Porta* (*Banco Nacion*), R. H. Crexell (*Jockey Club Rosario*); M. Aguirre (*Alumni*), A. Cubelli (*Belgrano Ath.*), D. M. Cash

234

(*SIC*), P. Garreton (*Tucuman Univ.*), G. Llanes (*La Plata*), P. Sporieder (*Curupaytí*), E. Ezcurra (*Newman*), M. J. S. Bertranou (*Los Tordos*).
Replacement: A. Scoini (*Alumni*) for H. Porta (16 min.).
Referee: F. Burger (*South Africa*).

Try by A. Stanger (4-0); penalty goal by A. G. Hastings (7-0); try by A. Moore, conv. by A. G. Hastings (13-0); try by K. Milne (17-0). (H.T.). Penalty goal by S. Meson (17-3); try by A. Stanger, conv. by A. G. Hastings (23-3); try by G. Armstrong (27-3); try by C. Gray, conv. by A. G. Hastings (33-3); try by A. G. Hastings (37-3); try by K. Milne, conv. by A. G. Hastings (43-3); try by C. Chalmers, conv. by A. G. Hastings (49-3).

The winning margin of 46 points set a new record for Scotland. Gavin Hastings' haul of 17 points for the match (1 try, 5 conversions, 1 penalty goal) promoted him to become Scotland's leading points scorer (286 in 26 matches). The previous best had been set by A. R. Irvine (Heriot's FP), 273 in 51 appearances. The gilt was removed somewhat by the poor quality of opposition supplied by Argentina although it should be remembered that, from four penalty attempts, Meson hit the posts with three of them.

A win – but not an entirely satisfactory one.

FRANCE 15   SCOTLAND 9
Parc des Princes, Paris
19 January 1991

France: S. Blanco* (*Biarritz*); J-B Lafond (*Racing Club*), F. Mesnel (*Racing Club*), D. Charvet (*Racing Club*), P. Lagisquet (*Bayonne*); D. Camberabero (*Béziers*), P. Berbizier (*Agen*); G. Lascubé (*Agen*), P. Marocco (*Montferrand*), P. Ondarts (*Biarritz*), X. Blond (*Racing Club*), M. Tachdjian (*Racing Club*), O. Roumat (*Dax*), M. Cecillon (*Bourgoin*), L. Cabannes (*Racing Club*).
Scotland: A. G. Hastings (*Watsonians*); A. G. Stanger (*Hawick*), S. Hastings (*Watsonians*), S. R. P. Lineen (*Boroughmuir*), A. Moore (*Edin. Acad.*); C. M. Chalmers (*Melrose*), G. Armstrong (*Jedforest*); D. M. B. Sole* (*Edin. Acad.*), K. S. Milne (*Heriot's FP*), A. P. Burnell (*Lond. Scot.*), D. J. Turnbull (*Hawick*), C. A. Gray (*Nottingham*), D. F. Cronin (*Bath*), J. Jeffrey (*Kelso*), D. B. White (*Lond. Scot.*).
Referee: E. F. Morrison (*England*).

Penalty goal by D. Camberabero (3-0); dropped goal by C. Chalmers (3-3); dropped goal by S. Blanco (6-3); penalty goal by D. Camberabero (9-3). (H.T.). Two penalty goals by C. Chalmers (9-9); two dropped goals by D. Camberabero (15-9).

Starting a new international season as Five Nations champions, this was a disappointing performance from the Scots. The game was remarkable in that four dropped goals were scored (three to France and one to Scotland): this was most unusual in any match, let alone an international. Otherwise, an undistinguished game which France thoroughly deserved to win. Serge Blanco became the world's most capped player in this, his 82nd appearance for France.

SCOTLAND 32   WALES 12
Murrayfield
2 February 1991

Scotland: A. G. Hastings (*Watsonians*); A. G. Stanger (*Hawick*), S. Hastings (*Watsonians*), S. R. P. Lineen (*Boroughmuir*), A. Moore (*Edin. Acad.*), C. M. Chalmers (*Melrose*), G. Armstrong (*Jedforest*); D. M. B. Sole* (*Edin. Acad.*), J. Allan (*Edin. Acad.*), A. P. Burnell (*Lond. Scot.*), D. J. Turnbull (*Hawick*), C. A. Gray (*Nottingham*), D. F. Cronin (*Bath*), J. Jeffrey (*Kelso*), D. B. White (*Lond. Scot.*).
Replacement: K. S. Milne (*Heriot's FP*) for J. Allan (47 min.).
Wales: P. H. Thorburn* (*Neath*); I. Evans (*Llanelli*), M. Ring (*Cardiff*), S. Gibbs (*Neath*), S. P. Ford (*Cardiff*); N. R. Jenkins (*Pontypridd*), R. Jones (*Swansea*); B. Williams (*Neath*), K. Phillips (*Neath*), P. Knight (*Pontypridd*), A. J. Carter (*Newport*), G D. Llewellyn (*Neath*), G. O. Llewellyn (*Neath*), G. M. George (*Newport*), P. Arnold (*Swansea*).
Replacement: A. Clement (*Swansea*) for P. Thorburn (67 min.).
Referee: D. J. Bishop (*New Zealand*).

Penalty goal by C. Chalmers (3-0); penalty goal by P. Thorburn (3-3); try by D. White (7-3); try by G. Armstrong, conv. by C. Chalmers (13-3); penalty goal by P. Thorburn (13-6); dropped goal by C. Chalmers (16-6). (H.T.). Try by C. Chalmers (20-6); try by S. Ford, conv. by P. Thorburn (20-12); two penalty goals by A. G. Hastings (26-12); try by D. White, conv. by A. G. Hastings (32-12).

This 95th international between Scotland and Wales saw the Scots notch up their 41st victory in the series, against Wales' 52 wins with 2 matches drawn. In a rampant Scottish performance several new records were set: (a) it was Scotland's largest-ever winning margin against Wales; (b) both fullbacks, each scoring 8 points, increased their already-held points scoring records for their respective countries: Gavin Hastings having scored 294 points for Scotland and Paul Thorburn 288 for Wales.

It had been an overwhelming Scottish victory with the Scots having given the most devastating display of forward power that they had shown for many years. The team had shaken off the defeat by France and, following this victory, were now fired up for the visit to Twickenham in two weeks time.

ENGLAND 21   SCOTLAND 12
Twickenham
16 February 1991

England: S. D. Hodgkinson (*Nottingham*); N. J. Heslop (*Orrell*), W. D. C. Carling* (*Harlequins*), J. C. Guscott (*Bath*), R. Underwood (*Leicester*); C. R. Andrew (*Wasps*), R. J. Hill (*Bath*); J. Leonard (*Harlequins*), B. C. Moore (*Harlequins*), J. A. Probyn (*Wasps*), P. J. Ackford (*Harlequins*), W. A. Dooley (*Preston Grasshoppers*), M. C. Teague (*Gloucester*), P. J. Winterbottom (*Harlequins*), D. Richards (*Leicester*)
Scotland: A. G. Hastings (*Watsonians*); A. G. Stanger (*Hawick*), S. Hastings (*Watsonians*), S. R. P. Lineen (*Boroughmuir*), A. Moore (*Edin. Acad.*); C. M. Chalmers (*Melrose*), G. Armstrong (*Jedforest*); D. M. B. Sole* (*Edin. Acad.*), K. S. Milne (*Heriot's FP*), A. P. Burnell (*Lond. Scot.*), C. A. Gray (*Nottingham*), D. F. Cronin (*Bath*), D. J. Turnbull (*Hawick*), J. Jeffrey (*Kelso*), D. B. White (*Lond. Scot.*).
Referee: S. R. Hilditch (*Ireland*).

Two penalty goals by S. Hodgkinson (6-0); two penalty goals by C. Chalmers (6-6); Penalty goal by S. Hodgkinson (9-6). (H.T.). Try by N. Heslop, conv. by S. Hodgkinson (15-6); two penalty goals by C. Chalmers (15-12); two penalty goals by N. Hodgkinson (21-12).

Just as the Scottish pack had dominated in the previous international against Wales, so the England pack outplayed the Scots in this match. Following their victory over the Welsh, this was a disappointing performance by the Scots. Surprisingly, with the scores at 6-6, 9-6 and 15-12, Scotland were commendably close but they were always playing catch-up and never at any stage really looked like penetrating the English defence. That all Scotland's points came from the boot of Craig Chalmers, who scored four penalty goals, tells its own story.

Following this match, England had their sights on Triple Crown and, possibly, the Grand Slam. Scotland were left to lick their wounds.

SCOTLAND 28   IRELAND 25
Murrayfield
16 March 1991

Scotland: A. G. Hastings (*Watsonians*); A. G. Stanger (*Hawick*), S. Hastings (*Watsonians*), S. R. P. Lineen (*Boroughmuir*), I. Tukalo (*Selkirk*); C. M. Chalmers (*Melrose*), G. Armstrong (*Jedforest*); D. M. B. Sole* (*Edin. Acad.*), J. Allan (*Edin. Acad.*), A. P. Burnell (*Lond. Scot.*), C. A. Gray (*Nottingham*), D. F. Cronin (*Bath*), D. J. Turnbull (*Hawick*), D. B. White (*Lond. Scot.*), J. Jeffrey (*Kelso*)
Replacement: P. W. Dods (*Gala*) for I. Tukalo (32 min.).
Ireland: J. E. Staples (*Lond. Irish*); S. P. Geoghegan (*Lond. Irish*), B. J. Mullin (*Blackrock Coll.*), D. M. Curtis (*Lond. Irish*), K. D. Crossan (*Instonians*); B. A. Smith (*Leicester*), R. Saunders* (*Lond. Irish*); J. J. Fitzgerald (*Young Munster*), S. J. Smith (*Ballymena*), D. C. Fitzgerald (*Lansdowne*), B. J. Rigney (*Greystones*), N. P. J. Francis (*Blackrock Coll.*), P. M. Matthews (*Wanderers*), B. F. Robinson (*Ballymena*), G. F. Hamilton (*N. of Ireland*).

Replacement: K. J. Murphy (*Cork Const.*) for J. Staples (70 min.).
Referee: K. V. J. Fitzgerald (*Australia*).

Two penalty goals by C. Chalmers (6-0); try by K. Crossan, conv. by B. Smith (6-6); dropped goal by B. Smith (6-9); penalty goal by A. G. Hastings (9-9); try by B. Robinson, conv. by B. Smith (9-15); try by A. G. Hastings, conv. by C. Chalmers (15-15). (H.T.). Try by S. Geoghegan (15-19); try by A. Stanger, conv. by C. Chalmers (21-19); penalty goal by C. Chalmers (24-19); try by S. Hastings (28-19); try by B. Mullin, conv. by B. Smith (28-25).

For a team to concede four tries (three of them converted) and still win the match takes a bit of doing and believing – but Scotland contrived to do just that in this game. Both countries had had a poor Five Nations series: this final match put Scotland in third place with four points and Ireland in fourth place with only one point. Compared with their winning of the championship the previous season, Scotland had had a particularly lean time. Ireland were still team-building.

Scotland twice came from behind to go on to win but the Irish won many admirers for their swashbuckling style of play.

The after-match comment by the Irish coach, Ciaran Fitzgerald, perhaps summed up a somewhat confused but thrilling match: 'If I thought morale was dropping and defeats were weighing heavily on people, I would be concerned. But that is not the case. I would be concerned if they were concerned, but they are not concerned, so we do not concern ourselves either'.

Some newspaper headlines said it all:
'To Scotland the spoils but to Ireland the glory' (Sunday Times).
'Ireland do everything but win' (The Times).

Five Nations Championship 1990-91

	P	W	L	D	F	A	Pts
England	4	4	0	0	83	44	8
France	4	3	1	0	91	46	6
Scotland	4	2	2	0	81	73	4
Ireland	4	0	3	1	66	86	1
Wales	4	0	3	1	42	114	1

UNITED STATES OF AMERICA 12   SCOTLAND XV 41
Hartford, Connecticut
18 May 1991

U.S.A.:R. Nelson; R. Lewis, J. Burke, K. Higgins, C. Williams; M. De Jong, B. Daily; C. Lippert, A. Flay, N. Mottram, K. Swords, W. Leversee, A. Ridnell, B. Vizard*, R. Farley.
Replacement: C. O'Brien for C. Williams (71 min.).
Scotland: P. W. Dods (*Gala*); A. G. Stanger (*Hawick*), D. S. Wyllie* (*Stewart's-Melville*), A. G. Shiel (*Melrose*), M. Moncrieff (*Gala*); C. M. Chalmers (*Melrose*), G. H. Oliver (*Hawick*); D. F. Milne (*Heriot's FP*), J. Allan (*Edin. Acad.*), A. G. J. Watt (*GH-K*), A. E. D. Macdonald (*Heriot's FP*), G. W. Weir (*Melrose*), D. J. Turnbull (*Hawick*), S. J. Reid (*Boroughmuir*), G. R. Marshall (*Selkirk*).
Referee: G. Gadjovich (*Canada*).

In this first-ever rugby Test between the two countries, Scotland scored five successful penalty awards by Peter Dods and these were answered by four from M. De Jong (12-15); try by A. Macdonald (12-19); try by S. Reid (12-23); try by A. Stanger, conv. by P. Dods (12-29); try by A. Stanger, conv. by P. Dods (12-35); try by S. Reid, conv. by P. Dods (12-41).

Scotland dominated for most of the game which purveyed an injury-strewn first half. The Scotland XV scored five tries to the home side's nil and won the lineouts 22-12. Three of the Scottish tries were scored in the final ten minutes by which time the American 'Eagles' were a beaten side.

CANADA 24 SCOTLAND XV 19
Saint John, New Brunswick
25 May 1991

Canada: M. Wyatt*; S. Gray, C. Stewart, J. Locky, T. Woods; G. Rees, J. Graf; E. Evans, M. Cardinal, D. Jackart, A. Charron, N. Hadley, G. Mackinnon, G. Ennis, D. Brean.
Replacement: I. Gordon for A. Charron (76 min.).
Scotland XV: P. W. Dods (*Gala*); A. G. Stanger (*Hawick*), D. S. Wyllie* (*Stewart's-Melville*), A. G. Shiel (*Melrose*), M. Moncrieff (*Gala*); C. M. Chalmers (*Melrose*), G. H. Oliver (*Hawick*); D. F. Milne (*Heriot's FP*), J. Allan (*Edin. Acad.*), A. G. J. Watt (*GH-K*), A. E. D. Macdonald (*Heriot's FP*), G. W. Weir (*Melrose*), D. J. Turnbull (*Hawick*), S. J. Reid (*Boroughmuir*), R. Kirkpatrick (*Jedforest*).
Referee: S. V. Griffiths (*England*).

Two penalty goals by P. Dods and two by M. Wyatt (6-6). (H.T.). Four penalty goals by M. Wyatt (24-6); penalty goal by P. Dods (24-9); try by S. Reid, conv. by P. Dods (24-15); try by A. Stanger (24-19).

In this first-ever Test between the countries, Scotland disappointed by committing so many errors – but full marks to Canada for a fine aggresive display of spirited and ardent rugby. Canada's fullback, Mark Wyatt, made eight successful penalty kicks – a world record which may not be ratified because of this being a non-cap match.

The Canadians were very successful at robbing initial Scottish possession.

This was the only reverse suffered by the Scots on this tour.

ROMANIA 18 SCOTLAND 12
23 August Stadium, Bucharest
31 August 1991

Romania: D. Piti; C. Sasu, G. Sava, A. Lungu, L. Colceriu; F. Ion, D. Neaga; G. Leonte, G. Ion, C. Stan, C. Cojocariu, S. Ciorascu, G. Dinu, H. Dumitras*, A. Guranescu.
Scotland: P. W. Dods (*Gala*); A. G. Stanger (*Hawick*), S. R. P. Lineen (*Boroughmuir*), D. S. Wyllie (*Stewart's-Melville*), I. Tukalo (*Selkirk*); C. M. Chalmers (*Melrose*), G. Armstrong (*Jedforest*); D. M. B. Sole* (*Edin. Acad.*), J. Allan (*Edin. Acad.*), A. P. Burnell (*Lond. Scot.*), G. W. Weir (*Melrose*), D. F. Cronin (*Bath*), D. J. Turnbull (*Hawick*), D. B. White (*Lond. Scot.*), F. Calder (*Stewart's-Melville*).
Referee: A. Ceccon (*France*).

Penalty goal by P. Dods (0-3); try by S. Ciorascu, conv. by P. Ion (6-3); penalty goal by P. Dods (6-6); penalty goal by P. Ion (9-6). (H.T.). Try by C. Sasu, conv. by F. Ion (15-6); penalty goal by P. Ion (18-6); try by I. Tukalo, conv. by P. Dods (18-12).

This was the first of four matches arranged by the S.R.U. as a build-up to the forthcoming Rugby World Cup series of matches. That the Scots were rusty and short of match practice was lamentably clear: they were ponderous in the pack and showed indifferent form at half-back. In contrast, the Romanians were sharp and showed flair and adventure in their play.

The final scoreline did not accurately reflect the Romanians superiority. Had they had a reliable goal-kicker their points score could have been embarrassingly high for the Scots.

SCOTLAND 16 BARBARIANS 16
Murrayfield
7 September 1991

Scotland: A. G. Hastings (*Watsonians*); A. G. Stanger (*Hawick*), S. Hastings (*Watsonians*), A. G. Shiel (*Melrose*), M. Moncrieff (*Gala*); C. M. Chalmers (*Melrose*), G. H. Oliver (*Hawick*); D. M. B. Sole* (*Edin. Acad.*), K. S. Milne (*Heriot's FP*), K. P. Burnell (*Lond. Scot.*), D. F. Cronin (*Bath*), G. W. Weir (*Melrose*), J. Jeffrey (*Kelso*), G. R. Marshall (*Selkirk*), F. Calder (*Stewart's-Melville*).
Replacement: D. B. White (*Lond. Scot.*) for G. Marshall (75 min.).

Barbarians: A. Joubert (*Old Greys*); A. Harriman (*Harlequins*), S. Pierce (*N. Shore*), E. Blanc (*Racing Club*), T. Underwood (*Camb. Univ.*); S. Barnes* (*Bath*), P. Berbizier (*Agen*); G. Kebble (*Durban Collegians*), T. Lawton (*Durban HSOB*), E. Rodriguez (*Warringah*), A. Macdonald (*Heriot's FP*), A. Copsey (*Llanelli*), W. Bartmann (*Durban Harlequins*), K. Tapper (*Enkoping*), E. Rush (*Otahuhu*).
Replacements: Q. Daniels (*Cape Town Police*) for T. Underwood (65 min.); C. Stephens (*Llanelli*) for A. Joubert (77 min.).
Referee: F. A. Howard (England).

Try by E. Rush (0-4); penalty goal by C. Chalmers (3-4); try by E. Rush, conv. by S. Barnes (3-10); penalty goal by C. Chalmers (6-10). (H.T.). Try by K. Milne (10-10); try by F. Calder, conv. by C. Chalmers (16-10); try by Q. Daniels, conv. by S. Barnes (16-16).

This second match in the pre-Rugby World Cup preparations found the Scots to be sharper and more attuned than they were against Romania. Despite giving away a lot of weight to the Barbarians, the Scottish pack did very well and did not buckle although the scrummage count went 29-13 against them.

RUGBY WORLD CUP – POOL 2
The second competition for the Webb Ellis Trophy
in France, England, Ireland, Scotland and Wales

SCOTLAND 47 JAPAN 9
Murrayfield
5 October 1991

Scotland: A. G. Hastings (*Watsonians*); A. G. Stanger (*Hawick*), S. Hastings (*Watsonians*), S. R. P. Lineen (*Boroughmuir*), I. Tukalo (*Selkirk*); C. M. Chalmers (*Melrose*), G. Armstrong (*Jedforest*); D. M. B. Sole* (*Edin. Acad.*), J. Allan (*Edin. Acad.*), A. P. Burnell (*Lond. Scot.*), C. A. Gray (*Nottingham*), G. W. Weir (*Melrose*), J. Jeffrey (*Kelso*), D. B. White (*Lond. Scot.*), F. Calder (*Stewart's-Melville*).
Replacements: D. S. Wyllie (*Stewart's-Melville*) for C. Chalmers (68 min.); D. F. Milne (*Heriot's FP*) for D. Sole (73 min.).
Japan: T. Hosokawa; T. Masuho, E. Kutsuki, S. Hirao*, Y. Yoshida; K. Matsuo, W. Murata; C. Ohta, M. Kunda, M. Takura, T. Hayashi, E. Tifaga, H. Kajihara, S. Latu, S. Nakashima.
Referee: E. F. Morrison (England).

Try by A. G. Hastings (4-0); penalty goal by C. Chalmers (7-0); dropped goal by T. Hosokawa (7-3); try by A. Stanger (11-3); try by C. Chalmers, conv. by A. G. Hastings (17-3); try and conv. by T. Hosokawa (17-9). (H.T.). Penalty try, conv. by A. G. Hastings (23-9); two penalty goals by A. G. Hastings (29-9); try by D. White, conv. by A. G. Hastings (35-9); try by I. Tukalo, conv. by A. G. Hastings (41-9); try and conv. by A. G. Hastings (47-9).

After a series of rather stuttering build-up matches, the Scottish team 'came good' in this first pool match in the World Cup. In the first quarter, the Scots played it tight but when they brought their backs into the play and started to spread the ball a bit, the scoreboard started to move with ominous regularity for the Japanese: it became a question of 'how many?'.

Japan never gave up and ran the ball and tackled right to the end but the final scoreline was a brutally accurate measure of the superiority of the Scots. A hugely successful opening game for Scotland.

The introduction of David Milne as a Scottish replacement gave the player his first full cap and completed a remarkable hat-trick for his family: his brothers, Iain and Kenny had each already played in the international side.

International Rugby Union

RUGBY WORLD CUP

SCOTLAND 51   ZIMBABWE 12
Murrayfield
9 October 1991

Scotland: P. W. Dods* (*Gala*); A. G. Stanger (*Hawick*), S. Hastings (*Watsonians*), S. R. P. Lineen (*Boroughmuir*), I. Tukalo (*Selkirk*); D. S. Wyllie (*Stewart's-Melville*), G. H. Oliver (*Hawick*); A. P. Burnell (*Lond. Scot.*), K. S. Milne (*Heriot's FP*), A. J. G. Watt (*GH-K*), D. F. Cronin (*Bath*), G. W. Weir (*Melrose*), D. J. Turnbull (*Hawick*), D. B. White (*Lond. Scot.*), G. R. Marshall (*Selkirk*).
Replacement: C. M. Chalmers (*Melrose*) for A. Stanger (78 min.).
Zimbabwe: B. S. Currin*; W. H. Schultz, R. U. Tsimba, M. S. Letcher, D. A. Walters; C. Brown, E. A. MacMillan; A. H. Nicholls, B. A. Beattie, A. C. Garvey, M. L. Martin, H. Nguruve, D. G. Muirhead, B. W. Catterall, B. N. Dawson.
Replacements: R. N. Hunter for A. Garvey (46 min.); E. Chimbima for D. Walters (56 min.); C. P. Roberts for R. Hunter (78 min.).
Referee: D. Reordan (*U.S.A.*).

Try by I. Tukalo, conv. by P. Dods (6-0); try by A. Garvie, conv. by B. Currin (6-6); penalty goal by P. Dods (9-6); try by D. Turnbull, conv. by P. Dods (15-6); try by A. Garvie, conv. by B. Currin (15-12); try by S. Hastings, conv. by P.Dods (21-12). (H.T.). Try by A. Stanger (25-12); dropped goal by D. Wyllie (28-12); penalty goal by P. Dods (31-12); try by I. Tukalo, conv. by P. Dods (37-12); try by I. Tukalo, conv. by P. Dods (43-12); try by G. Weir (47-12); try by D. White (51-12).

That Scotland had made nine team changes from the previous match against Japan was obvious in an error-prone first-half. Indeed, had Zimbabwe kicked their goals (place and drop), then the score could well have been level-pegging instead of the rather flattering 21-12 that Scotland enjoyed. However, the Scots moved up a gear in the second half and put in a strong finish in the last quarter.

Highlights (few in this match) were Iwan Tukalo's hat-trick of tries – raising him to second place in the list of Scottish try scorers with 15. Derek White's try brought his tally to 10 for Scotland – a record for a Scottish forward.

For Zimbabwe, Ewan MacMillan (son of a Scottish father from Perth) had an excellent game at scrum half as did his partner, Craig Brown, at stand-off.

RUGBY WORLD CUP

SCOTLAND 24   IRELAND 15
Murrayfield
12 October 1991

Scotland: A. G. Hastings (*Watsonians*); A. G. Stanger (*Hawick*), S. Hastings (*Watsonians*), S. R. P. Lineen (*Boroughmuir*), I. Tukalo (*Selkirk*); C. M. Chalmers (*Melrose*), G. Armstrong (*Jedforest*); D. M. B. Sole* (*Edin. Acad.*), J. Allan (*Edin. Acad.*), A. P. Burnell (*Lond. Scot.*), C. A. Gray (*Nottingham*), G. W. Weir (*Melrose*), J. Jeffrey (*Kelso*), D. B. White (*Lond. Scot.*), F. Calder (*Stewart's-Melville*).
Replacement: A. G. Shiel (*Melrose*) for C. Chalmers (42 min.).
Ireland: J. E. Staples (*Lond. Irish*); S. P. Geoghegan (*Lond. Irish*), L. J. Mullin (*Blackrock Coll.*), D. M. Curtis (*Lond. Irish*), K. D. Crossan (*Instonians*); R. P. Keyes (*Cork Const.*), R. Saunders (*Lond. Irish*); N. J. Popplewell (*Greystones*), S. J. Smith (*Ballymena*), D. C. Fitzgerald (*DLS Palmerston*), D. G. Lenihan (*Cork Const.*), N. P. J. Francis (*Blackrock Coll.*), P. M. Matthews* (*Wanderers*), B. F. Robinson (*Ballymena*), G. F. Hamilton (*Ballymena*).
Referee: F. A. Howard (*England*).

Penalty goal by R. Keyes (0-3); penalty goal by A. G. Hastings (3-3); penalty goal by R. Keyes (3-6); dropped goal by C. Chalmers (6-6); penalty goal by A. G. Hastings (9-6); penalty goal by R. Keyes (9-9); dropped goal by R. Keyes (9-12). (H.T.). Penalty goal by R. Keyes (9-15); try by G. Shiel, conv. by . G. Hastings (15-15); penalty goal by A. G. Hastings (18-15); try by G. Armstrong, conv. by A. G. Hastings (24-15).

For long spells in this thrilling end-to-end match, Scotland were playing 'catch-up'. They were never in the lead in the first half and trailed Ireland 9-12 at the interval. At 9-15 in the second half, and having lost Craig Chalmers through injury, in the 42nd minute, they looked to be in real trouble. Chalmers' replacement, Graham Shiel, was making his international debut and, after 13 minutes on the pitch, scored a try. Truly a memorable day for the 21-year old.

With the Scotland fly-half off injured and the visitors leading by 6 points, the Irish must have fancied their chances but a tackle on Staples left the Irish fullback groggy. He had still not fully recovered when Gary Armstrong hoisted a huge up-and-under which the Irish fullback failed to gather. Tony Stanger caught the ball and progressed almost to the Irish line before giving the scoring pass to Graham Shiel to score his debut try. From that point on, Scotland never looked like losing. Their table-topping of Pool 2 assured them of a home quarter-final tie against Western Samoa.

Pool 2

	P	W	D	L	F	A	Pts
Scotland	3	3	0	0	122	36	9
Ireland	3	2	0	1	102	51	7
Japan	3	1	0	2	77	87	5
Zimbabwe	3	0	0	3	31	158	3

The two top teams in each pool went forward to the quarter-finals. Ireland were due to meet Australia.

RUGBY WORLD CUP – QUARTER-FINAL

SCOTLAND 28   WESTERN SAMOA 6
Murrayfield
15 October 1991

Scotland: A. G. Hastings (*Watsonians*); A. G. Stanger (*Hawick*), S. Hastings (*Watsonians*), A. G. Shiel (*Melrose*), I. Tukalo (*Selkirk*); C. M. Chalmers (*Melrose*), G. Armstrong (*Jedforest*); D. M. B. Sole* (*Edin. Acad.*), J, Allan (*Edin. Acad.*), A. P. Burnell (*Lond. Scot.*), C. A. Gray (*Nottingham*), G. W. Weir (*Melrose*), J. Jeffrey (*Kelso*), D. B. White (*Lond. Scot.*), F. Calder (*Stewart's-Melville*).
Western Samoa: A. A. Aiolupo; B. Lima, T. Vaega, F. E. Bunce, T. D. L. Tagaloa; S. J. Bachop, M. M. Vaea; P. Fatialofa*, S. Toomalatai, V. Alalatoa, M. L. Birtwhistle, E. Iaone, S. Viafole, P. R. Lam, A. Perelini.
Referee: W. D. Bevan (Wales).

Penalty goal by M. Vaega (0-3); penalty goal by A. G. Hastings (3-3); try by A. Stanger (7-3); try by J. Jeffrey, conv. by A. G. Hastings (13-3). (H.T.). Penalty goal by A. G. Hastings (16-3); dropped goal by S. Bachop (16-6); penalty goal by A. G. Hastings (19-6); try by J. Jeffrey, conv. by A. G. Hastings (25-6); penalty goal by A. G. Hastings (28-6).

Western Samoa had earned a place in the quarter-finals by defeating Wales 16-13 and Argentina 35-12; their only pool-match loss being to Australia, 3-9. Their second place in Pool 3 brought them to Murrayfield.

Scotland chose to face a gusty and unreliable wind in the first half. The Scottish pack proved immense, their work-rate being first-class. John Jeffrey scored two tries and, but for a fumble from a Tony Stanger pass, might have had a third.

The Western Samoans tackled tenaciously throughout and the strong running of Tagaloa, Lima and Bachop perhaps merited more than was delivered. That the visitors did not score more points was due, in no small measure, to the fact that the Scots had tackled like demons.

Scotland progressed to the semi-final and a confrontation with England at Murrayfield. It had been the Western Samoans first visit to Murrayfield but they departed Scotland, not as 6-28 losers, but with their heads held high and the appreciative plaudits of the Scottish crowd of 54,000 ringing in their ears such had been their open friendliness. Despite their defeat, they accorded the crowd a lap-of-honour, following no-side.

RUGBY WORLD CUP – SEMI-FINAL

SCOTLAND 6   ENGLAND 9
Murrayfield
26 October 1991

Scotland: A. G. Hastings (*Watsonians*); A. G. Stanger (*Hawick*), S. Hastings (*Watsonians*), S. R. P. Lineen (*Boroughmuir*), I. Tukalo (*Selkirk*); C. M. Chalmers (*Melrose*), G. Armstrong (*Jedforest*); D. M. B. Sole* (*Edin. Acad.*), J. Allan (*Edin. Acad.*), A. P. Burnell (*Lond. Scot.*), C. A. Gray (*Nottingham*), G. W. Weir (*Melrose*), J. Jeffrey (*Kelso*), D. B. White (*Lond. Scot.*), F. Calder (*Stewart's-Melville*).
England: J. M. Webb (*Northampton*); S. J. Halliday (*Harlequins*), W. D. C. Carling* (*Harlequins*), J. C. Guscott (*Bath*), R. Underwood (*Leicester*); C. R. Andrew (*Wasps*), R. J. Hill (*Bath*); J. Leonard (*Harlequins*), B. C. Moore (*Harlequins*), J. Probyn (*Wasps*), P. J. Ackford (*Harlequins*), W. A. Dooley (*Preston Grasshoppers*), M. G. Skinner (*Harlequins*), M. C. Teague (*Gloucester*), P. J. Winterbottom (*Harlequins*).
Referee: K. V. J. Fitzgerald (*Australia*).

Two penalty goals by A. G. Hastings (6-0); penalty goal by J. Webb (6-3). (H.T.). penalty goal by J. Webb (6-6); dropped goal by R. Andrew (6-9).

After all the pre-match hype, this game turned out to be a disappointing spectacle. The England pack took full advantage of their superior weight and controlled the set pieces admirably throughout. Labelled the 'English juggernaut', that pack rolled on and took England into the final of the Rugby World Cup, against Australia at Twickenham.

With the score at 6-6, Gavin Hastings contrived to miss what should have been a kickable penalty. Despite that, England deserved their win – although the manner of it did the game of rugby no favours. The English threequarters hardly received a pass all afternoon and it was left to their pack to dominate at lineouts and scrummages.

The media pundits were not all complimentary in their reportage of the game. One *Scotsman* headline summed it up thus: 'England bore their way to Twickenham'.

In the second semi-final, Australia defeated New Zealand 16-6 (1 goal, 1 try, 2 penalty goals to 2 penalty goals).

RUGBY WORLD CUP – Play-off for Third and Fourth Places

SCOTLAND 6   NEW ZEALAND 13
Cardiff Arms Park
30 October 1991

Scotland: A. G. Hastings (*Watsonians*); A. G. Stanger (*Hawick*), S. Hastings (*Watsonians*), S. R. P. Lineen (*Boroughmuir*), I. Tukalo (*Selkirk*); C. M. Chalmers (*Melrose*), G. Armstrong (*Jedforest*); D. M. B. Sole* (*Edin. Acad.*), J. Allan (*Edin. Acad.*), A. P. Burnell (*Lond. Scot.*), C. A. Gray (*Nottingham*), G. W. Weir (*Melrose*), J. Jeffrey (*Kelso*), D. B. White (*Lond. Scot.*), F. Calder (*Stewart's-Melville*).
New Zealand: T. Wright; J. Kirwan, C. Innes, W. Little, V. Tuigamala; J. Preston, G. Bachop; S. McDowell, S. Fitzpatrick, R. Loe, I. Jones, G. Whetton*, A. Earl, Z. Brooke, M. Jones.
Replacement: S. Philpott for V. Tuigamala (40 min.).
Referee: S. R. Hilditch (Ireland).

Penalty goal by A. G. Hastings (3-0); two penalty goals by J. Preston (3-6). (H.T.). Penalty goal by J. Preston (3-9); penalty goal by A. G. Hastings (6-9); try by W. Little (6-13).

This play-off provided a pulsatingly hard but fair match. Scotland's defence withstood massive pressure by the All Blacks and held them to a 6-3 lead at the interval. An exchange of penalties in the second half brought the score to 9-6 in New Zealand's favour but it was in the third quarter of the game that Scotland were suddenly galvanized. That they did not score at that stage proved to be crucial. The All Blacks scored the only try of the match in the 80th minute. To have withstood so much New Zealand pressure, and given the amount of possession that the All Blacks enjoyed, it was a great achievement by the Scots to have denied their opponents a try until the final minute.

To have finished in fourth place in the Rugby World Cup was no mean achievement: Scots everywhere could hold their heads high.

John Jeffrey and Finlay Calder announced their retirement from international rugby as did Jim Telfer the assistant coach. Derek White let it be known that he, too, would be departing the international scene following the 1991-92 Five Nations matches. With these departures, a new era was about to dawn for Scottish international rugby.

In the Rugby World Cup final at Twickenham, Australia defeated England 12-6 to become the world champions.

SCOTLAND 7   ENGLAND 25
Murrayfield
18 January 1992

Scotland: A. G. Hastings (*Watsonians*); A. G. Stanger (*Hawick*), S. Hastings (*Watsonians*), S. R. P. Lineen (*Boroughmuir*), I. Tukalo (*Selkirk*); C. M. Chalmers (*Melrose*), A. D. Nicol (*Dundee HSFP*); D. M. B. Sole* (*Edin. Acad.*), K. S. Milne (*Heriot's FP*), A. P. Burnell (*Lond. Scot.*), N. G. B. Edwards (*Harlequins*), G. W. Weir (*Melrose*), D. J. McIvor (*Edin. Acad.*), I. R. Smith (*Gloucester*), D. B. White (*Lond. Scot.*).
England: J. M. Webb (*Bath*); S. J. Halliday (*Harlequins*), J. C. Guscott (*Bath*), W. D. C. Carling* (*Harlequins*), R. Underwood (*Leicester*); C. R. Andrew (*Toulouse*), C. D. Morris (*Orrell*); J. Leonard (*Harlequins*), B. C. Moore (*Harlequins*), J. A. Probyn (*Wasps*), M. C. Bayfield (*Northampton*), W. A. Dooley (*Preston Grasshoppers*), M. G. Skinner (*Harlequins*), P. J. Winterbottom (*Harlequins*), T. A. K. Rodber (*Northampton*).
Replacement: D. Richards (*Leicester*) for T. Rodber (62 min).
Referee: W. D. Bevan (*Wales*).

Penalty goal by A. G. Hastings (3-0); two penalty goals by J. Webb (3-6); try by R. Underwood (3-10); try by D. White (7-10). (H.T.). Two penalty goals by J. Webb (7-16); dropped goal by J. Guscott (7-19); try by D. Morris, conv. by J. Webb (7-25).

This was England's 33rd visit to Murrayfield and the final score reflected the widest margin in any of their 12 previous victories at the stadium. The final scoreline slightly flattered England: had the Scots backs played with the fire and commitment of the forwards, the score could have been much closer – or the result reversed!

Andy Nicol, whose grandfather, George Ritchie, had played for Scotland at Twickenham in 1932, was making his cap debut and was exempted from much of the criticism: he had played a splendid all-round game. Scotland's three new forwards, Dave McIvor, Ian Smith and Neil Edwards, played well. Derek White's 11th try for Scotland equalled the record for a forward, held by John Jeffrey.

England found extra impetus in the third quarter when Dean Richards replaced Tim Rodber. England's grandstand finish saw off the Scottish challenge.

IRELAND 10   SCOTLAND 18
Lansdowne Road
15 February 1992

Ireland: K. J. Murphy (*Cork Const.*); R. M. Wallace (*Garryowen*), B. J. Mullin (*Blackrock Coll.*), P. P. A. Danaher (*Garryowen*), S. P. Geoghegan (*Lond. Irish*); R. P. Keyes (*Cork Const.*), L. F. P. Aherne (*Lansdowne*); N. J. Popplewell (*Greystones*), S. J. Smith (*Ballymena*), G. F. Halpin (*Lond. Irish*), M. J. Galway (*Shannon*), N. P. J. Francis (*Blackrock Coll.*), P. M. Matthews* (*Wanderers*), B. F. Robinson (*Ballymena*), M. J. Fitzgibbon (*Shannon*).
Replacements: D. C. Fitzgerald (*DLS Palmerston*) for G. Halpin (29 min.); D. M. Curtis (*Lond. Irish*) for S. Geoghegan (half-time).
Scotland: A. G. Hastings (*Watsonians*); A G. Stanger (*Hawick*), S. Hastings (*Watsonians*), S. R. P. Lineen (*Boroughmuir*), I. Tukalo (*Selkirk*); C. M. Chalmers (*Melrose*), A. D. Nicol (*Dundee HSFP*); D. M. B. Sole* (*Edin. Acad.*), K. S. Milne (*Heriot's FP*), A. P. Burnell (*Lond. Scot.*), N. G. P. Edwards (*Harlequins*), G. W. Weir (*Melrose*), D. J. McIvor (*Edin. Acad.*), D. B. White (*Lond. Scot.*), I. R. Smith (*Gloucester*).
Replacement: R. I. Wainwright (*Edin. Acad.*) for N. Edwards (77 min.).
Referee: A. J. Spreadbury (*England*).

Penalty goal by R. Keyes (3-0); try by A. Stanger, conv. by A. G. Hastings (3-6); penalty goal by A. G. Hastings (3-9). (H.T.). Try by A. Nicol, conv. by A. G. Hastings (3-15); try by R. Wallace (7-15); penalty goal by R. Keyes (10-15); penalty goal by A. G. Hastings (10-18).

This is one match the Irish will want to forget. The team gave a most inept performance and were booed off the field by their own supporters. The play of this Scottish team was, at times, wayward but the Scots were at a rebuilding stage and deserved credit for the application and discipline shown. The Scottish forwards won the lineouts battle 18-6 and were untroubled in the scrummages.

SCOTLAND 10   FRANCE 6
Murrayfield
7 March 1992

Scotland: A. G. Hastings (*Watsonians*); A. G. Stanger (*Hawick*), S. Hastings (*Watsonians*), S. R. P. Lineen (*Boroughmuir*), I. Tukalo (*Selkirk*); C. M. Chalmers (*Melrose*), A. D. Nicol (*Dundee HSFP*); D. M. B. Sole* (*Edin. Acad.*), K. S. Milne (*Heriot's FP*), A. P. Burnell (*Lond. Scot.*), N. G. B. Edwards (*Harlequins*), G. W. Weir (*Melrose*), D. J. McIvor (*Edin. Acad.*), D. B. White (*Lond. Scot.*), R. I. Wainwright (*Edin. Acad.*).
France: L. S. Sadourny (*Colomiers*); J-B Lafond (*Racing Club*), P. Sella* (*Agen*), F. Mesnel (*Racing Club*), P. Saint-Andre (*Montferrand*); A. Penaud (*Brive*), F. Galthie (*Colomiers*); L. Almary (*Lourdes*), J-P Genet (*Racing Club*), P. Gallart (*Beziers*), M. Cecillon (*Bourgoin*), O. Roumat (*Dax*), J. F. Tordo (*Nice*), A. van Heerden (*Tarbes*), I. Cabannes (*Racing Club*).
Referee: F. Burger (*South Africa*).

Try by N. Edwards (4-0); penalty goal by J-B Lafond (4-3). (H.T.). Penalty goal by J-B Lafond (4-6); two penalty goals by A. G. Hastings (10-6).

Compared with some previous encounters between these two nations, this was a fairly drab and dull affair: it was neither memorable nor an intense spectacle.

Following some disgraceful events in their previous match with England, France tried to play this game as disciplined and within the laws. That they failed to defeat Scotland was due in part to incessant rain, a gusting wind and Scotland's resolute defence. That and a lack of French bite and honed edges saw Scotland stand up to intense French pressure and steal the game.

This win by Scotland levelled the series between the countries at 30 wins each with three matches drawn. The match signalled the farewell appearances at Murrayfield of David Sole and Derek White.

WALES 15   SCOTLAND 12
Cardiff Arms Park
21 March 1992

Wales: A. Clement (*Swansea*); I. C. Evans* (*Llanelli*), R. A. Bidgood (*Newport*), I. S. Gibbs (*Swansea*), M. R. Hall (*Cardiff*); N. R. Jenkins (*Pontypridd*), R. N. Jones (*Swansea*); M. Griffiths (*Cardiff*), G. R. Jenkins (*Swansea*), H. Williams-Jones (*S. Wales Police*), G. O. Llewellyn (*Neath*), A. H. Copsey (*Llanelli*), E. W. Lewis (*Llanelli*), S. Davies (*Swansea*), R. E. Webster (*Swansea*).
Scotland: A. G. Hastings (*Watsonians*); A. G. Stanger (*Hawick*), S. Hastings (*Watsonians*), S. R. P. Lineen (*Boroughmuir*), I. Tukalo (*Selkirk*); C. M. Chalmers (*Melrose*), A. D. Nicol (*Dundee HSFP*); D. M. B. Sole* (*Edin. Acad.*), K. S.Milne (*Heriot's FP*), A. P. Burnell (*Lond. Scot.*), N. G. B. Edwards (*Harlequins*), G. W. Weir (*Melrose*), D. J. McIvor (*Edin. Acad.*), D. B. White (*Lond. Scot.*), I. R. Smith (*Gloucester*).
Replacement: P. M. Jones (*Gloucester*) for A. Burnell (53 min.).
Referee: M. Desclaux (*France*).

Penalty goal by M. Jenkins (3-0); penalty goal by A. G. Hastings (3-3); dropped goal by C. Chalmers (3-6); try by R. Webster, conv. by N. Jenkins (9-6). (H.T.). Penalty goal by N. Jenkins (12-6); penalty goal by C. Chalmers (12-9); penalty goal by N. Jenkins (15-9); penalty goal by C. Chalmers (15-12).

Scotland ended the season's Five Nations matches on a rather flat note. It was an inglorious farewell to international rugby for Derek White. The fact of the matter was that both Wales and Scotland were poor teams on the day.

The nearest the Scots got to scoring a try was when, following a rather wild Scott Hastings pass which had eluded Ian Smith, Iwan Tukalo charged down Robert Jones' attempted clearing kick and dived over the Welsh line only to be judged to have knocked on by the referee.

The match was too error-ridden to sparkle in any way and this ensured that the usual snap and crackle was missing from this fixture.

Five Nations Championship 1991-92

	P	W	L	D	F	A	Pts
England	4	4	0	0	118	29	8
France	4	2	2	0	75	62	4
Scotland	4	2	2	0	47	56	4
Wales	4	2	2	0	40	63	4
Ireland	4	0	4	0	46	116	0

AUSTRALIA 27   SCOTLAND 12
Football Ground, Sydney
13 June 1992

Australia: M. Roebuck; D. Campese, R. Tombs, T. Horan, P. Carozza; M. Lynagh, N. Farr-Jones*; T. Daly, P. Kearns, E. MacKenzie, J. Eales, R. McCall, W. Ofahengaue, D. Wilson, T. Gavin.
Replacement: P. Jorgensen for P. Carozza (70 min.).
Scotland: A. G. Hastings (*Watsonians*); A. G. Stanger (*Hawick*), S. Hastings (*Watsonians*), S. R. P. Lineen (*Boroughmuir*), I. Tukalo (*Selkirk*); C. M. Chalmers (*Melrose*), A. D. Nicol (*Dundee HSFP*); D. M.B. Sole* (*Edin. Acad.*), K. S. Milne (*Heriot's FP*), P. H. Wright (*Boroughmuir*), G. W. Weir (*Melrose*), N. G. B. Edwards (*Harlequins*), C. D. Hogg (*Melrose*), I. R. Smith (*Gloucester*), R. I. Wainwright (*Edin. Acad.*).
Replacement I. Corcoran (*Gala*) for K. Milne (10 min.).
Referee: L. McLachlan (*New Zealand*).

Penalty goal by A. G. Hastings (0-3); penalty goal by M. Lynagh (3-3); try by D. Campese (7-3); try by R. Wainwright, conv. by A. G. Hastings (7-9). (H.T.). Try by by P. Carozza (11-9); two penalty goals by M. Lynagh (17-9); penalty goal by A. G. Hastings (17-12); try by M. Lynagh (21-12); try by D. Campese, conv. by M. Lynagh (27-12).

There were first caps for Peter Wright and Carl Hogg and also for Ian Corcoran who came on as a replacement for Kenny Milne.

With Scotland leading 9-7 at half-time, it seemed that they might be in with a chance of pulling off a surprise win. However, mis-cued kicks and wayward passes, early in the second half, saw the Scots practically gift 10 points to their opponents in the first 11 minutes and, although Gavin Hastings kicked a penalty to make the scores 17-12, two further tries and a conversion saw Australia through as worthy winners.

Plusses for Scotland were the displays of Scott Hastings, Ian Smith, Rob Wainwright and Peter Wright. It was a match the Scots will want to forget.

AUSTRALIA 37   SCOTLAND 13
Ballymore, Brisbane
21 June 1992

Australia: M. C. Roebuck; D. I. Campese, R. C. Tombs, T. J. Horan, P. V. Carozza; M. P. Lynagh, N. C. Farr-Jones*; A. J. Daly, P. N. Kearns, E. J. A. MacKenzie, R. J. McCall, J. A. Eales, V. Ofahengaue, B. T. Gavin, D. Wilson. Replacement: P. Jorgensen for D. Campese (78 min.).
Scotland: K. M. Logan (*Stirling County*); A. G. Stanger (*Hawick*), S . Hastings (*Watsonians*), S. R. P. Lineen (*Boroughmuir*), I. Tukalo (*Selkirk*); C. M. Chalmers (*Melrose*), A. D. Nicol (*Dundee HSFP*); D. M. B. Sole* (*Edin. Acad.*), M. W. Scott (*Dunfermline*), P. H. Wright (*Boroughmuir*), D. F. Cronin (*Lond. Scot.*), G. W. Weir (*Melrose*), C. D. Hogg (*Melrose*), R. I. Wainwright (*Edin. Acad.*), I. R. Smith (*Gloucester*).
Referee: C. J. Hawke (*New Zealand*).

Four penalty goals by M. Lynagh (12-0); penalty goal by C . Chalmers (12-3) try by P. Carozza (16-3). (H.T.). Try by T. Horan (20-3); penalty goal by M. Lynagh (23-3); try by T. Horan (27-3); try by S. Lineen, conv. by C. Chalmers (27-9); try by P. Carozza (31-9); try by J. Eales, conv. by M. Lynagh (37-9); try by D. Sole (37-13).

Scotland's weaknesses were cruelly exposed in this Second Test, the final match of the tour. The difference between the two sides was palpable and the try-count of 5-2 in Australia' s favour did not in any way flatter the host country. At lineouts and scrummages the Scots forwards struggled to compete. Scotland's backs were forced to defend for most of the game and the fact that Scotland scored two tries in the second half was credit to their stubborn refusal to throw in the towel against opponents who were superior in all departments.

This was David Sole's last international and it was fitting that he should score a late try and so put his signature on the match.

SCOTLAND 15   IRELAND 3
Murrayfield
16 January 1993

Scotland: A. G. Hastings* (*Watsonians*); A. G. Stanger (*Hawick*), S. Hastings (*Watsonians*), A. G. Shiel (*Melrose*), D. A. Stark (*Boroughmuir*); C. M. Chalmers (*Melrose*), G. Armstrong (*Jedforest*); A. G. Watt (*GH-K*), K. S. Milne (*Heriot's FP*), A. P. Burnell (*Lond. Scot.*), A. I. Reed (*Bath*), D. F. Cronin (*Lond. Scot.*), D. J. Turnbull (*Hawick*), G. W. Weir (*Melrose*), I. R. Morrison (*Lond. Scot.*).
Ireland: C. R. Wilkinson (*Malone*); S. P. Geoghegan (*Lond. Irish*), V. J. G. Cunningham (*St Mary's Coll.*), P. P. A. Danaher (*Garryowen*), R. M. Wallace (*Garryowen*); N. G. Malone (*Oxford Univ.*), M. T. Bradley* (*Cork Const.*); N. J. Popplewell (*Greystones*), S. J. Smith (*Ballymena*), P. D. McCarthy (*Cork Const.*), P. S. Johns (*Dungannon*), R. A. Costello (*Garryowen*), P. J. Lawlor (*Bective Rangers*), N. P. S. Mannion (*Lansdowne*), W. D. McBride (*Malone*).
Referee: E. F. Morrison (*England*).

Penalty goal by A. G. Hastings (3-0); try by D. Stark, conv. by A. G. Hastings (10-0); try by A. Stanger (15-0). (H.T.). Penalty goal by N. Malone (15-3).

Gavin Hastings captained Scotland for the first time and the Scots introduced three new caps: Derek Stark, Andy Reed and Ian Morrison. This match saw, for the first time in an international, five points being awarded for a try.

On a day of strong, gusty wind, Ireland won the toss and chose to play against the elements. In an uninspiring match, Scotland dominated the lineouts, taking the touchline count 27-10. Both Scotland's wing threequarters scored tries (Stark's on his international debut) – something that had last happened when Scotland were defeated 21-18 by New Zealand in 1990.

The final score did not truly reflect the Scots superiority. In difficult conditions, the hosts were well worthy of their victory.

FRANCE 11   SCOTLAND 3
Parc des Princes, Paris
6 February 1993

France: J-B Lafond (*Begles*); P. Saint-Andres (*Montferrand*), P. Sella (*Agen*), T. Lacroix (*Dax*), P. Hontas (*Biarritz*); D. Camberabero (*Beziers*), A. Hueber (*Toulon*); L. Armary (*Lourdes*), J-F Tordo* (*Nice*), L. Seigne (*Merignac*), A. Benazzi (*Agen*), C. Roumat (*Dax*), P. Benatton (*Agen*),M. Cecillon (*Bourgoin*), L. Cabannes (*Racing Club*).
Scotland: A. G. Hastings* (*Watsonians*); A. G. Stanger (*Hawick*), S. Hastings (*Watsonians*), A. G. Shiel (*Melrose*), D. A. Stark (*Boroughmuir*); C. M. Chalmers (*Melrose*), G. Armstrong (*Jedforest*); P. H. Wright (*Boroughmuir*), K. S. Milne (*Heriot's FP*), A. P. Burnell (*Lond. Scot.*), D. F. Cronin (*Lond. Scot.*), A. I. Reed (*Bath*), D. J. Turnbull (*Hawick*), G. W. Weir (*Melrose*), I. R. Morrison (*Lond. Scot.*).
Referee: W. D. Bevan (*Wales*).

Penalty goal by D. Camberabero (3-0); penalty goal by A. G. Hastings (3-3). (H.T.). penalty goal by D. Camberabero (6-3); try by T. Lacroix (11-3).

On recent previous visits to the Parc des Princes, Scottish teams had found it difficult to secure good ball. In this match they won an abundance of ball but still lost the encounter. The Scots scorned chances to put points on the board. Gavin Hastings scored but one penalty goal from six attempts. In the periods immediately prior to and following the interval the Scots shunned gilt-edged opportunities to score tries. Had either of these been made to count, the French would have been forced to play catch-up.

With no-side impending, Derek Stark intercepted Hueber's attempted pass to Roumat and crossed the French line only for the referee to judge him to have been offside. Had it counted and had the try been converted, the final result would not have been affected but the scoreline would have been a truer reflection of Scotland's efforts in this match.

Gavin Hastings' penalty goal raised his international points tally to 400, making him the first Five Nations player to achieve that figure.

SCOTLAND 20   WALES 0
Murrayfield
20 February 1993

Scotland: A. G. Hastings*(*Watsonians*); A. G. Stanger (*Hawick*), S. Hastings (*Watsonians*), A. G. Shiel (*Melrose*), D. A. Stark (*Boroughmuir*); C. M. Chalmers (*Melrose*), G. Armstrong (*Jedforest*); P. H. Wright (*Boroughmuir*), K. S. Milne (*Heriot's FP*), A. P. Burnell (*Lond. Scot.*), A. I. Reed (*Bath*), D. F. Cronin (*Lond. Scot.*), D. J. Turnbull (*Hawick*), G. W. Weir (*Melrose*), I. R. Morrison (*Lond. Scot.*).
Wales: M. A. Rayer (*Cardiff*); I. C. Evans* (*Llanelli*), M. R. Hall (*Cardiff*), I. S. Gibbs (*Swansea*), W. T. Procter (*Llanelli*); N. R. Jenkins (*Pontypool*), R. N. Jones (*Swansea*); R. L. Evans (*Llanelli*), N. Meek (*Pontypool*), H. Williams-Jones (*S. Wales Police*), G. O. Llewellyn (*Neath*), A. H. Copsey (*Llanelli*), E. W. Lewis (*Llanelli*), S. Davies (*Swansea*), R. E. Webster (*Swansea*).
Referee: J. Dumé (*France*).

Three penalty goals by A. G. Hastings (9-0); try by D. Turnbull (14-0). (H.T.). Two penalty goals by A. G. Hastings (20-0).

Two penalty goals and an unconverted try saw the Scots 14-0 ahead at the interval. The Welsh, who had been playing into the wind, must have been looking forward to having it in their favour in the second half, but the malevolent elements dictated otherwise. Straight from the restart, Gary Armstrong hoofed a ball all of 70 metres thus putting the Welsh on the defensive immediately. That kick must have given the Scots a tremendous psychological boost and they proceeded to dictate play just as they had done in the first half.

In this, their 31st visit to Murrayfield, the Welsh sampled only the third shut-out by Scotland (1951, 19-0; 1961, 3-0). In this match, the scoreline of 20-0 did not truly reflect Scotland's control and dominance. The Scots thrilled the crowd with their relentless driving in the loose and with their sheer hunger for the game, The wonder was not only that Scotland did not score more points but that this Welsh team had defeated England in Cardiff two weeks previously.

247

The Scots had set themselves up for a possible Triple Crown clash with England at Twickenham which, if successful, would be their third in ten years.

Some newspaper headlines said it all:

'Dynamic Scots' (The Scotsman).

'Absolute control' (The Herald).

'Hastings' knights slay the dragon' (Sunday Times).

'Hastings blows hot to leave Wales becalmed' (The Times).

'A nearly perfect performance' (Scottish Rugby).

ENGLAND 26 SCOTLAND 12
Twickenham
6 March 1993

England: J. M. Webb (*Bath*); T. Underwood (*Leicester*), W. D. C. Carling* (*Harlequins*), J. C.Guscott (*Bath*), R. Underwood (*Leicester*); S. Barnes (*Bath*), C. D. Morris (*Orrell*); J. Leonard (*Harlequins*), B. C. Moore (*Harlequins*), J. A. Probyn (*Wasps*), M. C. Bayfield (*Northampton*), W. A. Dooley (*Preston Grasshoppers*), M. C. Teague (*Moseley*), B. B. Clarke (*Bath*), P. J. Winterbottom (*Harlequins*).

Scotland: A. G. Hastings* (*Watsonians*); A. G. Stanger (*Hawick*), S. Hastings (*Watsonians*), A. G. Shiel (*Melrose*), D. A. Stark (*Boroughmuir*); C. M. Chalmers (*Melrose*), G. Armstrong (*Jedforest*); P. H. Wright (*Boroughmuir*), K. S. Milne (*Heriot's FP*), A. P. Burnell (*Lond. Scot.*), A. I. Reed (*Bath*), D. F. Cronin (*Lond. Scot.*), D. J. Turnbull (*Hawick*), G. W. Weir (*Melrose*), I. R. Morrison (*Lond. Scot.*).

Replacements: G. J. P. Townsend (*Gala*) for C. Chalmers (22 min.); K. M. Logan (*Stirling County*) for S. Hastings (62 min.). **Referee:** B. W. Stirling (*Ireland*).

Penalty goal by A. G. Hastings (0-3); penalty goal by J. Webb (3-3); dropped goal by C. Chalmers (3-6); try by J. Guscott (8-6); penalty goal by J. Webb (11-6). (H.T.). Try by R. Underwood (16-6); try by T. Underwood, conv. by J. Webb (23-6); penalty goal by A. G. Hastings (23-9); penalty goal by J. Webb (26-9); penalty goal by A. G. Hastings (26-12).

Stuart Barnes, the England stand-off, was the principal architect of this home win thus seeing off the Scottish challenge. In the opening exchanges, the Scots held their own and gave as good as they got. However, after 22 minutes, and with the score at 6-3 in Scotland's favour, they suffered a crippling blow when stand-off Craig Chalmers was seriously injured (he sustained a double fracture of his right forearm). Gregor Townsend came on as a replacement to win his first cap, going to inside centre with Graham Shiel moving to stand-off. This disruption seriously upset the Scottish team.

Nor was Chalmers' departure the end of Scotland's ill-fortune. Another set-back came just after the hour when Scott Hastings had to depart with an ankle injury, Kenny Logan coming on for only his second cap. By that time, however, England were leading 23-6 and on the way to a well-deserved victory.

So ended Scotland's Calcutta Cup and Triple Crown aspirations for another season.

Five Nations Championship 1992-93

	P	W	L	D	F	A	Pts
France	4	3	1	0	73	35	6
Scotland	4	2	2	0	50	40	4
England	4	2	2	0	54	54	4
Ireland	4	2	2	0	45	53	4
Wales	4	1	3	0	34	74	2

FIJI 10   SCOTLAND XV 21
Suva
29 May 1993

Fiji: T. Vonolagi; W. Komaitai, V. Raulini, E. Nauga, T. Lovo; E. Rowkowailoa, W. Serevi; M. Taga*, A. Rabitu, I. Naituku, P. Naruma, A. Naololo, I. Tawake, E. Tuvunivono, S. Vololagi.
Scotland: K. M. Logan (*Stirling County*); N. J. Grecian (*Lond. Scot.*), S. A. Nichol (*Selkirk*), I. C. Jardine (*Stirling County*), M. Moncrieff (*Gala*); A. Donaldson (*Currie*), A. D. Nicol* (*Dundee HSFP*); G. R. Isaac (*Gala*), J. A. Hay (*Hawick*), S. W. Ferguson (*Peebles*), C. A. Gray (*Nottingham*), R. Scott (*Lond. Scot.*), D. J. McIvor (*Edin. Acad.*), G. W. Weir (*Melrose*), I. R. Smith (*Gloucester*).
Referee: B. M. Kinsey (*Australia*).

Try by J. Hay, conv. by A. Donaldson (0-7); penalty goal by A. Donaldson (0-10). (H.T.). Try by E. Rokowailowa, conv. by W. Serevi (7-10); penalty goal by W. Serevi (10-10); try by K. Logan (10-15); two penalty goals by A. Donaldson (10-21).

This was Scotland's third match of their tour of the South Seas and saw them remain undefeated. With only six previously-capped players in the team, the Scots did very well under the circumstances and thereby confounded those critics who had written them off before the tour started.

The Scottish pack played well as a unit and drove and pummelled their opponents, especially in the last quarter.

Although satisfying in itself, the victory was not as clear-cut as the Scots would have wished. The Fijiians pulled back to 10-10 in the third quarter and the tourists had to dig deep into their reserves to secure the victory.

TONGA 5   SCOTLAND XV 23
Nuku'alofa
5 June 1993

Tonga: I. Tapueluelu; A. Uasi, T. Tu'ineau, M. Lavaka, T. Va'enuku; E. Vunipola, A. Tulikali; V. Moa, F. Masila, E. Talaki, T. Loto'ahea, I. Fatani, F. Fakeonjo, M. Manukia*, I. Fennkitau.
Scotland: A. C. Redpath (*Melrose*); M. Moncrieff (*Gala*), S. A. Nichol (*Selkirk*), I. C. Jardine (*Stirling County*), K.M. Logan (*Stirling County*); G. P. J. Townsend (*Gala*), A. D. Nicol* (*Dundee HSFP*); G. R. Isaac (*Gala*), J. A. Hay (*Hawick*), S. W. Ferguson (*Peebles*), C. A. Gray (*Nottingham*), R. Scott (*Lond. Scot.*), D. J. McIvor (*Edin. Acad.*), G. W. Weir (*Melrose*), I. R. Smith (*Gloucester*).
Replacement: C. D. Hogg (*Melrose*) for R. Scott (53 min.).
Referee: L. McLachlan (*New Zealand*).

Try by G. Weir (0-5); try by M. Lavoko (5-5); penalty goal by G. Townsend (5-8). (H.T.). Penalty try, conv. by G. Townsend (5-15); penalty goal by G. Townsend (5-18); try by K. Logan (5-23).

After four exciting performances, the Scots appeared to have gone off the boil in this fifth match of the tour. The Tongans gave the impression that they had the flair but not the finishing ability to defeat a rather lethargic Scottish team.

The Scottish pack, for the first time in this tour, failed to dominate as they had done in earlier matches. The Tongans appeared to be sharper to the 50-50 ball and their forwards moved smartly and swiftly, and threatened the Scottish line on several occasions: only some resolute tackling by the Scots prevented some Tongan scores.

WESTERN SAMOA 28   SCOTLAND XV 11
Apia
12 June 1993

Western Samoa: A. Aiolupo; L. Koko, T. Vaega, A. Ieramia, B. Lima; D. Kellett, J. Tonu'u; P. Fatialofa*, T. Leasamaivao, A. Lenu, P. Leavasa, L. Falaniko, S. Vaifale, D. Kaleopa, M. Iupeli.
Scotland: N. J. Grecian (*Lond. Scot.*); M. Moncrieff (*Gala*), S. A. Nichol (*Selkirk*), I. C. Jardine (*Stirling County*), K. M. Logan (*Stirling County*); G. P. J. Townsend (*Gala*), A. D. Nicol* (*Dundee HSFP*); G. R. Isaac (*Gala*), J. A. Hay (*Hawick*), S. W. Ferguson (*Peebles*), D. S. Munro (*GH-K*), R. Scott (*Lond. Scot.*), D. J. McIvor (*Edin. Acad.*), G. W. Weir (*Melrose*), I. R. Smith (*Gloucester*).
Replacements: A. E. D. Macdonald (*Heriot's FP*) for R. Scott (24 min.); I. Corcoran (*Gala*) for J. Hay (78 min.).
Referee: L. McLachlan (*New Zealand*).

Try by T. Vaega, conv. by D. Kellett (7-0); try by A. Nicol (7-5); try by D. Kaleopa (12-5); penalty goal by G. Townsend (12-8). (H.T.). Three penalty goals by D. Kellett (21-8); penalty goal by G. Townsend (21-11); try by L. Lima, conv. by D. Kellett (28-11).

In this final match of the tour, the Scots suffered their only defeat. Scotland's hopes of a clean sweep on the tour evaporated in the sweltering conditions encountered at Apia. For the first time on the tour, the Scots pack found themselves being out-jumped at the lineout and forced on to the back foot in the scrum.

The Scottish backs did not escape criticism, missing vital tackles which helped the Samoans to a 3-1 try advantage.

Following the match, Andy Nicol, scrum-half and captain, was informed that he had been called up to join the British Isles squad (The Lions) in New Zealand as cover for Robert Jones (Wales). Nicol had finished the tour as top try scorer with four tries and was recovering, exhausted, in the dressing room when given the news. Afterwards, he said: 'I had dreamed about a Lions call-up and where I would be if it materialised. Little did I know I would be sitting on a dressing-room floor, too knackered to even say anything!' In New Zealand, the player was called on to the field as a substitute during a Lions mid-week match.

SCOTLAND 15   NEW ZEALAND 51
Murrayfield
20 November 1993

Scotland: A. G. Hastings* (*Watsonians*); A. G. Stanger (*Hawick*), I. C. Jardine (*Stirling County*), A. G. Shiel (*Melrose*), S. Hastings (*Watsonians*); C. M. Chalmers (*Melrose*), A. D. Nicol (*Dundee HSFP*); A. G. J. Watt (*GH-K*), K. S. Milne (*Heriot's FP*), A. P. Burnell (*Lond. Scot.*), D. F. Cronin (*Lond. Scot.*), A. E. D. MacDonald (*Heriot's FP*), D. J. McIvor (*Edin. Acad.*), G. W. Weir (*Melrose*), R. I. Wainwright (*Edin. Acad.*).
Replacements: D. S. Wyllie (*Stewart's-Melville*) for C. Chalmers (56 min.); C. D. Hogg (*Melrose*) for D. Cronin (60 min.). Temporary replacements: B. W. Redpath (*Melrose*) for A. Nicol (7-8 min.); K. M. Logan (*Stirling County*) for A. G. Hastings (35-40 min.).
New Zealand: J. K. R. Timu (*Otago*); J. W. Wilson (*Otago*), F. E. Bunce (*N. Harbour*), M. J. A. Cooper (*Waikato*), V. L. Tuigamala (*Auckland*); M. C. G. Ellis (*Otago*), S. Forster (*Otago*); C. Dowd (*Auckland*), S. B. T. Fitzgerald* (*Auckland*), O. M. Brown (*Auckland*), I. D. Jones (*N. Auckland*), S. B. Gordon (*Waikato*), J. W. Joseph (*Otago*), A. R. B. Penc (*Otago*), Z. V. Brooke (*Auckland*).
Replacement: E. Clarke (*Auckland*) for M. Cooper (75 min.).
Referee: F. Burger (*South Africa*).

Penalty goal by M. Cooper (0-3); try by M. Ellis (0-8); penalty goal by A. G. Hastings (3-8); try by J. Wilson, conv. by M. Cooper (3-15); penalty goal by A G. Hastings (6-15); try by Z. Brooke, conv. by M. Cooper (6-22); penalty goal by C. Chalmers (9-22). (H.T.). Try by F. Bunce (9-27); penalty goal by A. G. Hastings (12-27); penalty goal by M. Cooper (12-30); penalty goal by A. G. Hastings (15-30); try by J. Wilson, conv. by M. Cooper (15-37); try by M. Ellis, conv. by M. Cooper (15-44); try and conv. by J. Wilson (15-51).

The whole of Scotland winced at the final scoreline. Not since the 0-44 thrashing by South Africa in 1951 had a Scotland rugby team been so humiliated. The All Blacks were not particularly spectacular or intricate in the demolition of this Scotland team: but they played with power and pace which Scotland could not match.

Scotland took the lineouts 15-14 – but the All Blacks took cleaner ball. Scotland had to contend with the ball being peppered back, meaning that they had to try to clean up from an untidy base. Scotland's points were all from penalties; the All Blacks ran in seven tries – a depressing comparison. It must have been a humbling experience for Ian Jardine winning his first cap for Scotland – on the other hand, Jeffrey Wilson, just turned 20 at the start of the tour, scored a hat-trick of tries on his debut for New Zealand. He goaled the third of these to give him a haul of 17 points in his first international.

Although the All Blacks scored 51 points in this match, the 44-0 hiding from South Africa made more depressing reading in 1951 in that they had scored nine tries, each valued at only three points. If the 1994 points valuations had been in vogue in 1951, the South Africans score would have reached 60 points. Alternatively, application of the 1951 points valuation to the 1994 match would have meant a New Zealand win of 37-15!

WALES 29   SCOTLAND 6
Cardiff Arms Park
15 January 1994

Wales: A. Clement (*Swansea*); I. Evans* (*Llanelli*), M. Hall (*Cardiff*), N. Davies (*Llanelli*), N. Walker (*Cardiff*); N. Jenkins (*Pontypridd*), R. Moon (*Llanelli*), R. Evans (*Llanelli*), G. Jenkins (*Swansea*), J. Davies (*Neath*), P. Davies (*Llanelli*), G. Llewellyn (*Neath*), E. Lewis (*Llanelli*), S. Quinnell (*Llanelli*), M. Perego (*Llanelli*).
Replacement: M. Rayer (*Cardiff*) for N. Walker (11 min.).
Scotland: A. G. Hastings* (*Watsonians*); A. G. Stanger (*Hawick*), G. P. J. Townsend (*Gala*), I. C. Jardine (*Stirling County*), K. M. Logan (*Stirling County*); C. M. Chalmers (*Melrose*), A. D. Nicol (*Dundee HSFP*); P. H. Wright (*Boroughmuir*), K. S. Milne (*Heriot's FP*), A. P. Burnell (*Lond. Scot.*), N. G. B. Edwards (*Northampton*), D. S. Munro (*GH-K*), D. J. Turnbull (*Hawick*), R. I. Wainwright (*Edin. Acad.*), I. R. Morrison (*Lond. Scot.*).
Replacements: G. W. Weir (*Melrose*) for I. Morrison (18 min.); D. S. Wyllie (*Stewart's-Melville*) for C. Chalmers (55 min.); B. Redpath (*Melrose*) for A. Nicol (79 min.).
Referee: P. Robin (*France*).

Penalty goal by N. Jenkins (3-0); penalty goal by A. G. Hastings (3-3); two penalty goals by N. Jenkins (9-3). (H.T.). penalty goal by N. Jenkins (12-3); try by M. Rayer (17-3); penalty goal by A. G. Hastings (17-6); try by M. Rayer, conv by N. Jenkins (24-6); try by I. Evans (29-6).

A depressing match for Scottish rugby: this Scottish team had weaknesses shown up on every front. This defeat by Wales equalled the record points margin of 23 in matches between these two countries. The match was played in torrential rain throughout. On the day, one of the Scots' major weaknesses was failure to retain and recycle the ball when tackled. Two of the Welsh tries resulted from pirated Scottish ball.

Scotland's forwards gave a poor display in the loose and in the set pieces, leaving much to be desired. This was a match which posed the question for the Scots: 'Where do we go from here?' – and with England to face two weeks later there were not going to be any easy answers.

SCOTLAND 14   ENGLAND 15
Murrayfield
5 February 1994

Scotland: A. G. Hastings* (*Watsonians*); A. G. Stanger (*Hawick*), S. Hastings (*Watsonians*), D. S. Wyllie (*Stewart's-Melville*), K. M. Logan (*Stirling County*); G. P. J. Townsend (*Gala*), G. Armstrong (*Jedforest*); A. V. Sharp (*Bristol*), K. S. Milne (*Heriot's FP*), A. P. Burnell (*Lond. Scot.*), D. S. Munro (*GH-K*), A. I. Reed (*Bath*), P. Walton (*Northampton*), G. W. Weir (*Melrose*), R. I. Wainwright (*Edin. Acad.*).
Replacements: I. R. Smith (*Gloucester*) for R. Wainwright (67 min.); I. C. Jardine (*Stirling County*) for S. Hastings (72 min.). Temporary replacement: B. W. Redpath (*Melrose*) for G. Armstrong (49-51 min.).
England: J. Callard (*Bath*); T. Underwood (*Leicester*), W. D. C. Carling* (*Harlequins*) P. R. de Glanville (*Bath*), R. Underwood (*Leicester*); C. R. Andrew (*Wasps*), K. Bracken (*Bristol*); J. Leonard (*Harlequins*), B. C. Moore (*Harlequins*), V. E. Obogu (*Bath*), M. C. Bayfield (*Northampton*), M. O. Johnson (*Leicester*), J. P. Hall (*Bath*), B. B. Clarke (*Bath*), N. A. Back (*Leicester*).
Referee: L. McLachlan (*New Zealand*).

Penalty goal by J. Callard (0-3); try by R. Wainwright (5-3). (H.T.). Penalty goal by A. G. Hastings (8-3); penalty goal by J. Callard (8-6); penalty goal by J. Callard (8-9); penalty goal by A. G. Hastings (11-9); penalty goal by J. Callard (11-12); dropped goal by G. Townsend (14-12); penalty goal by J. Callard (14-15).

This was the match that restored Scotland's pride and esteem. Prior to the match the scribes and pundits gave them little or no chance; one former English international player was quoted as suggesting that the margin of an England win might be as much as 70 points! Of such thoughts are paper dreams made – but this Scotland team had other ideas and made their critics think again.

The fact that the lead changed hands six times (five in the last quarter) gives every indication of the huge drama of this match. Although England opened the scoring, the Scots, quickly aware of England's defensive frailties, pumped Garryowens at their dithering opponents. The Scots created havoc in the attempted-orderliness of the English ranks – harrying them into all kinds of nervous errors, only heeding the offside line when the referee did.

The Scots came more and more into the game: the lineouts were evenly divided by the end of the match (Scotland were 4-12 down on lineout count at half-time). The only try of the game was scored by Rob Wainwright, the best forward on view. The Scots looked to have won the game when Gregor Townsend lofted a high drop kick between the posts at the Ice Rink end in the last minute of normal time – but they had reckoned without fate. An attempted drop kick by Rob Andrew was charged down by Gregor Townsend but, with the seconds of injury time ticking away, a last ruck was formed and the referee ruled that a Scottish hand had illegally played the ball on the deck and, from the resulting penalty award, Jonothan Callard made no mistake with the kick.

The fact that subsequent television replays showed the referee to have apparently erred (it transpired that it had been an *English* hand on the ball), did nothing to placate all disappointed Scots – the fact only rubbed salt into the wound and increased the feeling that they had been 'Doubly robbed'. For all their superior technique and handling skills, England had not deserved to win. Their success had all the hallmarks of an act by Dick Turpin!

Despite all the excitement and emotion, in time to come the records will show a win for England – a 'steal' if ever there was one.

IRELAND 6   SCOTLAND 6
Lansdowne Road
5 March 1994

Ireland: C. M. P. O'Shea (*Lansdowne*); R. M. Wallace (*Garryowen*), M. J. Field (*Malone*), P. P. A. Danaher (*Garryowen*), S. P. Geoghegan (*Lond. Irish*); E. P. Elwood (*Lansdowne*), M. T. Bradley* (*Cork Const.*); N. J. Popplewell (*Greystones*), T. J. Kingston (*Dolphin*), P. M. Clohessy (*Young Munster*), B. F. Robinson (*Ballymena*), M. J. Galwey (*Shannon*), N. P. J. Francis (*Old Belvedere*), W. D. McBride (*Malone*), P. S. Johns (*Dungannon*).
Scotland: A. G. Hastings* (*Watsonians*); A. G. Stanger (*Hawick*), S. Hastings (*Watsonians*), D. S. Wyllie (*Stewart's-Melville*), K. M. Logan (*Stirling County*); G. P. J. Townsend (*Gala*), G. Armstrong (*Jedforest*); A. V. Sharp (*Bristol*), K. S. Milne (*Heriot's FP*), A P. Burnell (*Lond. Scot.*), P. Walton (*Northampton*), D. S. Munro (*GH-K*), A. I. Reed (*Bath*), I. R. Smith (*Gloucester*), G. W. Weir (*Melrose*).
Temporary replacement: M. Dods (*Gala*) for A. G. Hastings (39-40 min.).
Referee: E. F. Morrison (*England*).

Penalty goal by E. Elwood (3-0). (H.T.). Penalty goal by A. G. Hastings (3-3); penalty goal by A. G. Hastings (3-6); penalty goal by E. Elwood (6-6).

The Scottish pack had to dig deep into their reserves of fitness when facing a gale-force wind in the first-half and displayed heroics in doing so, rucking and driving with great control and determination. The lineouts were fairly evenly contested, Scotland being just ahead at 16-15.

The Scots tackled like demons and thwarted any threatening Irish moves. Gregor Townsend, the Scots new stand-off, had a fine game and showed blazing acceleration on the break. The return of scrum-half Gary Armstrong seemed to work wonders for Scottish morale. He exuded class in all he did and posed a constant threat to the Irish.

The Scots had the better of the first half exchanges and should have made certain of victory in the second. That they did not could be attributed to stout Irish defence. A draw was just right in this match of shared fortunes – but the Scots may well look back and think of it as 'the one that got away'.

SCOTLAND 12   FRANCE 20
Murrayfield
19 March 1994

Scotland: A. G. Hastings* (*Watsonians*); A. G. Stanger (*Hawick*), S. Hastings (*Watsonians*), D. S. Wyllie (*Stewart's-Melville*), K. M. Logan (*Stirling Co.*); G. P. J. Townsend (*Gala*), B. W. Redpath (*Melrose*); A. V. Sharp (*Bristol*), K. S. Milne (*Heriot's FP*), A. P. Burnell (*Lond. Scot.*), D. S. Munro (*GH-K*), A. I. Reed (*Bath*), P. Walton (*Northampton*), I. R. Smith (*Gloucester*), G. W. Weir (*Melrose*).
France: J-L Sadourny (*Colomiers*); P. Saint-Andre* (*Montferrand*), P. Sella (*Agen*), Y. Delaigue (*Toulon*), W. Techoueyres (*SPUC*); T. Lacroix (*Dax*), A. Macabrau (*Perpignan*); L. Benezech (*Racing Club*), J-M Gonzalez (*Bayonne*), L. Seigne (*Merignac*), O. Brouzet (*Grenoble*), O. Merle (*Grenoble*), P. Benetton (*Agen*), L. Cabannes (*Racing Club*), A. Benazzi (*Agen*). Replacement: P. Montlaur (*Agen*) for T. Lacroix (52 min.).
Referee: W. D. Bevan (*Wales*).

Penalty goal by T. Lacroix (0-3); try by J-L Sadourny, converted by T. Lacroix (0-10); three penalty goals by A. G. Hastings (9-10); penalty goal by T. Lacroix (9-13). (H.T.). Try by P. Saint-Andre, converted by P. Montlaur (9-20); penalty goal by A. G. Hastings (12-20).

The Hastings' brothers, Gavin and Scott, each played his 50th international for Scotland in this match, albeit their caps were won by slightly different routes. This game also saw Gavin raise his points total for Scotland to 466.

These landmarks apart, Scotland had little to enthuse over following this match. France were not a great team but they were just that little bit better than Scotland. The Scottish pack again played splendidly and this season's newcomers, Peter Walton, Shade Munro and Alan Sharp, showed up well. Scotland won the lineouts by 27-15 but the backs had a less productive match.

A number of the senior international players pronounced themselves unavailable for selection for the forthcoming tour to Argentina. Some of those will enjoy a well-earned rest from rugby and give themselves a chance to recharge their batteries and be fully fit for the 1994-95 season and the Rugby World Cup in South Africa in 1995.

Five Nations Championship 1993-94

	P	W	L	D	F	A	Pts
Wales	4	3	1	0	78	51	6
England	4	3	1	0	60	49	6
France	4	2	2	0	84	69	4
Ireland	4	1	2	1	49	70	3
Scotland	4	0	3	1	38	70	1

ARGENTINA 16   SCOTLAND 15
Buenos Aires
4 June 1994

Argentina: S. E. Meson; M. J. Teran, D. Cuesta Silva, M. H. Loffreda*, G. M. Jorge; G. del Castillo, N. Fernandez Miranda; M. Corral, J. J. Angelillo, E. P. Noriega, P. L. Sporleder, G. A. Llanes, R. Martin, P. Camerlinckx, C. Viel Temperley.
Scotland: M. Dods (*Gala*); C. A. Joiner (*Melrose*), I. C. Jardine (*Stirling Co.*), A. G. Shiel (*Melrose*), K. M. Logan (*Stirling Co.*); G. P. J. Townsend (*Gala*), B. W. Redpath (*Melrose*); A. V. Sharp (*Bristol*), K. D. McKenzie (*Stirling Co.*), A. P. Burnell (*Lond. Scot.*), D. S. Munro (*GH-K*), A. I. Reed* (*Bath*), P. Walton (*Northampton*), I. R. Smith (*Gloucester*), C. D. Hogg (*Melrose*).
Referee: W. J. Erickson (*Australia*).

Penalty goal by S. Meson (3-0); penalty goal by M. Dods (3-3); penalty goal by S. Meson (6-3). (H.T.). Try by M. Teran, conv. by S. Meson (13-3); penalty goal by S. Meson (16-3); four penalty goals by M. Dods (16-15).

Running rugby seemed to be a lost art as this match developed into a procession of set pieces. Scotland's tactics backfired because of their indifferent kicking – especially from hand.

The Pumas looked a very ordinary side but the Scots were unable to take advantage of the apparent shortcomings of their opponents. The visitors failed to play the kind of dynamic game which must surely have overcome such opposition.

All of Scotland's points came from the boot of Michael Dods who scored five penalty goals from ten attempts.

ARGENTINA 19   SCOTLAND 17
Buenos Aires
11 June 1994

Argentina: S. E. Meson; M. J. Teran, D. Cuesta Silva, M. H. Loffreda*, G. M. Jorge; G. del Castillo, N. Fernandez Miranda; F. E. Mendez, J. J. Angelillo, E. P. Noriega, P. L. Sporleder, G. A. Llanes, R. Martin, J. Santamarina, C. Viel Temperley.
Scotland: M. Dods (*Gala*); C. A. Joiner (*Melrose*), I. C. Jardine (*Stirling Co.*), A. G. Shiel (*Melrose*), K. M. Logan (*Stirling Co.*); G. P. J. Townsend (*Gala*), B. W. Redpath (*Melrose*); A. V. Sharp (*Bristol*), K. D. McKenzie (*Stirling Co.*), A. P. Burnell (*Lond. Scot.*), D. S. Munro (*GH-K*), A. I. Reed* (*Bath*), P. Watson (*Northampton*), I. R. Smith (*Gloucester*), C. D. Hogg (*Melrose*). **Referee:** W. J. Erickson (*Australia*).

Two penalty goals by G. Shiel (0-6); try by R. Martin, conv. by S. Meson (7-6); two penalty goals by S. Meson (13-6). (H.T.). Penalty goal by S. Meson (16-6); dropped goal by G. Townsend (16-9); try by K. Logan (16-14); penalty goal by M. Dods (16-17); dropped goal by G. del Castillo (19-17).

Scotland did not deserve to lose this second Test of their tour of Argentina. The Scottish forwards were much more effective than in the first Test, being faster in the loose and rucking more positively. However, as in the first Test, the Scots missed a number of scoring opportunities. Goal kicking was entrusted to Graham Shiel but, after a promising start by kicking two early penalty goals from two attempts, he then missed with a further three kicks.

Scotland did well to recover from a 6-16 deficit just after half-time to take a 17-16 lead, but a dropped goal by G. del Castillo near the end, denied them a victory which they deserved.

SCOTLAND 17   BARBARIANS 33
Murrayfield
9 May 1970

Scotland: I. S. G. Smith (*London Scot.*); M. A. Smith (*London Scot.*), J. N. M. Frame (*Gala*), J. W. C. Turner (*Gala*), A. G. Biggar (*London Scot.*); I. Robertson (*Watsonians*), D. S. Paterson (*Gala*); N. Suddon (*Hawick*), F. A. L. Laidlaw* (*Melrose*), A. B. Carmichael (*West of Scot.*), P. K. Stagg (*Sale*), G. L. Brown (*West of Scot.*), T. G. Elliot (*Langholm*), P. C. Brown (*Gala*), R. J. Arneil (*Leicester*)
Barbarians: J. P. R. Williams (*Wales*); A. T. A. Duggan (*Ireland*), J. S. Spencer (*England*), D. J. Duckham (*England*), K. J. Fielding (*England*); P. Bennett (*Wales*), G. O. Edwards (*Wales*); D. B. Llewelyn *(Wales)*, J. V. Pullin (*England*), P. O'Callaghan (*Ireland*), M. G. Molloy (*Ireland*), S. Gallacher (*Wales*), M. L. Hipwell (*Ireland*), J. F. Slattery (*Ireland*), T. M. Davies (*Wales*). **Referee:** R. P. Burrell (*Gala*)

Two pen. goals by P. Brown (6-0); try by K. Fielding, conv. by J. Williams (6-5); try by D. Duckham (6-8). (H-T). Try by D. Duckham, conv. by J. Williams (6-13); try by J. Spencer, conv. by J. Williams (6-18); try by M. Molloy, conv. by J. Williams (6-23); try by G. Edwards, conv. by J. Williams (6-28); try by T. Elliott, conv. by P. Brown (11-28); try by D. Llewelyn, conv. by J. Williams (11-33); two pen. goals by P. Brown (17-33).

This was the Barbarians first-ever visit to Murrayfield. The Scots, about to set off on a tour to Austrialia, were soundly beaten by a very good Barbarians team. The try count of 7-1 tells its own story. The Scots were immediately handicapped when Mike Smith was injured after only three minutes play and took no further part in the match. They also lost scrum-half Dunc Paterson fifteen minutes from the end. This disruption brought about an unusual solution in Peter Brown's moving to scrum-half. The thirteen players gave a good account of themselves in the final quarter of an hour. Despite taking a lot of ball at lineouts, the Scots were out-gunned by the Barbarians attacking play.

IV

The Calcutta Cup, Triple Crowns and Grand Slams

The formation of a unique club

British émigrés in Calcutta in the 1870s expended their sporting energies in playing polo and tennis but some rugby followers and players yearned for an outlet for their particular sporting interest. Their frustrations brought about some agitated letter-writing to the editors of *The Englishman* and the *Indian Daily News* to try to drum up interest and support in the idea of an organised rugby match. The campaign bore fruit and, on Christmas Day 1872, a match between a XX representing England and XX representing Scotland, Ireland and Wales, was played. The match was a great success, so much so that it was repeated a week later: the game of rugby football had reached India!

Those rugby enthusiasts, who had been instrumental in planning and arranging the matches had been encouraged and were keen to take their idea a step further and form a club. – and so it was that the Calcutta Football Club was founded in January 1873. The club's first year was most successful: 137 members, a free bar (described in the Centenary History of the Rugby Football Union as being '... a slight sop to Cerberus ...'), and an interesting fixture list: Calcutta FC v. The Calcutta Volunteers (the second club to be formed in the area), Calcutta Club v. The Military, Scottish and Irish v. English and Welsh, Griffs v. The Rest, and other unusual team names.

The Calcutta Club were admitted to membership of the Rugby Football Union in 1874. The Indian climate was not ideal for the playing of rugby but, during that first year, the club prospered. In the second year, however, the free bar had to be discontinued, resulting in an appreciable drop in membership. Another stumbling block proved to be the lack of opponents.

Playing members did not, it would appear, present a problem. Officers of the Buffs and of the 62nd Regiment coached and trained 'other ranks' and officers in the playing of the game. (This was in direct contrast with the actions of the then organisers of the Inter-Services Tournament in the U.K.: over thirty years were to pass before that tournament was opened up to 'other ranks').

255

Among their members the club had B. H. Burns, a Scot who had played in the England XX in the first international in 1871. They had other international players, too, in Stephen Finney (England) and an Irishman, G. St Leger Fagan who was to be capped for his country at a later date. Stephen Finney was to be knighted in 1913.

The Calcutta Club was not lacking for funds but finding suitable opponents did pose a problem. Sports such as tennis and polo, which were considered to be more suitable for the local climate, were making inroads into the numbers of gentlemen available. This state of affairs forced the Club to close down after only four years in existence.

The question then arose as to what to do with the club funds. Suggestions were many and varied: a 'beano' in the form of a gymkhana, a ball, and a dinner were all suggested and discarded. The Club Captain, G. A. James Rothney (who was also Honorary Secretary and Treasurer) pointed out that the celebrations suggested would be but transient and quickly forgotten. He then made a suggestion, with a great sense of history (whether intentional or not), which was carried by the members and which was to be instrumental in keeping alive for ever the memory of the Calcutta Football Club.

Rothney's suggestion was that the funds be used to have made a trophy of ornate Indian craftsmanship and that this be offered to the RFU in London. A letter to this effect was sent to the Honorary Secretary and Treasurer of the RFU. The letter, dated December 20th 1877, stated:

... as the best means of doing some lasting good for the cause of Rugby Football and as a slight memento of the Calcutta Club that the funds remaining to the credit of the Club should be devoted to the purpose of a Challenge Cup and presented to the Rugby Union to be competed for annually in the same way as the Association Cup or in any other way the Committee of the Rugby Union may consider best for the encouragement of Rugby Football ... beg their kind acceptance of a Cup and also to enquire if the Committee would prefer one of Indian workmanship, or the money remitted for the purchase of a cup at home? The sum of money at my disposal at the present rate of Exchange is about £60 sterling ...

Rothney's letter, charming yet to-the-point, related the background, the birth, the life and the death of the Calcutta Football Club. The club had been enthusiastic when in existence and, at the end, determined to do good for the advancement of rugby. The advent f the Calcutta Cup opened the way for keen competition, between England a   otland, on the field of international rugby, adding an incentive to matches u ween the two countries.

The RFU's response was positive. A. G. Guillemard, President of the RFU, wrote:

The Committee accept with very great pleasure your generous offer of the cup as an international challenge cup to be played for annually by England and Scotland – the cup remaining the property of the Rugby Football Union.

This acceptance saw the Calcutta Club officials close their bank account, withdrawing the balance due in silver rupees. These they had melted down and crafted by the finest Indian workmanship into what is an original, elegant and distinguished trophy. Known world-wide as the Calcutta Cup, it is 18 inches high, has three handles in the form of cobras and has a handsome lid surmounted by an elephant.

The inscription on the Cup's wooden base (which was added later) reads:

THE CALCUTTA CUP

PRESENTED TO THE RUGBY FOOTBALL UNION

BY THE CALCUTTA FOOTBALL CLUB

AS AN INTERNATIONAL CHALLENGE CUP

TO BE PLAYED FOR ANNUALLY BY ENGLAND AND

SCOTLAND

1878

Attached to the base are plates which record the date of each match played, with the name of the winning country and the names of the two captains.

The first Calcutta Cup match was played at Raeburn Place, Edinburgh, on 10 March 1879, and ended in a draw – Scotland scoring a dropped goal and England a goal. Including that match in 1879, England and Scotland have, up to 1994, contested the Calcutta Cup on 103 occasions, England having won the trophy 52 times, Scotland 37, with 14 matches having been drawn. In Rugby World Cup ties, if the two countries meet, the Calcutta Cup is not up for competition.

The records on the base of the Cup carry an anomaly. The Cup was first competed for in 1879 but an inspection of the plinth shows records extending back to the first international in 1871 – eight years before the Calcutta Cup came into being.

The original Cup is seldom seen by the public. Whether held in London or in Edinburgh, it is stored securely in a safe vault and withdrawn, usually, only on match days. However, in 1990, the Bovis Construction Group very generously donated full-size replicas of the Calcutta Cup to the Rugby Museums at Murrayfield and at Twickenham. This enables visitors to admire the rare beauty and craftsmanship of the original. The replicas were produced by making use of modern technology.

The Calcutta Club's letter to the RFU, in December 1877, stated that the members desired to '... do some lasting good for the cause of Rugby Football...'. We are left to wonder if the members had any inkling as to just how prophetic those words were to become. The Calcutta Cup: the catalyst that spawned the still-growing world-wide brotherhood of rugby football which, today, spans the five continents and allows opportunity for all, who may wish, to enjoy the camaraderie that comes from playing the game in spirited but friendly competition.

The Triple Crown

This rather mythical accolade is thought to have been coined by newspaper journalists. A Home country (England, Ireland, Scotland or Wales) is said to have won the Triple Crown when they have defeated each of the three other Home countries in the Five Nations Championship series of matches, in any one international season. There is no trophy, cup, flag or other reward for achieving the Triple Crown: merely the prestige of having done so.

Scotland have won the Triple Crown on 10 occasions.

The Grand Slam

This equally-mythical accolade is probably also the invention of journalists. A Grand Slam is achieved when one of the countries taking part in the Five Nations series of matches (the four Home countries plus France) defeats each of the other four in any one international season. Again, there is no tangible reward for achieving a Grand Slam: merely the prestige that goes with such success.

Scotland have had Grand Slam successes on only three occasions: 1925, 1984 and 1990.

The Five Nations series

Scotland and France first met in an official rugby international in 1910. From that date, war years and disputes apart, the five competing nations have played each other in this series of matches. Although it was not officially intended at the outset, inevitably newsmen compiled the match results into a league table. It is possible to win the series (the 'championship') without necessarily achieving a Grand Slam: a country could be champions even if they were defeated in one match but unlikely if they lost two.

Up to, and including, 1992 there was no material reward for a country's being champions. However, for the 1993 series of matches, a handsome cup, known as 'The Five Nations Championship Trophy' was presented for competition. France were the first winners in 1993 and Wales in 1994.

Scotland have been Five Nations Champions on 19 occasions and wooden spoonists (the least successful country in a series) on 24 occasions.

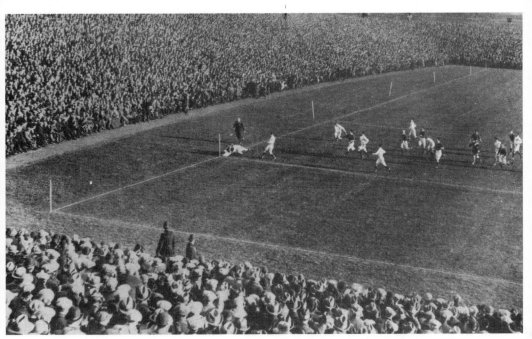

1. 1925 Scotland *v* England. The opening match at Murrayfield. A.C. Wallace, the Scottish winger, dives under the attempted tackle by T.E. Holliday the English full-back to score a vital try which was converted by A.C. Gillies to make the score 10-11. Later, H. Waddell dropped a goal to win the match for Scotland (14-11) and thus secure Scotland's first-ever Grand Slam success. [See page 88].

2. 1925 Scotland *v* England: the successful team.
Standing (l. to r.): D. J. MacMyn *(Cambridge Univ.)*, J. W. Scott *(Stewart's College FP)*, A. C. Gillies *(Carlisle)*, J. C. H. Ireland *(Glas. HSFP)*, R. Howie *(Kirkcaldy)*, I. S. Smith *(Oxford Univ.)*.
Seated: G. G. Aitken *(Oxford Univ.)*, D. S. Davies *(Hawick)*, J. M. Bannerman *(Glas. HSFP)*, G. P. S. Macpherson *(Oxford Univ., Capt.)*, D. Drysdale *(Heriot's FP)*, A. C. Wallace *(Oxford Univ.)*, H. Waddell *(Glas. Acad.)*. *In front:* J. B. Nelson *(Glas. Acad.)*, J. R. Paterson *(Birkenhead Park)*.

3. An artist's impression of medieval street football. Played on feast days by enthusiastic students and other youths, it was abhorred by officialdom and other would-be keepers of the peace. [See page 2].

4. Trophy cap and jersey badge, 1871. These belonged to J. W. Arthur *(Glas. Acad.)*. Initially, in international rugby, players bought their own trophy caps and paid to have them dated. The SFU decided that, from season 1891-92, trophy caps would be presented by the Union. Early caps, like the one illustrated, were of the plain skullcap type. A front peak was added around 1880.

5. 1879 Scotland v England. The first Calcutta Cup match: the Scotland XV.
Back row (L. to r.): R. Ainslie *(Edin. Inst. FP)*, E. N. Ewart *(Glas. Acad.)*, H. M. Napier *(West of Scot.)*, D. R. Irvine *(Edin. Acad.)*, J. B. Brown *(Glas. Acad.)*.
Middle: N. J. Finlay *(Edin. Acad.)*, R. W. Irvine *(Edin. Acad., Capt.)*. A. G. Petrie *(RHSFP)*, J. H. S. Graham *(Edin. Acad.)*, J. A. Neilson *(Glas. Acad.)*.
Front: N. T. Brewis *(Edin. Inst. FP)*, J. E. Junor *(Glas. Acad.)*, M. Cross *(Glas. Acad.)*, W. E. MacLagan *(Edin. Acad.)*, J. A. Campbell *(Merchistonians)*. [See page 20].

6. 1938 England v Scotland. The Scottish captain, R. W. Shaw, after a brilliant solo run, beats the attempted tackle by G. W. Parker, the English full-back on the touch-line, to score the first of his two tries and make the score 12-9 at half-time. As 'no-side' approached he scored a second individual try to make the final score 21-16 in Scotland's favour, thus securing the Triple Crown for the Scots. [See page 110].

7. 1963 France *v* Scotland. Right on 'no-side', Iain Laughland's attempted drop goal fell short of the left-hand post and bounced over P. Besson's head. R. H. Thomson, the Scotland *right* winger gathered the ball in full cry and scored in the *left*-hand corner. Ken Scotland's conversion made the score 11-6 for Scotland as the final whistle sounded. [See page 152].

8. 1971 Having defeated England in a Five Nations match at Twickenham the previous Saturday, Scotland again faced the 'Auld Enemy' at Murrayfield a week later in a match to mark the Centenary of the first-ever international in 1871 [See pages 7-14]. From the kick-off, the English backs made a mess of a passing move, the ball being dropped. John Frame pounced on the loose ball and crossed the line – 10 to 12 seconds from kick-off! This was one of the quickest tries ever scored in international rugby. Scotland won the match 26-6. [See page 174].

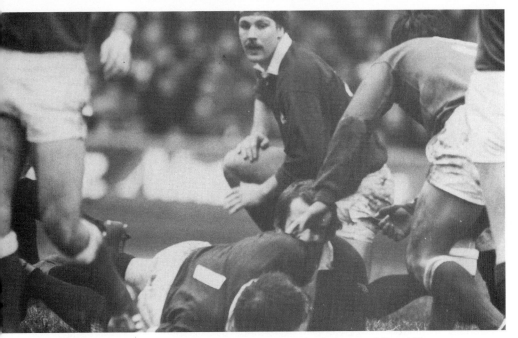

9. 1984 Wales *v* Scotland. En route to what was to prove to be their second Grand Slam success, Scotland defeated Wales 15-9 in Cardiff. With the scores even at 9-9, Jim Aitken scored this captain's try which gave Scotland the victory. [See page 208].

10. 1984 Scotland *v* France. The scoreline was 12-12, the time was twenty-three minutes past four: 'no-side' was approaching when Jim Calder plunged over the French line for this try which was converted by Peter Dods who was also to kick another penalty goal (his fifth in the match). The sheer joy on Jim Calder's face is unmistakable: Scotland had secured their second Grand Slam success. [See page 210].

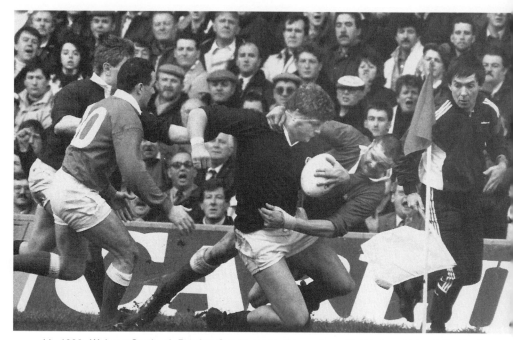

11. 1990 Wales *v* Scotland. Damian Cronin opens the scoring with this try which set the Scots on their way to victory, and a grandstand finale to the season at Murrayfield two weeks later. [See page 232].

12. 1990 Scotland *v* England. Tony Stanger, having scored a try in the opening minute of the second half to make the score 13-4 for Scotland, turns to receive the congratulations of his team-mates, leaving a dejected Rory Underwood on the ground whilst Micky Skinner turns away. [See page 232].

13. 1990 Scotland v England. Happiness is ... the sheer joy in the realisation that the 'Auld Enemy' have been defeated and that the Calcutta Cup, the Triple Crown, the Grand Slam and the Five Nations Championship have been secured for your country. Following 'no-side', Tony Stanger punches the air in delight whilst John Jeffrey and Gavin Hastings race up the field with new-found energy following a hard eighty minutes of play.

14. The way it was. This post-1936 photograph of Murrayfield shows the North and East terracings, complete with score box, and the original West Stand with the North Wing Stand which was added in 1936. [See page 269].

15. The nearly-complete Murrayfield in 1994. The terracings have gone as can be seen from this aerial view which shows the new North and South Stands with the corners having also been completed, and the almost-ready new West Stand. The refurbished stadium was opened with a match v. South Africa on 19th November 1994.

V

The Webb Ellis Trophy:
Rugby World Cup

Whilst the leading rugby-playing countries in Europe – England, France, Ireland, Scotland and Wales – competed on a regular annual basis, matches with other countries were only possible when teams were either taken on tour to another country (outwith the Five Nations) or when a touring team visited one or more of the European countries.

The opportunity for rugby-playing countries from around the world to meet together in a truly international competition was first made possible in 1987 when the inaugural competition for the Webb Ellis Trophy (Rugby World Cup) took place. The leading rugby-playing countries were seeded to take part in the final stages of the competition.

The finals were played in Australia and New Zealand with sixteen countries, playing in four groups, with four countries playing a round-robin competition in each group. Scotland were drawn in Group 4 along with France, Romania and Zimbabwe. The Scots finished top equal in their group along with France but, the French having scored three tries to the Scots' two in their 20-20 opening match, the French went on to meet Fiji in the quarter finals whilst the Scots had to face the formidable All Blacks. New Zealand eliminated the Scots but France went on to contest the final with New Zealand, the All Blacks being the victors and thus the first winners of the new trophy.

Accounts of Scotland's matches can be found on pp 221-223.

The second Rugby World Cup competition was played in Europe in 1991 with matches played in each of the Five Nations countries. It was organised and run on similar lines to that of the 1987 competition. On this occasion, Scotland were drawn in Group 2 along with Ireland, Japan and Zimbabwe. Scotland's matches, throughout the initial stages of the competition, were played at Murrayfield. By topping their group, Scotland met Western Samoa in a quarter-final tie, also at Murrayfield, and by achieving success in that match they progressed to the semifinals. In that match they were defeated by England at Murrayfield.

The team then went to Cardiff to contest the play-off for third and fourth places with New Zealand. The All Blacks won the tie, leaving Scotland to occupy fourth place in the competition – and that was no mean achievement for a small country.

Accounts of all Scotland's matches in the 1991 Rugby World Cup are on pp 239-243.

The third competition for the Webb Ellis Trophy is scheduled to take place in South Africa in 1995.

VI

Touring Teams: Scotland to other countries – other countries to Scotland

The first touring teams

The first rugby touring team was one taken to Australia and New Zealand during the home summer of 1888 by Messrs Shaw and Shrewsbury, two professional cricketers who had just returned from a successful cricket tour of Australia. Three Scots were included in the party: W. Burnet, R. Burnet and A. J. Laing, all from Hawick, and, on their return, were promptly interviewed by the SFU about the terms, management and conduct of the tour. However, they were able to give satisfactory assurances about any alleged professionalism and the matter was dropped.

There followed a tour of Britain by the 'Maori' team during the 1888-89 season but only one match was played in Scotland when Hawick, playing on their new ground at Mansfield Park, were beaten by 3-5.

With the IB dispute behind them, the Home Unions began to co-operate in staging a succession of rugby tours to the Colonies – South Africa in 1891, 1896, 1903, and Australia/New Zealand in 1899 and 1904. The inevitable return visit was first sought by New Zealand in 1902 but this did not materialise until the 1905-6 season while the first South African visit took place during the following season.

The first New Zealand tour did not pass without controversy. Firstly the visitors adopted a novel formation of seven forwards packing two-three-two and always tried to pack down not on the opposition middle man but on one of the flank forwards so leaving the other 'prop' with no one to push against. This not only gave them the loose head but provided an extremely rapid heel. This was made good use of by having three half backs. One put the ball into the scrum but generally remained at his mid-way position to become what most considered to be a quite illegal offside obstruction. The second half played in the scrum half position with the third 'standing off'. The result was an extremely rapid and unobstructed supply of the ball to their very efficient backs.

261

Well before the tour was even begun the SFU had made it clear that they would not accede to the New Zealand request for a guaranteed sum from each match but offered instead the nett gates, after deduction of expenses, from their two matches. Later comments by J. Aikman Smith, as Treasurer, revealed that his committee, while genuinely anxious to do everything possible to assist the visitors, was faced with a fairly hefty Debenture Debt and Bond on the new ground at Inverleith, so was not prepared to ask its Trustees to undertake a further guarantee. However, as a result of the agreement reached the tourists received nearly £1700, a sum something like four times the amount a guarantee would have given them and as a result the SFU was later frequently made the butt of sarcastic humour over the outcome. It is only fair to make two points here: first, a committee which contained men of the professional background and quality such as W. Neilson, J. D. Dallas, J. C. Findlay (a barrister, Sheriff and solicitor), Robin Welsh (gentleman farmer), A. B. Flett, J. W. Simpson (doctors) and steered by J. Aikman Smith (Chartered Accountant), lacked neither legal, financial nor business sense. These men knew what they were doing and, secondly, showed this by offering precisely the same terms to the South Africans for their visit in the following season.

Nevertheless the SFU remained perturbed about the amateur status of the New Zealand players, making it known that they did not feel justified in handing over money without knowing what was to be done with it and once the South African tour was over asked for copies of the accounts of both tours. Those for the South African tour soon arrived and were accepted but the New Zealand set came much later and at once the SFU queried an entry therein of 3s (15p) per day for players' expenses. When they learned that this had been authorised by the RFU they were so disturbed that they wrote cancelling the next Calcutta Cup match. The whole question was at once laid before the IB who ruled: (1) that Scotland were not entitled to cancel the fixture without reference to the Board; (2) that the question of those daily payments to players should not be pressed; (3) that in future no such allowances be made to any player. These findings the SFU accepted, feeling that it would be in the best interests of the game that they should do so. Yet it had been noted that the Scottish motion on the payments had failed by a vote of six-six so it was no surprise to find the SFU making a request to the IB for equal representation of the four countries for all purposes. This was debated and eventually, in 1910, a compromise was achieved by England reducing its representation to four thus permitting the other countries to have a majority vote if desired.

In 1960, Scotland was the first country to introduce and experiment with a short tour. The Scots played South Africa in Fort Elizabeth, being defeated 10-18. The tour was deemed to have been very successful and laid the groundwork for similar tours in years to come.

With the spread of rugby's popularity as a game, and with world travel becoming more readily available, Scotland's rugby opponents, from other countries, have increased in number. Following the Second World War, and certainly since the 1960s, the international fixtures list, for Scotland's tours and for touring teams visiting Scotland, has expanded rapidly. The following lists give a breakdown of all Scotland's tours and touring teams visiting Scotland, including non-cap matches played by Scotland XVs.

Scotland on Tour

To New Zealand: 1975, 1981, (RWC 1987), 1990
To South Africa: 1960
To Australia: 1970, 1982, 1992
To Romania: 1984,
To Argentina: 1994

Scotland XVs on tour

To Canada: 1964
To Canada and U.S.A.: 1985, 1991
To France: 1980
To Argentina: 1969
To Fiji, Tonga and Western Samoa: 1993
To France: 1986
To Japan: 1977, 1989
To Zimbabwe: 1988

Touring teams in Scotland

New Zealand: 1905, 1935, 1954, 1964, 1967, 1972, 1978, 1979, 1983, 1993
South Africa: 1906, 1912, 1932, 1951, 1961, 1965, 1969, 1994
New South Wales: 1927
Australia: 1947, 1958, 1966, 1968, 1975, 1981, 1984, 1988
Romania: 1981
Argentina: 1990
Fiji: 1989
RWC: 1991

Touring teams versus Scotland XVs

Spain: 1987
Argentina: 1973
France XV:1987
Japan: 1976, 1986
Tonga: 1974
Fiji: 1982

VII

The Scottish Football Union: The Scottish Rugby Union: The International Rugby Football Board

The Scottish Football Union

In May 1872 the Grange Cricket Club, having settled into their new ground just across the lane from the Academy field at Raeburn Place, opened it with a grand match 'Edinburgh v Glasgow' and this was so successful that it may well have been the reason why the rugby men staged two inter-city matches, one in Glasgow in December 1872 and a return in Edinburgh in January 1873. Certainly the cricket and rugby fraternities of these days were closely linked, because they shared not only many players but also playing areas. Indeed, most of Scotland's early international rugby matches were played on cricket fields.

The two inter-city matches and the trials for the 1873 International in Glasgow were arranged by the quondam Scottish Committee but obviously the aims and success of the new English Union had not gone unnoticed, and sometime during the autumn or early winter of 1872 the first steps to form a Scottish Union were taken at a small dinner session in the University Club in Edinburgh. Those present were Dr John Chiene, James Wallace, R. Craigie Bell and Harry Cheyne (Edinburgh Academicals), B. Hall-Blyth (Merchistonians) and Albert Harvey (Glasgow Academicals) – a group of players of considerable professional standing which was later to provide the first three Presidents, one Vice-President and the first Secretary of the future Scottish Football Union. All, except Harvey, were graduates of Edinburgh University: Chiene finished as a very distinguished Professor of medicine; Wallace, an Advocate, became a Sheriff; Bell and Cheyne were Writers to the Signet; Hall-Blyth was a noted Civil Engineer, whilst Harvey, from a family of distillers, was a prominent merchant in Glasgow.

The eventual outcome of their discussion was a notice calling a meeting on Monday, 3 March 1873 to be held in the old Glasgow Academy in Elmbank Street at 4.30 pm (i.e. immediately after the end of the Scotland v. England match at Hamilton Crescent) to consider 'the propriety of forming a Football Union in Scotland on a similar basis to the Rugby Union in England'.

This meeting duly took place with Dr Chiene called to the Chair and it was agreed that such a Union should be created with the objects of (1) providing funds for a Cup (2) bringing into closer connection the clubs then playing (3) the formation of a committee by whom the Scotch International team might in future be chosen.

A provisional committee consisting of the Captain and one other member from each of the following clubs: Edinburgh, Glasgow and St Andrews Universities, Edinburgh and Glasgow Academicals, West of Scotland, Royal High School FP and Merchistonians, with James Wallace as Secretary, was nominated to draw up the Bye-Laws of a Union to be submitted at a General Meeting to be held before the opening of the next season. There must have been little doubt about the outcome of this meeting for the International dinner card for that same evening not only carried a toast to the Rugby Football Union but also one for this embryonic Scottish Football Union.

Eventually the First AGM of the Scottish Football Union was held in Keith & Co's Rooms, 65A George Street, Edinburgh at 4.30pm on Thursday, 9 October 1873. Harry Cheyne, WS, was in the Chair and the meeting first approved and passed the Bye-Laws of the new Union. The idea of providing a Cup had been discarded—a decision that was to be maintained for many years to come. It was, however, agreed that the new Union should co-operate with the Rugby Football Union but this was a relationship that, after some ten years, became badly strained. It was also decided that the working committee should consist of a President, Vice President, Honorary Secretary and Treasurer with the Captains of all the member clubs.

The Bye-Laws having been passed, the meeting then admitted the Wanderers FC (Edinburgh) and Warriston FC as members, so whilst the eight original clubs may be termed founder members those two additional clubs now joined them as original members of the Union.

Here we may look ahead and review briefly the changes in the composition of the committee that were to follow up to the war in 1914. The original set-up remained until 1876 by which time the number of member clubs had risen to 21, and it was then passed that the committee should consist of the three office bearers with two representatives from both the Eastern and Western Districts – a number that was increased to three each in 1880. By then the game had become firmly established in areas outside the two cities and recognition of this came in 1889 when the Northern and Southern Districts both added a single member to the committee. Not content with this the Borders (who, to put it bluntly, had their reservations about being controlled by the Old School Tie Brigade) succeeded in 1894 in raising the South representation to two while reducing the West to the same number. The proposer stated: 'This was not dictated by any hostility to Glasgow but from a sense of justice to the South who boasted as many clubs as the West and who were not deficient in play'. Needless to say the Western contingent protested vigorously, even more so when in 1896 the London District were granted a single representative, and the question of numbers was raised and voted on without result until 1905 when a sub-committee produced a report on the matter. This report, amongst other points, suggested that the East and South representation should drop to two and one respectively. Again for two years these numbers were discussed without result until in 1908 when they were accepted in spite of the continued opposition of the South who maintained that one man could not do justice to the needs of their scattered community. The next significant change came in 1910 when it was decided to appoint A.D. Flett, CA (Edinburgh Wanderers) as Treasurer — the first paid official of the Union. Finally, in March 1914, with no knowledge of the disruption that lay ahead, J. Aikman Smith, acting on medical advice, announced his intention to demit office at the next AGM. So a new Constitution was prepared which retained the seven District representatives, proposed the addition to the committee of five Special Representatives who, without vote, would serve for a period of five years and allowed the engagement of a paid Secretary. At the AGM, changed to a new date in May, this Constitution was passed and A.D. Flett was appointed to the dual position of paid Secretary and Treasurer. At the Union's AGM in 1924, some decisions were made to change some of the Bye-Laws. One alteration that was proposed and accepted was to change the name of the Union to 'The Scottish Rugby Union'. The original name had been used for over fifty years.

The International Rugby Football Board

Since Kindersley's disputed try (England v. Scotland, 1.3.1884) was destined to start discussions which led to the formation of the International Rugby Football Board, the course of events may be set out now.

Two versions of the incident may be quoted, the first by G. Rowland Hill, the Secretary of the RFU: 'In the course of play the ball was knocked back by a Scotsman (C. W. Berry), one of the English team secured it and a try was obtained. The Scots claimed that 'knocking back' was illegal; the English held that it was not an illegal act and even though it had been, the act was done by a Scotsman and as no Englishman claimed for it, the Scotsmen could not claim for or profit by their own infringement.'

The other account came from A. R. Don Wauchope who played in the game: 'In those days there were two umpires who carried sticks, not flags, and a referee without a whistle. The ball was thrown out of touch, an appeal was made, the umpire on the touch line (J.H.S. Graham) held up his stick, all the players with the exception of four Englishmen and two Scotsmen, stopped play-ing and England scored a try. The only question of fact decided by the referee was that a Scotsman knocked the ball back. This, according to the Scottish view of the reading of the rule, was illegal and the whole question turned on the interpretation. The point that no Englishman had appealed was never raised at the time and to judge by the fact that eleven of the English team ceased play, it would appear that their idea was that the game should stop.'

If we note that the Advantage Law was not introduced until 1896, some of the Scottish resentment over the try may be better understood and the basic cause of the trouble revealed as a lack of uniformity in the interpretation of the rules.

Following the match the SFU entered into a correspondence with the RFU and while maintaining that the try was invalid, eventually offered to have the question adjudicated by some neutral body. The RFU, while more or less agreeing that a difference in interpretation existed, would not accept arbitration, maintaining that the referee, having made a decision on a question of fact, must have his authority on the field upheld. These two views could not be reconciled and as a result the fixture for 1885 was not arranged.

At their AGM in 1885 the Irish Union suggested that the four Unions should meet to discuss the possible formation of a body which would be useful for the settling of International disputes. Such a meeting did take place in Dublin in February 1886 and one outcome was that Scotland agreed to cede the 1884 game to England on the understanding that the latter would join an International Board composed of equal numbers of representatives of each Union and whose duty would be to decide on such points of law that might arise in International matches. This Board was duly inaugurated in Manchester in early 1886 but the RFU were not represented and later refused to accept the constitutional terms agreed on. At their own AGM in October 1886 they decided to alter their scoring system only to find the other Unions passing the decision to the new IB, which met in Liverpool in early 1887 and decreed that all International games should use the RFU Rules of 1885.

By now it was clear that England was not prepared to yield her position as lawmaker for the game and in March 1887 the RFU offered to allow representation from each Union to attend and vote at any committee meeting dealing with possible alterations in the rules. They received no replies but were faced by an IB ultimatum in December 1887 which decreed that the IB Rules must be used in all International games and that no English matches would be arranged unless the RFU accepted this by joining the IB. This was not taken up and as a result England played no International games in 1888 and 1889.

The IB's views were splendidly summed up in a manifesto issued in September 1888 but there was no reaction from the RFU until December 1889 when they took the decisive step of offering to submit the dispute to arbitration before two persons, one nominated by the IB and one by the RFU. As a result Lord Kingsburgh, the Lord Justice Clerk (whom we last met as Mr Macdonald taking the gate money at Raeburn Place in 1871), and Major Marindin, President of the Football Association, were nominated, met and by April 1890 produced their judgment which established the present International Rugby Football Board.

Basically the new constitution satisfied the Unions by establishing that all Internationals should be played under one Code of Laws maintained and administered by the new board, while the RFU were satisfied by having six members on the board as compared with two each from the other Unions.

VIII
Scotland's International Grounds

The very first rugby international was played at Raeburn Place, Edinburgh, on Monday, 27 March 1871, on the cricket field of the Edinburgh Academy. Indeed, Scotland's first nine home internationals were all played on established cricket fields. The second match was played at Hamilton Crescent, Glasgow, the home of West of Scotland CC. Both fields were used for rugby trial matches and internationals up until 1895. The SFU rented the fields on a match-to-match basis, paying a rental of £25 in 1875, a sum which gradually rose to £30 in 1881 by which year the gate money had more than doubled. A temporary stand, costing £45, was erected at Raeburn Place.

In time, Edinburgh Academy became increasingly unhappy with the arrangement; the field was in constant use by pupils of the school, including Saturdays, and there was little time left to prepare the ground for the international matches which were played on Monday afternoons – the field having been in use by the school in the forenoon!

Search for a suitable ground

The cricket clubs began to raise objections to the SFU about that body's applying for the use of their grounds. The complaints included the crowds swarming over their field, the erection of temporary stands and the SFU's insistence that cricket club members should pay for entry to watch the rugby internationals. On the other hand, the SFU were unhappy about the ground being used on the morning of a match and the loss of revenue created by cricket members and others gaining entry without payment.

Things came to a head in October 1895 when the Edinburgh Academical Club let it be known that they were no longer prepared to lease the field to the SFU. This blow forced the Union's hand and they entered into an arrangement for the use of Old Hampden Park, Glasgow, in time for the 1896 match v. England. District and Trial matches were also affected and these were played at Merchiston Castle School and the Newington ground of The Royal High School FPs.

Inverleith: the first purpose-built international rugby ground

The Union's search for a suitable ground was long and fraught with difficulties, disappointments and frustrations. The public raised many objections: they simply did not want an international rugby ground in their locality. Eventually, in 1897, the Union was successful in purchasing land at Inverleith, Edinburgh. The purchase cost was £3,800: the money was raised by means of a debenture issue. With this piece of business successfully completed, the SFU became the first of the Home Unions to own its rugby ground complete with stand.

To bridge the gap between moving from Raeburn Place and into Inverleith, the SFU made arrangements for the playing of two internationals at Powderhall Sports Ground in Edinburgh – v. Ireland in 1897 and v. England in 1898. The opening of Inverleith suffered an immediate setback with the planned first match, v. Wales in January 1899, having to be postponed because of inclement weather. This resulted in the first visitors being Ireland on 18 February 1899. The match result was not one that had been hoped for: Scotland 3 Ireland 9. The rescheduled Welsh match was played on 4 March 1099, Scotland 21 Wales 10.

The First World War (1914-18) saw Inverleith little used apart from some military rugby matches but little by way of maintenance was carried out. By the end of hostilities, the general condition of the ground, the buildings and fitments, were the cause of some concern to the SFU. In addition to these difficulties, the Union had other problems to address and solve. Rugby had increased in popularity and it became clear that Inverleith could not satisfactorily cope with the larger crowds at internationals. In addition, the public demand for stand seats could not be met.

The dilemma for the Union was compounded by the clubs in the west of Scotland making increasing demands for some international matches to be played in Glasgow. The only suitable ground there was Hampden Park, the home of Queens Park FC.

A new name and a new ground: Murrayfield

The SFU showed interest in land at Corstorphime, previously occupied by The Royal High School FP Club, but the opportunity was lost when the land was taken over by the City in 1921. Concurrently with these enquiries, the Union had looked into the possibility of leasing land to the east of Inverleith, belonging to the Fettes Trust. Estimates were sought and obtained for the building of a second stand should the application be successful.

Whilst all of this exploratory activity was taking place, the then Honorary Secretary and Treasurer of the SFU announced that there was an opportunity to possibly acquire 19 acres of land at Murrayfield. Negotiations were entered into with the Edinburgh Polo Club and, by the end of 1922, the purchase of the ground had been completed.

A special debenture issue raised the capital necessary for the preparation of the land and the construction of a purpose-built rugby stadium. Preparations were in full swing when the Union decided on a name-change for itself: in season 1924-25 it became known as The Scottish Rugby Union.

Scotland played their last international match at Inverleith on 25 January 1925, the game recording a result befitting Burns' Day: Scotland 25 France 4.

Murrayfield was officially opened on a sunny day on 21 March 1925. England were the visitors and a more fitting climax to the international rugby season, and the handselling of a new stadium, could not have been better scripted: it was pure *Boys' Own* stuff!

Scotland already had victories over France at Inverleith (25-4), Wales in Swansea (24-14) and Ireland in Dublin (14-8) England, the Grand Slam champions of the two previous seasons, already had a win over Wales (12-6) and a drawn game with Ireland (6-6) – both matches played at Twickenham; they were to go on to defeat France in Paris (13-11) in April. The 70,000 spectators at the newly-opened Murrayfield were treated to a stupendously exciting match in which the lead changed hands three times before Scotland came from behind at 10-11 to secure victory by means of a dropped goal by stand-off Herbert Waddell. The final score of 14-11 meant that Scotland had achieved their first-ever Grand Slam. Fifty-nine years were to pass before they successfully performed the feat for a second time.

Improvements and expansion

Over a period of time improvements were made to the stadium and its surrounds. Land to the west was purchased (1927) to prepare additional pitches for use by junior clubs, and two access bridges were built over the Water of Leith. A car park was prepared.

The Union's audaciousness in moving to Murrayfield proved to be fully justified. There was an increasing demand for stand tickets and, attempting to alleviate this difficulty, the Union had two wing extensions built on to the West Stand (1936), thereby increasing the seating capacity to 15,228.

The War Memorial Arch, erected at Inverleith in 1921, was transferred to Murrayfield (1936) and improvements were carried out to the dressing rooms and to the Committee Room, with a Committee Box within the stand also being created. Past-President Sir David McCowan gifted a clock tower, still a landmark today, in 1929; Past-President J. Aikman Smith presented the first score box and Sheriff Watt, K.C., presented a flagstaff and flag (1931).

The war years

During the Second World War, Murrayfield was offered to the nation and was used as an army supply depot. War-time England v. Scotland Services Internationals were arranged on a home-and-home basis each year, the Scotland matches being played at Inverleith. In 1944 Murrayfield was derequisitioned and handed back to the SRU.

The post-war years

Following the reorganisation of the game in 1945, Murrayfield was the venue for a number of 'Victory' international matches in 1946, no caps being awarded to participating players. Full international matches at Murrayfield were resumed on 1 February 1947, Scotland 8 Wales 22 – a result not exactly to the liking of Scots!

Five years of wartime neglect had taken its toll of the ground, the stand and terraces. The metalwork, the roof and the seating of the stand all underwent major overhaul. The terracing had to be cleared of overgrown grass and weeds, 2-3 feet high in places.

The Union's offices in Coates Crescent were transferred to new accommodation at the Stadium in 1964. Extra office staff were taken on to meet the increasing workload.

Undersoil heating: the first electric blanket

In the early 1950s investigation was made into the possibility of installing an undersoil heating system for the playing area. The estimated cost of such a system proved to be prohibitive and the idea was shelved. Wintry conditions posed a constant threat to matches and the then existing contingency arrangements to protect the playing surface were somewhat Heath-Robinson and not entirely satisfactory. If hard frost threatened, the playing area had tent-like canopies pitched over it with tall paraffin heaters within – supplemented by tons of straw. The remarkable thing about these arrangements was that they did work but were very costly of time, manpower and materials. Then, in 1959, Dr C. A. Hepburn magnanimously offered to meet the cost (£10,000) for the installation of an undersoil electric blanket. The Union gratefully accepted the offer.

A new undersoil heating system

The original electric blanket served the Union well for over thirty years but, by the end of the 1980s, it was beset by recurring maintenance problems and a decision was made to have it replaced (1991). The opportunity was taken to switch to a more modern system of gas-heated water pipes laid below the playing surface. The new system included drainage, sand-slitting and irrigation of the pitch and was costed at £250,000. Work went ahead and the pitch was ready in time for the Rugby World Cup matches in October 1991.

Crowd problems and a new stand

Murrayfield had played host, comfortably, to 70,000 spectators at many of the internationals played there but the match against Wales in 1975 (Scotland 12 Wales 10) saw 104,000 spectators in attendance – a world record for a rugby international. Hundreds, many of them ticket holders, could not gain entry to the ground. Following that match a decision was made that all future internationals would be all-ticket with attendance restricted to 70,000.

In July 1981 the Union decided to build a new stand in place of the East Terracing. The new East Stand cost £3.15 million and was ready for use for the matches against Ireland and Wales early in 1983. The official opening ceremony was performed by the then HRH The Princess Anne prior to the match v. The Barbarians on 26 March 1983.

The building of the East Stand necessitated the demolition of the old scorebox and the installation of two electric scoreboards, one on each stand. Mrs G. P. S. Macpherson, widow of one of Scotland's most prominent international rugby players, graciously contributed toward the cost of a clock at the rear of the new stand, in memory of her husband.

New office and Committee accommodation was built at the rear of the West Stand (1985) and a rugby Library and Museum was established within an area of the West Stand in 1986.

An all-seated stadium

By 1990 plans were drawn up to explore the feasability of building stands to replace the North and South Terracings. This action came about partly because of government legislation (The Taylor Report) which demanded that major sporting venues attain certain laid-down criteria by season 1994-95. All-seated stadia was one of the recommendations. To meet the cost of this major refurbishment, the Union launched what turned out to be a successful debenture scheme, and reconstruction work, at an eventual cost of £41 million, started after the Five Nations series of matches in 1992 with a target date for completion of the entire plan by 1995. Whilst work on the terracings went ahead, fresh plans were drawn up for the West Stand. The original decision had been to refurbish and extend the stand but it was then decided to demolish entirely the West Stand and replace it with a completely new purpose-built stand which would match in with and complement the new North and South Stands.

The work is on schedule for completion in time for the visit of South Africa in November 1994 at which time Scotland will be able to boast one of the finest sports stadiums in Europe: an all-covered, all-seated Murrayfield capable of hosting 67,500 spectators.

Early Laws and Rules of Play

Laws of Football at Rugby School 1846

1. Kick off from Middle must be a place kick.
2. Kick out must not be from more than 25 yards out of goal, nor from more than 10 yards if a place kick.
3. Fair catch is a catch direct from the foot.
4. Charging is fair, in the case of a place kick, as soon as the ball has left the ground; in the case of a kick from a catch, as soon as the player offers to kick, but he may always draw back, unless he has actually touched the ball with his foot.
5. Offside – A player is off his side if the ball has touched one of his own side behind him until the other party kick it.
6. A player being off his side is to consider himself as out of the game, and is not to touch the ball in any case whatever (either in or out of touch); or in any way to interrupt the play, and is, of course, incapable of holding the ball.
7. Knocking on, as distinguished from throwing on, is altogether disallowed under any circumstances whatsoever. In case of this rule being broken, a catch from such a knock on shall be equivalent to a fair catch.
8. It is not lawful to take the ball off the ground, except in touch, either for a kick or throw on.
9. First of His Side is the player nearest the ball on his side.
10. Running In is allowed to any player on his side, provided he does not take the ball off the ground, or through touch.
11. If, in the case of a run in, the ball is held in a scrummage, it shall not be lawful for the holder to transmit it to another of his own side.
12. No player may be held, unless he is himself holding the ball.
13. It is not fair to hack and hold at the same time.
14. No hacking with the heel, or unless below the knee is fair.
15. No one wearing projecting nails or iron plates on the soles or heels of his shoes or boots shall be allowed to play.
16. Try at Goal – A ball touched down between the goal posts may be brought up to either of them but not between.
17. The ball when punted must be within, and when caught without the line of goal.
18. The ball must be placed kicked and not dropped and if it touches two hands the try will be lost.
19. It shall be a goal if the ball goes over the bar (whether it touches or not) without

having touched the dress or person of any player; but no player may stand on the goal bar to interrupt it going over.

20. No goal may be kicked from touch.
21. Touch – A player may not in any case run with the ball in touch.
22. A player standing up to another may hold one arm only, but may hack him or knock the ball out of his hand if he attempts to kick it, or go beyond the line of touch.
23. No agreement between two players to send the ball straight out shall be allowed.
24. A player having touched the ball straight for a tree and touched the tree with it, may drop from either side if he can, but one of the opposite side may oblige him to go to his own side of the tree.
25. In case of a player getting a fair catch immediately in front of his own goal, he may not retire behind the line to kick it.
26. No player may take the ball out of the Close.
27. No player may stop the ball with anything but his own person.
28. If a player takes a punt or drop when he is not entitled to it, the opposite side may take a punt or drop, without running (after touching the ball on the ground) if the ball has not touched two hands, but such a drop may not be a goal.
29. That part of the Island which is in front of the line of goal is in touch, that behind is in goal.
30. The discretion of sending into goal rests with heads of sides and houses or their deputies.
31. Heads of sides, or two deputies appointed by them, are the sole arbiters of all disputes.
32. All matches are drawn after 5 days or after 3 days if no goal has been kicked.

Laws 33–37 are of local interest only.

Some amendments of 1847

4. Charging is fair, in the case of a place kick, as soon as the ball has touched the ground.
5. Off side – A player is off his side, if the ball had been kicked or thrown on by one of his own side behind him, until the other party kick it, thrown it on or run with it.
26. No player may take the ball out of the Close, i.e. behind the line of trees beyond the goal.

Edinburgh Academicals FC Rules 1858

A foreword states 'The following Rules are taken from the Book of Rules used at Rugby'.
I. KICK OFF must be from MIDDLE and a place kick.
2. When the ball is touched down behind goal, if touched by the side behind whose goal it is, they have a KICK OUT; but if by the opposite side, they may have a TRY AT GOAL.
3. KICK OUT must not be from more than 25 yards out of goal .
4. FAIR CATCH is a catch direct from the foot, or a knock on from the HAND of the opposite side only.
5. A CATCH from a throw on is not a fair catch.
6. CHARGING is fair, in the case of a place kick, as soon as the ball has touched the ground; in case of a kick from a catch, as soon as the player offers to kick, but he may always draw back unless he has actually touched the ball with his foot.

7. OFFSIDE. A player is off his side when he is behind all the players on the opposite side, or in front of the kicker of his own side.
8. A player being off his side is to consider himself as out of the game and is not to touch the ball in any case whatever (either in or out of touch) or in any way to interrupt the play, and is of course incapable of holding the ball.
9. It is not lawful to take the ball off the ground, except in touch, for any purpose whatsoever.
10. It is not lawful to take the ball when rolling as distinguished from bounding.
11. RUNNING IN is allowed to any player on his side, provided he does not take the ball off the ground, or through touch.
12. RUNNING IN: If, in the case of a run in, the ball be held in a maul, it shall be lawful for a player on either side to take it from the runner in.
13. No player out of a maul may be held, or pulled over, unless he is himself holding the ball.
14. Though it is lawful to hold any player in a maul, this holding does not include attempts to throttle or strangle, which are totally opposed to all the principles of the game.
15. No one wearing projecting nails or iron plates on the soles or heels of his boots or shoes shall be allowed to play.
16. TRY AT GOAL: A ball touched between the goal posts may be brought up to either of them, but not between; but if not touched between the posts must be brought up in a straight line from where it is touched.
17. The ball, when punted, must be within, and when caught, without the line of goal.
18. The ball must be place kicked or dropped, but if it touches two players' hands the try will be lost.
19. It shall be a goal if the ball goes over the bar (whether it touch or no) without having touched the dress or person of any player; but no player may stand on the goal bar to interrupt it going over.
20. No goal may be kicked from touch or by a punt at any time.
21. TOUCH: A ball in touch is dead; consequently the first player on his side must in any case touch it down, bring it to the edge of touch and throw it suraight out, but may take it himself if he can.
22. No player may stop the ball with anything but his own person.
23. Heads of sides, or two deputies appointed by them, are the sole arbiters of all disputes.

Blackheath Club Rules 1862

1. That the ball be started from the centre of the ground by a place kick.
2. A fair catch is a catch direct from the foot or a knock on from the hand of one of the opposite side, when the catcher may either run with the ball or make his mark by inserting his heel in the ground on the spot where he catches it; in which case he is entitled to a free kick.
3. It is not lawful to take the ball off the ground, except in touch, for any purpose whatever.
4. A ball in touch is dead, and the first player who touches it down must kick it out straight from the place where it entered touch.
5. A catch out of touch is not a fair catch, but may be run off.
6. Running is allowed to any player on his side if the ball be caught or taken off the first bound.
7. Any player holding the ball unless he has made his mark after a fair catch, may be

hacked; and running is not allowed after the mark is made.

8. No player may be hacked and held at the same time – and hacking above or on the knees or from behind is unfair.
9. No player can be held or hacked unless he has the ball in his hands.
10. Though it is lawful to hold a player in a scrummage, this does not include attempts to throttle or strangle, which are totally opposed to the principles of the game.
11. A player whilst running or being held may hand the ball to one of his own side who may continue to run with it, but after the ball is grounded it must be hacked through, not thrown or lifted.
12. When a player running with the ball grounds it, it cannot be touched by anyone until he lifts his hand from it.
13. If the ball goes behind the goal it must be kicked out by the party to whom the goal belongs from in a line with the goals; but a catch off a kick behind goal is not a fair catch, but may be run off.
14. No player is to get before the ball on the side furthest from his own goal; but if he does he must not touch the ball as it passes him until touched by one of the opposite side, he being off-side.
15. A goal must be a kick through or over and between the poles, and if touched by the hands of one of the opposite side before or whilst going through, is no goal.
16. No one wearing projecting nails, iron plates or gutta-percha on the soles or heels of his boots be allowed to play.

Laws of Blairgowrie, Rattray and Neighbourhood 1865

1. The maximum length of the ground shall be 200 yards, the maximum breadth shall be 100 yards; the length and breadth shall be marked off with flags; and the goal shall be defined by two upright posts, 8 yards apart, without any tape or bar across.
2. The game shall be commenced by a place kick from the centre of the ground by the side winning the toss; the other side shall not approach within 10 yards of the ball until it is kicked off. After a goal is won the losing side shall be entitled to kick off.
3. The two sides shall change goals after each goal is won.
4. A goal shall be won when the ball passes over the space between the goal posts (at whatever height), not having been thrown, knocked on or carried.
5. When the ball is in touch, the first player who touches it shall kick or throw it from the point on the boundary line where it left the ground, in a direction at right angles with the boundary line.
6. A player shall be out of play immediately he is in front of the ball, and must return behind the ball as soon as possible. If the ball is kicked past a player by his own side, he shall not touch or kick it, or advance until one of the other side has first kicked it or one of his own side on a level with or in front of him has been able to kick it.
7. In case the ball goes behind the goal line, if a player on the side to whom the goal belongs first touches the ball, one of his side shall be entitled to a free kick from the goal line at the point opposite the place where the ball shall be touched. If a player of the opposite side first touches the ball, one of his side shall be entitled to a free kick from a point 15 yards outside the goal line opposite the place where the ball is touched.
8. If a player makes a fair catch he shall be entitled to a free kick, provided he claims it by making a mark with his heel at once; and in order to take such a kick he may go as far back as he pleases, and no player on the opposite side shall advance beyond his mark until he has kicked.
9. A player shall be entitled to run with the ball towards his adversaries' goal if he

makes a fair catch or catches the ball on the first bound; but in the case of a fair catch, if he makes his mark, he shall not then run.

10. If a player shall run with the ball towards his adversaries' goal, any player on the opposite side shall be at liberty to charge, hold, trip or hack him, or to wrest the ball from him; but no player shall be held and hacked at the same time.
11. Neither tripping nor hacking shall be allowed and no player shall use his hands or elbows to hold or push his adversary, except in the case provided for by Law 10.
12. Any player shall be allowed to charge another, provided they are both in active play. A player shall be allowed to charge even if he is out of play.
13. A player shall be allowed to throw the ball or pass it to another if he makes a fair catch, or catches the ball on the first bound.
14. No player shall be allowed to wear projecting nails, iron plates, or gutta-percha on the soles or heels of his boots.

Some definitions of terms follow, of which the most interesting are:

HACKING: Is kicking an adversary on the front of the leg below the knee.
CHARGING: Is attacking an adversary with the shoulder, chest or body, without using the hands or legs.
TRIPPING: Is throwing an adversary by the use of the legs without the hands, and without hacking or charging.
KNOCKING ON: Is when a player strikes or propels the ball with his hands, arms or body without kicking or throwing it.

These extracts are from W. P. Ireland & Isaac Donald: *Handbook to Blairgowrie, Rattray and Neighbourhood*, 1865

Kilmarnock FC Rules of Play 1869

1. The length of the ground shall be 200 yards, the breadth 100 yards, and the distance between the goal posts 15 feet.
2. Before the commencement of the Game, the Captain of each side, or their representatives, shall toss for choice of goals and the kick off. They shall also fix the time for leaving off playing.
3. In a Match, when half the time agreed upon has elapsed, the sides shall change goals the next time the ball is out of play. In ordinary games the change shall be made after every goal.
4. The ball shall be put in play as follows:
a. At the commencement of the game, and after every goal, by a place kick, from a point 25 yards in advance of the goal, by either side alternately.
b. If the ball has been played behind the goal line, the side owning the goal shall have a free kick from behind the goal line, at their discretion. But it is not permissable for one of a side wilfully to play the ball behind his own goal.
c. If the ball has been played across the side line, the player first touching it with his hand shall have a free kick from the point at which the ball crossed the line; the ball must be kicked into the ground at right angles to the side line.
5. In all the above cases the side starting the ball shall be out of play until one of the opposite side has played it; and in the last two, the ball shall not be considered in play until it has touched the ground.
6. When any player catches the ball by a fair and full catch, he is entitled to a free kick; and if caught when bouncing above the knee, he may, if he chooses, take a run with it.

7. Any player may hold, push with his hands, or trip any player of the opposite side, when within 4 yards of the ball.
8. Though it is lawful to hold any player with the ball, this holding does not include attempts to throttle or strangle, which are, of course, opposed to all the principles of the game.
9. It is not lawful to pick up the ball for any purpose whatever (except in touch, or after it has been touched down in goal, to take it out).
10. No player may wear iron plates or projecting nails on his boots or shoes.
11. No hacking allowed.
12. A goal is gained when the ball is kicked in between the two flags which mark out the goals.
13. In case of any distinct and wilful violation of these rules of play, by one of either side, the opposite side may claim a fresh kick off.

Definition of terms

A 'place kick' is a kick at the ball while it is at rest on the ground.
'Touch' is that part of the field on either side of the ground, which is beyond the line of flags.
'Hacking' is kicking an adversary intentionally.

These extracts are from J. F. T. Thomson: *More Than a Game: Kilmarnock R. F. C. Centenary History 1868-1973*

APPENDIX 2

Reports and Hark-backs to Early Games

Extract from a letter to the Editor.

Many years ago, when I had occasion to hunt for the origin of Rugby, I discovered that the High School played a carrying game round about 1810. This fact I mentioned to some of my old English football friends and others when we gathered at Rugby in 1923 as representatives of the carrying game to help to celebrate the centenary-so-called. When told that they had given the name 'Rugby' to the game, but that they certainly did not invent it as it had been played in Scotland for unknown years before 1823 and by the High School about 1810, some of them were very annoyed.

I am not an old High School boy and in fact was one of her 'enemies' in the football world and only wish I could claim that my old school was as close to the origin of rugby as was the High School.

H. J. Stevenson

Harry Stevenson W. S. (Edin. Acads.) was one of the most outstanding backs of his time, playing fifteen times for Scotland between 1888 and 1893.

The Scotsman November 1937

Comments on the first Edinburgh Academy-Merchiston match

Football at Merchiston this year is very different and superior to the game as played last year (i.e. 1857-58). For this improvement we have to thank the Rugby rules and those who introduced them. Last year there was no order in the game whatever; it was each for himself, each kicking recklessly ahead, very little running with the ball and 'off side' scarcely heard of. Now it is far different, each one has that place assigned to him for which he is most suited, whether goalkeeper, muddler, dodger or as a member of that useful body, thé light brigade.

Last year we were disappointed in playing the Academy but now it was fixed as the first match of the season. Accordingly, at about 11 a.m. of Saturday, 11th December last an omnibus drew up at the gate of the Academy field and discharged the 20 Merchistonians eager for the fight and a few who had come as spectators.

... we could not help observing that the Academy goals were a good deal easier to kick over than ours, being both lower and broader ...

Lyall ... runs into touch right behind our goal. Here an expostulation was made on the plea that the rules prohibited running into touch but finding that it only related to side touch, we were obliged to yield and allow the try at goal.

We had always been accustomed to play over the area of the whole field, our only boundaries being the goals and the school wall on one side and the paling at the bottom of the field on the other.

... we thought we had a goal, for McFie kicked the ball easily over, but it stood for nothing as it was handed to him 'off his side'.

... Willie Tennent comes in for his share of kudos ... the agility he displayed in leaping through the wires round the cricket ground after the ball (in touch!)

Our captain must not be forgotten, his way of ridding himself of those who press upon him too closely in a maul by stamping on their toes is admirable.

The Merchistonian, January 1859

Comments on the second Edinburgh Academy-Merchiston match

'The Academy had two Academicals on their side, Merchiston confining itself strictly to the residents at the school. This was, perhaps, the best way of settling an amicable controversy we have had for some time with the Academy, relative to the right of playing masters.'

The Merchiston XX is known and included Mr Almond.

The Merchiston Chronicle, February 1859

APPENDIX 3

Postponements, Abandonments and Disputes

There were various reasons for certain international matches not being played. In 1878, the Scotland v. Ireland match, scheduled to be played in Glasgow, did not take place because the two Irish Unions (the Irish Football Union and the Northern Football Union of Ireland) were in dispute with each other. The disagreements ended with the formation of a single body, the Irish Rugby Football Union in 1879.

The 1885 match in Belfast was abandoned after 20 minutes play because of very extreme inclement weather – gale force winds and heavy rain. The two countries agreed to play a second match, at Raeburn Place in Edinburgh, a month later. These two matches, played in 1885, posed something of a rugby conundrum to historians and record-keepers. The Irish decided that the abandoned match would not count as an international and did not award caps to their players. By contrast, Scotland took the view that, as the players had taken the field, and play did commence, then the game should count as a match – and the Scottish players were, accordingly, credited with caps. Thus, some Scottish players were awarded two caps against Ireland in 1885, whilst some Irish players had none to their credit.

This state of affairs did not seem to matter very much – until the playing of the 100th match neared. Scottish records showed that the match due to be played in Edinburgh in 1989 would be the 100th; the Irish point-of-view was that that milestone would be reached in Dublin in 1990. This raised the question: 'When is one hundred perhaps not one hundred?' Fortunately, good sense prevailed and both Unions agreed that, in fact, the 1989 match was, indeed, the 100th between the two countries.

Matches against England in 1885, 1888 and 1889 did not take place because of a dispute arising from the 1884 match. The discussions arising from this dispute led to the formation of the IB in 1890.

Wales found themselves in dispute with the IB and withdrew from that body in 1897-98. This meant that matches with that country were cancelled for these years.

Disputes with France meant that no internationals were played with that country between 1932 and 1939 .

Two World Wars (1914-18 and 1939-45) meant the discontinuation of all rugby internationals, although 'Services Internationals' were played during, and immediately following, the Second World War.

In 1972, the political situation in Ireland led to the cancellation of the Ireland v. Scotland fixture due to have been played in Dublin.

APPENDIX 4

Scoring Systems and Schemes

Matches played prior to the 1891 season were won by the majority of goals scored. 'Goals' included converted tries, dropped goals, goals from a mark and the rarely-achieved field goal. That particular scheme meant that tries had no scoring value in themselves: the try was merely the means by which a team was allowed an attempt to convert the try. If successful, the team was credited with having scored a goal. The scheme, as described, created some rather anomalous situations. For example, the Royal High School FPs drew their match with Edinburgh University in 1872: RHSFP scored one goal and seven tries against one goal and one try by the University. The University converted their try with the last kick of the game, thus drawing the match. However, had RHSFP not converted their seventh try, they would have been deemed to have lost.

A points scoring scheme, which would have credited 10 points for each goal scored, 5 points for a try and one point for a touch down, was discussed at the SFU's AGM in 1875. The scheme, as suggested, was rejected.

Then, In November 1875, a revised scheme was put forward, thus:

A match shall be decided by a majority of goals but if the number of goals be equal, or no goal be kicked, by a majority of tries; if no goal be kicked or try obtained, the match shall be drawn.

A month later, in December 1875, the Committee of the SFU voted for the adoption of this scheme and announced that it should be given effect to from the start of the next season.

In 1882, a rule was introduced which awarded a penalty kick for offside - but no goal could be dropped or placed from the award. In 1888, the RFU decided that a goal could be scored from a penalty kick but it was 1891 before this new ruling was adopted by the IB.

For international matches, a uniform points scoring system was introduced in 1890-91 when the IB system was adopted. Previously, various experiments in scoring had been tried but different scoring values in the Home countries had resulted in confusion.

The following table indicates the scoring values from season 1890-91. The introduction of the free kick, in season 1977-78, saw the discontinuation of the goal from a mark.

	Goal from mark	Conversion	Dropped goal	Penalty goal	Try
1889-90	3	2	3	2	2
1890-91	3	2	3	2	1
1891-92 to 1892-93	4	3	4	3	2
1893-94 to 1904-05	4	2	4	3	3
1905-06 to 1947-48	3	2	4	3	3
1948-49 to 1970-71	3	2	3	3	3
1971-72 to 1976-77	3	2	3	3	4
1977-78 to 1991-92	void	2	3	3	4
1992-93 to present	–	2	3	3	5

APPENDIX 5

Scottish Captains

A = Australia; Ar = Argentina; Barb = Barbarians; C = Canada; E = England; F = France; Fj = Fiji; I =Ireland; J = Japan; NZ = New Zealand; NSW = New South Wales; P = SRU President's XV; R = Romania; *RWC* = Rugby World Cup; SA = South Africa; Sp = Spain; T = Tonga; USA = United States of America; W = Wales; WS = Western Samoa; Z = Zimbabwe

* =   Non-cap international   ** = Services and Victory Internationals

F. J. Moncreiff	Edin. Acads	(3)	1871: E 1872: E 1873: E
W. D. Brown	Glas. Acads.	(2)	1874: E 1875: E
R. W. Irvine	Edin. Acads.	(8)	1876: E 1877: I.E. 1878: E 1879: I.E. 1880 I.E.

J. H. S. Graham	Edin. Acads.	(2)	1881: I.E.
R. Ainslie	Edin.Inst. F.P.	(1)	1882: I
D. Y. Cassels	West of Scot.	(4)	1882: E 1883: W.I.E.
W. E. Maclagan	London Scottish	(8)	1884: W.I.E. 1885: W.I (2) 1890: W.E.
J. B. Brown	Glas. Acads.	(3)	1886: W.I.E.
C. Reid	Edin. Acads.	(4)	1887: W.I.E. 1888: W.
A. R. Don Wauchope	Fettesians-Lorettonians	(1)	1888: I.
D. S. Morton	West of Scot.	(2)	1889: W.I.
M. C. McEwan	Edin. Acads.	(4)	1890: I. 1891: W.I.E.
C. E. Orr	West of Scot.	(3)	1892: W.I.E.
R. G. Macmillan	London Scottish	(6)	1893: W 1894: W 1895: I.E. 1897: I.E.
J. D. Boswell	West of Scot.	(4)	1893: I.E. 1894: I.E.
W. R. Gibson	RHSFP	(1)	1895: W
G. T. Neilson	West of Scot.	(3)	1896: W.I.E.
A. R. Smith	Oxford Univ.	(2)	1898: I.E.
W. P. Donaldson	West of Scot.	(1)	1899: I.
M. C. Morrison	RHSFP	(15)	1899: W.E. 1900: W.E. 1901: W.I.E. 1902: W.I.E. 1903: W.I. 1904: W.I.E.
T. Scott	Hawick	(1)	1900: I.
J. R. C. Greenlees	Cambridge Univ.	(1)	1903: E
W. P. Scott	West of Scot.	(2)	1905: W.I.
A. B. Timms	Edin. Univ.	(1)	1905: E
D. R. Bedell-Sivright	Edin. Univ.	(1)	1905: NZ
L. West	Hartlepool; L. Scot.	(3)	1906: W.I.E.
L. L. Greig	Glas. Acads.; Un. Services	(4)	1906: SA 1907: W 1908: W.I.
P. Munro	London Scot.	(5)	1907: I.E. 1911: F.W.I.
I. C. Geddes	London Scot.	(1)	1908: E
J. M. B. Scott	Edn. Acads.	(2)	1909: W.I.
G. Cunningham	Oxford Univ.	(4)	1909: E 1910: F.I.E.
G. M. Frew	Glas. HSFP	(1)	1910: W
J. C. MacCallum	Watsonians	(5)	1911: E 1912:F.W.I.E.
F. H. Turner	Liverpool; Oxford Univ.	(5)	1912: SA 1913: F.W.I.E
D. M. Bain	Oxford Univ.	(1)	1914: W
E. Milroy	Watsonians	(2)	1914: I.E.
A. W. Angus	Watsonians	(1)	1920: F
C. M. Usher	London Scot.; Edn. Wrs.	(7)	1920: W.I.E 1922: F.W.I.E
A. T. Sloan	Edn. Acads.	(1)	1921: F
J. Hume	RHSFP	(3)	1921: W.I.E.
A. L. Gracie	Harlequins	(4)	1923: F.W.I.E.
J. C. R. Buchanan	Stewart's Coll. FP	(4)	1924: F.W.I.E

283

G. P. S. Macpherson	Oxford Univ. Edin. Acads.	(12)	1925: F.W.E 1927: F.W.I 1930: F.W.I.E 1931: E 1932: E
D. Drysdale	Heriot's F.P.; Oxford Univ. London Scot.	(11)	1925: I 1926: F.W.I.E. 1927: E.NSW 1928: F.I.E. 1929: F
J. M. Bannerman	Glasgow HSFP	(4)	1928: W 1929: W.I.E.
W. N. Roughead	London Scottish	(3)	1931: F.W.I.
W. M. Simmers	Glas. Acads.	(3)	1932: SA.W.I
I. S. Smith	London Scottish	(3)	1933: W.E.I
H. Lind	Dunfermline	(1)	1934: W
M. S. Stewart	Stewart's Coll. FP	(2)	1934: I.E
K. C. Fyfe	Camb. Univ.	(1)	1935: W
R. W. Shaw	Glasgow HSFP	(9)	1935: I.E.NZ 1938: W.I.E. 1939: W.I.E.
R. C. S. Dick	Guy's	(2)	1936: W.I
J. A. Beattie	Hawick	(1)	1936: E
W. R. Logan	Edn. Wndrs.	(3)	1937: W.I.E
C. L. Melville	Army	(*4)	**1942: E. (2) **1943: E (2)
J. A. Waters	Selkirk	(*2)	**1944: E (2)
K. I. Geddes	RAF; Wasps; London Scots.	(*6+2)	**1945: E (2) **1946: NZ.W.I.E 1947: F.W
D. W. Deas	Heriot's FP	(*2)	**1946: W.E
W. H. Munro	Glas. HSFP	(1)	1947: I
C. R. Bruce	Glas. Acads.	(1)	1947: E
J. R. S. Innes	Aberdeen GSFP	(5)	1948: A.F.W.I.E
D. H. Keller	London Scot.	(4)	1949: F.W.I.E
W. I. D. Elliot	Edn. Acads.	(7)	1950: F.W.I 1954: NZ.I.E.W
P. W. Kininmonth	Richmond	(8)	1950: E 1951: F.W.I.E 1952: F.W.I
A. Cameron	Glasgow HSFP	(9)	1951: SA 1953: I.E 1955: W.I.E. 1956: F.W.I
A. F. Dorward	Gala.	(3)	1952: E 1953: F.W
J. N. G. Davidson	Edn. Univ.	(1)	1954: F
J. T. Greenwood	Dunfermline: Perth Acads.	(9)	1955: F 1956: E 1957: F.W.E. 1958: E 1959: F.W.I
A. R. Smith	Camb. Univ: Gosforth	(15)	1957: I 1958: F.W.A.I 1960: F.W.
	Ebbw Vale: Edn. Wrs.		1961: SA.W.I.E. 1962: F.W.I.E
G. H. Waddell	Cam. Univ.	(4)	1959: E 1960: I.E.SA
K. J. F. Scotland	Heriot's FP	(4)	1963: F.W.I.E
J. B. Neill	Edn. Acads.	(6)	1964: F.NZ.W.I.E 1965: F
M. J. Campbell-Lamerton	London Scottish	(2)	1965: W.I
S. Wilson	London Scot.	(4)	1965: E.SA 1966: F.W

284

l. H. P. Laughland	London Scot.	(2)	1966: I.E
J. P. Fisher	London Scot.	(9)	1966: A 1967: F.W.I.E.NZ. 1968: F.W.I
J. W. Telfer	Melrose	(*2+10)	1968: E.A 1969: F.W.I.E.SA. *1969: Ar. (2) 1970: F.W.I.
F. A. L. Laidlaw	Melrose	(2)	1970: E.A *Barb
P. C. Brown	Gala.	(9)	1971: F.W.I.E 1972: F.W.E.NZ 1973: F
J. McLauchlan	Jordanhill	(*2+19)	1973: W.I.E.P *Ar. 1974: W.E.I.F. *T 1975: I.F.W.E.NZ.A. 1976: F.W.E.I. 1979: NZ
I. R. McGeechan	Headingley	(9)	1976: *J 1977: E.I.F.W. 1978: NZ. 1979: W.E.I.F.
D. W. Morgan	Stew.-Mel. FP	(4)	1978: I.F.W.E
M. A. Biggar	London Scottish	(3)	1980: I.F.W.
A. R. Irvine	Heriot's FP	(15)	1980: E. 1981: F.W.E.I.NZ (2). R.A. 1982: E.I.F.W.A(2).
R. J. Laidlaw	Jedforest	(*1+5)	1982: *Fj. 1983: I.F.W.1984: A. 1985: I.
J. Aitken	Gala	(7+*1)	1983: E.*Barb.NZ. 1984: W.E.I.F.R.
D. G. Leslie	Gala	(3)	1985: F.W.E.
C. T. Deans	Hawick	(13+*2)	1986: F.W.E.I.R. *J 1987: I.F.W.E.*Sp. RWC: F.Z.R.NZ.
G. J. Callander	Kelso	(5+*1)	1987: *F. 1988: I.F.W.E.A.
P. W. Dods	Gala	(1+*2)	1988: *Z(2). 1991: RWC: Z.
F. Calder	Stewart's-Melville	(4)	1989:W.E.I.F.
A. Brewster	Stewart's-Melville	(*1)	1989: *J
D. M. B. Sole	Edinburgh Acad.	(25+*1)	1989: Fj.R. 1990: I.F.W.E. NZ(2). Ar. 1991: F.W.E.I.R. *Barb. RWC: J.I.WS.E.NZ. 1992: E.I.F.W.A (2)
D. S. Wyllie	Stewart's Melville	*2	1991: *USA.*C.
A. G. Hastings	Watsonians	9	1993: I.F.W.E.NZ. 1994: W.E.I.F.
A. D. Nicol	Dundee HSFP	*3	1993: *Fj.*T.*WS.
A. I. Reed	Bath	2	1994: Ar (2)

Captain with first cap

F. J. Moncreiff 1871: E   **D. H. Keller** 1949: F

Relatives Capped for Scotland

Father & Son

J. B. Waters (1904); F. H. Waters (1930)
H. T. S. Gedge (1894); P. M. S. Gedge (1933)
J. H. Bruce Lockhart (1913); R. B. Bruce Lockhart (1937); L. Bruce Lockhart (1948)
R. A. Gallie (1920); G. H. Gallie (1939)
I. C. Geddes (1906); K. I. Geddes (1947)
A. T. Sloan (1914); D. A. Sloan (1950)
H. Waddell (1924); G. H. Waddell (1957)
W. M. Simmers (1927); B. M. Simmers (1965)
A. T. Fisher (1947); C. D. Fisher (1975)
J. J. Hegarty (1951); C. B. Hegarty (1978)
M. J. Campbell-Lamerton (1961); J. R. E. Campbell-Lamerton (1986)

Brothers

G. T. Neilson (1891); W. Neilson (1891); W. G. Neilson (1894); R. T. Neilson (1898)
J. F. Finlay (1871); A. B. Finlay (1875); N. J. Finlay (1875)
J. W. Arthur (1871); A. Arthur (1875)
W. Cross (1871); M. Cross (1875)
R. W. Irvine (1871); D. R. Irvine (1878)
T. R. Marshall (1871); W. Marshall (1872)
J. H. McClure (1872); G. B. McClure (1873)
J. Reid (1874); C. Reid (1881)
R. Ainslie (1879); T. Ainslie (1881)
R. Maitland (1881); G. Maitland (1885)
A. Walker (1881); J. G. Walker (1882)
A. R. Don Wauchope (1881); P. H. Don Wauchope (1885)
M. C. McEwan (1886); W. M. C. McEwan (1894)
C. E. Orr (1887); J. E. Orr (1889)
J. H. Dods (1895); F. P. Dods (1901)
D. R. Bedell-Sivright (1900); J. V. Bedell-Sivright (1902)
J. E. Crabbie (1900); G. E. Crabbie (1904)
J. Ross (1901); E.J. Ross (1904)
L. M. MacLeod (1904), K. G. MacLeod (1905)
A. B. H. L. Purves (1906); W. D. C. L. Purves (1912)
D. G. McGregor (1907); J. R. McGregor (1909)
C. D. Stuart (1909); L. M. Stuart (1923)
J. D. Dobson (1901); J. Dobson (1911)
D. D. Howie (1912); R. A. Howie (1924)
G. M. Murray (1921); R. O. Murray (1935)
J. C. Dykes (1922); A. S. Dykes (1932)
J. M. Henderson (1933); I. C. Henderson (1939)
R. W. Shaw (1934); I. Shaw (1937)
R. B. Bruce Lockhart (1937); L. Bruce Lockhart (1948)
T. F. Dorward (1938); A. F. Dorward (1950)

D. D. Valentine (1947); A .R. Valentine (1953)
A. Cameron (1948); D. Cameron (1953)
R. W .T. Chisholm (1955); D. H. Chisholm (1964)
C. Elliot (1958); T. G. Elliot (1968)
T. O. Grant (1960); D. Grant (1965)
A. C. W. Boyle (1963); A. H. W. Boyle (1966)
P. C. Brown (1964); G. L. Brown (1969)
B. M. Gossman (1980); J. S. Gossman (1980)
I. G. Milne (1979); K. S. Milne (1989); D. F. Milne (1991)
J. H. Calder (1981); F. Calder (1986)
A. G. Hastings (1986); S. Hastings (1986)
P. W. Dods (1983); M. Dods (1994)

Half Brothers

P. Turnbull (1901); G. B. Crole (1920)

Cousins

R. W. Irvine (1871); D. R. Irvine (1878); T. W. Irvine (1885)
R. Welsh (1895); W. H. Welsh (1900)
E. D. Simson (1902); J. T. Simson (1905)
A. G. Biggar (1969); M. A. Biggar (1975)

Uncles & Nephews

A. Buchanan (1871); F. G. Buchanan (1910)
D. Patterson (1896); W. Burnet (1912)
J. M. Dykes (1898); J. C. Dykes (1922); A. S. Dykes (1932)
G. Thom (1920); J. R. Thom (1933)
J.W. Allan (1927); J. L. Allan (1952)
J. G. Watherston (1934); W. R. A. Watherston (1962)
C. McDonald (1947); D. M. Rose (1951)
H. F.McLeod (1954); C. M. Telfer (1968)

Grandfather and Grandson

G. F. Ritchie (1932); A. D. Nicol (1992)
J. M. Bannerman (1921); D. S. Munro (1994)

Ages Comparisons of Scottish Players

Youngest First Cap

	School	Date of Birth	Date of Match	Age
N. J. Finlay*	Edin. Academy	31.1.1858	8.3.1875	17y 36 days
C. Reid*	Edin. Academy	14.1.1864	19.2.1881	17y 36 days
W. G. Neilson*	Merchiston	1.10.1876	17.3.1894	17y 5m
W. Neilson*	Merchiston	18.8.1873	7.2.1891	17y 5m
K. G. MacLeod	Fettes	2.2.1888	18.11.1905	17y 9m
L. M. Balfour	Edin. Academy	9.3.1854	5.2.1872	17y 10m
A. Arthur	Glas. Academy	3.4.1857	8.3.1875	17y 11m
R. W. Irvine	Edin. Academy	19.4.1853	27.3.1871	17y 11m
W. M. C. McEwan	Edin. Academy	24.10.1875	3.2.1894	18y 3m

The reader is invited to check why N.J. Finlay is placed ahead of C. Reid. The first four marked by an asterisk, were capped while still at school, as were the following five players:

	School	Date of Birth	Date of Match	Age
W. StC. Grant	Craigmount	c.1853	3.3.1873	c.20y
J.A. Campbell	Merchiston	c.1858	4.3.1878	c.20y
T. Anderson	Merchiston	17.5.1863	18.2.1882	18y 9m
M.F. Reid	Loretto	3.8.1864	17.2.1883	18y 5m
D. M. Grant	Elstow	c.1893	4.2.1911	c.18y

Oldest First Cap

T. Gray (*33y.2m*): C. J. G. Mackenzie (*32y.1m*): F. O. Turnbull (*31y.7m*): R. H. D. Bryce (*31y.3m*): R. J. C. Glasgow (*31y.2m*)

Oldest Cap

J McLauchlan (*37y.6m*): A. F. McHarg (*34y.7m*): R. J. C. Glasgow (*34y.3m*): T. Gray (*34y.2m*)

Scottish International Players: Rugby plus other Sports

Cricket: Pre-1909

T. Anderson: A. G. G. Asher: L. M. Balfour-Melville: E. M. Bannerman: A. Buchanan: J. S. Carrick: T. Chalmers: W. St.C. Grant: F. Hunter: W. E. Maclagan: T. R. Marshall: G. MacGregor: D. Somerville: H. J. Stevenson: J. G. Walker: A. R. Don Wauchope

Cricket Post-1909

A. W. Angus: D. L. Bell: G. B. Crole: J. N. G. Davidson: M. R. Dickson: A. W. Duncan:
T. M. Hart: A. B. M. Ker: J. R. Kerr: J. H. Bruce Lockhart: R. B. Bruce Lockhart:
W. R. Logan: I. J. M. Lumsden: A. S. B. McNeil: N. G. R. Mair: K. W. Marshall:
K. J. F. Scotland: J. M. Tennent

Other Sports

Athletics
R. H. Lindsay-Watson (*Hammer Throw*) (Olympic Team): F. G. Buchanan;
G. P. S. Macpherson; D. J. Whyte (*Long Jump*): E. H. Liddell (*Track Events*) (OlympicTeam):
P. M. S. Gedge (*Fencing*): D. D. Mackenzie (*Relay Team*)
Basketball: J. P. Fisher (Olympic Team): T. J. Smith
Curling: D. S. Davies
Golf: G. Roberts
Hockey: W. E. Bryce
Water Polo: J. M. Ritchie

This list is nowhere near complete and I should welcome additional entries.

APPENDIX 9

Scottish International Players
whose Careers Bridged the Wars

1914-1919

A. W. Angus (1910-1920): A. S. Hamilton (1914-1920): J. Hume (1912-1922):
A. D. Laing (1914-1921): J. H. Bruce Lockhart (1913-1920): J. B. Macdougall
(1913-1921): G. H. H. P. Maxwell (1913-1922): A. T. Sloan (1914-1921): C. M. Usher
(1912-1923): A. Wemyss (1914-1922)

1939-1945

I. C. Henderson (1939-1948): J. R. S. Innes (1939-1948): W. C. W. Murdoch
(1935-1948): R. W. F. Sampson (1939-1947): W. B. Young (1937-1948)

APPENDIX 10

Scotland's Most Capped Players

52	J. M. Renwick, 1972-84	40	D. M. B. Rollo, 1959-68
52	C. T. Deans, 1978-86	37	J. M. Bannerman, 1921-29
51	A. R. Irvine, 1972-82	37	I. Tukalo, 1985-92
50	A. B. Carmichael, 1967-78	36	I. A. M. Paxton, 1981-88
50	A. G. Hastings, 1986-94	35	A. G. Stanger, 1989-94
50	S. Hastings, 1986-94	34	F. Calder, 1986-91
48	A. J. Tomes, 1976-87	33	A. R. Smith, 1955-62
47	R. J. Laidlaw, 1980-88	32	F. A. L. Laidlaw, 1965-71
44	I. G. Milne, 1979-90	32	D. G. Leslie, 1975-85
44	K. W. Robertson, 1978-89	32	I. R. McGeechan, 1972-79
44	D. M. B. Sole, 1986-92	32	I. S. Smith, 1924-33
43	A. F. McHarg, 1968-79	31	N. S. Bruce, 1958-64
43	J. McLauchlan, 1969-79	31	I. H. P. Laughland, 1959-67
42	J. Y. Rutherford, 1979-87	31	K. S. Milne, 1989-94
41	D. B. White, 1982-92	30	G. Armstrong, 1988-94
40	J. Jeffrey, 1984-91	30	G. L. Brown, 1969-76
40	H. F. McLeod, 1954-62		

APPENDIX 11

Scotland's International Records

ENGLAND

Played 111: Scotland 39, England 55. drawn 17

IRELAND

Played 106: Scotland 55, Ireland 45, drawn 5, abandoned 1

WALES

Played 98: Scotland 42, Wales 54, drawn 2

FRANCE

Played 65: Scotland 30, France 32, drawn 3

NEW ZEALAND

Played 17: New Zealand 15, drawn 2

SOUTH AFRICA

Played 8: Scotland 3, South Africa 5

NEW SOUTH WALES

Played 1: Scotland 1

AUSTRALIA

Played 13: Scotland 6, Australia 7

Appendix 11 Scotland's International Record

ROMANIA

Played 6: Scotland 4, Romania 2

JAPAN

Played 1 Scotland 1

WESTERN SAMOA

Played 1: Scotland 1

ZIMBABWE

Played 2: Scotland 2

ARGENTINA

Played 3: Scotland 1, Argentina 2

FIJI

Played 1: Scotland 1

SRU PRESIDENT'S XV

Played 1: Scotland 1

Scotland XVs (no caps awarded)

CANADA

Played 1 Canada 1

UNITED STATES OF AMERICA

Played 1: Scotland 1

BARBARIANS

Played 3: Barbarians 2, drawn 1

SPAIN

Played 2: Scotland 2

ARGENTINA

Played 3: Scotland 2, Argentina 1

FIJI

Played 2: Scotland 2

FRANCE XV

Played 2: Scotland 1, drawn 1

JAPAN

Played 4: Scotland 3, Japan 1

TONGA

Played 2: Scotland 2

WESTERN SAMOA

Played 1: Western Samoa 1

ZIMBABWE

Played 2: Scotland 2

'A' Internationals

IRELAND 'A'

Played 2: Scotland 2

FRANCE 'A'

Played 2: Scotland 1, France 1

SPAIN

Played 3: Scotland 3

ITALY

Played 2: Scotland 1, Italy 1

NEW ZEALAND

Played 1: New Zealand 1

'B' Internationals

FRANCE

Played 20: Scotland 8, France 12   Cancelled 1 (Snow)

IRELAND

Played 7: Scotland 2, Ireland 4, drawn 1

ITALY

Played 4: Scotland 4

Under 21 Internationals

WALES

Played 8: Wales 8

IRELAND

Played 2: Ireland 2

FRANCE

Played 2: France 2

ITALY

Played 4: Scotland 1, Italy 2, drawn 1

NETHERLANDS

Played 2: Scotland 2

NEW ZEALAND RUGBY NEWS YOUTH XV

Played 1: New Zealand Youth 1

Under-19 Internationals

ENGLAND

Played 5: Scotland 1, England 4

WALES

Played 4: Wales 4

ITALY

Played 4: Scotland 2, Italy 2

ROMANIA

Played 1: Romania 1

AUSTRALIAN SCHOOLS

Played 1: Australian Schools 1

Under-18 Internationals

IRELAND

Played 3: Scotland 2, Ireland 1

BELGIUM

Played 1: Scotland 1

ITALY

Played 2: Scotland 1, drawn 1

JAPAN SCHOOLS

Played 1: Scotland 1

NETHERLANDS

Played 3: Scotland 3

SPAIN

Played 4: Scotland 1, Spain 3

SWEDEN

Played 3: Scotland 3

WEST GERMANY

Played 3: Scotland 2, West Germany 1

APPENDIX 12

Roll of Honour

The Boer War 1899-1902

1900: D. B. Monypenny

The 1914-1918 War

1914: R. F. Simson: J. L. Huggan: J. Ross: L. Robertson
1915: F. H. Turner: J. Pearson: D. M. Bain: W. C. Church: E. T. Young: P. C. B. Blair: W. M. Wallace: D. R. Bedell-Sivright: W. M. Dickson
1916: D. D. Howie: A. Ross: C. H. Abercrombie: J. S. Wilson: R. Fraser: E. Milroy
1917: J. G.Will: T. A. Nelson: W. T. Forrest: A. L. Wade: J. Y. M. Henderson: J. A. Campbell: S. S. L. Steyn
1918: G. A. W. Lamond: W. R. Hutchison: R. E. Gordon: W. R. Sutherland

The 1939-45 War

1940: D. K. A. Mackenzie

1941: T. F. Dorward: A. W. Symington

1942: P. Munro: J. M. Ritchie: R. M. Kinnear: W. A. Ross: J. G. S. Forrest: D. St. C. Ford

1943: G. Roberts: W. M. Penman

1944: A. S. B. McNeil: W. N. Renwick: G. H. Gallie

1945: E. H. Liddell

Acknowledgements

The following publications were consulted by the author when researching and writing the match reports from 1980 onwards:

Rothmans Rugby Year Book; Edinburgh Evening News; The Glasgow Herald (now The Herald); The Guardian; The Independent; The Observer; Scotland on Sunday; The Scotsman; Sunday Express; The Sunday Times; The Times, Rugby News; Rugby World; Scottish Rugby.